A

A

VULNERABILITY TO PSYCHOPATHOLOGY

VULNERABILITY TO PSYCHOPATHOLOGY

A Biosocial Model

MARVIN ZUCKERMAN

American Psychological Association
Washington, DC

Published by
American Psychological Association
750 First Street, NE
Washington, DC 20002

Copies may be ordered from
APA Order Department
P.O. Box 92984
Washington, DC 20090-2984

In the U.K., Europe, Africa, and the Middle East, copies may be ordered from
American Psychological Association
3 Henrietta Street
Covent Garden, London
WC2E 8LU England

Typeset in Goudy by EPS Group Inc., Easton, MD

Printer: Braun-Brumfield, Inc., Ann Arbor, MI
Cover Designer: Minker Design, Bethesda, MD
Technical/Production Editor: Catherine R. W. Hudson

Library of Congress Cataloging-in-Publication Data
Zuckerman, Marvin.
    Vulnerability to psychopathology : a biosocial model / Marvin Zuckerman.
      p.   cm.
    Includes bibliographical references and index.
    ISBN 1-55798-566-9 (acid-free paper)
    1. Psychology, Pathological.   2. Mental illness—Risk factors.
   3. Mental illness—Etiology.   I. Title.
    RC454.Z93   1999
    616.89'071—dc21
                                        98-33296
                                              CIP

British Library Cataloguing-in-Publication Data
A CIP record is available from the British Library.

Printed in the United States of America
First Edition

To April, Steve, and Paula, my family "shrinks,"
who are out on the front lines struggling
with psychopathology, not just talking
about strategy like their father.

CONTENTS

PREFACE

This book should be useful to researchers and teachers of psychopathology and to students in graduate courses on the subject or physicians in resident training programs. I have been teaching a graduate psychopathology course for over 30 years and have missed having a text of sufficient depth, that incorporates the most current research findings and is based on some kind of consistent framework, rather than on the eclectic mixture of biosocial, psychodynamic, behavioral, and cognitive interpretations found in undergraduate texts. Most teachers of graduate courses in psychopathology do not use a text, but instead use photocopies of articles that are selected according to their own predilections, as I have done. The problem with this approach is the lack of a single source presenting basic information on research findings on history of the disorders, diagnosis, prognosis, course, prevalence, demographic characteristics, comorbidities, genetics, neurological and pharmacological studies, and social factors. Using articles on each of these subjects for every form of psychopathology covered in the course would lead to such extensive reading that students would rebel and passively aggress against the instructor in their teaching evaluations. One has to be selective or waste a lot of class time in presenting basic facts. The recent enforcement of copyright laws has also made a reprint text difficult, unless one decides well ahead of time what articles to use in the course and obtains permissions. If *this* book is used in a course, instructors can still select reprints in special areas of interest, but fewer of them will be needed, and instructors can be confident that the students will be informed of the basic findings reported in the text.

But this book is not written just for graduate students. Over the years I have been developing a model for psychopathology that I want to offer to theorists and researchers. I have become convinced that Meehl's (1962, 1989) diathesis–stress model for schizophrenia, or other versions of it, can be used for all forms of psychopathology. Meehl also included personality (the schizotypic) in his model. Because of my own central interest in personality, I decided that the pathological response to stress depends on pre-existing personality traits. The *Diagnostic and Statistical Manual of Mental Disorders* (American Psychiatric Association, 1994) (DSM) regards personality as a separate dimension from clinical disorders, but I regard it as an intrinsic part of clinical disorders.

I approach the diathesis first in terms of the genetic or biological bases of the disorders. My book, the *Psychobiology of Personality* (Zuckerman, 1991) included two chapters on psychopathology: one for the anxiety disorders as developments from the neuroticism dimension of personality, and the other on disinhibitory disorders (antisocial personality disorder and substance abuse) as an extension of the major dimension of personality from my "Alternative Five" structural model for personality, Impulsive Unsocialized Sensation Seeking. These chapters focused on the biological bases for the disorders and the personality traits associated with them. Their treatment, however, and the treatment of other disorders here is much broader, covering social factors as well as biological ones. *Psychobiology of Personality* provides more detail on genetic, neurological, psychopharmacological, and psychophysiological methods, which could be helpful to readers of this volume who have no familiarity with these areas.

After finishing *Psychobiology of Personality*, I began to think about the logical sequel on the psychobiology of psychopathology. At the time I had a more urgent project: to update my 1979 book, *Sensation Seeking: Beyond the Optimal Level of Arousal* by incorporating the hundreds of new studies and changes in theoretical outlook occurring in the intervening years. Another reason for delaying the start of this book was the impending revisions in diagnostic definitions in the *Diagnostic and Statistical Manual* (DSM) of the American Psychiatric Association. The *DSM-III-R* revision had appeared in 1987, and *DSM-IV* was not scheduled until 1994. There was no point in describing disorders in terms of *DSM-III-R* if those definitions were going to be changed right after the publication of my book, therefore, I began this book soon after the publication of *DSM-IV* in 1994.

In order to achieve the depth I wanted, I decided to focus first on the major disorders rather than try to describe all of the narrow or less prevalent ones. I selected anxiety, mood, antisocial personality, substance abuse, and schizophrenic disorders for my subjects. There is no separate chapter for the personality disorders except for the one on antisocial personality. Some are treated in relevant chapters, such as the Class C (avoidant, dependent, and obsessive–compulsive) disorders in chapter 3, and the Class A (paranoid, schizotypal, and schizoid) disorders in chapter 7 on schizophrenia. I also decided not to attempt a systematic coverage of psychodynamic, behavioral, or cognitive theories and research for all disorders, except where there was a substantial body of research on them (excluding therapy research). One cannot discuss anxiety or depression, for instance, without attention to the cognitive viewpoint and the research it has stimulated. The only theoretical viewpoint systematically treated in this book is the biosocial one incorporated in my diathesis–personality–stress model. I also did not provide systematic coverage of therapy except where it was relevant to theories of etiology. Drug treatments, for instance, are the sources of psychopharmacological theories for some of the disorders. The effectiveness of treatments has not been discussed. In most schools, the issues of psychopathology and therapy are dealt with in separate courses. Anyway, the outcomes of therapies are not reliable proofs of the theories of etiology behind them. Many different kinds of therapies, based on different theoretical assumptions and employing different techniques, are equally effective for the treatment of many disorders.

Chapter 1 discusses the diathesis–stress models and the construct of *vulnerability*. Some of the problems in defining diathesis and stress are discussed. Chapter 2 deals with diagnosis, first with its history from the time of the ancient Greeks to the present, and then with the reliability and validity of the current *DSM*-defined diagnoses from *DSM-I* to *DSM-IV*. Because I advocate a dimensional view to psychopathology, my organization of the book around the categorical definitions of the *DSM* might be questioned. The answer is simple. Nearly all of the clinical research is organized using these definitions. One of the main purposes of the *DSM-III* changes was to clarify these definitions so that researchers and clinicians were talking about the same patients when they used diagnostic terms. More of the impetus for change came from the researchers than from the clinicians. The danger is that once these definitions are "engraved in stone," the validity of the research may be compromised by errors in the constructs. But this is not a unique problem for psychiatry. Most sciences change their definitions and constructs from time to time, sometimes resulting in the irrelevance of older research and theory. The frequent changes in the *DSM* have been condemned by some, but if they are based on new research evidence rather than political pressures, they should be welcomed. The more recent revisions have been largely based on the research findings of "task groups" rather than compromises between clinical and research pressure groups within the American Psychiatric Association.

Chapters 3 through 8, dealing with clinical and personality disorders, are organized in the following manner. First, there is a summary of the *DSM-IV* descriptions of the disorder and its subcategories and specifiers. Next, the data on comorbidities with other disorders, prevalence rates, demographics, and course of the disorder are discussed. The prevalence rates are largely based on two recent large-scale community surveys in the United States and surveys in other countries for cross-cultural comparisons. The diathesis for the disorder is then discussed: first, in terms of genetic studies, including twin, adoption, prevalence in relatives, and molecular studies searching for specific genes for the disorder; and then in terms of the biological factors implicated in the disorder. The latter includes brain imaging, neurological, and psychopharmacology studies. Personality background to the disorder is then discussed with a concentration on longitudinal, predictive studies of so-called high risk children. Studies of concurrent personality traits are always suspect because of the confounding effects of the psychopathology itself.

Stress is treated in terms of distal sources that long precede the clinical disorder, and proximal sources, or stressful events, occurring just prior to the disorder. Parental death during the early childhood of the person is an example of distal stress, whereas recent separation or divorce of the patient occurring in the month or two before the manifestation of the disorder might be a proximal stressor. Although the book does not deal with theories of family or social etiology based on retrospective accounts from psychotherapy, prospective studies or those based on records during childhood prior to the development of the disorders are reviewed for possible etiological relevance. The emotional quality of the home environment and the interactions of parents and children are reviewed in this section.

Chapter 3 deals with the anxiety disorders, chapter 4 with the mood disorders, chapter 5 with the antisocial personality disorder, chapter 6 with substance abuse and dependence (primarily of alcohol, heroin, and cocaine), and pathological gambling disorder. Because gambling disorder is grouped in a separate category of *DSM-IV*, one might question why I have included it in the chapter on substance abuse. The answer, briefly, is that except for the absence of a substance, gambling disorder has many of the same phenomenal characteristics, biological correlates, and personality types as substance abuse. Chapter 7 is on schizophrenia. The first diathesis–stress model was developed in regard to this baffling and complex disorder. This is the longest chapter in the book, primarily because it has been the most researched of all of the disorders and readers need to survey the broad range of this research to draw any meaningful conclusions. Finally, chapter 8 is a discussion of the problems in the study of psychopathology, a discussion of the fit of different diathesis–stress models to the disorders discussed in this volume, and prognostications for future developments in the field.

This book gives primary importance to the more recent literature, particularly that of the past decade. It is not that earlier research is not informative, but that it was based on earlier and less reliable definitions of the disorders and did not have the advantages of developments in the field such as structured interviews for diagnosis, imaging techniques for brain studies, and the results of long-term longitudinal studies which are just coming to fruition. The recent literature has been extensively surveyed as apparent in the length of the reference section at the end of the book.

Although case histories can be useful for students, there are none in this book because they are available from many other sources, including books and videotapes. Important insights and hypotheses may emerge from clinical case work, but I believe that only controlled research can sort out the false from the true. In this age of relativism it may seem a little old-fashioned to speak of *truth* without using quotation marks. But to the extent that ideas can be supported or refuted in the real world (and I am a realist, although not a naive one) I believe that scientific method is the way to do this. My son, an anthropologist, tells me that medical psychiatric and psychological science is just another belief system, no more valid than that of a New Guinea tribal shaman. But witch doctors do not usually discover antibiotics (although they may occasionally find a useful herb), antipsychotics, antidepressives, or antianxiety drugs (other than opiates and alcohol), and although they may be quite skilled at hypnotherapy and suggestion, they are not likely to use systematic desensitization to eliminate a phobia. I admit my Western cultural–scientific bias.

ACKNOWLEDGMENTS

The University of Delaware provided support for some of the incidental expenses such as copying and library work during the first 3½ years of this project. Robert Plomin provided a good work facility at the Social, Genetic, and Developmental Psychiatry Research Center of the Institute of Psychiatry in London during my 1997–1998 sabbatical year in which I was able to finish the last chapters of the book. He also stimulated my interest in molecular genetics, read the genetic sections of the book, and provided constructive suggestions for these. The excellent psychiatric library at the Institute and the librarians there were a great help in this final push. Selected chapters were read by Avshalom Caspi and Terrie Moffitt, currently at the Institute in London, and the chapter on anxiety disorders was read by David Barlow. All of these readers were quite helpful. Irving Gottesman reviewed the entire book and made many helpful suggestions for revision and additions. He also introduced me to Paul Meehl via e-mail to discuss Meehl's diathesis–stress model of schizophrenia. Paul Meehl patiently guided me through his latest model for schizophrenia and his philosophy of science. Colleagues like these make writing a book an adventure in learning.

As with all of my books, the greatest thanks must go to Mary E. Hazard who tried to bear with me, even during bearish moods and neglectful periods when I was preoccupied with the book, which came to be informally known as the "albatross" (that dead bird around the neck of Coleridge's "Ancient Mariner"). Fortunately, this albatross is taking flight.

VULNERABILITY TO PSYCHOPATHOLOGY

1

DIATHESIS–STRESS MODELS

GENERAL DEFINITIONS

Diathesis

A definition of *diathesis* is "constitutional disposition, or predisposition, to some anomalous or morbid condition 'which no longer belongs within the confines of normal variability, but already begins to represent a potential disease condition'" (Campbell, 1989, p. 202). The word is derived from the ancient Greek idea of *disposition* related to the humoral (body fluids) theory of temperament and disease, for instance, an excess of black bile was regarded as the diathesis for depression or "melancholia." In the modern sense the biological traits produced by the genetic disposition are the diathesis. Some have broadened the use of the term *diathesis* to include cognitive or social predispositions that make a person vulnerable to disorders such as depression (Monroe & Simons, 1991). In this broader sense the diathesis is simply the necessary antecedent condition for the development of a disorder, whether biological or psychological. In most models the diathesis alone is not sufficient to produce the disorder but requires other potentiating or releasing factors to become pathogenic. The diathesis, in this case, includes the vulnerability to stress.

"These various diathetic conditions are distinguished by the fact that diathetic individuals respond with abnormal or truly pathological reactions

3

to physiological stimuli . . . or the ordinary conditions of life . . . that are borne by the majority of individuals without injury" (Campbell, 1989, p. 202).

This concept of diathesis, developed by Meehl (1962), Gottesman and Shields (1967), and Rosenthal (1967), suggests a vulnerability factor that makes some persons more susceptible to particular degrees of stress than others. Zubin and Spring (1977) describe the construct of vulnerability as one that connects genetic, brain function, ecological, learning, developmental, and psychosocial models. Their vulnerability model (see Fig. 1.1) suggests that each person has a degree of vulnerability or threshold effect for the development of schizophrenia. But the vulnerability model may be applicable to all types of psychopathology. Vulnerability is a trait, whereas the psychopathological episode is a state (albeit one which may last for months or years). A pathological episode may be provoked in a vulnerable person by relatively minor stresses or "hassles," whereas only a major catastrophic event might induce a similar reaction in a nonvulnerable person. In the case of the nonvulnerable individual, the episode would likely be brief or acute, rather than chronic, and would not last long beyond the stress situation itself. Vulnerability may be a function of biological factors, but Zubin and Spring suggest that it is also influenced by *coping* and *confidence* (similar to Bandura's, 1977, "efficacy expectation") or the belief that one can cope with the stressful life situation.

Of course there are simple single-gene neurological diseases, such as Huntington's chorea, where the genetic diathesis alone can and will produce the pathological brain condition and the resulting behavioral disorder without any influence of external stress. But all of the conditions to be

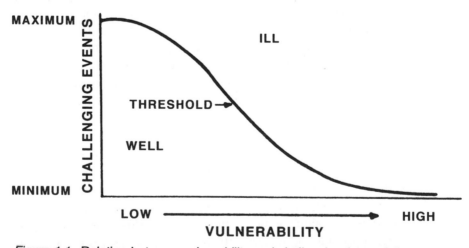

Figure 1.1. Relation between vulnerability and challenging (stressful) events. From "A New View of Schizophrenia," by J. Zubin & B. Spring, 1977, *Journal of Abnormal Psychology, 86*, p. 110. Copyright 1977 by American Psychological Association.

discussed in this volume seem to be polygenic, and the diathesis does not invariably result in its expression in the disorder. If the diathesis were sufficient, identical twins would always be concordant for the disorder; if one had it, the other would also manifest it. This is not the case for any of the disorders discussed in this book.

Behavior genetics is a science that attempts to determine the role of genes and postconception biological or social environmental conditions in explaining variations in behavior (Bouchard, Lykken, McGue, Segal, & Tellegen, 1990; Plomin, Owen, & McGuffin, 1994). In animals the approach may be an experimental one, using the methods of selective breeding, inbreeding, and crosses between inbred strains to shape specific behaviors and thus determine their amenability to genetic control. The pure strains resulting from such "unnatural" selection may be compared in behavior; the members of each inbred strain are like an extended set of identical twins. In humans the researchers must rely on the experiments of nature to study genetic control of behavior. One well-known method is to compare the similarities or differences between identical and fraternal twins in order to estimate the heritability for some trait. Identical twins have all of their genes in common, whereas fraternal twins have only an average of half in common. Given that both kinds of twins are the same age and raised in a shared family environment, these shared environmental differences are controlled, and the differences in concordance between identical and fraternal pairs are due to heredity. If identical twins are separated shortly after birth and reared without contact in different and uncorrelated environments, then their similarity can only be attributed to their common genes. Adoption studies of nontwins are also useful in estimating the relative influences of heredity and shared environment. Assuming they have no contact with their biological relatives, adopted children's resemblance to their adoptive parents can only be due to shared environment, and their resemblance to their biological parents can only be a function of the genetic relationship or the prenatal environment of the womb. Studies of incidence of disorders in intact families do not control for shared environments, but if the rate of the disorder is not higher than in the relatives of controls without the disorder or with other disorders, then this argues against a genetic influence specific to the disorder. If disorders do run in families and show the expected genetic relationships depending on degree of biological relatedness, there is some evidence of a possible genetic diathesis.

When a trait is measured in continuous quantitative form, the relationship between sets of twins may be expressed as a correlation. But when the variable is a dichotomous one as in diagnoses (i.e., disorder present or absent), then the usual statistic is a concordance ratio. The probandwise concordance expresses the percentage of cases where if one twin has the disorder, the other one also does. The pairwise concordance is the percentage of pairs in which both twins have the disorder. Phi correlations based on 2 × 2 frequency tables are commonly used to calculate heritabilities from concordance data.

The other aspect of diathesis concerns the question of what is inherited that produces the predisposition toward the disorder. Although we may speak in terms of an inherited trait or behavioral disposition, we do not inherit traits or dispositions as such. Neurological structures and some aspects of their physiology are more directly related to the protein products of genes. The science of psychopharmacology looks to these inherited biological traits for clues as to the cause of disorders and keys to their treatment through drugs. The belief that something that is strongly genetically influenced is irremediable is one of the fallacies that provokes negative attitudes toward genetics among the ill-informed. Anxiety, depression, and even psychotic behavior are all genetically influenced, but are often alterable by various kinds of psychotherapies as well as by drug treatments.

One must distinguish between biological correlates of disorders, which accompany the disorder but are not abnormal before or after the disorder, and biological variables, which are predictive of the disorder and do not return to normal levels after remission of the disorder. It is primarily biological variables of the last type that offer clues to the diathesis of the disorder. Some biological variables are quite stable over long periods of time and do not change much with the emotional state of the patient. Others vary markedly with the clinical and emotional state of the disorder, for instance falling in a depressive state and rising in a manic state in the bipolar disorder. The latter type may play a role in the changing states of the disorder, or may simply be a consequence of the mood change.

A *vulnerability marker* is a behavioral or biological characteristic that does not change with the clinical state and is abnormal when the patient is in remission as well as when he is in the active state of the disorder (Nuechterlein et al., 1992). Since such markers are often found in the well relatives who do not manifest the disorder, it is obvious that these markers by themselves are not sufficient to produce the disorder. *Episode markers* are abnormal during the acute stage of the disorder, but return to normal levels when the patient is recovered. One of the more reliable vulnerability markers for schizophrenia is a deficit in eye-tracking, although it is only found in 20–80% of schizophrenics, depending on the types of criteria used (Iacono, 1993). The inability to pursue a moving object smoothly cannot explain the cognitive, emotional, and behavioral deficits in schizophrenia, but an understanding of the neurology and pharmacology of eye-tracking could lead us to the core of the brain deficit in the schizophrenic diathesis. Nuechterlein et al. (1992) also distinguish a "mediating vulnerability marker," which is deviant during remission but becomes even more abnormal during the episodes. Such factors could play a more direct causal role in the onset of episodes.

Treating cognitive schemas or self-attitudes as diatheses stretches the original sense of the term but this is not the basic problem. If the diathesis is a cognitive trait, such as a tendency to blame oneself for negative events, what is the origin of this trait? It could be a typical expression of a biological disposition toward depression, or a tendency learned by observation and reinforcement within the family. If social learning were the sole explanation, both identical and fraternal twins would have high but equal concordance rates for the attitude. If the biological diathesis was the origin of the cognitive trait, the identical twins should have higher concordance than the fraternal twins. Is attribution a trait that precedes depression or one that increases as a function of depression and subsides when depression does? Does clinical depression occur in the context of a preexisting depressive personality? These are the kinds of questions that must be addressed if cognitive schemas are to be regarded as diatheses for the disorder rather than as symptoms of the disorder. In this volume the term *diathesis* will be restricted to genetic and biological factors in the nervous system that influence the likelihood of developing a disorder either directly or through the mediation of personality and cognitive trait factors.

Personality

Personality may be defined as the organization of traits that characterize individuals. *Traits* are relatively enduring dispositions of persons to react in relatively consistent ways in certain kinds of situations which are prototypical for the trait. As such, a trait is a hypothetical construct based on the observation of certain consistencies in behavior across a limited range of situations. Traits are also relatively enduring across time in contrast to *states*, which may vary from moment to moment, hour to hour, or day to day. A trait does not imply consistency of response across all situations. Only patients who have catatonia or severe depression demonstrate such global rigidity of response. A relatively strong rigidity of response characterizes much psychopathology. A person with a disorder is one who reacts inappropriately or with an abnormal exaggeration of response to situations that would not elicit such a response or such an intense or prolonged response in others. A person with depressive personality may respond to a failure or rejection experience with a severe and prolonged depressive reaction, whereas the same situation would produce only a moderate depression of more limited duration in someone without the depressive personality. The responses of adjusted persons are in response to the specifics of the situations eliciting them and are proportional to those situations. The responses of maladjusted persons involve much more than the situation itself, which is interpreted in an idiosyncratic manner. This is not to say that adjusted persons do not show any consistency of behavior across situations. If that were so there would be no such thing as personality traits, and indeed, some colleagues have maintained this nihilistic viewpoint. In general, personality psychologists have conceded that a totally person-centered approach is equally impossible and that much of personality emerges in person–situation interactions. The diathesis–stress approach is the embodiment of person–situation interaction in the realm of psychopathology.

The definitions of some disorders imply consistency of abnormal reactions. A *dysthymic disorder* is defined as "a chronically depressed mood that occurs for most of the day more days than not for at least 2 years" (American Psychiatric Association, *Diagnostic and Statistical Manual of Mental Disorders*, 4th ed. [DSM-IV], 1994, p. 345). A *generalized anxiety disorder* (GAD) is described as "excessive anxiety and worry (apprehensive expectation), occurring more days than not for a period of at least 6 months, about a number of events or activities" (*DSM-IV*, 1994, p. 435). Although 6 months is the minimum period of time required for this diagnosis, patients with GAD reported generalized anxiety for more than half of their lives (Barlow, Blanchard, Vermilyea, Vermilyea, & DiNardo, 1986). In contrast, a *panic disorder* may be diagnosed after as few as two panic attacks (lasting minutes). But patients diagnosed as having panic disorder typically report experiencing this condition for several years (Barlow et al., 1986). Whereas both generalized anxiety and panic may occur in a wide range of situations, phobic reactions occur only in the presence of a phobic object or in a phobic-type situation. The abnormality is defined in terms of consistent response to that object or situation and not as a generalized response trait across many situations. Despite the relatively consistent abnormal behavior displayed in some disorders, for most cases people with neuroses, psychoses, and extraverted people do not behave neurotically, psychotically, or in an extremely extraverted manner at all times and in all situations. The parameters of consistency of abnormal and normal traits are an interesting area of study, but consistency depends on aggregation of responses across time and situations. This fact does not preclude the use of trait or diagnostic constructs. Aggregation of observations produces increased reliability for normal and abnormal traits (Epstein, 1979).

Not all diathesis–stress theories incorporate personality in the sense of broad traits that distinguish one disorder from another. In some theories the traits are relatively narrow ones such as a cognitive style or a symptom tendency. For those who view clinical disorders as quantitative extensions of relatively stable personality traits, an intermediate range of syndromes of traits is represented in the personality disorders. In DSM-III, III-R, and IV, these personality disorders are diagnosed on a separate axis from clinical disorders (see *Diagnostic and Statistical Manual of Mental Disorders*, 3rd ed., 3rd ed. rev., American Psychiatric Association, 1980, 1987). One of their distinguishing characteristics from clinical disorders is that they are supposed to be long-standing. If a personality disorder is comorbid with a clinical disorder, it usually preceded the more severe clinical disorder, and it persists after the clinical disorder has subsided. Unlike the clinical disorders, which are defined in terms of narrow symptoms of varying duration, the personality disorders are defined by clusters of personality traits of long duration. But it is by no means clear that all clinical disorders emerge from preexisting personality disorders. Whether a clinical disorder grows out of a personality disposition or disorder is a question that will be addressed for each disorder considered in this volume.

Stress

The term *stress* as used in psychology is borrowed from physics where it refers to an "applied force that tends to strain or deform a body," or "the internal resistance of a body to such an applied force . . ." (*American Heritage Dictionary*, 3rd ed., p. 1778). A psychiatric definition is "the imposition of strain on a person or the effects of the strain on him; both physical and psychological factors can be stressful. Prolonged stress may impair functioning or trigger mental illness" (Sutherland, 1989, p. 428). These definitions from both physics and psychology include an external factor (a stressor) and an internal stress response to the stressor. However some colleagues prefer to define stress primarily in terms of the internal response, for example Selye (1956), who describes a "general adaptation syndrome" by the sympathetic nervous system and pituitary–adrenal cortical response to environmental and psychological changes; whereas others, for example Spielberger (1966), prefer to limit the definition of stress to the external conditions producing strain or anxiety. Walton (1985) defines stress as "an interference or change in conditions affecting the individual which has an adverse effect, such as worry or hostility, especially when prolonged; also external conditions producing anxiety" (p. 157). But if stress is defined in terms of conditions that produce anxiety or other unpleasant or dysphoric states, then one must consider individual differences. The reaction is a function of both the force or intensity of the stressor and the resistance or other properties of the stressed object or subject. The term *stress* is commonly used to describe the situation affecting persons, their internal reactions to the situation in terms of physiological arousal and subjective emotional responses, and their behavioral reactions. In this volume I restrict the use of the word *stress* to the objective situations. Of course, how do you know a situation or experience is stressful if you do not assess the subect's reactions to it? Part of the answer is the use of objective life stress scales on which particular life experiences have been rated for stressfulness by many other people. It is important not to confuse the independent stress, defined by the normative reactions to a given situation, with individual reactions to it. The impact of stress in producing major depression is greater for individuals of high genetic risk than for those at low genetic risk (Kendler, Kessler, et al., 1995). Psychopathology may be a disproportionate response to stress, but in order to evaluate the role of stress in the psychopathology, the two factors must be independently assessed. The death of a loved one constitutes a stressor for most persons, but the individual reaction to it may be assessed as the persistent depression or other psychopathological or physiological responses to that event. Of course, the effects of stressors may be cumulative, so that a series of milder stressors occurring in a short time interval may produce an aggregated effect equivalent to a single severe stressor.

Psychodynamic theories of psychopathology suggest that a particular kind of stress produced by intrapsychic or interpersonal conflict produces psychopathology. Diathesis theories often do not specify a particular kind of stress as prepotent for psychopathology. Losing one's job may be just as stressful as losing one's spouse, particularly for a "workaholic." Psychodynamic theories usually suggest that stress operating on the developing personality during infancy or childhood and involving significant others on whom one is dependent may make the person less resistant to later stress, particularly stress which reactivates the earlier conflicts. The stress produced by rejection in an adult is magnified in effect by a previous rejection by a parent or other significant figure during childhood. In contrast, the stress in diathesis–stress theories is that which occurs just prior to the manifestation of a disorder or its reactivation. If a person becomes clinically depressed following a rejection, it is assumed that the rejection was the stressor, but if the rejection occurred a year or more earlier, and there are no obvious persisting effects of that rejection, it is not considered a stressor. In psychodynamic theories family stress early in life is a "diathesis" for the later developing disorder, but in diathesis–stress theories, stress interacts with the diathesis factors to produce the disorder. Stress is the event or events occurring in close temporal proximity to the appearance of psychopathology.

There are some classes of disorder described in the *DSM-IV* in which stress is assumed to be the major cause if not the sole cause, for example "reactive depressive disorder," "brief reactive psychosis," or "acute stress disorder." One in which there is persisting reaction to an external life stress or the reactivation after the passage of months or years is called post-traumatic stress disorder (PTSD). Even Freud (1922/1961), despite his emphasis on repressed conflict as the source of adult anxiety, noted the large number of cases following World War I in which the usual defenses against trauma never developed, and the anxiety persisted in relation to its traumatic source in the form of thoughts, fantasies, and nightmares.

Can stress alone produce a disorder in the absence of a diathesis for that disorder? Although many types of severe stress such as war, rape, and catastrophic experiences produce many persistent disorders, only a minority of those people exposed to such experiences develop a PTSD or more severe condition.

One cannot imagine any more prolonged intense stress than confinement in a German concentration camp during World War II. Eitinger (1972) and Eitinger and Strom (1973) followed psychiatric outcomes in Norwegian and Jewish prisoners confined in concentration camps during World War II for 20 years postwar and compared the incidence of various psychological and medical disorders with controls in the Norwegian group. Whereas the figures for neurosis and substance abuse were high, that for psychosis was low, although still significantly higher than that for controls. Nervousness and substance abuse are common symptoms of PTSD, but still less than half and probably a third (assuming comorbidity of the two categories) of the persons exposed to the stress developed a PTSD. Can a severe stress of this type produce a persistent psychosis? After eliminating those cases of schizophrenia in which there was evidence of a hereditary background for the disorder and those who showed suspicious personality abnormalities preceding the concentration camp experience, Eitinger concluded that for slightly more than half of the cases the patients' schizophrenia developed as a function of the horrendous camp experiences (1972). Although many of these patients may not have had schizophrenia by current diagnostic standards, and allowing for hidden diatheses not apparent or reported, it is possible that some of the cases were produced by the stress of the experience alone. But one may always ask, why them and not others exposed to the same extreme conditions? The converse question is this: How can anyone endure such severe and prolonged stress and not show some kind of subsequent psychopathology?

The fact that stress alone is usually not sufficient to explain psychopathology argues for the necessity to introduce personality into the equation. A personality structure develops from the interactions of genetics and experience during the formative years probably extending to young adulthood, at which time personality stabilizes and becomes quite reliable (Zuckerman, 1991). Personality, including both broad general traits and narrower cognitive traits, probably functions as a moderator of response to stress and may explain why two persons exposed to the same stress may have such remarkably different outcomes. It is a mistake, however, to describe personality as the diathesis, because personality itself is a function of its own genotypes and life experiences.

DIATHESIS–STRESS MODELS

Diathesis–stress models may take different forms depending on assumptions made about the roles of the diathesis and stress, such as whether they are necessary, sufficient, or contributing but not necessary causes.

Meehl's first model for schizophrenia is shown in Figure 1.2 (1962). The specifics of this and later models will be discussed again (see chap. 7, this volume, on schizophrenia). As shown here the model may be described as an *interactive model with a dichotomous diathesis*. The diathesis is a single dominant "schizogene" which produces a *schizotaxic* neural integrative defect. The schizotaxic condition produces a *schizotypic* personality "on all existing social learning regimes" (Meehl, 1962). Only some schizotypes go on to develop a full-blown schizophrenic disorder. Most remain compensated schizotypes. Stress produced by a so-called schizophrenogenic type of mother who is ambivalent and inconsistently aversive to the schizotypic child is the most important type of stress pushing the schizotype into schizophrenia according to Meehl (1962). A single gene and the neural (schizotaxic) condition it produces constitute the diathesis that is a necessary cause of schizophrenia, that is, if the diathesis is absent, one cannot become a schizophrenic with any kind of rearing or stress exposure. The gene inevitably produces the schizotaxic neural condition, which is common to all forms of schizophrenia regardless of the symptoms.

The schizotaxic condition is a sufficient cause for the development of a schizotypic personality. There are no social child-rearing factors influencing the development of this personality trait. Presumably all schizophrenics must develop from a schizotypic personality. Stress, in the form of inconsistent and aversive–controlling child rearing, is an environmental variable that influences whether the schizotype decompensates into schizophrenia. Given a normal affectionate mother and consistent child

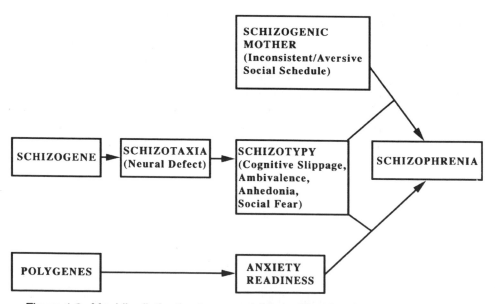

Figure 1.2. Meehl's diathesis-stress model for schizophrenia. Data from "Schizotaxia, Schizotypy, Schizophrenia," by P. E. Meehl, 1962, *American Psychologist, 12,* 827–838.

rearing, the individual with this schizotype will not develop schizophrenia according to Meehl's theory.

Meehl's model (1989, 1990, & personal communications, 1998) was changed drastically at the beginning of this decade. Whereas in 1962 he maintained that the dominant "schizogene" and the resultant schizotaxic brain pathology were necessary but not sufficient causes of schizophrenia, he now theorizes that there is another pathway, the SHAITU genophenocopy. The SHAI part of the acronym stands for personality trait extremes (submissive, hypohedonic, anxious, & introverted) of polygenic origins which may increase the potential for schizotaxia to develop into schizotypy, and for schizotypy to decompensate into schizophrenia. The TU part of the acronym stands for environmental risk factors: T for major or frequent minor traumas during development, and U for unlucky events in adult life which also increase the risk for schizophrenia. Another major factor is a mixed social learning schedule on the part of parents, particularly the mother. But apart from the potentiating role of SHAITU in the schizotaxic type of schizophrenia, it can produce a schizophrenic disorder *even in individuals who do not carry the schizogene and have the schizotaxic brain pathology.* Meehl calls this type a genophenocopy because the personality traits are polygenic, but the stress factors are environmental. The "true" schizophrenia (with a schizotaxic origin) accounts for the great majority (85–90%) of cases, whereas only a minority (10–15%) are genophenocopies (SHAITU). Patients with the "true" schizophrenia are more likely to show the severe negative and disorganized symptomatology, whereas those patients with pure SHAITU are more likely to have disturbances in the content (delusions) rather than the form (disorganization) of thought. Meehl (1990) believes that "delusions in general, do not require an abnormal brain" (p. 82).

Gottesman (1993) and Gottesman and Shields (1982) proposed that a polygenic model best accounts for the schizophrenic disorder with both specific and general (similar to Meehl's "potentiators") genetic and general environmental factors contributing to a *liability threshold.* Fowles (1992) suggested that persons already genetically above the threshold do not require any stress to develop schizophrenia, those near threshold will develop the disorder in most environments, those lower below threshold require a significantly stressful environment, and those far below the threshold would require unusually severe environments and then would be most likely to develop a brief reactive psychosis. Finally, there is a group so far below the threshold that no amount of environmental stress can produce a psychosis.

Fowles (1992) has incorporated the concepts of Gray (1982, 1987) and Depue (1988) on the behavioral approach system (BAS) and behavioral inhibition systems (BIS) as nonspecific sources of liability to schizophrenia. These systems affect the particular types of symptomatic expression in a disorder like schizophrenia. The balance between BAS and BIS systems, for instance, could determine whether schizophrenia is primarily expressed in passivity and withdrawal (BIS) or by delusional and hallucinatory symptoms (BAS). At another level these tendencies are manifested in affect: positive affect as a BAS trait and negative affect as a BIS trait.

The theories of Gray and Fowles are directed at an explanation for schizophrenia but this type of diathesis–stress model, which incorporates genetic, personality, motivational, and emotional traits and stress could be applied to other types of psychopathology as well. This extension is the framework for the present volume.

The *additive model of diathesis–stress interaction* (Monroe & Simons, 1991; Fig. 1.3) suggests that stress may have some influence in producing the disorder, but that it takes much more stress in a person with a low diathesis than in someone with a high diathesis. A level of stress (*bx*) which is sufficient to produce a disorder (level *a*) in an individual (*x*) with a high diathesis will not result in the disorder in another person (*y*) with a low diathesis. Only extreme stress (*by*) can make it probable that this person will develop the disorder. If this model were applied to schizophrenia, a severe stress or extremely ambivalent and aversive parenting could produce a disorder even in a person with no diathesis for the disorder.

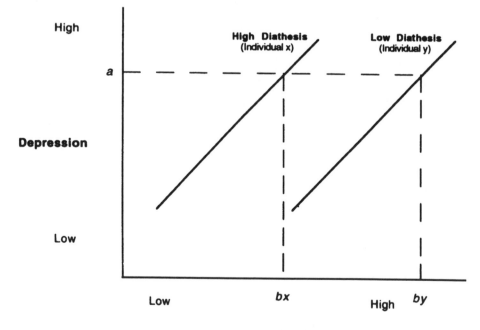

Figure 1.3. Additive model of diathesis–stress interaction with a dichotomous diathesis for depression. From "Diathesis-Stress Theories in the Context of Life-Stress Research: Implications for the Depressive Disorders," by S. M. Monroe & A. D. Simons, 1991, *Psychological Bulletin, 110,* p. 414. Copyright 1991 by the American Psychological Association.

Both of the preceding models assume a dichotomous diathesis, that is, either one has it (a gene, a unique combination of genes, or a particular structural brain pathology) or one doesn't have it. The evidence for most disorders suggests polygenic models that allow for varying dosages of the diathesis agent. Variations in neurotransmitter activity levels, rather than a specific structural neural deficit, would also allow for degrees of diathesis. Figure 1.4 shows the interaction of diathesis stress with a quasicontinuous diathesis. Although a minimal level of diathesis may be insufficient to produce the disorder even under high stress, the probability of the disorder increases as a function of both level of stress and strength of the diathesis beyond this minimal level.

Thus far the models described have treated the diathesis and the stress as independent factors. Certain kinds of stress, such as natural disasters or death of kin due to medical causes, may be unrelated to the diathesis. But other types of stress, such as those produced by defective interpersonal skills or the consequences of substance abuse, may have a direct relationship with the diathesis. Schizotypic or antisocial personalities, for instance, may elicit rejection by family and society, producing the stress which interacts with the diathesis itself. In this model (Monroe & Simons, 1991; Fig. 1.5) the disorder is a result of both diathesis and stress, but the diathesis itself influences at least one type of stress (1) but is independent of the other

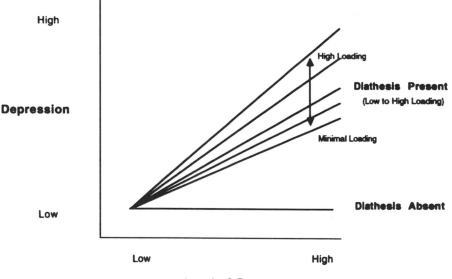

Figure 1.4. Interactive model of diathesis–stress interaction: Quasicontinuous diathesis for depression. From "Diathesis-Stress Theories in the Context of Life-Stress Research: Implications for the Depression Disorders," by S. M. Monroe & A. D. Simons, 1991, *Psychological Bulletin, 110*, p. 415. Copyright 1991 by the American Psychological Association.

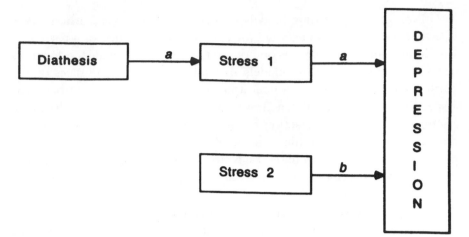

Figure 1.5. Diathesis–stress interactions. Stress 1 = stress related to diathesis; Stress 2 = stress unrelated to diathesis. From "Diathesis–Stress Theories in the Context of Life-Stress Research: Implications for the Depressive Disorders," by S. M. Monroe & A. D. Simons, 1991, *Psychological Bulletin, 110,* p. 420. Copyright 1991 by the American Psychological Association.

(2). A schizotype may have a father who is highly intolerant of the passive behavior of the child, but this stress may be counteracted by a loving and sympathetic mother who shields the child from the aversiveness of the father. The mother's sudden death from natural causes could create a stress that not only interacts with the diathesis but isolates the child and intensifies the stress from the paternal influence.

In another model shown in Figure 1.6, stress is not a necessary condition for the disorder and may be produced solely by the diathesis, the disorder, or both. Thus there is a direct pathway between the diathesis and the disorder without a necessary addition of stress as a contributing cause. I have added a double arrow to pathway c in the original model to suggest

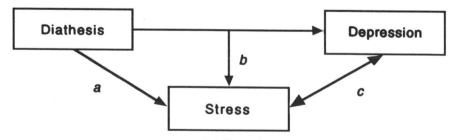

Figure 1.6. Diathesis–stress interactions. Stress is either a minor factor, a result of the diathesis's expression (pathway a), or simply a consequence of the emerging disorder (pathway b or c). From "Diathesis-Stress Theories in the Context of Life-Stress Research: Implications for the Depressive Disorders," by S. M. Monroe & A. D. Simons, 1991, *Psychological Bulletin, 110,* p. 420. Copyright 1991 by the American Psychological Association.

that in some cases stress produced by the diathesis may also play a causal role in the symptoms. The converse model (Fig. 1.6) is that stress alone, without a diathesis, can produce the disorder in some cases in which there is no diathesis.

Personality in the Diathesis–Stress Models

In Meehl's earlier model (see Fig. 1.2), a person develops a schizotype personality as an invariable consequence of the diathesis. The characteristics of this personality, such as interpersonal aversiveness and cognitive slippage, predispose to the disorder and play a role in the interpersonal stress contributing to the disorder. There is a direct line of causation between the schizogene, the schizotaxic neural condition, and the schizotypic personality. This is not the only possible model however. The premorbid personality may be independent or partially independent of the diathesis producing the disorder. A "schizogene" or genes may produce the cognitive disturbances, but other genes may produce the potentiators such as anxiety and social withdrawal. Some of the latter may be necessary as well as potentiators for the development of the schizotypic personality or schizophrenia. Only some schizophrenics show evidence of a schizotypic personality in the developmental period leading to the manifestation of the full-blown disorder. Furthermore social learning and stress may play roles in the development of the premorbid personality. The premorbid personality may influence the form that the disorder will take and the prognosis and outcome of the disorder, even though it may not be a function of the same diathesis that produced the disorder. There may be two diatheses to the etiology of some disorders, one mediated by a personality type and one more directly underlying the specific symptoms of the disorder.

The usual model for diathesis stress does not distinguish between the genetic aspect of the disorder and the biological basis in the nervous system, assuming that the latter is a function of the former. Biological influences on the nervous system can originate from nongenetical external sources during the prenatal, perinatal, and postnatal periods of life. The developing brain is particularly vulnerable to biological stress or other influences such as hormones during the prenatal period. Brain damage can occur in the form of anoxia or direct traumatic insult during the birth process itself. Disease, diet, and trauma can create the diathesis condition in the brain during the postnatal period of development.

Most models do not distinguish between distal and proximal stressors. Early stress, whether directly biological or social in nature, may make the child more vulnerable to later stress. This idea is a basic tenet of psychodynamic theory. Cognitive theories imply an early social origin for the schemas that provide the background or vulnerability for disorders. Behavioral, cognitive, and emotional traits may be regarded as part of the premorbid personality or personality disorder. Habitual ways of coping with stress constitute part of the personality and determine the impact of later stress and adaptive or maladaptive outcomes of such stress. Figure 1.7 shows a single pathway system that is similar to Meehl's but distinguishes between genetic and nervous system diatheses and the points at which stress may affect the likelihood of developing a disorder. An aversive or inconsistent social reinforcement schedule may be a source of stress in itself, but the social learning influence may also play a role in the learning of stress-coping mechanisms and the direct modeling of abnormal behavior.

Let us take a hypothetical case of a somatoform disorder as an example. A man inherits an overreactive brain system (the diathesis), producing a general disposition toward neurosis. During the early postnatal period the man suffers an infectious illness. The parents' realistic anxiety during this period is translated into excessive and persistent concern over any sign of illness in the child. The child's somatic symptoms elicit sympathy and provide a rationalization for any behavior that would elicit parental punishment or withdrawal of love under other circumstances. Denial of emotional conflicts is abetted by the somatization of such conflicts. Illness becomes a mode of avoiding conflict, reducing anxiety, and a cognitive rationalization for avoidant social tendencies. Whereas these personality characteristics produce a certain amount of inefficiency for the individual, they are not sufficient to prevent the attainment of an education, a spouse, and a job. However at some point in later adult life, through no individual fault, the job is lost. Somatoform reactions tend to restrict job-seeking efforts. The spouse assumes more of the social and financial responsibilities of the family, but the passivity of the patient draws increasing aversive reactions from the spouse which cause the patient's somatoform reactions to increase in severity to the level of a full-blown somatoform disorder.

The diathesis toward neurosis may have played some role in the disorder, but the early childhood illness and the parental reactions to it may

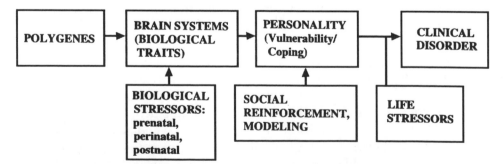

Figure 1.7. Single pathway model showing nongenetic biological stressors acting on brain systems in early development, social reinforcement and modeling to influence personality. Life stressors are the proximal releasing conditions for a clinical disorder.

have influenced the form the disorder eventually took. The proximal stressor was the loss of the job, but the patient's method of coping with the loss and the consequences in the family dynamics potentiated the stress, and, acting on the preexisting personality, produced the particular form of the disorder.

A person with a different diathesis, a different kind of stress in childhood, or a different kind of parental reaction to the same stress, might have developed an agoraphobic or generalized anxiety disorder, a depressive mood disorder, or no disorder at all in reaction to the same proximal stressor.

A somewhat more complicated model (see Fig. 1.8) assumes that whereas some personality development is a function of the same diathesis as that involved in the disorder, this is not necessarily the case. The diathesis for the disorder may be based on a different set of genetic and nervous system factors than those shaping the personality. Another possibility is that there is some overlap in the genotype for some traits but not for others. A genotype for neuroticism–anxiety trait may be common to the disorder and personality but the genotypes for extraversion (vs. introversion) or impulsivity (vs. inhibition) may be unrelated to the genotype for the disorder. The premorbid personality may still interact with the disorder in determining the form it takes and its prognosis, but it is not in a direct causal pathway with the general disorder itself. A normal introversive personality combined with a diathesis of a brain system disposed toward neu-

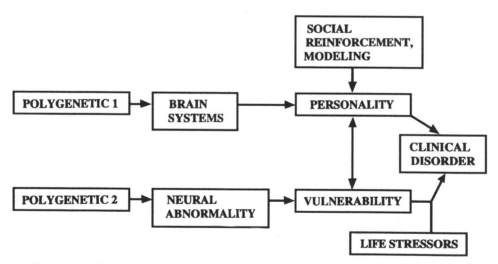

Figure 1.8. Dual pathway model with particular genes influencing specific brain system, while other genes cause a neural abnormality. The first pathway, together with the results of social reinforcement and modeling, results in an abnormal personality, whereas the second pathway creates the vulnerability. The personality and the vulnerability acted on by life stressors create the clinical disorder.

rosis may result in a (socially) avoidant personality disorder, whereas an extraverted personality combined with the same diathesis may develop a histrionic personality disorder. Under stress the avoidant personality may develop a social phobic disorder and the histrionic personality a somatoform disorder.

ANIMAL MODELS

If one assumes that the manifestations and causes of psychopathology are unique to our species, then animal models are useless. But if one assumes an evolutionary continuity in emotional reactions to stress, then animal models are useful in examining the diathesis–stress theories. Different strains of mice or rats, representing specific diatheses (e.g., emotional reactivity or capacity for behavioral inhibition), can be exposed to powerful stress situations involving important biological motivators (e.g., food and pain) and conflicts of a sort which cannot ethically be used with humans. Psychopathology can be induced in animals, but laboratory induced psychopathology in humans must be confined to brief and easily reversible forms. The diathesis itself may be experimentally changed in animals by selective lesioning or chemical alteration of the brain, but in humans, researchers must rely on natural biological variations or drug interventions in those participants who enter their study as "abnormal."

The limitation of comparative research on psychopathology is that we cannot study the role of cognition in the disorders. The rat or monkey cannot tell us how they feel, but characteristic species expressions (facial, behavioral, autonomic) for emotions are fair substitutes for the lack of verbal communication. Of course, it is a leap from animal models to human psychopathology, but if we can identify common biological markers for disorders across species, we have some indication that the disorder may have an evolutionary history.

A species generality in these disorders or in their prototypes would suggest that some of the theories that rely solely on human species-specific attributes, such as repression, Oedipus complexes, cognitive schemas, and so forth cannot be completely accurate. On the other hand, some of the theories derived from humans, such as the role of separation stress or of threat on anxiety and depression, may be compatible with animal models. The theory of "learned helplessness" (Seligman, 1975) was developed from research with dogs and rats but was applied with success to humans, where it provides an explanation of some depressive cognitions and the depressive patient's passivity in response to stressful life situations. Learned helplessness may be translated into cognitive terms in humans and may be useful in psychotherapy with them, but it is fully compatible with a strictly behavioral version seen in animals.

RELEVANT DATA FOR HUMAN MODELS

These and other models will be considered in evaluating the evidence concerning each disorder covered in this volume. Different disorders may be best fitted by different models. The models suggest crucial kinds of information to be sought in the research literature including the following objectives:

1. Ascertain the comorbidity of the disorder with other disorders, including personality disorders, both in the individuals themselves and in their families. The findings on these questions could indicate the breadth of the diathesis and whether the clinical disorder is preceded by a long-standing personality disorder.

2. Ascertain the concordance of the disorder (genetic diathesis) in identical and fraternal twins, as well as the concordance of the disorder between adopted children and their biological and adoptive relatives. These standard biometric methods may be used to estimate whether a genetic diathesis plays a role in the disorder and, if so, its strength relative to the influence of environment. Adoption studies are useful in estimating the influence of a shared environment (particularly within the family), and the influence of common stressors on the disorder.

3. Examine possible prenatal, perinatal, and postnatal conditions that might affect the nervous system diathesis independent of the genetic diathesis.

4. Study biological markers associated with the disorder for clues to the nature of the diathesis. Associations of the markers with personality traits and disorders and other clinical disorders may be indications of a shared diathesis.

5. Focus on concurrent data collected in longitudinal studies on social stress and family interactions during development. Retrospective data may be useful in forming hypotheses, but current data are more reliable sources of information on the role of stress in the eventual disorder because they are less susceptible to a negative bias in recall. Longitudinal studies of high-risk children start with a group of children at risk for a disorder, such as children whose parents have that disorder, and look for factors that differ in the children who develop the disorder and those who do not.

6. Ascertain whether disorders are characterized by particular kinds of personality types or traits, including cognitive and emotional traits. For instance, is there a depressive personality type that is an antecedent of a dysthymic or major mood disorder? Would such a personality type show evidence of depressive cognitive schemas prior to the onset of a depressive disorder? Personality characteristics may change during a disorder, therefore such data should be collected prior to the onset of the disorder or after its remission. The latter is less preferable than the former because some

changes in personality that have developed as a concomitant of the disorder may persist even after recovery from the acute phase of the disorder.

7. Determine whether there is evidence for a proximal effect of stress in the precipitation of the disorder or its relapse after a period of remission. Can stress alone without the presence of an obvious diathesis, predisposing personality, or a history of disorder itself, account for a current disorder? Is there a particular kind of stress that is characteristic in the provocation of the disorder? Do those people with particular disorders respond differently to stress than others? Many theorists propose that it is not the stress per se that is important, but the personality-related modes of adaptation or defense that lead to particular forms of psychopathology. Life stress scales provide a method for evaluating the strength and types of stressors and comparing those who develop the disorder or suffer relapse from those who do not.

8. Refer to treatment insofar as it might suggest some particular etiology of the disorder rather than systematically review treatment. For instance, a drug that has specific effects on a particular neurotransmitter or its receptors and that ameliorates the disorder may suggest the involvement of that system in the etiology of the disorder or some of its symptoms.

SUMMARY

The *diathesis* for a disorder is defined as the genetic predisposition and the biological traits produced by the genetic programming, biological stressors, or both. The diathesis produces a vulnerability to stress. The biological traits that are part of the diathesis do not necessarily have a genetic origin but may be produced by biological stressors during the prenatal, perinatal, or postnatal periods. Others have used diathesis to refer to cognitive predispositions for a disorder, but in this model these cognitive predispositions are relegated to personality predispositions, which may be a function of the diathesis for the disorder or may have their own genetic and environmental origins. *Stress* is often used to refer to both external sources of negative feelings and physiological arousal and to the internal reactions themselves. In this model, it refers only to the external sources or *stressors*. Diathesis–stress models specify the kinds of interaction between the diathesis and stress. The interactive model with a dichotomous diathesis postulates that the diathesis is a necessary but not sufficient condition for the disorder. In the additive model, stress may produce the disorder in a person with a weak or absent diathesis, but it takes much more stress than in a vulnerable person with a strong diathesis.

A third model proposes a quasicontinuous diathesis rather than a dichotomous one and is more compatible with most polygenetic additive models for disorders. Other models differentiate between independent diathesis and the stress that is produced by the diathesis itself. New models are proposed that will incorporate personality and distinguish between distal stressors occurring during development and those that occur in proximity to the disorder. The diathesis–personality–stress model suggests specific questions to be asked of the research literature for each disorder. Models of psychopathology using other species may be useful, particularly in investigating biological bases for the disorders, although they cannot explore the more subjective emotional and cognitive aspects of the disorder, which are accessible only by human self-report.

I have been speaking of *disorders* to designate the subject of this volume. But how do we define a disorder and how do we distinguish one from another? The topic of the next chapter is *diagnosis*. The term itself derives from the medical model of classifying diseases, but also from the biological model of taxonomy. The dimensional model is discussed along with the question of continuity between disorders and traits of personality.

Before we can address questions of causation, we must define the phenomena in question in terms that can be agreed upon. The changing definitions of disorders such as "schizophrenia," and the complete abandonment of "neurosis" as a supraordinate classification emphasize that these disorders are constructs, not tangibles like cancers or elephants. But scientific constructs, as opposed to philosophical or religious ones, must be ultimately defined by physical phenomena no matter how complex the relationships between the phenomena and the construct. To the extent that our provisional definitions are unreliable or inaccurate in describing the phenomena of psychopathology, the explanations of etiology are bound to be erroneous.

2

DIAGNOSIS

The need to classify is not unique to science or to obsessive pedants. Categorization is an essential aspect of human cognition that enables us to connect and organize the complex perceptual world into relative constancies and react to it with the advantage of learned generalizations. But even the simplest categories may be difficult to define in terms of their structural elements. The prototypical image of a chair includes four legs, a seat, and a back support, but the category of chairs can encompass everything from bean-bag chairs to rockers. Definitions based on function also are not free of ambiguities. Chairs are for sitting and beds are for lying, but a bed may be used for sitting and a lounge chair for lying. If a simple concept such as "chair" is difficult to define, what can be expected with a concept such as "schizophrenia?"

There is an invariable loss of information in categorization that does an injustice to the uniqueness of the thing or person being classified, but classification is not necessarily prejudicial. If the categories themselves are not arbitrary, inaccurate, or overgeneralized, they may furnish a base from which to explore the uniqueness of the individual case. Assuming the class can be reasonably defined to fit most—if not all—instances, and assuming there are useful generalizations one can make about members of the class, the concept of categorization can serve a useful function.

Some concepts are based on the degree of a continuous trait and therefore have no meaning outside of reference to some norm. One cannot

25

define *tall* or *short*, for instance, without reference to some standard height, which is further specified by gender and population. A short member of the Watusi tribe might be considered tall, or at least average in height by American standards, and a tall member of the Pygmy tribe would still be short by the same standards. Disorders that are primarily defined by the degree of a single trait, such as anxiety or depression, have a similar problem of arbitrariness unless characteristics other than intensity of affect are used to define them. The medical model is largely a disease model, which usually regards disorders as unique, each with its own underlying causes. Although some symptoms, such as fever, are shared by many different disorders, each disorder has a particular syndrome, or combination of symptoms, by which the clinician may recognize the disorder. Particular signs may then be used to validate the syndromal diagnosis. A clinician may recognize a syndrome such as urinary complaints, use a prostate antigen blood test as a second test, and if that test is positive, use a sonar imaging and a biopsy to validate the diagnosis. Most of the major psychiatric disorders, however, have no final biological criteria to establish a diagnosis, and therefore, must be based primarily on symptoms. A generalized anxiety disorder would be the equivalent of a "fever" disorder in ancient medicine. Of course most medical diagnoses were in the same position prior to the advances made in biology in the 19th and 20th centuries. It is a matter of faith that the psychological disorders described in the *Diagnostic and Statistical Manual of Mental Disorders* (DSM) of the American Psychiatric Association will ultimately be anchored in specific etiological factors, whether biological or psychological. Thus far, many contributing but no necessary causes have been found for any of these disorders.

HISTORY OF MEDICAL DIAGNOSIS

Ancient Greece and Rome

The description of mental disorders within the medical model began in the ancient world (Roccatagliata, 1986). Throughout history most physicians interpreted mental and physical disorders as natural phenomena with both biological and environmental etiologies, as opposed to the result of demonic possession, divine punishment, or other supernatural causes. A natural explanation for illness should reduce stigma and lead to more humane treatment, but this is not always the case. Leprosy and madness were stigmatized in the ancient world just as autoimmune deficiency syndrome (AIDS) and psychosis are today. Some religious institutions such as the Temples of Apollo in ancient times and hospitals providing "moral treatment" sponsored by the Quakers in the 19th century provided more humane treatment than most of the medical asylums of the 19th and 20th centuries. Until the 19th century medical science was based on erroneous theories that led to ineffective and even harmful treatments such as bleeding, purging, and "non-injurious torture" for persons with mental illness.

Hippocrates, known as the father of medicine, was a pioneer in the description of mental disorders. Born 460 B.C., he was the son of a priest in a temple for healing, but he came to oppose divine and supernatural explanations of illness and characterized the priest–practitioners as "swindlers, charlatans, and magicians" who preyed upon hysterical women, professing to cure them with spells and prayers (Roccatagliata, 1986).

In the Hellenistic period, three types of psychosis were diagnosed: mania, melancholia, and phrenitis (Jackson, 1986). The latter was an acute disease associated with fever, whereas mania and melancholia were regarded more as chronic diseases. The descriptions of the delusions of people with mania and melancholia suggest that these diagnoses included some patients who would be regarded as having schizophrenia today. Hippocrates was among those who first suggested that all mental disorders are brain disorders. He distinguished mania and melancholia from disorders following a direct head trauma. In the former, the brain disorder was produced by the action of "humors" (natural body fluids) on the brain.

The humoral theory suggested four vital humors in the body: blood, phlegm, black bile, and yellow bile (see Fig. 2.1). The theory of temperaments related to humors was elaborated several centuries later by Galen, who explained, for example, that black bile had the natural properties of coldness and dryness, and when out of balance with the other humors, produced fear, depression, or torpor. Hippocrates, however, suggested that black bile could also become overheated, producing maniclike symptoms. When the brain is hot, as while drinking or during sex, mood is cheerful, but when it cools, people tend to become depressed (Jackson, 1986). Yet an excess of yellow bile was thought to produce mania through an overheating of the brain with symptoms of motor excitement, euphoria, rage, violent actions, grandiosity, and religious fanaticism. Although Hippocrates conceived of mania and melancholia as opposite states, he did not link them into a single bipolar disorder as modern theorists have done.

Hippocrates associated another disease, *stupiditas*, with an excess of cold and wet phlegm that was produced in the brain itself. Some of the symptoms of this disease—inappropriate laughter, autism, apathy, abulia, aberrant thoughts, and mutism—sound like the primary symptoms of schizophrenia, as described by E. Bleuler (1911/1950).

Like other physicians of his time, Hippocrates regarded hysteria as a female disorder because it was supposedly caused by the uterus and the humors it contained that served the functions of sex and procreation. When these "natural" needs were unfulfilled, as in virgin, sterile, and barren women or young widows, the uterus became dilated and "savage" because of an accumulation of its humors, and the uterus was thought to

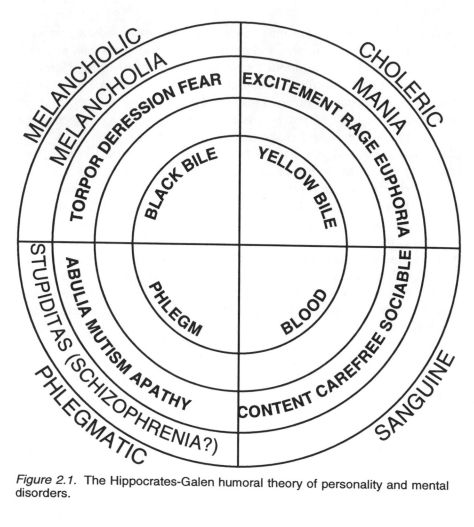

Figure 2.1. The Hippocrates-Galen humoral theory of personality and mental disorders.

wander through the body producing symptoms wherever it lodged. Despite this physiological explanation, Hippocrates advocated a simple behavioral treatment: sexual satisfaction through marriage (the only acceptable outlet for a respectable Greek woman of that era). If this solution was not possible, then the physician could treat the symptoms with purgatives or opium in order to "cool the heated humors." Many centuries later, Freud rejected the uterine theory but came to a similar conclusion about the role of sexual frustration in hysteria, whether in women or men (Breuer & Freud, 1895/1955).

Hippocrates used dream interpretation, not in the fashion of priests as a clue to divine or supernatural signs, but rather as an indication of the current problems in life which might be a source of melancholia. He acknowledged two types of melancholia: one precipitated by stress and emotional reactions, and the other by endogenous changes in humors. The treatment of humors resulted in bleeding and purging to reduce the bad humors, procedures for mental illnesses that persisted through the 18th century. Another holistic approach involved diet, baths, exercise, massage, opiates, moderate doses of wine, and sometimes, a genuine psychological analysis of the patient's sources of emotional upset. As an illustration of the psychological approach, Hippocrates diagnosed a king's secret love for the concubine of his deceased father from the king's dreams. He cured the king's melancholia by getting the king to admit his love for the woman, and by arranging a match between them (no oedipal complications were reported).

Galen, born in 131 A.D. in Pergamum, a Roman city in what is now Turkey, systematized the humoral theory and extended it to normal dimensions of temperament and what we would now call personality disorders (Jackson, 1986). Figure 2.1 shows the system, the four humors, their organ sources, and the traits and disorders associated with them. Three of the humors—black bile, yellow bile, and phlegm—existed in normal and abnormal forms. The ideal temperament contained a balance of all four. A constitutional imbalance of the humors produced a tendency toward certain traits or disorders if extreme. The theory provides a view of continuity between normalcy, personality, and clinical disorders along both biochemical and behavioral dimensions, with the biochemical (humoral) dimension regarded as etiological.

Galen rejected the so-called wandering uterus theory of hysteria but felt that a blocking of the female "semen" produced toxic substances which in turn provoked the hysterical symptoms. He reported curing a woman with melancholia after the death of her husband by manual manipulation of her vagina and clitoris, producing a discharge of "semen" and some great pleasure. But his more conventional treatment used drugs or stimulation of the senses to unblock the sexual humors. He felt that sexual outlet in coitus was necessary for health purposes for both men and women. Unlike Hippocrates, who felt that melancholia could be produced by lack of love, Galen felt that it was blocked sexual expression alone that produced the disorder. Centuries later, the latter concept recurred in Freud's idea of the "actual neuroses." In his initial formulations pure anxiety states were produced by blocked or frustrated sexual outlet, whereas neurasthenia was a consequence of excessive sexual outlet, usually in the form of masturbation.

Medieval and Renaissance Periods

The humoral theory basis for mental disorders persisted for over 2,000 years and was not seriously challenged until the 17th century. Debates continued about which humors or forms of humors were responsible for disorders. Mania in ancient Greece was a description of disordered thought and behavior generally called "madness" and probably included what is today called schizophrenia. Melancholia included what today would be called mood and anxiety disorders. Beginning in the post-Hippocratic times, and during the Middle Ages and Renaissance, a number of physicians noted a form of melancholia that turned into mania. Some regarded mania as an extreme form of melancholia that was produced by the same humor or altered form of black bile. Hypochondria was differentiated from melancholia and was regarded as the male form of hysteria.

The standard treatments for humoral-based disorders continued: purging, vomiting, bleeding, diet, and warm baths. At times the medical viewpoint was mixed with the religious, and prayer supplemented or substituted for medical prescriptions. Divine punishment and demonic possession were competing supernatural theories in explanations of madness or melancholy. Burton's *Anatomy of Melancholy*, published in 1621, classified causes of melancholy as either supernatural (from God, the devil, magicians, witches, stars) or natural (cited in Jackson, 1986). Natural causes of "head melancholy" were further classified as inner and outer. Inner causes included humors, a hot brain, "an excess of venery," agues, and fumes from the stomach. Outer causes are listed as heat of the sun; blows to the head; overuse of wine, garlic, onions, and spices; idleness; solitariness; excessive study and passions (emotions), and perturbations. Hypochondriacal melancholy is listed with its own inner and outer causes.

Eighteenth Century

Following Harvey's discovery of the circulation of blood, the blood became the primary humor, and black and yellow bile and phlegm were regarded as metabolites to be separated by the blood rather than active causal agents. Melancholia was thought to be due to a thick accumulation of blood in the brain and sluggish circulation. Later in the century, scholars' attention shifted to the brain and nervous system. Neural transmission was thought to be a function of neural fluids or gases (animal spirits). The discovery of electricity led to the idea that the nervous system worked through this physical medium. Despite these new theories, the Galenic humoral remedies remained as treatments with perhaps a greater emphasis on bleeding, sedative drugs for sleeping, and the drinking of spa waters to strengthen the "nervous juice." In diagnosis, the definition of hypochondria was broadened to include categories of nonpsychotic disorders (neuroses?) and monodelusional states (paranoid disorders), which were distinguished from melancholia and mania.

Nineteenth Century

In the early 19th century, traditional notions of etiology and treatment were challenged by Pinel and other reformers in the so-called moral treatment movement. Moral causes of melancholia and other disturbances included strong emotions generated by frustrated ambition or love, religious fanaticism, and "domestic misfortunes." The recognition of such causes required a thorough case history on a patient. Diagnoses were simplified to four possibilities: mania, melancholia, dementia, and idiotism. Skeptical about the efficacy of traditional medical treatments like bloodletting, purging, and medications in general, Pinel advocated a kind of moral persuasion (cognitive therapy?) in a hospital atmosphere of pleasant surroundings with entertainments and diverting activities for patients. But traditional medical treatment and theories persisted, as in the ideas of Benjamin Rush, the "father of American psychiatry." Rush believed that the vascular system in the brain was the main source of madness and advocated the usual methods of bloodletting, purging, emetics, reduced diet, and blistering. Psychotherapy at that time consisted of reassuring the patient or challenging delusional thinking with reasoning or ridicule.

From the time of the ancient Greeks to the 19th century, the distinction between delusional and mood disorders was not clear except in subclassifications of mania and melancholia. What would be called schizophrenia today was probably regarded as a kind of chronic mania or melancholia. Henry Maudsley in England made a distinction between two broad diagnostic divisions: affective and ideational. Although Maudsley believed that the distinction was relative rather than absolute, his dichotomy presages the current one between mood disorders and schizophrenia and other delusional disorders. Among etiological factors he included hereditary predisposition, cerebral blood flow disorder, brain disease, alcohol, and opium, as well as overwork and disturbing emotions.

The antecedents of what came to be called "psychoneurotic disorders" included hysteria and hypochondriasis. The success of Mesmer's "animal magnetism" treatment for hysteria (hypnotism and suggestion) in the last part of the 18th century had challenged the traditional medical views of that disorder. Mesmer was labeled a charlatan, and indeed he was, but so were his medical critics from a retrospective view. The theory of neurasthenia, literally regarded as an "exhaustion of the nervous system," came into prominence in the latter part of the 19th century and was treated with mild electrotherapy (to stimulate the nerves) and various baths, tonics, and other treatments based on the assumed etiology of nervous exhaustion.

Kraepelin

Toward the end of the 19th century, German psychiatrists became interested in the systematic description and classification of psychiatric disorders. The most influential of these was Emil Kraepelin. His classifications and definitions of disorders, particularly schizophrenia and mood disorders, are influential in the most recent diagnostic systems embodied in *DSM-III* and *DSM-IV* (Blashfield, 1984). One of the major influences on Kraepelin was the founder of experimental psychology, Wilhelm Wundt. Kraepelin worked in Wundt's laboratory for a time and later applied some of the laboratory measures to the study of psychiatric disorders. Although Kraepelin shared a neurological view of psychiatric disorders with other physicians, he felt that diagnoses should rest primarily on observations of behavior and symptoms.

Other 19th century psychiatrists had described catatonic, paranoid, and hebephrenic types of disorders. Kraepelin grouped all of these as subcategories of what he regarded as a primary brain disease: *dementia praecox*. The *dementia* part of the label referred to his belief that this was a progressively deteriorative brain disease, and the term, *praecox*, indicated that the disorder, in contrast to senile dementias, began early in life (adolescence or early adulthood). He also made the connection between mania and melancholia explicit in the diagnosis: manic–depressive psychosis. Among the involutional psychoses, such as senile dementia, he listed involutional melancholia and presenile delusional psychosis, on the assumption that these were all due to physiological changes associated with aging. He also listed paranoia, a pure delusional disorder without the disorganization of paranoid *dementia praecox*. The psychogenic neuroses included epileptic psychosis; hysterical psychoses; and war neurosis (probably what is now called Posttraumatic Stress Disorder). His category of psychopathic conditions included what we would now call personality and impulse disorders, as well as paraphilic sexual disorders. In addition to these diagnoses, he described psychoses due to infection, intoxication, thyroid conditions, syphilis, other obvious organic sources, and mental deficiency.

Although most of his diagnoses, such as *dementia praecox* and involutional melancholia, were based on an assumed etiology, Kraepelin (1919) admitted that there was wide variation in the symptomatology among actual cases within a particular diagnosis. The process of diagnosis was seen as the matching of an individual case to an ideal prototype for a disorder. He also admitted the uncertainty of the underlying pathology and etiology of the disorders. But he felt that the advance in science would validate or correct the diagnoses. Diagnostic formulations were regarded as hypotheses or starting points for research. This view prevails today among Kraepelin's descendants among the constructors of recent psychiatric classification systems described by Blashfield (1984) as neo-Kraepelinians. But the neo-Kraepelinians have one major departure from Kraepelin. They refuse to use assumed etiology for a disorder as a basis for classification unless there is sufficient evidence to establish the connection between the etiological factor and the current syndrome. This has led to the dropping of some Kraepelinian diagnoses, such as involutional melancholia and psychogenic neuroses, which were differentiated from other disorders on the basis of an unproven etiology.

Freud

Freud was born the same year as Kraepelin, but his approach to psychiatry was quite different. Kraepelin operated from a vague organic theory of etiology. Freud began as a neurologist, but after some success in the study of aphasia turned away from an academic career and began to practice with a particular interest in the disorder called hysteria. After a period in Paris studying with Charcot, he became disillusioned with the neurological explanations for the disorder and began to develop a theory of psychopathology based on a developmental model and emphasizing the continuity of the normal and abnormal. Freud attributed psychopathology to intense conflicts developed in childhood as a consequence of parental suppression of children's sexual and aggressive drives, and children's fear of punishment. Repression and other defenses are subsequently used to avoid anxiety. The fixation at the developmental points of these conflicts weakens the ego and increases the chances of neurotic expressions if the conflicts are reactivated by later events in life. Freud, however, never completely repressed his own biological interests, and his metapsychology used many mechanistic metaphors such as *libido* and *cathexis*. He postulated a constitutional factor in disorders that created a disposition toward fixation at early phases of development and the inability of the ego to defend itself.

Because of his interest in the psychoneurotics, who unlike persons with psychotic symptoms were treatable by the methods of psychoanalysis, he developed diagnostic concepts differentiating among this group. The more severe disorders, such as schizophrenia and manic–depressive psychoses, developed from conflicts at the earliest or oral phase of development when object relations were not secure and ego boundaries with reality were permeable. Obsessive–compulsive disorders developed from the anxiety-driven need for self-control in the anal stage of development. Anxiety-hysteria, conversion-hysteria, and dissociative disorders originated in oedipal conflicts during the phallic phase of development. In addition to symptomatic neuroses, Freud and his disciples described personality types related to personality traits developed during the psychosexual periods. The oral-erotic type is primarily a dependent personality; the anal character is a compulsive or a sadistic type with strong inhibition of emotional expression; the phallic type is egocentric, narcissistic, and aggressive. These theoretical conceptions of psychoneuroses and personality disorders had a marked effect on the first formalized diagnostic system of American psychiatry, which was developed after World War II.

EVOLUTION OF THE *DSM*: *DSM-I* TO *DSM-IV*

Most psychoanalytic and other psychodynamic theorists showed little interest in classification because they felt it was static rather than dynamic and did not do justice to the complex motives and conflicts underlying disorders. Classification has traditionally been linked to a structural medical approach with an assumed organic basis for disorders that psychodynamic followers rejected. The psychodynamic view was not prominent in American psychiatry until the Nazi persecution of the Jews during the 1930s and World War II led to an influx of psychoanalysts from Europe who became influential in training young American psychiatrists in their tradition.

Adolf Meyer, the major influence in American psychiatry in the first part of this century, used the term *psychobiology* to emphasize the complex interaction of biological and environmental (including parental treatment) causes of disorders. Meyer did not regard diagnosis as important and said that it is often used as a substitute for a real understanding of the psychological events and biological mechanisms contributing to the disorder in an individual patient. The behavioral influence on Meyer is apparent in his view of psychiatric symptoms as "faulty reaction patterns" which were the outcome of progressive "habit formations."

Kirk and Kutchins (1992), critics of the *DSM*, describe the history of the psychiatric classification system in America. There was little concern about classification of psychiatric disorders in the middle of 19th century America, and it was done only for statistical or census purposes. In 1840, there was only one diagnosis: idiocy (inclusive of mental deficiency and insanity). But by 1880, the European medical influence is apparent in that there are seven categories: melancholia, mania, monomania, paresis, dementia, dipsomania (alcoholism), and epilepsy. A group of the emerging specialty of medical-psychologists (psychiatrists) produced the forerunner of the *DSMs* in a *Statistical Manual for the Use of Institutions for the Insane* released in 1918. The manual contained 22 primary categories. In 1933, the American Psychiatric Association incorporated most of these categories into the *Standard Classified Nomenclature of Diseases*, which had a total of 24 categories.

DSM-I

During World War II, psychiatrists found the old classification system inadequate for most of the disorders encountered in the military. Only 10% of the disorders encountered in the military fitted the standard categories developed from mental hospital populations (see *Diagnostic and Statistical Manual of Mental Disorders*, 1st ed., American Psychiatric Association [DSM-I], 1952). The Army, Navy, and Veterans Administration each developed their own system, and these were used along with the Standard. Psychiatrists using different systems had difficulties in communication. The first function of a classification system is to provide a field with a means of communication, and the older system was not serving this function. The

American Psychiatric Association, therefore, formed the task force that created the first edition of the *Diagnostic and Statistical Manual of Mental Disorders* (1st ed., American Psychiatric Association [DSM-I] 1952).

The process the association followed in developing the first *DSM* is similar to that in subsequent editions and represents an attempt to guarantee consensus among practitioners. A select committee formulates an initial draft of the manual and submits it to a representative sample of the profession, inviting commentary and suggestions for change. Over 90% of the professionals sampled approved the initial draft, although many suggested changes in specific sections.

Table 2.1 shows selective categories of *DSM-I*—omitting the organic disorders—and traces these categories through the subsequent editions, *DSM-II, III,* and *IV.* The revision of *DSM-III* (*DSM-III-R,* 1987) is omitted because changes from *DSM-III* were not major, and the revised version was recognized as a temporary step on the way to *DSM-IV.*

The major categories in *DSM-I* were labeled disorders, and the subcategories were called reactions. A major category, Psychoneurotic Disorders, for instance, had seven subcategories such as anxiety reaction, dissociative reaction, phobic reaction, and so forth. The term *reactions* was probably derived from Adolf Meyer's diathesis–stress view of the origins of mental disorders. The 1952 manual was notable for the increase in categories of psychoneurotic and personality disorders, reflecting the interests of the postwar practicing clinicians and the growth of outpatient clinics. The addition of a category for psychophysiologic autonomic and visceral disorders, subdivided by organ systems involved, was for the newly emerging field of psychosomatic medicine. A category of transient situational personality disorders was created to accommodate the transient disorders of adjustment to stress common in military personnel during wartime and in the civilian population as well. A primary purpose of the DSMs is to provide terms that reflect the interests, practices, and theories of a particular generation of clinicians. *DSM-I* reflected a shift away from the organically oriented clinicians of the 19th century to the post-Freudian psychodynamic schools of psychiatry. This first *DSM* was driven more by the pragmatics of clinical practice than by scientific data.

DSM-II

The *Diagnostic and Statistical Manual of Mental Disorders* (2nd ed., American Psychiatric Association [DSM-II], 1968) was impelled by the need to make the American classification more compatible with the eighth revision of the *International Classification of Diseases.* Again, a committee was formed to develop the new *DSM,* and it was tested for approval by submitting it to a sample of psychiatrists. There was also input from two consultants, Morton Kramer and Robert L. Spitzer, who represented the

TABLE 2.1
DSM-I to DSM-IV: Selected Diagnoses Tracked Through DSM Versions

DSM-I (1952)	DSM-II (1968)	DSM-III (1980)	DSM-IV (1994)
PSYCHOTIC DISORDERS	PSYCHOSES	SCHIZOPHRENIC DISORDERS	PSYCHOTIC DISORDERS
Schizophrenic Reactions	*Schizophrenia*		*Schizophrenia*
Hebephrenic Type	Hebephrenic Type	Disorganized Type	Disorganized Type
Catatonic Type	Catatonic Type	Catatonic Type	Catatonic Type
Paranoid Type	Paranoid Type	Paranoid Type	Paranoid Type
Residual Type	Residual Type	Residual Type	Residual Type
Chronic Undifferentiated	Chronic Undifferentiated	Undifferentiated	Undifferentiated
Acute	Acute Schizophrenic Episode	*Other Psychotic Disorders*	*Other Psychotic Disorders*
Undifferentiated		Schizophreniform & Brief Reactive Psychosis	Schizophreniform & Brief Psychotic Disorder
Schizoaffective Type	Schizoaffective Type	Schizoaffective Disorder	Schizoaffective Disorder
Simple Type	Simple Type	(Schizotypal Personality Disorder)	(Schizotypal Personality Disorder)
	Latent Type	(Borderline Personality Disorder)	(Borderline Personality Disorder)
Paranoid Reactions	*Paranoid States*	PARANOID DISORDERS	*Delusional Disorders*
Paranoia	Paranoia	Paranoia	(classified by type of delusion)
Paranoid State	Other Paranoid State	Acute Paranoid Disorder	
		Shared Paranoid Disorder	(Shared Psychotic Disorder)
Involutional Psychotic Reaction	Involutional Paranoid State, Involutional Melancholia		
Affective Reactions	*Major Affective Disorders*	AFFECTIVE DISORDERS	MOOD DISORDERS
Manic–Depressive Reactions	Manic–Depressive Illness	Bipolar Disorder	Bipolar Disorders
depressed type	depressed type	Major Depression	Major Depressive Disorder
manic type	manic type	Bipolar Disorder, Manic	Bipolar Disorder, Manic
mixed or circular	circular type	Bipolar Disorder, Depressed	Bipolar I Disorder
		Bipolar Disorder, Mixed	Bipolar II Disorder

Column 1	Column 2	Column 3	Column 4
Psychotic Depressive Reaction	(Psychotic Depressive Reaction)	Major Depression Single Episode Major Depression Recurrent Dysthymic Disorder	Major Depressive Disorder Single Episode Major Depressive Disorder Recurrent Dysthymic Disorder
(Neurotic Depressive Reaction)	(Depressive Neurosis)		
(Cyclothymic Personality) PSYCHONEUROTIC DISORDERS	(Cyclothymic Personality) NEUROSES	Cyclothymic Disorder ANXIETY DISORDERS	Cyclothymic Disorder ANXIETY DISORDERS
Anxiety Reactions	Anxiety Neurosis	Panic Disorder, Generalized Anxiety Disorder	Panic Disorder, Generalized Anxiety Disorder
Obsessive–Compulsive Reaction	Obsessive–Compulsive Neurosis	Obsessive–Compulsive Disorder	Obsessive–Compulsive Disorder
Phobic Reaction	Phobic Neurosis	Simple Phobia, Social Phobia, Agoraphobia Posttraumatic Stress Disorder, Acute or Chronic SOMATOFORM DISORDERS	Specific Phobia, Social Phobia, Agoraphobia Acute Stress Disorder, Post-traumatic Stress Disorder SOMATOFORM DISORDERS
Conversion Reaction	Hysterical Neurosis, Conversion Type	Conversion Disorder	Conversion Disorder
Psychoneurotic Reaction Other	Hypochondriacal Neurosis	Psychogenic Pain Disorder Hypochondriasis	Pain Disorder Hypochondriasis
		Somatization Disorder Atypical Somatoform Disorder	Somatization Disorder Body Dysmorphic Disorder
Dissociative Reaction	Neurasthenic Neurosis Hysterical Neurosis, Dissociative Type	DISSOCIATIVE DISORDERS Psychogenic Amnesia, Fugue Multiple Personality Depersonalization Disorder	DISSOCIATIVE DISORDERS Dissociative Amnesia Fugue, Identity Disorders Depersonalization Disorder

Table continues

TABLE 2.1 (Continued)

DSM-I (1952)	DSM-II (1968)	DSM-III (1980)	DSM-IV (1994)
PERSONALITY DISORDERS	PERSONALITY DISORDERS	PERSONALITY DISORDERS (AXIS II)	PERSONALITY DISORDERS (AXIS II)
Personality Pattern D			
Schizoid Personality	Schizoid Personality	Schizoid Personality Disorder Schizotypal Personality Disorder	Schizoid Personality Disorder Schizotypal Personality Disorder
Paranoid Personality Cyclothymic Personality Inadequate Personality Personality, Other	Paranoid Personality Cyclothymic Personality Inadequate Personality Other Personality Disorders	Paranoid Personality Disorder (Cyclothymic Disorder)	Paranoid Personality Disorder (Cyclothymic Disorder)
		Avoidant Personality Disorder Borderline Personality Disorder	Avoidant Personality Disorder Borderline Personality Disorder
Personality Trait Disturbance	Dependent Personality Disorder	Dependent Personality Disorder Narcissistic Personality Disorder	Dependent Personality Disorder Narcissistic Personality Disorder
Emotionally Unstable Compulsive Personality	Hysterical Personality Obsessive–Compulsive	Histrionic Personality Disorder Compulsive Personality Disorder	Histrionic Personality Disorder Obsessive–Compulsive Personality Disorder
Passive–Aggressive	Passive–Aggressive	Passive–Aggressive Personality Disorder	
Sociopathic Personality Disorder			
Antisocial Reaction Dyssocial Reaction	Antisocial Personality Dyssocial Behavior	Antisocial Personality Disorder	Antisocial Personality Disorder
Sexual Deviations, 8 types including homosexuality	Sexual Deviations, 8 types including homosexuality	PSYCHOSEXUAL DISORDERS sexual dysfunctions, 7 paraphilias ego-dystonic homosexuality	SEXUAL & GENDER IDENTITY DISORDERS 8 paraphilias
			sexual disorders not otherwise specified

		SUBSTANCE USE DISORDERS	SUBSTANCE-RELATED DISORDERS
Alcoholism (addiction)	Episodic excessive drinking	Alcohol abuse	Alcohol abuse
	Habitual excessive drinking		Alcohol intoxication
			Alcohol withdrawal
Drug addiction	Alcohol addiction	Alcohol dependence	Alcohol dependence
	Drug dependence, 8 drugs specified	Drug dependence, 5 drugs listed by abuse and dependence, 3 by abuse only, tobacco by dependence only	Drug dependence, abuse, intoxication, withdrawal specified for 11 drugs
Transient Situational Personality Disorders	TRANSIENT SITUATIONAL DISTURBANCE	ADJUSTMENT DISORDERS	ADJUSTMENT DISORDERS
Gross Stress Reaction	Adjustment Reaction of adult life	with depressed mood	with depressed mood
Adult Situational Reaction	Adjustment Reaction of infancy	with anxious mood	with anxious mood
	Adjustment Reaction of childhood	conduct disturbance	conduct disturbance
	Adjustment Reaction of adolescence	with work inhibition	with work inhibition
	Adjustment Reaction of late life		
PSYCHOPHYSIOLOGICAL DISORDERS	PSYCHOPHYSIOLOGICAL DISORDERS	PSYCHOLOGICAL FACTORS AFFECTING PHYSICAL CONDITION (AXIS III)	GENERAL MEDICAL CONDITIONS (AXIS III)
10 systems (e.g., skin reaction) specified	10 systems (e.g., skin reaction) specified		

biometric interests. This time the committee "tried to avoid terms which carry with them *implications* regarding either the nature of a disorder or its causes and has been explicit about causal assumptions when they are integral to a diagnostic concept" (p. viii). Psychoneurotic *reactions* in *DSM-I* were changed to *neuroses* in *DSM-II*. Arguably *neuroses*, derived from Freud, carries much more causal implication than the term *reactions*, which can include biological vulnerability as well as biological and environmental stress as sources of psychopathological reactions. Similarly, the change from manic–depressive *reactions* in *DSM-I* to manic–depressive *illness* in *DSM-II* seems contrary to the goal of etiological neutrality, because the term *illness* suggests biological causes.

As with *DSM-I*, science played little role in the construction of the categories for *DSM-II*. Few changes other than semantic ones can be seen in the disorders listed in *DSM-II*. The classification of personality disorders into personality pattern disorders, personality trait disturbances, and sociopathic personality disorders, was dropped, but the same personality disorders were listed under the general heading. A new schizophrenic diagnosis, schizophrenia, latent type, and a new neurotic diagnosis, neurasthenic neurosis, were added. These diagnoses were short-lived and were eliminated or transformed in the subsequent *DSM-III* version.

Despite the disclaiming of theoretical influence, the dominance of the psychodynamic view in American psychiatry was apparent in the terminology and descriptions of the syndromes. As in the *DSM-I*, no clear criteria were given for diagnosis. The diagnostic process involved matching a particular patient's symptoms with the prototypical descriptions of the disorders in a paragraph. The weighting of symptoms was left to the discretion of the clinician.

DSM-III

The *Diagnostic and Statistical Manual of Mental Disorders* (3rd ed., American Psychiatric Association [*DSM-III*], 1980) was a marked change, both in conception and form, from *DSM-I* and *DSM-II*. It represented a shift in the dominance of the American Psychiatric Association from the psychoanalytic to the biological and from practicing therapist to research scientist. The reliability studies of both *DSM-I* and *II* revealed a level of reliability that was appalling, at least to the researchers. Not only were there wide disagreements between England and America in prevalence rates, but within the United States, there were wide disparities between states or even hospitals within states. Investigation of the English–American disparity revealed that American psychiatrists, using broad Bleuler-type definitions, were diagnosing schizophrenia in cases that were diagnosed as mood disorders in England (Kendell et al., 1971). Using objective critieria, the English diagnoses seemed to be more on the mark.

Psychiatrists in America could not agree on the major diagnostic category in about 50% of the cases, and agreement on the specific categories was much less (Kreitman, 1961). Ward, Beck, Mendelson, Mock, and Erbaugh (1962) investigated the reasons for disagreements on diagnoses among clinicians. Surprisingly, little of the disagreement among interviewers was due to inconsistency in the behavior of the patients. Rather, a major part was due to differences in the interviewing technique of the clinicians. But the largest proportion of the disagreement was due to the deficiencies of the diagnostic system (*DSM-I*). These deficiencies were carried over virtually unchanged to *DSM-II*. Spitzer and Fleiss (1974), using a reliability statistic (Kappa) developed by J. Cohen (1960), found low reliabilities for the major diagnostic categories of the *DSM-II*.

Researchers began to devise their own diagnostic systems, such as the Feighner et al. criteria (1972) incorporating explicit rules for the diagnosis of 16 categories of disorder. Blashfield (1984) described this group as the "Neo-Kraepelinians" because of their return to the idea of discrete medical disorders, primarily based on underlying biological variations. These psychiatrists advocate the use of modern scientific methods to establish objective diagnostic categories and to improve the reliability and validity of diagnoses (Klerman, 1978). One of their group, Spitzer became the organizer of the *DSM-III* approach to diagnosis.

Spitzer described the basic assumptions of the new approach, disavowing other assumptions (1980). He defined a mental disorder as "a clinically significant behavioral or psychological syndrome or pattern that occurs in an individual and that is typically associated with either a painful symptom (distress) or impairment in one or more important areas of functioning (disability)" (Spitzer, 1980, p. 6). Social deviance alone is denied as a basis for diagnosis.

The establishment of categories of disorder does not assume sharp boundaries between disorders or between disorders and what is considered normalcy. Although this allows for compatibility between dimensional and categorical approaches, it is difficult to see how these two are reconcilable. If boundaries between disorders are fuzzy and the goal is to increase reliability, then arbitrary distinctions must be made to codify discriminations.

All individuals described as having the same disorder are not necessarily alike in all important ways. In fact using the *polythetic* system, sometimes described as the "Chinese menu," two persons with totally different sets of symptoms can receive the same diagnosis. If 4 symptoms in a list of 10 are required, and there is no necessary symptom, then one person can have 4 of these, and another person a different 4, and both can earn the same diagnosis. Specifying a specific number of symptoms required for diagnosis helps reliability, but if that number is arbitrary, it may result in reduced validity due to an unwarranted exclusion of cases falling below that threshold.

For some organic and stress disorders the etiology is known, but for many it is not. The *DSM-III* is claimed to be atheoretical with regard to etiology, and the classifications of disorders with unknown etiologies should not be classified in terms of etiology. The major consequence of this is that the major category of neuroses (based on Freudian theory) in *DSM-II* was eliminated, and its constituent categories each became an independent major category: anxiety, somatoform, and dissociative disorders. Some researchers, like Millon (1991), would argue that it is impossible to develop a taxonomic system that has no theoretical assumptions. If the system had developed from a purely inductive approach and was subjected to neutral statistical methods, such as factor or cluster analysis to define categories, then the only theory would have been in the sampling of symptoms to analyze. In actuality, most of the categories are simply a resorting and renaming of categories recognized in the earlier *DSMs*. For instance, neurotic depressive reaction in *DSM-I* was renamed depressive neurosis in *DSM-II*, but was shifted to the mood disorder category in *DSM-III*, and renamed dysthymic disorder. *DSM-III* and *IV* make a major distinction between mood and anxiety disorders. But from another theoretical viewpoint, and with some empirical support, a case could be made for a major dysphoric disorder classification, combining the two negative affects that are usually found in some combination. Purer cases of anxiety and depression could be subcategories of dysphoria.

The major innovation in *DSM-III* is the multiaxial system. One of the sources of diagreement in the old system was that one had to choose between diagnostic alternatives that were not all incompatible. For instance, one might have an obsessive–compulsive personality disorder preceding but coexistent with an obsessive–compulsive neurosis, *and* a psychophysiological ulcer aggravated by obsessive worrying. The *DSM-III* solves this problem by putting clinical disorders on one axis (I), longstanding personality disorders in adults or developmental disorders in children, on another axis (II), and physical (somatic or physiological) disorders on yet another axis (III). The clinician can make diagnoses on all three or on only one or two of these axes. Axis IV was for the severity of psychosocial stressors, and Axis V was a rating of the highest level of adaptive functioning in the past year. Both of these represent factors which may be predictive of outcome of treatment and the type of treatment needed within any diagnosis on Axes I or II.

A hierarchical system is used so that broad disorders that include many types of symptoms (e.g., schizophrenia) are given a diagnostic priority over narrow disorders (e.g., anxiety disorder, agoraphobia). This strategem increases reliability, but ignores the problem of comorbidity between disorders (Clarkin & Kendall, 1992). If comorbidity is high, as it is between certain disorders, it challenges the validity of the system.

DSM-III describes disorders in terms of information provided by research on factors such as essential features, age of onset, typical course or courses, impairment, complications, predisposing factors, prevalence, sex ratio, familial pattern, and differential diagnosis. More than any preceding volume, the *DSM-III* relied on empirical studies in preference to clinical lore. It did not, however, provide information about theories or research on etiology or treatment.

DSM-III-R

The *DSM-III* was widely accepted in the United States and even in Europe and parts of Asia (Maser, Kaelber, & Weise, 1991). The expansive textbook-like descriptions were useful in teaching and were adopted by many researchers as criteria for definition of research groups. Only 3 years after publication of the *DSM-III*, the American Psychiatric Association formed a work group to begin a revision (American Psychiatric Association, *DSM-III-R*, 1987). The association classifiers have two harsh taskmasters: scientific researchers and clinical practitioners. Some adjustments in the *DSM-III* were dictated by new research findings, but others were made to placate practitioners who wanted distinctions made for treatment or insurance purposes, or simply to calm the outrage over ignoring of their theoretical convictions. The elimination of the term *neurosis* upset the psychoanalytic members of the association, so the solution was to include the term *neurosis* in parentheses. Thus, obsessive–compulsive disorder became obsessive–compulsive disorder (or obsessive–compulsive neurosis). Most of the changes in *DSM-III-R* were simply a fine-tuning of *DSM-III*, changing duration requirements for a disorder, adding new specifications (e.g., primary or secondary, early or late onset for dysthymic disorder), or adding a new symptom. Because of the poor reliability of the personality disorders in Axis II, more behavioral descriptors were added to the general trait descriptors. Some decisions reflect pressures from organized minority groups within the association. For instance, the number of symptoms required for somatization disorder was made the same for men and women (in *DSM-III* fewer were required for men). Ego-dystonic homosexuality was dropped as a diagnosis. The history of the diagnosis of homosexuality throughout the *DSMs* is discussed below.

DSM-IV

Scientific data were more influential in the *Diagnostic and Statistical Manual of Mental Disorders* (4th ed., American Psychiatric Association [DSM IV], 1994) than in any of the previous volumes. Planning for the *DSM-IV* began almost immediately after publication of the *DSM-III-R* (Frances, Widiger, & Pincus, 1989). No longer were the pressures from groups of practitioners sufficient for decisions about the addition or deletion of diagnoses or criteria. Critical reviews were conducted using computer searches of the scientific literature, and positions were argued from data rather than theory or clinical experience. The literature review identified gaps in the knowledge. Researchers undertook 12 field trials at 70 sites to determine whether proposed revisions would actually improve the reliability or validity of diagnoses and their criteria. Parsimony was urged in adding new categories as the DSM constructors recognized that no system can incorporate all the variations of categories or borderline conditions. Unfortunately, there was no move to reduce the already excessive number of categories by statistical analyses.

Among the changes in the *DSM-IV* concerning adult disorders are the following:

1. The term *organic mental disorders* has been eliminated because of the implication of an outmoded dichotomy between organically caused disorders and purely psychogenic disorders. Instead disorders almost certainly due to a simple organic cause are classified by symptom category, for example, *amphetamine induced anxiety disorder*.

2. Various changes were made in duration and nature of symptom requirements for some disorders, presumably on the basis of the literature review and field trials.

3. In the mood disorders, *hypomanic episode* was added with its own criteria set, distinguishing it from mania. Bipolar II disorder has been added and distinguished from bipolar I. Various specific types of bipolar I disorder, classified by the nature of the most recent episode, have been added.

4. In the anxiety disorders, the term *simple phobia* was changed to *specific phobia* and a requirement was added that the phobia stimulus, if unavoidable, elicits intense anxiety or distress "that is excessive or unreasonable." This change illustrates a major problem with nondimensional definitions. What is "excessive" and how much is "intense anxiety?"

5. Acute stress disorder was added to fill in the temporal gap left by the definition of posttraumatic stress disorder, which requires a duration of at least 1 month. Acute stress disorder requires a duration of only 2 days to 1 month after the trauma. Why is it necessary to name a new disorder when the symptoms are identical and the only issue is one of duration? Does the person suffering from acute stress disorder have a different disorder than the one suffering from posttraumatic stress disorder, even though the immediate cause (the traumatic event) is the same for both? Arbitrary temporal distinctions may increase reliability, but their validity is dubious.

6. In the dissociative disorders, psychogenic amnesia and fugue disorders are changed to *dissociative amnesia* and *dissociative fugue* disorders, and multiple personality disorder has been changed to *dissociative identity disorder*, with only slight changes in symptom definitions. The authors of the DSM note the controversy about this last disorder: whether it is a genuine disorder, underdiagnosed in the past, or whether it is one created

by the media publicity for famous cases and overzealous practitioners. The *DSM* does not take a stand on the issue.

7. The paraphilias, dealing with deviant forms of sexuality, have been one of the more contentious areas of the *DSM*s. The *DSM-III-R* did not include homosexuality as one of this group of disorders. Table 2.2 shows how the classification of homosexuality and the other paraphilias has changed through publication of subsequent volumes. In *DSM-I* sexual deviations, including homosexuality, was a subcategory of sociopathic personality disturbance, which was a subcategory of personality disorders. The persons exhibiting such deviations "are ill primarily in terms of society and of conformity with the prevailing cultural milieu, and not only in terms of personal discomfort and relations with other individuals" (DSM-I, 1952, p. 38). *DSM-I* included psychopaths (antisocial reaction) and career criminals (dyssocial reaction) in the same category. In *DSM-II*, no distinctions were made between types of personality disorders, and sexual

TABLE 2.2
The Devolution of Homosexuality in the *DSM*s

DSM-I (1952)
  Personality disorders
    Sociopathic personality disorders
      Sexual deviations
        Homosexuality (others: transvestism, pedophilia, fetishism, sexual sadism, masochism)
DSM-II (1968)
  Personality disorders
    Sexual deviations
      Homosexuality (& others as above)
DSM-III (1980)
  Psychosexual disorders
    Gender identity or role disorders (i.e., transsexualism)
    Paraphilias (i.e., pedophilia, voyeurism, exhibitionism)
    Other psychosexual disorders
    Ego-dystonic homosexuality
DSM-III-R (1987)
  Sexual disorders
    Paraphilias
    Sexual dysfunctions (e.g., inhibited orgasm)
    Sexual disorder not otherwise specified
      1. marked feelings of inadequacy about size of sex organs, sexual performance
      2. distress about promiscuity
      3. persistent and marked distress about sexual orientation
DSM-IV (1994)
  Sexual and gender identity disorders
    Sexual dysfunctions
    Paraphilias
    Gender identity disorder (transsexualism)
    Sexual disorder not otherwise specified
      1, 2, & 3 (as above) [3 = ego-dystonic homosexuality]

---

deviations including homosexuality were simply another type of personality disorder and not grouped with antisocial personality or dyssocial behavior.

In the 1970s the Gay Rights movement began to campaign for a removal of the stigma of psychiatric diagnosis from what they regarded as an alternate lifestyle. This was resisted by psychoanalytically trained psychiatrists and some of the neo-Kraepelinians as well. Kirk and Kutchins (1992) related the inside story of this debate in the American Psychiatric Association as a case study of the political influences in the construction of the *DSMs*. The compromise in the *DSM-III* was that homosexuality was removed from the category of paraphilias. Ego-dystonic homosexuality was listed under the category of other sexual disorders, and defined as a category reserved for those in whom homosexuality "is unwanted and a persistent source of distress [and] . . . for whom changing sexual orientations is a persisting concern" (*DSM-III*, 1980, p. 281). The compromise was still unacceptable to the advocates for gay rights as well as for those who felt that diagnoses should not be based solely on deviance from societal norms or values.

Homosexuality does not appear as such in *DSM-III-R* and *DSM-IV*, but under the category of "sexual disorder not otherwise specified" is description 3. "persistent and marked distress about sexual orientation" (*DSM-IV*, 1994, p. 538). This description is clearly the remnants of ego-dystonic homosexuality. However, the removal of the specific designation seems to have stilled the political protest, even if the issue is unresolved. After all, everything that causes "persistent and marked distress" is not a disorder, and how persistent does the distress have to be? The basic idea for inclusion in the *DSM* is that any complaint that might bring a person to a psychiatrist for treatment should have a number somewhere in the *DSM*. The issue is more insurance than science.

Many of the remaining paraphilias still pose a problem for a system that claims to exclude disturbances representing only a conflict between an individual and society. For the writers of *DSM-I*, deviant sexuality per se was sufficient grounds to diagnose a disorder. *DSM-II* added the idea of compulsion: "Even though many find their practices distasteful they remain unable to substitute normal sexual behavior for them" (*DSM-II*, 1968, p. 44). *DSM-III* states that mere social deviance "may or may not be commendable, but is not by itself a disorder" (*DSM-III*, 1980, p. 6). But in regard to the paraphilias, the writers of *DSM-III* admit that: "frequently those individuals assert that their behavior causes them no distress and that their only problem is the reaction of others to their behavior" (*DSM-III*, 1980, p. 267). So, if there is no distress how can a deviant pattern of sexual behavior be classified as a disorder? In *DSM-IV* (1994) the criteria for every paraphilia state that: "the fantasies, sexual urges, or behaviors cause clinically significant distress or impairment in social, occupational, or other important areas of functioning" (pp. 526–538). Of course this would exempt from diagnosis those whose sexual activity is with consenting partners and has not (as yet) brought them into difficulty with the law, their coworkers and employers, spouses, or families, or caused serious physical harm to themselves or others. The behavior itself does not warrant a diagnosis. But how do such "problems in living" of persons who are different qualify them for a diagnosis? Many persons who behave differently, dress differently, or have different opinions have problems with the law, employers, and their families. Why should a sexual type of deviance be singled out for diagnosis? The DSM is still not value-free, and it cannot be claimed that scientific description is the sole source of its classifications.

Overview of the DSM Evolution

Table 2.1 shows that most of the basic diagnoses have been retained through the nearly half century of the DSMs. Changes in terminology and classifications of specific disorders occur, but the essence of the disorder is identifiable. The major category of neurosis disappears in DSM-III, but most of its constituent disorders are still there under new headings organized by symptoms. The increase in numbers of disorders has been largely due to subdivisions of inclusive categories. For instance, phobic reaction in DSM-I is subdivided into categories of specific phobia, social phobia, and agoraphobia in DSM-III and IV. The conversion reaction in DSM-I is subdivided into conversion disorder, psychogenic pain disorder, hypochondriasis, somatization disorder, and body dysmorphic disorder in DSM-IV. In a deliberate effort to be specific about diagnostic criteria and descriptions in these volumes, DSM-III and IV have subdivided disorders and given very explicit descriptions of symptoms, exclusions, differential diagnostic criteria, and other features of disorders. This expansion of descriptions is reflected in the number of pages of the respective volumes: DSM-I, 130; DSM-II, 134; DSM-III, 494; DSM-III-R, 565; DSM-IV, 886. The purpose of specification is to make diagnosis more reliable. To what extent has the revolution that began with DSM-III accomplished this goal?

RELIABILITY

Although reliability does not guarantee validity, one cannot have a valid diagnostic system in which diagnoses are unreliable, that is, one where clinicians cannot agree on the diagnoses assigned to patients (Spitzer & Fleiss, 1974). One of the major criticisms of DSM-I and II was their lack of reliability. Researchers interested in studying reliably defined groups of patients could not depend on the diagnoses of clinicians and had to devise their own criteria for diagnosis. These more objective systems were the starting points for *DSM-III*.

The idea that reliability is a prerequisite for validity is accepted by psychometricians, with some exception as in retest reliability for state tests (Zuckerman, 1983a). However, is it possible to have too much reliability, or can an emphasis on reliability work to the detraction of validity? The answer is "yes." Internal reliability, for instance, is a measure of factor homogeneity within a test. The more items are alike the more the respondent is likely to endorse them in the same way. This means that a more reliable test is likely to be more restrictive in terms of content area, and therefore less likely to be valid in measuring a broader construct. Similarly, diagnoses may be made more explicit by specifying detailed and concrete criteria on which clinicians can easily agree, but these criteria may be arbitrary and irrelevant to the disorder. We may specify that a patient must have the symptoms for 6 months and be at least 20 years of age, but does a 19-year-old who has had the symptoms for 5 months have some other disorder or no disorder? The specification of duration and age requirements makes for greater reliability but doubtful validity. Similarly, specifying the minimum number of symptoms from a list of symptoms qualifying for the diagnosis is arbitrary, unless based on statistical evidence that this is an optimal cutting point for validity. What is good for reliability can be bad for validity.

The tests for reliability and validity used for psychometric measures are generally applicable to psychiatric diagnosis (Nelson-Gray, 1991), but there are some differences that require different methods. Most psychometric measures involve continuous measurement on ordinal scales, but psychiatric diagnosis is categorical, and, therefore, ordinary correlation methods cannot be used in measuring agreement between diagnosticians (observer reliability) or retest reliability. Short-term retest reliability is obviously important for diagnosis. If a patient is diagnosed as having an anxiety disorder on one day and as having schizophrenia on the next day, it could be due to inconsistency in the diagnostician, or the patient, or ambiguity in the diagnostic criteria; but it does pose a problem in reliability. However, longer term retest reliability may not be applicable to many psychiatric disorders. A personality trait is assumed to be stable over long periods of time during adult life, but a clinical disorder (Axis I) may last only weeks or months. Although it may recur, the time of that recurrence is not predictable. Retest reliability should be more applicable to personality disorders (Axis II), which are conceptualized as long-standing conditions based on extremes of normal traits.

Internal reliability in a test is based on the correlations between responses to the items of that test, or scores based on half of the items compared to scores based on the other half of the items. This assumes that all items are equal as measures of the test construct and that there is only a single factor involved in the scale. Although some diagnoses have lists of symptoms, the assumption of equipotentiality of symptoms is usually not tenable. Some symptoms may be more crucial or weighted more than others. Specific clusters of symptoms may represent alternative forms of the same underlying disorder. Paranoid and catatonic symptoms in schizophrenia, for instance, may not appear together at a given time in the course of the disorder. This would produce low internal reliability for the syndrome. However, internal reliability has not been a matter of much concern to the constructors of the DSMs. The more immediate concern has been interobserver reliability, and the system was redesigned to enhance agreement on diagnoses by making the diagnostic criteria more specific. To what extent have they been successful? Before answering this question I must describe the measure used to assess such reliability:

Kappa

In the older reliability studies, reliability of diagnoses was usually expressed as percentages of cases in which clinicians agreed on the presence of the disorder as opposed to some other disorder or no disorder. This figure is actually a composite of the agreement on the presence of a disorder or *sensitivity* of diagnosis, and the agreement on the absence of a disorder or *specificity* of diagnosis. The problem with this simple statistic was that a certain percentage of those agreements could reflect chance rather than diagnostic sensitivity. If the particular disorder was prevalent in 50% of the cases in a particular hospital, clinicians could attain 50% agreement just by flipping a coin to determine whether or not a patient had that diagnosis. Sometimes clinicians feel they are achieving moderate success with a method that is not really better than chance. After all, they are hitting many of the cases even if not all of them! When base rates become extreme, say 90%, clinicians can attain very high agreement indeed, if they diagnose everyone with the prevalent disorder. However, even if they try to pick out the 10% of cases in which patients do not have the disorder but are operating no better than chance, they will still have an impressively high rate of agreement by chance alone. When base rates are very low, it is nearly impossible to beat the odds no matter how sensitive the procedure (Meehl & Rosen, 1955). Even a small percentage of false positives will add up to a huge number of subjects without the disorder diagnosed as positive. Spitzer, Cohen, and Endicott (1967) suggested the use of the statistic kappa to quantify the reliability of categorical diagnosis controlling for the effects of chance agreement and base rates.

The formula for kappa together with an example is given in Table 2.3. Essentially, kappa is the difference between the achieved level of agreement of two diagnosticians on the presence or absence of a particular disorder and the level of agreement that would be achieved by chance, ex-

TABLE 2.3
Formula for Kappa (κ) Measure of Reliability With Hypothetical Example of Application

$$\kappa = \frac{po - pc}{1 - pc}$$

Diagnostician A	Diagnostician B				Total Proportion	
	Psychotic		All Others			
Psychotic	106 (.53)	(.39)	14 (.07)	(.21)	120	(.60)
All Others	24 (.12)	(.26)	56 (.28)	(.14)	80	(.40)
Total Proportion	130 (.65)		70 (.35)		200	(1.00)

Note. From "Quantification of Agreement in Psychiatric Diagnosis," by R. L. Spitzer, J. L. Cohen, & J. Endicott, 1967, *Archives of General Psychiatry, 17,* p. 86. Copyright 1967 by American Medical Association. Reprinted by permission. $po = 53 + .28 = .81$; $pc = .39 + .14 = .53$; κ for psychosis = $\frac{.81 - .53}{1 - .53} = \frac{.28}{.47} = .596$. κ = Kappa; po = observed proportion of agreement; pc = chance expected proportion of agreement (p placed in category by Diagnostician A × p placed in category by Diagnostician B).

pressed as a proportion of the possible proportion of agreement beyond chance. The kappa statistic has been criticized on a number of grounds (see Blashfield, 1984, and Kirk & Kutchins, 1992, for summaries and illustrations) including its influence by the base rates of the actual disorder in the population. Critics have argued that the statistic is not applicable when base rates of disorders are low as in community studies, but alternative measures that have been proposed do not solve the base-rate problem and are less interpretable than kappa (Shrout, Spitzer, & Fleiss, 1987). Despite criticisms of kappa, it has become the nearly universal reliability statistic in the field of psychiatric diagnosis, and therefore, the only one that can be used for comparability of outcomes of the reliability studies done using the pre-*DSM-III* criteria and the *DSM-III* and *III-R* criteria.

Comparisons of Reliabilities of DSM-I and II Versus DSM-III and III-R

The first field trials of the *DSM-III* were reported in the manual (1980, Appendix F). The trials were done in two phases (see I & II in Tab. 2.4). The reliability studies in the second phase may have benefited from some tightening of the criteria based on the Phase 1 study. Each patient evaluation was conducted by two clinicians; about two thirds of the interviews were done separately, and about one third were done jointly. Reliabilities for some types of disorder such as schizophrenia were the same

TABLE 2.4
Comparisons of Reliabilities of Diagnoses in *DSM-I* and *II*-based Studies and Studies Based on *DSM-III* and *DSM-III-R*

Diagnoses	Spitzer & Fleiss (1974)	Field Trials		Robins et al. (1981)	Hyler et al. (1982)	Williams et al. (1992)	Rice et al. (1992)[a]
		Phase 1	Phase 2				
Mental deficiency	.72	.80	.83	—	—	—	—
Organic brain disorder	.77	—	—	.79	.55	—	—
Alcoholism/Substance abuse	.71	.86	.80	.86	—	.75	.70
Schizophrenia	.57	.81	.81	.60	.69	.65	.57
Affective disorders	.41	.69	.83	—	—	—	—
MD	.24	—	—	.63	—	.64	.61
Dysthymia	.26	—	—	—	—	.40	—
Mania	.33	—	—	—	—	.84	.60
Anxiety disorders	.45	.63	.72	.67	.66	.56	.30
Agoraphobia	—	—	—	.47	—	.43	—
Simple phobia	—	—	—	—	—	.52	.34
PD	—	—	—	.40	—	.58	.37
OCD	—	—	—	.60	—	.59	.27
Somatoform disorders	—	.54	.42	.50	.64	.57	—
Personality disorders	—	.56	.65	—	—	—	—
APD	—	.87	.65	.63	—	—	.33
Paranoid/Delusional	—	.66	.75	—	.65	.69	—
Overall Kappa	.54	—	—	—	.67	.61	—

Note. MD = major depression; PD = panic disorder; OCD = obsessive–compulsive disorder; APD = antisocial personality disorder. Data from "Reliability in the *DSM-III* Field Trials," by S. E. Hyler et al., 1982, *Archives of General Psychiatry, 39*, p. 1276. Copyright 1982 by American Medical Association; "Stability of Psychiatric Diagnoses," by J. P. Rice et al., 1992, *Archives of General Psychiatry, 49*, p. 826. Copyright 1992 by American Medical Association; "National Register of Mental Health Diagnostic Interview Schedule," by L. N. Robins et al., 1981, *Archives of General Psychiatry, 38*, p. 386. Copyright 1981 by American Medical Association; "Research Diagnostic Criteria: Rationale and Reliability," by R. L. Spitzer et al., 1978, *Archives of General Psychiatry, 35*, p. 779. Copyright 1978 by American Medical Association; "The Structured Clinical Interview for *DSM-III-R (SCID)* II. Multisite Retest Reliability," by J. B. W. Williams et al., 1992, *Archives of General Psychiatry, 49*, p. 635. Copyright 1992 by American Medical Association. All of the above adapted and reprinted by permission.
[a]6-year interval between diagnostic interviews.

for both types of interview, but the kappas for affective and anxiety disorders were much lower when separate interviews were done (Spitzer, Forman, & Nee, 1979). Table 2.4 shows the reliabilities for the field trials on *DSM-III* compared with those for similar disorders defined by *DSM-I* and *DSM-II* (Spitzer & Fleiss, 1974). The reliabilities for most of the major disorders on Axis I were quite good, especially in the Phase II studies, and markedly improved for affective and anxiety disorders compared to the older *DSM* studies. Somatoform disorders on Axis I and personality disorders on Axis II showed less than satisfactory reliabilities, and those for specific personality disorders, with the exception of antisocial PD, were quite low, with kappas ranging from .26 to .75.

Structured interview methods combined with computer programs were developed to increase reliability. Robins, Helzer, Croughan, and Ratcliff (1981) used the Diagnostic Interview schedule which is easily scored and can be entered into a computer where diagnostic programs are applied. This method was used in a retest design in which trained lay interviewers and psychiatrists interviewed the patients separately on two different occasions. The authors compared the *DSM-III*, Feighner, and research diagnostic criteria (RDC) criteria for the disorders diagnosed. The resulting kappas for agoraphobia, schizophrenia, obsessive–compulsive disorder, antisocial personality, and depression were in the satisfactory .60–.67 range; but those for panic disorder, simple phobia, and somatization were poorer (.40–.50). Since the interviews were interpreted by computer the disagreements could have been a function of interviewers or patients. Kappas were highest for alcohol abuse, drug abuse, and alcohol and drug dependence and lowest for some of the anxiety disorders and somatization disorder, in which symptoms are more varied and less behaviorally obvious.

Hyler, Williams, and Spitzer (1982) compared the interview and case history as sources of diagnoses using *DSM-III* criteria. In the case of most disorders, the case summary method of diagnosis yielded lower kappas than the interview method, the one exception being the affective disorders in which kappas were nearly the same. The overall kappa for the interview method was .67 and that for the case summary was .47. There was no difference in reliabilities of interviews done jointly or consecutively (retest).

Williams et al. (1992) used the Structured Clinical Interview for *DSM-III-R* (SCID) in a multisite test–retest reliability study. As in other studies, reliabilities for alcoholism and drug abuse disorders are high, schizophrenic and major mood disorders moderate, and those for anxiety and dysthymic disorders poor to fair. An overall kappa was .61, indicating no improvement in reliability of the *DSM-III-R* over the *DSM-III*. Comparing their results with the studies of RDC, *DSM-III* with or without structured interviews, the authors were surprised that their reliabilities were not higher.

Rice, Rochberg, Endicott, Lavori, and Miller (1992) used the term *stability* rather than reliability to describe their 6-year blind reinterview-based diagnoses of first degree relatives of patients who had mood disorder diagnoses. Instability of diagnosis may reflect a true change in diagnostic state rather than merely error in the instrument, observers, or inconsistency in the patients reporting. However, since they used a lifetime version of the schedule for affective disorders and schizophrenia (SADS) on both occasions, the failure to report past states sufficient to meet the criterion could reflect an instrument or patient recall problem. The most stable diagnoses with the highest kappas were alcoholism, major depression, and mania, with kappas of .70, .61, and .60, respectively. Of those diagnosed with alcoholism at Time 1, 80% still received that lifetime diagnosis 6 years later. The percent of stable diagnoses was 74% for major depression. Two factors independently predicted stability of diagnosis for major depressive disorder: number of symptoms at the initial evaluation and whether or not the relative was hospitalized and received medication or electroconvulsive therapy. There was a linear relationship between number of symptoms and stability of diagnosis from three symptoms (53% stable) to 8 symptoms (91% stable). Hypomania showed the same kind of relationship between number of symptoms and stability of diagnosis. Those who were hospitalized and treated were more stable in diagnosis. In other words, those with the more severe expressions of the disorder at Time 1 were most likely to receive the same lifetime diagnosis at follow-up. The authors assume that underlying the diagnostic dichotomy (presence or absence) is a continuum of liability to the disorder with diagnosis merely reflecting agreement on a threshold value. This *latent dimensional approach*, often used in genetic models, is discussed later in this chapter.

Comparing the reliabilities (kappas) reported in the pre-1974 era (Spitzer & Fleiss, 1974) with those reported since the use of more specific criteria and structured diagnostic interviews, it is apparent that there has been some improvement in every category of diagnosis except organic brain syndrome (in which the criteria were more specific in the *DSM-II*). However the studies of the 1980s and 1990s showed less dramatic increases than those of Helzer et al. (1977) and Spitzer, Endicott, and Robins (1978) done using the Feighner and RDC criteria. Some diagnoses such as schizophrenia and anxiety disorders are still less than optimal in reliability. In the typical psychiatric setting the diagnoses are made without a structured interview and less systematic application of the criteria in the *DSM* manual; therefore, the reliabilities reported in these studies are probably maximum values to be expected in common clinical practice.

Reliabilities of Personality Disorders (Axis II)

Reliability of the presence or absence of any personality disorder (PD) in the *DSM-III* field trials was .61 (kappa) based on a joint interview and

.54 based on a test–retest situation. Reliabilities were not provided for specific personality disorders. Since that time several structured interviews have been developed to facilitate the diagnoses of PDs. Zimmerman (1994) reviewed the studies of PD reliabilities done using these instruments. His results are summarized in Table 2.5. Fifteen studies using a joint interview technique yielded an average kappa of .75 for the presence of any personality disorder and average kappas ranging from .62 for the paranoid PD to .77 for the antisocial PD; 59% of the kappas for all of the studies were at or above .70; and 79% were at or above .60. Four studies using a short-interval retest method yielded much lower reliabilities. The average kappa for presence of any PD was .56; only 28% of the kappas were at or above .70, and only 42% were at or above .60. For the longer interval studies ranging from 1 week to 3 years between interviews, the average kappa for any PD was .57; only 11% of the kappas were above .70, and only 22% were at or above .60. The reliabilities of PD diagnoses do show a considerable attrition with time in seeming contradiction to the idea that these are the long-standing disorders in contrast to the clinical disorders on Axis I. The only PD that held up over time was the antisocial PD. Paranoid PD did not show much change in reliability from the joint interview value, which was somewhat low already. PDs such as schizotypal and narcissistic,

TABLE 2.5
Reliability Studies of *DSM-III* and *DSM-III-R* Personality
Disorders (PDs)

	Mean PD Kappa Coefficients		
	Joint Interviews	Short Interval Test–Retest	Long Interval Test–Retest
Number of studies	15	4	5
Any PD	.75	.56	.56
Paranoid PD	.62	.56	.57
Schizoid PD	.74	—	—
Schizotypal PD	.75	.69	.11
Obsessive–compulsive PD	.69	.35	.52
Dependent PD	.75	.59	.15
Antisocial PD	.77	.77	.84
Narcissistic PD	.69	.54	.32
Histrionic PD	.76	.59	.40
Borderline PD	.73	.60	.56
Passive–aggressive PD	.70	.45	.16
Avoidant PD	.68	.63	.41

Note. From "Diagnosing Personality Disorders," by M. Zimmerman, 1994, *Archives of General Psychiatry, 51*, p. 231. Copyright 1994 by the American Medical Association. Adapted with permission.

which would be expected to be enduring, showed dramatic drops in reliability in the long-interval test–retest studies. We cannot blame the instruments for this instability because in the joint interview method, the reliabilities were high. Just as anxiety disorders may represent states rather than traits, many of the personality disorders may be more changeable than previously thought. If personality disorders are no more stable than clinical disorders, then they may be quantitative variations of clinical disorders challenging the whole rationale for the separation of Axis I and Axis II. Thus, reliability studies may also have implication for the validity of *DSM* diagnosis.

VALIDITY

Robins and Guze (1970), in a now classic paper, outlined five phases of validation for diagnostic systems. The term, *phases*, may be misleading because there is no particular ordering of the phases beyond the first one, and research in most disorders proceeds in a parallel fashion rather than in a sequence across these areas. The first phase is agreement on what is to be included in the clinical description of a disorder. In psychometrics this is called "content validity." Constructors of the *DSMs* resolved this through committees or task forces assigned to particular diagnoses. *DSM-III-R* and *IV* have increasingly depended on clinical research findings for deciding on which diagnostic criteria to include in a disorder category.

The second phase consists of researchers conducting laboratory studies looking for biological or psychological tests that show a high degree of sensitivity to specific disorders and high specificity in discrimination of other disorders. This goal has not yet been achieved for most of the disorders. If such reliable tests could be found, the existing symptomatic criteria could be modified to maximize prediction of the test rather than the other way around. Meehl calls this the "bootstrap approach." Assessment of validity in reference to a fixed standard is called "criterion validity" in psychometrics, but is not considered appropriate for tests intended for a broad range of applications. In medicine, there are definitive laboratory tests for certain conditions, such as biopsy for cancer, but as yet, there are no "gold standards" against which most psychiatric diagnoses can be compared. Even if laboratory tests do not show sufficient sensitivity or specificity to use them as diagnostic criteria, they may contribute to our understanding of the etiology of the disorder through the association with biological traits. The testing of hypotheses relevant to etiology would be called "construct validity" in psychology.

The third phase is delimitation from other disorders. In psychology, this necessary step is called "discriminant validity" in contrast to "convergent validity." In psychiatry, it corresponds to "specificity" in contrast to "sensitivity,"or "true negatives" in contrast to "true positives." Assigning a diagnosis that is not correct, in terms of eventual definitive evidence, is a "false positive," and incorrectly concluding that the diagnosis is absent or some other diagnosis is present is a "false negative." In deciding whether to attempt to minimize false positives or false negatives, researchers and clinicians need to consider the relative risks involved in either choice. False positives, for instance, can result in the wrong treatment being given to too many people, and false negatives may lead to needed treatment being withheld for too long.

The fourth phase consists of follow-up studies to test the homogeneity of prognosis for persons diagnosed with the disorder. In psychology this is called "predictive validity." If prognoses are variable for persons with the same diagnosis, it could indicate that more than one disorder is subsumed under the diagnosis, and at least the designation of subsidiary diagnoses should be considered. However, a variable outcome by itself is not necessarily the indication of more than one disorder subsumed under a diagnosis. A medical disease such as cancer may have a variable outcome, particularly if treated. Individual variations in the strength of immune systems and other factors could account for the different outcomes.

The fifth phase is family studies. Whether causes are genetic or environmental, the tendency of a specific disorder to occur with greater than chance frequency in close relatives of a patient is evidence of diagnostic validity. If other disorders are also found in the same families, then there is a possibility that these disorders are related through some kind of superordinate diagnoses. These studies are a starting point for "construct validity," because they begin to address theories of the etiology of the disorder in either genetic transmission or family environment. More specific separation of the genetic and shared environmental influences can be obtained through twin and adoption studies. Family studies using genetic linkage markers are even more specific and have the potentiality of finding a specific gene responsible for a disorder. These studies require large families with some members affected by the disorder. All diseases where linkage studies were successful relied on a simple Mendelian model with a single gene locus. Most psychiatric disorders appear to be polygenic and perhaps too complex for these models at present. The identification of major genes involved in a polygenic disorder or trait, however, is now possible (Plomin, 1995) with some results for some forms of psychopathology described in subsequent chapters.

Robins and Guze (1970) did not include outcome of treatment as a sixth type of validity study. One of the main functions of diagnosis is to provide a means of selecting the most appropriate treatment for a case. Some treatments are supposedly specific for certain disorders, such as anxiolytic drugs for anxiety disorders, antidepressants for mood disorders, antipsychotics for schizophrenic disorders, and lithium as a prophylaxis for bipolar mood disorders. Many psychotherapies, particularly psychodynamic ones, have been nonspecific, and essentially the same methods are applied to different types of disorders. In contrast, the current trend is to design particular types of behavioral, cognitive, or interpersonal treatments for specific kinds of disorders. A valid diagnostic system should maximize prediction of outcome of specific treatments.

This approach is somewhat complicated by the findings that what are regarded as specific treatments may cross diagnostic lines. For instance, certain antidepressants have been found to be more effective than the standard anxiolytic drugs in treating some of the anxiety disorders such as panic and obsessional disorders. Does this mean that these anxiety disorders really belong in the major category of mood disorders, or simply that anxiety and depression have some common as well as some specific etiologies? These kinds of questions carry us from questions of utility into the area of construct validity.

The ultimate criterion for a medical model "disease" is one directly related to the etiology. Cold, flu, and pneumonia may have many symptoms in common, as do the various anxiety disorders (T. A. Brown & Barlow, 1992). Yet in the case of medical disorders, each illness has a distinctive necessary cause, and only a test that is sensitive and specific to the source of the illness can be completely valid. Unfortunately, the specific etiology, whether it be a gene or child abuse, is unknown for most of the disorders considered in this book. Indeed, it is possible that there is no one specific causal agent for many, most, or all of them. A diathesis–stress theory suggests that both biological and environmental factors are necessary to produce a disorder.

Of course, physicians have diagnosed and treated diseases for countless centuries, during which various theories based on immature science and flawed practice prevailed. In the absence of an accurate understanding of etiology, such diagnoses were inaccurate and treatment was ineffective if not fatal. Indeed, many disorders defined solely by clinical description of onset and symptoms were valid long before their etiology was understood. Paresis was differentiated from schizophrenia and mania before its specific etiology in a syphilitic infection of the brain was known. Will the same kind of success be obtained for *DSM* diagnoses such as panic disorder, schizophrenic disorder, and bipolar mood disorder? Perhaps, but in the meantime, we must proceed with an imperfect construct based on what we can observe.

Comorbidity

Kendell (1989) raises a question regarding the medical categorization approach to mental disorders:

One important possibility is that the discrete clusters of psychiatric symptoms we are trying to delineate do not actually exist but are as much a mirage as discrete personality types. We are reluctant to take this possibility seriously, partly because the whole weight of medical history is against it. Even so, we ignore the possibility at our peril. . . . The old aphorism that classification is "the art of carving nature at its joints" loses its force if nature has no joints. (pp. 314–315)

The widely acknowledged comorbidity of many psychiatric disorders questions the whole notion of discrete psychiatric disorders or at least the current basis for establishing these categories. *Comorbidity* is usually defined as the co-occurrence of two or more disorders in the same individual (T. A. Brown & Barlow, 1992). The term, however, may be used in the the sense of occurrence of the disorders at the same period of time or at different points in time. The designation of a primary and secondary diagnosis may depend on chronological (which occurs first), causal (which is presumed to be causal), or severity (which causes more distress or disability) criteria. Much of the comorbidity may be due to overlapping criteria for different disorders in the *DSMs* (Shea, Widiger, & Klein, 1992). However, some may be due to shared etiologies.

Earlier theories have suggested that anxiety is a basis for many kinds of other symptoms, so it is not surprising that it is a diagnosable component of other disorders. The common components in many disorders may have accounted for much of the diagnostic unreliability of *DSM-I* and *II*. The *DSM-III* attempted to eliminate this source of disagreement by establishing exclusionary rules. For instance, if symptoms meeting the criteria for panic disorder occur in the context of a schizophrenic episode, as is often the case in acute schizophrenia, the diagnosis of panic disorder is not made because the panic is considered an expression of the more serious disorder rather than a comorbid disorder. But suppose a schizophrenic with only residual symptoms experiences panic attacks. Does this mean that the patient should be treated with increased dosages of antipsychotic medication or the antidepressants shown to be effective in the treatment of panic attacks?

Kendell (1989) suggests a natural hierarchy of symptoms based on chronology. Kendell's hierarchy begins with mood changes, such as anxiety and depression, followed by phobias, obsessional rituals, agitation, severe insomnia, apathy, anhedonia, retardation, and attention difficulties. The exclusion criteria for the *DSMs* are generally the reverse of these, going from schizophrenia and major mood disorders, to anxiety and less severe mood disorders such as dysthymia. Undoubtedly there is more than one dimension of psychopathology, but the idea does suggest a dimensional approach that reduces the number of dimensions from the hundreds of categories in the *DSMs*.

Using the data from a large epidemiological community study, Boyd et al. (1984) found that when the exlusionary criteria of *DSM-III* were suspended, the presence of nearly any disorder increased the patient's chances of being diagnosable with another disorder. In those disorders where the connection was recognized by exclusionary criteria, the co-occurrence of the primary and excluded disorder was even more probable than for disorders where no exclusion was stated.

Extensive comorbidity of disorders was found in the two largest community epidemiological studies done in the United States. Robins, Locke, and Regier (1991) found that 60% of their interviewees who had at least one disorder during their lifetimes had at least one or more other disorders. Kessler et al. (1994) reported that 56% of their community respondents who had one disorder had at least one other disorder. Zimmerman and Coryell (1989) examined the comorbidity of personality disorders (PDs) in a nonpatient sample, most of whom were first-degree relatives of patient groups. Nearly all of the correlations between Axis II dimensional scores were significant, and comorbidity was the rule rather than the exception for nearly every PD except the schizoid and the dependent PDs, in which about 70% of the cases studied had no additional PD diagnoses.

Comorbidity is high among patient populations where most studies have been of particular disorders. High rates of comorbidity have been found among anxiety disorders and between anxiety disorders and mood disorders. Of patients diagnosed with an anxiety disorder using *DSM-III-R*, 70% received at least one additional Axis I disorder (Sanderson, DiNardo, Rapee, & Barlow, 1990). The most common additional diagnoses were social and simple phobias, but one third of the anxiety patients received an additional diagnosis of a depressive mood disorder (dysthymia or major depression). Sanderson and Wetzler (1991) reviewed studies of comorbidity in generalized anxiety disorder (GAD). These studies report comorbid diagnoses in 45–91% of GAD cases. Simple and social phobias were the most common comorbid Axis I disorders, and dysthymia and major depression were also frequent. The authors suggest that GAD might be regarded as a personality disorder because patients typically have life-long histories of anxiety proneness. Wetzler and Sanderson (1995) did a similar review of comorbidity for panic disorders. Comorbid diagnoses were found for 46–83% of patients with PDs, with simple and social phobias, GAD, and depressive disorders common. It should be noted that a majority of panic disorders are accompanied by agoraphobia, a common development of these disorders. T. A. Brown and Barlow (1992) noted that comorbid depressive disorders are more frequent in the more severe PD and agoraphobic disorders than in PD without agoraphobia, or in PD with mild agoraphobia. Conceivably, the depression could evolve from the life restrictions and feelings of helplessness engendered by the agoraphobic house confinement.

Sanderson, Beck, and Beck (1990) studied comorbidity when dysthymic or major depressive disorders are the primary diagnosis. Among patients with dysthymic disorders, 65% had at least one comorbid Axis I diagnosis, and among those with major depressive disorders, 59% had additional diagnoses. In nearly half the cases the additional diagnoses were anxiety disorders, most commonly GAD or social phobia. The next most common class of comorbid disorders (11–15%) was substance abuse or dependence, usually alcohol abuse. When depressive and anxiety disorders were comorbid, the depressive disorder preceded the onset of the anxiety disorder in 77% of the cases of patients with dysthymia and 60% of the cases of major depression. These chronological data should not be taken as evidence of etiological priority for depression. Apart from the fact that this was a group selected on the basis of a primary depressive disorder, the age of onset of dysthymia is earlier than that for anxiety disorders.

This comorbidity among anxiety disorders is not unexpected because all are assumed to be different expressions of the common component of anxiety. Nevertheless, anxiety and mood disorders constitute two major classes, presumably with distinctive phenomenologies, etiologies, and treatments. Their comorbidity poses a challenge to the validity of the categorical system of diagnosis. One solution is to propose a new diagnostic category: mixed anxiety–depression (Katon & Roy-Byrne, 1991). Although it preserves the categorical system, this solution may compound the problem and make the diagnostic process even more cumbersome. We can anticipate that this category, as with the schizoaffective, would require three subcategories: primarily depressive, primarily anxious, and equally mixed.

Clark and Watson (1991) studied the phenomenological overlap between depression and anxiety in self-report tests and clinical ratings. As expected, the overlap is extensive, particularly for the self-report measures, which usually reveal a factor of general negative affect and a relatively independent factor of positive affect. Actually, Zuckerman and Lubin (1985) were able to distinguish subfactors of anxiety, depression, and hostility among the adjectives of the revised *Multiple Affect Adjective Check List* (MAACL-R). They also found a positive affect factor. The three negative affect factors were highly intercorrelated, but corrections for the response set of number of items checked reduced the correlations to a moderate level. Other methods have also succeeded in distinguishing anxiety and depression in self-reports, although scales based on these factors are usually correlated. Clark and Watson conclude that "anxious and depressive syndromes share a significant nonspecific component that encompasses general affective distress and other common symptoms, whereas these syndromes are distinguished by physiological arousal (specific to anxiety) versus the absence of PA [positive affect] (specific to depression)" (1991, p. 331).

It is not clear that physiological arousal distinguishes anxiety from all types of depression. Patients with agitated depression, but not those with retarded depression, exhibit levels of physiological arousal that are as high as that in the most severe anxiety cases (Kelly, 1980; Lader, 1975). The absence of positive affect is useful in differentiating depressive and anxious patients. Zuckerman and Lubin (1985) used the MAACL-R score of *depression minus positive affect* to differentiate patients with depression from other patients, with considerable success. The use of the depressive scale rather than the general negative affect score (including anxiety and hostility as well as depression) enhanced the discrimination of the depressive disorder group from the other patients, including anxiety disorders (Lubin, Van Witlock, & Zuckerman, in press).

Clark and Watson propose two *mixed anxiety–depression* diagnoses: (a) *mild* (or moderate), with general negative affectivity but without physiological arousal or anhedonic symptoms, and (b) *severe*, with both physiological arousal and anhedonic symptoms (presumably the agitated depressives). Whatever the criteria, the problems of comorbidity could be more parsimoniously resolved by a dimensional system rather than by adding mixed categories to accommodate the fuzzy boundaries between the major disorders. Clark and Watson identify three such dimensions that could be used: negative affect, positive affect, and physiological arousal.

One of the vexing diagnostic problems that is still not completely resolved is the comorbidity of schizophrenia and the bipolar mood disorders. Narrowing the definition of schizophrenia to concrete symptoms such as experiencing delusions, hallucinations, and thought disorder has helped but not resolved the problem because some patients with mood disorders also present psychotic symptoms. Boyd et al. (1984) showed that when exlusionary rules are suspended, manic episodes are very frequently diagnosable in schizophrenics. Other significantly comorbid diagnoses include panic disorder, major depressive episode, and agoraphobia. The compromise diagnosis of schizoaffective disorder was introduced to accommodate the large number of patients who were sometimes manic or depressed, with or without accompanying psychotic symptoms, and those who were sometimes simply psychotic without manic or depressive mood states. Although sharing some of the features of both disorders, the diagnosis of schizoaffective was separated from these two major classes of disorder and described under "other psychotic disorders."

Substance abuse and dependent disorders are also highly comorbid for schizophrenia (Mueser, Bellack, & Blanchard, 1992). Substance abuse and dependence (lifetime prevalence) in the general population is about 17%; in those with anxiety disorders it is 24%; in those with affective disorders, 32%; and in patients with schizophrenia, 47% (Regier, Farmer, et al., 1990). The chronological sequence of schizophrenia and substance abuse is important in making inferences about etiology because many drugs, especially stimulants, as well as alcohol can produce psychoses and weaken controls in those people already predisposed to psychosis. Regardless of causality, drug abuse and dependence require special kinds of treatment, and a comorbid diagnosis should not be minimized. Similarly, the drug abuse problem comorbid with other disorders should be recognized as one demanding treatment regardless of its etiological role.

Comorbidity of Axis I and Axis II Disorders

Axis I and Axis II disorders are regarded as independent in the DSMs, so that comorbidity between disorders across the two axes is acceptable. Since some Axis I disorders closely resemble some of the personality disorders (e.g., social phobia and avoidant personality disorder), they may be regarded as mutually exclusive or a matter of cronology or severity. Apart from this type of problem, such comorbidity is of interest from the viewpoint of a diathesis–personality–stress model that suggests a continuum between normal personality traits, personality disorders, and clinical disorders. According to this view one should find some preexisting personality disturbance in most clinical disorders, although the manifestations may not always be strong enough to meet the diagnostic criteria for personality disorders. It follows that the pattern of association between particular clinical and personality disorders is not a random one, and clinical disorders would be associated with particular personality disorders or classes of disorders.

Table 2.6 shows the prevalence of personality disorders in patients with anxiety (Sanderson, Wetzler, Beck, & Betz, 1994) and depressive disorders (Sanderson, Wetzler, Beck, & Betz, 1992). Both studies were conducted at the same center (an outpatient clinic for cognitive therapy) and used structured interviews analyzed on the basis of DSM-III-R diagnoses. The pattern of association between clinical and personality disorders was similar for anxiety and depressive disorders except for the higher prevalence of PDs in the depressive disorders. About 35% of the patients with anxiety disorders were also diagnosed with at least one PD, whereas 53% of the patients with depressive disorders also had a PD. The strongest association of both clinical disorders was with the Cluster C personality disorders (27–36%) describing neurotic mechanisms (avoidant, dependent, obsessive–compulsive, and passive–aggressive). Few cases of PDs in Cluster A (odd or eccentric) were found (1–3%); and only slightly more (6–13%) were found in Cluster B (emotional, dramatic, impulsive).

The anxiety disorders included panic disorder, panic disorder with agoraphobia, generalized anxiety disorder, social phobia, simple phobia, obsessive–compulsive disorder (OCD), and anxiety disorder, not otherwise specified (NOS). Social phobia had the highest percentage (61%) of associated PDs, and simple phobia had the lowest (12%). Panic disorder,

TABLE 2.6
Personality Disorder (PD) Diagnosis (%) Among Patients With Anxiety and Depressive Disorders

	Anxiety Disorders (n = 347)	Depressive Disorders (n = 197)
Any PD	35	53
Two PDs	11	15
Any Cluster A PD	1	3
Paranoid	1	2
Schizoid	0	0
Schizotypal	0	1
Any Cluster B PD	6	13
Antisocial	0	2
Borderline	2	6
Histrionic	3	3
Narcissistic	3	4
Any Cluster C PD	27	36
Avoidant	13	15
Dependent	8	14
Obsessive–compulsive	11	10
Passive–aggressive	3	5
PD not otherwise specified	4	8

Note. The data on anxiety disorders are adapted from *Psychiatry Research, 51*, W. C. Sanderson, S. Wetzler, A. T. Beck, & F. Betz, "Prevalence of Personality Disorders Among Patients With Anxiety Disorders," p. 169, copyright 1994, with permission from Elsevier Science. The data on depressive disorders are adapted from *Psychiatry Research, 42*, W. C. Sanderson, S. Wetzler, A. T. Beck, & F. Betz, "Prevalence of Personality Disorders in Patients With Major Depression and Dysthymia," p. 96, copyright 1992, with permission from Elsevier Science.

with or without agoraphobia, simple phobia, and OCD showed about an equal distribution among the five types of PDs within Cluster C. On the basis of theory relating panic disorder to separation anxiety (D. F. Klein, 1981) Klein expected that panic disorder would be associated with dependent PD, but in the Sanderson et al. (1994) study, the highest association of this PD was with social phobia. Social phobia showed a primary association with avoidant PD (37%) and a secondary association with dependent personality (18%). The frequent association of social phobia with avoidant PD is not surprising given the overlap in their phenomenological descriptions. It is surprising, however, that obsessive–compulsive PD was found more often in GAD (38%) than in OCD (9%). A large-scale community study also found a relationship between compulsive PD and GAD and specific phobia as well (Nestadt, Romanski, Samuels, Folstein, & McHugh, 1992). Alcohol use disorders, however, varied inversely with compulsive PD. Apparently OCD symptoms can develop in a person without an obsessive–compulsive personality. OCD seems more likely to develop from a background of generalized anxiety, and the obsessive and compulsive mechanisms may represent late developing attempts to deal with this anxiety. The authors suggest that GAD may actually be an early developing PD rather than an acute condition.

The depressive disorders represented in the second study were major depression (MD), dysthymia (Dys), and double depression (DD, dysthymia plus major depression). Estimates of the rate of PDs in MD in previous studies (Sanderson et al., 1992), range from 9% to 92%, but those in the lower end of the range were based on chart reviews, and those at the higher end of the range were based on self-report tests. The estimate of 53% in the Sanderson et al. study is almost exactly at the middle of the range (34–82%) of those studies using structured interviews. Patients with PDs had significantly higher scores than those without PDs on the Beck Depression Inventory (Beck, 1967). Avoidant and dependent PDs within the Cluster C PDs are found most associated with MD and DD, but avoidant and obsessive–compulsive PDs are most closely associated with dysthymia. Despite the claim that borderline PD is a form of mood disorder, the incidence of borderline PD among the depressives in this study was small (6%).

Sullivan, Joyce, and Mulder (1994) studied the specific relationship between borderline PD and major depression (MD). They used a structured interview with *DSM-III-R* criteria. Of their cases, 53% had a PD diagnosis (close to the 50% of the MDs in the Sanderson et al., 1992 study), but in this study, 19% met the criteria for BPD as opposed to only 4% in the Sanderson et al. study. The BPDs had a remarkably high incidence of childhood conduct disorder (65%) compared to the two other groups. Childhood conduct disorder is closely associated with adult antisocial PD. Zanarini (1993) reviewed the comorbidity studies of BPD and found no association with schizophrenic spectrum disorders, but a high comorbidity with both mood disorders and impulse spectrum disorders.

The findings from these studies strongly suggest that BPD is a PD involving sporadic major depression occurring in an unstable, impulsive personality with antisocial dispositions. Despite these traits, which might be poor prognostic signs for treatment, the patients with borderline PD in the Sullivan et al. study (1994) responded as well as the other two groups to treatment with antidepressant drugs. Many studies have shown that major depressive disorders with any PD have poorer outcomes in treatment with antidepressant drugs or most forms of psychotherapy, with the exception of cognitive therapy (Shea et al., 1992). However, depression occurring in the context of psychotherapy aimed at drug-dependent, or borderline individuals was a positive prognostic sign. Patients diagnosed with MDs with PD responded quite positively to a specific antidepressant, phenelzine, an MAO inhibitor, suggesting a biological difference between ordinary depression and that occurring within a BPD. The influence of PDs on treatment outcome may depend on the focus of the treatment. In a drug treatment aimed at depression, clearing of the depression may uncover the underlying primary problems of the PDs resulting in stress-instigated relapse. On the other hand, when the treatment is of the behavior problems resulting in drug abuse or self-harmful behaviors, the presence of depression is a motivation for psychotherapeutic attempts aimed at self-change.

Most studies have found a high rate of comorbidity between antisocial personality disorder (APD) and substance abuse or dependence, particularly among males (Koenigsberg, Kaplan, Gilmore, & Cooper, 1985; Lewis, Rice, & Helzer, 1983; Lewis, Robins, & Rice, 1985). Nestadt et al. (1992), using dimensionally scaled scores in a general population survey, found that there was a strong linear relationship between an antisocial PD score and the probability of an alcohol abuse diagnosis. Most drug and alcohol abusers are not APDs, but most APDs abuse alcohol or drugs. This relationship may be due to the overlap in criteria for the PD and the clinical disorder, but it is also likely to be due to the impulsive and hedonistic characteristics of psychopathy, which make these persons seek immediate gratification without regard for consequences. There are important behavioral differences between alcoholics with and those without APD. Although alcoholics with APD drink no more than those without APD, the former are more likely to lose their jobs, be involved in auto accidents, abuse drugs other than alcohol, and exhibit violence toward children and spouses (Bland & Orn, 1986; Jaffe & Schukit, 1981; Lewis et al., 1983).

Schizotypal PD was introduced in *DSM-III* and was related to the diagnosis of latent schizophrenia in *DSM-II*. Phenomenology, family studies, and biological markers suggest that schizotypal PD and the related paranoid PD may be subclinical forms of schizophrenia. Some researchers have suggested that the diagnosis be moved back to Axis I because it may simply represent a long prodromal phase of schizophrenia (Klerman, 1990; Rutter, 1987). If schizotypal personality inevitably progressed to schizophrenia an argument could be made that the distinction between the two is unnecessary. However, many cases of schizotypy remain at this level and are found in the seemingly well relatives of schizophrenics. Meehl's (1962) diathesis–stress theory maintains that schizotypes only become schizophrenic when exposed to certain kinds of stress, and that most remain compensated during their lifetimes. Schizotypal and paranoid PDs are also found in clinical disorders other than schizophrenia in the general population, most notably obsessive–compulsive and panic disorders, and substance abuse disorders (Zimmerman & Coryell, 1989).

Obviously, there is considerable overlap between particular Axis I and Axis II diagnoses in the *DSMs*. Much of this may be due to the overlapping criteria for placement on the two axes. The basic idea that long-standing disorders are placed on Axis II, and acute or episodic disorders belong on Axis I is not consistently adhered to in the *DSM*. Disorders such as GAD and social phobia are usually long-term disorders but are placed on Axis I. Similarly, cyclothymic and dysthymic disorders could easily be regarded as PDs rather than as Axis I disorders. The unreliability of many of the PDs over time suggests that they may not be as long standing or stable as suggested by their placement on Axis I. Widiger and Shea (1991) proposed several different ways of remedying the overlap between the personality and clinical dimensions:

1. *Add exclusion criteria.* This is the least likely solution because it would be artifactual in many cases. Actually, the *DSM-III-R* and the *DSM-IV* have moved in the opposite direction by reducing exclusionary criteria and allowing multiple diagnoses.

2. *Shift the placement of the disorders.* This would include moves such as cyclothymic and dysthymic (depressive personality) from Axis I to Axis II, and schizotypy (as a variant of schizophrenia) from Axis II to Axis I. Every disorder could be examined in terms of its age of onset and chronicity and these factors given priority over simple symptom phenomenology in assignments to Axes I or II. In view of their common origin, a dysphoric or neurotic personality might replace depressive or anxious personalities.

3. *Delete overlapping criteria.* This might help in some instances such as deleting substance abuse from the definition of antisocial personality, but in many cases removing a central component from one disorder to avoid overlap with another may destroy the validity of that disorder and necessitate its removal from the list altogether.

4. *Adding differentiating criteria.* Instead of the polythetic format where overlap in symptoms produces artifactual correlations between syndromes, one could specify a single core criterion that is specific to each disorder from among the other additive criteria. It is unlikely that a consensus could ever be obtained on a single necessary criterion for any disorder, nor is there any evidence that a single criterion could distinguish all members of any diagnostic category from members of all other categories.

5. *Convert to a dimensional format.* It is obvious that many of the distinctions between Axis I and Axis II, as well as between some Axis II disorders is one of severity of the disorder rather than a qualitative difference between disorders. A dimensional approach would first ask: What are the basic dimensions underlying the diverse symptoms present in disorders? Then, how many of these could be defined along continuous, quantitative dimensions of psychopathology? Finally, how may typical combinations of dimensions could be described in diagnostic terms? Dimensions could be quantified by some of the structured interview and self-report methods now in existence or by newly devised ones. Perhaps case history factors such as duration of symptoms could be built into the dimensional systems. Although many psychologists and some psychiatrists would prefer this kind of system, it would probably be too unfamiliar to most clinicians and too much a departure from the medical model for those who have so much invested in the *DSM* approach. These arguments, however, are no reason to ignore the dimensional approach. For those interested in objective, rational, and theoretically relevant methods of diagnosis, it could provide an

alternative method. For those interested in retaining the categorical model, translations from one system to the other could be developed. In time, the advantages of the dimensional model may produce a change.

Dimensional Approaches

The first question that must be asked is do all categories of diagnosis simply represent extremes of continuous dimensions of personality or psychopathology, or do some of them constitute objective taxons that have qualitative distinctiveness from both normal variations and other disorders? Meehl (1986) states that schizophrenic, manic–depressive, unipolar major depressive, and antisocial personality are all probably genuine taxons, whereas psychoneuroses are not. How does one distinguish a "disease" from a "deviation" short of discovering a sensitive and specific marker for the etiological factor such as a gene or biological abnormality? Assuming one has a quantitative index based on symptoms alone, one might think that bimodality in the frequency distribution of the index would indicate a discontinuity based on a taxon, or the existence of two different populations. But bimodality may be an artifact of the class intervals selected, the representativeness of the larger population sample, or a function of observer bias (Grove & Andreasen, 1989). Intelligence is normally distributed in the general population, but at the low end of the curve are a number of infrequent but discrete disease-produced mental deficiencies. Furthermore, a disorder might occur as a critical threshold effect in a continuous, normal distribution. Meehl (1995) has proposed a taxometric statistical procedure to test the taxonomic hypothesis, but like all such methods it relies on very large and representative samples and reliable and valid quantitative indicators of wide range. Taxometric methods have not been widely applied, but several studies have shown that schizotypy meets the criteria for a taxon (Lezenweger & Korfine, 1992; Lezenweger & Moldin, 1990; Tyrka et al., 1995), whereas dysthymia and borderline personality disorder do not (Trull, Widiger, & Guthrie, 1990). This is a promising approach, which could resolve the endless debate between advocates of dimensional and categorical approaches and lead to a change in the diagnostic systems in future DSMs.

H. J. Eysenck (1986) has advocated a dimensional approach to psychiatric diagnosis for the past 50 years but has gone unheeded by the psychiatric community. With his wife and colleague (S. B. Eysenck), Eysenck showed that a small battery of performance tests could be used to sort out patients diagnosed as normal, neurotic, and psychotic (including both those with schizophrenia and manic–depression) into distinct groups within two dimensions of a discriminant function. Factor analyses of symptoms suggested three factors, which they called Neuroticism, Psychoticism, and Extraversion–Introversion. The first two represented continua in which one extreme was psychopathology. Although extraversion was a normal dimension, it could be used to differentiate hysterical (extraverted-neurotic), from dysthymic (introverted-neurotic) neurotic disorders (Eysenck, 1947, 1957). Similarly, schizophrenics (introverted-psychotic) could be differentiated from manic–depressive patients (extraverted-psychotic; Verma & Eysenck, 1973). The Eysencks developed questionnaire measures for extraversion and neuroticism, but one for psychoticism was not developed until much later.

The neuroticism (N) dimension has emerged in every model of personality based on questionnaire measurement (Zuckerman, Kuhlman, & Camac, 1988; Zuckerman, Kuhlman, Joireman, Teta, & Kraft, 1993) and also in analyses of ratings of psychiatric symptoms where anxiety and depression emerge in a general dysphoric or negative affect factor (Clark & Watson, 1991). The correlations of N with most trait anxiety tests are high enough to equate these two dimensions. A large body of literature attests to the construct validity of extraversion (E) and neuroticism or negative affectivity (Eysenck, 1967; H. J. Eysenck & Eysenck, 1985). But the diagnostic significance of the disinhibition (P) dimension is more problematical.

Eysenck (1992; Eysenck & Eysenck, 1976) conceived of the dimension as a latent trait with altruistic and highly socialized, conventional "normals" at one end, and psychotics, schizophrenics, major mood disorders, and aggressive psychopaths at the other (see Fig. 2.2). People with psychotic symptoms should score highest on the scale, but in actuality, the highest scoring clinical groups are psychopaths, delinquents, and criminals; schizophrenics score only slightly higher than "normals," and endogenous depressives score near the normal level. Rated psychopathy is correlated with P. Actually, the highest scoring groups on the P scale are artists, art students, and creative writers (Eysenck & Eysenck, 1976). This is congruent with Eysenck's idea that creativity is associated with P, but also suggests that the P measures some normal trait like asocialization, or disinhibition, rather than psychoticism per se. Eysenck said that the super trait is an amalgam of narrower traits: aggression, coldness, egocentricity, impersonal affect, impulsivity, antisocial personality, empathy (lack of), toughmindedness, and creativity. Factor analyses of scales in "normals" have shown that the P scale is the best marker for a factor defined by scales of impulsivity and sensation seeking at the high end, and scales of socialization, responsibility, and conformity at the low end; consequently, the factor was named *Impulsive–Unsocialized Sensation Seeking* (Zuckerman et al., 1988). I have suggested that if the P scale measures any trait of psychopathology, it is psychopathy (antisocial personality; Zuckerman, 1989). I also question the Eysencks' argument that psychopathy, severe mood disorders, and schizophrenia share a common underlying diathesis (Zuckerman, 1989).

Three dimensions are probably too few to accommodate the full range

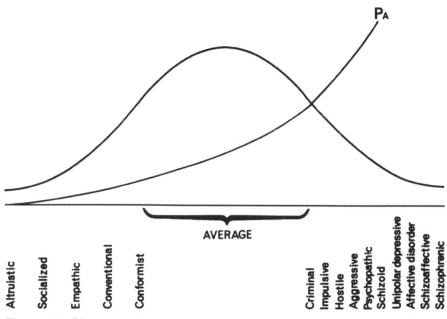

Figure 2.2. Diagrammatic representation of the continuity theory of
"psychoticism." From "The Definition and Measurement of Psychoticism," by
H. J. Eysenck, 1992, *Personality and Individual Differences, 13*, p. 758.
Copyright 1992 by Elsevier Science. Reprinted by permission.

of psychiatric symptoms. Lorr, Klett, & McNair (1963) pursued the dimensional approach by developing standardized rating scales for psychiatric
symptoms and subjecting them to factor analyses. Factors confirmed in at
least three of four independent studies (described in Lorr, 1986) include:
Excitement, Paranoid Projection, Anxious-Depression, Retardation, Conceptual Disorganization, and Depression. Other factors confirmed in only
one or two studies include: Hostile Belligerence, Grandiosity, Perceptual
Distortion, Obsessive–Compulsive, Disorientation, Motor Disturbances,
Somatic Concern, and Phobic Anxiety. Lorr's work was primarily concentrated on defining subtypes among schizophrenics. He described six syndrome types defined by characteristic profiles on 10 symptom scales: ex-
cited-grandiose, excited-hostile, retarded, intropunitive, hostile-paranoid,
and disorganized (Lorr et al., 1963). Some of these correspond directly to
DSM-IV schizophrenic subtypes: disorganized with disorganized (hebephrenic), hostile paranoid with paranoid, and retarded with catatonic, but
others, such as excited and intropunitive types are not so readily identifiable with *DSM* subtypes of schizophrenia. They could represent manic or
depressive states within either bipolar or schizoaffective disorders. The
schizophrenic classification in the United States was much broader at the
time Lorr did this work. Lorr (1986) points out the advantages of a dimensional approach in preserving information beyond the categorical label.

For instance, one could differentiate diagnoses of depression into anxious, hostile, and retarded types. This kind of differentiation may provide important information to the treating practitioner in the choice of drug to administer. Quantitative ratings can be used to evaluate precisely the course of the disorder and the outcome of therapy, in place of the crude "unimproved, improved, or recovered" designations routinely used in case records. Although Lorr's syndromes of psychosis are less relevant to current definitions of psychotic disorders, the approach and methods he used to define them could furnish a model for future attempts to develop diagnostic criteria for the *DSMs*.

The personality disorders (PDs) are almost dimensional by definition. Widiger (1991, 1992) reviewed the arguments and evidence relating to the dimensional versus the categorical approaches to PDs and concluded that the data consistently favor the dimensional model. Reviewing 16 studies comparing dimensional and categorical methods in studies of reliability and validity of PDs, Widiger found all but one of the studies showed that reliability and validity were better using the dimensional approach (1992).

The *DSM-IV* defines PDs as extremes of personality traits characterized by their inflexibility, pervasiveness across situations, stability, and their result in significant distress or impairment in functioning. The *DSM-IV* lists 10 such disorders, although as we have seen, there is considerable comorbidity among and between them and clinical disorders suggesting that a smaller number of dimensions could account for the variance among the PDs. Actually, the *DSM* categorizes the 10 PDs in three classes on a rational basis: Class A, odd-eccentric; Class B, dramatic-emotional; Class C, anxious-fearful. Class A represents primarily those disorders showing a cognitive disturbance and inappropriate social behavior most related to the psychotic disorders on Axis I. The disorders in Class B are characterized by impulsive, sensation seeking behavior, with labile emotionality. The disorders in Class C resemble the so-called character neuroses and are closest to the anxiety and mood disorders on Axis I. The comorbidity studies largely support these assumptions.

Using multidimensional scaling of the 11 PDs in the *DSM-III*, Widiger and his colleagues (Widiger, Trull, Hurt, Clarkin, & Frances, 1987) found three dimensions:

1. A desire for social involvement dimension with schizoid and paranoid at the low end, and dependent, avoidant, borderline, and histrionic at the other.
2. An assertiveness dimension with narcissistic and histrionic at one end, and schizoid, passive–aggressive, avoidant, and dependent at the nonassertive end.
3. Anxious rumination (schizotypal, compulsive, paranoid, avoidant) at one end, and external behavioral "acting-out" (antisocial, borderline, passive–aggressive) at the other.

A great deal of interest has been expressed in the applicability of the five-factor model of personality called the Big Five to classification of the personality disorders (Costa & Widiger, 1994). However, the questionnaire and rating scales devised for the Big Five do not incorporate many of the maladaptive forms of behavior and emotions described in the DSM PDs. A new instrument based on the actual personality traits described in the DSM was clearly needed. In a review of the literature on diagnosis and classification, Clark (1995) advocated a switch from the categorical to the dimensional model of psychopathology, beginning with the personality disorders. Clark (1993) developed the Schedule for Nonadaptive and Adaptive Personality (SNAP) for this purpose. Clark's work represents the best information we now have on the dimensions of personality disorders.

A series of psychometric procedures were used to develop 12 primary scales based on the actual symptoms described for the PDs in the DSM-III and DSM-III-R as well as for some of the symptoms described for the more stable long-term DSM-I disorders such as cyclothymia and dysthymia. Three additional scales incorporating general temperament dimensions from another instrument were also incorporated into the SNAP: positive affectivity, negative affectivity, and disinhibition. Factor analyses of the 15 scales in a college population yielded three factors that accounted for nearly all of the common variance in both men and women: Negative Affectivity, including scales for negative temperament, mistrust, self-harm, aggression, manipulativeness, eccentric perceptions, and dependency; Positive Affectivity, including scales for exhibitionism, entitlement (narcissism), and detachment (negative loading); and Disinhibition, including scales for impulsivity, propriety, and workaholism (the latter two loading negatively). The factor constructs are based on Tellegen's (1985) model, but also fit Eysenck's as well: N = Negative Affectivity, E = Positive Affectivity, and P = Disinhibition. However, the Disinhibition factor resembles Zuckerman's (1994a) concept of impulsive unsocialized sensation seeking (ImpUSS) and does not include the kinds of psychotic thinking thought to be characteristic of high P scorers. The subscale called Eccentric Perceptions loads on the Negative Affectivity factor, not the Disinhibition one. High disinhibition scorers are described in terms that sound very much like psychopathy (antisocial personality disorder).

Harkness and McNulty (1994) constructed a "personality psychopathology" dimensional model in which two of the five dimensions are psychoticism and constraint. The psychoticism dimension has to do with reality contact, whereas the constraint dimension describes recklessness, risk-taking, impulsivity, amorality, and unreliability. The separation of psychotic and psychopathic traits is additional evidence that schizotypy is not on the same dimension as antisocial tendency as was maintained by Eysenck (1992).

Clark (1993) also developed diagnostic scales specifically related to the 11 PDs in the *DSM-III*. She correlated the personality trait and diagnostic scales with interview-based clinical ratings of the PDs in a group of patients (see Table C.16 in Clark, 1993). Each diagnosis correlated with several trait scales congruent with the concepts of the disorders. *Paranoid* PD correlated most highly with aggression and mistrust; *schizoid* PD with self-harm, mistrust, and detachment; *schizotypic* PD with mistrust, self-harm, and eccentric perceptions; *antisocial* PD with disinhibition, aggression, manipulativeness, and impulsivity; *borderline* PD with self-harm, aggression, disinhibition, and negative temperament; *histrionic* PD with exhibitionism, aggression, and disinhibition; *narcissistic* PD with disinhibition and aggression; *avoidant* PD with detachment; *dependent* PD with dependency and negative temperament; *obsessive–compulsive* PD with negative temperament, workaholism, and propriety; and *passive–aggressive* PD with disinhibition and aggression. With the exception of obsessive–compulsive and passive–aggressive PDs, the highest correlations were in the range of .4 to .6. Clearly, there is overlap between the PDs in terms of their scale correlates, just as there is in their symptoms described in the DSM.

The scales specifically designed to measure the DSM PD diagnoses showed remarkable convergent and discriminant validities (Clark, 1993). In convergent validity correlations between SNAP diagnostic scales and their respective diagnostic ratings, 9 of 11 were the highest correlations in their columns, and 8 of the 11 were higher than .50. The SNAP can be used either to identify the particular personality traits making up a disorder or to facilitate diagnoses in the traditional PD categories. The SNAP scales also correlate highly with the normal personality dimensions in the five- or three-factor models. Thus this instrument furnishes a bridge between personality and personality disorder, which should be useful in developing a dimensional model of diagnosis. Further studies should be done to see if a three-factor PD diagnostic system would work as well as the current 10-PD system. A profile of symptoms similar to that obtainable on the SNAP would convey more than a diagnostic label, and there would be greater reliability of diagnoses and less need for multiple diagnoses in a simplified system.

Thus far, I have dealt with only two of the Robins and Guze (1970) criteria for validity of a diagnostic system, that is, what is to be included (content validity), and delimitation of disorders (discriminant validity). The other validity methods include laboratory studies demonstrating sensitive and specific biological or psychological criteria for the disorders (criterion validity); family and twin biometric as well as molecular genetic studies of the disorders (construct validity); and prognostic studies demonstrating the usefulness of the system in prediction of outcome of treatment (predictive validity). The applications of these methods to the particular classes of disorders will be done in subsequent chapters. For now I outline the general approaches to validity of the present diagnostic system and provide some examples.

Laboratory Tests

A medical disease model suggests that there is a specific pathology associated with each disorder. In the diagnosis of medical disorders, laboratory tests play an increasingly important role. The rectal examination for prostate cancer can only detect about 20% of the cases with cancer because at the early stages the growth of the cancer is not palpable. The prostate specific antigen (PSA) test is a blood test that has a higher sensitivity but a lower specificity because temporary prostatic infections can produce an elevated PSA, and a benignly enlarged prostate can also produce values above the normal range. Ultrasonic visualization can much improve the sensitivity and specificity, but the ultimate criterion is the biopsy in which actual cells from the prostate are examined under the microscope. Analogous difficulties face any biological test for a psychiatric disorder. The purposes of a laboratory test are (a) to confirm a diagnosis reached on the basis of clinical signs (sensitivity), (b) to rule out or confirm alternative psychiatric diagnoses or medical conditions which could produce the symptoms (specificity), and (c) to advance research on biological hypotheses of etiology (Kupfer & Thase, 1989). The test is only a "surrogate" for the underlying disorder (Carroll, 1989). There is as yet no biopsy "gold standard" for psychiatric disorders, even assuming that there are specific biological bases for these disorders. But there are a number of candidates for laboratory surrogate tests. Just as a transient infection can produce an abnormal PSA, a brief psychosis or a reactive depression may mimic the symptoms of schizophrenia or major endogenous depression. Carroll points out that no biologic measure can do better than the independent variable against which it is observed. In regard to the dexamethasone suppression test (DST), which he developed for the diagnosis of endogenous type major depression, the sensitivity and specificity have varied with the particular diagnostic system used with the same group of patients. Unfortunately, the *DSM-III* resulted in the lowest accuracy for the test (about chance), whereas the ICD-9 gave an accuracy of 92% for the DST. If a laboratory test fails to confirm clinically based diagnoses, one cannot discount the validity of the test, but we must first consider the reliability and validity of the clinical criteria. Carroll says that the DST works with a particular type of depression called *endogenous depression* (*DSM-IV* melancholia) and not with other types. Cronbach and Meehl (1955) referred to this problem of trying to validate objective psychological diagnostic tests against imperfect criteria as "the bootstrap approach," meaning that we improve the construct validity of the test until eventually the test could prove more valid than the fallible criteria used in its initial appraisal. Carroll (1989) suggests that apart from its correlation with clinical diagnosis (criterion validity), a test for depression should show a gradual reduction as clinical recovery occurs, an association with suicide, and a relationship to other biological variables associated with depression (construct validity). A test of endogenous depression should also predict the response to biological treatments but not the response to placebos or psychotherapy (predictive validity). This latter indicates the author's specific construct which seems to rule out a two-way interaction between biological and psychological variables.

Like other biological tests for psychiatric disorders, the DST has significant sensitivity to the target diagnosis, but it also shows some lack of specificity in that it may be influenced by temporary stress, harsh dieting, and alcohol withdrawal. In addition, the DST shows intermediate results in other disorders such as obsessive–compulsive, schizophrenic, and manic disorders (Kupfer & Thase, 1989). These kinds of errors occur in many medical diagnostic tests. This is why most tests cannot be used in a mechanical fashion but must be integrated as part of the information given to the practitioner. Sometimes more than one test or measure is required for maximal accuracy (Mason, Kosten, & Giller, 1991; Shagass, Roemer, Straumanis, & Josiassen, 1985). Mason et al., for instance, found that a combination of hormonal measures increased diagnostic accuracy in discrimination of paranoid schizophrenic from bipolar manic-state patients from 70% (using a single hormone measure) to 95% using five hormones. Shagass et al. found that patients with schizophrenia could be differentiated from those diagnosed as nonpsychotic using factors consisting of multiple EEG measures. Other markers for depression and other disorders are discussed in the following chapters.

Genetic Studies

The comorbidity of disorders within individuals could reflect either a real overlap in the genetic and biological determinants of the comorbid disorders or mistakes in the conception of the diagnostic categories and their relationships. A high comorbidity between disorders could be due to common genetic or environmental factors shared by these disorders. If either type of shared background is true, clinicians would expect to find many GAD cases as well as MD cases in the near relatives of MD disorder cases. Twin and adoption studies can sort out which type of shared factors (genetic or environmental) account for the comorbidity at the phenomenal level.

The percentage of panic disorder patients who experience a major depression in their lifetimes is estimated at 63–68% (Wetzler & Sanderson, 1995). Relatives of patients with panic disorder showed significantly increased risk for panic disorder and social phobia but not for MD (Goldstein et al., 1994). Similarly, MD cases occur with increased frequency in the relatives of MD probands, but not in the relatives of patients with panic disorder. Dysthymia and substance abuse (particularly alcoholism) also appeared with above chance frequency in relatives of MD patients, but not in relatives of panic disorder patients. Goldstein et al.'s results suggest that panic disorder and major depressive disorder are discrete disorders, despite the fact that one or the other often occurs in the subsequent history of the same individuals. Generalized anxiety and bipolar disorders, cyclothymia, and simple phobia cases were not found in relatives of either panic disorder or major depressive disorder patients, suggesting that their separate categorizations in the DSMs are also appropriate.

Kendler, Walters, et al. (1995) used a biometric analysis of a large population of twins to analyze the genetic and environmental risk factors for six major psychiatric disorders in women: specific phobia, generalized anxiety disorder (GAD), panic disorder, bulimia, major depression (MD), and alcoholism. DSM-III-R criteria were used for diagnosis, but for bulimia, panic disorder, and alcoholism, the definitions were broadened in order to increase low prevalence rates in the interest of statistical power. All disorders could have been entirely genetically specific, or one set of genetic risk factors could have been common to all or some of the disorders. Similarly, nonspecific environmental factors (such as life stress) could have been responsible for all disorders, or specific kinds of factors could have accounted for each disorder.

Their results suggested that neither complete generality nor complete nonspecificity explained the data. For GAD, specific phobias, and bulimia, total heritability was low (30–35%). MD and panic disorder showed moderate heritability (41–44%), and heritability was high for alcoholism (59%). One genetic factor accounted for the genetic components in phobia, panic disorder, and bulimia, and another genetic factor accounted for most of the genetic component of GAD and MD. In contrast, most of the genetic component of alcoholism was unique to that disorder. Their methods allowed the analysis of environmental factors into those shared by members within families and those specific to individuals within families. The shared family environments was a minimal influence in all of the disorders except for bulimia in which shared family environments had a substantial role. One individual-specific environmental factor was shared by GAD and MD, while the others were specific to the other disorders. The highest influence of specific environmental factors was found for phobias. This latter finding supports the theory that specific phobias are often the result of particular conditioning experiences affecting individuals with a genetic disposition to anxiety.

Adoption studies provide a natural separation of heredity and environment. Providing that the separation of the child from its biological family took place soon after birth, and there was no further contact, and assuming that the adoptive family was unrelated to the biological family, then the relationships of the adoptee's traits or disorders to those in the biological family are due to genetic influences and those to the adopting family are due to shared environmental factors. The major studies have been conducted in Scandinavia because of the complete medical and legal records on the total population and their accessibility to investigators.

Many more twin and adoption studies have been conducted on single disorders or disorders within particular classes of diagnoses such as anxiety disorders. These studies will be discussed in the relevant chapters. The twin study just discussed illustrates how genetic–environmental analyses go beyond comorbidity based on symptoms to examine the underlying etiological bases for such comorbidity. Despite the placement of generalized anxiety disorder and major depressive disorder in two different diagnostic groups, they seem to share some of the same genetic and environmental etiological factors. Perhaps a common disposition toward negative affectivity expressed in a neurotic or dysphoric personality type underlies both disorders. Schizophrenia and major depressive disorders are shown to be independent in diathesis confounding theories, suggesting that they are part of a common psychotic continuum (Eysenck, 1992). Schizotypic and paranoid PDs and some schizoaffective disorders do share a genetic diathesis with schizophrenia and may represent points on a continuum of severity.

Recent developments in molecular genetics promise to unravel the relationships between diagnoses in terms of the genes that underlie them (Gelernter & Gershon, 1989; Todd & Reich, 1989). *Linkage markers* are distinguishable forms of enzymes, proteins, and blood groups that can be associated with the presence of a disorder in a particular individual within a family. Such markers may not themselves be related to the disorder but are associated with the genes controlling the disorder and are located in proximity to those genes. The new generation of linkage markers are thought to be the differences in the DNA itself. They are mostly bits of the DNA with no known function. The establishment of a linkage locus may narrow the search for the gene candidates from about 100,000 possibilities to a few hundred within the section of the DNA. Once the gene or genes involved are identified, their particular functions in metabolic or neural pathways can be established and even corrected.

One drawback is that classical linkage studies were based on simple Mendelian models, whereas biometric studies suggest that most disorders have a polygenic basis. The task of isolating all genes associated with a disorder may be daunting within the scope of present methods. However, the markers may reveal genes of modest effect sizes (Quantitative Trait Loci, Plomin et al., 1994) involved in the disorder, perhaps even necessary genes, whereas other genes of weak effect sizes may be merely potentiating in their cumulative effects. Another possibility is that there are different forms of a disorder with different genetic bases. There are, for instance, three different linked markers for bipolar disorder, which could be related to three different forms of the disorder (Todd & Reich, 1989) such as bipolar I and II, hypomanic disorder, cyclothymic, and others.

Belmaker and Biederman (1994) have an interesting viewpoint on the direction of future research on genetic markers. They suggest "that it may be more heuristic to look for genetic markers for temperamental traits rather than to look for markers of specific . . . disorders" (p. 71). Plomin (1995), in an address on molecular genetics, made a similar prediction to the effect that we will discover major genes involved in basic personality traits underlying disorders before we will find genes specifically controlling those disorders. He particularly pointed to the evidence on the D2 dopamine receptor gene implicated in various kinds of drug abuse and wondered if this gene could be involved in the trait of sensation-seeking. This kind of hypothesis is exciting because it provides a basis for the diathesis–personality–stress approach of the present work.

Prognosis and Course of Disorder

Diagnosis should have some predictive value for the outcome of a disorder, but diagnosis cannot be based solely on this factor. Cancers have varying outcomes depending on the locus of the cancer, its stage, the patient's response to treatment, and individual differences, perhaps related to strength of the autoimmune systems. Psychiatric disorders also have varying outcomes related to severity of the disorder, acuteness or chronicity of its development, premorbid personality, a rather nebulous quality called *ego strength*, intelligence, socioeconomic level, level of premorbid functioning, social support, and treatment. But given these sources of variation within diagnostic categories, the diagnoses per se have prognostic implications. Mood disorders in general have a better outcome for the episode than schizophrenic disorders. Most patients with mood disorders return to their previous level of functioning after the episode of the disorder is in remission, but most patients with schizophrenia are left with residual symptoms even after the acute episode is in abeyance.

As a general rule early developing disorders have a poorer outcome than more acute disorders, and this is particularly true of schizophrenia, alcoholism, drug abuse, and mood disorders. Patients with mood disorders without preexisting personality disorders generally have a better outcome than those without PDs (Reich & Green, 1991).

Response to Treatment

One of Freud's distinctions between psychoses and neuroses was that the former could not benefit from psychoanalytic treatment. Although this assumption was later challenged by Harry Stack Sullivan (1953) and his students, studies of the effects of psychotherapy without drug treatment show poor results with schizophrenics, confirming Freud's view. The initial studies of drug success with different diagnostic groups seemed to validate the usefulness of the classic diagnoses. Antianxiety drugs, such as the benzodiazepines, benefit anxiety disorders (or GAD at least); antipsychotic medications, such as the phenothiazines, reduce or eliminate psychotic symptoms; antidepressants, such as the tricyclics and MAO inhibiters, benefit the mood disorders; and lithium has a remarkable effect on bipolar disorders. Psychopharmacological theories of the etiology of these disorders were built on the basis of the actions of particular therapeutic drugs in the brain. On the basis of the theories new drugs were designed and predictions made for experimental tests of the theories (construct validity).

The situation in psychopharmacology has now become more complicated, and findings in the past 2 decades challenge the neat specificity of drugs for disorders (Klein, 1989). The process and reactive (poor and good prognostic types) schizophrenia patients referred to earlier, respond differently to antipsychotic medication such as chlorpromazine. Those with process, asocial type schizophrenia did not improve in response to medication, and many worsened and showed neurological signs. Those with reactive type schizophrenia (acute development, more social) improved as shown by reduction of delusions, hallucinations, and cognitive disorganization (Klein & Rosen, 1973). The differential response of the two types of schizophrenia patients to medication, and other features distinguishing the two groups, have been the basis of the idea that there are two types of schizophrenia with different etiologies (Crow, 1985). Klein claims that panic attacks are reduced or eliminated by the antidepressant drug imipramine, but are not helped by the antianxiety benzodiazepines. On this basis he suggested that GAD and panic attacks are not simply degrees of anxiety, but represent two distinct disorders. He suggests similar validation by pharmacological "dissection" for narrow and generalized social phobic disorders, and different types of depression and personality disorders. As he points out, most clinical trials involve diagnostically homogeneous groups and preclude discovery of different drug effects in subcategories of the disorder or other disorders.

Inferring different latent diagnoses on the basis of responses to drugs is a challenging approach with many complications (as admitted by Klein). We must be wary of inferring cause from effect even in placebo-controlled studies. A drug or psychotherapeutic technique may work for reasons having little to do with the primary effect of the drug or the particular technique of psychotherapy. The challenge of research is to isolate the particular action of the drug or the essential aspect of the psychotherapy that effects the changes.

Cultural, Class, and Gender Considerations

The constructors of the American *DSM* have attempted to keep their diagnostic categories in some accord with the *International Classifications of Disorders* (ICD) with the idea that diagnoses should be generalizable beyond national boundaries. A cross-national survey has found that psychiatrists in 24 countries were generally satisfied with the *DSM-III* and a clear majority considered the diagnostic definitions appropriate and preferable to other definitions in their own countries (Helzer & Canino, 1989). Lifetime prevalence rates of *DSM-III* diagnoses were highly correlated across 11 cultural regions. Even the frequencies of symptoms of one disorder, major depression, correlated very highly across regions. This simply means that psychiatrists around the world who have been strongly influenced by the Western countries in their concepts and practices, use the *DSM* in the same way. Anthropologists have pointed out that what are regarded as symptoms in our culture may be culturally sanctioned and normative beliefs and even perceptual experiences in others (Lewis-Fernández & Kleinman, 1994). What is paranoia in one culture may be self-evident reality in another. The *DSM-IV* (1994) recognizes this in regard to delusional disorders for which it cautions:

> An individual's cultural and religious background must be taken into account in evaluating the possible presence of Delusional Disorder. Some cultures have widely held and culturally sanctioned beliefs that might be considered delusional in other cultures and subcultures. (pp. 298–299)

Many would argue that all psychiatric diagnoses are not fixed physical entities but cultural constructions depending on a particular context of biological–medical constructs (Fabrega, 1994). Cultures have their own concepts of disorders affecting behavior and emotions. In recognition of this, the *DSM-IV* (1994) describes 25 "culture-bound syndromes" in a glossary (pp. 844–849). One of these is neurasthenia. In China, this diagnosis describes a condition characterized by mental and physical fatigue, pain and somatic symptoms, sexual dysfunction, dizziness, insomnia, and other symptoms which in the *DSM-IV* might meet the criteria for somatoform, anxiety, or mood disorder. In Japan, *neurasthenia* is often used as a euphemism for schizophrenia (Machizawa, 1992). Japanese psychiatrists are reluctant to use schizophrenia because of the stigma attached to that diagnosis. However, they do not regard neurasthenia as a neurosis. Neurasthenia was a popular diagnosis in western Europe in the latter part of the 19th century and was regarded as due to literal nervous exhaustion. Freud regarded neurasthenia as an actual neurosis due to excessive libidinal discharge through masturbation. Neurasthenic neurosis was introduced into the *DSM-II* in 1968, but dropped in the *DSM-III* in 1980. It survives in the advertisement world in America as "tired nerves." In the 1980s a new medical condition appeared in America called chronic fatigue syndrome (CFS; Greenberg, 1990). Some physicians believe it is due to a virus, whereas others feel it is just a new manifestation of the old neurosis. A study of patients with chronic fatigue complaints found that 60% of them had *DSM-III* disorders, and half of this group had major depression (Manu, Lane, & Matthews, 1988). All of this underlines the point that most psychiatric diagnoses for which the etiology is not fully understood are psychological "constructs." But this does not mean that the syndrome itself is a myth or is culturally specific. There have always been and will always be people who complain of fatigue beyond what is explainable by their physical exertions. Cultures will differ in how this symptom is interpreted. Some will have a purely medical explanation, some a psychological one, and some will attribute it to religious or other supernatural causes.

Previous studies of social class have generally found that rates of psychotic disorders are most frequent in the lowest socioeconomic classes. However, many of these studies were based on patients seeking treatment rather than real community studies and used nonstandard interviews or hospital records that could have been affected by the biases of upper-middle-class psychiatrists. A large community study in the United States (Kessler et al., 1994) found that rates of nearly all disorders declined monotonically with income and education, the highest rates being in the lowest social classes. Anxiety disorders and antisocial personality disorder showed particularly strong relationships with social class, as indexed by income and education.

Nonaffective acute remitting psychosis (NARP or brief psychotic disorder in *DSM-IV*) is a disorder with psychotic symptoms similar to those in schizophrenia, but unlike typical schizophrenia, this disorder lasts only a short time, and on recovery, the patient returns to the full premorbid level of functioning. This kind of disorder is rare in Western industrial countries, but its rate in developing countries is 10 times that in the industrial countries sampled, despite the fact that the rate of schizophrenia (after omitting the acute remitting psychosis cases) did not differ (Susser & Wanderling, 1994). Unlike schizophrenia, where rates for men and women are nearly the same, the rate of NARP was twice as high for women as for men in the developing countries. Does this represent a cultural difference, perhaps reflecting the greater stress for women in these societies, or simply cultural differences in the expression of neuroses?

Because Blacks in America tend to be represented disproportionately in the lower socioeconomic classes, one would expect higher rates of disorders in this group as compared with Whites. But there was no disorder where either lifetime or active prevalence rates were higher in Blacks than in Whites, and on two categories, mood and substance-use disorders, the proportion of affected Blacks was significantly lower than in Whites (Kes-

TABLE 2.7
Prevalence (%) of Major Categories of *DSM-III-R* Disorders (NCS)

Disorders	Lifetime Prevalence			12-Month Prevalence		
	Male	Female	Total	Male	Female	Total
Any mood disorder	14.7	23.9	19.3	8.5	14.1	11.3
Any anxiety disorder	19.2	30.5	24.9	11.8	22.6	17.2
Any substance disorder	35.4	17.9	26.6	16.1	6.6	11.3
APD	5.8	1.2	3.5	—	—	—
NA psychoses	0.6	0.8	0.7	0.5	0.6	0.5
Any disorder	48.7	47.3	48.0	27.7	31.3	29.5

Note. *n* = 8,098; NCS = National Comorbidity Survey; NA = nonaffective psychoses; APD = antisocial personality disorder. From "Lifetime and 12-Month Prevalence of DSM-III-R Psychiatric Disorders in the United States," by R. C. Kessler et al., 1994, *Archives of General Psychiatry, 51*, p. 12. Copyright 1994 by American Medical Association. Adapted by permission.

sler et al., 1994). Differences were not affected by controlling for income or education. Hispanics, in contrast to Blacks, had significantly higher prevalences of current mood disorders. In view of the high crime rate for Blacks, it is interesting that there was no significant difference in the diagnosis of antisocial personality disorder, and the disorder was actually diagnosed somewhat less frequently in Blacks than in Whites.

Table 2.7 shows lifetime and 12-month prevalences of disorders for men and women. As in previous surveys, women had higher rates of anxiety and mood disorders (with the exception of mania). Men had higher rates of all substance-abuse and dependence disorders and antisocial personality disorder. Feminist critics of the DSM suggested that some of the diagnoses are written in a way that creates gender disparities. It is difficult to see how this is true for affective and anxiety disorders, but it could very well be true for some of the personality disorders such as dependent, histrionic, or borderline PDs. The larger number of women with anxiety and depressive mood disorders is congruent with the general finding that women score higher on measures of neuroticism, trait anxiety, or negative affectivity. The differences in diagnostic prevalence have been explained in terms of both biological and socialization differences. Regardless of the explanations for the gender (or sex) differences in particular disorders, they are real and not a function of biases in diagnosticians.

Prevalence

Prevalence is the proportion of the population who have had a disorder during a specified portion of their lives. *Morbidity risk* is the risk for a person's developing the disorder. The overall prevalence rates of disorders in Table 2.7 are quite high. If we accept the adequacy of the community survey, one out of two Americans will experience one of the disorders listed in the table sometime during their lives, and almost one out of three is currently or has recently (within the past year) had one of these disorders. Not included in these figures are those for the more common personality and sexual disorders. One out of three men will manifest an alcohol or drug-abuse or dependence problem, almost one out three women will have an anxiety disorder, and one out of four will have a mood disorder during their lifetimes. The prevalence figures are higher than those reported for the Epidemiological Catchment Area (ECA) study done a decade previously (Robins et al., 1984; Robins & Regier, 1991). In that survey, the lifetime prevalence of any of the disorders was 33% rather than the current 48%. The current National Comorbidity Study (NCS) sample is a national one, whereas the ECA sample was centered in several urban communities. The NCS used a younger age range, and most disorders decrease with age. The NCS used the *DSM-III-R*, whereas the ECA survey was based on the *DSM-III*. There were also some differences in the interview schedules used in the two studies, for example more extensive probes in the NCS interview, which could have produced more diagnoses in the NCS study. But even allowing for possible overdiagnosis in the surveys, the prevalence of psychopathology in the general population is sobering and underlines the importance of understanding its sources.

SUMMARY

The impetus for the changes from *DSM-II* to *DSM-III* was the embarrassing lack of reliability in psychiatric diagnoses. Researchers wanted clear-cut criteria for definition of a disorder, so they began to devise their own methods, for example, the Feighner and the Research Diagnostic criteria. *DSM-III* evolved from these methods. For a time it seemed that reliabilities of clinical disorders were markedly improved by the new methods. Reliabilities for personality disorders were still low, probably because they were less clearly defined and overlapped considerably. But more recent studies of *DSM-III* and *DSM-III-R* show an attrition in reliabilities of the clinical disorders so that many are still unsatisfactory.

The DSM has been more concerned with interjudge reliability than with consistency of symptoms within diagnoses or the "fuzzy" borders between diagnoses. Exclusionary rules hid some of the high comorbidity between diagnoses. When these rules were suspended, high rates of comorbidity were found. In the general population those people who have one diagnosable disorder are about 60% likely to have another concomitant diagnosis. High comorbidities are found between anxiety and depressive disorders, and between schizophrenia, mania, and substance abuse. High comorbidities are also found between clinical and personality disorders. The similarity of disorders such as avoidant personality disorder on Axis II and generalized social phobia on Axis I create differential diagnostic problems and unreliability. Still, the associations between Axis I and Axis II disorders are not random. Anxiety and depressive disorders are associated more with avoidant, dependent, and obsessive–compulsive PDs, suggesting their continuity with a general neuroticism personality factor. Schizotypic and paranoid PDs are associated with schizophrenia, and antisocial PD is most closely associated with substance abuse.

The continuity of diagnoses along a continuum of severity suggests that a dimensional approach would have greater reliability, validity, and flexibility. Three dimensional approaches are discussed: Eysenck's three-factor, Lorr's 10 dimensions of psychosis (which combine into six types), and Clark's 12 primary-symptom scales for personality disorders, which form three primary dimensions: negative affectivity (neuroticism and anxiety), positive affectivity, and disinhibition (impulsive, unsocialized sensation-seeking or psychopathy).

Laboratory tests involving biochemical or psychophysiological reactions associated with disorders hold some promise for more definitive criteria for diagnosis, but as yet, none have achieved a level of validity that would allow them to replace the clinical syndrome definitions of disorders. Many, however, suggest subcategories of major diagnoses, such as endogenous versus reactive depression, which may have different etiologies.

Family prevalence, twin, and adoption studies have suggested co-morbidities that reflect common underlying genetic or environmental factors. For example, they suggest some common genetic factor in generalized anxiety disorder and major depressive disorder, and between disorders within the schizophrenic spectrum. The newer methods of molecular genetics promise even more diagnostic resolution through the isolation of linkage markers and even specific genes for disorders.

Differential response to different kinds of drug therapies could show which disorders share a common diathesis, but without careful "pharmacological dissection," such studies can be misleading. Differential prognoses of the various disorders could also be a basis for classification, particularly for subtypes within major diagnoses.

Cultural differences may limit the applicability of diagnoses outside of Western cultures, but psychiatrists around the world are generally finding the DSM categories appropriate. Differences within the American population are found in prevalences of particular diagnoses as a function of class, ethnicity, and gender. More women than men have anxiety and mood disorders, whereas more men manifest substance-abuse disorders and antisocial personality. The sources of these pervasive differences are unclear, but they do not necessarily show a bias in diagnosticians or invalidate the diagnostic system.

3

ANXIETY DISORDERS

The anxiety disorders in the *Diagnostic and Statistical Manual of Mental Disorders* (4th ed., American Psychiatric Association, 1994) may be described in terms of the situations, objects, or thoughts provoking anxiety, the particular expressions of anxiety (autonomic, motoric, and cognitive), and the typical patterns of maladaptive behaviors used to deal with anxiety. Table 3.1 summarizes the criteria for the 11 anxiety disorders, without the exclusion criteria and other specifics. The question, "what is feared?" must go beyond the statement of the situation to ask "why is it feared?" Some people may fear going to restaurants because it would be difficult to get out in case of a panic attack (panic disorder with agoraphobia), or because they are afraid of embarrassment due to imperfect table manners (social phobia), or because they fear contamination from tainted food or dirt (obsessive–compulsive), or because they were once traumatized in a restaurant by a hold-up (posttraumatic stress disorder), or because they are unduly worried about their general health or finances (generalized anxiety disorder). In some disorders anxiety is expressed primarily in physiological reactions such as heart palpitations or breathing difficulties (panic disorder), in others primarily by avoidance (phobias), and still others by cognitive symptoms such as obsessions, worries, or distractiveness (generalized anxiety disorder), or detachment, apathy, and numbness (posttraumatic stress disorder). Avoidance, compulsion, and detachment are usually inadequate ways of dealing with anxiety, although for some narrow disorders

TABLE 3.1
Sources, Expressions, and Symptoms of Anxiety in the Anxiety Disorders (DSM-IV)

Disorder	Situational or Cognitive Sources of Anxiety	Expressions of Anxiety
PDA	Concern about having panic attack. Dying, losing control, going "crazy," having heart attack.	Panic attacks: heart palpitations, breathing difficulties, choking, nausea, dizziness, faintness, sweating.
Ag (without PD)	Being in places or situations from which escape might be difficult or embarrassing, e.g., crowds, bridges, highways, stores.	Avoidance of many or all situations or distress in such situations, especially when without a close companion.
PD with Ag	Both PD and Ag, as described above.	
SP	One or more social or performance situations involving unfamiliar people. Being humiliated, embarrassed, or appearing foolish or inadequate.	Avoidance of feared situations and distress or panic when exposed to such situations. Hypersensitivity, low self-esteem, inferiority feelings.
SpPs	Specific animals, insects, natural environments, i.e., storms, heights, water. Blood, injections, physicians, dentists. Flying, driving, tunnels, bridges, elevators, or other enclosed places.	Avoidance of feared situation(s) and distress or intense anxiety when exposed to situation(s). Person recognizes fear as excessive or unreasonable.
OC	Obsessive fears: contamination by dirt, germs. Harming others; leaving doors unlocked, disorder; unwanted intrusive thoughts or images, e.g., obscene.	Compulsions: excessive and repetitive hand-washing, praying, counting, checking, meaningless rituals, e.g., order of dressing. (Anxiety if not performed.)
GAD	Excessive, shifting worries about many dire possibilities, e.g., job, finances, health, misfortunes to children or spouse, or minor daily obligations or hassles.	Restlessness, fatigue, difficulty in concentration, muscle tension, sleep disturbance, irritability. (More days than not for at least 6 months.)
PTSD	Reexperiencing the original traumatic situation. (Persists for more than 1 month after the trauma.)	Avoidance of thoughts, feelings, places, people associated with the trauma. Amnesia, feelings of detachment, estrangement, restricted affect, irritability, hypervigilance, insomnia.
Acute SD	Same as PTSD except that it occurs within 4 weeks after the trauma.	
AD due to general medical condition	May be with generalized anxiety, panic attacks, obsessive-compulsive symptoms.	
Substance-induced AD	May be with generalized anxiety, panic attacks, obsessive-compulsive, phobic symptoms.	

Note. PD = panic disorder; PDA = panic disorder with agoraphobia; SP = social phobia; OCD = obsessive–compulsive disorder; GAD = generalized anxiety disorder; PTSD = posttraumatic stress disorder; Ag = agoraphobia; SpPs = specific phobias; SD = stress disorder; AD = anxiety disorder.

such as specific phobias, the avoidance may not incur much distress or interfere "significantly with the person's daily routine, occupational . . . functioning, or social life or relationships" (*DSM-IV*, 1994, p. 405). A snake phobia in a person living in a large city would not necessarily be a phobic disorder by this criterion.

Acute and posttraumatic stress disorders are assumed to have their origins primarily in being in, witnessing, or hearing of an extreme traumatic event involving actual or threatened death or injury to others, especially family members, or oneself. War and catastrophies such as explosions, fires, and criminal assaults are typical sources of trauma. The last two disorders in the *DSM-IV* anxiety list, anxiety disorder due to a medical condition and substance-induced anxiety disorder, are assumed to be a direct result of the organic processes involved in specific medical disorders (e.g., hyperthyroidism), or substance intoxication or withdrawal.

COMORBIDITY

Among Anxiety Disorders and Between Anxiety and Depressive Disorders

Although there are distinctions between the anxiety disorders described in Table 3.1, there is extensive comorbidity among them when exclusionary rules are suspended. Among patients given a principal anxiety disorder diagnosis, half have at least one other clinically significant anxiety or depressive disorder diagnosis (T. A. Brown & Barlow, 1992). Generalized anxiety disorder (GAD) and panic disorder with agoraphobia (PDA) had the highest comorbidity rates, and GAD and social phobia had the highest rates of assignment as additional diagnoses for other disorders.

It has been argued that the extensive comorbidity among anxiety disorders and between anxiety disorders and unipolar depressive disorders (major depression and dysthymia) argues for the existence of a general neuroticism dimension for anxiety and depressive disorders (Andrews, Stewart, Morris-Yates, Holt, & Henderson, 1990).

The highest loading disorders on the general neuroticism factor in the Andrews et al. (1990) study were major depression and dysthymia. About 68% of major depressive disorders and 58% of dysthymic disorders had a lifetime secondary diagnosis of GAD. A high comorbidity of major depression with anxiety disorders has been found in many other studies (Sanderson & Wetzler, 1991).

Of Anxiety and Personality Disorders

If anxiety and depressive disorders share a common neuroticism trait, we would expect that they also share a similar comorbidity with the Cluster

C subgroup of personality disorders characterized in *DSM-IV* as "anxious-fearful." Cluster C includes the following:

1. *Avoidant Personality Disorder.* This disorder is characterized by fears of criticism, rejection, ridicule or shame, leading to avoidance of social and certain occupational situations and avoidance or restraint in intimate relationships because of these fears. The disorder is also characterized by chronic feelings of inferiority, and self-perceptions of social ineptness and unattractiveness.

2. *Dependent Personality Disorder.* Like the avoidant personality, the dependent personality type is characterized by fears of rejection and feelings of inadequacy, but unlike the avoidant personality the dependent personality type responds by seeking nuturance and support from others, especially those in a close relationship. Because of their lack of self-confidence, people with dependent personality have difficulty in making everyday decisions or assuming responsibilities, preferring to let others take charge of these things and make decisions for them. They are afraid and feel helpless when alone. They fear asserting themselves lest they lose the support or approval from others, particularly those on whom they are most dependent.

3. *Obsessive–Compulsive Personality Disorder (OCD).* Although not necessarily overtly fearful, those people with OCD are overly concerned about control of themselves and their environments. They are preoccupied with order and perfectionistic to the point of inability to complete projects because of failure to meet rigid standards. They may also try to impose their strict standards of order and perfection on others, and they may become petulant when others do not meet these standards or when they are questioned about their demands. They tend to be overconscientious and inflexible about morality, ethics, and values, even by the standards of those within their own religious or cultural group. They seem to lack the capacity to relax or be spontaneous even in leisure time or with family and friends. They tend to be stingy about both money and expression of affectionate feelings. They tend to hoard worn-out possessions and useless papers.

Anxiety and depressive disorders on Axis I tend to be associated with the Cluster C of personality disorders far more than the other two clusters: Cluster A, the "odd-eccentric" (paranoid, schizoid, schizotypal), and Cluster B, the "dramatic-emotional" (antisocial, borderline, histrionic, narcissistic; Oldham et al., 1995; Sanderson, Wetzler, Beck, & Betz, 1992, 1994). Oldham et al. also found some association between anxiety disorders and borderline PD from Cluster B. Social phobia, GAD, and panic disorder were the anxiety disorders most highly associated with Cluster C personality disorders, whereas specific phobic disorders showed little association with personality disorders of any type.

There is a great deal of conceptual similarity between the diagnoses of generalized social phobia (GSP) and avoidant personality disorder (APD). In *DSM-III* one could not make a diagnosis of social phobia (SP) if the criteria for APD were met. This rule was suspended in *DSM-III-R*, which introduced the distinction between SP and GSP. Herbert, Hope, and Bellack (1992) found that of subjects from the community with a diagnosis of GSP, 61% also met the criteria for APD. All subjects with APD met the criteria for GSP. The authors conclude that "GSP and APD represent different points on a continuum of severity" (p. 338).

The continuity of the obsessive–compulsive disorder (OCD) in the general population was demonstrated by Nestadt et al. (1991) using interviews from the ECA prevalence study. They rated the severity (0–3) of each of five OCD traits from the *DSM-III*, and from this calculated a compulsivity score ranging from 0 to 15. Figure 3.1 shows the distribution of the trait in a survey among the general population. The shaded zone of the distribution represents those people meeting the diagnostic criterion of severe expression on four or more traits. A similar approach to other personality disorders would probably yield the same type of continuity, showing the arbitrariness of some of the distinctions between clinical (Axis I) and personality (Axis II) disorders.

The presence of a personality disorder diagnosis along with a clinical (Axis I) diagnosis implies a chronicity of the traits underlying the disorder and perhaps a stronger constitutional factor in the disorder than in one which appears with little predisposition. Anxiety and depressive disorders with comorbid personality disorders have more severe symptoms of anxiety and depression than those without PDs (Flick, Roy-Byrne, Cowley, Shores, & Dunner, 1993).

Prevalence and Demographic Characteristics

Table 3.2 shows the lifetime and 12-month prevalences of the anxiety disorders from the NCS survey (Kessler et al., 1994). The figures for posttraumatic stress disorder were added after the initial publication (Kessler, Sonnega, Bromet, Hughes, & Nelson, 1995). One quarter of the population was estimated to develop an anxiety disorder at some time in their lives, and about 17% were diagnosed as having one currently or during the past 12 months. The most frequent kind of anxiety disorder (lifetime prevalence) was social phobia (13%) followed closely by specific phobia (11%). These rates are higher than those found in the ECA study (Regier, Narrow, & Rae, 1990), the other large recent study done in the United States, where a 1-month prevalence of 7.3% was found for anxiety disorders. However, the ECA study used the *DSM-III* and was not based on a representative national sample.

Both major studies found that women have about twice the incidence of anxiety disorders as men. This is true for all of the anxiety disorders except social phobia where women still outnumber men but not at the 2:1 ratio characteristic of other anxiety disorders. Anxiety disorders (12-

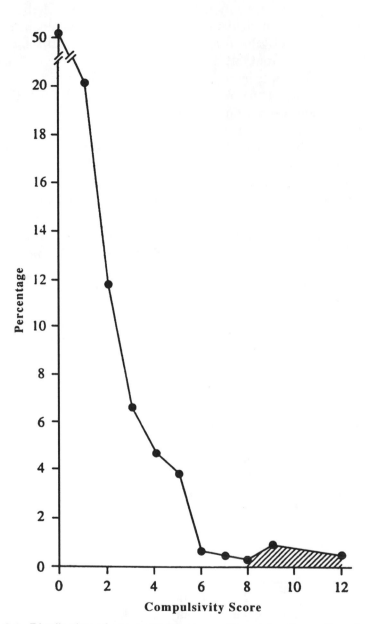

Figure 3.1. Distribution of compulsivity scores (from interview ratings in the ECA study) in the general population (hatched portion of curve are those persons with diagnosed *DSM-III* compulsive personality disorder). From "DSM-III Compulsive Personality Disorder: An Epidemiological Survey," by G. Nestadt et al., 1991, *Psychological Medicine, 21*, p. 465. Copyright 1991 by Cambridge University Press. Reprinted by permission.

TABLE 3.2
Prevalence (%) of *DSM-III-R* Anxiety Disorders (NCS)

Disorders	Lifetime Prevalence			12-Month Prevalence		
	Male	Female	Total	Male	Female	Total
PD	2.0	5.0	3.5	1.3	3.2	2.3
Ag no PD	3.5	7.0	5.3	1.7	3.8	2.8
SP	11.1	15.5	13.3	6.6	9.1	7.9
SpPs	6.7	15.7	11.3	4.4	13.2	8.8
GAD	3.6	6.6	5.1	2.0	4.3	3.1
PTSD	5.0	10.4	7.8			
Any anxiety disorder	19.2	30.5	24.9	11.8	22.6	17.2

Note. $n = 8,098$. NCS = National Comorbidity Survey; PD = panic disorder; Ag = agoraphobia; SP = social phobia; SpPs = specific phobias; GAD = generalized anxiety disorder; PTSD = posttraumatic stress disorder. From "Lifetime and 12-month Prevalence of DSM-III-R Psychiatric Disorders in the United States," by R. C. Kessler et al., 1994, *Archives of General Psychiatry, 51,* p. 11. Copyright 1994 by American Medical Association. Adapted by permission.

month prevalence) are highest in the youngest age groups (15–24 years) and tend to decline with increasing age in the NCR study; in the ECA study, they peak in the 25- to 44-year-old range and decline after that in the two older groups. Anxiety disorders decline as a function of increasing income and social class, with rates twice as high in the lowest income group as in the highest one. Similarly, rates decline as a function of education. Ethnicity (African American, European American, and Hispanic) was not related to incidence of anxiety disorders when income and education were controlled. In the ECA study, rates of anxiety disorders were higher in those who were separated or divorced than in those who were married, single, or widowed. Similar results were found for GAD in the NCS study (Wittchen, Zhao, Kessler, & Eaton, 1994).

Prevalence statistics indicate possible sources of stress or other etiological factors, but they are not at all definitive. What is the significance of the higher rate of anxiety disorders in women? The finding is consistent with the nearly universal finding of higher scores of women on neuroticism and anxiety trait scales in questionnaires, but does it indicate a socially learned difference in the expression of negative emotions, a greater stress in the lives of women, or a biological vulnerability that is different in men and women? Does the high rate of anxiety disorder in separated or divorced persons indicate that the stress of separation is a causal factor in anxiety disorder, or that persons with anxiety disorders are more likely to have marital problems? Similarly, the inverse relation between social class and anxiety could mean that the economic stresses of low social class and poverty are a factor in anxiety disorders, or that persons with anxiety disorders tend to be at a disadvantage in educational and vocational pursuits.

There are ways to test these alternative explanations for demographic differences, but unfortunately, most studies are not designed for this kind of hypothesis testing. In contrast, many of the genetic studies of disorders are designed to compare different etiological possibilities. These studies may also provide some answers to the problems of diagnostic comorbidity. Common genetic or environmental factors take us beyond the fact of a mere similarity in symptom phenomenology.

DIATHESIS

Genetics

Twin Studies

Concordance studies of twins are a crude way of estimating the genetic influences in a particular disorder. If a disorder were totally genetic, we would expect that if one of a pair of identical twins had the disorder then in all cases the other twin would also have the disorder, because identical twins have identical genes. However, in fraternal twins, who only share 50% of their genetic makeup, the concordance in the presence or absence of the disorder should be 50% in the case of total genetic determination, or about half of whatever the concordance rate is for identical twins. However, if the phenomenal comorbidity of disorders is actually a function of a partially shared genetic factor, then more genetic influence may be found for the broad class of disorders (rather than for the specific disorders within that class). Table 3.3 gives some concordance rates for the broad class of anxiety disorders and for the specific disorders within that class. Note that the low ns, particularly for some of the specific disorders, make a percentage statistic highly unreliable.

In general there is evidence of some heritability for both the broad category of anxiety disorders and the specific disorders such as panic disorder, agoraphobia, social phobia, and obsessive–compulsive disorder. In the Torgersen (1983) study, however, the concordance rates for GAD were about the same for identical and fraternal twins, and in the Carey and Gottesman (1981) study, the rates of concordance for specific phobia were only slightly different in identical and fraternal twins, suggesting a lack of genetic influence. Studies of identical twins separated at or near birth and raised in different families and environments provide a more stringent test of the influence of heredity because it is the only factor shared by the twins which could make them alike (assuming no selective placement). In the Minnesota separated-twin study (Lykken, 1982), nine pairs of identical twins reared apart were found in which at least one of the pair had a specific phobia (Eckert, Heston, & Bouchard, 1981). In six of these nine cases (67%), the other twin had a phobia, and in some cases, it was the same kind of phobia. This would indicate a stronger influence of heredity in the specific phobia than indicated by the Carey and Gottesman (1981) study.

TABLE 3.3
Twin Studies of Anxiety Disorders

		Concordance			
Authors	Diagnoses	Identical Twins *n*	Fraternal Twins *n*	Identical Twins %	Fraternal Twins %
Slater & Shields (1969)	Anxiety disorders	17	28	42	4
Torgersen (1983)	All anxiety disorders	32	53	34	17
	PD	5	6	60	33
	Ag	11	15	36	13
	SP	1	3	100	0
	GAD	12	20	17	20
	OCD	3	9	33	11
Rasmussen & Zahn (1984)[a]	OCD	51	—	57	—
Carey & Gottesman (1981)[b]	OCD	15	15	33	7
	Phobic disorders	8	13	13	8
Ekkert et al. (1981)[c]	Phobic disorders	9	—	67	—

[a]Data from 10 other studies. [b]Data from Maudsley twin register in cooperation with Shields.
[c]Identical twins separated at or near birth.

Toward the end of the 1980s and in the 1990s, more precise studies of twins were done by Kendler and his colleagues using large samples of twins who were found to have disorders, selected from the general population. These studies used multivariate techniques, which specified the proportional influences of shared and specific genetic factors and shared and specific environmental factors in the disorder. They also allowed an examination of the influence of comorbid disorders and specified which share common influences, whether genetic or environmental.

In analyses of anxiety and depressive symptoms (Kendler, Heath, Martin, & Eaves, 1987) or diagnoses (Kendler, Neale, Kessler, Heath, & Eaves, 1992b; Kendler, Walters, et al., 1995), it was found that GAD and major depression shared a common genetic factor (neuroticism?), but environmental factors determined whether the common diathesis would take the direction of a predominance of anxiety or depression.

The types of environment or life events that predispose toward anxiety are not the same as those that create a vulnerability to depression. These results are interesting because they are so counterintuitive. Previous notions suggested a different genetic basis for anxiety and depression with a common stressful environment releasing either according to the specific genetic vulnerability.

Kendler, Walters, et al. (1995) found another genetic factor that in-

TABLE 3.4
Estimated Heritabilities of Anxiety Disorders

Primary Disorder	Identical Twins (r)	Fraternal Twins (r)	Parameter Estimates From Models		
			h	s	ns
GAD (1 month)	.35	.12	.30	—	.67
GAD (6 months)	.28	.28	—	.23	.72
PD (1 month)	.35	.09	.29	—	.68
PD (6 months)	.29	.15	.23	—	.68
Ag	.41	.15	.39	—	.61
SP	.31	.12	.30	—	.70
Animal Phobia (specific)	.38	.04	.32	—	.68
Situational Phobia (specific)	.27	.27	—	.27	.73

Note. h = additive genetic effects; s = shared environmental effects; ns = nonshared environmental effects; GAD = generalized anxiety disorder; PD = panic disorder; Ag = agoraphobia (going out of house alone, being in crowds, being in open spaces); SP = social phobia (meeting new people, giving a speech, using public bathrooms, eating in public); Animal phobias (insects, spiders, mice, snakes, bats); Situational phobias (tunnels, other closed places, bridges, airplanes, other high places). From "The Genetic Epidemiology of Phobias in Women," by K. S. Kendler et al., 1992a, *Archives of General Psychiatry, 49,* p. 277. Copyright 1992 by American Medical Association; and "Major Depression and Generalized Anxiety Disorder: Same Genes (Partly) Different Environments?" by K. S. Kendler et al., 1992b, *Archives of General Psychiatry, 49,* p. 277. Adapted by permission.

cluded phobia, panic disorder, and bulimia. Alcoholism was based upon a specific genetic factor, not common with the other disorders. Table 3.4 shows the results from two studies (Kendler et al., 1992a, 1992b) of anxiety disorders diagnosed from personal interviews in a population-based register of adult female twins.

In the first study of generalized anxiety disorder (GAD), GAD was diagnosed using both the *DSM-III* 1-month duration and the *DSM-III-R* 6-month criterion (Kendler et al., 1992a). The second study (Kendler et al., 1992b), based on the same sample of twins, analyzed the genetic and environmental effects for *DSM-III*-based diagnoses of agoraphobia, social phobia, and specific phobias divided into situational types (tunnels, bridges, airplanes, closed spaces) and animal types (spiders, mice, snakes, bats, insects).

Modest heritabilities (23–39%) were found for all of the anxiety disorders except 6-month GAD and situation–specific phobias. For these two disorders a small but significant shared environment effect and a larger nonshared environment effect accounted for most of the variance in the best-fitting models. In the other disorders only nonshared environmental effects were significant.

A twin study of the broad trait of neuroticism (N) in females of about the same age and using a similar method of analysis (L. J. Eaves & Young, 1981), yielded a heritability of 51%, higher than any of the disorders in the Kendler et al. studies. Most twin studies of N trait in the normal population yield heritabilities around 50%. Perhaps the modest hereditary component shared by anxiety disorders is of the broad dispositional type encompassed in the trait of neuroticism. As Belmaker and Biederman (1994) suggest, "it may be more heuristic to look for genetic markers for temperamental traits rather than to look for markers of specific anxiety disorders" (p. 71).

Family Aggregation Studies

In most family studies, investigators examine the rates of the disorder in a proband group against the rates of that disorder and other disorders in their first-degree relatives (parents, children, and siblings). Unless the study compares rates of the disorder in biological and adoptive relatives of adoptees, it does not separate the effects of shared environment from genetic ones. Although an above chance rate of aggregation of a disorder in the relatives of probands cannot demonstrate whether this is due to genetic or shared environmental factors, the absence of an increased rate argues against the influence of either. Given the general lack of influence of shared environment in most of the studies of twins already discussed, it is unlikely that it is a strong influence in family studies; however, that possibility cannot be dismissed.

The high lifetime comorbidity of panic disorder with major depression plus the fact that the same drugs (tricyclic antidepressants) are often effective in treatment of both disorders have led some researchers to suggest a common genetic diathesis in the disorders. Four studies examined the prevalence of major depression and other disorders in the relatives of patients with panic disorders (R. B. Goldstein et al., 1994; Horwath et al., 1995; Mendlewicz, Papadimitroiu, & Wilmotte, 1993; Weissman et al., 1993). In all four studies the rates of panic disorder (with or without agoraphobia) in first-degree relatives of patients with panic disorder have been remarkably consistent, ranging from 13% to 16%, compared with rates in relatives of disorder-free controls of 1–2%, and relatives of patients with major depression and no history of panic disorder of 2–4%. The high lifetime comorbidity of panic disorder with major depressive disorder cannot be attributed to genetic or shared environmental factors, a similar conclusion to that reached in the twin study by Kendler, Walters, et al. (1995).

It has been argued that panic disorder is simply a more severe form of generalized anxiety disorder (GAD). The distinction between the two disorders was not made until DSM-III (1980). The results of twin and family studies (discussed below) support the legitimacy of the diagnostic distinction.

PERSONALITY

In the previous section on comorbidity it was noted that certain personality disorders were often found co-occurring with anxiety disorders. The problem with most studies of the role of personality in disorders is that one can seldom be sure that the current assessment of personality traits is not influenced by the disorder itself. This is particularly true of the trait of neuroticism, which tends to vary during the course of an anxiety or mood disorder. Longitudinal studies are most useful in showing the effects of temperament or personality in the disorders. The focus of this section, therefore, will be primarily on studies in which observations were made prior to the development of an anxiety disorder.

Temperament

Temperament may be distinguished from personality in that it concerns early appearing individual differences in emotional and behavioral reactivity, some of which may develop into basic personality characteristics. A significant body of prospective research has emerged from the work of Kagan (1994) and his colleagues (Kagan, Reznick, & Snidman, 1988) on inhibited and uninhibited children studied from 20 months of age to adolescence. In an earlier longitudinal study, Kagan and Moss (1962) found significant predictions from ratings of children's spontaneity in social interactions at ages 6–14 to ratings of social interaction anxiety in young adulthood. Those who were more inhibited at these earlier ages showed more social anxiety as young adults. Ratings of infants and children's reactions at ages younger than 6 were not generally predictive of adult anxiety reactions.

Later studies used more direct measures, such as observations of 21-month-old children's reactions to situations involving sudden exposures to unfamiliar adults, other children, or objects in an unfamiliar laboratory setting (Kagan, Reznick, & Snidman, 1988). These groups were again studied at 4, 5.5, and 7.5 years of age (Kagan et al., 1990).

The inhibited children from the 21-month-old cohort tended to have more than one anxiety disorder and had more phobic disorders at age 7, and the uninhibited children had more oppositional disorders at that age. Another study showed that the consistently inhibited children across all assessments from ages 4–7.5 had higher rates of all anxiety disorders, multiple anxiety disorders, and phobic disorders than nonstable inhibited and all uninhibited children (D. R. Hirshfeld et al., 1992). The parents and siblings of inhibited children in the Kagan cohort had a higher incidence of multiple anxiety disorders and social phobia, as well as childhood avoidant and overanxious disorders than parents of uninhibited children and normal controls (Rosenbaum et al., 1991).

Chess and Thomas (1984) also distinguished two types of babies who are inhibited in novel situations with strangers: those with a "difficult" temperament, that is, is fearful and distressed in novel situations and with new persons, and those with a slow-to-warm-up temperament, showing little distress but cautious about interactions and needing more time to adjust to new situations than less inhibited children. They report that 71% of the difficult temperament types of children were found to be at risk for the development of behavior disorders, contrasted with 50% of the "slow-to-warm-up" type and 10% of those with an "easy" temperament.

Gray (1982) describes a behavioral inhibition system (BIS) as a central factor in anxiety disorders (see Fig. 3.2). An overactive BIS is especially sensitive to signals of punishment and nonreward (frustration or deprivation), ambiguous or novel stimuli, and stimuli having an innate capacity to elicit fear, such as heights, animals, or other stimuli that are the sources of specific phobias. Individual differences in BIS reactivity may be the basis of the trait of anxious behavioral inhibition.

Personality Traits and the Anxiety Disorders

Studies using Eysenck's scales of neuroticism (N) and extraversion (E; Andrews et al., 1990; Kelly, 1980) and Costa and McRae's NEO (cited in Trull & Sher, 1994) found that people with anxiety disorders, with the exception of those with specific phobias, scored higher on N and lower on E than controls. People with specific phobias show essentially normal test profiles, while those with major depressive disorders show a profile similar to that for anxiety disorders.

These results are in accord with H. J. Eysenck's prediction that anxiety neurotics fall into the neurotic-introverted quadrant of his two-factor dimensions (1967). Gray (1982) has maintained that anxiety is a primary dimension of personality that lies between Eysenck's dimensions of N and E (but closer to N than to E). Can the anxiety disorders be conceptualized as simply the extreme of neuroticism or anxiety? This is a recurring question throughout this chapter.

Long-Term Outcome

If there is a personality component underlying anxiety disorders, then we would expect complete remissions to be less common over long periods of time and recurrences to be more common. Even psychotherapists admit that basic personality traits are difficult to change. Most outcome studies are evaluations of therapy, and for most of the anxiety disorders, the results are good for many types of therapy. But few evaluations are done beyond a year posttherapy. One study re-evaluated a group diagnosed with anxiety neurosis and a surgical control group after a period of 6 years posttreatment

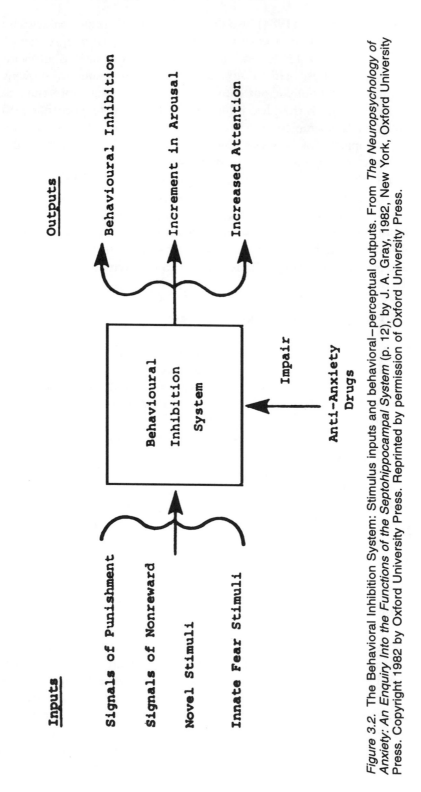

Figure 3.2. The Behavioral Inhibition System: Stimulus inputs and behavioral–perceptual outputs. From *The Neuropsychology of Anxiety: An Enquiry Into the Functions of the Septohippocampal System* (p. 12), by J. A. Gray, 1982, New York, Oxford University Press. Copyright 1982 by Oxford University Press. Reprinted by permission of Oxford University Press.

(Noyes, Clancy, Hoenk, & Slymen, 1980). At follow-up, only 23% of the anxiety group showed no impairment as contrasted with 59% of the control group: Nearly half of the anxiety group still had moderate to severe anxiety symptoms as compared to 17% of the controls. Two thirds of the anxious patients were initially classified as having personality disorders as well as anxiety disorders. The presence of premorbid personality disorders predicted negative outcomes in terms of symptoms.

Another study evaluated neurotic depressives and other neuroses over a 15-year period (Andrews, Neilson, Hunt, Stewart, & Kiloh, 1990). Only 14–18% of the neurotic groups were classified as "recovered and continuously well" over the 15-year period. The modal classification (38–48%) was "recovered and further episodes." "Never completely well but not incapacitated" (24–28%) and "incapacitated for more than 2 years or dead by suicide" (16–20%) characterized the outcomes for the remaining patients. Personality assessments predicted 20% of the variance in long-term outcome in neurotic groups. The effects of treatment for anxiety disorders may be less permanent than commonly thought. There is a core of personality that is not permanently changed for most patients, but remains as a vulnerability to future stress.

STRESS

Many people tend to regard stress as a function of the "slings and arrows of outrageous fortune," and therefore, as independent of genetic and shared environmental factors. But there are different kinds of stress. Some types, such as being in a bomb explosion or a natural disaster, are entirely fortuitous, and a function of being in the wrong place at the wrong time (specific environmental factor). Other types such as the death of a parent, may be shared by all members of the family (shared environmental factor). In still other types, the source of the stress itself may lie in the personality makeup of the individual, which depends in part on the genetic makeup of that person. A neurotic may have difficulties in interpersonal relationships and thus incur rejection from others.

Another way to classify stress situations is by danger or loss. *Loss* includes loss of a person (by separation, divorce, or death) or resources (loss of job) or a "cherished concept" (such as a spouse's fidelity); whereas danger is the threat of a future loss or a serious threat to life (G. W. Brown, 1993). Brown showed that pure anxiety cases are primarily associated with danger situations, whereas pure depressive cases are predominantly associated with loss.

A study conducted on a large number of twins drawn from a normal population examined the roles of genes, shared environments, and specific environmental factors on reported stressful experiences of the twins (Kendler, Neale, Kessler, Heath, & Eaves, 1993a). This experiencing of stressful life events could be explained by genetics (26%), shared familial environmental factors (18%), and nonshared or specific environmental factors (57%). However, the results varied as a function of the types of life-event difficulties. Events which involve death, serious illness or injury, or personal crises that happen to close relatives or friends in one's network have no genetic involvement, but relatively strong shared or specific environmental determinants. In contrast, interpersonal events, marital difficulties, personal illness or injury, financial problems, and the experience of being assaulted, involve primarily genetic and specific environmental factors. Whatever the sources of distress, it is apparent that some forms of life stress are not simply fortuitous environmental events but depend in part on what the individual defines as stressful (the data were obtained entirely from self-reports), and upon involvement of personality factors, which may have moderate genetic determinations.

One type of anxiety disorder is defined by persistent reactions to traumatic experiences: posttraumatic stress disorder (PTSD). PTSD may have many features in common with other kinds of disorders. Jordan et al. (1991) examined the lifetime and current (6 months) prevalence rates for specific psychiatric disorders—other than PTSD—among male and female veterans who were in Vietnam during the 1964–1975 war period, other veterans from that era who did not serve in Vietnam, and civilians matched with the veterans on relevant demographic factors. A further analysis was done by dividing the Vietnam veterans into those who had been exposed to severe war-zone stress such as combat, or for the females—mostly nurses—exposure to wounded and dead persons as well as to abusive violence, or even enemy fire.

More than 20 years after the war, 30% of the male veterans and 16% of the female veterans who had been exposed to extreme stress were currently suffering from some disorder, contrasted with 13–14% of the males and 5% of the females in the other groups. The prevalence in the high-stress-exposed male group significantly exceeded the rates for the low-stress-exposed group of war-zone veterans for six of the nine disorders, including panic disorder, obsessive–compulsive disorder, and GAD. Nonanxiety disorders that were higher in the high-stress group included depressive episode, alcohol abuse or dependence, and antisocial personality disorder. There was a more limited range of disorders in the female veterans, and the high-stress group had higher prevalence rates for only two of the disorders: depressive episode and panic disorder. Jordan et al. (1991) conducted a preliminary investigation of age of onset of disorders and concluded that "most of the disorders observed developed during or after Vietnam service" (p. 214). There is little doubt that the stress of war leaves residual psychopathology, particularly anxiety disorders among its sufferers. The role of stress in psychopathology does not seem to be a linear one.

The higher incidence of disorders was seen only in the group exposed to the extreme stresses of combat in Vietnam. Other troops in Vietnam who were not exposed to such extreme stress had rates of disorder that were not higher than those of veterans who did not serve in Vietnam at all and in those of civilians of the same age cohort.

Whereas war veterans may have been exposed to many stressful events over relatively longer periods of time, civilian stress involving traumatic life-threatening events is usually confined to a single major incident. One group of investigators examined survivors of a dam collapse (B. L. Green, Lindy, Grace, & Leonard, 1992). PTSD was initially diagnosed in 59% of the sample and comorbid lifetime prevalences of major depression (36%), GAD (18%), and simple phobia (16%) were also high. Fourteen years later, 25% of the civilian group exposed to the trauma still suffered from PTSD with continued high rates of major depression (19%), GAD (18%), and simple phobia (16%). Their rates of PTSD and comorbid depressive and anxiety disorders were quite similar to those found in Vietnam veterans in the same community.

Most civilians who exhibit anxiety disorders are not reacting to a traumatic event, but many relate their anxiety to marital or relationship sources of stress. It is difficult to separate the causal roles of the disorder itself and the marital stress because they are usually interactive. McLeod (1994) studied the marital quality among couples in which either or both members of the pair suffered from an anxiety disorder. Marital stress was associated with GAD in wives, with phobic disorders in husbands, and with panic disorder in both husbands and wives. McLeod attempted to estimate whether the disorder preceded or accompanied the marital stress. Only GAD in the wives seemed to be a clear consequence of the marital stress. In the other types of disorders the disorder preceded the marital stress. Although the marital problems may have exacerbated the already existing disorder, they could not be blamed for it. The disorder itself may have been a factor in the marital stress. Panic disorder and phobias, particularly agoraphobia, can make strong dependency demands on the well partner, leading to separation threats.

Both the genetic studies and those of marital relationships suggest that personality may influence the likelihood of encountering certain types of life stress, namely those which are a function of the individual's own behavior. The personality trait most closely associated with anxiety disorders is neuroticism, so it is not surprising to find that this trait is also associated with interpersonal types of stressors. Poulton and Andrews (1992) divided stressful life events reported by subjects into those that could be regarded as caused by chance and those more likely to be generated by the subjects or significant others. This longitudinal study included repeated measures of neuroticism as well as of life events. Subjects with high aggregated neuroticism (N) scores on the EPQ reported many more stressful interpersonal life events, but did not differ on reports of chance life events compared to those low on N.

Thus far this chapter has been concerned with anxiety disorders in general. What follows will focus on specific disorders: the validity of their diagnoses, their biological and cognitive sources, and their outcomes.

PANIC DISORDER (PD)

In *DSM-II* (1952), no distinction was made between panic disorder (PD) and generalized anxiety disorder (GAD); both were subsumed under the psychoneurotic disorder "anxiety reaction." Similarly, no distinctions were made between agoraphobia, social phobia, and specific phobia in the *DSM-II* category of "phobic reaction." The distinction between panic disorder and GAD owes much to the work of D. F. Klein (1967, 1981), who concluded on the basis of differential effectiveness of two classes of drugs, benzodiazepines and antidepressants, that the two disorders had different biological bases as well as phenomenal expressions.

Not all psychopathologists have accepted the distinction between panic and more moderate anxiety expressions, insisting they are merely points on a continuum ranging from mild apprehension to extreme panic reactions (Marks, 1987; Turner, Beidel, & Jacob, 1988). Others feel that the distinction is based on the different cognitive reactions to physiological arousal and its meanings to the person (Beck, Emery, & Greenberg, 1985; Chambless, 1988; D. M. Clark, 1988; Lang, 1988).

Phenomenology

Barlow (1988; Barlow, Brown, & Craske, 1994) maintains that the panic attack is an acute fear reaction that differs from the normal reaction of fear in that it appears at inappropriate or unexpected times with no apparent stimulus. The PD includes such attacks with the added development of anxiety based on the apprehension of future attacks. Panic attacks are defined in *DSM-IV* (1994) as "a discrete period of intense fear or discomfort in which four (or more) . . . symptoms develop abruptly and reach a peak within 10 minutes" (p. 395). The four symptoms are any of a list of 14, including symptoms of autonomic system arousal such as palpitations, smothering, and sweating; subjective sensations such as dizziness; and general fears such as losing control, dying, or "going crazy." These reactions may appear in other types of anxiety disorders in which they are cued by specific stimuli or situations (specific or social phobias). This may be one reason for the high comorbidity of panic disorder with other anxiety disorders. Panic disorder is defined by recurrent *unexpected* (uncued) panic attacks where at least some of the attacks are followed by 1 month or more of persistent worry about having more such attacks, about the implications of the attacks, or about a significant change of behavior related to the attacks (e.g., restricting activities). Agoraphobia may be one of the latter complications.

Panic attacks are not synonymous with PD if there is no persisting concern about the attacks. In fact, about a third of the nonclinical population reported having at least one such attack in the previous year, although these attacks were generally less severe than those experienced by panic disorder patients and may have been triggered by specific cues (Wilson, Sandler, Asmundson, Ediger, & Larsen, 1992).

People diagnosed with PDs were compared with a group of nonclinical panickers who reported panic attacks in the past but had not sought treatment for these attacks (McNally, Hornis, & O'Donnell, 1995). The PDs and nonclinical panickers showed similar symptom profiles, but the PDs reported greater severity of most of the symptoms. The three symptoms with the largest effect sizes were cognitive: fears of dying, of having a heart attack, or of losing control. Among the physiological symptoms, the one with the largest effect size was "choking or smothering sensations." The major distinction between the specific symptoms of panic in PD patients and the larger group of nonclinical panickers was in the intensity and frequency of symptoms and the percentage of the groups that experienced unexpected attacks.

Barlow and Craske (1988) reached similar conclusions in comparing PD with other anxiety and depressive disorders. The PD patients reported more intense symptoms than those in most of the groups, but the only symptoms distinguishing the PD from the GAD group were the cognitive ones, that is fear of going crazy or losing control.

An important distinction between the panic attack and other anxiety expressions is that at least some of the panic attacks are "unexpected," in contrast with specific phobias or social phobias where the panic may be cued by a predictable situation or object. Although the cues for the panic attacks may be clear in the patient's mind, the cue or situation does not always elicit the attack, and the patient does not know when to expect the panic attack (Barlow et al., 1994). Unpredictability, by definition, is one difference between panic disorder and phobic disorders. The cue for the panic attack seems less important.

Another important difference between panic attacks and general anxiety is the duration and intensity of the attack. Panic attacks are sudden, rise to a peak quickly, and subside rapidly. General anxiety periods are less intense but more prolonged. Panic attacks have been assessed using heart rate (HR) measures in the laboratory (e.g., Barlow et al., 1994) and in the field using ambulatory heart rate monitors (e.g., Freedman, Ianni, Ettedgui, & Puthezhath, 1985). During a period reported by the subject as a panic attack, HR peaks within 1–5 min of the onset, considerably shorter than the *DSM-IV* 10-min rise-time criteria. But the subjective effects could last a little longer than the actual heart rate rise. The increase in HR during panic attacks was greater than during high-anxiety states without panic attacks (Freedman et al., 1985).

Comorbidity

About 60% of patients with PD have an additional diagnosis, most frequently agoraphobia, specific phobia, or social phobia. The other phobias may be components of the general agoraphobic reaction. In clinical samples nearly all cases (84%) of patients with PD have some agoraphobic complications, but a majority of agoraphobic symptoms are mild and limited to specific situations such as tunnels, bridges, or highways (T. A. Brown & Barlow, 1992). Panic attacks in with severe cases of agoraphobia who are housebound occur less often. However, higher rates of agoraphobia without PD have been found in community studies (Kessler et al., 1994; Regier et al., 1990). The reasons for this discrepancy between clinic and community studies will be discussed in the section on agoraphobia.

Prevalence

The lifetime prevalence of PD in the U.S. community (NCS study) is 3.5%, and the 12-month prevalence is 2.3% (Kessler et al., 1994). Women have a rate more than twice as high as men. A large survey using the ICD-10 criteria for a current panic disorder *or* agoraphobia, with interviews of screened patients from general health care centers in 15 countries across 4 continents, found rates of 1.5% for men and 2.8% for women (Gater et al., 1998). There was no significant center by gender interaction, suggesting that the overall gender ratio (women:men) of 1.63 was relatively constant across the diverse countries and cultures.

Genetics

The genetics of PD were discussed in the section on diatheses. There is a modest heritability for PD. Although PD shares a genetic factor with some other phobias, particularly agoraphobia, the genetic factors are different for PD and GAD or depression (Kendler, Walters, et al., 1995).

Neuropsychology

Neuroimaging methods, including magnetic resonance imaging (MRI) and positron emission tomography (PET), have allowed investigators to study the structure (MRI) and activity (PET) of all brain areas. Previously, brain structure could only be studied by autopsy and brain function by EEG. The electrical potentials of the EEG are limited to the cortical areas immediately below the electrodes. Neurological theories of psychopathology usually involve areas of the limbic brain, which are only now accessible in living humans through the neuroimaging methods. Figure 3.3 shows some of these structures, including the parahippocampal gyrus and the anterior temporal lobe, which are discussed below. Note that the limbic brain areas (stippled in the figure) lie under and inside the lobes of the cerebrum.

Reiman (1990; Reiman et al., 1989) conducted a series of studies on patients with panic disorder using the PET method of assessing cerebral blood flow (CBF) to image the brain and lactate infusion to provoke panic attacks. Prior to provocation of the panic attack, there was a significant difference between patients who subsequently panicked and those who did not as well as between the panickers and normal controls. The panic patients who panicked during the lactate procedure showed a relatively higher level of CBF in the right parahippocampal gyrus prior to the provocation of the attack and an increased CBF in the anterior ends of the temporal lobes during the attack itself.

Reiman concludes that the parahippocampal abnormality may represent a predisposition to anxiety mediated by projections to other regions, for instance the temporal lobe poles. Supporting the importance of the temporal lobe part of this hypothesis is the MRI finding that 43% of a lactate-sensitive panic group showed temporal lobe dysmorphias contrasted with only 10% of normal control subjects (Ontiveros, Fontaine, Breton, Fontaine, & Dery, 1989).

Psychopharmacology

The dorsal ascending noradrenergic system (DANA) originating in the locus coeruleus (Fig. 3.4) has been described as mediating anticipatory anxiety or "sensitivity to signals of punishment" (Gray, 1982), and as an alarm system responsible for panic attacks at the higher levels of activity (Redmond, 1987). Figure 3.5 shows the mechanisms of synaptic action for the noradrenergic neuron. Transmission of the nerve impulse across the synapse occurs when beta-1 receptors are occupied by norepinephrine (NE). Alpha-2 receptors on the presynaptic nerve terminal detect the NE in the synapse and trigger a negative feedback mechanism that inhibits the production process of NE within the neuron. Yohimbine blocks the alpha-2 receptor and thereby increases the level of NE and the activity in the system. It is as if a broken thermostat fails to shut off the furnace, and it continues to send up heat into an already overheated room. Clonidine has the reverse effect on the alpha-2 receptor thereby tending to reduce activity in the system.

Support for the Gray–Redmond hypothesis comes from the studies of Charney et al. (1990) who use yohimbine to provoke panic attacks in

VULNERABILITY TO PSYCHOPATHOLOGY

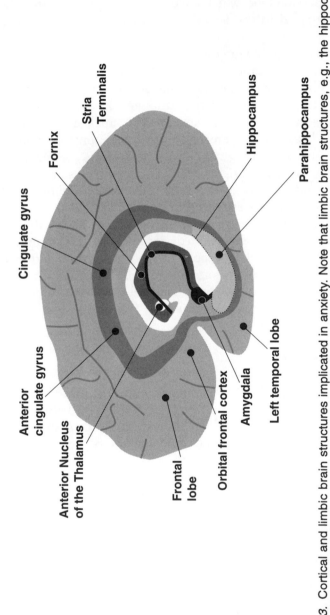

Figure 3.3. Cortical and limbic brain structures implicated in anxiety. Note that limbic brain structures, e.g., the hippocampus (stippled) lie under and inside the lobes of the cerebrum.

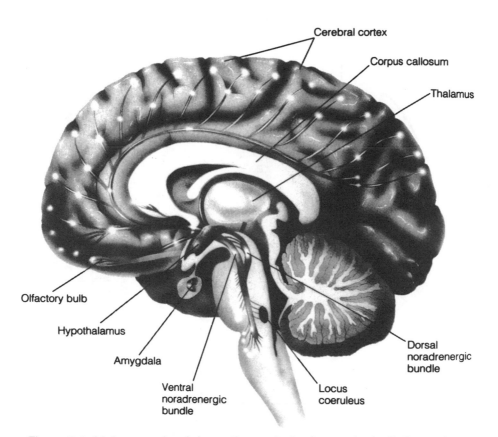

Cerebral cortex

Corpus callosum

Thalamus

Olfactory bulb

Hypothalamus

Amygdala

Ventral
noradrenergic
bundle

Locus
coeruleus

Dorsal
noradrenergic
bundle

Figure 3.4. Major norepinephrine pathways in the human brain. Pathway 1. Dorsal noradrenergic bundle originating in locus coeruleus and extending to cerebellum, thalamus, hippocampus, amygdala, the forebrain, and the entire neocortex. Pathway 2. The ventral noradrenergic bundle, originating in the medulla and pons and ending in the hypothalamus and limbic system. From *Biological Psychology,* by J. W. Kalat. Copyright 1998, 1995, 1992, 1988, 1984, 1981 by International Thomson Publishing Inc. Figure 10.20, p. 374. By permission Brooks/Cole Publishing Co. Originally published in C. Valzelli (1980). *Psychology of Aggression and Violence* (p. 46). New York: Raven Press.

patients with panic and other types of disorders and clonidine to reduce anxiety. They compared PD, GAD, OCD, major depression, and schizo-phrenic patients in response to yohimbine. In the panic disorder group, 54% had a full-blown panic attack compared to 13% of the normal controls and few of the other patient groups. The PD patients who panicked showed a greater increase in MHPG (the NE metabolite) than the PD group who did not panic, the normal controls, *and* the GAD group. Increase in anxiety ratings and peak increases in MHPG were significantly correlated ($r = .37$). Blood pressure (BP) also showed greater increases in panic disorder patients who panicked than in control patients, but these results were less specific in that other diagnostic groups also showed equivalent increases compared

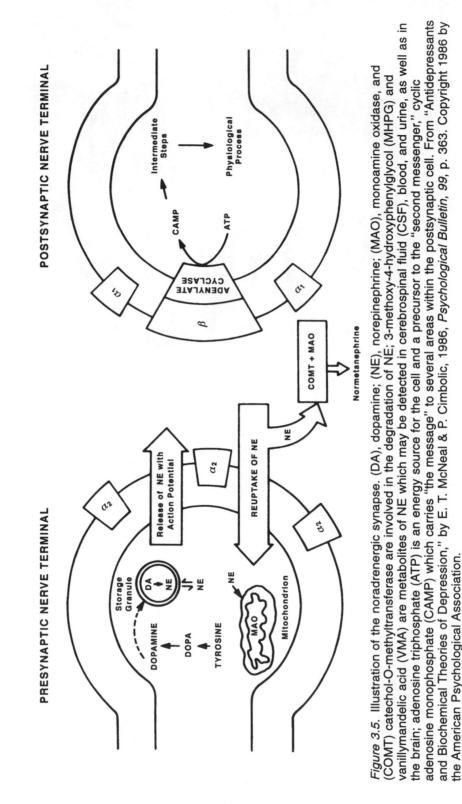

Figure 3.5. Illustration of the noradrenergic synapse. (DA), dopamine; (NE), norepinephrine; (MAO), monoamine oxidase, and (COMT) catechol-O-methyltransferase are involved in the degradation of NE; 3-methoxy-4-hydroxyphenylglycol (MHPG) and vanillymandelic acid (VMA) are metabolites of NE which may be detected in cerebrospinal fluid (CSF), blood, and urine, as well as in the brain; adenosine triphosphate (ATP) is an energy source for the cell and a precursor to the "second messenger," cyclic adenosine monophosphate (CAMP) which carries "the message" to several areas within the postsynaptic cell. From "Antidepressants and Biochemical Theories of Depression," by E. T. McNeal & P. Cimbolic, 1986, *Psychological Bulletin, 99,* p. 363. Copyright 1986 by the American Psychological Association.

with controls. Intravenous administered clonidine reduced MHPG levels, BP, and cortisol more in panic disorder patients than in controls, but there was no difference in anxiety reduction (Charney & Heninger, 1986).

Whereas significant anxiety and NE response to yohimbine is specific to a subgroup of the PD patients, the autonomic arousal was common to nearly all patient groups. The studies of yohimbine tend to confirm the role of the DANA in panic disorders and validate the distinction between panic disorder and GAD. However, there are other drugs and procedures that can provoke panic attacks in panic disorders, but which do not have direct effects on the noradrenergic systems. Table 3.5 shows the rates of panic provoked by other drugs, CO_2 inhalation, and voluntary hyperventilation, as well as the panic effects of yohimbine.

Uhde (1990) found that two thirds of PDs had given up coffee compared to about one fifth of depressive patients or normal controls. In fact, caffeine is a strong panicogenic substance, stimulating panic attacks in 71% of PD patients but in none of the normal control groups (Charney, Heninger, & Jatlow, 1985; Uhde, 1990). Caffeine is an antagonist for adenosine receptors in the brain. Adenosine produces sedation, hypotension, and has anticonvulsant properties. Caffeine effects are the opposite: behavioral activation, decreasing fatigue, increasing BP and heart rate, and inducing or

TABLE 3.5
Panic Reactions in Response to Drugs, CO_2, and Hyperventilation

Treatment	PD Patients (%)	Controls (%)	Study
Yohimbine	54	13	Charney et al. (1990)
Caffeine	71	0	Charney et al. (1985)
	38	0	Uhde (1990)
MCCP	52	32	Charney et al., 1987
	60	0	Kahn et al. (1988)
CCK			
low dose	91	17	Bradwejn et al. (1992)
high dose	100	47	
Flumazenil			
infusion	80	0	Nutt et al. (1990)
oral administration	40	0	Woods et al. (1991)
Isoproterenol	66	9	Pohl et al. (1988)
Sodium lactate	71	9	Sandberg & Liebowitz (1990) 6 studies
	67	13	Cowley & Arana (1990)
CO_2 inhalation			
5%	39	8	Gorman et al. (1988)
35%	51	2	Perna et al. (1995)
50%	63		Rapee et al. (1992)
Hyperventilation	37	16	Whittal & Goetsch (1995)
	23		Gorman et al. (1988)

Note. MCCP = metachlorophenylpiperazine; CCK = cholecystokinin.

augmenting seizures. There are also indirect effects of caffeine through other systems. Caffeine stimulates firing of the locus coeruleus (LC) and thus the NE alarm systems in the brain.

Metachlorophenylpiperazine (m-CPP), a serotonin agonist, induces panic attacks in a majority of PD patients in two studies, in none of the controls in one study (Kahn et al., 1988), and in one third of them in another (Charney et al., 1987). M-CPP stimulates postsynaptic serotonergic receptors and also increases release of prolactin, an index of serotonergic function, and cortisol.

CCK (cholecystokinin) is a neuropeptide that functions as a neurotransmitter and is often secreted with dopamine in the brain. It has produced the highest rates of panic reaction in PD patients of any drug (91% at low dosage, 100% at high dosage), but at high dosage it also produces panic in nearly 50% (higher in other studies) of normal control subjects (Bradwejn, Koszycki, & Covetoux-de-Terte, 1992). The drug produces intensely distressing somatic effects, including nausea, which might account for the high rates of panic even in normal controls.

Flumazenil is a GABA antagonist, and by reducing GABAnergic function, might release noradrenergic alarm reactions from GABAnergic inhibition. GABA is linked to the benzodiazepine receptors, and therefore, is a medium of action for these antianxiety drugs. The infusion of flumazil induced panic attacks in 80% of PDs, but not in controls (Nutt, Glue, Lawson, & Wilson, 1990). Oral administration was less provoking of panic but still produced a 40% rate of panic in PDs and none in controls. Participants reported that the attacks resembled their spontaneous attacks with one exception: There were no severe respiratory symptoms. The results were said to implicate altered benzodiazepine receptor function in panic disorder, but they raise the question of whether respiratory distress is an essential link in the panic disorder as suggested by many researchers.

Isoproterenol is a stimulant of the peripheral sympathetic nervous system through its agonistic action on beta-receptors. Peripheral catecholamines, particularly epinephrine, could be a direct source of many of the panic symptoms such as the accelerated heart rate and breathing difficulties. Isoproterenol provoked panic attacks in two thirds of a group of PD patients in comparison to 9% of normal controls (Pohl, Yeragani, Balon, Ortiz, & Aleem, 1990).

Sodium lactate infusion effects in six studies summarized by Sandberg and Liebowitz (1990), involving 133 PD patients and 53 controls, are combined to yield a rate of 71% of panic reactions in PD patients compared to 9% in normal controls. Infusion of a placebo such as glucose or saline rarely results in panic in PD patients and almost never in controls. Goetz et al. (1993) found that only 6% of the patients in 355 anxiety cases manifested a situationally produced panic attack (SPP) during a placebo infusion. The increase in ventilation preceding the panic in these SPPs was even more profound than in the lactate-produced panic reactions. Studies of obsessive–compulsive patients (Gorman et al., 1985) and social phobia patients (Liebowitz et al., 1985) revealed little panic response to lactate in these groups, but a study of GAD patients showed the same degree of panic response as in those patients with PDs (Cowley, Dager, McClellan, Roy-Byrne, & Dunner, 1988).

Most of the physiological symptoms of spontaneous panic attacks and lactate-induced attacks are quite similar. Lactate increases heart rate to levels similar to those seen in spontaneous panic attacks. Drugs that block panic attacks, such as the tricyclic antidepressants and aprazolam, also block lactate-induced anxiety.

Although lactate does not increase MHPG (the brain NE metabolite), lactate does increase peripheral plasma NE in both PD patients and controls (Carr et al., 1986). This suggests that lactate could induce panic through peripheral rather than central noradrenergic mechanisms. Supporting this notion is the fact that infusion of isoproterenol, an NE beta-receptor agonist, produces a high rate of panic attacks (80%) in PD patients. Isoproterenol does not cross the blood–brain barrier and therefore is assumed to affect peripheral NE receptors (Pohl et al., 1988).

Gorman and Papp (1990) suggest that lactate produces a state of peripheral alkalosis and is metabolized to CO_2. CO_2 crosses the blood–brain barrier and acts on ventral medullary chemoreceptors, which increase ventilation. The symptoms produced by hyperventilation then produce the panic reaction. This theory is supported by the provoking of panic through CO_2 inhalation. Either a 20-min breathing of 5% CO_2 (95% O_2) or a brief inhalation of 35 or 50% CO_2 may precipitate panic attacks in 31–63% of PD patients, contrasted with only 2–8% of controls (Papp et al., 1993; Perna, Cocchi, Bertani, Arancio, & Bellodi, 1995; Rapee, Brown, Antony, & Barlow, 1992). CO_2-produced panic in other anxiety disorders ranges from zero in mixed anxiety disorders (Gorman et al., 1988) to 30% in social phobics (Rapee, 1986). Although CO_2 inhalation is a potent stimulant for anxiety attacks in PD patients, voluntary hyperventilation is less so, producing a panic rate of only 23–37% in PDs and of 8% in other anxiety disorder patients (Gorman et al., 1988; Whittal & Goetsch, 1995). However, PD patients show greater increases in brain lactate than do normal controls in response to controlled hyperventilation (Dager et al., 1995).

Nearly all studies show that PD patients are more likely to panic in response to CO_2 inhalation or hyperventilation than are healthy controls or patients with other types of anxiety disorders. What is the basis of this specific mode of reaction, which partially defines the disorder? Klein (1993) has proposed that there are differences in threshold for the firing of an evolved suffocation alarm system. The cerebral production of lactate, shown to be greater in PD patients in the Dager et al. (1995) study, could be a trigger for this mechanism as could detectors for CO_2 levels.

Klein's theory does not rule out psychological factors in panic disorder, and he has emphasized the background of childhood and adult separation anxiety in the patients with panic and agoraphobic disorder. The role of such factors is suggested in a study by Carter, Hollon, Carson, and Shelton (1995). They found that PD patients experiencing a CO_2 challenge alone reported greater distress, catastrophic cognitions (e.g., having a heart attack or dying), and showed stronger heart rate increases (up to 96 bpm!) compared to PD patients with spouses or other safe persons present during the procedure. The latter group did not differ significantly from controls on most measures.

One of the fears patients with PD experience is a lack of control during a panic attack. The influence of a subjective feeling of control was shown in an experiment in which PD patients were exposed to 15 min of 5.5% CO_2 after they were told that the illumination of a dial indicated that they could reduce the CO_2 by turning the dial (Sanderson, Rapee, & Barlow, 1989). In actuality, the dial was inoperative; however, it was illuminated for half the subjects. In the group who thought they had control over the inhalation, only 20% panicked, but in the group who felt they had no control, 80% panicked. The results of both of these studies argue against a purely biological theory of panic disorder. Although there may be individual differences in the biological mechanisms underlying panic disorder, the thresholds for panic are clearly subject to the psychological influences discussed below.

Conditioning

Classical or Pavlovian conditioning provides a paradigm that lies between the biological and behavioral forms of explanation, because it is based on the extension of reflexive responses to conditioned stimuli (CS) by association between CS and unconditioned stimuli (UCS). According to these theories, the internal sensations, particularly cardiorespiratory ones, associated with panic attacks become the CSs for subsequent panic attacks (A. J. Goldstein & Chambless, 1978; Wolpe & Rowan, 1988). Although the classical conditioning models use external CSs and UCSs, these theories of panic are based on Razran's (1961) model of interoceptive conditioning in which internal stimuli could be used as CS to be associated with either internal or external UCSs. Cognitive and conditioning explanations often lead to the same predictions except that cognitions are deemed necessary in the cognitive account but are superfluous in the conditioning account. After all, animals show conditioned fear reactions but whether they have *cognitions* in the human sense of the term is questionable. McNally (1994) and others have invoked the notion of *automaticity* in some information processing, that is to say processing without expending deliberate or conscious effort or intent. This is the kind of processing that guides us home along a well-practiced route while our mind is engaged elsewhere. But McNally (1990, 1994) and others have pointed out the ambiguities in the conditioning model. According to the conditioning model, the internal sensations in the first panic attack provide the CS for subsequent attacks which are the CRs. But the panic attacks are primarily defined by these same internal sensations. So is the internal sensation, such as a missed heartbeat, dizziness, or breathlessness, a CS, a CR, or a UCS? Given the fact that sudden increases in these sensations occur in many conditions of arousal, why do they become CSs only for PD patients and why do they only elicit the full-blown panic reaction on some occasions?

These kinds of objections to conditioning theory have been answered by a broader view of conditioning (Mineka & Zinbarg, 1995). According to this view, all cues present during conditioning contribute to the strength of the conditioned response. Thus a safety cue such as a trusted companion may counterbalance an anxiety cue such as the facemask in CO_2 injection or the internal cues of smothering sensations. Lang (1988) describes a similar view. Emotions are described as conceptual networks involving representations of stimuli, responses, and meanings. Any of the representations may activate the network or enhance the effects of another representation.

Cognitive Theories

During the panic attacks, patients often have catastrophic cognitions such as "I am having a heart attack," or "I am going crazy." These are particularly prevalent in the first attacks, but they may also persist despite subsequent reassurances that these interpretations of their sensations are inaccurate. D. M. Clark (1988) maintains that catastrophic interpretations of body sensations during panic attacks are an essential causal link in the panic attack. These thoughts may become automatic, and therefore, not conscious. Catastrophic cognitions are both a state (at the time of the attack) and a trait, shown by a persisting tendency to regard certain body sensations as harbingers of doom. Critics of Clark's model (e.g., Seligman, 1988) have questioned the scientific validity or falsifiability of an approach that postulates unconscious cognitions but generates the same predictions as a more parsimonious conditioning approach.

An *anxiety trait* or neuroticism is generally involved in most anxiety disorders, but panic attacks are relatively specific to a subgroup of these disorders, the PDs. McNally (1990) proposes a trait of *anxiety sensitivity* (AS) defined as "fears of anxiety symptoms that are based on beliefs that these symptoms have harmful consequences." He differentiates AS from trait anxiety on the basis that AS refers to fear of anxiety symptoms themselves, whereas trait anxiety refers to fears of external stressors, such as social rejection. Persons with high AS do not necessarily interpret their cardiac sensations as a heart attack, but they may believe that the long-term consequence of cardiac dysregulation in panic attacks could produce a heart attack. They find intense arousal aversive and frightening.

McNally (1996) and his colleagues have shown that AS and trait anxiety have different but moderately correlated traits. AS is measured by a questionnaire, the Anxiety Sensitivity Index (ASI) which correlates moderately with measures of trait anxiety, but shows an incremental prediction of the frequency of panic attacks in phobic patients and surpasses trait anxiety indices in the prediction of fear responses to CO_2 inhalation and hyperventilation. Although PD and GAD patients score equally high on measures of trait anxiety, panic patients score higher on the ASI. However, high ASI is not synonymous with PD, and two thirds of high ASI scorers in a general college population reported that they had never experienced a panic attack.

There are many cognitive factors that determine the likelihood of panic in a given situation, including predictability, expectancies, sense of control, and information-processing biases (McNally, 1990). Most of these are probably influenced by the interaction between traits such as AS and elements of the situation or information provided to the participant in experiments. The question is: Are these panicogenic factors produced by the disorder, or did they precede the disorder? A second question is whether they are secondary to more fundamental biological traits or do they constitute the diathesis itself?

Barlow's integrative view of biological and psychological factors in panic disorder (1988; M. M. Antony & Barlow, 1996), shown in Fig. 3.6 is most compatible with the diathesis—stress viewpoint expressed in this volume. Barlow regards the panic reaction as similar to the biologically based mechanism of the primary emotion of fear. Panic is an alarm reaction, ordinarily seen in response to immediate threats to the survival of the organism, in contrast to anxiety, which is the response to anticipated threats. The PD sufferer is predisposed by a biological vulnerability (diathesis) to react to stress due to negative life events with a so-called false alarm that occurs in the absence of a real threat. The reactions in the alarm are associated with its internal sensations, leading to a learned or conditioned alarm reaction. It is at this point that cognitive factors, which constitute the psychological vulnerability, lead to the anxious apprehension of future alarms (panics) and the triggering of future alarms by conditioned autonomic and cognitive components of these alarms. In some PD patients, the avoidance reaction leads to the agoraphobic disorder the parameters of which are determined by the presence or absence of safety signals.

D. F. Klein (1981) offers another model that links panic with separation anxiety. Freud (1926/1959) originally suggested that the basic anx-

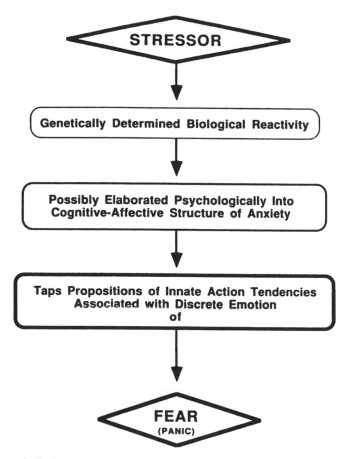

Figure 3.6. A diathesis–stress model for panic disorder. From *Anxiety and Its Disorders* (p. 178), by D. H. Barlow, 1988, New York: Guilford Press. Copyright 1988 by Guilford Press. Reprinted by permission.

iety is rooted in the vulnerability of the infant to maternal separation, which threatens its survival. Klein suggests that the biological vulnerability to panic is based on differences in threshold for the firing of an innate "separation alarm." The reaction, observable in the young of many species, consists of a typical protest reaction to the absence of the parent. Klein maintains that agoraphobic reactions are based on fear of panic attacks and that childhood separation anxiety is found in excess in the background of patients diagnosed with panic disorders with agoraphobia. Childhood events, such as prolonged maternal separations, parental divorce, or death were found in a higher proportion of agoraphobics than in normal control participants in some studies, but other studies have failed to confirm this or have found that the early separation experiences in agoraphobic patients did not exceed those found in other types of anxiety or mood disorders (McNally, 1994).

GENERALIZED ANXIETY DISORDER (GAD)

Phenomenology

The *DSM-IV* (4th ed., American Psychiatric Association, 1994) defines GAD as "excessive anxiety and worry. . . . occurring more days than not for at least 6 months, about a number of events or activities (such as work or school performance)" (p. 435) and adds the requirement that the person finds it difficult to control such worries. In addition to this cognitive component the diagnosis requires three or more of symptoms of somatic tension: restlessness, fatigue, difficulty concentrating, irritability, muscle tension, or sleep disturbance. As previously noted, there is a difference between GAD and PD in both cognitive and somatic symptoms. The anxiety in GAD is largely anticipatory of future threat (worry) as opposed to immediate threat (panic) in PD. The worries concern various threats in GAD but in PD are focused on having a panic attack. The somatic symptoms in GAD are primarily focused on the central nervous system and muscular tension, whereas in PD they are largely autonomic or cardiorespiratory. The condition must have been extant for at least 6 months in GAD in contrast with the 1-month requirement for PD. In *DSM-III* (1980) the criterion for GAD was set at only 1 month, but this shorter limit increased the possibility of including temporary adjustment reactions and GAD was conceptualized as a more chronic condition.

Actually the GAD condition is usually a long-standing one: the majority of patients report an onset before the age of 20, although a substantial minority report that the disorder began in adulthood (T. A. Brown, Barlow, & Liebowitz, 1994). The early onset patients report a history of childhood fears and inhibitions and a background of marital or sexual disturbances, whereas the adult onset patients often report that their GAD began after a stressful life event. Marital stress is a significant factor for GAD in women (McLeod, 1994). The condition tends to be a chronic one, but fluctuates markedly with the current levels of stress in the patient's life. The full remission rate at 2 years in one study was only 25%, despite the fact that most of the patients had received both some form of psychosocial and psychopharmacological treatment (Yonkers, Warshaw, Massion, & Keller, 1996). GAD patients have tended to respond less favorably to cognitive–behavioral treatments than patients with other kinds of anxiety disorders, perhaps because their symptoms are less specific, and these kinds of treatments tend to be targeted at specific kinds of symptoms (T. A. Brown et al., 1994).

The major worries GAD patients experience concern family, finance, work, and illness; although, a large proportion (23–31%) called "miscellanious" are unique to the individuals and not classifiable under these major categories (Borkovec, Shadnick, & Hopkins, 1991). Worry is not intrinsically an abnormal activity, and actually can be useful in preparations to cope with a realistic and anticipated negative event. A person who is worried about his job may plan job alternatives in the eventuality of being laid off. GAD patients do not differ much from normal control participants in the content of their worries. What distinguishes the worrying in GAD patients from that of normals is the percentage of the day that is taken up with worry, whether there are recognizable precipitants to the worry, the controllability of the worry, the realistic nature of the worry, and the ability to reduce the worry (Craske, Rapee, Jackel, & Barlow, 1989). The GAD patients cannot stop worrying, and therefore, spend a large portion of the day in this activity, which makes them more distractible and less efficient in other activities requiring attention.

Comorbidity

About two thirds of the patients with GAD have additional concurrent diagnoses, a comorbidity higher than that for any of the other anxiety disorders (Sanderson & Wetzler, 1991). In the NCS community survey, two thirds of GAD cases had at least one other comorbid disorder, and the lifetime comorbidity rate for GAD was 90% (Wittchen et al., 1994). The highest current comorbidity rates were with major depression (39%), but high rates were also found with nearly all other anxiety disorders. GAD is given as a secondary diagnosis in other anxiety and mood disorders less frequently, occurring most often in addition to dysthymic and major depressive diagnoses. Comorbidity of GAD and mood disorders would be higher if not for the DSM-III-R rule that GAD cannot be diagnosed if it appears only during the course of a mood disorder (T. A. Brown et al., 1994). However, the comorbidity data do establish the relative independence of GAD as a disorder and perhaps as the one from which other anxiety disorders emerge.

About half of the GAD patients have some comorbid personality disorder, the most common of these being obsessive–compulsive and avoidant personality disorders (Sanderson et al., 1994). However these disorders were diagnosed in only 13–16% of the GAD patients. In view of the fact that both obsessive–compulsive disorder (OCD) and GAD emphasize cognitive types of anxiety symptoms, their comorbidity might be expected.

Sanderson and Wetzler (1991) say that GAD is more like a personality disorder than a clinical disorder and suggest including an "anxious personality disorder" among the Axis II disorders. T. A. Brown et al. (1994) propose that GAD may represent a vulnerability to developing additional anxiety or even mood disorders. However conceptualized, GAD appears to be on a continuum of the general anxiety trait or higher than other anxiety disorders in a hierarchy of traits starting with negative affectivity (neuroticism).

Prevalence

The change in the temporal criterion for GAD from 1-month duration in *DSM-III* to 6 months in *DSM-III-R*, markedly decreased the prevalence rates of the disorder (Barlow & DiNardo, 1991). The lifetime prevalence for GAD in the United States is 6.6%, and the 12-month prevalence is 3.1% (Kessler et al., 1994). Women have rates about twice as high as those for men. In a community survey in England, the current prevalence rate of GAD was exactly what it was in the United States, 3.1%, and higher in women than in men (Mason & Wilkinson, 1996). The large study of rates of prevalence of current GAD conducted in health centers in 15 countries found average rates of 5.7% for men and 9.2% for women (Gater et al., 1998). There was a significant Sex × Center interaction. In most centers, the rate was higher among women than men, but in three centers, there was a tendency for men to have higher rates. There was no culturally obvious pattern distinguishing centers with very high female predominance ratios from those in which women had lower rates than men.

Genetics

Torgersen's (1983) study of identical and fraternal twins where one twin had a GAD showed equal concordance of identicals and fraternals, and therefore, no influence of heredity in this disorder. However, the numbers of twins were relatively small. As discussed previously, Kendler and his colleagues (Kendler, Walters, et al., 1995), using twins from a community survey, found evidence of a modest heritability for GAD and a genetic link between GAD and major depression. Curiously, the diagnosis of GAD based upon a 1-month duration had a significant genetic effect, whereas the diagnosis based on a 6-month criterion (as in *DSM-III-R* and *DSM-IV*) showed only environmental effects (see Table 3.4). Using the 1-month duration definition with broad diagnostic criteria, Roy and colleagues found a significant heritability of 49% for GAD in a community based sample of Swedish twins where one had been diagnosed with GAD (Roy, Neale, Pedersen, Mathé, & Kendler, 1995). Like Kendler et al., they also found that GAD and major depression shared the same genetic factors, but had specific nonshared environmental determinants. They suggest that GAD is primarily related to so-called danger events, whereas major depression is more a response to loss events.

Respondents to the NCS community survey were asked about the history of GAD in their parents (Kendler, Davis, & Kessler, 1997). The lifetime prevalence among parents of patients with GAD (34%) was more than twice that for parents of those cases not diagnosed with the disorder.

The odds ratio of 1.70 remained substantial even when controlled for the presence of other disorders.

Studies confirm the specificity of aggregation in the PD and GAD disorders. PD is found to a significant extent among the relatives of PD patients, but GAD is not (R. B. Goldstein et al., 1994; Mendlewicz et al., 1993). GAD is found among the relatives of GAD patients, but PD is not (Noyes, Clarkson, Crowe, Yates, & McChesney, 1987).

Biology of GAD

Some of the biological factors described for PD could be applicable to GAD, but the phenomenology and genetics of the two disorders suggest differences. The PD patients describe more autonomic arousal than those with GAD, whereas GAD is characterized more by factors of cognition and muscle tension, suggestive of central nervous system rather than autonomic nervous system involvement. Confirming the subjective symptoms, GAD patients showed more baseline muscle tension (EMG) than controls but did not differ in levels of autonomic arousal measured in the laboratory (Hoehn-Saric, McLeod, & Zimmerli, 1989). In the yohimbine and lactate challenge studies, there is much less response in GAD than in PD patients of either subjective symptoms, or physiological measures such as heart rate, blood pressure, or plasma MHPG.

Cowley and Roy-Byrne (1991) suggest that GAD patients may have decreased functional sensitivity of the benzodiazepine-GABA receptor complex in the brain. Weizman et al. (1987) found a 24% reduction in benzodiazepine binding sites in a group of GAD patients compared with controls. After treatment with diazepam, the maximum binding capacity of patients was similar to that of the normal controls. Buchsbaum et al. (1987) used the positron emission tomography (PET) scan to examine the effects of benzodiapines on regional glucose metabolism rates for GAD in baseline and stressful conditions. Benzodiazepine (BZ) produced decreases in the right frontal and visual cortex, and these decreases were correlated with the receptor density of these areas. The right frontal area has been implicated in anxiety reactions. Unfortunately, the GAD patients were not compared with control participants in this study, so that it does not constitute a test of the BZ-receptor hypothesis.

If the BZ-receptor GABA density is low in critical brain areas in GAD patients, this might predispose them to general anxiety. An anxious strain of rats has been shown to suffer from lowered density of BZ receptors. GABA receptors on the locus coeruleus (LC) may inhibit the firing of this structure, the source of the ascending noradrenergic system involved in panic attacks. Thus PD might arise from a general background of GAD through weakened inhibition over the spontaneous or provoked firing of the LC.

Analyses of questionnaires assessing GAD symptoms show a subset of items in the tension scale describing "vigilance and scanning," which are strongly predictive of overall measures of GAD (T. A. Brown et al., 1994). The concept is quite similar to Gray's (1982) description of a function of the septohippocampal system as continually checking the environment for novel signals incongruent with expected stimuli, or for signals associated with punishment. If such signals are detected, the system moves from the "checking" mode to a "control" mode, resulting in the inhibition and arousal characteristic of anxiety. The hypervigilance in the first mode resembles worry activity and may be an expression of an overactive septohippocampal system.

Cognition in GAD

In conflicts between neutral stimuli and stimuli with threat connotations, GAD patients allot more attention to threat stimuli and are biased toward threat stimuli in their recall (Rapee, 1991). The question is this: Are such interference factors as found in these patients simply a manifestation of the anxiety state they are in "more days than not," or are these preexisting and predisposing cognitive traits for GAD? Studies of the effects of cognitive therapy on laboratory measures of cognitive bias show a reduction of the bias to a level not differing from that of nonanxious controls (Mathews, Mogg, Kentish, & Eysenck, 1995; Mogg, Bradley, Millon, & White, 1995). Such studies suggest that the bias in information-processing is a state-dependent phenomenon, of the same kind that can be produced in normal control participants by stress or threat. If there are biological mechanisms underlying these cognitive tendencies, they could be modifiable by psychological treatments. However, one would expect that if the cognitive mechanisms were preexistent and predisposing, they would result in anxiety in childhood as well as in adult life and might be a function of an unstable and threatening family environment. All anxiety disorders probably have some childhood antecedents, but these factors cannot explain the specificity of the worry and tension symptoms of GAD.

Another cognitive explanation is that GAD patients perceive threat as uncontrollable, and therefore, it provokes more fear (Barlow, 1988, 1991). An attitude of helplessness has been postulated as a cause of depression, and Barlow suggests that the perception of uncontrollability and the consequent feelings of helplessness are also characteristic of GAD with mixed anxiety and depression. The more the sense of uncontrollability of dire events and helplessness, the greater the relative preponderance of depression. As previously discussed, GAD and major depression are highly comorbid and share some common genetic factors, so that it would not be surprising if they were distinguished by some of the same psychological mechanisms. Barlow (1991) suggests that negative life events during childhood over which the child had little or no control might lead to adult GAD *if* combined with a biological vulnerability.

SOCIAL PHOBIA (SP)

Phenomenology

Social phobia (SP) is defined in *DSM-IV* (1994) as "marked and persistent fear of one or more social or performance situations in which the person is exposed to unfamiliar people or to possible scrutiny by others" (p. 416). Panic or severe anxiety attacks may occur when exposed to the specific phobic situations, but spontaneous attacks or responses to non-evaluative or social situations are usually not seen. The fear is not of the panic attacks per se but of being shamed or embarrassed by one's poor performance or social impression in these situations. Such fears are not uncommon in the general population, but in SP they interfere significantly with relationships or occupational and academic functioning. Generalized social phobia (GSP) is a specifier which is used when fears are related to most social–interactional situations such as attending social affairs and parties, talking to strangers, and dealing with authority figures (Hazen & Stein, 1995). Nongeneralized social phobia (NGSP) is restricted to typical performance situations and the fear of being scrutinized closely, critically, or both: for example, speaking in public, eating or drinking in front of others, urinating in a public bathroom, or entering a room where people are already seated.

The symptoms of situationally induced panic in social phobia are like those seen in PD in many respects but differ in some specific reactions (Hazen & Stein, 1995). Reactions of dizziness, choking, numbness or tingling, feeling faint, and fear of dying are more severe in PDs, whereas muteness or "being unable to speak" is more common in SP panic attacks.

Comorbidity

In the ECA community study (using *DSM-III*), the most common lifetime comorbidities for SP were specific phobia (59%) and agoraphobia (45%) (Schneier et al., 1992). In two clinical samples, the most common lifetime comorbidity for SP was major depression (57–70%) with GAD, PD, and alcohol abuse or dependence also frequent (Mannuzza et al., 1995; Van Ameringen, Mancini, Styan, & Donison, 1991). GAD was also a frequent comorbid diagnosis, occurring in a third of SP patients in two studies (Turner, Beidel, Borden, Stanley, & Jacob, 1991; Van Ameringen et al., 1991).

The criteria for avoidant personality disorder (APD) on Axis II and

SP on Axis I are very similar. The *DSM-III* did not allow a diagnosis of both SP and APD, but this exclusion criterion was removed in *DSM-III-R*, resulting in a larger comorbidity of the personality and clinical disorders. In most studies avoidant personality disorder was the highest comorbid diagnosis with SP, as high as 75% if subthreshold diagnoses are allowed, but the other Cluster 3 personality disorders, dependent personality disorder, and OCD were also frequent (Jansen, Arntz, Merckelbach, & Mersch, 1994; Turner et al., 1991). If cases just below the threshold for diagnosis were considered, close to 90% of SP cases showed avoidant or obsessive features (Turner et al., 1991).

Prevalence and Demographic Characteristics

The NCS community survey (Kessler et al., 1994) found a lifetime prevalence of 13.3% and a 12-month prevalence of 7.9% for SP. The lifetime rate is very much higher than the ECA survey rate of 2.4% (Schneier et al., 1992), perhaps because of the change in diagnostic criteria for SP between *DSM-III* and *DSM III-R* and the more comprehensive structured interview questions used for SP in the more recent survey (J. R. Walker & Stein, 1995). The NCS data make SP the most prevalent (lifetime) diagnosis among the anxiety disorders, exceeded only by major depression and alcohol dependence in the full range of diagnoses. Could this be because the criteria include too large a range of persons who merely suffer from shyness? J. R. Walker and Stein (1995) claim that about a third of these cases are severely impaired so that the disorder as diagnosed is not a trivial one.

The NCS prevalence rates for the other anxiety disorders are about twice as high for women as for men, but the ratio is not as extreme for SP: Lifetime prevalence is 15.5% for women and 11.1% for men. In the ECA survey the ratio of women to men (3:2) was about the same as in the NCS study, but the absolute percentages for both sexes were much lower. Clinical samples of SP also reveal only a slightly higher preponderance of females (Mannuzza et al., 1995).

A review of 15 studies shows mean onsets between the ages of 13 and 20 years, with an earlier onset for the GSP than for the specific SP (Hazen & Stein, 1995). The ECA study found a mean age over all sites of about 15 years. In the ECA study, SP showed a declining frequency with age. Apparently, SP begins early in life and has even earlier antecedents in social anxiety disorders and inhibited temperament in young children (Francis & Radka, 1995). In the ECA study a bimodal distribution of age of onset was noted, with one peak from birth to 5 years of age and another from 11 to 15 years of age. The youngest group may represent a temperamental form of behavioral inhibition often expressed as fear of strangers (Kagan, 1994). A marked age difference was found between generalized and nongeneralized SP: The mean age of onset for GSP was 11 years, and for NGSP it was 17 years (Mannuzza et al., 1995).

Not surprising, considering the social inhibition implicit in the SP diagnosis, is the high proportion of patients who have never married: about 50% in clinical samples (Mannuzza et al., 1995) and about 30% in the ECA community sample (Schneier et al., 1992). In the clinical sample nearly two thirds of the GSP patients and only about one third of the NGSP patients were single and never married (Mannuzza et al., 1995). In the ECA community study, SP was related to both socioeconomic (SE) status and education; the highest rates were found in the lower SE and less educated groups.

Genetics

Although several studies of twins suggest a moderate heritability for broad social anxiety traits or social fears, only one has specifically used the SP diagnosis as defined in *DSM-III* (Knowles, Mannuzza, & Fyer, 1995). Kendler et al. (1992a) found a modest heritability of 30% for the disorder with concordance rates of 24.4% for identical and 15.3% for fraternal twins. Genetic factors specific to the disorder accounted for 21% of the variance, and another 10% came from a factor common to all types of phobic disorders. Specific (nonshared) environmental factors accounted for twice the variance as genetic factors. Family studies of SP show significantly higher rates of SP in the relatives of SP patients than in relatives of normal control participants or panic disorder patients and no differences are found in rates of other types of anxiety disorders (Fyer, Mannuzza, Chapman, Liebowitz, & Klein, 1993; Knowles et al., 1995). Fyer et al. found SP in 16% of the relatives of SP patients compared with 5% of control relatives.

Biological Factors

Some of the biological challenges used for PD described above have also been tried for SP (Tancer, Lewis, & Stein, 1995). Lactate infusion, for instance, resulted in a panic attack in only 1 of 15 SP patients compared with nearly half of the PD patients tested (Liebowitz et al., 1985), suggesting that the alarm mechanism involved in panic disorder may not be the same as the one triggered by social situations. Carbon dioxide (35%) inhalation produced panic in 72% of PD cases, 30% of SP cases, and none of the control subjects. The SP patients were more prone to panic than control participants but less so than PD patients. Studies of cortisol secretion and the dexamethasone suppression test show that the HPA axis is not involved in SP. A study of clonidine challenge, a probe directed at the central noradrenergic system, showed that SP patients shared a noradrenergic system reactive dysfunction with panic disorder patients, specifically an underreactivity of alpha-2 receptors to stress. This characteristic would result in an undampened alarm reaction because the alpha-2 receptors regulate the noradrenergic production. However, beta-receptor density appears to be normal in people with social phobias, suggesting that the sensitivity of the peripheral receptors mediating noradrenergic arousal is not a factor in SP.

Because the anxiety reactions of SP patients are in response to certain social situations, the testing of psychophysiological responses to these situations could show a particular susceptibility and reactivity of peripheral autonomic systems. Two studies failed to find differences in heart rate or catecholamine (epinephrine and norepinephrine) responses of SP patients and normal controls to a speech-giving situation, although patients reported greater subjective anxiety symptoms during the speech (Levin et al., 1993; Naftolowitz, Vaughn, Ranc, & Tancer, 1993). However, two other studies found differences between subjects with public-speaking NGSP and those with GSP or those with SP and APD (Heimberg, Hope, Dodge, & Becker, 1990; Hoffman, Newman, Ehlers, & Roth, 1995). Both specific and generalized types of SP showed higher levels of state anxiety and more inhibited speech production than control participants, but only the specific SP type showed higher heart rates than controls during the speech. The greater physiological reactivity of the specific SPs to the relevant situations could suggest conditioned reactions underlying these SPs as opposed to more general life experiences and biological vulnerabilities in the GSP and APD types.

Conditioning

Conditioning has been discussed in relation to other types of anxiety disorders. Mineka and Zinbarg (1995) have theorized about the role of conditioning and the evolution of specific vulnerabilities to social threat. Research has shown that viewing pictures of angry, head-on viewed faces as CSs in conditioning where shock is the UCS results in quicker conditioning and more resistance to extinction than when happy or neutral faces are used (Öhman, 1986). If threat expressions are biologically prepared stimuli for eliciting fear, then social anxiety may be influenced by individual differences in the biological mechanisms underlying such reactivity as well as experiences in which CRs were established in social threat situations. Hoffman, Ehlers, and Roth (1995) found that 89% of a group of speech phobic people recalled a traumatic experience associated with their phobias, but in most cases, these events occurred long after the phobia began so that they cannot be considered causal conditioning events. However, the most common fear in the social situation was of having a panic attack, followed by fears of extremely unpleasant outcomes and negative evaluations by others. Only 1 of 10 subjects who attributed their fears of giving a speech to fear of panic attack met the criteria for a panic disorder.

Although SPs may have "repressed" the traumatic conditioning origins of their social fears, perhaps broader social experiences and cognitive biases in perception, expectations (of failure in performance), and memories might account for SP.

Cognitive Factors

Mineka and Zinbarg (1995) have pointed to the role of inescapable punishment in general, and social defeat in particular, in creating social avoidance in primates. Such experiences can produce increased levels of submissiveness and a susceptibility to fear conditioning. SP persons have shown a sense of lack of control, as well as expectations and biased perceptions of negative evaluations that could stem from analogous experiences during development. Rapee and Lim (1992) had SP patients and control participants present a brief, impromptu speech to a small audience. Although global ratings of performance made by others revealed no differences in actual performance of SPs and controls, SP persons rated their overall performance as worse than did controls, and the SPs had a greater discrepancy between self and other ratings of performance. A Fear of Negative Evaluation trait scale predicted the discrepancy. A similar study demonstrated a negative bias in self-evaluations of people with SPs during a social interaction situation (Alden & Wallace, 1995). Real social behavioral deficits in those with SPs were observed: They were rated as less warm and less interested in the other person, as more visibly anxious, and as making fewer positive verbal responses. The question is this: Are these deficits in social skills fixed traits in SP persons or are they produced by their exaggerated fears of negative evaluations? The subjects in the Alden and Wallace study overestimated their negative behaviors and underestimated their positive behaviors during the interaction, suggesting the possibility of a negative memory bias which could cumulate into a negative expectation bias over time. However, studies of memory bias in SP persons compared to nonanxious control participants have shown no evidence of a memory bias for threat-related stimuli in either free-recall or recognition tasks (Cloitre, Cancienne, Heimberg, Holt, & Liebowitz, 1995; Rapee, McCallum, Melville, Ravenscroft, & Rodney, 1994). Perhaps the deficit is more the result of a generalized negative self-concept than of specific memory biases.

AGORAPHOBIA (Ag)

Agoraphobia (Ag) was first identified as a disorder in the 19th century. Psychiatrists described it as anxiety appearing when walking through empty spaces or empty streets. The *agora* was the marketplace in ancient

Greece, so the term literally means fear of the marketplace or plaza (today it would read "mallophobia" or fear of the mall). However, from what we know of the phobia today and the fears involved, a crowded marketplace or mall would be a more likely provoker of anxiety than an empty one. Ag is defined in *DSM-IV* (1994) as "anxiety about being in places or situations from which escape might be difficult (or embarrassing) or in which help may not be available in the event of having an unexpected or situationally predisposed panic-attack or panic-like symptoms" (p. 396). The typical situations feared are many that include being outside the home alone, particularly those from which one cannot extricate oneself easily such as being in a crowd, a restaurant, a theater, an elevator, in a line, or stalled in a traffic jam on a highway, bridge, or tunnel. Eventually the specific situations may combine so that the only option is to stay in the home or close to it, because one cannot drive or use public transportation. However, short of this result "the situations are avoided (travel is restricted) or else are endured with marked distress or with anxiety about having a Panic Attack or panic-like symptoms, or require the presence of a companion" (*DSM-IV*, p. 396).

Many of the situations people fear, such as elevators or bridges, could be the basis for a specific phobia if they were the *only* feared situation, and a fear of crowds or parties could be a social phobia if that class of situations were the only ones feared. What makes sense of the multiple-phobic situations avoided in Ag is the basic fear of *any* situation from which escape is difficult or embarrassing in the event of a panic attack or an anxiety attack short of a full-blown panic attack. Ag is now defined not as the fear of open spaces but as the "fear of fear," or the unpleasant symptoms of fear, which are the symptoms used to define a panic attack. Much of the fear is anticipatory, as when a person starts to go out and then thinks, "What if I should have an attack in (or at) __, could I easily get away without making a scene?" Usually the home is the safest place, but even that place may not be safe under some circumstances.

Thus the key to the avoidance patterns evidenced in Ag is the *source* of the fear. The major primary fear given by patients in one study was that of fainting or collapsing, and the most frequent secondary fear was of "causing a scene" (Mathews, Gelder, & Johnston, 1981). The primary fear is fear of a panic attack, and the secondary fear explains many of the avoidance patterns in public places.

Comorbidity

The close link of Ag with PD has resulted in one *DSM-IV* diagnosis for "panic disorder with agoraphobia," in which both disorders are diagnosable by the *DSM-IV* criteria, and it is assumed that the Ag has developed from the fear of panic attacks and their complications. The other diagnosis, which is more controversial, is "agoraphobia without history of panic disorder." The view of many (e.g., D. F. Klein, 1981), but not all (e.g., Marks, 1987), researchers is that Ag always develops as an avoidance reaction to panic attacks.

A survey of clinical studies involving 1,521 patients seeking help for Ag found only 6.5% of the cases involved agoraphobia without panic attacks, whereas in community studies involving 1,206 participants identified as having Ag, nearly two thirds reported no experience of panic attacks at or before the time they first experienced Ag (Horwath, Lish, Johnson, Hornig, & Weissman, 1993). However follow-up studies of cases diagnosed as agoraphobia without panic disorder showed that most cases were either misdiagnosed cases of specific or social phobia, or just missed the diagnostic threshold for PD by one panic symptom (Goisman et al., 1995). Nearly all patients had catastrophic cognitions characteristic of panic attacks. The problem is the dichotomous nature of medical diagnosis. A dimensional approach would not have the problem.

Prevalence and Demographics

In the NCS community prevalence study (Kessler et al., 1994) panic disorder with agoraphobia is subsumed under PD and not otherwise differentiated. Agoraphobia without panic disorder had an overall lifetime prevalence of 5.3% and a 12-month prevalence of 2.8%. Note that this figure is higher than that for panic disorder (see Table 4.2), which includes PD with and without Ag, illustrating again the discrepancy between community and clinical studies. The prevalence among women is twice the prevalence among men. The most typical age of onset is in the middle to late 20s, although there may be a bimodal distribution with one peak in late adolescence and another around age 30 (Mathews et al., 1981).

Cox, Endler, and Swinson (1995) compared groups with four levels of severity of Ag among PD patients based on levels of avoidance: none, mild, moderate, and severe. The definitions of these were not given, but in *DSM-III-R*, *severe* means completely housebound. There were no differences among the four levels on age, marital status, or gender. However, the PD group without Ag had a higher educational level than the PD groups with moderate and severe Ag. The less educated groups were more prone to have extreme agoraphobic avoidance.

Genetics

Torgersen (1983) found a 36% rate of concordance among identical twins with Ag compared with a 13% concordance among fraternal twins, indicating a moderate degree of genetic influence in the disorder. Ag had the highest heritability (39%) of all of the anxiety disorders in the larger scale twin study by Kendler et al. (1992a). The remainder of the variance (61%) was due to nonshared environment and error.

Noyes et al. (1986) found that the relatives of PD patients without Ag showed higher incidence of PD than controls and Ag was rare in this group. In a group of patients with Ag and a history of panic attacks, there was a higher incidence of both PD and Ag. The results tend to validate the idea that Ag is genetically as well as phenomenologically linked to PD, but pure PD may have a distinctive genetic makeup.

Biological Bases

If Ag is as closely linked to PD as the current literature suggests, then the biological factors already discussed in relation to PD would also play a role in Ag. However, not all PD patients develop agoraphobic avoidance reactions, and biological factors beyond those involved in PD could play a role in agoraphobia. The genetic factors in Ag are specific to that disorder and not shared with other phobic disorders (Kendler et al., 1992b), unlike PD which shares a genetic factor with specific phobias (Kendler, Walters, et al., 1995). These specific genetic factors could control discrete biological mechanisms. On the other hand, the extension of PD to agoraphobia could be a fortuitous conditioning factor based on the occurrence of panic attacks in particular situations.

Woods, Charney, McPherson, Gradman, & Henninger (1987) used situations that Ag patients thought would elicit their panic and found greater reports of panic symptoms and heart rate increases in these patients than in controls, but changes in blood pressure and plasma MHPG did not exceed those in controls. This pattern of response in the Ag patients suggests a greater response in the sympathetic nervous system and adrenal medulla, but not a greater response of the central or peripheral noradrenergic systems. Ag patients show higher heart rate levels and spontaneous skin conductance responses than normal control participants and patients with specific phobias under baseline conditions, indicating a generally heightened level of sympathetic system arousal even when not exposed to provocative situations.

Conditioning and Cognitive Factors

Conditioning theory of Ag suggests that the situations avoided by Ag patients are those in which they experienced a panic attack. But the common Ag situations share a conceptual similarity not an experiential one: They are situations in which escape would be difficult or embarrassing. Cox et al. (1995) found no evidence of a differential degree of situational experiences with panic attacks in severe, moderate, mild, or non-Ag panickers. The most common experience was characterized as "spontaneous" by this group or as not associated with a situation, and there were no differences between groups in the occurrence of spontaneous panic. The first attack, which would have been the basis for conditioning, was described by most as spontaneous. Patients often recall a generally stressful background in the development of Ag, but few of them recall a traumatic event associated with the Ag situation (Mathews et al., 1981).

In the Cox et al. (1995) study there were no differences between the Ag groups in the severity of panic symptoms (source of UCS), another factor that might facilitate conditioning. However, patients with more severe Ag anticipated panic in more situations than those without or those with mild Ag, and these anticipations were the most powerful predictor of agoraphobic severity. Sufferers of Ag were more prone to anticipate panic in novel situations, which may be why they find the familiarity of home reassuring. Those with more severe Ag were also more likely to use escape as a coping mechanism and to find it efficacious. Thus, they had negative efficacy and outcome expectations for these situations.

Cognitive factors seem more significant than conditioning in the development of Ag out of panic. If this is true, one would expect that breaking the cognitive link between panic and Ag avoidance, whether by direct exposure or cognitive therapy, or both, would be effective. Training in coping with panic without escaping should also be useful.

Trait anxiety and depression were related to the continuum of agoraphobia in the Cox et al. study, suggesting that the agoraphobia is an expression of general neurotic disability. The use of escape as a coping method is a common expression of neurosis. Low education might also limit coping skills, accounting for its relationship to agoraphobic severity.

Separation Anxiety

D. F. Klein's (1981) theory of the panic reaction is based on an evolved biological alarm reaction to separation in neonates. There are similarities between the Ag reaction and separation anxiety in children. The child with separation anxiety is distressed when leaving the home without the protective presence of a parent or other support figure. School phobia is a frequent expression of the disorder, although there may be other reasons for a fear of school. The adult Ag similarly depends on a trusted companion—often a spouse—for responsibilities such as shopping, and often cannot leave the house without the companion. Klein originally asserted that a history of school phobia was reported by half of a group of adult Ag patients. Follow-up studies reveal less impressive findings. A history of separation anxiety during childhood and adolescence is reported significantly more frequently in the background of agoraphobic patients than in patients with specific phobias or controls, but male Ag patients do not report this kind of history with any significant frequency (Gittleman

& Klein, 1985). Other studies describe histories of separation anxiety in parents of children with school phobias as well as a relatively high frequency of school phobia in children of agoraphobics.

Klein would explain these family similarities in terms of a genetically influenced, evolved biological separation mechanism. Gittleman and Klein (1985) note that the antidepressant drugs used to treat patients with PDs and Ag are also effective in treatment of school phobia. However, it is also possible that particular parental patterns, such as overprotection, might foster dependency in children and insecurity in social situations outside of the home. A review of studies of the parents of Ag patients shows a mixture of "confused and contradictory" results (Mathews et al., 1981). Whatever the mechanism, there is some evidence of a link between childhood separation anxiety and Ag.

SPECIFIC PHOBIAS (SpPs)

DSM-IV (1994) describes SpP as "marked and persistent fear that is excessive and unreasonable, cued by the presence or anticipation of a specific object or situation" (p. 410). The manual further specifies that exposure to the phobic stimulus almost invariably provokes an anxiety response, which may take the form of a panic attack, but one that is specific to the phobic situation. The phobic person usually recognizes that the fear is excessive or unreasonable but either avoids the stimulus or situation or else endures it with intense anxiety or distress. The fear and resultant avoidance pattern must interfere with the person's normal routine or occupational functioning or must cause marked distress to qualify as a diagnosable disorder. Many persons develop fears of certain situations, such as fear of flying, which cause little disruption in their lives because there is little need to confront the situation on a regular basis.

The *DSM-IV* classifies SpPs into five subtypes:

1. *Animal type*, cued by animals or insects.
2. *Natural environment type*, cued by situations in the natural environment such as storms, bodies of water, or heights (acrophobia).
3. *Blood-injection-injury type*, triggered by seeing blood or an injury, or invasive medical procedures such as an injection.
4. *Situational type*, stimulated by specific situations, such as public transportation, elevators, bridges, tunnels, flying, driving, or being in enclosed places (claustrophobia).
5. *Other type* for phobias not fitting into the first four types.

SpP patients may have more than one phobia within a given type or across types. A factor analysis of phobias within a general community sample yielded three factors: Animal Fears (like 1 above), Mutilation Fears (like 3 above), and Situational Fears (a combination of 2 and 4) (Frederikson, Annas, Fischer, & Wik, 1996). Although conditioning theory in its original form suggests that anything could become a conditioned stimulus for fear, there is actually a very limited range of common specific phobias. The argument is that evolutionary selection has made certain objects or situations prepotent for the acquiring of fears (Marks & Tobeña, 1990; Seligman, 1971).

Comorbidity

The only anxiety disorder showing much comorbidity (29%) with SpP is social phobia (Sanderson, DiNardo, et al., 1990). Unlike other anxiety disorders, there is hardly any comorbidity between SpP and personality disorders, even those in the anxious-fearful type.

Prevalence and Demographic Characteristics

SpPs are the second more common type of anxiety disorder found in the NCS study (Kessler et al., 1994) with a lifetime prevalence of 11.3% and a 12-month prevalence of 8.8%. The lifetime prevalence of SpP is slightly lower, but the 12-month prevalence is higher than that for social phobia. The lifetime prevalence for women is two times higher than that for men, and the 12-month prevalence is three times higher for women. A community study done in Stockholm, Sweden, found a total-point prevalence of 19.9%, with a greater than 2:1 ratio of women to men. Situational phobias were the most common type in both countries. In the Swedish study, women scored higher than men in animal and situational types but not in mutilation type (injections, dentists, injuries). Among the situational types women and men had equivalent rates for fears of heights and flying. Comparing older (mean age 53) and younger (mean age 29) subjects, researchers found the rate of situational phobias, particularly fears of lightning and heights, were higher in the older group.

Comparing age of onset in five classes of phobias, Öst (1987) found that people with animal phobias were the youngest (M = 6.9 years) at onset, those with injection and blood phobias next (M = 8.1, 8.6 years), followed by dental phobics (M = 11.7 years). Claustrophobia sufferers usually had onset as young adults (M = 20.2 years). The literature on children shows a large number of animal phobias, but most of these are outgrown, judging by the relatively lower incidence in adults.

Genetics

The genetic influence of specific phobias varies with the type of phobia. In the Kendler et al. (1992b) twin study, animal phobias showed a moderate genetic influence, close to that for social phobias and other anxiety disorders, but situational phobias showed no genetic influence, some shared environmental influence, and a stronger influence of nonshared environment. A family history of the same type of phobia was reported in a remarkably high percentage (60.5%) of relatives of blood phobics, in a high percentage of relatives of injection phobics (28.8%), but only in a low percentage of relatives of animal phobics (8%), and claustrophobics (5%) (Öst, 1992). A higher than expected incidence of specific phobias is found in the relatives of specific phobics, but there is no higher incidence of other anxiety disorders, suggesting a specific and narrow genetic basis for this kind of phobia (Fyer et al., 1990). Perhaps the factor is what H. J. Eysenck calls "conditionability" (1967).

Biological Factors

Few studies have found any differences between specific phobic patients and control participants during baseline or resting conditions on any neurophysiological variable, indicating no evidence of a generalized arousal such as that found in PD and GAD. However, when confronted with their phobic stimulus, these people often show strong activation. Rauch et al. (1995) used PET to show significant increases in blood flow in left medial orbitofrontal cortex, left insular cortex, right anterior-temporal cortex, anterior cingulate cortex, and left somatosensory cortex during presentation of the phobic stimulus. The results for orbitofrontal cortex and cingulate cortex resembled those seen in obsessive–compulsive patients during symptom provocation (Rauch et al., 1994). However, these studies use patients as their own controls without normal controls, so although they identify some of the brain circuits activated by provoked anxiety reactions, they do not indicate differences in the physiology of these circuits, which might be of etiological significance.

Nesse et al. (1985) reported strong increases in plasma norepinephrine and epinephrine, pulse rate, and blood pressure, as well as cortisol in patients with SpP when they were exposed to their particular phobic stimuli. There were no significant changes in plasma MHPG, and the panic attacks were less severe than those seen in PD patients with Ag who do show increases in MHPG when Ag symptoms are provoked by situations (Ko et al., 1983).

Baseline levels of heart rate, blood pressure (Kelly, 1980), and skin conductance levels (Lader, 1975) are no higher in those with specific phobias than in normal control participants, and Kelly found that they also did not differ from "normals" in questionnaire measures of general trait anxiety. Their robust response to laboratory stressors that were not relevant to their phobias was the same as that seen in normals. However, in response to specific phobia provocations, animal and dental phobics showed strong increases in heart rate, and claustrophobics showed moderate increases in comparison to controls. However, blood and injection phobics showed very little increase in heart rate, despite the fact that they had high self-ratings of anxiety (Öst, 1992).

Perhaps some types of SpPs represent very circumscribed anxiety disorders that are closer to normal fears than other anxiety disorders. The explanation might be that these disorders represent specific conditioning experiences unique to the individual and not requiring a strong genetic or biological predisposition. Specific phobias are more easily remedied by standard behavioral procedures such as desensitization than are other disorders such as agoraphobia or social phobias. What is the evidence for the origin of these disorders in conditioned or cognitive reactions?

Conditioning and Cognitive Sources

Contrary to the ubiquitous impression that Watson and Rayner (1920) demonstrated the establishment of a phobia through conditioning in the laboratory, conditioned fears in humans have been difficult to create in the laboratory (Rachman, 1977). Perhaps the problem is that ethical restraints prevent the use of intense UCSs (Siddle & Bond, 1988). Watson's experiment would have problems passing a current ethics review committee. But intense pain is rarely the UCS in natural human conditioning of fear. Traumatic fear-producing conditions are more common, but these do not fit the usual classical conditioning model. Rachman suggested three types of learning involved in the acquisition of phobias: direct classical conditioning, vicarious conditioning (observation), and information transmission (instruction). He hypothesized that the direct conditioning is more closely associated with physiological symptoms of fear, whereas indirect conditioning (observational and informational) is more closely related to cognitive symptoms.

Many studies document phobics' recollections of the origins of their phobias. Naturally, such recollections are fallible, particularly for phobias that originated in childhood. About 7–27% of people with phobias say they have no recollection of the origin of their phobias, and about half of them in most studies say that they have always had the fear. Only 10–22% of those with spider phobias attribute the origin of their phobias to direct conditioned experiences such as a painful spider bite (Kirby, Menzies, Daniels, & Smith, 1995; Merckelbach, Arntz, Arrindel, & De Jong, 1992; Merckelbach, Arntz, & De Jong, 1991). Contrary to Rachman's (1977) hypotheses, there was no relationship between the mode of acquisition and the type of phobic symptom (physiological vs. cognitive) or the intensity of symptoms. Furthermore, comparisons with a control nonphobic group revealed no differences in the types of actual experiences with spiders. The same experiences that supposedly caused the acquisition of a phobia in the phobics failed to leave an enduring fear effect in the controls!

A similar study of acrophobia (fear of heights) showed similar results (Menzies & Clarke, 1995). Only 11% of those with the phobias reported an experience that could be interpreted as direct conditioning. A larger percentage reported indirect or vicarious conditioning. No difference was found in severity or distress or symptom response patterns between directly and indirectly conditioned cases. There was no difference between phobics and controls in the types of negative experiences with heights, direct, indirect, or informational.

Direct conditioning origins are more common in blood and injection phobias (Kleinknecht, 1994; Öst, 1991). About half of these groups report the origin of the phobia in a traumatic experience, but for about one third of those with blood phobias and about one half of those with injection phobias, their experiences involve the classical S-S association of the CS with the UCS of pain, whereas the others involve intense fright.

Origins of fears in young children have been studied using reports by their mothers. A majority of parents (56%) believed that their children showed fear of water from their very first contact, 26% report vicarious conditioning experiences, but only 2% could identify a direct conditioning episode as the origin of the fear (Menzies & Clarke, 1993). Both direct and indirect conditioning (as estimated by mothers' own dental fears) were significant predictors of children's dental fears (Milgram, Mancl, King, & Weinstein, 1995).

Vicarious conditioning involves conditioned reactions caused by the observation of fear reactions in a model. From the studies described above, it is apparent that at least as much human conditioning of fear is mediated through vicarious conditioning as through direct conditioning. Monkeys may be conditioned by observing other monkeys' fear reactions to snakes, even though the conditioned monkey has no prior experience with snakes (Mineka, Davidson, Cool, & Kier, 1984). Acrophobics described their sources of vicarious conditioning as their fathers, mothers, or other sources (Menzies & Clarke, 1995).

Trait anxiety of children was related to trait anxiety in both their fathers and mothers, but fearfulness in children was only related to fearfulness in the mother (Muris, Steeneman, Merckelbach, & Meesters, 1996). The latter relationship depended on how much the mothers expressed or concealed their fears. Children of mothers who said that they openly expressed their fears in the presence of the children had the highest levels of anxiety, whereas children of mothers who concealed their fears from their children were low in fearfulness. This fearfulness extended across a variety of specific fears.

The biological preparedness hypothesis (Seligman, 1971) is an evolutionary explanation of the prepotency of certain stimuli in conditioning, such as animals and insects; or situations, such as heights. Öhman (1986) demonstrated that slides of snakes and spiders are more easily conditioned to aversive UCSs than neutral stimuli and are more difficult to extinguish once conditioned. Conditioning can be accomplished using direct association with shock UCS, or mere threat of a shock, or vicariously through watching a model display fear. Telling a participant that no more shocks will occur and removing the shock electrodes before extinction, results in immediate extinction of responses to neutral stimuli, but responses to prepared stimuli persist, suggesting the irrational nature of prepared phobias and the rapid and automatic responses to their stimuli (Soares & Öhman, 1993).

SpP, Ag, OCD, and normal participants were compared on avoidance (reaction time to turn off slide) and physiological (skin conductance) CRs to the slides of snakes or spiders during acquisition and extinction (Foa, McNally, Steketee, & McCarthy, 1991). Diagnostic groups did not differ in conditioning. Since people with Ag and OCD usually have higher levels of general anxiety and arousal than those with SpP, the results suggested that general level of anxiety, as opposed to specific conditioning, does not exert a significant influence on these biologically prepared responses.

The common mechanism of direct or indirect conditioning influences in phobias is the *learning of expectations of outcome*, whether personally experienced, witnessed, or informed. A group of people with height phobias showed stronger anticipation of harm before entering a situation where they would be asked to climb a ladder than during or after the situation (Andrews, Freed, & Teeson, 1994). Cognitive or behavioral therapy can change these expectations. After a conditioning experiment, untreated spider phobics overestimated the strength of the association between the slides of spiders (CS) and shock (UCS), but they did not exhibit a bias in regard to neutral CSs, and they did show the bias in association of spiders with simple tones (De Jong, Merckelbach, Arntz, & Nijman, 1992). Treated spider phobics did not show this memory bias, suggesting the role of exposure in removing expectations of harm even if these biases stem from biologically prepared associations.

A problem with the idea that phobics are persons with irrational fears of harm from the phobic situation or object is the fact that what they most fear is not harm from the object as much as their unpleasant anxiety or panic reactions to it. In this respect, they are not that different from patients with panic disorder. About one third of a group of spider phobics had a high level of belief in the idea that a spider might harm them, but the majority had strong expectations that they would either make a fool of themselves, be hysterical, act foolish, or scream if exposed to a spider (Thorpe & Salkovkis, 1995).

Bandura (1977) described two kinds of expectations involved in fear and avoidance: efficacy and outcome expectations. *Efficacy* concerns the ability to cope with the feared situation, and *outcome* concerns what is expected to happen if one is exposed. In the case of phobias, both kinds of expectations are negative. A person with a spider phobia might say, "I will become hysterical," "I will faint," or "the spider will bite me." Therapy must demonstrate to the patients that they can cope and that no harmful outcomes are likely to occur as a consequence of exposure.

OBSESSIVE–COMPULSIVE DISORDER (OCD)

Phenomenology

The *DSM-IV* (1994) defines obsessions as "recurrent and persistent thoughts, impulses, or images that are experienced . . . as intrusive and inappropriate and that cause anxiety or distress" (p. 422). They are not worries about real-life problems, as seen in GAD. The individual recognizes them as his or her own thoughts, unlike the delusional ideas in schizophrenia, which the patient believes have an origin in external reality. They are experienced as incongruous with the self-concept, as when someone has a thought of harming someone they love, or engaging in a sexual act which they regard as abhorrent. The most common obsessions concern the possibilities of contamination and repeated doubts about whether or not one has performed some routine act such as locking a door, or whether one has inadvertently hit someone while driving a car.

Compulsions are defined as "repetitive behaviors . . . that the person feels driven to perform in response to an obsession, or according to rules that must be applied rigidly" (*DSM-IV*, 1994, p. 423). Some compulsions are attempts to deal with the anxiety produced by the obsession. An obsession with contamination leads to excessive hand-washing, obsessive doubt leads to checking—even at great inconvenience or time lost—undesired ego-dystonic thoughts may be countered by ritualistic counter-thoughts. A survey of 601 cases of patients in treatment showed that the most common kind of compulsions were cleaning ones (48%), followed by checking compulsions (27%; S. G. Ball, Baer, & Otto, 1996). In only 14% of the cases were obsessions not accompanied by behavioral or cognitive rituals. Some rituals may have no obvious connection with an obsession, such as having to dress or do some other activity in a rigidly prescribed order and starting over if there is a mistake or doubt about the precision of the sequence.

Having doubts and performing checking rituals are not uncommon among persons without disorders (e.g., "Did I lock the door . . . turn off the lights . . . the gas . . . remember to take the file?, etc.). To meet the diagnostic criterion, the obsessions or compulsions must "cause marked distress" or significantly interfere with functioning in work, routine, occupational, or social functioning, or simply be excessively time-consuming. The criteria also note that the recognition that the obsessions and compulsions are unreasonable will vary among persons with the disorder. The diagnosis specifier "with poor insight" may be added if a person does not recognize that the obsessions and compulsions are unreasonable.

Although OCD and obsessive–compulsive personality disorder (OCPD) sound alike, the person with OCPD does not have actual obsessions and compulsions, but is characterized by traits of excessive orderliness, perfectionism, and control. They are usually not distressed by their traits and are more likely to regard them as virtues than as symptoms. Their zeal and perfectionism may result in inefficiency and impaired interpersonal relationships, but they do not recognize this. However, when OCD has developed from a long-standing OCPD, they may both be diagnosed.

A factor analysis of an OC inventory in patients with OCDs, panic disorders, and social phobias and normal control participants yielded five OCD symptom factors:

1. Impulses (ego-dystonic)
2. Washing
3. Checking
4. Rumination, and
5. Precision (ritualistic order, compulsive counting, etc.). (Van Oppen, Hoekstra, & Emmelkamp, 1995).

The OCD group had significantly higher scores on all of these factors than both normals and the other two anxiety disorder groups with one exception: The differences between OCD and the other two anxiety disorder groups were not significant on the ego-dystonic impulse factor. The impulse items mostly concern suicidal, homicidal, or violent thoughts. Apparently this kind of anxiety-provoking impulse is common in the other kinds of anxiety disorders as well.

Comorbidity

The most common clinical disorders (Axis I) given as additional diagnoses to OCD are major depression, dysthymia, and specific phobia. Like other anxiety disorders, OCD has its highest rates of comorbidity with the Cluster C personality disorders, but surprisingly, it is about as frequently found in association with avoidant and dependent personality disorders as with OCPD (Baer et al., 1992; Sanderson et al., 1994). Enright (1996) raises the question of whether OCD is an anxiety disorder or a schizotypal disorder. In a study using *DSM-III* criteria, schizotypal personality was the most frequent comorbid personality disorder for OCD, found in 26% of the cases together with almost 9% of paranoid personality types (Zimmerman & Coryell, 1989). But using the *DSM-III-R*, Sanderson et al. (1994)

found no cases where schizotypal or paranoid personality disorders were comorbid with OCD.

Prevalence and Demographics

The NCR study does not provide community prevalence figures for OCD. The ECA study gave a lifetime prevalence of 2.5% and a 1-year prevalence of 1.4–2.3% (Karno, Golding, Sorenson, & Burnham, 1988). Unlike the other anxiety disorders, the prevalence rate is about the same in men and women. Age at onset is about 23 for both. The disorder is more prevalent among persons who are young, divorced or separated, and of lower socioeconomic class.

Genetics

Rasmussen and Tsuang (1984) found a concordance rate of 57% for obsessive–compulsive neurosis among identical twins aggregated from 10 small studies. The rates for fraternal twins are not given, but the rate for identical twins is the highest reported for any anxiety disorder. Carey and Gottesman (1981) reported a rate of only 33% concordance for this disorder among identical twins, but this rate was still almost five times the rate found for fraternal twins. The concordance rates were higher for both types of twins, using broader definitions of the OC trait, but the ratio was not as high. The aforementioned studies found rates of about 7% for parents and of 5% for siblings of OCD patients. OCD was found to have a relatively higher rate among relatives of people with early onset OCD (by age 14) than among relatives of those with late onset OCD (Bellodi, Sciuto, Diaferia, Ronchi, & Smeraldi, 1992). Although anxiety disorders in general were found to be higher in frequency among relatives of OCD patients, the specific OCD itself did not differ in frequencies between relatives of OCDs and those of controls (Black, Noyes, Goldstein, & Blum, 1992). However, broadly defined, OCD was more frequent among the relatives of OCDs. Apparently OCD is inherited as part of a vulnerability to a broader OC type of anxiety. The dimensional nature of OCD was demonstrated by Nestadt et al. (1991).

Neuropsychology

OCD, particularly the childhood onset type, has much in common with Tourette's syndrome (TS), a genetically transmitted disorder characterized by involuntary motor and verbal tics. OCD is a complication in 30–50% of TS cases, and tics occur in many cases of OCD. A family prevalence study suggests a genetic link between the two disorders (Pauls, Towbin, Leckman, Zahner, & Cohen, 1986). Since Tourette's is considered a neurological disorder that is probably related to a dysfunction in the basal ganglia, the possibility of a neurological basis for OCD has been considered. Hollander, Schiffman, et al. (1992) found that OCD patients showed significantly more total soft signs of neurological disorder than did controls. There was an excess of findings on the left side of the body, suggesting a right hemisphere dysfunction, at least in some OCD patients. Soft signs correlated with the severity of obsessions.

A number of brain scan studies of OCD using X-ray or MRI imaging methods have revealed little difference in the brain structures of OCDs and those of controls (Pigott, Myers, & Williams, 1996). Although a few studies showed reduced caudate nucleus volume in brains of OCD patients, the most recent study failed to confirm this finding and also found no differences in the size of other basal ganglia structures, or in the brain as a whole (Aylward et al., 1996).

The relatively new method of functional magnetic resonance imaging has allowed studies of sequential conditions and their effects on the brain. Breiter et al. (1996) stimulated patients with OCD under control conditions and when provoked by stimuli associated with their fearful obsessions. Under provocation conditions, OCD patients but not controls showed significant increases in activity in paralimbic (medial orbitofrontal lobes, the anterior cingulate, the temporal and insular cortex), amygdala, and caudate nuclei. Many of the paralimbic areas have been implicated in provocation studies of OCD and other anxiety disorders (e.g., Rauch et al., 1995; Reiman, 1990). These findings tend to validate the inclusion of OCD among the anxiety disorders. The basic pathway of fears—whether phobic, panic, or obsessional—is from the orbital frontal cortex around the cingulate gyrus to the caudate and temporal inputs into the limbic systems (see Fig. 3.3).

The finding of pathways and nuclei that are operative during obsessive anxiety does not answer the "chicken or egg" problem regarding whether these physiological differences are consequences or causes of OCD. PET studies have shown that orbitofrontal brain activity, which correlates with OCD symptoms, is reduced by successful treatment, whether by drugs (Baxter et al., 1992; Swedo et al., 1992) or behavior therapy (Baxter et al., 1992). In both studies the extent of right orbitofrontal metabolism change was correlated with measures of OCD improvement. Regardless of which is chicken and which egg, the physiological and behavioral phenomena are interdependent.

Although prefrontal lobotomies are no longer performed, cingulotomies have been used in cases of OCD which were unresponsive to other treatments (Jenike et al., 1991). About 25–30% of the patients showed marked improvement at follow-up over 25 years. A study of cingulotomy done on patients treated unsuccessfully with behavioral methods or with serotonin drugs or both yielded a 28% marked improvement rate, indicating that cingulotomy may have had some effectiveness as a treatment of last resort (Baer et al., 1995). But then again the same was said for lobotomies as a treatment for chronic schizophrenia before research showed that improvement rates for this drastic procedure did not exceed those of custodial care and time.

Neuropsychological tests showed that OCD patients were impaired on measures of spatial working memory, spatial recognition, speed of motor initiation and execution, and attentional set shifting (Purcell, Maruff, Kyrios, & Pantelis, 1998). None of these cognitive deficits were found in patients with panic disorder or major depression except for the deficit in attentional shift setting, which was even worse in patients with depression. The authors suggest that the pattern of findings is indicative of a disturbance in the dorsolateral prefrontal cortex, an area associated with spatial working memory. However, PET studies have not as yet shown a specific disturbance in this brain area for OCD patients.

Psychopharmacology

Effectiveness of therapy is not proof of etiology but, as with other disorders, the hypothesis about the role of the neurotransmitter serotonin in OCD is partly a function of the relative success of treatment with the selective serotonin reuptake inhibitor, clomipramine. A large multicenter study of patients with OCD who were treated with clomipramine or a placebo showed that clomipramine reduced symptoms by 38–44% compared with 3–5% for placebo-treated patients (Clomipramine Collaborative Study Group, 1991). Treatment with clomipramine produced a decrease in OCD patients of 5-HIAA, the metabolite of serotonin (Altemus et al., 1994).

M-CCP, the potent serotonin agonist, exacerbates obsessional symptoms in OCD patients (Hollander, DeCaria, et al., 1992; Zohar, Mueller, Insel, Zohar-Kadovich, & Murphy, 1987). Low levels of 5-HIAA in child and adolescent OCDs were related to high levels of global OCD symptoms and 5-HIAA was unrelated to anxiety; in contrast, MHPG, the norepinephrine metabolite, was positively related to ratings of global anxiety but unrelated to OCD symptoms (Swedo et al., 1992). Perhaps OCD symptoms are not merely expressions of anxiety, but represent something else (e.g., a dysregulation of cognitive control) more closely related to serotonergic than to noradrenergic function, whereas anxious arousal could be more closely related to noradrenergic function. I will return to this question in discussion of the psychophysiology of OCD below.

Arginine vasopressin (AVP) is a neurohormone that is stress responsive and that slows extinction of aversively conditioned responses in rats. AVP also promotes repetitive self-grooming behavior in rats, a possible analogue of compulsive hand-washing in humans. Altemus et al. (1992)

found elevated levels of AVP in the CSF of OCD patients. AVP decreased in patients given clomipramine therapy (Altemus et al., 1994). However, Leckman et al. (1994) found no difference in AVP levels among patients with OCD or TS, and controls. Instead, this group found elevated levels of a related neurohormone, oxytocin (OT). OT was elevated in the OCD group compared to either the TS or to control groups. OT is also related to grooming plus a variety of sexual, affiliative, and cognitive behaviors in animals. In the study of children and adolescents with OCD, OT was positively related to symptoms of depression, whereas AVP was negatively related to OCD symptoms (Swedo et al., 1992). The reliability and significance of these neurohormone findings are somewhat obscure at present.

Psychophysiological Arousal

Some researchers have questioned the identification of OCD as an anxiety disorder (Enright, 1996; Insel, Zahn, & Murphy, 1985). If OCD is primarily a cognitive disorder, one would not expect to find high tonic levels of psychophysiological arousal like those found in most other anxiety disorders. Kelly (1980) found elevated levels of heart rate, blood pressure, and forearm blood flow, and Insel et al. (1985) reported higher levels of heart rate and skin conductance, and spontaneous fluctuations of skin conductance in OCD patients as compared to controls. However, a more recent study found no differences between an OCD group and controls in heart rate, skin conductance, or blood pressure (Hoehn-Saric, McLeod, & Hipsley, 1995). The earlier studies found that "normals" had a greater response to stress based on the simple difference between stress and basal levels. However these differences were due to the higher baseline levels of the anxiety disorders and the "law of initial limits." In the Hoehn-Saric et al. study, the baselines were equivalent, and the OCD patients still exhibited smaller increases in skin conductance and heart rate than controls during stressful tasks. However, their blood pressure increased more than that of the control participants following a "risk-taking" task. Considering the risk aversiveness in OCD patients, the latter task may have been particularly relevant to their problems. Perhaps the difference between these findings and earlier ones is attributable to the authors' exclusion of OCD patients with comorbid anxiety disorders other than GAD or specific phobias. Anxiety in uncomplicated OCD may be a product rather than a cause of the obsessions. However, the same could be said of SpP sufferers in that they are not generally aroused but only show panic-like anxiety when confronted with the phobic stimulus or situation. The difference is that OCD patients must cope with their frightening obsessions on a daily basis and cannot avoid them.

Personality

In contrast to the lack of physiological arousal in the OCD patients studied by Hoehn-Sacric et al., measures of anxiety trait, phobic fears, somatic symptoms, and neuroticism in the OCDs were significantly higher than those of controls in the questionnaire. They were also higher on personality scales of harm avoidance and reward dependence and lower on a scale of mastery (vs. powerlessness). They did not differ from controls on extraversion–introversion. The OCD patients in this study resemble other patients with anxiety disorders in personality traits with the exception of extraversion, on which most other anxiety disorder groups score in the direction of introversion.

Conditioning and Cognitive Factors

According to the two-factor conditioning model (Mowrer, 1950) the obsessions are CSs for anxiety CRs, and the compulsions are temporary anxiety reducers. As with most conditioning theories, the source of the conditioning process by which obsessions become CSs is obscure. Freudian psychoanalysts maintain that fears of contamination stem from overly severe and punitive toilet training, but evidence for this hypothesis is scarce. Behavioral treatment relies on exposure to the feared situation with prevention of the usual anxiety reducing compulsive response. For instance, patients might be asked to handle feces and be restrained from washing their hands. The nature of most OCD symptoms, however, represents cognitive distortions, and most OCD sufferers realize this. The probability of serious contamination from doorknobs or shaking hands does not justify the avoidance patterns in reaction to such situations.

The cognitive approach starts with the assumption that obsessive ideas are normal intrusive thoughts that occur frequently in most of the general population (Salkovkis, 1996). In the non-OCD person, the intrusive thoughts are quickly or automatically appraised as irrelevant, and there is no further processing. The OCD patient, however, interprets intrusions in a catastrophic fashion, believing that thoughts of harm can lead to harm, and if harm occurred to oneself or loved ones, then one would be responsible unless one took some preventive action. Attempts to suppress thoughts may actually increase them, and ritualistic thought substitutions or compulsive actions only temporarily reduce the anxiety. Furthermore, if the neutralizing activity, such as hand-washing, is based on a feeling of contamination, it is difficult to stop it until all anxiety is absent. In a peculiar way, the psychoanalytic interpretation of ego-dystonic thoughts as representing the patient's own unconscious impulses breaking through repression enhances the responsibility that the OCD patients feel for their obsessions and could be countertherapeutic.

OCD patients seem to have a greater difficulty suppressing irrelevant thoughts, even those not directly connected with their obsessions. In one experimental paradigm subjects are told to try *not* to think about a white bear either before or after they had been primed to think about white bears. Enright (1996) reports an experiment in which OCD subjects were compared with subjects with other anxiety disorders in their ability to suppress thoughts of white bears. The OCD group showed more white-bear intrusions than did the other anxiety disorder patients. Those OCD patients who exhibited checking type compulsions exhibited more intrusions than did noncheckers.

POSTTRAUMATIC STRESS DISORDER (PTSD)

Stress is assumed to play some role in anxiety disorders other than PTSD, either in predisposing, precipitating, or exacerbating the disorders (Mazure, 1995). The categories of "gross stress reaction" and "transient situational disturbance" in *DSM-I* and *DSM-II* covered short-term reactions to stress, but if such reactions persisted they were reclassified under the other diagnoses such as anxiety or depressive neuroses on the assumption that the stressor simply released or exacerbated the predisposed disorder. The introduction of PTSD into *DSM-III* is based on the assumption that chronic reactions to traumatic experiences represent a distinctive type of anxiety disorder, with stress in the form of traumatic experiences playing a primary role in its development (Yehuda & McFarlane, 1995). Of course the stress cannot account entirely for the disorder because no matter how severe or prolonged it is, only some individuals will develop an enduring disorder. Although psychopathologists have emphasized the vulnerabilities of humans to stress, what is remarkable is the resilience of most people after the horrors of traumatic events, tragedy, and loss. But as Freud (1922/1961,) noted, sometimes a stress is so severe that it cannot be sealed over with defenses, and the original anxiety symptoms persist in painful recollections and dreams for many years in defiance of the "pleasure principle."

Phenomenology

The *DSM-IV* (1994) defines PTSD in terms of four categories of criteria: (a) the traumatic event, (b) psychological reexperiencing of the traumatic event, (c) avoidance mechanisms in relation to stimuli or thoughts associated with the event, and (d) persistent symptoms of increased arousal which were not present prior to the traumatic event.

1. *The traumatic event* must have involved the experiencing, witnessing, or being confronted with "an event or events that involved actual or threatened death or serious injury to the physical integrity of self or others"

(p. 427). In addition, "the person's response involved intense fear, help-lessness or horror" (p. 428).

2. The traumatic event is *persistently reexperienced* in recollections, dreams, "flashbacks" (reliving the experience), intense distress or physio-logical arousal on exposure to cues associated with the event.

3. *Persistent avoidance* of trauma-related stimuli and numbing of emo-tions, lack of recall of some aspects of the trauma, diminished interest in significant activities, feelings of detachment from others, restricted range of positive feelings, and a feeling of impermanence and lack of hope.

4. *Persistently elevated arousal* as indicated by sleep difficulties, irrita-bility, concentration difficulty, hypervigilance, and exaggerated startle re-sponses.

The *DSM-IV* requires that the disturbance must have persisted for at least a month beyond the end of the trauma for a PTSD diagnosis. If less than a month has passed, the disorder is diagnosed as acute stress disorder and changed to PTSD if it is still persisting after a month. The PTSD is termed *acute* if the duration is 1–3 months posttrauma, and *chronic* if 3 months or more have passed.

Comorbidity

The most common sources of trauma for PTSD in the community (NCS study) were war experiences for men and rape for women (Kessler et al., 1995). Both men and women with PTSD had a high rate (close to 50%) for comorbid depressive episodes. Specific phobia, social phobia, and dysthymic disorders were next prevalent as comorbid disorders. Male PTSD cases also showed very high rates (52%) of comorbid alcohol abuse and the rate of this disorder in women was also significantly elevated. Drug abuse was common in both sexes.

Severity of Stress as a Determinant of PTSD

Some developers of vulnerability theories have maintained that if the stress factor is severe enough, nearly all those exposed to the trauma will be left with PTSD, albeit in a milder form. In a small sample of Bosnian refugees exposed to some of the horrendous experiences of "ethnic cleans-ing" by Serbians, PTSD was diagnosed in 65% (Weine et al., 1995). Among American prisoners of war during World War II, 71% had a history of PTSD, and 35% were diagnosed as suffering from PTSD at the time of the study 45 years after the end of the war (Eberly, Harkness, & Engdahl, 1991). One study of male veterans from World War II found that only 11% had PTSD symptoms on returning to civilian life, but 71% of these had been engaged in heavy combat (Lee, Vaillant, Torrey, & Elder, 1995). The intensity of level of combat is a highly significant predictor of PTSD symptoms among Vietnam veterans as well. The incidence of PTSD symptoms ranges from 7% of those not exposed to much combat to 50–60% among those involved in the most intense combat experiences (True et al., 1993). Among a sample of graves-registration troops, those exposed to actual body handling during the Desert Storm conflict had a current PTSD rate of 48% and a lifetime rate of 65%, as opposed to those who stayed stateside, none of whom developed PTSD (Sutker, Uddo, Brailey, Vasterling, & Errera, 1994).

Exposure to traumatic events in the civilian population is not uncommon. About 40% of the sample in one survey reported exposure to one or more traumatic events, as these are defined in the *DSM*, and 24% of those exposed to such events had *DSM-III-R* defined PTSD (Breslau, Davis, Andreski, & Peterson, 1991). The specific type of trauma did not affect the rate except for a lower rate for sudden injury or serious accidents (12%) and a markedly higher rate for rape (80%). A 3-year follow-up of this sample showed that further traumatic incidents combined with past ones increased the odds of developing PTSD by an odds ratio of 1.75 (Breslau, Davis, & Andreski, 1995). Perhaps more notable than the typical one quarter of PTSD in the survivors was that, with the exception of rape, three quarters of those exposed to traumatic events did not have PTSD sequelae. Although the severity, duration, and frequency of traumatic events are important in determining who will develop PTSD, there are obviously preexisting risk factors that play a role. What are these risk factors?

Genetics

Some of the resilience or vulnerability to stress may reside in genetically influenced traits. True et al. (1993) studied a large group of twins who served in the armed forces during the Vietnam War period. After adjusting for differences due to extent of combat exposure (stress), heredity accounted for up to a third of the variance in symptoms.

Individual Risk Factors

Apart from the extent of the stress itself, demographic, family, and personality factors have been related to the outcome of traumatic events. Age and gender have not shown consistent prediction effects across studies. Family background variables, such as warmth, predicted neuroticism at age 65 but did not predict PTSD outcomes in World War II veterans (Lee et al., 1995). A family history of psychiatric disorders and early separation was predictive of PTSD in those people exposed to trauma in a civilian population (Breslau et al., 1991).

Personality variables have been related to PTSD outcomes, but in most studies these measures were not obtained prior to the traumatic incidents, and therefore, might have been influenced by them. In the Lee et al. (1995) study of World War II veterans, ratings of the maturity of the veterans' defenses during the postwar years predicted the occurrence or absence of PTSD. In the Persian Gulf War, a measure of hardiness, particularly the subscale of commitment (sense of meaning and purpose), seemed to insulate soldiers against PTSD, whereas an avoidance coping mechanism was related to vulnerability to PTSD (Sutker, Davis, Uddo, & Ditta, 1995). Since these measures were taken after soldiers returned from the war, their confounding with stress reactions to the war is possible. Both neuroticism (N) and extraversion (E) scores predicted the likelihood of being exposed to traumatic events in a civilian population, but only N predicted the likelihood of developing PTSD after exposure to trauma (Breslau et al., 1991). Both E and N continued to predict subsequent traumatic events in the next 3 years, showing the constant interplay of personality and environment in producing psychopathology (Breslau et al., 1995).

Biological Factors

Can severe stress produce gross structural brain changes? PTSD patients showed a significantly (8%) smaller volume of the right hippocampus than did control participants (Bremner et al., 1995). Furthermore, the size of this structure was positively related to a verbal memory score on a memory scale, a scale on which PTSD patients had shown a deficiency in earlier studies by these investigators. It is possible, of course, that the loss of hippocampal volume represents a premorbid risk factor, but a more likely explanation is that certain glucocorticoids, released by stress and associated with brain changes, are responsible.

A variety of monoamine, opiate, and other neurochemical factors have been implicated in PTSD. The fear-potentiated startle response, a conditioned reaction often associated with the sounds of battle, is a characteristic frequently seen in PTSD cases. N-methyl-D-aspartate (NMDA) receptors, and noradrenergic and opiate transmitters are involved in the pathways between amygdala, locus coeruleus, thalamus, and hippocampus activated by the startle reaction (Charney, Deutch, Krystal, Southwick, & Davis, 1993). NMDA antagonists infused into the amygdala prevent extinction of the fear-potentiated startle. A failure to extinguish conditioned fear reactions is a characteristic of PTSD as shown by the persistence of images (flashbacks), painful memories, and arousal.

Arousal mediated by the noradrenergic system, implicated in panic disorder, may also play an important role in PTSD. Significantly elevated levels of 24-hour urinary NE excretion have been found in PTSD cases along with a reduction in the density of alpha-2 receptors, which modulate the production of NE in response to activity (Charney et al., 1993). Yohimbine, an alpha-2 receptor antagonist, has been used as a provoker of panic attacks in studies of panic disorder and other anxiety disorders, as previously described. Yohimbine provoked panic attacks in 70% of a group of PTSD patients and in none of a group of controls, an effect exceeding that seen in panic disorder patients (Southwick et al., 1993). Furthermore, 40% of the PTSD patients had flashbacks in response to the yohimbine. The PTSD group had larger increases in plasma MHPG (the NE metabolite), blood pressure, and heart rate than did the controls. In both patients and controls, there were significant correlations between baseline levels of MHPG and reports of previous symptoms of panic attacks. In the patients the peak effects of yohimbine on MHPG were significantly correlated with their symptoms of panic during yohimbine infusion.

Since stimulation of noradrenergic receptors in the amygdala after a learning experience has a memory enhancing effect, it is possible that a high state of noradrenergic activity during and after a traumatic incident could be responsible for the "fixing" of the traumatic memory in PTSD patients. The persistent arousability of PTSD patients could be due to a sensitization of the NE system, which is then easily triggered by conditioned external or internal (cognitive) stimuli.

Psychophysiological studies compared World War II and Korean War veterans with a PTSD history and other veterans with equal levels of combat exposure but no PTSD reactions (Orr, Pittman, Lasko, & Herz, 1993). Scripts based on personal combat memories elicited stronger heart-rate and skin conductance responses in the PTSDs than in the controls, even though the controls' subjective ratings of arousal and negative emotions did not differ from those of the PTSD veterans. Physiological reactions to neutral scenes did not differentiate the groups, showing the relative specificity of arousability in PTSD. But in contrast to this study, another of Vietnam war veterans with PTSD showed that they had higher levels of heart rate and blood pressure than veterans of the same era with no combat experience. Measurements were made while the subjects were simply awaiting a physical examination, a relatively low stressful experience (Gerardi, Keane, Cahoon, & Klauminzer, 1994). Perhaps the difference in results of the two studies is due to the relatively greater recency of the Vietnam war experience compared to the World War II and Korean wars.

Both Israeli veterans of Israel's wars and American Vietnam veterans with PTSD showed higher heart-rate responses to loud tones than non-PTSD veterans or those with other anxiety disorders (Orr, Lasko, Shalev, & Pittman, 1995; Shalev, Orr, Peri, Schreiber, & Pittman, 1992). Loud sounds are UCSs for startle reflexes. In both studies there was slow or little decline in the skin conductance responses of the PTSD cases. The Vietnam veteran study (Orr et al., 1995) also showed increased muscle tension startle reflexes in the PTSD subjects, and the Israeli study (Shalev et al., 1992) showed increased skin conductance reflexes in their PTSD veterans. Apparently the PTSD arousability is not limited to trauma-relevant stimuli but reflects a general sensitization to any intense noise with an intense startle reaction that does not readily habituate.

Cognitive Factors

The Stroop color-naming task has been used to study PTSD as well as other anxiety disorders. The subject is required to name the colors used in the print for different words. Words that are related to the particular kind of trauma are used along with general threat words and neutral words. Inhibition in relation to a particular semantic category is revealed in longer latencies to name the colors of those words.

Even years after the traumatic events, those participants with PTSD exhibit a special interference effect connected with words directly associated with the trauma. This phenomenon has been demonstrated for PTSD patients among rape victims (Foa, Feske, Murdock, Kozak, & McCarthy, 1991), war veterans (McNally, Kaspi, Riemann, & Zeitlin, 1990), survivors of motor vehicle accidents (Bryant & Harvey, 1995), and survivors of a ferry accident (Thrasher, Dalgesh, & Yule, 1994). The cognitive bias is not shown by those who were exposed to the same traumatic event or like events but who did not develop PTSD. The effect can be conceptualized in terms of conditioning. The words eliciting inhibition are those associated through meaning with the traumatic events, and therefore, those that elicit some of the conditioned anxiety responses such as arousal and inhibition.

SUMMARY

The extensive comorbidity among anxiety disorders is not a surprise considering the many symptoms that are common among the disorders. Analyses suggest a common factor corresponding to the older concept of "neuroticism" underlying these disorders. What is surprising is that the comorbidity of most of the anxiety disorders extends into the mood disorders. Major depression is a highly co-occurring disorder with GAD, SP, OCD, and PTSD. Anxiety and mood disorders are not as distinctive as the diagnostic system suggests. Many of the problems of distinguishing one disorder from another are a function of the categorical diagnostic system. Several studies have shown the continuity of the distribution between personality traits, personality disorders, and clinical anxiety disorders. The heritabilities for most of the anxiety disorders are quite modest and not as high as those found for the general personality traits such as neuroticism. Broad forms of disorders such as OCD and SP seem to be more heritable than specific symptom-defined forms. Perhaps the inherited vulnerability for all anxiety and mood disorders is the trait of neuroticism, and the specific forms that the disorder takes depend on narrower genetic factors, like those causing autonomic instability in panic disorders, or specific environmental events, such as threats or losses in GAD and depression, respectively.

Given the arbitrariness of many criteria for the disorders, we must look at more basic phenomena to assess the relatedness of the disorders: genetic covariance and common biological and cognitive mechanisms. GAD and major depression share one common genetic factor, whereas PD and phobias share another. PD has a clear heritability, whereas the heritability of GAD depends on the duration criteria for the disorder. The 1-month criterion for GAD is modestly heritable; the 6-month for PD is not. Panic attacks probably involve a disinhibition of an arousal mechanism involving the ascending and descending pathways from the locus coeruleus, although other pathways may also affect the peripheral adrenergic mechanisms and thus trigger attacks. GAD seems to involve less of the autonomic type of peripheral arousal and more central nervous system and muscular tension. The vigilance seen in GAD cases could be a function of the septohippocampal system described by Gray (1982). In the cognitive realm, PD fears are more directly a function of the helplessness felt during the panic attack (going crazy, losing control) and less directly concern the social embarrassment of attacks in public places. GAD anxieties are less immediate and concern chronic worries about more everyday concerns such as jobs, relationships, finances, and so forth.

The personality disorders most closely linked to the anxiety disorders are the avoidant, dependent, and the obsessive–compulsive types. The avoidant defense mechanism is what turns a panic disorder into agoraphobia, or an acute stress disorder into a posttraumatic stress disorder. The use of the avoidance mechanism is one of the few predictors of PTSD in longitudinal studies. Threats to dependency in relationships may be one of the factors that turn an anxious personality into a general anxiety disorder, particularly in women. Dependency threat is involved in the separation anxiety beginning in childhood and may develop into panic disorder with agoraphobia in the adult. Social inhibition is manifested early in life, and extreme cases are at risk for developing anxiety disorders in general and probably avoidant personality and social phobia disorders in particular.

Specific phobias appear to have little in common with the other anxiety disorders. They have little comorbidity with personality disorders, and although they often appear as a secondary feature in other anxiety disorders, they are not comorbid as a primary disorder. People with these phobias do not score high on tests for neuroticism or general anxiety. Although some types, such as animal phobias, show a modest degree of heritability, others, such as situational phobias, show little evidence of genetic and much of specific environmental source. Patients with specific phobias show little general autonomic arousal except when exposed to their specific phobic stimulus. Their etiology may be conditioning of biologically prepared stimuli at a time when there is a background of heightened arousal.

Stress may be the crucial factor in concert with preexisting vulnerabilities—both for the biological and the resultant personality development—in producing anxiety disorders. PTSD in reaction to traumatic stress is clearly a function of that stressor, but even the most traumatic kinds of experience do not yield rates of disorders beyond 70%. Vulnerability factors determine the long-term consequences of stress. But stress and vulnerability are not totally independent. Genetic factors influence not only the response to stress, but also the likelihood of encountering certain types of stress, particularly those involving interpersonal relationships. The latter effect is probably through personality and coping abilities. Intelligence and education are also factors that influence stress vulnerability.

Conditioning has been used as an explanation for anxiety disorders, particularly the phobic ones. But on closer examination, classical conditioning can explain only a minority of the phobias. However, if we include vicarious conditioning and broader conceptions of conditioning which include the influence of stimuli associated with safety as well as with punishment, and if we allow the possibility of panic symptoms becoming conditioned stimuli for later attacks, then conditioning theory can be accommodated. But as conditioning theory is broadened, it begins to sound more like cognitive theory without the necessity for postulating conscious or unconscious cognitive processes. Still conditioning theory becomes somewhat strained when dealing with factors such as the sense of control or helplessness. Cognitive biases have been demonstrated for most of the anxiety disorders. But these attentional and memory biases may very well be symptoms of the disorder rather than its causes. Longitudinal studies must be done to demonstrate that they have predictive rather than just concurrent validity.

Anxiety disorders have been shown to have much in common with mood disorders at every level from the phenomenal to the genetic. As dimensions of mood traits or states, anxiety and depression are highly correlated, although they can be distinguished in mood scales (Lubin et al., in press; Zuckerman & Lubin, 1985) and symptom ratings (Moras & Barlow, 1992). Chapter 4 will delve into the theories and research on the mood disorders to find what is unique and what is common to both kinds of emotional disturbance.

4

MOOD DISORDERS

Mood disorders and their symptoms were diagnosed in antiquity (see chap. 2, this volume), but their popularity as medical diagnoses has waxed and waned over the centuries, probably as much a function of changes in their definitions and treatments as of any real changes in their actual prevalences. Cynics such as Szasz (1961) suggest that changes in diagnostic styles are entirely a function of their arbitrary definitions because they are all nothing but "illness myths." I do not agree with this viewpoint, but there is no question that changes in diagnostic definitions will affect the prevalence of any disorder.

Since Kraepelin distinguished manic–depressive and dementia praecox (schizophrenia) psychoses in the 19th century, the two have been rivals for diagnostic status. Figure 4.1 shows the changing diagnostic frequencies at six North American psychiatric hospitals in the years between 1972 and 1991 (Stoll et al., 1993). Until 1979, schizophrenia was the most common diagnosis, but beginning in 1979 the diagnosis of schizophrenia showed a gradual decline while the diagnosis of major mood disorders showed a dramatic increase. The rates of the two disorders over the years of the study were nearly perfectly correlated ($r = -.94$), indicating an inverse interdependence. Of course, 1980 was the year of publication of *DSM-III*, in which the diagnostic criteria for schizophrenia were narrowed, and the criteria for major mood disorders were broadened. The introduction during the 1970s of lithium for bipolar disorder and antidepressant drugs for major

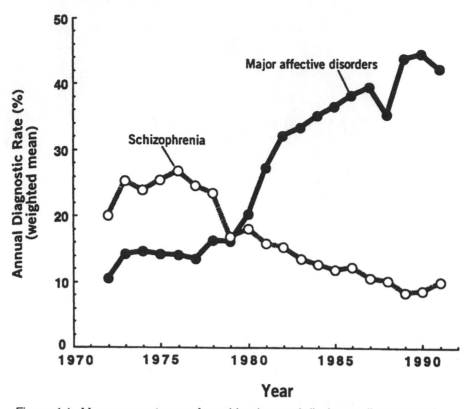

Figure 4.1. Mean percentages of combined annual discharge diagnoses of schizophrenia and major affective disorders from six psychiatric treatment centers, weighted for the total number of annual diagnoses at each site. From "Shifts in Diagnostic Frequencies of Schizophrenia and Major Affective Disorders at Six North American Psychiatric Hospitals, 1972–1988," by A. L. Stoll et al., 1993, *American Journal of Psychiatry, 150,* Figure 2, p. 1671. Copyright 1993, the American Psychiatric Association. Reprinted by permission.

depressions may also have contributed to the increasing popularity of that diagnosis, as well as to the formalization of the bipolar–unipolar major diagnostic distinction in *DSM-III* (1980).

Throughout this century, psychiatrists have debated whether depression represents a single continuum of severity or is a blanket for two or more different disorders with different etiologies (Boyce & Hadzi-Pavlovic, 1996). Prior to the adoption of the bipolar–unipolar classification, other types of distinctions among the mood disorders carried assumptions of etiology, for instance endogenous (genetic–biological) versus reactive, or neurotic versus psychotic depressions. Manic–depressive "illness" and involutional melancholia were assumed to be endogenous (biological etiology). Psychotic and neurotic depressive reactions were assumed to be precipitated by life stressors. Neurotic depressive reactions were also assumed to be more chronic and long-standing, but of less severity than psychotic ones. Some researchers claimed that neurotic and psychotic depressions were distinctive disorders, but others maintained that the distinction was simply one of severity of symptoms. Beck (1967) found no symptoms present in people with psychotic depressions that were not also found in some neurotic depressions, even if less commonly.

Factor and cluster analyses of symptoms have not resolved the taxonomic debates (Parker, Hadzi-Pavlovic, & Boyce, 1996). Most of these studies analyze symptoms at a given time and do not consider the history and course of the disorders as factors. The DSM defines the current episode in terms of symptoms (e.g., manic or major depressive episode) and the disorder in terms of past episodes as well as of the present one (e.g., bipolar or cyclothymic disorder, major depressive or dysthymic disorder). Diagnoses of major depressions on first admissions may be rediagnosed as bipolar cases because of manic episodes on subsequent admissions (Perris, 1992). However, most of these studies have found some evidence for a severe, psychotic, or endogenous depression (Grove & Andreasen, 1992; Parker et al., 1996). A recent large-scale twin study found three types of depression: mild typical depression, severe typical depression, and atypical depression (Kendler et al., 1996). The first two differ primarily in number and severity of symptoms. Two thirds of the mild typical group and nearly all of the severe typical group were diagnosed as having major depression by DSM-III-R criteria. The atypical depression was different from the other two groups in the direction of the "vital signs:" these showed increased rather than decreased appetite, gained rather than lost weight, and had hypersomnia rather than insomnia.

DESCRIPTIONS

DSM Definitions

The major classifications of DSM-III (carried over to DSM-III-R and IV) are whether the disorder manifests itself only in depression (unipolar) or in both mania and depression (bipolar), and its intensity and chronicity. Table 4.1 shows five primary disorders classified within the four combinations of the dimensions.

TABLE 4.1
Classification of Mood Disorders by Polarity and Intensity

Intensity of Episodes	Bipolar	Unipolar
Moderate	Cyclothymia Bipolar II	Dysthymia
Severe	Bipolar I	Major depression

Dysthymia is a less severe but more chronic form of major depression, and *cyclothymia* is a form of bipolar disorder in which the mood-swing symptoms have never reached the severity of either a major depressive or a manic episode (*DSM-IV*). Both dysthymic and cyclothymic disorders require at least a 2-year period during which the symptoms have never been absent for longer than a 2-month period. A *major depressive episode* requires a duration of at least 2 weeks. A *manic episode* is defined by a minimum of 1 week, and a *hypomanic episode* by only 4 days.

The list of symptoms for a major depressive episode and a dysthymic disorder are similar. Both include depressed mood for most of the day, significant weight loss (poor appetite) or weight gain (overeating), insomnia or hypersomnia, low energy or fatigue, feelings of worthlessness or low self-esteem, and poor concentration or indecisiveness. The major depressive episode, however, also includes four symptoms not specifically mentioned under dysthymic disorder: (a) "markedly diminished interest or pleasure in all or almost all activities," (b) psychomotor agitation or retardation, (c) "excessive or inappropriate guilt (which may be delusional)," and (d) recurrent thoughts of death or suicide or an actual suicide attempt (*DSM-IV*, 1994, p. 327). The depressive episode requires at least 5 of 9 listed symptoms, whereas the dysthymic disorder requires only 2 of 6 symptoms in addition to depressed mood. Except for these symptoms, the distinction between dysthymia and depression is primarily a polythetic, quantitative one. The temporal distinctions are not invariable since some dysthymic disorders tend to be episodic and some major depressions tend to be chronic.

The symptoms of major depression vary somewhat across cultures, but two symptoms were found to be relatively consistent across countries around the world: insomnia and energy loss were manifested by more than 60% of those people diagnosed with major depression (Negrao, 1997).

F. K. Goodwin and Jamison (1990) describe clinical differences between depressive episodes in the unipolar and bipolar disorders drawn from the literature. The *unipolar depression* is more likely to be characterized by anxiety and overt anger, psychomotor agitation, physical complaints, pain sensitivity, and weight loss. The *bipolar depression* is more likely to exhibit psychomotor retardation, low activity level, mood lability and symptomatic variability within the episode, excessive sleep, and fragmented REM sleep. People with unipolar depression are more likely to have a later age of onset and a more chronic depressive disorder. Females with bipolar depression are more likely to make suicide attempts with serious intentions and to have psychotic depressions. Females with bipolar II are more likely to have secondary alcoholism and premenstrual dysphoria. Further differences between bipolar and unipolar disorders in prevalence, demographics, genetics, personality, and biological characteristics are described below. Most of these findings tend to validate the distinction in the *DSM*.

The only difference between the *DSM-IV* definitions of manic and hypomanic episodes is that the manic episodes are sufficiently severe to cause marked impairment in occupational or social functioning or hospitalization, whereas hypomanic episodes are not severe enough to cause any of these consequences, and there are no psychotic features (delusions or hallucinations) associated with the mood elevation. A *bipolar I disorder* requires both major depressive and manic episodes, whereas a *bipolar II disorder* requires only a history of a hypomanic episode in addition to one or more major depressive episodes. Both manic and hypomanic episodes may include elevated, expansive, or irritable mood, inflated self-esteem or grandiosity, decreased need for sleep, increased talkativeness or pressure of speech, flight of ideas or racing thoughts, distractibility, increase in goal-directed activity (e.g., work or sex) or in psychomotor agitation, and impulsive pursuit of pleasure without regard for consequences as in buying sprees, sexual affairs, and risky investments. The only requirement for a *cyclothymic disorder* is that for the first 2 years of the disorder, the symptoms never reach the thresholds required for a manic or depressive episode.

A major depressive episode is classified as *major depressive disorder, single episode* if it is the first episode, and *major depressive disorder, recurrent,* if there have been at least one or more previous episodes of depression. Bipolar I and II disorders are classified as such even if there has been only the one manic or hypomanic episode. Further episodes are classified by type.

In addition to the primary diagnoses episode specifiers are used to describe additional features of the episode. Depressive or manic episodes may be described in terms of severity: mild, moderate, severe, or severe with psychotic features, in partial remission, or in full remission. Psychotic features are only associated with the severe category and are defined in the narrow sense by the presence of delusions or hallucinations. The delusions or hallucinations are further classified into those that are "mood congruent" and those that are "mood incongruent." *Mood congruent* delusions or hallucinations are those whose content is consistent with the mood in which they occur. Examples are the delusion during a depressive episode that one is condemned to suffering or death because of one's sins, or the delusion during a manic episode that one is chosen to be president, or to win the Nobel prize (assuming these are totally implausible).

A major depressive episode may be described as *chronic* if it lasts more than 2 years. A depressive episode may also be specified as catatonic if it is expressed in total immobility, rigidity, posturing, or excessive and purposeless motor activity. The *melancholic specifier* describes a severe form of major depression characterized by complete anhedonia and lack of reactivity to pleasurable stimuli, the severe quality of depressed mood, a depression worse in the mornings, early morning awakenings, psychomotor retardation or agitation, anorexia or weight loss, and excessive and inappropriate guilt.

Atypical features specifier includes increase in appetite (as opposed to a decrease), hypersomnia (as opposed to insomnia), leaden paralysis of limbs, and long-standing sensitivity to interpersonal rejection resulting in significant social or work impairment.

The melancholic specifier represents a compromise in the historical debate between proponents of a dimensional view and those who believe the melancholic or endogenous depression represents a specific subtype rather than a severe type of major depression. Parker and Hadzi-Pavlovic (1996) developed their own rating system (CORE) for diagnosing melancholia, consisting of items describing behavioral and verbal retardation, behavioral agitation, or stereotypy. It differs from the *DSM-IV* melancholic specifier in that it does not include "vital signs" such as disturbances of sleep and appetite or guilt and sensitivity to rejection. They acknowledge that this represents a more severe kind of depression but maintain that it is also a qualitatively distinct type, probably with its own organic etiology. A variety of validity evidence is presented to support the claim that their definition is better than the one in *DSM-III-R*.

One problem with their definition is that it confounds psychotic and melancholic features. Although psychotic symptoms are only found in a subgroup of melancholics, they rarely appear in nonmelancholic depressions. Another problem is the strong relationship of melancholic depression to age. Not only are current melancholics older, but the age of onset is much later than in nonmelancholic depressions (41 years vs. 26 years). They would appear to represent the group called "involutional melancholia" prior to the publication of the *DSM*. The symptoms of melancholia also resemble those seen in organic disorders associated with advanced age, such as Parkinson's disease and Alzheimer's disease, as well as functional depressions of older age (Austin & Mitchell, 1996). Scores on the CORE index of melancholia and incidence of psychoticism increase dramatically in depressed patients over 60 years old.

The *postpartum specifier* is a substitute for the older diagnosis of "postpartum psychosis." It represents a severe expression of "postpartum blues," which occur in many women after giving birth and usually last only 3 to 7 days postpartum. Postpartum reactions in the past were assumed to be due to the decreasing levels of circulating hormones such as estradiol and progesterone after giving birth, but psychoendocrinological studies have been inconclusive as they were for involutional melancholia, also thought to be associated with hormonal changes. The postpartum specifier is used if the onset of a depressive or manic episode is within 4 weeks postpartum. It may or may not be accompanied by suicidal thoughts and obsessions or delusions regarding the newborn.

Disorder course specifiers describe interepisode recovery from a major depressive episode, which may be a full-blown one or a continuation of the depressed baseline of a dysthymic disorder. A *seasonal pattern specifier* refers to major depressive episodes that occur only during certain seasons of the year, usually fall and winter. The depressive episode usually disappers in the spring. A *rapid-cycling specifier* describes bipolar reactions occurring at least four times in 12 months. Some even occur on a daily or weekly basis.

In addition to the mood disorders already described there are "*depressive disorder not otherwise specified*" (NOS) and "*bipolar disorder not otherwise specified.*" These categories are for subclinical disorders that fall just short of meeting the temporal or number of symptoms criteria for either kind of disorder. A special category for subthreshold disorders would not be unnecessary in a dimensional system. Also included in the NOS categories are major mood disorders that occur in the aftermath or during the course of other psychotic disorders, such as schizophrenia or delusional disorder. These are sometimes called "secondary depressions." There are also diagnoses of *mood disorders due to a general medical condition* and *substance-induced mood disorders* for use when the mood disturbance is thought to be due to the condition or substance. An NOS diagnosis may be used when the clinician suspects but is not sure of the medical or drug cause.

Schizoaffective disorder (SAD) is not classified with either schizophrenia or the mood disorders because it contains elements of both of these disorders. Instead, it is listed in the *DSM-IV* after schizophrenia under the major heading of "other psychotic disorders." Just as the boundaries of anxiety and mood disorders are fuzzy, the line between schizophrenia and mood disorders is blurred when psychotic symptoms are present in a mood disorder or when mood symptoms are present in a schizophrenic disorder. The distinction between "mood disorders with psychotic features" and SAD is that there are also periods (of at least 2 weeks) when the delusions or hallucinations are present in the absence of prominent mood symptoms. SAD may be further specified as bipolar or depressive type by the mood symptoms.

The DSM diagnostic system for mood disorders is not without its critics. Van Praag (1993) questions the distinction between dysthymic disorder and major depressive disorder, claiming that severity, duration, or preexisting personality disorders do not really distinguish the two types except by fiat. Many milder cases of major depression, which might otherwise be called dysthymic disorder, display an episodic rather than a chronic pattern. Others have suggested that a depressive personality disorder diagnosis is needed to describe the less intense, more chronic form of depression not adequately described by dysthymic disorder (D. N. Klein & Miller, 1993; R. M. A. Hirschfeld, 1994; Schraeder, 1994). In response, a provisional description of a diagnosis of depressive personality disorder has been included in *DSM-IV*. This diagnostic concept will be described further in the later section on personality.

Comorbidity

The comorbidity of depressive and anxiety disorders, particularly of GAD, was discussed in chapter 3. Nearly half of all dysthymic and major depression disorders have a concurrent anxiety diagnosis, most typically social phobia or GAD (Sanderson, Beck, & Beck, 1990). In 77% of the cases, the onset of the depressive disorder preceded the onset of the anxiety disorder. When an anxiety disorder precedes the onset of a depressive disorder, it is generally GAD. Whereas depression may emerge from a background of general anxiety, phobic disorders tend to develop out of the depression. Major depression has a high lifetime comorbidity (43%) with posttraumatic stress disorder (PTSD). Analyses of the temporal relationships between the two disorders show that major depression is both a significant antecedent and a significant sequela of PTSD (Breslau, Davis, Peterson, & Schultz, 1997).

Anywhere from 50–95% of patients with mood disorders are also diagnosed with personality disorders, usually avoidant and dependent personality disorders (Alnaes & Torgersen, 1991; Sanderson et al., 1992). Patients who had a personality disorder scored higher on tests of depression and anxiety than those who did not have a comorbid disorder, indicating greater severity of symptoms during the Axis I episode. Patients with any personality disorder, but particularly those with paranoid or schizoid personality disorders, were less likely to remit after drug therapy (Sato, Sakado, Sato, & Morikawa, 1994).

Patients with bipolar disorders have relatively fewer personality disorders than patients with unipolar disorders, and more of their disorders tend to be of the Cluster B variety, that is, antisocial, histrionic, narcissistic, or borderline subtypes (F. K. Goodwin & Jamison, 1990; Turley, Bates, Edwards, & Jackson, 1992). Patients with early onset dysthymic disorder also exhibit a greater number of personality disorders than late onset cases, particularly Cluster B disorders such as borderline personality.

Borderline personality disorder represents a mixture of impulsive self-damaging behavior and unstable mood with agitated depressive features, unstable and ambivalent interpersonal relationships, suicidal threats or attempts, intense inappropriate displays of anger, and transient stress-related paranoid or disorganized symptoms. In some ways it is like a bipolar disorder except that the two phases are mixed and more reactive to interpersonal problems.

A field test of the provisional depressive personality disorder in *DSM-IV* found that 45% of those patients with major depression, and 58% of patients with dysthymia had comorbid depressive personality disorder, and 75% of those with the personality disorder had current major depression or dysthymia. The overlap between depressive personality disorder and dysthymia, and between dysthymia and major mood disorder suggests that these disorders constitute a continuum of severity along which patients may move up or down at different times.

Prevalence and Demographics

The prevalence rates for the mood disorders from the NCS survey (Kessler et al., 1994) are shown in Table 4.2. About 1 in 5 persons (19%) is likely to develop a mood disorder during his or her lifetime, and about 1 in 10 (11%) has been suffering with a mood disorder during the past year. The most predominant type of mood disorder in the population is major depressive disorder (17%). The lifetime rate for dysthymia (6.4%) is considerably less. Only 1.6% of the population is likely to experience a manic episode, and therefore, incur a diagnosis of bipolar disorder. The rates for mood disorders (*DSM-III*) for the six communities in the ECA study were much lower: 2.9–5.8% for major depression, 2.1–4.2% for dysthymia, and 0.6–1.7% for bipolar disorder. The possible reasons for the discrepancy in rates of the two community surveys were mentioned in chapter 3.

A worldwide study in 10 countries using the *DSM-III* criteria found lifetime prevalence rates ranging from 1.5% in Taiwan to 19% in Beirut (Negrao, 1997). High rates were also found in Paris, Florence, and New Zealand. Relatively speaking, American rates, based on the ECA study, were not that high, ranking only seventh out of the 10 countries. Lifetime prevalence rates for bipolar disorder varied within a much smaller range, from 0.3% in Taiwan to 1.5% in New Zealand. Rates of current prevalence of major depressive episodes in 15 countries averaged 7.1% for men and 12.5% for women (Gater et al., 1998). The Gender × Center interaction was not significant, showing that the odds ratio preponderance of women to men (1.6) was universal among the nations and cultures in the study. The findings suggest that the higher incidence of unipolar depression among women cannot be attributed to local social conditions for women. In fact, three Western countries (England, France, & the Netherlands) are

TABLE 4.2
Prevalence (%) of *DSM-III-R* Mood Disorders (NCS)

Disorders	Lifetime Prevalence			12-Month Prevalence		
	Male	Female	Total	Male	Female	Total
Major depressive	12.7	21.3	17.1	7.7	12.9	10.3
Manic episode	1.6	1.7	1.6	1.4	1.3	1.3
Dysthymia	4.8	8.0	6.4	2.1	3.0	2.5
Any Mood Disorder	14.7	23.9	19.3	8.5	14.1	11.3

Note. n = 8,098; NCS = National Comorbidity Survey. From "Lifetime and 12-month Prevalence of Major Disorders," by R. C. Kessler et al., *Archives of General Psychiatry, 51*, p. 12. Copyright 1994 by American Medical Association. Adapted by permission.

among those with the highest rates of depression in women, and Greece, China, Italy, Nigeria, and Japan are the countries with the lowest rates of depression in women.

In most surveys women show higher rates than men for all of the disorders except mania. These gender differences are generally consistent with those found in other countries and cultures (Culbertson, Smith, & Weissman, 1992; Negrao, 1997). In the cross-national study the female to male ratio of major depressive disorder ranged from 1.6:3.1 across countries. In the United States, it was 2.6. However, in nondeveloped nations, particularly those in Africa, findings are mixed, and most studies show no significant gender differences in the prevalence of mood disorders (Noelen-Hoeksemi, 1990). Equal male and female prevalences for both bipolar *and* unipolar disorders were found in the Amish community in an extended family study using RDC criteria for diagnosis (Egeland, 1994).

In the NCS survey, mood disorders declined as a function of increasing incomes. Blacks had lower rates and Hispanics had higher rates of mood disorders than did non-Hispanic Whites. Prevalence did not vary with education, urbanicity of residence, or region of the country. In the ECA study, socioeconomic status was not related to any of the three mood disorders, and race was not a significant factor. Currently married persons had lower rates of mood disorders than divorced, separated, or never-married persons. In both studies higher rates were found in the younger age groups. In the cross-national study separated or divorced persons had rates of major depression 2–4 times higher than married persons, although the risk was somewhat greater for divorced or separated men than for women in most countries (Negrao, 1997).

A comparison of four generational cohorts beginning with those born before 1917 and ending with those born 1953–1966 shows a progressive increase in the rates for major depressive episodes, particularly in the 15- to 19-year-old group (Burke, Burke, Rae, & Regier, 1991). The post-World War II generation (baby-boomers) had very high rates of depression onset in their adolescent years compared with post-World War I generations. Bipolar disorders did not show this trend but drug and alcohol abuse disorders did, suggesting the possibility that these latter disorders may have played some role in the increase of depression in more recent cohorts or that depression may have influenced drug use for this cohort.

Comparisons of older people (over 60) with unipolar major depression and younger people with the same diagnosis showed that the older patients were more likely to be psychotic (delusional), agitated, and guilty, and more severely depressed than their younger counterparts (Brodarty et al., 1991). The older patients were less likely to have personality disorders or a family history of mood disorders. Comparisons of early and late onset elderly depressives revealed no differences in symptoms, but a family history of mood disorder was found more often in early onset than in late onset patients.

This might suggest a greater role of stress (relative to diathesis) in the late occurring depression. However, comparisons of older and younger depressives on life event stressors in the year prior to the episode revealed no overall differences, although breakups of relationships were more frequent in the younger group, and loss through death tended to be more frequent in the older subjects.

DIATHESIS

For many years before controlled biometric studies were done, physicians and others observed the tendency of major mood disorders to occur with high frequency in members of certain families. Biometric studies have confirmed these observations. Most of the earlier studies did not classify patients by what is now the major diagnostic subclassification: bipolar or unipolar. The genetic studies to be discussed next are a crucial test for the validity of the distinction between these two types of disorders. To the extent that there is a genetic basis for the disorders we would expect to see similarities in diagnoses of twins and first degree relatives, not only for the presence of major mood disorder, but for the bipolar or unipolar specification of the disorder.

GENETICS

Twin Studies

Nurnberger and Gershon (1992) have described the evidence from eight studies of twins with major mood disorders done between 1930 and 1986. The concordance rate for 183 pairs of identical twins was 60% and that for 343 pairs of dizygotic twins was 14%. More recent studies using more current diagnostic criteria found about the same concordance as did the older studies for identical twins (53–61%) but somewhat higher concordances for fraternal twins (28–31%) (Kendler, Pederson, Johnson, Neale, & Mathe, 1993; McGuffin & Katz, 1989).

Studies that contrasted the concordance rates for people with major mood disorders and bipolar disorders and unipolar diagnoses have found higher rates of concordance for those with a bipolar diagnosis (Bertelson, Harvald, & Hauge, 1977; Kendler et al., 1993). Granted the higher heritability for major mood disorder in the bipolar group, to what degree is the genetic disposition specific to the subtype? Table 4.3 shows the concordances in the Kendler et al. study classified by the polarity of the twin as well as the polarity of the proband. In cases where the proband identical twin was diagnosed as bipolar, about a third of their cotwins were also

TABLE 4.3
Probandwise Concordance for Bipolar and Unipolar Major Mood Disorders

Proband Diagnosis	Identical Cotwins		Fraternal Cotwins	
	Bipolar	Unipolar	Bipolar	Unipolar
Bipolar	35.7	35.7	0.4	21.1
Unipolar	0.6	53.0	0.2	29.4

Note. Combines data from those diagnosed by broad and narrow definitions of diagnoses according to definiteness of responses on the Structural Clinical Interview for *DSM-III-R*. From "A Pilot Swedish Twin Study of Affective Illness, Including Hospital and Population-Ascertained Subsamples," by K. S. Kendler et al. (1993), *Archives of General Psychiatry, 50*, pp. 699–706; 703. Copyright 1993, American Medical Association. Adapted by permission.

bipolar, and an equal proportion were unipolar. In contrast, in cases where the identical proband twin was unipolar, half of the cotwins had unipolar diagnoses and practically none had a bipolar diagnosis. Bipolar disorder was rare in both groups of fraternal twins in whom nearly all of the cases diagnosed with any major mood disorder were also unipolar. The pattern is suggestive of some kind of autosomal or epistatic genetic mechanism for bipolar disorder and an additive genetic one for unipolar disorder, because the specific concordance of the bipolar disorder is only found in identical twins who have all of their genes in common. However, these kinds of data have also been interpreted as evidence that unipolar and bipolar disorders are on the same continuum, with the latter representing the more severe form of mood disorder (Karowski & Kendler, 1997).

Nearly all of the studies reviewed in the literature until recently used pre-*DSM-III* criteria. A recent twin study compared the effect of different diagnostic criteria for major depression (unipolar)—including those for the *DSM-III-R*—on the heritability, and compared different models of genetic–environmental influence (Kendler et al., 1992). This study used female twins from a community screened for major depression. The *DSM-III-R* criterion showed relatively higher heritability (.42) than all of the others except one (the RDC). The best model was one that attributed all of the remaining variance (58%) to specific environmental factors and error. Age, Shared Environment, and Dominant Genetic Effects were not important factors in the results. The lack of any influence of shared environment was surprising, considering all of the theories suggesting family influences in depression. However, these theories may be more relevant for mood disturbances of a less severe type.

Another twin study showed that the influences of shared environment depended on the breadth or inclusiveness of the diagnostic definition (McGuffin & Katz, 1993). Using the narrow definition of *DSM-III-R* major depressive disorder, these investigators found a high figure of 79% of variance for genetic sources with all of the remainder due to specific environmental factors. When the authors used a criterion with a broader definition of depressive disorder, however, the additive genetic variance was 39% (closer to Kendler's result), but the shared environment accounted for 46%, and the nonshared environment accounted for only 15% of the variance! Perhaps the broader definition included patients with dysthymic disorder or less severe depressions, which might show more influence of shared family environment factors.

The twin study of male veterans from the Vietnam era showed that only severe or psychotic major depressions (*DSM-III-R*) were affected by heredity, with genetic variances of 36% and 39%, but they were not affected by shared environment (Lyons et al., 1998). Dysthymia and mild and moderate major depression showed no significant genetic influence, but both showed moderate effects of family (shared) environment and stronger effects of nonshared environment. Early onset cases (first episode before age 30) were affected by genetic factors (.47), late onset cases showed a significant but weaker genetic influence (.10), and both showed only effects of nonshared environmental influence.

Another study using *DSM-III-R* and *DSM-IV* criteria for major depression was based on a hospital sample of twins of both sexes in which the proband twins were hospitalized for depression (McGuffin, Katz, Watkins, & Rutherford, 1996). The concordance was 46% in identical and 20% in fraternal twins, yielding a heritability of between .48 and .75, depending on the assumptions about prevalence rates in the community. But when the sample was divided into those with an endogenous and those with a neurotic type of depression (using the ICD-9 criteria), the endogenous showed marked heritability (concordances of .54 and .22 for identical and fraternal twins), whereas the neurotic type showed no significant evidence of heritability (concordances of .33 and .22 for identical and fraternal twins). Twins with longer and fewer episodes (typical of neurotic depressions) had nonsignificant heritability, whereas those with shorter and more frequent episodes had stronger evidence of heritability. Model testing showed no significant effects of gender or shared environment for the group as a whole. This study suggests that the current diagnostic criteria for major depression may actually subsume an older dichotomy (endogenous-neurotic), which has more validity by genetic criteria. Episodic major depression has a strong genetic basis, whereas the more chronic, less severe type does not. To some extent this distinction may be captured as that between dysthymic and major depressive disorders.

Of three studies of neurotic depression or dysthymia (Lyons et al., 1998; Shapiro, 1970; Torgersen, 1986), only one (Shapiro, 1970) showed any evidence of heritability. A study of Swedish twins analyzed symptoms of depression rather than diagnoses and compared twins raised separately as well as those raised together (Gatz, Pederson, Plomin, Nesselroade, & McClearn, 1992). The symptoms were assessed by a depression questionnaire with three subscales: psychomotor retardation and somatic complaints, depressed mood, and well-being. Although mood and lack of well-being could describe either dysthymia or major depression, psychomotor retardation is more characteristic of major depressive episodes. Retardation was the only scale showing the influence of a significant genetic effect (19%). Shared environmental effects were significant in all factors, particularly depressed mood (41%), and nonshared environmental influences were strong in all three types of symptoms.

The twin studies suggest that heredity and specific environmental factors, such as a stress affecting one of the twins but not the other, are important in major depressive disorders with endogenous and episodic characteristics, but shared environmental factors, such as parents and family environment, are not important. Shared environmental factors do appear, however, to be a more important factor in less severe mood disturbance and dysthymic disorder.

Family Studies

Nurnberger and Gershon (1992, p. 132) use a table to summarize the family prevalence of unipolar and bipolar disorders in the relatives of bipolar probands (14 studies), unipolar probands (9 studies), and normal probands (3 studies). The studies occur from 1966 to 1987 and use different kinds of diagnostic criteria and populations, so the variability in results is not surprising. Table 4.4 summarizes their table results, giving the range and median values for the bipolar and unipolar cases among the relatives of bipolar and unipolar probands. Added to their list is the ECA study. The others used pre-*DSM-III* criteria.

A greater lifetime prevalence of bipolar disorders (6.1%) is found among the first-degree relatives of patients with bipolar disorders, but a prevalence of bipolar disorder is not found to any significant degree in the relatives of those with unipolar disorders (2.1%). However, unipolar dis-

TABLE 4.4
Family Prevalence (Lifetime) Studies in Relatives of Patients With
Bipolar and Unipolar Disorders: Medians and Ranges of Results

Probands	Morbid Risk Median (%)	
	Bipolar	Unipolar
Bipolar (14 studies)	6.1 (2.5–17.7)	12.4 (0.5–23.1)
Unipolar (9 studies)	2.1 (0.1–4.1)	14.2 (5.9–28.6)
Controls (3 studies)	0.5 (0.2–1.8)	5.6 (0.7–5.8)
ECA study, U.S.	1.2 (0.7–1.6)	4.4 (2.9–5.8)

Note. From "Genetics," by J. I. Nurnberger and E. S. Gershon, in *Handbook of Affective Disorders* (p. 132), edited by E. S. Paykel, 1992, New York: Guilford Press. Reprinted with permission.

orders are found among the relatives of patients with bipolar (12.4%) and unipolar (14.2%) disorders. These results are similar to those for the previously mentioned twin studies.

Kendler, Davis, and Kessler (1997) reported a high incidence (34%) of lifetime prevalence of major depression in the parents of patients with that disorder as compared with parents of other patients and of controls without the disorder (16%). The findings remained significant even when the comorbid presence of other disorders in the patients and their parents was controlled.

Gershon et al. (1982) found a relatively large prevalence of both bipolar and unipolar mood disorders among schizoaffective probands. In fact, unipolar depression was found far more frequently than schizophrenia or schizoaffective disorders in relatives of schizophrenics and schizoaffectives, and at about the same prevalence as among relatives of bipolar and unipolar mood disorders (Maier et al., 1993). Bipolar disorder, however, was as rare among the relatives of schizophrenics as it was among the relatives of patients with unipolar mood disorder. Among schizoaffectives with bipolar characteristics it reaches the 6% level noted in older studies and 4.4% in the the Maier et al. study. When schizoaffectives are subtyped as bipolar or depressive, their relatives follow the bipolar unipolar characteristics previously outlined (Winokur, Coryell, Keller, Endicott, & Leon, 1995). Relatives of either those with bipolar disorder or schizoaffective mania had a 22% rate of bipolar disorder, whereas relatives of those with major depression or schizoaffective depression had a bipolar rate of only 5%. Relatives of both types had high rates of unipolar disorders (60–65%).

Some studies suggest that alcoholism might be part of a depressive spectrum, at least in males (Winokur, 1991). Female relatives of patients with early onset depression were more likely to be depressed, but male relatives of these patients were more likely to be either alcoholic or to have antisocial personality disorder. The idea of the spectrum was tested in a study of depression in adoptees whose biological parents were either alcoholic or had antisocial personality disorder. A genetic–environmental interaction was found for females only (Cadoret et al., 1996). Females who had a biological parent who was alcoholic (genetic influence) were at risk for depression only if there was also some behavioral disturbance in their adoptive parent (environmental influence). Antisocial personality in a parent only influenced females through environment; growing up in an adoptive family with an antisocial parent creates a risk for depression in adopted daughters. Males had neither a genetic nor an environmental link between alcoholism or antisocial personality in parents and depression. There was one confounding factor in this study. Fetal alcohol exposure from a biological alcoholic mother was related to depression in both male and female adoptees.

Studies by D. N. Klein and his colleagues showed significant numbers of cyclothymic disorders in offspring of parents with bipolar disorders (D. N. Klein, Depue, & Slater, 1986). In addition there were more dysthymic disorders of the early onset type (*DSM-III-R*) and major depressive disorders in the offspring of patients with unipolar major depressive disorders (D. N. Klein, Clark, Dansky, & Margolis, 1988).

D. N. Klein et al. (1995) later contrasted prevalence rates of disorders in relatives of patients with dysthymic disorder (DD), relatives of episodic major depression (EMD), and relatives of normal controls (NC). A majority of the DD patients had concurrent major depression, and 77% had a lifetime history of major depression, typical of the high comorbidity between the two diagnoses. Those identified as having dysthymias without a history of major depression are more appropriate for comparisons with the pure major depression group, so that only these two groups and the controls are included in Table 4.5. Relatives of DDs exceeded the relatives of NCs on incidence of all mood disorders except bipolar disorder, and both DD and EMD relatives exceeded the NC relatives on all three clusters of personality disorders. The DD and EMD relatives differed only on prevalence of DD. The EMD relatives had a low rate, which did not differ from the rate in relatives of controls, whereas the prevalence in DDs was higher than in either EMDs or controls. The results suggest a strong familial influence between dysthymia and episodic major depression. Considering the high proportion of "double-depression" (both disorders in the same persons), it is not surprising that they share much of a common diathesis. However, the specific aggregation of dysthymics in the relatives of patients

TABLE 4.5
Rates (%) of Lifetime Mood and Personality Disorders in Relatives of Patients With Dysthymia (No History of Major Depression), Episodic Major Depression (No History of Dysthymia), and Normal Controls

	Proband Diagnoses		
Disorders in Relatives	Dysthymia (No MD) (*n* = 103)	EMD (No Dys.) (*n* = 207)	Normal Controls (*n* = 229)
Mood disorders	34.0*	27.1*	16.6
Bipolar disorder	0.0	2.4	0.4
Major depression	24.3*	23.7*	15.3
Dysthymia	12.6*†	2.9	1.3
Personality disorders			
Cluster A, odd–eccentric	9.7*	10.1*	2.6
Cluster B, impulsive–egocentric	28.2*	19.3*	7.0
Cluster C, anxious–rigid	18.4*	17.4*	8.3

Note. MD = major depression; EMD = episodic major depression; Dys = dysthymia. From "Family Study of Early-Onset Dysthymia" by D. N. Klein et al., 1995, *Archives of General Psychiatry, 52,* p. 491. Copyright 1995 by American Medical Association. Reprinted by permission.
*(*p* < .05) significantly higher than normal controls.
†(*p* < .05) dysthymics significantly higher than episodic major depressives.

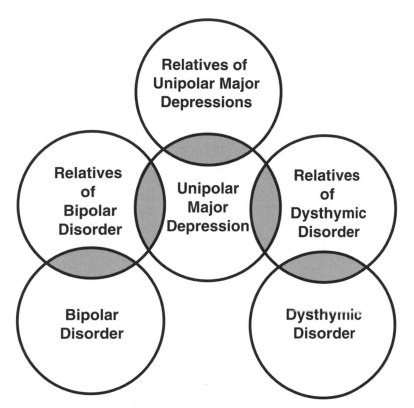

Figure 4.2. Occurrence of bipolar disorder, unipolar major depression, and dysthymic disorders in relatives of probands with these disorders.

with pure dysthymia, but not in those of the patients with major depression, suggests that there is also a specific factor in dysthymia that is not necessarily present in pure episodic mood disorders. Figure 4.2 shows the relationships between bipolar, unipolar, and dysthymic disorders in family studies. Unipolar major mood disorders are found in the relatives of all three disorders, but bipolar disorders are only found in the relatives of patients with bipolar disorder, and dysthymic disorders only in the relatives of patients with other dysthymic disorders.

A family study comparing the comorbidities of early onset (before age 18) and late onset dysthymia with Cluster B personality disorders (most borderlines) in relatives and probands concluded that dysthymia and personality disorders co-occur because of shared etiological factors, which are either genetic–biological or shared-environmental (Riso et al., 1996).

Molecular Genetic Studies

Recent developments in molecular genetics provide the exciting possibility of finding major genes for psychiatric disorders, including the mood disorders (Papolos & Lackman, 1994). Most biometric studies have concluded that there is a substantial genetic influence in the major mood disorders, particularly the bipolar disorder. These studies, however, do not specify the mode of genetic transmission involved in bipolar or unipolar disorders. Possibilities include a single major gene, a limited number of genes, or many genes, none of which are necessary or sufficient to produce the disorder (additive polygenic model). Model-fitting biometrics provide no strong support for any of these models for mood disorders (M. T. Tsuang, Faraone, & Green, 1994).

In order to narrow the genetic search, investigators have looked for linkages between the disorders and genetic markers where the loci are known. The concept of *linkage* is that if two traits are inherited together and each has a different gene associated with it, then these genes will be found in the same region on a chromosome (Lackman, 1994). Linkages can be examined within families with a high incidence of the disorder by contrasting the DNA of those individuals with the disorder with that of nonaffected individuals, or by contrasting the DNA of patients diagnosed with and without the same disorder across families.

Linkages for bipolar mood disorder have included the human leukocyte antigen on chromosome 6, color-blindness on the X chromosome, an insulin marker and an oncogene on the short arm of chromosome 11, the dopamine-2 receptor gene on the long arm of chromosome 11, and hemophilia B and a subunit of the GABA receptor on the long arm of the X chromosome (Mendlewicz, 1994). Only the last of these has received a preponderance of replications in other pedigrees (family lines). Mendlewicz feels that there is substantial evidence for an X-linkage in bipolar disorder. Such a linkage would explain the 2:1 prevalence of females to males with unipolar major depression found in community studies in America and elsewhere, because females have two X chromosomes, one from each parent, whereas males only receive one, from their mothers. If only a dominant gene on the X chromosome were involved, then males could not inherit bipolar disorder from their fathers. Cases of father to son inheritance for both major depression and bipolar disorder are common, and therefore, refute this theory (Plomin, DeFries, McClearn, & Rutter, 1997). Perhaps an X-linked bipolar disorder is only one subtype.

A major study is being conducted in an Amish community in Pennsylvania (Egeland, 1994). The community was selected because it is genetically and socially isolated from the surrounding communities and has many large multigenerational families, including some with high rates of mood disorders. The community also has a cultural uniformity, which reduces environmental variations existing in the outside world. Initial results were consistent with the model that theorizes a single dominant gene for a spectrum that includes bipolar, schizoaffective, atypical bipolar, and major depressive disorders. Unfortunately, the initial results linking loci on chromosome 11 to bipolar disorder could not be replicated using new pedigrees. Recent studies of this population suggest that inheritance in the bipolar spectrum disorder is multifactorial or polygenic rather than Mendelian, with genes on chromosomes, 6, 13, and 15 implicated (Ginns et al., 1996).

A number of families containing members with bipolar disorder have been studied in Scotland (Blackwood et al., 1996). A locus on chromosome 4p has been identified in affected family members in several families. The locus has also been found in a linkage study of families with mainly schizo-phrenic and schizoaffective diagnoses, suggesting the possibility of a shared genetic basis for psychosis in both disorders (Asherton et al., in press). The family in which the 4p linkage was found showed a mixture of schizo-phrenic and manic symptoms. The dopamine D5 receptor site lies within the region identified by the linkage studies, but neither study could find an association between bipolar or schizoaffective disorders and DRD5-M. A Mendelian single-gene model has been used for these studies, but as yet, no replicated linkages have been reported for the major mood disorders.

The single-gene hypothesis may be untenable, and a limited number of major genes may be another possibility, but one more difficult to dem-onstrate. Such approaches are being used for personality traits, and one success has been achieved with alleles of the D4 dopamine receptor gene associated with the trait of sensation- or novelty-seeking (Benjamin et al., 1996; Ebstein et al., 1996; Ebstein & Belmaker, 1997; Ebstein, Nemarov, Klotz, Gritsenko, & Belmaker, 1997). However, some failures of replication have also been reported, and the stability of the finding has been ques-tioned (Baron, 1998). Even if the association is valid, this gene would account for only 10% of the genetic variance and 3–4% of the total var-iance of the trait, so there is the possibility that other genes will be found. Sensation-seeking is a trait that has been associated with bipolar disorder (Zuckerman, 1994b). Plomin (1995) suggested that genes may be found for personality traits underlying psychiatric disorders before any are found for the disorders themselves.

NEUROPSYCHOLOGY

Brain Imaging Studies

The discovery of lateral ventricular enlargement and sulcal widening, indicative of loss of brain tissue, in many patients with schizophrenia has raised the question of specificity of the finding for schizophrenia (Pearlson & Schlaepfer, 1995). Since major depression is usually episodic rather than chronic, investigators did not expect to find such CNS damage in mood disorders. However, it soon became clear that such findings were nearly as pronounced in mood disorders as in schizophrenia. Meta-analyses of magnetic resonance imaging (MRI) studies, most of which used unipolar depressives, revealed that patients with mood disorders do have increased ventricular enlargement and sulcal space compared to control participants (Elkis, Friedman, Wise, & Meltzer, 1995). Schizophrenia patients had even greater ventricular enlargements than did patients with mood disorders, but the effect size of the difference was smaller than that between mood disorders and controls. MRI studies have also shown more specific losses of brain volume in several areas including the frontal lobes (Coffey et al., 1993), subcortical white matter, and the caudate nuclei (Krishnan et al., 1992; Husain et al., 1991). The findings are similar to those of patients with head injury, stroke, Parkinsonism, and Huntington's disease, many of whom also suffer from mood disorders (Mayberg, 1994; Pearlson & Schlaepfer, 1995). A study of patients with head injuries found that major depression developed more often in patients with left basal ganglia and left dorsolateral frontal cortex lesions (Fedoroff, Starkstein, Forrester, Geisler, & Jorge, 1992).

MRI scans of patients with bipolar disorders revealed a significant incidence of signal hyperintensities in white matter, most involving the frontal lobes, in about half of the bipolar patients and in none of the control participants (DuPont, Jernigan, Butlers, Delis, & Hesselink, 1990). These abnormalities were persistent in the MRIs taken a year later. The patients were relatively young so that organic disorders associated with age were unlikely. Birth complications are one source of brain damage revealed by MRI. An analysis of birth records of patients with bipolar disorders revealed a significantly greater number of obstetrical complications as compared with the birth records of their well adult siblings (Kinney et al., 1993). Such birth damage could create a vulnerability factor as has been shown for schizophrenia.

Functional studies using cerebral blood flow (CBF) methods have generally shown widespread reductions in blood flow in the frontal, temporal, and parietal regions of the brains of patients with major depressive disorders (Lesser et al., 1994; Nobler et al., 1994; Sackheim et al., 1990), and these differences are not reduced by successful treatment with ECT, suggesting that the differences are trait, not state, in nature (Nobler et al., 1994). PET studies have shown reduced activity of the prefrontal dorsolateral cortex (Baxter, 1991) and the caudate nucleus (Mayberg, 1994). Decreased metabolism in the caudate has also been shown in depressed patients with Parkinson's syndrome, and there is a high prevalence of mood disorders in patients with lesions of the basal ganglia in general. Mayberg (1994) developed a brain model for depression based on the similarities of brain imaging studies in primary and secondary (to brain injury or disease) depressions (see Fig. 4.3). Essentially the model suggests two major pathways involved in mood disorders. The first is an orbitofrontal-basal ganglia-thalamic circuit, and the second is a basotemporal-limbic circuit that con-

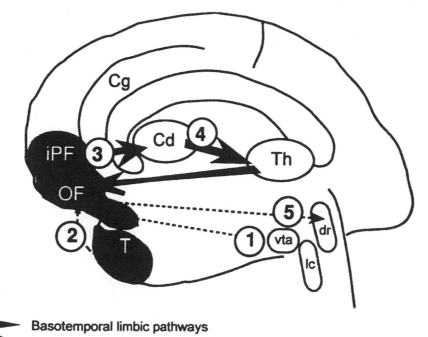

---▶ Basotemporal limbic pathways
▶ BG-thalamo-cortical pathways

Figure 4.3. A brain model for depression. Possible mechanisms for common paralimbic cortex hypometabolism in primary and secondary depressions include (1) degeneration of mesencephalic monoamine neurons (vta, dr, lc) and their cortical projections; (2) remote changes in basotemporal limbic regions, with or without involvement of the amygdala; (3) and (4), anterograde or retrograde disruption of cortico-basal ganglia circuits from striatal degeneration or injury; and (5) secondary involvement of serotonergic neurons via disruption of orbital–frontal outflow to the dorsal raphe. Cg = anterior cingulate; Cd = caudate; iPF = inferior prefrontal cortex; T = temporal cortex; Th = thalamus; vta = ventral tegmental area; dr = dorsal raphe; lc = locus coeruleus; BG = basal ganglia. From "Frontal Lobe Dysfunction in Secondary Depression," by H. S. Mayberg, 1994, *Journal of Neuropsychiatry, 6,* p. 431. Copyright 1994, the American Psychiatric Association. Reprinted by permission.

nects the orbitofrontal cortex with the anterior temporal cortex. Either organic lesions in these pathways or biochemical state changes could initiate mood changes. Interestingly, Baxter et al. (1992) suggested an involvement of the orbitofrontal-caudate nucleus-thalamic circuit in obsessive–compulsive disorder (OCD), except that in OCD there is an increased activity of the orbitofrontal cortex, particularly during provocation of OCD symptoms, and in depression there is reduced activity. However in OCD, as in depressive disorders, there is reduced caudate nuclei volume (Robinson et al., 1995).

The circuits involved in depression, as well as in anxiety, are pharmacologically mediated by the monoamine systems, and damage to these systems is implicated in the depressions of Parkinson's disease (Torack & Morris, 1988). Dopamine neurons are strongly represented in the basal ganglia. Degeneration of these neurons in the ventral tegmental area has been associated with depression in Parkinson's disease. The psychopharmacological approach to mood disorders has been focused on the role of the monoamine systems, norepinephrine, serotonin, and dopamine, discussed below.

PSYCHOPHARMACOLOGY OF MOOD DISORDERS

Those researchers and clinicians who believe that there is greater certitude in the biological than in the psychological approaches to psychopathology would be sobered to read the reviews in areas of clinical psychopharmacology which appear after each "generation of progress" (Bloom & Kupfer, 1995). Qualifying phrases such as "although not all studies agree," "in many but not all studies," and "at least in a subgroup of patients" follow or precede nearly every claim of a positive finding linking some specific biological factor to some form of psychopathology. There is much speculation on why results are found in one study and not another, often blaming population, method, and procedural differences, which of course may be the sources of replication failures. But the basic problem may be that single biological factors in etiology, whether they are specific genes, neurotransmitters, receptors, enzymes, or hormones, are not sufficient causes. Rarely does a study focus on more than one neurotransmitter at a time, even though the monoamines are known to interact extensively. Following this regrettable strategy, the following three sections will each deal with one monoamine.

Norepinephrine

The initial hypothesis on the psychopharmacology of mood disorders was called the "catecholamine hypothesis" even though it dealt primarily with norepinephrine (NE) and not the other major catecholamine in the brain, dopamine. Schildkraut (1965) proposed that major depression was produced by depletion of brain NE and mania by an overactivity of NE systems. The activity of brain NE was first assessed by the NE metabolite, MHPG, measured from 24-hour urine samples. The problem with the urinary MHPG measure is that only 25% appears to derive from NE metabolism in the brain. The rest comes from peripheral NE.

Using this measure, researchers determined that MHPG was significantly lower in patients with bipolar depression than in either those with unipolar depression or in controls. "Several but not all" attempted replications supported the finding (Schatzberg & Schildkraut, 1995). Further studies restricted the finding of low urinary NE to bipolar I and not bipolar II disorders. Plasma and CSF measures of NE and MHPG usually failed to discriminate bipolar from unipolar patients, except that bipolars with melancholic type reactions during their depressed phase had lower plasma NE and MHPG levels than unipolars, and the unipolars had higher levels than controls (Roy, Jimerson, & Pickar, 1986). Plasma NE (a peripheral measure) tends to be elevated in unipolar patients compared with bipolar patients and control participants. Even with the urinary measure there appears to be more heterogeneity in MHPG in the unipolars, with some patients showing very low values, such as those with bipolar disorder, and some very high values. The source of the variability could be in the clinical states of the patients. Bipolar patients exhibit high levels of urinary MHPG in the manic state and lower levels in the depressed state. But if the level of NE shifts with the mood changes it is simply a correlated state variable and the chicken in the chicken–egg problem raises its head. Patients in the manic state are very active both mentally and physically, but when they are depressed, they tend to show more of the retarded type of depression than the agitated type more typical of unipolar patients. Exercise can temporarily raise MHPG levels in depressive patients (but not in normals). Do the raised or lowered NE states produce the mania or depression or are they a function of either the activity or the behavioral retardation characteristic of the states of mania and depression? Experimental approaches are better able than correlational studies to answer questions of etiological priority.

The popularity of the catecholamine hypothesis stemmed partly from the success of the tricyclic antidepressant drugs, such as imipramine, in relieving depression in a significant proportion of depressives. Such drugs inhibited reuptake of NE, thereby potentiating NE activity. Added to this was the finding that depressives with low MHPG levels responded better to these drugs than patients with high levels of MHPG (Maas et al., 1984). Amphetamines also increase catecholamine activity but have only brief effects on mood and little lasting therapeutic value.

The catecholamine hypothesis was tested using a drug that inhibits tyrosine hydroxylase (TH), the enzyme that converts tyrosine to L-dopa, the first step in the production of the catecholamines (see Fig. 4.4). The drug produced increases in depressive symptoms in patients who were being treated with a norepinephrine reuptake inhibitor but not in patients being treated with a serotonergic reuptake inhibitor, suggesting a specific depressogenic effect caused by interference with catecholamine production (H. L. Miller et al., 1996).

Much of the current interest in the monoamines has shifted from the gross activity of the systems, as estimated from metabolites, to receptor functions. Figure 3.5 (this volume) shows receptors and functions in the NE neuron. The beta-1 receptors trigger the adenylate cyclase response in

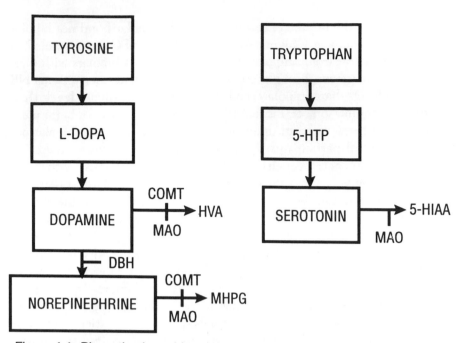

Figure 4.4. Biosynthesis and breakdown of the monoamines dopamine, norepinephrine, and serotonin. 5-HTP = 5-hydroxytryptamine, COMT = catechol-O-methyltransferase, MAO = monoamine oxidase, HVA = homovanillic acid, DBH = dopamine-beta-hydroxylase, MHPG = 3-methoxy-4-hydroxyphenylglycol, DBH = dopamine-beta-hydroxylase. From *Psychobiology of Personality* (p. 177) by M. Zuckerman, 1991, Cambridge, England: Cambridge University Press. Copyright 1991 by Cambridge University Press. Reprinted by permission.

the postsynaptic neuron. "Numerous" studies found fewer beta receptors in the lymphocytes or leukocytes of depressed patients than in controls, but "many studies have failed to find similar differences" (Schatzberg & Schildkraut, 1995, p. 917). Other studies have found decreased responses of adenylate cyclase activity to beta agonists in depressives, and hyporesponsiveness in the NE neuron decreases with treatment. Alpha-2 receptors on the presynaptic neurons may play an important role in anxiety (see chap. 3, this volume), since they act as a "brake" on NE production and release.

One might expect to find a plethora of these receptors in depression according to the catecholamine hypothesis, but studies have failed to show differences between patients and controls in alpha-2 receptor numbers. Another approach has been to measure growth hormone (GH) release in response to clonidine, a measure of alpha-2 receptor activity. Blunted GH responses to clonidine have been found "in many but not all studies" (Schatzberg & Schildkraut, 1995). The blunted GH response to clonidine tends to persist in depressed patients after recovery, suggesting it is a trait- rather than a state-limited factor.

Despite the evidence already described supporting the catecholamine hypothesis, its limitations have become evident. Although it predicts NE activity in a subset of bipolar patients and some unipolar patients, it does not predict NE in many unipolar patients, and some are clearly characterized by an overreactivity in the NE system, similar to some of the anxiety disorders. Furthermore both biochemical (Veith et al., 1994) and psychophysiological (Lader, 1975) studies show increased sympathetic nervous system (SNS) activity in most depressives, even those of the melancholic type (Veith et al., 1994). The effectiveness of serotonin reuptake inhibitors in depression, particularly for the patients who do not respond to NE reuptake inhibitors such as imipramine, suggests that serotonin deficit may be as basic to depression as is NE status.

Serotonin

There are two alternative views of the role of serotonin (5-hydroxytryptophan, or 5-HT) in depression. The first is that a deficit in 5-HT is a direct cause of depression. There may be two types of depression, one caused by a deficit in NE and the other by a deficit in 5-HT (Maes & Meltzer, 1995). Supporting this "two-disease" notion is the finding that low MHPG predicts positive response to NE-potentiating drugs, and low 5-HIAA predicts response to 5-HT potentiating drugs. The second is that deficits in brain serotonergic activity constitute a vulnerability to major depression rather than a direct cause (Meltzer & Lowry, 1987). The second view suggests that the deficits constitute a trait and should be found to some degree in prospective studies of depressive patients prior to their first episode and should be found in diminished but still elevated degree in those who have recovered from depression. Recovered patients should be vulnerable to relapse by any depletion of 5-HT. Prospective studies on 5-HT could not be found, but some studies of recovered patients and the effects of 5-HT depletion in depressed patients will be described. Serotonin is a good etiological candidate for major depression because it has been shown to play a role in some of the major symptoms of depression, particularly the vital signs of appetite, sleep, activity, and sexual desire as well as mood dysfunction and suicidal risk.

The first studies, as with those testing the catecholamine hypothesis, simply compared levels of the transmitter metabolites in depressed patients and controls. The serotonin metabolite 5-HIAA did not show any consistent differences (Maes & Meltzer, 1995). Studies of tryptophan (TRP), the precursor of 5-HT (see Fig. 4.4), have yielded more positive findings including lower availability of plasma TRP to the brain, prediction of positive response to 5-HT antidepressive treatments from lower TRP levels, and lower TRP as well as 5-HT and 5-HIAA in the brains of some types of depressed suicides.

Interestingly, lower TRP levels are found in fasting female control participants and depressed patients than in male controls and patients, and males show a smaller response to TRP infusion than females (Delgado et al., 1990; Maes et al., 1990). This could have something to do with the higher rates of major depression found in women. 5-HT receptors are estrogen sensitive. A negative correlation between plasma TRP and self-rated depression was found in female depressed patients. These results support the vulnerability interpretation of the role of 5-HT in depression. But the most impressive findings are on the experimental effects of TRP depletion.

Just as the interference with catecholamine production produced an increase in depressive symptoms in recovering depressed patients (H. L. Miller et al., 1996), TRP depletion produces an increase in depression in patients in remission (Delgado et al., 1990, 1994). A technique involving a low-TRP diet and a rapid depletion by a 16-amino-acid drink reduced TRP levels by about 90% and caused a temporary relapse in two thirds of a group of remitted depressed patients (Delgado et al., 1990). Free TRP levels were highly negatively correlated with ratings on the Hamilton Depression Rating scale after depletion. Melancholic type patients were particularly susceptible to relapse. A subsequent study by the same group found increases in depression as a function of TRP depletion only in patients who had been nonresponders to previous treatment with imipramine (Delgado et al., 1994). The same kinds of symptom worsening in the treatment of nonresponders was found as in the previous study. Patients with personality disorders showed a greater worsening of symptoms than patients without such disorders. The depletion procedure was applied to a group of normal men with a family history of mood disorders and another group without such a history (Benkelfut, Ellenbogen, Dean, Palmour, & Young, 1994). About a third of the group with a family history but none of the group without a family history of depression reacted with an increase in self-reported depression and loss of confidence after TRP depletion. The results support a vulnerability interpretation for 5-HT in that depletion affected mood only in those with a genetic risk factor, even though they were not currently ill. In a control condition there was no difference in depressive mood between the two groups.

As with the research on NE, current research on 5-HT has increasingly focused on receptors. This is a daunting task because there are currently some 15 known 5-HT receptor types. Although studies of rats show that traditional antidepressant treatments, including drugs and electroconvulsive therapy (ECT) increase 5-HT1A receptor binding sites and postsynaptic sensitization in rats, the evidence in humans is mixed (Maes & Meltzer, 1995). However, the evidence is firmer for an increased number, affinity, and responsivity of central postsynaptic 5-HT2 receptors. High 5-HT2 binding in platelets was found in the prefrontal cortex of major depressed suicides.

Maes and Meltzer (1995) are sanguine about the role of 5-HT in depression:

> Indeed it seems doubtful than any one neurotransmitter is entirely responsible for the pathogenesis of pathophysiology of depression because of the extensive interactions between neurotransmitters at the level of cell bodies as well as terminal regions. Nevertheless, 5-HT appears to be the most important monoamine relevant to the pathophysiology of depression and the action of antidepressant drugs. (p. 934)

Dopamine

Serotonin seems to have a strong role in depression, but it does not provide a reasonable hypothesis for bipolar disorder. A deficit in serotonin production or of primary receptors may explain depression, but an excess of serotonin does not produce mania. If anything it is likely to produce sedation rather than arousal, and inhibition rather than impulsivity. The swing from low to high levels of NE in bipolar disorder provides a partial explanation of manic arousal, but excessive activity in the other catecholamine, dopamine, might provide a basis for a number of other manic symptoms including euphoric mood, excessive activity, and unbridled sensation-seeking. To use Freud's (1917/1957) pithy observation, "He [the manic] runs after new object-cathexes [love objects] like a starving man after bread" (p. 136).

There are two major branches of the forebrain ascending dopamine system, as shown in Figure 4.5. The part originating in the substantia nigra nucleus ascends to the striate structures, the caudate and the putamen, where it is involved in regulation of motor functions. A deficit of dopamine in this branch could be related to the behavioral retardation in depression, and an excess of dopamine might underlie the hyperactivity of mania. An association of dopamine depletion, behavioral retardation, depressive mood, and loss of interest in activities is seen in Parkinson's disease. The other mesocorticolimbic system innervates the nucleus accumbens, amygdala, ventral hippocampus, and prefrontal cortex. This latter system is crucial in the reward or pleasure functions at its terminus in the nucleus accumbens. The psychostimulants, such as amphetamine and cocaine, produce their euphoric effects through this system. A deficit in dopamine could produce the anhedonia and loss of motivation that are basic symptoms of depression, and an excess could produce the frantic hedonic excesses of mania. A third branch (not shown in the figure), the tuberloinfudibular projection, is involved in neuroendocrine functions and may play a role in disturbances of these functions seen in depression.

The CSF, NE, and dopamine metabolites, MHPG and HVA, showed little evidence of deficit function in depression, but the CSF dopamine

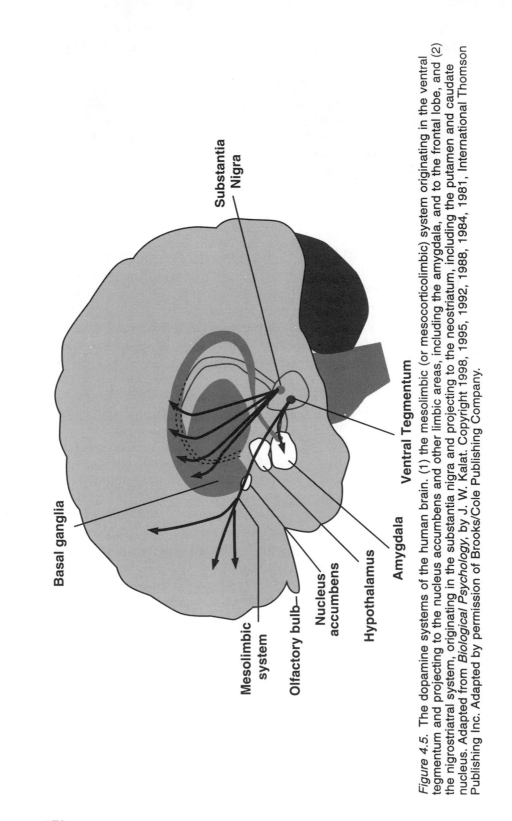

Substantia
Nigra

Basal ganglia

Mesolimbic
system

Olfactory bulb

Nucleus
accumbens

Hypothalamus

Amygdala   Ventral Tegmentum

Figure 4.5. The dopamine systems of the human brain. (1) the mesolimbic (or mesocorticolimbic) system originating in the ventral tegmentum and projecting to the nucleus accumbens and other limbic areas, including the amygdala, and to the frontal lobe, and (2) the nigrostriatral system, originating in the substantia nigra and projecting to the neostriatum, including the putamen and caudate nucleus. Adapted from *Biological Psychology*, by J. W. Kalat. Copyright 1998, 1995, 1992, 1988, 1984, 1981, International Thomson Publishing Inc. Adapted by permission of Brooks/Cole Publishing Company.

metabolite, homovanyllic acid (HVA) has been found in decreased quantities in depressed patients, particularly in those with psychomotor retardation (Willner, 1995). Low levels of both CSF and urinary HVA have been found in depressed suicide attempters (Roy, Karoum, & Pollack, 1992). The unanswered question is the extent to which the low level of activity in the dopamine systems, suggested by the metabolite studies, is a cause or a result of the low level of physical activity typical in the melancholic depressives. PET imaging studies show a hypometabolism of the caudate nucleus in both unipolar and bipolar depressed patients (Baxter et al., 1989), suggesting low dopamine activity in this motor regulation area of the brain. Another imaging study found an increased density of D2-like dopamine receptors in the caudate of patients with bipolar disorder who also had psychotic symptoms, but not in nonpsychotic patients with bipolar disorder (Pearlson et al., 1995). The psychotic bipolar patients had dopamine receptor densities as high as those found in schizophrenics in the study, but the densities in nonpsychotic bipolar patients did not differ from levels found in normal controls. The index of receptor density was correlated with ratings of psychotic symptoms, but not with ratings of mood and other nonpsychotic depressive symptoms.

The findings for mania explain why antipsychotic drugs such as Haloperidol, which block D2 receptors, are also effective with acute mania. But these drugs are usually given to those patients in psychotic, out-of-control states. There is no evidence of a link between bipolar disorder and the D1 or D2 receptor genes. However, the D4 receptor gene, recently associated with the trait of sensation-seeking (novelty) (Ebstein et al., 1996), has not been explored for a linkage to bipolar disorder. Sensation-seeking is a trait found in bipolar patients, even in the euthymic state, as well as in their offspring and may constitute a vulnerability trait for bipolar disorder as well as for other disorders involving disinhibition (see chap. 5, this volume). The D4 is found in greater density in the mesolimbic pathway than in the striate, and this may be where the action is in bipolar disorder.

Both dopa, the precursor of dopamine, and other drugs that enhance dopaminergic activity may have a therapeutic effect on depression, but in bipolar depressions, they may provoke a manic phase. This suggests a dysregulation of a dopaminergic system in bipolar disorder. One source of this dysregulation may be the enzyme MAO-B type, which is primarily dedicated to regulation by deamination of dopamine with dopamine neurons. Low levels of platelet MAO-B have been found in patients with bipolar disorders as well as in normal sensation-seekers and others in disorders characterized by disinhibition (Zuckerman, 1994b). Since the MAO does not vary much with the clinical state of bipolar disorder, is relatively stable and reliable, and shows strong genetic determination, it may be a trait marker for vulnerability to bipolar disorder or to the impulsive sensation-seeking trait also typical in the bipolar personality.

Hormones

The so-called humors in ancient medicine, such as black bile thought to produce melancholia, resemble hormones more than neurotransmitters of modern psychopharmacology, because they were believed to affect the brain and body moving freely throughout the body. Hormones are biochemicals that affect distant cells usually through travel through the bloodstream. Figure 4.6 shows three hormonal systems, two of which are thought to play a direct role in mood disorders, cortisol and thyroxin. The third, the gonadal hormones, may play an indirect role through their effect on neurotransmitter systems. Hypothalamic centers release hormones which reach the pituitary gland, which is situated at the base of the brain, through

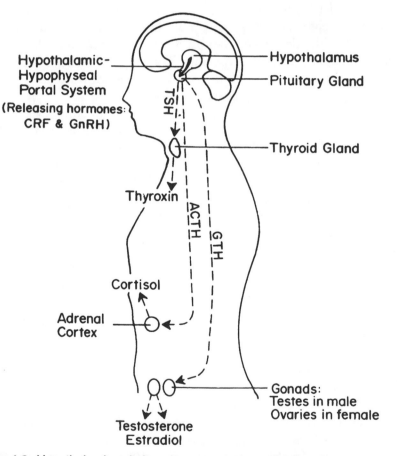

Figure 4.6. Hypothalamic–pituitary hormone systems for thyroid, gonadal, and adrenocortical hormones. ACTH = adrenocorticotropic hormone; GTH = gonadotropic hormone; TSH = thyroid-stimulating hormone. From *Psychobiology of Personality* (p. 182) by M. Zuckerman, 1991, Cambridge, England: Cambridge University Press. Copyright 1991 by Cambridge University Press. Reprinted by permission.

a direct portal system. Each hormone is associated with a specific releasing hormone, such as corticotropin-releasing hormone (CRH) in the case of cortisol, thyrotropin-releasing hormone (TRH) in the case of thyroxin, and gonadotropin-releasing hormone (GRH) in the case of gonadal hormones. These releasing hormones, in turn, release tropic hormones which have as their targets the glands in the body that release their hormones. CRH stimulates the anterior pituitary gland to release adrenocorticotropic hormone (ACTH), which travels to the adrenal cortex where it releases a number of corticosteroid hormones including cortisol. TRH similarly produces a release of thyroid-stimulating hormone (TSH) from the pituitary, which releases thyroxin (T4) from the thyroid gland, which is then converted to triiodothyronine (T3). GRH likewise releases gonadotropic hormone (GTH), which releases the gonadal hormones, testosterone from the male testes and estradiol from the female ovaries. The entire system involving all the hormones is called the hypothalamic-pituitary-adrenal (HPA) system.

The hypothalamus is the nexus of the interactions between the monoamines and hormonal systems because it initiates the hormonal reactions in the form of the releasing hormones. Both systems are responsive to stress, so it is not surprising to find that there are relationships between the monoamines and cortisol. Both MHPG and measures of peripheral catecholamines have been repeatedly found to be positively correlated with cortisol measured in CSF, blood, and urine (Schatzberg & Schildkraut, 1995). Other than the common effect of stress on both systems, the association could be due to an effect of CRH on the ascending noradrenergic system originating in the locus coeruleus (LC) and a positive feedback effect of the LC on the hypothalamus producing CRH. Whatever the source of the association, many patients with unipolar depression show increased HPA activity in ACTH and cortisol (Holsboer, 1995) as well as increased NE as indexed by MHPG. This increased and dysregulated cortisol release may be responsible for the sleep disorder characterized by early morning awakening in depression, because the cortisol cycle is one factor regulating the sleep cycle. The elevated cortisol activity is the basis for a laboratory test for major depression: *the dexamethasone suppression test* (DST; B. J. Carroll et al., 1981).

Dexamethasone suppresses ACTH and cortisol release for more than 24 hours in most normal subjects, with only 7% showing nonsuppression (Arana & Baldessarini, 1987). Only 8% of patients with anxiety disorders, 13% of patients with schizophrenic disorders, and 23% of patients with dysthymic or minor depression show nonsuppression. In contrast, 43% of adult patients with major depression, and 69% of those whose major depression (bipolar or unipolar) is accompanied by psychosis, show nonsuppression.

Patients diagnosed as depressive with melancholia, as defined by the

CORE criteria (Parker & Hadzi-Pavlovic, 1996), showed greater nonsuppression on the DST than melancholic patients, whereas melancholia as defined by *DSM-III-R* criteria did not differentiate the two groups on DST response (Mitchell, 1996). Melancholic patients were older than control participants, and DST nonsuppression increased with age, but the index of melancholia retained significant predictive variance even after the effects of age and weight loss were controlled.

Characteristics differentiating cortisol suppressors from nonsuppressors among unipolar major depressive patients include age (nonsuppressors are older), higher incidence of marital separation and divorce, preexisting personality disorders, dysfunctional attitudes, and stressful life events (Zimmerman, Coryell, & Pfohl, 1986). Those categorized as *suppressors* were rated as more depressed, even though they described themselves to be as depressed as the nonsuppressors. The *nonsuppressors* seem to show a more endogenous type of depression in which depressive cognitions and stress play a lesser role than in the suppressors. However, there was no difference in the incidence of family history of depression in suppressors and nonsuppressors. The nonsuppressors had a higher incidence of alcoholism and antisocial personality disorder in their relatives, perhaps indicating something other than pure depression in their diathesis.

Nonsuppressors have a slightly better outcome than cortisol suppressors, although the test could not be used as an effective predictor of outcome (Arana & Baldessarini, 1987). DST suppression changes to nonsuppression during the course of therapy in therapy responders, and those whose DST did not change had a poorer long-term prognosis. Although the DST now appears sensitive to only a subset of more severe depressive disorders and is less specific than originally thought, it does suggest a dysregulated cortisol system in depression possibly originating in hypothalamic CRH or pituitary ACTH. Spuriously abnormal DST readings have been obtained during hospital admissions or when surgery is imminent, such that it has been suggested that the test is a measure of stress rather than of major depression. However, Blouin et al. (1992) found that depressed patients had higher cortisol levels on the DST than generalized anxiety disorder patients, but the level of stress in both groups was not related to DST results.

Abnormalities of the thyroid system have also been found in one fifth to one third of patients with mood disorders (Holsboer, 1995). There is increased TRH in the CSF of depressed patients. When TRH is stimulated, the TSH response to it is blunted in about one fourth of the cases even though T3 and T4 levels are not changed (Prange, Garbutt, & Loosen, 1987). Hypothyroidism has been found in 60% of a group of patients with rapid-cycling bipolar disorder (Bauer, Whybrow, & Winokur, 1990). It might account for the rapid shift from mania to depression as a function of sheer overtaxing of the thyroid system and a defect in the homeostatic mechanism during recovery.

PERSONALITY

R. M. A. Hirschfeld and Shea (1992) describe four different models for the relationship between personality and mood disorders. Personality characteristics that are concurrently correlated with depression may represent: (a) a vulnerability to depression; (b) a part of a depressive spectrum on a continuum with more symptomatic forms; (c) a consequence of depression, assuming that depression may cause a personality change; or (d) traits that are not etiological for the depression, but that influence the expression and course of the disorder. Because the correlation between personality and depression during a depressive episode cannot narrow these possible interpretations, this section focuses on longitudinal predictive studies or studies of recovered patients. The personality assessment of recovered patients cannot help us decide between (a) and (b), and longitudinal studies cannot differentiate between (a) and (d), but a correlation during the clinical state cannot differentiate between (a), (b), (c), or (d).

The clinical state of the subject has been shown to influence trait measures of emotional strength and stability, neuroticism, and dependency; scores on such scales are generally reduced when the patient has recovered from the episode (R. M. A. Hirschfeld et al., 1983). Depressed patients will often say that they have always felt this miserable, and they just put up a good facade in years past. These retrospections are probably influenced by the depressive state.

Personality scores are not always affected by changes in depressed states. A study of patients with major depression before and after therapy showed that their elevated scores on a dependency scale did not change after drug therapy even though depressed mood was markedly reduced (Bagby et al., 1994). A study of the trait of sensation seeking (Zuckerman, 1979, 1994b) showed that patients with major depressive disorder scored significantly lower than normal population controls both before and after recovery (Carton, Jouvent, Bungener, & Widlöcher, 1992).

Comparisons of bipolar patients in remission with normal control participants show little difference in extraversion or neuroticism; however, recovered bipolar depressive patients do score higher on extraversion than recovered unipolar depressive patients (F. K. Goodwin & Jamison, 1990).

Mania represents a behavioral caricature of sensation-seeking, and therefore, it is interesting that the hypomania scale of the MMPI is the most consistent correlate of the sensation-seeking scale in normal college students and patients (Zuckerman, 1979). Cronin and Zuckerman (1992) studied patients diagnosed with bipolar disorders in a hospital setting. Although some of these patients were in the manic state and some in the depressed phase of the disorder, all scored higher than normal controls regardless of current state. Nurnberger et al. (1988) found that the "at risk" offspring of patients with bipolar disorder scored higher on sensation-seeking than the offspring of controls, suggesting a genetic link between the personality trait and bipolar disorder. High scores on "novelty-seeking" predicted poor outcome at a 6-month follow-up of a first episode of mania (Strakowski, Stoll, Tohen, Faedda, & Goodwin, 1993).

Jamison (1993) has developed the thesis that bipolar disorder is associated with creativity in artists and what is loosely called "the artistic temperament." There is evidence of an excess of bipolar disorder in British and American writers, poets, and artists. Most of these artists report periods of high productivity characterized by "enthusiasm, energy, self-confidence, speed of mental association, fluency of thoughts, euphoric mood, decreased need for sleep, impulsiveness, and other traits characteristic of hypomania. Depressive periods are characterized by creative blocks and diminished productivity. Jamison presents many individual cases and relates their creativity to manic periods, including Byron, Tennyson, Schumann, and Van Gogh. She then presents geneologies showing the presence of bipolar and other mood disorders in their ancestors and descendants. Although the emphasis is on artists, one suspects that certain tycoons and persons in other fields have their work regulated by mood swings.

Although measures of personality after recovery from a disorder may represent the predisorder personality, they may also be influenced by residual effects of the disorder. Prospective studies in which personality is assessed prior to the onset of the disorder are better for drawing conclusions about personality as a vulnerability factor.

The longest follow-up study started with children first assessed at 3 years of age and then diagnosed 18 years later by *DSM-III-R* criteria at age 21 (Caspi, Moffitt, Newman, & Silva, 1996). Inhibited children were more likely to be diagnosed with depressive disorder (major depressive or dysthymic disorder) at age 21 than children classified as well-adjusted or undercontrolled. As children, the future depressives were rated as socially reticent and fearful in the presence of strangers, and as inhibited and distracted in the testing situation. Studies discussed in chapter 3 showed that anxiety and inhibition in childhood also predicted future anxiety disorders.

The NIMH Psychobiology study followed a large group consisting of relatives and spouses of depressives for 6 years (R. M. A. Hirschfeld et al., 1989). The relatives had no previous histories of depression or other disorders at the time of initial assessment. The younger adults who became depressed in the interim did not differ from their age controls on any personality measures, but the older (31–41 years) group who became depressed were more neurotic and less emotionally stable, more dependent, and less resilient on the first assessment prior to their first episode. The difference in results of the two age groups could have been because the younger group had not passed sufficiently far through the age of risk, and therefore, included many false negatives.

A second study by the NIMH group investigated the "scar" hypothesis (i.e., personality changes produced by a depressive episode) in the group of relatives (Shea et al., 1996). Those who had no previous history of depression but developed a major depression in the 6-year interval showed no negative changes in personality from the pre- to postepisode tests. Participants who became depressed during the study scored higher on neuroticism both before and after the episode, but did not increase on this trait after the episode.

Angst and Clayton (1986) tested a more homogenous age group consisting of 19-year-old Swedish Army conscripts. A follow-up study 12 years later revealed 16 cases of bipolar disorder and 19 cases of unipolar disorder. The bipolar patients did not differ from disorder-free controls on any pre-existing personality traits, although they showed a tendency to be less stable. Unipolar depressives scored higher on measures of aggressivity and tended to score higher in nervousness prior to the onset of their disorder.

A 1-year follow-up of the community onset cases in the study by G. W. Brown and his colleagues showed that self-esteem, as assessed from a screening interview, predicted who would have a depressive reaction to a subsequent severe life event (G. W. Brown, Andrews, Bifulco, & Veiel, 1990). Severe negative self-evaluations were characteristic of 73% of the group who became cases, 52% of the group who were judged borderline cases, and only 19% of the group who were not cases.

A scale of "interpersonal sensitivity," developed specifically to measure depression proneness and including items assessing sensitivity to the opinion of others about oneself, need for approval from others, separation anxiety, lack of assertiveness, and fear of rejection or ridicule, was given to women in the second trimester of pregnancy. Postpartum depression was assessed at 1, 3, and 6 months postnatally (Boyce, Parker, Barnett, Cooney, & Smith, 1991). Interpersonal sensitivity predicted postpartum depression, and so did neuroticism but to a lesser degree.

Lewinsohn and his colleagues assessed volunteers from the community on two occasions with an average interval of 29 months (Rohde, Lewinsohn, & Seely, 1990). Measures of depressive mood, life stress, health, personality, social support, and other variables were obtained at both testing times. Subjects who became distressed after experiencing stressful situations differed from other subjects who experienced stress but did not become seriously depressed on first occasion measures of need for attachment and dependency on others.

A longitudinal study of twins enabled the investigators to answer more than the question of the predictive value of personality such as the extent to which the relationship of personality to depression represents shared genetic or environmental factors (Kendler, Neale, Kessler, Heath, & Eaves, 1993b). Personality and diagnostic assessments were made twice in a sample of 1,733 twins. The personality measures used were neuroticism (N) and extraversion (E) measured from a questionnaire. The first measure of N strongly predicted a new onset of major depression in the subsequent year and an onset of major depression significantly increased the level of N in the postepisode measure. No predictive or change measures of E were significant. Genetic analyses indicated that neuroticism is a major part of the diathesis for major depression, but there is also another genetic factor specific to the depressive disorder. Both genetic factors contribute about equally to major depression. But on the environmental side, the specific environmental events involved in major depression, such as loss, prolonged life stressors, and interpersonal problems, are specific to depression and not shared with the neuroticism liability. There is a residual "scar" effect of a depressive episode on neuroticism, but this effect is small relative to the liability effect of N on depression. From this study, introversion does not appear to be a predisposing trait for major depression or a consequence of the disorder.

D. N. Klein (1990) proposed the diagnosis of *depressive personality*, arguing that the dysthymic disorder is a more severe disorder than implied by the concept of a depressive personality. The *DSM-IV* (1994) describes a depressive personality disorder in the section for proposed diagnoses for further study. The personality is characterized by depressive mood and cognitions beginning by early adulthood and occurring in a variety of contexts. The traits include a usual mood characterized by dejection and unhappiness, low self-esteem, a critical and a negativistic approach toward self and others, pessimism, and guilt. The *DSM-IV* states that the distinction between dysthymic disorder, which also often has its origins in adolescence or early adult life, and depressive personality disorder is still in question. Klein claims that only 30% of the cases qualify for both diagnoses of depressive personality and dysthymia, but recent field tests suggest a much higher comorbidity. Diagnostic screening of young college students yielded a group with depressive personality (DP) (D. N. Klein & Miller, 1993). When compared with the larger group without this personality, the DP group had a significantly higher prevalence of current and lifetime mood disorders including major depression and dysthymia. Their relatives also had higher rates of major depression than the relatives of controls. This would make DP part of a spectrum (or continuum) of unipolar mood disorder. But the real question may be the extent to which depressive personality overlaps with the trait of neuroticism, or negative affectivity. Mood disorders are highly comorbid with avoidant and dependent personality disorders, and these disorders are comorbid with mood disorders in 68–95% of the cases (Alnaes & Torgersen, 1991).

Neuroticism has been shown to be a strong predictor of depression and to share a substantial common genetic variance with the depressive disorder. Inhibition and anxiety in early childhood predict depression almost 2 decades later. The same kind of childhood traits predict later onset of anxiety disorders. Emotional dependency is a personality risk factor for depression. What need is there to add to another personality disorder? Depressive personality, dysthymia, and major depression seem to represent points on a single intensity dimension. The comorbidity of anxiety and unipolar depressive disorders and their shared genetic variance suggest that the personality vulnerability for both is neuroticism.

STRESS

Stressful Events

Severe stress events often leave a residue of depression in their aftermath. The most common disorders—other than PTSD and GAD—in the study of Vietnam veterans exposed to severe stress in that war were major depressive episodes and dysthymia (Jordan et al., 1991). Major depression was also a frequent sequela of assault or rape in a civilian population of women (Breslau et al., 1997). Nearly every study relating negative life events to the onset of depressive episodes finds that there is an excess of such events occurring prior to the depressive episode as compared with their incidence in nondepressed control groups (Paykel & Cooper, 1992). The most common types of events are loss due to separation and discords in important interpersonal relationships. Although the study by G. W. Brown and Harris (1978) predates the DSM classifications, the careful way in which life stressors were defined in the context of the subjects' lives, and the testing of specific hypotheses about interactions between factors makes their results of continuing interest. The populations were both women patients from several London hospitals diagnosed and confirmed with cases of depression, and women from the Camberwell community in south London who were found on interview to have had a major depressive episode or who developed one during the course of the study (onset cases). Only severe events, such as long-term threats to the women, to someone close to them, or both were associated with the onset of depression. Over 60% of the depressive patients and only 19% of the control participants from the community had at least one severe event occurring in the 9 months prior to the interview, with the major difference occurring in the 3 weeks immediately prior to the episode. The most frequent types of events were loss or threat of loss, disappointment in personal relationships, or threats to economic security. Severe events were cumulative in effect. The occurrence of one such event in a 9-month period was not uncommon in the normal group, but the occurrence of two or three events was rare. In the patient group, however, 40% of the participants experienced two or more such events, and 23% had three or more. Minor negative events, however, did not cumulate to produce depression. A critical bale, but not a stalk, of straw may "break the camel's back."

G. W. Brown and Harris distinguish chronic "difficulties" from events. *Difficulties* are chronic problems that have gone on for a month or longer but that do not result from a specific event. These are problems producing chronic stress, typically involving work, housing, health, children, marriage, and money. Major difficulties, excluding health problems, were found in two thirds of the women who became depressed during the study and only one fifth of the others. Either a severe event, a major difficulty, or both were found in 75% of the patients and 89% of the onset cases as contrasted with 30% of the normal or borderline women. Many of the patients who did not experience a severe event or major difficulty did experience minor events and overreacted to them in contrast to the normal controls who also experienced many such events. What explains the 30% of the normal group who experienced severe events or major life difficulties but did not become seriously depressed as a consequence? The difference may be in the strengths or vulnerability factors, which may attenuate or amplify the effects of stress.

Do all depressions have to involve stress provocation? Distinctions have been made between endogenous and reactive depressions in the past on the assumption that endogenous depressions do not require much stress to become manifest. The distinction between neurotic and psychotic depression also carried similar etiological assumptions. G. W. Brown and Harris (1978) had their depressed patients independently classified as neurotic or psychotic and found no difference in the proportions of the groups experiencing severe events or major difficulties. In a more recent study, Brown and his colleagues (G. W. Brown, Harris, & Heyworth, 1994) did not find a significant difference in severe events between patients classified as endogenous and other depressed patients, but another study using similar criteria for classifying events and diagnoses did find a significant difference with a higher incidence of severe events in the nonendogenous subtype (Frank, Anderson, Reynolds, Ritenour, & Kupfer, 1994). The actual figures for the two studies were not that different.

The DSM attempts to avoid diagnosis on the basis of assumed etiology but does distinguish specifiers for melancholic and psychotic depression, described in a previous section. Melancholic depression has many features, such as behavioral retardation and sleep and appetite problems, which are associated with what has been called endogenous depression. Both melancholic and psychotic depressions are regarded as more severe forms. G. W. Brown et al. (1994) found a significantly lower proportion (40%) of melancholic-psychotic depressed patients who had experienced a severe event prior to the depression than among other depressives, 73% of whom had a severe event provocation. However, for the first depressive episode the proportion of melancholic-psychotic depressives reacting to a severe event was nearly as high as that of other depressives. From the second episode to subsequent episodes, the involvement of severe stress in the melancholic group diminished as if the threshold of provocation was lowered by the disorder itself.

In another study, patients with a major depressive episode were more likely to identify stressful events as precipitants of the episode, particularly interpersonal stressors, including experiences of loss, divorce, or troubles in love relationships (Alnaes & Torgersen, 1993). However, these events did not exceed the numbers experienced by patients with other mental disorders (mainly anxiety and adjustment) in the incidence of interpersonal stress.

Interaction of Genetic Diathesis and Stress

Many conceive of stress as an independent causal factor interacting in an additive fashion with the genetic diathesis (see Fig. 1.4, this volume). However, in another model the genetic diathesis influences depression directly or predisposes the reactions to stress with a greater impact of stress on those with more genetic vulnerability (see Fig. 1.5, this volume). Kendler et al. (1995) compared the two models in predicting the impact of stressful life events and genetic vulnerability on the onset of major depression in female twins.

The diathesis–stress influence model best fit the data. The risk for a severe stressor in producing depression was 2.4 times greater for those at the highest genetic risk than for those at lowest genetic risk. Genetic factors influence the susceptibility of persons to the depressive effects of stressful events. According to their findings, even in the absence of either strong genetic disposition or significant stress, either one of these factors may influence risk for depression independently of the other.

Major stressful events have been found to be provokers or releasers of depressive disorders in first and subsequent episodes of major depression (Dohrenwend, Shrout, Linki, Skodol, & Stueve, 1995; Lewinsohn, Hoberman, & Rosenbaum, 1988), and in bipolar disorder (Hammer, 1995). Severe stress is clearly a factor in the initial onset of major depression— regardless of the form it takes—and influences the likelihood of further episodes, particularly for the nonmelancholic types. But what are the risk factors that make stress more crucial for some than for others?

Risk Factors

In the NCS prevalence study, income influenced the rate of mood disorders with the highest rate among the lowest income group. Similarly in the G. W. Brown and Harris project (1978) there were large class differences, with diagnosed depression in 23% of working-class women, and only 6% of middle-class women. These differences, however, were most accentuated when there was a child less than 6 years of age at home. Of course the age of 6 is when the child starts school. Considering that many of these women had to cope with crowded, substandard housing, poverty, and indifferent husbands, it is not surprising that confinement at home with a young child would make one susceptible to depression. But an even higher risk for depression was found in widowed, divorced, and separated women of all classes. Lewinsohn et al. (1988) found that unemployment and children younger than 6 in the home were predictors of subsequent depressive episodes. Marital problems also predicted depression in this study.

The lack of a permanent source of social support was another important risk factor in the study. However, the authors define *intimacy* not as the mere presence of a husband but as a spouse or other relative or friend in whom the participants could confide. Among the cases who experienced a severe event or major difficulty but who also had a high intimate relationship, the rate of experiencing an onset of depression was only 10%, but among those encountering stress who had few or no intimate relationships, the rate was 41%! Dohrenwend et al. (1995) found an association between depressive episodes and the lack of intimate, confiding relationships even in a group consisting entirely of married subjects. A review of 24 studies on the role of social support in depressive disorder concludes that although there is definitely an association between the lack of social support and psychological distress or disorder, there is little evidence that social support buffers the effect of stress (Paykel & Cooper, 1992) as proposed by G. W. Brown and Harris (1978). Perhaps the difference is that most studies do not define social support in the psychological manner (intimacy) as do Brown and Harris.

Sexual abuse during childhood has been implicated in personality disorders such as borderline personality. A study of reported sexual abuse before the age of 17 in women living in London showed that among those reporting such abuse, 64% developed depressive disorder during the 3-year prospective study, compared to 26% of the rest of the women in the study (Bifulco, Brown, & Adler, 1991). The highest rates of depression were associated with the most severe kinds of abuse. Sexual abuse may have contributed indirectly as well as directly to later depression because it increased the chances for never marrying and for divorce and separation among the married.

Prospective rather than retrospective studies would be more useful, but hardly any of the ongoing longitudinal studies have assessed their subjects from a psychiatric viewpoint. One study which did so started with a study of college sophomores between 1940 and 1942, and assessed psychological and physical health by questionnaire at age 62 (Cui & Vaillant, 1996). Although many weak predictors of depression in later life were found, three variables independently contributed to prediction of an "affective spectrum" disorder: negative life events (preceding the first depressive episode), family history of depression, and psychosocial "soundness" in college. These variables could represent the three primary sources of psychopathology according to the model predicated in this book: diathesis (family history), negative life events (stress), and personality (psychosocial adjustment). The most powerful predictor was life events. Other variables predicted depressive outcome when considered singly but were subsumed under the last mentioned three in a multivariate analysis. These were mood fluctuations in college, relationship with father, and relationship with siblings. Mood fluctuations probably are a component of overall adjustment at the young adult age. Relationships with father and siblings could be contributors to the development of personality or a result of personality traits.

COURSE AND OUTCOMES

The *DSM-IV* describes four courses for recurrent major depressive course as a function of whether there is full interepisode recovery and whether the major depression is superimposed on a dysthymic disorder (double-depression), including: (a) full interepisode recovery with no dysthymic disorder; (b) without full interepisode recovery, but with no dysthymic disorder; (c) with full interepisode recovery, superimposed on dysthymic disorder; and (d) without full interepisode recovery, superimposed on dysthymic disorder.

Describing or predicting the "natural" course of disorders is difficult. Except for therapy trials in which patients are randomly assigned to treatments, different types of patients get different kinds of treatments that might affect their different outcomes. In a study comparing the course of melancholic and nonmelancholic major depressions, the melancholic patients were more likely to receive antidepressant drug and ECT treatment, whereas a higher proportion of the nonmelancholics received individual psychotherapy and cognitive therapy (Parker et al., 1992). Although the rate of change was related to the subtype diagnosis, and patients with melancholia showed more rapid improvement, both types ended with the same proportion of residual symptoms after 20 weeks. Bipolar patients usually have an earlier age of onset than do unipolar depressives. A family history of mania in bipolar patients was found to predict outcome in mania, but when age of onset was controlled, the prediction disappeared because those with a family history had a lower age of onset (Winokur, Coryell, Keller, Endicott, & Akiskal, 1993). Although earlier studies (e.g., Kraepelin,

1921) have suggested a high frequency of single-episode disorders, studies beginning in the 1970s found that single episodes are not common, occurring in only about one third of unipolar and even fewer bipolar patients (Coryell & Winokur, 1992; F. K. Goodwin & Jamison, 1990). Bipolar patients were more likely to have multiple episodes and, although a chronic course is not typical, unipolar patients were more likely to have a chronic course during a 5-year follow-up (Winokur et al., 1993). The earlier age of onset could account for the higher frequency of episodes in the bipolar disorders, but even a family history of bipolar disorder is predictive of a more severe course.

A follow-up study 1.7 years after hospitalization showed that manic patients had a poorer outcome than those with diagnoses of unipolar depression (Harrow, Goldberg, Grossman, & Meltzer, 1990). Lithium was much less effective in outcome than earlier clinical trials suggested. Effectiveness rates of lithium have decreased from the 80% reported in earlier studies to 33–60% in more recent studies (Gershon & Soares, 1997).

A 5-year longitudinal study of recovery in unipolar major depressive patients showed 3% recovered at 1 week, 19% at 4 weeks, 31% at 8 weeks, 41% at 13 weeks, 54% at 26 weeks, 70% within a year, and 88% within 5 years (Keller et al., 1992). This leaves 12% of long-term chronic cases lasting more than 5 years. The recovery rate of 70% at 1 year is comparable with other studies (Coryell et al., 1994, 80%; Parker et al., 1992, 67%; Sargeant, Bruce, Floris, & Weissman, 1990, 76%).

Not all cases of major depression are episodic. Chronicity is associated with discontinuation of treatment or the use of antidepressant drugs at lower dosage levels. It was usually the patient who gave up on treatment after less than optimal treatment duration who remained with moderate to low levels of depression for prolonged periods (Keller et al., 1992). Maintenance treatment with imipramine resulted in a 61% depression-free group after 1 year, and 46% after 3 years, whereas maintenance on placebo showed 22% "survival" after 1 year and only 9% after 3 years (Frank et al., 1990). The importance of maintenance treatment to prevent recurrence was also underlined by the results of a major study of treatments for depression conducted at a number of sites in an NIMH-sponsored collaborative research program (Shea, Elkin, et al., 1992). Patients with major depression were randomly assigned to 16 weeks of treatment with either cognitive behavior therapy, interpersonal therapy, the antidepressant imipramine with clinical management, or a placebo with clinical management. All treatments showed significant levels of recovery right after termination of treatment (ranging from 38% for drug treatment to 49% for cognitive behavior therapy) compared to placebo controls (31%). But at 18 months after the initiation of treatment, only 19–30% of the treated patients and 20% of the placebo controls had remained recovered without relapse. Of those who had recovered, one third of the patients in the cognitive and interpersonal psychotherapy groups and half of those in the drug treatment group relapsed in the year after discontinuation of therapy. At this point, there were no significant differences between those who had received treatments and those who had received placebo and minimal clinical contacts. This study and others emphasize that all treatments, including psychological ones, do not permanently reduce the chances of relapse, but must be maintained at some level to affect the natural episodic course of the disorder.

A 4-year prospective study after an episode of mania showed 64% of the participants in remission at 6 months postepisode with 36% suffering a relapse (Tohen, Waternaux, & Tsuang, 1990). At 1-year, 51% were still in remission without a relapse, but by the end of the 2nd, 3rd, and 4th years, 44%, 33%, and 28%, respectively still retained their episode-free remission status. Mania is highly episodic with other episodes of mania or depression.

Prediction of Outcome

Patients who met the *DSM-III* or RDC criteria for major depression in the ECA community study were followed up for 1 year (Sargeant et al., 1990). About one quarter of the group of depressed subjects were still depressed on follow-up. Women tended to have a higher rate of chronicity than men. Those with a greater number of prior episodes, with longer durations of prior episodes, and with a greater number of symptoms and comorbid diagnoses for the current episode were most likely to have a chronic course for the episode. Significant factors for prediction of chronicity among women (but not men) included older age (above 30 years), having divorced, separated, or widowed marital status, and having less education. Similar results were obtained in a 1-year follow-up study of adolescent depression (Lewinsohn et al., 1994). Women were more likely to have higher risk for persistent or future episodes. Past depression and suicide attempts, comorbid diagnoses with the current depression, internalizing behavior problems, and physical symptoms were predictive of negative outcomes. Patients with double-depression tend to revert back to their dysthymic baseline after abatement of the major depressive episode and remain vulnerable to future major depressive episodes (Keller et al., 1992).

In the Parker et al. (1992) study of 20- and 52-week outcomes of melancholic and nonmelancholic depressions, predictors of improvement in both groups of depressive patients included older age at first episode, less severe depressive symptoms, and extraversion. Those with an earlier age of onset, more severe symptoms, and personalities that were more introverted had a longer duration of depression. Neuroticism was not related to outcome.

In a longer follow-up study, previous history of depression, marital status, and level of education also had some predictive strength, but even when demographic variables were controlled, the number of symptoms at the time of entry into the study predicted the likelihood of subsequent diagnosed episodes as well as other psychiatric diagnoses during the period of follow-up, typically 12–13 years (Zonderman, Herbst, Schmidt, Costa, & McCrae, 1993).

Outcomes in bipolar patients 4 years after recovery from a manic episode were predicted by depressive symptoms during the manic episode, psychotic features of the episode, and a history of alcoholism (Tohen et al., 1990). All of these characteristics were associated with worse outcomes.

In both short- and long-term studies, past history of depression and severity of current symptoms predicted the likelihood of a chronic course or recurrence of depression in the future and the lack of recovery after treatment. This is not an unusual prognostic finding in many types of psychopathology. Not surprisingly, the sick get sicker and the relatively healthy get healthier. Other factors that probably contribute to both past and current psychopathology such as gender and education probably work through the material and psychological resources that enable the person to cope with the depression. Although neuroticism (N) was more predictive of future depression, extraversion (E) may affect outcome of current depression through social support. Extraverts are probably more able than introverts to seek and find social support, an effective way of coping and one affecting the outcome of the disorder (Paykel & Cooper, 1992).

COGNITION

Patients with major depression castigate and demean themselves. Everywhere they look they see evidence of their worthlessness. All they can recall from their past is futility and failure, and all they can see in the future is the same. It is this catastrophic loss of self-esteem and intrapunitiveness that distinguishes their sorrow from that of "normal" grieving for a loss or disappointment (Freud, 1917/1957). The content of depressive cognitions amplifies and justifies the depressive mood, but is it a cause or a consequence of the mood changes?

Beck's (1972) revolutionary approach was to regard depressive cognitions as mediating the mood change and a focus for therapy for mood disorders rather than as a symptom of aggression toward objects turned inward against the self (Freud, 1917/1957), or a simple epiphenomenon of the primary mood disorder. However, the depressive cognitions that appear during a depressive episode and usually disappear after the episode are not the diathesis themselves. Beck (1972) suggests that the diathesis consists of cognitive traits, or *schemas*, that precede the first depressive episode and make the depressive patient vulnerable to future episodes precipitated by loss, failure, or other stressors. Under stress the schemas trigger the typical depressive cognitions. The three major depressive schemas are as follows:

1. Negative views of the self (low self-esteem)
2. Negative views of experience (cognitive distortions)
3. Negative views of the future (hopelessness)

These schemas, particularly numbers 1 and 2, bias the depression-prone individual toward typical errors in thinking, including the following:

1. *Arbitrary inference.* Erroneous conclusions drawn from little or no perceptual evidence.
2. *Selective abstraction.* Recalling only one negative detail of a series of positive events.
3. *Overgeneralization.* Overgeneralization based on a single specific nonsignificant failure.
4. *Magnification and minimization.* Underestimating the significance of positive experiences and maximizing the significance of negative ones.
5. *Personalization.* Blaming themselves without cause for the occurrence of negative events.

Beck (1983) distinguished two personality-linked modes that determine what kinds of stressors or negative life events are most likely to activate the latent schemas to produce depression. The *sociotrophic* personality type strongly values social acceptance, intimacy, and support, and therefore, is most threatened by the threat of rejection. In contrast, the *autonomous* personality type values independence, mobility, choice, and achievement, and is more stressed by failure in work and threats to independence.

Beck (1987) does not assert that depressive cognitions actually cause the depressive disorder. Rather, he says that "such statements would be akin to saying that 'delusions cause psychosis'" (p. 10). Instead he views "deviant cognitive processes as intrinsic to the depressive disorder, not a cause or a consequence" (p. 10). However, Beck does believe that depressive cognitions lead to, intensify, or prolong the depressive mood and behavioral inertia, and this is why they are the focus of his therapy. Thus, although depressive cognitions may play a proximal causal role in certain other symptoms of depression, they are not the diathesis for the disorder. The cognitive diatheses are the broader schemas which predispose individuals to respond to stress with both depressive cognitions and mood. Presumably these are variables such as self-esteem and attributional styles.

Seligman (1975) applied his construct of learned helplessness to explain the causes and symptoms of depression. *Learned helplessness* describes a phenomenon in which people (or laboratory animals) experience conditions where they have no control over the occurrence of negative events and then generalize this belief in their helplessness to other situations where they are not really helpless. Seligman recognized that the theory did not explain the loss of self-esteem in depression (Abramson, Seligman, & Teasdale, 1978). Why should people get depressed about events for which they were not responsible and had no control? Also, why should they generalize so much between specific experiences of helplessness and later situations, often quite different from the original ones? The new theory was applied to elaborate Beck's views of cognitive bias by describing three types of attribution or explanation for negative events: self vs. external, global vs. specific, and stable vs. unstable (Peterson & Seligman, 1984). When given an unpleasant event, the depression-prone individual has an *inferential style* characterized by self-, global, and stable attributions of cause. Although the model focused on negative events, there is a complementary picture for positive events. When good things happen to depressed persons, they are likely to interpret them as due to external, specific, and unstable causes such as luck rather than to their own efforts.

Table 4.6 illustrates the eight possible combinations of explanation for a hypothetical event. A therapist is treating a patient with a borderline personality. A day after a session the patient makes a serious suicide attempt. The eight types of explanation by the therapist are given in the table. According to Peterson and Seligman, it is primarily the first response that will lead to depression because (a) it attributes blame to the self; (b) it is highly generalized (global) across a significant part of the self-concept (ability in one's work); and (c) it indicates a personal defect which is unlikely to change in the future (stable).

Peterson and Seligman (1984) conceive of explanatory styles like Beck does of schemas: They are latent cognitive traits which may be activated by negative life events, biasing the explanations to depression-

TABLE 4.6
Examples of Causal Explanations for Event:
Patient Makes an Unanticipated Suicide Attempt;
Therapist's Attributions

	Internal	External
Stable/Global	"I'm an incompetent therapist."	"No one can help every patient."
Stable/Specific	"I'm not good with borderlines."	"Borderlines are difficult for everyone."
Unstable/Global	"I was stressed and had a difficult time with all my patients that week."	"There are times when patients are just unpredictable."
Unstable/Specific	"I missed a crucial hint she gave in the previous session."	"The patient just happened to experience an unexpected rejection that day."

inducing ones. They do concede some plasticity in the trait in that it may be changed by the depressive experience as well as play a role in its development. Depressive styles change for the better as the depression lifts. These styles are attributed to environmental influences, such as imitation of parents, particularly the mother or primary caregiver, criticisms of teachers, and early experiences of loss and helplessness. Mothers' explanatory styles for bad events and their depressive symptoms correlated with their children's depressive styles and depressive symptoms, but fathers' styles and symptoms did not (Seligman et al., 1984). Conceivably, the link between explanatory styles and depression in mother and child could be explained by genetic as well as by environmental causes. But the lack of correlation with the fathers' cognitive and mood traits suggests that it is primarily environmental unless depression was carried by an X-linked autosomal gene as has been suggested by some researchers.

Abramson, Metalsky, and Alloy (1989) incorporated Beck's theory of negative cognition bias and Seligman's theory of helplessness and attributional style within a type of *hopelessness depression* characterized by (a) attributing negative events to internal, stable, or global causes; (b) inferring negative consequences given the occurrence of negative life events; and (c) inferring negative characteristics about the self as a consequence of negative events. In their model, the attributional styles and negative outcome expectancies are only activated by negative life events to produce the condition of hopelessness, which in turn produces depression. Hopelessness is the proximal cause of depression, and the three negative styles are the diatheses, necessary but not sufficient causes of hopelessness depression.

Hopelessness depression is a particular subtype of depression characterized by retarded behavior, lack of energy, apathy, lack of motivation, sleep disturbance, difficulty in concentration, negative cognitions, sad affect, and suicide (Abramson et al., 1989). Although the authors say that this type of depression can be found in any of the *DSM* mood disorders, including dysthymia or personality disorders such as borderline personality, many of the symptoms, particularly psychomotor retardation, loss of energy, and suicidal preoccupation, describe a severe major mood disorder, especially of the melancholic type. Beck (1983), however, views cognitive dysfunction as a more important factor in *nonendogenous ("reactive") unipolar* types of depression.

Although Abramson concedes that interpersonal, developmental, and genetic and biological factors may influence whether a person will develop hopelessness after a negative life event, she does not seem to consider that these factors might be the real diathesis for the cognitive risk factors that precede hopelessness.

Measures of dysfunctional attitudes, expectations of positive outcomes, frequency of self-reinforcement, self-esteem, perceived control over one's life, and attributions of causality for negative and positive events were factor analyzed in a large sample of adolescents (Gotlib, Lewinsohn, Seely, Rohde, & Redner, 1993). Two major factors were found, one consisting of all of the negative cognition measures derived from the theories of Beck and Rehm, and the other of the attributional style measures derived from the theories of Seligman and Abramson et al. Currently depressed adolescents differed from remitted depressed adolescents and never-depressed adolescents on both of these factors. The depressed adolescents scored higher than adolescents with other types of psychiatric disorders (primarily substance abuse and behavior problems) on the negative cognitive function factor but not on the attribution factor, indicating some lack of diagnostic specificity for the attribution traits. The adolescents with remitted depression still had higher depressive mood scores than never-depressed participants, although lower depression scores than currently depressed participants. When differences on depression scores between groups were statistically controlled, all differences between groups on cognitive scores were eliminated, indicating that cognitive dysfunction was related to current mood dysfunction independent of diagnostic or recovery status. Mood and cognitive dysfunction are correlated, but the issue of causation can only be tested by prospective studies.

A study by Lewinsohn and colleagues used a variety of cognitive trait tests given to volunteers from the community two times with about a year interval (Lewinsohn, Steinmetz, Larson, & Franklin, 1981). Subjects were assessed for depressive mood and symptoms and cognitive traits at both times. The cognitive measures included locus of control, expectancies of positive and negative outcomes, irrational beliefs, perception of control, and self-esteem. They were also retrospectively assessed for depression prior to the first assessment. Individuals who had a history of previous depression did not differ from never-depressed subjects on any of the cognitive tests, arguing against a "scar" hypothesis. Persons who became depressed during the study were not characterized by depressive-type cognitions in the time before they became depressed, contrary to a cognitive-diathesis hypothesis. Subjects developed depressive cognitions at the same time they developed depressive symptoms, consistent with the idea that these cognitions are consequences rather than causes of depression. However, the depressed subjects who had more depressive cognitions were more likely to have a chronic depression persisting to the time the second test was administered. This might explain why cognitive therapy may have a positive effect on shortening depressive episodes even if these cognitions were not causal in the depression itself.

Although a few other studies, such as the one involving the prediction of onset of depression using self-esteem ratings derived from interviews (G. W. Brown et al., 1990), have predicted the onset of depression from cognitive measures assessed before the onset of the first depressive episode, most have failed to do so. Summarizing prospective type studies, Gotlib and McCabe (1992) concluded:

> Although some investigators have found currently depressed persons to be characterized by an elevated level of dysfunctional attitudes, there is no consistent evidence that these negative thoughts either predict subsequent levels of depression or remain elevated following recovery from a depressive episode, particularly in males. (p. 136)

Although McCabe says that this conclusion represents a disconfirmation of Beck's theory, it should be noted that Beck (1987) does not currently regard depressive cognitions as causal to depressive disorder, and he expects them to disappear after the remission of an episode. Indeed, using the Dysfunctional Attitude scale (DAS) developed by Beck and his colleagues, scores after recovery from a depressive episode fall to normal levels (I. W. Miller & Norman, 1986; Silverman, Silverman, & Eardley, 1984). In fact, patients diagnosed with major depression who were recovered scored significantly lower on the DAS than those diagnosed as recovered nonpsychotic/nonaffective and schizophrenic disorders (Silverman et al., 1984). However, a smaller study found that although scores on the DAS dropped in treated depressives, they remained higher than in controls (Eaves & Rush, 1984). Negative automatic thoughts dropped to normal levels after treatment in all but the unremitted depressive patients. On the other hand, attributional styles (internality, stability, globality, and their composite for attributions of negative events) did not change much with treatment and scores remained above those of controls. Only the attributional styles seemed to be unaffected by treatment, and therefore, were more likely candidates for a cognitive diathesis.

Assessing cognitive traits from questionnaires may not be ideal because they are too closely tied to mood and vulnerable to demand characteristics, that is, a respondent thinks, "if I feel better I must not believe these things anymore." Gotlib and McCabe (1992) used performance tests to assess reaction times, attention, and interference in the dichotic-listening task using depressive and neutral words as stimuli. They reasoned that depressive schemas would be reflected in inhibition and interference produced by words with negative connotations relative to neutral or positive words. As with most of the studies using questionnaires to assess cognitive types, the information-processing tasks revealed cognitive biases when the patients were depressed, but not after they had recovered from the depression. If these latent cognitive traits surface during the depression and disappear again when it dissipates, there seems to be no way to identify them during the latency periods.

Abramson et al. (1989) and Beck (1976) do not claim that all depressive patients are characterized by these cognitive styles. An attempt was made to define the characteristics of the cognitive style or hopelessness-type depressions in terms of diagnostic status, depressive severity and history, gender, and developmental history (Rose, Abramson, Hodulik, Halberstadt, & Leff, 1994). Personality disorders, family overcontrol, sexual abuse during development, and severe depression were characteristics of the depressed patients with the most extreme negative cognitive styles. No differences in cognitive styles were found between unipolar and bipolar or between psychotic and nonpsychotic patients with unipolar depression, but depressives with personality disorders exhibited worse cognitive styles than did dysthymic types.

EARLY ENVIRONMENTAL EXPERIENCES

This volume will not deal with psychodynamic theories of depression because nearly all are based on inferences from case studies of adults rather than from prospective studies beginning with observations in children and families and extending to adult years. Interested readers may read the chapter by Mendelson (1992) for a summary of these theories beginning with Freud's (1917/1957) classic paper, "Mourning and Melancholia." However, a basic assumption of all theories is that a major part of the diathesis is early childhood experiences involving loss, separation, or lack of affection from parents. This assumption has led to statistically controlled, if retrospective, studies of childhood experiences of persons who became depressed (Parker, 1992). These studies developed hypotheses from Bowlby's (1951, 1977) studies of infants and caregivers. One of Bowlby's risk factors is discontinuities in parenting, which could be due to loss of a parent by death or separation.

Parker (1992) found 10 studies of adults who had experienced the death of a parent before the age of 16 and met other methodological criteria. Only 3 of the 10 studies found an association between parental death in childhood and depression in adulthood. Most other investigators of this literature have come to the same conclusion as Parker: There is little support for the hypothesized relationship between parental loss in childhood and subsequent depression in adult life. An exception to this conclusion is the G. W. Brown and Harris (1978) prospective study in which 47% of the women who had lost a mother before age 11 and also encountered a later major stress developed depression during the study compared to only 17% of those who did not experience early maternal loss. Loss of a father was not related to a depressive response to stress. Furthermore, past loss was associated with severity and psychotic features of the depression. The Brown and Harris study shows that a mere cross-tabulation of parental loss and depression is not sufficient to test the hypothesis. At a minimum, one must consider which parent was lost, age of the child at the loss, and later stress that may reactivate the feelings and interpretations of the loss. Freud

(1917/1952) suggested that the relationship of the child with the parent prior to the loss could be crucial in determining the melancholic outcome. According to Freud, the more ambivalent the relationship, the greater the likelihood of a pathogenic effect of loss.

Several studies suggest an effect of parental separation on depression, particularly those separations due to divorce or marital conflict (Parker, 1992). Patients with major depression have been found to suffer more losses, particularly the loss of a father through divorce, than patients with other disorders, primarily anxiety and adjustment disorders (Alnaes & Torgersen, 1993). The loss of a mother through divorce, however, was a significant factor in the bipolar group.

Lack of effects due to reasons other than marital conflict, such as evacuation of children in England during World War II, suggest that separation per se is not the risk factor (Tennant, 1988). The association of separation with feelings of rejection and self-blame, even if irrational, could set the stage for subsequent depression. Unfortunately, most studies do not attempt to explore the interaction of psychological factors with the separation experience. But even without actual separation, lack of affection from parents could be a risk factor in depression according to most psychodynamic theories. These theories have been developed from retrospective accounts of child–parent interactions given by the child years later in therapy. Obviously there is no way to compare such unstandardized data, which is so likely to be influenced by the therapist's theories. Development of standardized tests for children to report parental behavior are an advance in this area. Although still subject to the memory biases of the child (now adolescent or adult) and the influences of social desirability on descriptions of parents, these methods allow for the testing outside of therapy settings and for comparability of data.

Two factors usually found in all scales of reported parent–child interactions are affection and control. The first concerns the perceived affectionate expression and behavior of the parent, and the second concerns the degree to which the parent tried to exert control of the child or adolescent's behavior inside and outside of the home. Many, but not all, studies using such instruments found that those with unipolar, reactive type mood disorders reported a pattern of *affectionless control* in their parents, that is, low scores on scales of affection or emotional warmth and high scores on scales of control or overprotection (Gerlsma, Emmelkamp, & Arrindel, 1990; Parker, 1992). The same pattern of parental affectionless control is reported by anxiety patients as well as those suffering from depressive disorders. The pattern is found in those who have recovered as well as in those who are currently depressed, suggesting it is not the state of depression that colors their perceptions of their parents, although this could be a "scar effect." Although general neuroticism scores are related to reports of low parental affection (Kraft & Zuckerman, in press), statistical control of these scores did not eliminate the association between depression and reported parenting (Parker, 1979), indicating that the relationship is probably not entirely due to a personality bias in parent perception.

Patients with mood disorders of all types tended to remember their mothers as more dominating and both parents as more rejecting than patients without mood disorders (Alnaes & Torgersen, 1993). The mood disorder patients also reported poorer relationships between their parents and a generally unhappy home atmosphere. Within the family, they describe themselves as feeling inferior and isolated. Of course many of these perceptions could be due to a negative memory bias.

It is not difficult to conceive of how the lack of affection combined with overcontrol could lead to the cognitive factors implicated in depression. A lack of affection can lead to low self-esteem and generalized and stable self-attributions for negative events. Overcontrol may lead to guilt and feelings of helplessness in the face of negative events. Later experiences of rejection and overcontrol from spouses and other significant figures may reactivate the schemas developed during childhood. But conceivably mothers' lack of affection could be due to their own depression, and overcontrol to their own fears. There is moderate support for effects of depression upon mothering such as diminished sensitivity and responsivity to children's needs, increased hostility, and ineffective attempts at discipline and control. Are the relationships between parental practices and depression in their children a function of the common genetic bond or of the parental behavior itself and its effect on the developing personality of the child? The lack of influence of shared family environment in most personality traits would argue against the latter possibility. However, in the case of nontwin siblings, it is possible that the mother's depression coincided with a critical age in one sibling but not the other. It is interesting that the pattern of affectionless control from parents is not found in bipolar depressive disorder (Parker, 1979).

Perceptions of current intimate relationships for depressives show the same perception of lack of affection found in their descriptions of past relationships with parents. Nonmelancholic depressives described their current intimate partners as less affectionate and caring than do controls, but melancholic depressive types did not (Hickie et al., 1990). Perhaps loveless parenting and the quality of later relationships are risk factors for only the less biologically determined depressive disorders. The role of family influences, shared or specific, in depression should be studied in the context of genetic research to provide answers to these questions.

SUMMARY

Before the codification of diagnoses in the 20th century, the diagnosis of melancholia was a broad one which covered anxiety as well as depressive disorders and included all degrees of the disorder. In the *DSM-II* overall category of affective disorders there was only involutional melancholia and "manic–depressive illness" subdivided into manic, depressed, and circular types. The innovations of *DSM-III* included the division of major mood disorders into unipolar major depression and bipolar (manic–depressive) types. Depressive neurosis was moved from the anxiety disorders to the mood disorders and renamed "dysthymic disorder." Cyclothymic personality was moved from the personality disorder category in *DSM-II* to the mood disorders in *DSM-III* and renamed "cyclothymic disorder." By moving all of the disorders based on mood symptoms into one category, the DSM constructors seemed to recognize that there were milder and more severe forms of the disorders within the unipolar and bipolar types, but they maintained the categorical distinction between the less incapacitating and severe types (dysthymia and cyclothymia) and the more severe types (major depressive disorder and bipolar disorder).

Other distinctions that are based on severity of mood are those between hypomanic and manic episodes and between bipolar I and bipolar II disorders. Specifiers may directly address the severity continuum by differentiating between mild, moderate, or severe forms. Using an arbitrary number of symptoms to establish a threshold for diagnosis (polythetic) and specifying a lesser number for dysthymic as compared to major mood disorder also recognizes the dimensional nature of the disorder. At the other end of the continuum, there is a proposal to incorporate "depressive personality disorder" as a milder form of early onset dysthymia. But dysthymia is an extension of earlier personality disorders, such as avoidant and dependent types, and these in turn are extremes of the broader trait of neuroticism. They also represent maladaptive ways of dealing with anxiety or depression. Neuroticism represents a personality trait that evolves from an earlier childhood variation of temperament characterized by anxiety, behavioral inhibition, and fear of novel situations or unfamiliar persons. This same temperament is predictive of both anxiety and unipolar mood disorders in adulthood.

Figure 4.7 shows a suggested continuum for depression, representing both a developmental sequence and a range of severity. Of course, it can be argued that because the disorders are not always concordant and sequential, they are not on the same continuum. So-called double-depressions are more the rule than the exception (D. N. Klein et al., 1995). After remission of a major depression, the patient may revert to the preexisting dysthymic disorder rather than experiencing a full remission of depression. A personality or dysthymic disorder in the background of a depression is associated with a worse prognosis for recurrence of the major depressive condition.

What about these exceptions to the comorbidity majorities? The chances are that many of them simply fell a little below the arbitrary cutoff points for the disorders and represent subclinical cases. However, there

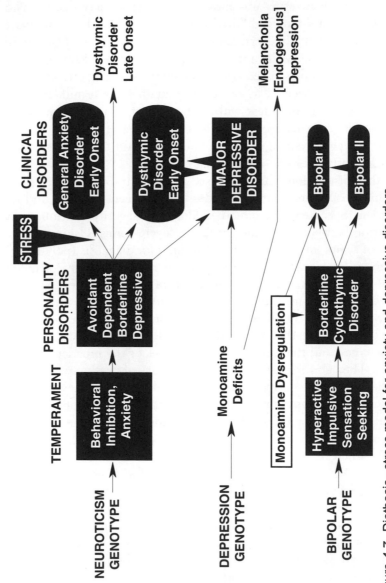

Figure 4.7. Diathesis–stress model for anxiety and depressive disorders.

is the possibility that there is another pathway for major depression in which biological factors create a vulnerability to stress without a developmental sequence passing through the personality trait, personality disorder, and milder forms of the disorder. Some of the more severe major depressions which have a late onset, such as the melancholic form, have less history of personality disorders, childhood stressors, and provoking stressors. What appears to be a continuum in severity could actually constitute two different developmental pathways. This alternate pathway to major depression is also shown in Figure 4.7.

The categorical diagnostic distinction between bipolar and unipolar disorder is probably a valid one, judging from the genetic data. Although bipolar disorders are found beyond chance only in relatives of bipolar probands, and dysthymic disorders only in relatives of dysthymic probands, unipolar major depression is found with high frequency in relatives of both dysthymic and bipolar disorders. Twin studies reveal similar results, although there is little evidence for genetic determination of dysthymic disorder. Major depression may be the result of the combination of a broad genetic diathesis, such as the one for general neuroticism trait, and a more specific genetic diathesis for major depression itself. Either dysthymic disorder is entirely due to environmental (shared and specific) factors, or the genetic factors are weak and undetectable by conventional biometric methods. The neuroticism diathesis may not be sufficient in a weak form to exceed the threshold for dysthymia or GAD without stronger environmental influences. The same may be true for milder forms of depression.

Bipolar disorder may have its own genetic diathesis, although there must be some cross-link with the unipolar major depressive diathesis, considering the great numbers of unipolar disorders found in the twins and families of bipolar patients. Although there are not many prospective studies of bipolar disorder, there may be a childhood disinhibitory temperament leading to the development of strong sensation seeking and impulsivity traits in the earlier background of patients who develop the disorder. This conclusion is reinforced by the finding of a strong sensation seeking trait in the offspring of bipolar patients who have not yet developed the disorder (Nurnberger et al., 1988). This can evolve into personality disorders such as antisocial, narcissistic, or borderline, which in turn may develop into cyclothymic disorder. From this baseline the cyclothymic disposition may evolve into bipolar II and finally into bipolar I disorder. It is arguable whether bipolar I and II represent distinctive disorders or are simply expressions of the developing severity of the manic component of the disorder.

The past 10 years have not seen much advance in our understanding of the biology of the mood disorders. Imaging studies have revealed evidence of brain damage and abnormalities of brain physiology in the major mood disorders similar to those seen in schizophrenia. This damage could represent a nonspecific vulnerability factor in both types of disorder. The first psychopharmacological evidence in major depression suggested a deficit in activity in the noradrenergic system. The evidence for the "catecholamine hypothesis" was limited to peripheral sources of norepinephrine metabolites in bipolar I disorders. Unipolar major depression seems to strike individuals with the same kind of deficit and others with overreactivity in the noradrenergic system, as in some anxiety disorders. Serotonin has also been implicated in mood disorders, and drugs that increase serotonergic activity by inhibiting its uptake have been effective in treating some depressive disorders. The serotonergic defect may represent an alternative type of cause to the noradrenergic one or perhaps a vulnerability to emotional dysregulation in response to stress. Depletion of serotonin through its precursor tryptophan can produce depression, arguing for a direct effect. However, the effect of serotonin depletion is found primarily in those with a family history of depression. This finding suggests a specific genetic effect mediated within the serotonergic system, perhaps through one of the receptors in the system.

Bipolar disorders may involve one or both of the previously mentioned neurotransmitters, but there is increasing influence for a role of a third monoamine, dopamine. Low serotonin activity may explain the disinhibition characteristic of mania, but excessive dopamine activity is known to directly increase the impulsive approach behavior and euphoric mood characteristic in hypomanic episodes. The association of a dopamine receptor gene with sensation-seeking, a personality trait related to bipolar disorder, reinforces the dopamine hypothesis of mania. The effectiveness of dopamine-receptor-blocking types of antipsychotic medication in mania also supports the connection.

Cortisol and thyroxin are hormones implicated in mood disorders, cortisol for the severe melancholic type of depression and thyroxin for the bipolar disorder. An overactivity of the cortisol system and hyporeactivity of the thyroid system have been demonstrated in these disorders. It is not clear whether these hormonal dysfunctions represent primary causes or are secondary effects of the monoamine disorders. Cortisol hyperactivity could be an effect of the high stress levels in the disorder, but evidence suggests that the effects of stress on the dexamethasone test cannot explain the cortisol response to this test in depressives.

Neuroticism, dependency, and separation anxiety are personality traits that increase the risk for depression in response to stress. Neuroticism is a broad trait that includes negative affect, low self-esteem, lack of self-assertiveness, pessimism, and guilt. It is about 50% heritable, but what kinds of environmental factors account for the rest of the variance?

Stressful life events and more chronic general stressful circumstances have been clearly demonstrated to be important provoking causes for depression for patients diagnosed as bipolar and unipolar for the first episode and for subsequent episodes among those with unipolar depression. The most common types of stressful events, particularly for women, are losses or threats of loss due to disturbed interpersonal relationships. However, a turn in economic circumstance, bad environmental conditions, and job loss can also be significant sources of stress. The effects of successive stressors are cumulative. But however severe the stress, there are always some who survive it without a prolonged or severe depressive reaction. Age and economic circumstances are risk factors that increase the likelihood of depression. Social support from intimate sources decreases the risk. Personality factors are another source of risks or strengths in coping with stress.

Loss of a parent through death during a patient's childhood has been suggested as a predisposing factor for later depression. Most studies do not support this connection. However, many studies do suggest that loss of a parent through separation or divorce is an important risk factor for depression. Separation per se is not a risk factor, but separation or loss in the context of abandonment are depressogenic. Even in intact families, the recalled lack of affection and overcontrol are associated with depression. The same kinds of familial factors are also correlated with anxiety disorders, so they are not specific for depression. But given the lack of evidence for shared family environment as an influence in anxiety or depression in the genetic studies, these familial factors may only operate through genetic–environment interactions: An emotionally deprived family environment may have its depressogenic effects only on those children who have a genetically predisposed vulnerability.

Just as the development of antidepressive drugs played a major role in the development of biological hypotheses about mood disorders, Beck's (1967) construction of cognitive therapy led to cognitive–behavioral explanations for depression. Beck suggested that schemas, or generalized negative views of self, led to negative cognitive processing biases in interpreting experience, as well as negative views of the future. These kinds of schemas are the diatheses that in stressful circumstances lead to depressive cognitions and mood disorder. According to recent formulations, depressive cognitions are not causal for the depressive episode but merely reinforce it once it has begun. Seligman amplified this approach with the learned-helplessness hypothesis and attribution theory. Depression-prone individuals feel helpless and unable to cope in the face of stressful circumstances because of prior experiences where they actually were helpless. They also attribute negative events with explanations that blame themselves rather than external influences and regard the negative conditions as generalized and stable rather than specific to a narrow set of circumstances and as impermanent. These kind of attributions lead to a type of "hopelessness depression" as described by Abramson and Seligman.

The research on depressive cognitions clearly supports the idea that these thoughts are part of the depressive syndrome in many depressives, particularly the nonmelancholic unipolar types, but there is not much evidence to suggest that they are causal. More important, the evidence for the etiological role of broader depressive schemas such as long-standing self-esteem or attributions is also scanty. There are information-processing biases demonstrable in persons who are depressed, but these disappear when they recover from the depression. The appeal to latent schemas which cannot be revealed by tests or behavior when the person is not depressed is a little like the postulation of unconscious forces by the psychodynamic school. Whatever the truth of the role of cognition in the etiology of depression, there is no question about the beneficial role of cognitive therapy in the treatment of depression and its effects on the outcome. But, as in other disorders, treatment does not prove etiology, particularly when various treatments—drug, interpersonal, and cognitive—seem to have equivalent effects on the outcome of the disorder.

In a comprehensive review of evidence on the "cognitive vulnerability to depression," Ingram, Miranda, and Segal (1998) summarize:

> There is no doubt that depression researchers have developed an impressive knowledge of the nature of cognition within the depressed state. What is less clear is how or whether this cognition relates to the onset and maintenance of depression. (p. 65)

Anxiety and mood disorders, with the exception of mania, are disorders that produce marked distress in the individuals affected and inhibitions of behavioral and social activity. The set of disorders discussed in chapter 5 are quite different because the persons affected are often not distressed, do not feel "sick," and their behavior is disinhibited and impulsive rather than inhibited and overcontrolled. Distress may occur when they are deprived of their freedom or valued rewards, such as substances, but is not typically part of their character.

5

ANTISOCIAL PERSONALITY DISORDER

Before the 19th century the disorders described in this and the following chapter were regarded as expressions of moral failure not as medical problems. The criminal, the drunk, and the compulsive gambler were seen as fallen characters, perhaps capable of redemption through religion, but not as sick or psychotic types in the same category as manics or other so-called mad persons. The first medical account of the "psychopath" near the beginning of the 19th century was given by Pinel, who described several patients as having "mania without delusion" (Pinel as cited in Pichot, 1978, p. 56). Pinel attributed the disorder either to bad upbringing *or* to a bad "disposition," an anticipation of the nature versus nurture debate on the causes of psychopathy.

The idea that a subgroup of the criminal population exhibited a different type of psychosis that was reflected in behavior rather than in disturbed cognition is illustrated in the labels given the disorder by other 19th century diagnosticians: "moral insanity," "moral imbecility," "lucid insanity," "mental degeneracy," "monomania" (a major category that included kleptomania, dipsomania, gambling mania, and "sexual peversions"), and "psychopathic inferiority." Cleckley (1976) described the disorder in his book title as "The Mask of Sanity." Most of these terms are probably based on an inability to understand the motivation of these criminals, which was basically a simple need for excitement, as opposed to the "profit motive" of the ordinary criminal. H. J. Eysenck and Eysenck (1976) identify chronic antisocial behavior on a dimension labeled "psychoticism," which includes schizophrenia and major mood disorders. Hare (1986) believes that there is a basic cognitive brain defect underlying the disorder. What is there that makes these seemingly lucid individuals impress so many clinicians as suffering from a variety of psychosis? Do other species show this kind of asocial behavior?

In her descriptions of the personalities of chimpanzees in her book, *The Chimpanzees of Gombe*, Jane Goodall (1986) describes two aberrant members of the chimpanzee social group that she studied. Goblin violated the "incest taboo" by raping his mother on many occasions. Passion, in collaboration with her adolescent daughter, Pom, forcibly seized newborn infants from their mothers and killed and ate them. Although cannibalism occurs across chimpanzee groups, this kind of infanticide within the group elicited horror among its members, and the perpetrators were attacked by other members of the group. Passion became asocial, associating only with her own family. These examples of extremely deviant types of aggression within a primate group could be a model for antisocial disorder within our own species. Normal types of aggression within the group occurred in the contexts of competition and dominance and rarely led to any severe harm. As with humans, murderous behavior toward members of other groups was not uncommon, but such behavior within the group was aberrant.

DESCRIPTION

Diagnosis

The antisocial personality disorder (APD) appeared in *DSM-I* (1952) as "antisocial reaction," subsumed in the major category of "sociopathic personality disturbances." The other members of the sociopathic classification were "dyssocial reaction" (ordinary professional criminals), "sexual deviation," and "addiction." The antisocial reaction was defined as:

> chronically antisocial individuals who are always in trouble, profiting neither from experience nor punishment, and maintaining no real loyalties to any person, group, or code. They are frequently callous and hedonistic, showing marked emotional immaturity, lack of judgment, and an ability to rationalize their behavior so that it appears warranted, reasonable, and justified. (p. 38).

In *DSM-II* (1968), the APD is described in similar terms, with the addition of a series of trait terms, for example, "grossly selfish, callous, irresponsible, impulsive" and "low frustration tolerance." The definition stressed the personality rather than the criminal history: "A *mere history of repeated legal or social offenses is not sufficient to justify the diagnosis*" (p. 43).

Although *DSM-III* (1980) listed APD on Axis II along with the other personality disorders, it described the disorder in specific behavioral terms rather than in personality traits. This kind of behavioral description contrasted with those used for the other personality disorders, which generally use trait terms. Another important change was the stipulation that the onset of the disorder must have occurred before the age of 15 years, as indicated by at least 3 of 12 specific antisocial behaviors associated with the diagnosis of *conduct disorder*. Nine major behavioral traits were listed for the adult form of the disorder (after reaching age 18), with many specific manifestations for each area:

1. Inability to sustain consistent work behavior
2. Lack of ability to function as a responsible parent
3. Failure to accept social norms with respect to lawful behavior
4. Inability to maintain enduring attachment to a sexual partner
5. Irritability and aggressiveness
6. Failure to honor financial obligations
7. Failure to plan ahead (impulsivity)
8. Disregard for the truth (repeated lying and "conning others" for personal profit)
9. Recklessness

As an example of the operational definitions, 4 was defined by "two or more divorces and/or separations (whether legally married or not), desertion of spouse, promiscuity (ten or more sexual partners within one year)" (p. 321). One wonders how the thresholds between two and three divorces or separations and between nine and ten sexual partners within a year were arrived at. Presumably, these numbers exceeded those in all members of the APA committee that formulated the criteria. Perhaps in recognition of the arbitrariness of such narrow definitions, this criterion in the *DSM-III-R* (1987) was changed to "has never sustained a totally monogamous relationship for more than one year" (p. 346). Finally, in *DSM-IV* (1994), sexual infidelity was removed from the list along with 2, "lack of ability to function as a responsible parent." After all, not all psychopaths have children.

The *DSM* definitions stress the history of delinquent and criminal behavior. But prior to *DSM-III*, the most influential definition was the one by Cleckley (1976) which consisted of 16 personality trait and behavioral characteristics, not including a history of criminal behavior and convictions. In fact, many of Cleckley's case examples were outwardly successful businessmen and professionals, including a psychiatrist! Cleckley stressed such characteristics as their "superficial charm" and their lack of strong negative or positive emotional responses in addition to their "fantastic and uninviting behavior with drink and sometimes without" (p. 408). Some of his other criteria, such as unreliability, untruthfulness, lack of remorse or shame, and impersonal sex life, are similar to those in some forms of the DSM.

Hare and Cox (1978) began with a single 7-point rating for psychopathy based on the Cleckley criteria. Subsequently, Hare (1986) developed the Psychopathy Check List (PCL) consisting of ratings on 22 items developed from the Cleckley criteria after extensive review of the case records and intensive interview with the offender. He emphasizes the untrustworthiness of the psychopath's self-report. The interview is an attempt to judge the self-attitudes and emotional reactivity of psychopaths, rather than to obtain an objective account of their behavioral histories.

Hare factor-analyzed the PCL items and found two consistent and replicable factors among them (Harpur, Hakistan, & Hare, 1988). Factor 1, "selfish, callous, and remorseless use of others," describes the cruelty, the absence of feelings of love, empathy, or guilt, and the egocentricity and exploitativeness of the psychopath. Factor 2 contains the more behavioral aspects of psychopaths in their "chronically unstable and antisocial lifestyle" and general "social deviance." Among the traits listed in Factor 2 are sensation-seeking ("need for stimulation and proneness to boredom"), impulsivity, and lack of socialization ("parasitic life style; irresponsibility, poor behavioral controls, juvenile delinquency") (Hare, 1991). This factor describes the extreme of a normal dimension of personality found in factor analyses of questionnaire scales: Impulsive Unsocialized Sensation Seeking, suggested as the basis for APD (Zuckerman, 1989).

Hare criticized the DSM-III and DSM-III-R criteria for APD as too detailed and specific and as focusing too much on antisocial behaviors rather than on the personality traits more central to the traditional concepts of psychopathy, as well as overdiagnosing APD in the prison populations (Hare & Hart, 1995; Hare, Hart, & Harpur, 1991). In response to these criticisms, a large group of 14 investigators (Widiger et al., 1996) undertook a field trial in preparation for DSM-IV.

Participants were from four different sites, including a prison, a methadone maintenance outpatient center, a homeless shelter, and an inpatient psychiatric unit. The criteria sets were from the DSM-III-R, the ICD-10, and a reduced criteria set from Hare's (1991) PCL-R, consisting of 10 of the original 20 rating items. The results confirmed the greater prevalence of the APD diagnosis using the DSM-III-R criteria than the PCL criteria, particularly in the prison setting in which the DSM diagnosed 70% of the inmates as APD in contrast to the PCL-R, which gave a prevalence of only 28%.

Interrater reliabilities were about the same for all three measures and, as might be expected, higher for the total scores than for the dichotomous diagnoses at three of the four sites. All three measures correlated about equally with clinicians' and interviewers' overall impressions and with relevant self-report measures of personality and psychopathy. Objective measures from the records, including numbers of arrests, convictions, marriages, and sex partners, and the longest time a job was held, correlated about equally with the three rating measures at the four sites, although most of the correlations were not very high (typically around .2 to .3).

The study showed that the more broadly defined criteria sets of the PCL and the ICD-10 could be as reliably assessed as the more specific ones in the *DSM-III-R*. Consequently, many of the specific examples of the behavioral traits listed in *DSM-III-R* were eliminated in *DSM-IV*, the list of items was shortened from 10 to 7 (deleting parental irresponsibility, failure to sustain a monogamous relationship), and inconsistent work and failure to honor financial obligations were collapsed into one item. There is also a recommendation to put more emphasis on personality items from the PCL-R in prison settings where criminal history itself may be less discriminating. Hare and Hart (1995) were disappointed in the minimal change in the *DSM* criteria and concluded that the personality of the psychopath is still not adequately emphasized in the *DSM*.

One of the drawbacks of the *DSM-III* emphasis on the criminal history of the psychopath is the identification of criminality, per se, with psychopathy. If the APD diagnosis has any value, it should be in making distinctions among the larger group of "criminals." Despite Cleckley's portrayal of the psychopath in society, most of the familial research uses criminal records as criteria, and most experimental research is done on incarcerated felons. The "successful" middle-class psychopath described by Cleckley is not well represented in the prison population.

Lykken (1995) not only distinguishes the normal offender from those with antisocial personalities, but he also makes distinctions within the "family of antisocial personalities." Unlike approaches taken by the *DSM* and Hare, Lykken bases his classifications on presumed etiology as well as on temperament. The terms *sociopathy*, *psychopathy*, and *antisocial personality* have been used more or less synonymously in the literature, but Lykken uses them as labels for different classifications.

The *sociopathic personality* describes those people who were never adequately socialized during childhood and adolescence. Their lack of socialization is attributed to family (weak parental bonding, control, and bad parental example) and subcultural environments. *Psychopathic personalities*, in contrast, are a development of temperament influenced by their genetics or pre- or postnatal brain damage. Although they may come from disordered families, like the sociopath, they are also found in traditional middle-class families, where they resist all attempts at socialization. He also uses an older distinction between the primary and secondary psychopath. The primary psychopath is closest to the type described by Cleckley, with a lack of anxiety, guilt, and depression as well as a general low arousal of all emotions, including the positive ones. The secondary psychopath has the aggressive, impulsive, sensation-seeking, and undersocialized traits of the primary type, but also shows anxiety, depression, guilt, and low self-esteem. To some extent, the newer classification of "borderline personality" resembles this mix of psychopathy, neuroticism, and mood disorder. The secondary type has also been characterized as introverted and withdrawn in contrast to the sociability of the primary type (Blackburn, 1979).

Lykken also speaks of other psychopathic personalities, based largely on their predominant mode of expression, such as the choleric (aggressive, short-tempered), hypersexual, and those with "pathological cravings" of drugs or with paraphilic sexual urges. He admits that much of his classification scheme is an armchair analysis. Within any group of alcoholics, drug addicts, or gamblers one will find some who fit the classical APD description and many others who do not. These expressions alone are not symptomatic of a class of psychopathy. Although they may share some traits with APD, such as sensation seeking, they lack other crucial characteristics such as lack of empathy, or their antisocial behavior is secondary rather than primary to their addiction.

In spite of objections from psychologist critics, the *DSM-IV* diagnostic criteria are likely to remain the basis for communication among researchers in the field until the next revision of the *DSM* or until psychologists become more active in formulating their own comprehensive dimensional systems for diagnosis. The *DSM-IV* criteria are given in Exhibit 1 below:

EXHIBIT 1
DSM Criteria for the Diagnosis of APD

A. There is a pervasive pattern of disregard for and violation of the rights of others occurring since age 15 years, as indicated by three (or more) of the following:
   1. failure to conform to social norms with respect to lawful behaviors as indicated by repeatedly performing acts that are grounds for arrest,
   2. deceitfulness, as indicated by repeated lying, use of aliases or conning others for personal profit or pleasure,
   3. impulsivity or failure to plan ahead,
   4. irritability and aggressiveness, as indicated by repeated physical fights or assaults,
   5. reckless disregard for the safety of self or others,
   6. consistent irresponsibility, as indicated by repeated failure to sustain consistent work behavior or honor financial obligations,
   7. lack of remorse, as indicated by being indifferent to or rationalizing having hurt, mistreated, or stolen from another.
B. The individual is at least 18.
C. There is evidence of conduct disorder with onset before age 15 years.
D. The occurrence of antisocial behavior is not exclusively during the course of a Schizophrenic or a Manic Episode. (APA, 1994, pp. 649–650)

Reliability and Validity of APD Diagnosis

The prevalences and reliabilities of the *DSM-III-R*, RDC, and restricted RDC methods of diagnoses were assessed in 399 adult cocaine abusers from inpatient, outpatient, and community centers (K. M. Carroll, Ball, & Rounsaville, 1993). The prevalences in this population varied markedly with the diagnostic system, with 53% diagnosed as having APD using the *DSM-III-R*, 29% using the RDC criteria, and 7% using the restricted RDC. Internal reliabilities (alphas) were respectable for all three methods (alpha for *DSM-III-R* was .74). Re-interview reliabilities were only moderate but much higher for the *DSM-III-R* (kappas = .61 for 1 month, .55 for 1 year) than for the RDC (kappas = .21 for 1 month and .14 for 1 year). Re-interview reliabilities were much higher for distinctive behavior items than for the classical trait items such as "lack of remorse" or "inability to sustain relationships." Hare (1991) also found higher retest correlations for his Factor 2 than for Factor 1, but the retest correlations were high for both.

Many of the criteria used for the diagnosis of APD are based on a past history of antisocial behavior, so correlations with past history are less relevant for diagnostic validity than predictions of behavior after the diagnosis. Prison inmates diagnosed as having APD are more likely than non-APD prisoners to have had at least one prior violent crime in their records and prior imprisonments as well (Stevens, 1993). APD prisoners were younger than non-APD prisoners at the times of their first arrest and institutionalization. Once in prison, the APD inmates had a higher number of disciplinary infractions and were more likely to spend more time in prison than other prisoners.

Using the PCL criteria, APD prisoners spend more of their lives in prison, have more new charges placed against them after they are released, and show less of the age decline in criminality characteristic of other prisoners (Hare & Jutai, 1983). Hare (1991) cites many studies showing that the PCL predicts outcome of parole from prison and usually improves prediction in multivariate studies. In one study, 24% of low PCL scorers, 49% of medium scorers, and 65% of high PCL scorers (considered psychopathic) violated their conditions of release. The probability of remaining out of prison for at least a year was .80 in the low group, .54 in the medium group, and only .38 in the high (psychopathy) group. The high-psychopathic group was almost four times as likely to commit a violent crime as those in the low-psychopathic group. Other studies are presented showing an association of the PCL with the prediction of violence after release, a notoriously difficult outcome to predict using clinical methods.

APD has an extensive comorbidity with alcohol and drug abuse (see chap. 6, this volume). Most studies show that substance abusers who are also diagnosed with APD have more severe histories of abuse and dependence and more involvement with criminal behavior than substance abusers who are not diagnosed with APD. Substance (alcohol and drug) abusers who were diagnosed as having APDs (*DSM-III*) reported more arrests, illegal behavior, chronic lying, trouble controlling violent behavior, and time spent in prison than non-APD substance abusers (Cacciola, Rutherford, Alterman, & Snider, 1994). Although alcoholics with APD do not drink more than primary alcoholics, they are more likely to be fired from their jobs, involved in auto accidents, arrested for alcohol-influenced behavior in public, and hospitalized for alcoholism (Jaffe & Shuckitt, 1981). APD alcoholics are more likely to use other drugs (Lewis, Rice, & Helzer, 1983) and to violently abuse their spouses or children (Bland & Orn, 1986).

APD diagnosed (*DSM-III-R*) cocaine abusers in treatment had more treatment involvement, but actually spent fewer days abstinent and had a poorer outcome (K. M. Caroll et al., 1993). However, they also had a more severe initial cocaine problem, an earlier age of onset, more legal, family, and psychological problems, and a greater incidence of other disorders, especially mood disorders. This author's experience with APDs among drug abusers in treatment in an inpatient therapeutic community, was that APDs did well in the first phase of the program in which they were strongly supervised by peers and paraprofessionals and required to express themselves in confrontation groups (Zuckerman, Sola, Masterson, & Angelone, 1975). But in the second phase of the program, where they were allowed to go out to a job during the day, they had a worse prognosis than others. They could respond to immediate rewards of good behavior for participation, but could not resist other rewards (drugs) once they were not under supervision. Like Oscar Wilde, they could "resist everything but temptation."

Comorbidity

Studies classifying APD by alcohol and drug abuse show a high prevalence of substance abuse in APDs. About two thirds of male and one third of female APDs also have a lifetime history of alcohol abuse or substance abuse in general (Koenigsberg et al., 1985; Lewis et al., 1983; Lewis, Robins, & Rice, 1985). These studies all used *DSM-III* criteria, and subjects were from the community or psychiatric departments of medical facilities. A study of male prison inmates, using the PCL to classify for psychopathy, revealed that nearly all (93%) of the psychopaths had a diagnosis of alcohol abuse, and nearly three fourths (74%) of the group had a drug abuse or dependency diagnosis during their lifetimes (Smith & Newman, 1990). The rates of these substance abuse diagnoses were also high in the nonpsychopathic prisoner groups (65% and 43%, respectively), but there were significantly more alcoholic and drug symptoms and higher frequencies of substance abuse diagnoses in the psychopathic prisoners.

The ECA community survey (Robins & Regier, 1991) found that prevalence rates for alcohol abuse were about 3 times as frequent in male and 13 times as frequent in female APDs as in persons without APD. Drug abuse was about 5 times as common in male APDs and 12 times as common in female APDs as in their non-APD counterparts. The higher ratio in females reflects the much lower rates of substance abuse in the general female population compared to the male population, and the greater atypicality of the female APD populations. Rates for other comorbid disorders, particularly for mania and schizophrenia, were also relatively higher in those with active APD.

Given the much higher prevalence of substance abuse than APD, one would expect that the majority of substance abusers do not have APD. Typically, about one fifth to one third of male and one tenth to one third of female substance abusers are diagnosed as having APDs, compared to the incidence of about 5% for males and 1% for females in the general population.

More than a majority of men with APD develop substance abuse problems, but only one fourth to one third of the larger substance abusing population have APD. Of course, mood disorders are even more prevalent than APD in substance abusers, but in a lifetime prevalence, it is difficult to distinguish the primary or secondary nature of the depression. Is it a cause or consequence of the substance abuse? APD almost always precedes substance abuse. By definition it must begin in conduct disorder before the age of 15, and the average age of onset for the first symptom is between 8 and 9 years of age for both men and women (Robins & Regier, 1991). The median ages of onset for drug abuse or dependence and alcohol abuse or dependence in the ECA data are 18 and 21, for males and females respectively, and the median ages of onset for bipolar disorder and unipolar depression are 19 and 25 years for males and females, respectively. The onset of antisocial personality far precedes these other disorders. APD is more prevalent in male alcoholics, whereas depression is more prevalent in female alcoholics (Hesselbrock, 1991).

Prevalence and Demographic Factors

Gender

The estimate of 2.6% for lifetime APD in the ECA study is an underestimate because certain questions regarding illegal activities had to be omitted from interviews in four of the five sites. A correction applied on the basis of data from the fifth site raised the nationwide estimate to 4.0% and markedly increased the estimate for males from 5.6% to 7.3% as shown in Table 5.1. The prevalence rates for APD in both the ECA and the NCA studies (see Table 5.1) both show large gender differences: About

TABLE 5.1
Lifetime Prevalence Rates (%) of Antisocial Personality Disorder in
General Population

Study	Males	Females	Both
DSM-III ECA	4.5	0.8	2.6
DSM-IV NCS	5.8	1.2	3.5

Note. ECA = Epidemiologic Catchment Area Study (Robins & Regier, 1991); NCS = National Comorbidity Study (Kessler et al., 1994). Data derived from *Psychiatric Disorders in America*, by L. N. Robins and D. A. Regier, 1991, p. 263. Copyright 1991 by American Medical Association. Reprinted with permission; and data derived from "Lifetime and 12-Month Prevalence of DSM-III Psychiatric Diagnoses in the United States," by R. C. Kessler et al., 1994, *Archives of General Psychiatry, 51,* p. 12. Copyright 1991 by American Medical Association. Reprinted with permission.

seven times as many men in the ECA (corrected data) and five times as many men than women in the NCA studies are diagnosed as having APD during their lifetimes. The ratios are similar for 1-year and 1-month prevalence rates. The preponderance of males with the diagnosis is true for every age and ethnic group.

Every problem associated with conduct disorders is more prevalent in men than in women (Robins et al., 1991). The childhood items relating to aggression and violence are much less frequently met by girls than by boys, and this may account for some of the gender differences in rates of APD (Rutherford, Alterman, Cacciola, & Snider, 1995). The *DSM-III-R* focused on these types of items more than *DSM-III.* The *DSM-IV* criteria for the APD diagnosis do not specify the childhood behaviors necessary for the diagnosis, merely stating: "There is evidence of Conduct Disorder with onset before age 15 years." But 9 of the 15 behavioral criteria for conduct disorder involve aggression to people and animals or destruction of property. However, even in the *DSM-III,* in which most childhood items do not describe aggression, male APDs exceeded females on every childhood behavior problem. For instance, the highest behavioral precursor of APD before the age of 15 was running away from home, an item that is neutral with regard to male aggressiveness. But nearly three times as many males (41%) as females with APD (15%) were runaways as children, whereas the item, "fighting," yielded only a ratio of 2:1, for males to females. For whatever reason, girls are more easily socialized than boys, and this is reflected in gender differences in behavioral traits such as aggression or incorrigibility.

Age

Although all APDs begin in childhood or early adolescence, many go into remission, in terms of the reduction of antisocial behaviors and arrests for crimes after the age of 45 (Robins & Regier, 1991). The average duration of the disorder is 19 years. Figure 5.1 shows the 1-year prevalence rates for men and women as a function of age. Note the sharp drop in the

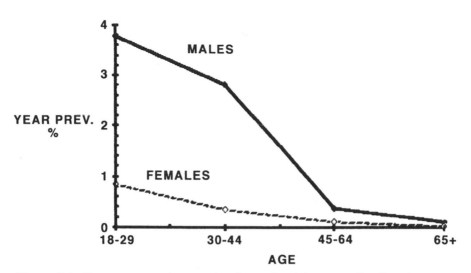

Figure 5.1. One-year prevalence rates for antisocial personality disorder as a function of age.

45- to 64-year-old age group. Arrest rates for crimes and rates of new male offenders show a similar peak in midadolescence and decline with age thereafter (Moffitt, 1993). Both cross-sectional and longitudinal studies using the PCL for diagnosing psychopathy show that overall, psychopaths have more convictions and spend more time in prison than nonpsychopaths between 16 and 40 years of age, but the psychopaths show a marked reduction to the level of the nonpsychopathic prisoners in convictions and time in prison after 40 years of age (Hare, McPherson, & Forth, 1988). However, it is the Factor 2 (antisocial behavioral) ratings that decline with age; the Factor 1 (antisocial personality) ratings remain level over time (Harpur & Hare, 1994).

Ethnicity

The ECA study found no significant differences in APD between three ethnic groups, Whites, Blacks, and Hispanics (Robins & Regier, 1991). This is an astounding lack of difference given the relatively higher proportion of Blacks arrested for crimes (Information Please Almanac, 1986). The ECA study used prison as well as community samples. They found that 1.8% of the Black male sample below age 45 was in prison, jail, or residential alcohol and drug treatment centers compared to 0.3% of Whites and Hispanics. The study investigated two hypotheses to explain the contradiction between the diagnostic and imprisonment rates. The first hypothesis is that Blacks are more likely to commit acts which may lead to arrest; the second is that Blacks may be more liable to arrest than Whites with the same pattern of behaviors. Blacks do tend to commit more crimes using weapons, which would increase their chances of being sent to prison and receiving longer sentences. But when types of crimes were equated, Whites were only half as likely to be sent to prison as Blacks (Robins & Regier, 1991). Among those offenders who used weapons, a smaller proportion of Blacks than Whites was classified as having APD, and fewer of the Black weapons-users met the childhood criteria for APD. Over all the crimes studied, fewer Blacks who were arrested met the criteria for APD than did Whites who were arrested.

Additional evidence that criminality is not as closely linked with APD in Blacks as in Whites is provided by studies that found less association between the PCL ratings of psychopathy and personality traits in Blacks than in Whites (Kosson, Smith, & Newman, 1990; Thornquist & Zuckerman, 1995). Although both studies found higher PCL ratings of psychopathy in Black than in White prisoners, there was a curious bimodal characteristic in the PCL distribution among the Blacks in the Kosson et al. study. The PCL cut-off points for high, medium, and low psychopathy showed that whereas the middle group was the largest one for Whites, it was smaller than the high and low groups for Blacks. It is as if there were two subpopulations of Blacks in prison: one a classic psychopathic group and the other a purely sociopathic one, to use the distinction by Lykken (1995). Both studies also found that a laboratory test of passive avoidance learning was related to psychopathy in Whites but not in Blacks.

The studies suggest a closer connection between crime and an antisocial type of personality in Whites than in Blacks. This could be a function of the poverty and high unemployment rates in the inner-city ghettos which foster a criminal career in so many young Black men. Lykken (1995) feels that crime is more a function of the family disruption produced by these social conditions than a direct effect of the social conditions. Intelligence is another factor that could produce lower educational achievement and fewer vocational alternatives to crime. How are these factors related to APD?

Employment, Education, Social Class, and Intelligence

In the ECA study a relationship between unemployment and APD diagnosis for Whites and Hispanics was shown, but not for Blacks; so many Blacks are unemployed that it is not a differentiating factor (Information Please Almanac, 1986). Similarly, although more Blacks received welfare or disability payments than Whites, this factor was not related to the incidence of APD. Quitting a job without another job prospect was more characteristic of Whites and Hispanics than of Blacks and more characteristic of those with an APD diagnosis among Whites.

The relation between education and APD is not a linear one. Those participants with less than an eighth-grade education have higher rates of APD than those with an eighth-grade education, but those who have some high school but are not high school graduates (dropouts) have the highest rates of APD. Similarly, those with some college have higher rates of APD than those who completed college, but they also have higher rates of APD than high school graduates. Interestingly, the same saw-toothed pattern, with peaks in high school and college dropouts, was found in a demographic study of the trait of sensation seeking (Zuckerman & Neeb, 1980). Could it be that the boredom and restlessness characteristic of high sensation seekers account for the poor educational history of those with APDs? Or is it a relationship with intelligence or academic aptitude that accounts for the relationship?

A short measure of intellectual functioning was related to the incidence of APD diagnoses in the ECA study, but the relationship was much stronger for Whites than for Blacks and Hispanics. However, summarizing many studies relating standard measures of intelligence to the PCL measure of psychopathy, Hare (1991) concluded that there was no relationship between psychopathy and intelligence.

Using the PCL, occupational level of prison inmates was related to their PCL Factor 2 scores, but the occupational level of the inmates' fathers was not (Hare, 1991). The results suggest that there is a "downward social drift" in psychopaths, at least as far as legal occupations are concerned. Psychopathic children of law-abiding middle-class parents are likely to end up in a lower social class than their parents due to their own lack of persistence in school or perseverance in legal occupations.

Marital Status

Because part of the DSM-III criteria for APD is "inability to maintain enduring attachment to a sexual partner," and divorces, desertions, separations, and promiscuity are given as examples, it is not surprising to find a relationship between marital status and APD in the ECA community study (Robins & Regier, 1991). Among men of all three ethnic groups, higher rates of APD are found in those who are nonmarried cohabitors than for single noncohabitors or those in a stable marriage. In White and Hispanic men who have had two or more divorces and separations, the rates of APD are higher than marrieds or those with only one divorce and separation, but for Blacks, the multiple-divorce criterion is not as discriminating. Cohabitation is less indicative of APD for Black or Hispanic women than for White women. As with men, rates are lowest in women in a stable marriage.

Criminal Behavior

Because both the DSM and PCL diagnoses use criminal behaviors as part of the definition of the APD or psychopathic personality, it is not surprising that criminal behaviors are characteristic in APD-diagnosed individuals. But the question is this: What kinds of crime and what characteristics of their criminal behavior distinguish APDs from other criminals?

The PCL-R measure of psychopathy given to a criminal population predicts total number of offenses, both violent and nonviolent types (Hare, 1991). Psychopathic criminals are more likely to engage in physical violence and other forms of aggressive behavior than nonpsychopathic criminals, both in and out of prison. A higher percentage of psychopathic criminals are convicted of weapon possession, robbery, assault, kidnapping, vandalism, and fighting. Violent crime convictions in general are found in 85% of the high psychopathic group, 64% of the medium group, and 54% of the low group (Hare & McPherson, 1984). Despite this difference in violent crime, convictions for murder and rape are not significantly related to degree of psychopathy, perhaps because these are often one-time offenses committed in a disinhibited state produced by alcohol or other drugs, and not symptomatic of a chronic personality disorder. Serial or professional murderers and serial rapists are probably more antisocial in personality, but these represent a minority of those persons arrested for murder or rape.

DIATHESIS

Genetics

Twin Studies

Most genetic studies of APD have defined the disorder by the criminal record, and more usually, in terms of having ever been convicted of a felony as an adult. Criminal conviction is a convenient and objective record, but no one claims it is synonymous with APD. There are many pathways to prison, and not all involve a genetically influenced antisocial temperament. The fact that both twin and adoption studies show some genetic influence in criminality causes controversy, because some use it to deny the social influences in crime. Evidence cited in the preceding section suggests that the high crime rate among Blacks in the United States does not translate into a higher rate for APD in Blacks. There is obviously something other than a genetically influenced temperament accounting for the statistics on crime. Evidence of a genetic influence within groups should *not* be used as an explanation of differences between groups.

Table 5.2 summarizes twin studies of juvenile delinquency and adult criminality from a listing of individual studies in the chapter by Cloninger & Gottesman (1987). Prior to 1962, most studies used small samples of twins with the proband twin selected from crime registers. Determinations

TABLE 5.2
Pairwise Twin Concordance Rates for Juvenile Delinquency and Crime

	IT Pairs		FT Pairs	
	n	% C	n	% C
Juvenile delinquency				
6 studies 1941–1977, M & F	83	87	61	72
Adult criminality				
6 studies 1931–1961, M & F	132	69	122	33
Scandinavian studies				
Dalgaard & Kringlen (1976), M	31	26	54	15
Christiansen et al. (1977), M	73	34	146	18
F	15	20	28	7
M & F	88	32	174	16

Note. IT = identical twins; FT = fraternal twins; M = male; F = female; C = concordance. Data adapted from "Genetic and Environmental Factors in Antisocial Behavior," by C. R. Cloninger and I. I. Gottesman, in *The Causes of Crime* (p. 98), edited by S. A. Mednick, T. E. Moffitt, & S. A. Stack, 1987, Cambridge, MA: Cambridge University Press. Reprinted with permission.

of zygosity were questionable and based on physical similarity alone. Definitions of criminality were fuzzy and subject to bias, and investigators were often not blind with respect to the criminal status of the proband. The Scandinavian studies (Christiansen, 1977; Dalgaarn & Kringlen, 1976) were population-based and used sounder methodology than the earlier studies.

The twin studies of juvenile delinquency show very high rates of concordance for both identical and fraternal twins and little difference between the two types of twins. These results suggest a strong familial shared environmental influence, not attributable to genetic similarity. In contrast, the early studies of adult criminality show a rate of concordance for identical twins (69%) that is about twice that for fraternal twins (33%), suggesting a strong genetic influence. The later Scandinavian studies for adult criminality show a much lower rate of concordance for criminal records in identical and fraternal twins, although the ratio remains at 2:1 for identical to fraternal concordance. The conclusion is that juvenile crime is not much influenced by heredity, but more a function of environmental influences, whereas a persistence of criminal tendencies into adult life does have some genetic influence.

There were two interesting sidelights to the Christiansen (1977) study. First, for the fraternal twins, the similarity in criminal behavior was much less among opposite sex twin pairs than among same sex pairs. Second, the hereditary dispositions for property and violent crimes were distinct, and the heritability for property crimes was higher than that for violent crimes. Both findings receive some support from adoption studies.

Despite the prominence of aggression in the criteria for APD, particularly in the childhood criteria, it may not be at the core of the genetic disposition toward crime. However, aggressive behavior items in both juvenile and adult *DSM-III-R* criteria for APD tend to show strong genetic determination in a twin study of males (Lyons et al., 1995).

An alternate explanation of the higher concordance among identical twins than among fraternal twins is that identicals influence each other toward criminal activity more than do fraternal twins. As a matter of fact, Rowe (1986) reported that adolescent twins are more likely to engage in the same antisocial acts together. Carey (1992) investigated the evidence for twin imitation using the follow-up data from the Christiansen study (Cloninger & Gottesman, 1987). Testing different models for the data, he found a pattern strongly suggesting reciprocal sibling influence in the development of criminal behavior. Models that ignored this factor had to be rejected. Since imitative sibling effects are confounded with genetic and shared environmental effects, genetic effects for criminal liability could be quite small. The traditional model assuming no imitation parameters yielded a heritability of .57 if shared environmental factors were assumed and of .71 if no such factors were assumed. Under the peer influence assumptions, heritability could vary anywhere from 0 to .45, depending on additional assumptions. Using a general model, assuming that the imitative influences are stronger in identical than in fraternal twins and no influence of shared environment, Carey calculated a heritability of .37. He rejected the assumption of no heritability on the basis of the adoption studies, which will be discussed in the next section.

A recent twin study used the *DSM-III-R* criteria for APD separating the juvenile from the adult criteria (Lyons, 1996). A structured interview for the *DSM-III-R* was given to a very large sample of pairs of male twins who were veterans from the Vietnam era. The correlations for early and later arrests and criminal behavior in identical and fraternal twins are shown in Table 5.3 along with the estimates of genetic and environmental factors. There is evidence for a shared environmental influence in juvenile arrests and early criminal behavior (before age 15), but later arrests show only the additive genetic influence. The results reinforce the conclusion from the earlier twin studies that shared environmental factors are of significance in juvenile delinquency, whereas genetic influences are more prominent in the adult criminal.

Perhaps as the twins leave the home and begin to lead their own lives, these shared influences are diminished. However, there does seem to be a genetic factor in a minority of delinquents that carries over into adult life and increases the liability for more chronic antisocial behavior in this later phase. Moffitt (1993) suggests that the large group of adolescent delinquents contains two distinct subgroups. The *adolescence-limited* antisocial group begins antisocial behavior during early adolescence but stops by their

TABLE 5.3
Twin Correlations for Arrest and Criminality Variables and Proportions
of Variance Due to Additive Genetics (G), Shared Environment (SE),
and Unique Environment (UE)

Variable	ITs (r)	FTs (r)	G	SE	UE
Early criminal behavior	.42	.37	.11	.32***	.58
Early arrest	.73	.53	.39***	.34*	.27
Later criminal behavior	.47	.32	.30*	.17	.53
Later arrested	.45	.30	.30*	.15	.55
Later multiple arrests	.47	.28	.39**	.08	.53
Felony	.59	.40	.38	.21	.41

Note. ITs = identical twins; FTs = fraternal twins. Data adapted from "A Twin Study of Self-Reported
Criminal Behavior," by M. J. Lyons in *Genetics of Criminal and Antisocial Behaviour*, edited by
G. R. Bock & J. A. Goode, 1996, Chichester, UK: Wiley. Copyright 1996. Reproduced by
permission of John Wiley & Sons Limited.
*p < .05, **p < .01, ***p < .001.

by their mid-20s. Moffitt attributes the large numbers of adolescents with
this type of delinquency in Western cultures to the delay between biological maturity and social-role maturity (getting a job and marrying) and to
susceptibility to peer modeling and reinforcement for rebellious, antisocial
behavior. The *life course-persistent* antisocial group is much smaller but accounts for a larger proportion of the crimes. They begin antisocial behavior
long before adolescence and persist long into adult life. Their development
is attributed to genetic and nongenetic anomalies in neural development,
resulting in speech and reading problems, poor verbal ability, and personality traits such as impulsivity and aggressiveness. Moffitt's distinction resembles earlier ones contrasting the socialized delinquent or "dyssocial reaction" with the "antisocial reaction" in *DSM-I*. Although Moffitt stresses
behavior patterns, her persistent antisocial type would meet the age criteria
for the *DSM-III, III-R*, and *IV*, whereas the adolescence- limited antisocial
type would not. The life course-persistent antisocial type is anticipated by
personality traits of impulsivity and aggression during childhood.

Adoption Studies

The twin studies rely on purely statistical criteria to separate genetic
and environmental factors. Conclusions based on them depend on a variety
of assumptions about shared environment and sibling interactive influences
that have been shown to be untenable. The adoption method cleanly sep-
arates the biological and social–environmental influences if separation occurs soon after birth. What are not controlled are prenatal influences, such
as alcohol or drug use by the biological mother during pregnancy, the possibility of selective placement, and the simple restriction of environmental
variance in the adopting population. Most of these studies were done in

Scandinavian countries, where there was much less economic variation in these welfare states after World War II. The selection of adopting parents makes this a much more law-abiding group than the biological parents, and even though a small number can be found who have criminal convictions, these are probably for less severe or persistent crimes.

This difference in rates of criminal convictions is apparent in the Danish adoption study in which about 29% of the biological fathers had at least one criminal conviction in contrast to about 6% of the adoptive fathers (Mednick, Gabrielli, & Hutchings, 1987). Nearly all of the offenders in the adoptive parents were one-time offenders and had committed their only offense at least 5 years before the adoption. In contrast, about 16% of the biological fathers had been convicted of two or more crimes. Table 5.4 shows the results of the cross-fostering analysis using the percentages of adoptive sons convicted of criminal law offenses as the dependent variable.

The results show a significant effect of the biological parents, increasing the risk of their sons' having a criminal record by a factor of about 50%, whereas criminality in the adopting parents (usually the father) had no significant effect on the risk for criminality. The combined influence of criminality in both the biological and adoptive parents had a small but significant effect over the effect of the biological parents alone, but only if the biological parent had a criminal record. The influence of biological parents with criminal records, who contributed only their genes and could have no social influence over their sons' criminality does not mean that genetic factors are more important than environmental ones in determining criminality. It must be remembered that the environment includes more than the parents, and in most analyses, it is the specific environmental factors, such as peer influences, which are most important. Furthermore, given the restrictions on adoption, it is likely that a criminal record in the adoptive parents does not mean that they actually provided a criminogenic environment.

The influence of the biological parents in this study varied directly

TABLE 5.4
Cross-Fostering Analysis: Percentage of Adoptive Sons Who Have
Been Convicted of Criminal Law Offenses

| | Biological Parents Criminal? | |
Adoptive Parents Criminal?	Yes	No
Yes	24.5% (n = 143)	14.7% (n = 204)
No	20.0% (n = 1,226)	13.5% (n = 2,492)

Note. Adapted from "Genetic Factors in Criminal Behavior: A Review," by S. A. Mednick, T. Moffitt, W. Gabrielli, Jr., & B. Hutchings in *Development of Antisocial and Prosocial Behavior: Research, Theories and Issues* (p. 40), edited by D. Olweus, J. Block, & M. Radke-Yarrow, 1986, New York: Academic. Copyright by Academic Press. Reprinted with permission.

with the number of convictions they had, suggesting that it is the more chronic offenders who transmit a biological vulnerability to their sons. The male adoptee offenders with biological parents who were convicted of three or more offenses comprised only 1% of the 3,691 adoptees, but they were responsible for more than 30% of the male adoptee convictions. The adoptees who had three or more convictions comprised 4% of the sample, but they accounted for 69% of the convictions in the group (Brennan, Mednick, & Jacobsen, 1996). Similar concentrations of convictions within a small percentage of the offending populations were described for English, Finnish (Pulkkinen, 1988), and Swedish populations (Magnusson & Bergman, 1988), suggesting that there may be a hard core of genetically influenced offenders who have a disproportionate influence on criminal activity.

The relationship between criminality in the biological parents and their sons was linear and significant for property crimes but not for violent crimes. Remember that the Danish twin study also showed more heritability for property crimes than for violent crimes. Similar results were obtained in the Swedish adoptee study: Crimes against persons and crimes against property come from distinctly different genetic predispositions with no significant genetic overlap between them (Cloninger & Gottesman, 1987). As in the Danish study, heritability was higher for property offenses. But a recent American study (Lyons et al., 1995) indicated a moderate genetic influence in both juvenile and adult APD traits of aggression. Certainly violence is more widespread in current American life and perhaps is a better index of APD than in Scandinavian culture. In Denmark and Sweden, violence may be more indicative of other kinds of psychopathology. Investigators in Denmark have found significant relationships between violence in the biological fathers and the rates of schizophrenia in their adopted-away children (Brennan et al., 1996).

The Swedish adoption study involved longitudinal data on a group of 1,775 Swedish adoptees representing the adoptees from the city of Stockholm born between 1930 and 1949 (Bohman, 1996; Cloninger & Gottesman, 1987). Table 5.5 shows a cross-classification like the one done for

TABLE 5.5
Cross-Fostering Analysis of Petty Criminality in Male Adoptees

Postnatal Predisposition	Congenital Predisposition	
	High	Low
High	40.0% (n = 10)	6.7% (n = 120)
Low	12.1% (n = 66)	2.9% (n = 666)
Total	n = 76	n = 786

Note. *Congenital* refers to variables derived from biological parents. *Postnatal* refers to variables derived from rearing experiences and adoptive placement. Adapted from "Predisposition to Criminality: Swedish Adoption Studies in Retrospect," by M. Bohman, in *Genetics of Criminal and Antisocial Behavior* (Au: Give p. no. here), edited by G. R. Bock and J. A. Goode, 1996, Chichester, UK: Wiley. Copyright John Wiley & Sons. Reproduced by permission of John Wiley & Sons Limited.

the Danish study (see Table 5.4). But in the Swedish study, congenital and postnatal factors were not restricted to the criminal records of the parents. *Congenital factors* refer to variables about the biological parents, whereas *postnatal factors* concern the rearing experiences such as the occupational status of the adopting father and multiple temporary placements prior to adoption. Unlike the Danish study where the adoptive parent (postnatal) factors showed only a minor additive effect to the biological parent (congenital) factor, the Swedish study showed a strong nonadditive interaction effect with the group having both congenital and postnatal predispositions to petty crime having a three times greater risk (males) or a five times greater risk (females) than the group having only a congenital disposition from the biological parents.

An American adoption study used children from four adoption agencies in the Midwest and followed their course to adulthood (Cadoret, Yates, Troughton, Woodworth, & Stewart, 1995). The study examined the effects of alcoholism and antisocial personality disorder in the biological parents, prenatal alcohol exposure, and an "adverse adoptive home environment" on childhood and adolescent aggressivity, conduct disorder, and adult APD in the adoptees. *Adverse home environment* included psychiatric disorders and alcohol or drug abuse or dependence in the adoptive parents, marital problems, separation, and divorce. Adoptees and adoptive parents were diagnosed (*DSM-III-R*) from interviews, whereas diagnoses of biological parents depended on records.

Regression analyses and model fitting showed that three of the independent variables predicted APD. In ascending order of importance they were APD in the biological parent, prenatal alcohol exposure, and an adverse adoptive home environment. Unlike the results of the Scandinavian studies, the adoptive home environment proved to be the strongest factor and the biologic parent APD the weakest one, and there was no interaction between the two factors for APD. However, the two factors did have significant interactions for childhood and adolescent aggressivity and conduct disorder. Apart from confirming the expectation that the environmental factor would be stronger in the United States because of the greater socioeconomic variability, the study points up the importance of a prenatal environmental factor that in most studies is added in with the genetic variance: exposure of the adoptee to alcohol during the pregancy of the biological mother. Alcoholism per se in the biological parents did not affect any of the dependent variables; it was only significant if the mother drank heavily during the fetal period of the adoptee.

Because there is such high comorbidity between APD and alcoholism, the question has been asked: Do they share a common genetic diathesis? The answer seems to be a confident "no!" Children of alcoholics who do not have APD are at risk for alcoholism but not for APD, and children of the APDs who are not alcoholics are at risk for APD but not for alcoholism

(Cadoret, O'Gorman, Troughton, & Haywood, 1985; Cloninger & Gottesman, 1987). Why then do so many APDs develop alcoholism? The answer must be that the APD personality type is impulsive, sensation seeking, disinhibited, and therefore, is likely to experience the effects of alcohol or other drugs as desirable early in life, in time to develop a lifelong dependency. The failure to learn from punishment is another trait of the APDs which makes them vulnerable to alcoholism.

Specific Genes

The revolutionary advances in molecular genetics have resulted in a search for genes underlying antisocial behavioral traits such as sensation seeking, impulsivity, and aggression. Two studies found an association between a particular form of the D4 dopamine receptor gene and the trait of novelty (sensation) seeking (Benjamin et al., 1996; Ebstein et al., 1996). A marker for the D2 receptor gene has been associated with substance abuse, although the specific association with alcoholism has not held up well on replication (Goldman, Lappalainen, & Ozaki, 1996). Serotonin receptor genes have been associated with the control of impulsive and aggressive behavior in mice and men. The MAO-type A enzyme specifically regulates serotonergic levels in the brain, whereas the MAO-type B enzyme is a more specific regulator of dopamine (Bruner, 1996). Little or no work has been done with gene variants for the MAO-B type despite the association of the enzyme with a number of disinhibitory disorders. Deficits in the MAO-A gene (resulting in the complete absence of MAO-A) were linked to a behavioral syndrome in the affected males in a Dutch family. The males with the genetic defect all showed borderline mental retardation and impulsive aggressive behavior. The gene is located on the X chromosome, but the defect was not linked to the behavioral syndrome in females, suggesting to the investigators that its effects are masked by the presence of the other X chromosome in females.

The functional significance of these genetic variations will be more apparent in a section to follow on the biochemical bases of antisocial personality. The monoamines, that is, dopamine, serotonin, norepinephrine, and epinephrine have all been implicated directly or indirectly in manifestations of antisocial behavior. The genetic influences on antisocial behavior may be mediated through genes involved in the personality traits that describe the disorder rather than being specific to the disorder itself.

Neuropsychology

L. N. Robins (1978) pointed out that one of the indirect effects of bad parenting, particularly neglect, was that the mother often provides a poor prenatal and postnatal environment through bad nutrition and health care and use of drugs during the prenatal period. The brain of the fetus and young infant is particularly susceptible to damage from such non-specific factors. Physical child abuse can also cause brain damage. Some theories of psychopathy suggest that brain damage, particularly to the frontal lobes, is a cause of psychopathy. Others suggest a developmental retardation of the brain in psychopaths resulting in an underaroused brain, particularly in the frontal lobes, which play an important role in the inhibition of behavior.

A study done on a large Danish cohort examined the effects of recorded birth complications and early (1 year of age) maternal rejection of the infant (Raine, Brennan, & Mednick, 1994). Neither factor alone resulted in an increased criminal record when the infants had reached young adulthood (17–19 years), but the interaction of the two factors did increase the rate of *violent offenses*: 47% of those with both birth complications and maternal rejection became violent criminals as contrasted with 20% of those with neither risk factor or with only one of them. At 1 year of age young infants' experience of maternal rejection probably had its greatest effect through defective physical and nutritional care or child abuse, all factors which could damage the brain further during this early period of development. However, the interaction of these factors did not increase the rate of nonviolent offenses in the children.

The same group then did a study of a broader group of social and biological variables in the cohort and isolated three clusters of variables: (a) *biosocial*, encompassing poverty, marital conflict, maternal rejection, family instability, parental crime, neurological problems during infancy, and slow motor development; (b) *obstetric*, comprised of pregnancy and birth complications and slow motor development; and (c) *poverty*, without marital discord and with faster motor development rather than slower (Raine, Brennan, Mednick, & Mednick, 1996). The children from the biosocial group had more academic and behavioral problems at ages 17–19, and more total crime, thievery, *and* violent crime when they were 20–22 years of age. The group with biosocial problems accounted for 70% of all the crimes committed by subjects in the sample! Poverty or obstetric problems alone could not account for later criminality.

The major hypothesis of brain dysfunction concerns the frontal lobes, which have been described as the "executive center" of the brain, and assign significance to incoming stimuli, integrate plans for action, and the process of checking on outcomes in conformance with plans (Luria, 1980). A pathway from the orbitofrontal cortex to the septum and from the septum to the hippocampus has been described as playing a role in the detection of signals of punishment or nonreward as well as the inhibition of behavior in response to such signals (Gray, 1982). Gorenstein and Newman (1980) described the behavior of rats in which this system is lesioned as the "septal syndrome." It consists of an enhanced response for positive reinforcement and a diminished capacity to inhibit responses that result in punishment or loss of reward. These rats also seem to show enhanced "stimulation seeking." In many respects the behavior of septal-lesioned rats resembles that of humans with "disinhibitory pathology." Gorenstein and Newman suggest that the human source of psychopathy may be a neurological deficit in the frontal cortex.

Gorenstein (1982) used neuropsychological tests that are particularly sensitive to demonstrated frontal lobe damage in neurological patients to test psychopathic and nonpsychopathic patients receiving psychiatric treatment for drug abuse. Psychopathic patients performed more poorly than controls on a number of these tests. Following this promising finding, several other studies failed to confirm such differences (Hare, 1984; Hart, Forth, & Hare, 1990; Sutker, Moan, & Allain, 1983).

Another hypothesis suggests that the brain disturbance in psychopathy is related to the functional relationships between the cerebral hemispheres and that psychopathy is associated with left-hemisphere dysfunction (Flor-Henry, 1976). Hare and McPherson (1984) further suggest that the left hemisphere is not as specialized for linguistic information processing as it is in "normals." They also suggest that the lack of lateralization is the source of the phenomenon in psychopaths that Cleckley (1976) called "semantic dementia," that is, using words to deceive without any emotional meaning attached to the words. Hare and his colleagues (Hare & Connolly, 1987; Hare & McPherson, 1984; Jutai, Hare, & Connolly, 1987) have done studies in which verbal or visual material is presented to the left or right hemispheres in psychopaths (PCL-defined) and controls. Most evidence supported their hypothesis of a relatively greater lateralization of the hemispheres in nonpsychopaths than in psychopaths. The significance of these findings to the disinhibition characteristic of psychopaths is not at all clear. Furthermore, the prediction that more psychopaths should be left-handed and show left eye preference was not supported, and the differences were in the opposite direction (Nachson & Denno, 1988). Males tend to be more lateralized, judging from hemispheric sizes, than females, but many more males are psychopathic than females. Perhaps the explanation for the lateralization differences among psychopaths lies in the emotional differences related to right and left hemispheres (R. J. Davidson, 1992) or to preferential inhibitory pathways between frontal cortex and the septohippocampal inhibition system.

Biochemical Factors

The enzyme MAO-B type seems to be more closely related to the catabolism of dopamine, rather than brain norepinephrine or serotonin (Murphy, Aulack, Garrick, & Sunderland, 1987). MAO-B is obtained from blood platelets in living humans, and its correlation with brain MAO is uncertain. Many studies have shown a weak but fairly consistent negative correlation of MAO with the trait of sensation seeking in normal and abnormal populations (Zuckerman, 1994b). High sensation seekers tend to have low levels of MAO. Low levels of MAO-B in males from the general population are associated with greater use of tobacco, alcohol, and illegal drugs, as well as convictions for criminal offenses. Low MAO-B in clinical populations has been found in 6- to 12-year-olds with ADHD (Shekim et al., 1986), and diagnosed antisocial (Lidberg, Modin, Oreland, Tuck, & Gillner, 1985) and borderline (Reist, Haier, DeMet, & Cicz-DeMet, 1990) personality disorders.

Low MAO is characteristic of a wide range of disinhibitory disorders, including substance abuse and personality traits such as impulsive sensation seeking in normals. Since the enzyme is a regulator of the dopamine system, the MAO deficit may result in a dysregulation of the dopamine system and thus a vulnerability to the impulsive sensation-seeking perhaps mediated by that approach system.

Both studies of animals and humans suggest that serotonergic brain systems are involved in behavioral inhibition, particularly in situations where there is competition between approach and avoidance motivations (Soubrié, 1986). Serotonin is also a factor in the capacity to delay response before acting. Lesioning of the serotonergic system originating in the Raphe nuclei typically results in disinhibition of exploratory, social, sexual, and aggressive behavior in animals. Because of these studies in animals and studies showing a relationship between the serotonin metabolite 5-HIAA and impulsive aggressive behavior in humans, Zuckerman (1991) suggested that a serotonergic deficit comprises a central part of the biological basis of the disinhibition in the impulsive sensation-seeking trait.

Evidence has been accumulating over the years linking low brain serotonin (5-hydroxytryptamine, 5-HT), or its precursor tryptophan, to impulsive violent behavior directed either toward the self (suicide) or others (homicide; Virkkunen, Goldman, & Linnoila, 1996).

Some studies of serotonergic function have used serotonergic agonists and indexed the serotonergic response by cortisol and prolactin increases. Moss, Yao, and Panzak (1990) compared men diagnosed as having APD with controls in their prolactin and cortisol responses to a serotonin agonist. The APD subjects showed a blunted prolactin response but a somewhat elevated cortisol response to the agonist. Prolactin response, but not cortisol response, correlated negatively with various self-report indices of antisocial traits such as sensation seeking ("search for highs" through substance use), egocentricity, and assaultiveness. Siever and Trestman (1993) found a similar blunting of prolactin response to another serotonin agonist in those with borderline personality disorders compared to "normals" and those with other personality disorders (not including APD). The borderline

PDs account for much of the association between impulsive suicide attempts and low serotonin levels.

Virkkunen et al. (1994) contrasted the levels of the serotonin metabolite 5-HIAA in CSF of a group of impulsive and alcoholic violent offenders and arsonists with nonimpulsve alcoholics and controls. About half of the impulsive offenders were diagnosed as having APD and the other half as having intermittent explosive disorder. Both impulsive-violent groups had CSF 5-HIAA levels that were below those of normal controls, whereas the nonimpulsive group had levels of the serotonin metabolite that were above those of normals.

A similar study in children and adolescents found lower 5-HIAA levels in a group diagnosed with disruptive disorders (most with conduct and oppositional disorder) than in a group with obsessive–compulsive disorder (Kruesi et al., 1990). No normal control group of children was used. Reduced numbers of platelet 5-HT transporter sites were found in a group whose personality disorders in the "dramatic" cluster, included APD and BPD as well as histrionic and narcissistic types (Coccaro, Kavoussi, Sheline, Lish, & Csernansky, 1996). The Bmax measure of number of uptake sites correlated negatively with measures of aggressiveness, particularly assaultiveness, in the personality disorders.

The association of low serotonin levels or responsivity with impulsivity and aggression is a fairly confirmed finding. The impulsivity may be part of an antisocial personality or the borderline or intermittently explosive types. In the case of the borderline, it is often associated with affective symptoms such as depression and impulsive suicide attempts.

Despite animal studies suggesting relationships between aggressiveness and dopaminergic and noradrenergic reactivity, little replicable evidence has been found on associations between the norepinephrine or dopamine metabolites (MHPG and HVA) and antisocial personality disorder or aggressiveness in humans. Previously cited studies on serotonin have also failed to find an association of these catecholamine metabolites with antisocial, aggressive, or impulsive traits (Fils-Aime et al., 1996; Kruesi et al., 1990; Virkkunen et al., 1994). Part of the problem may be methodological. Even the CSF measures appear to be problematical as measures of brain catecholamine activity. CSF HIAA and HVA metabolites correlate so highly that their effects cannot be separated.

The catecholamines epinephrine and norepinephrine, produced in the adrenal medulla and peripheral nerve endings and measured in urine, are low in men who have been arrested and also have strong psychopathic traits (Lidberg, Levander, Schalling, & Lidberg, 1978; Woodman, Hinton, & O'Neill, 1977). The differences between psychopathic prisoners and nonpsychopathic ones are particularly salient when these prisoners are in stressful situations such as awaiting a criminal trial (Lidberg et al., 1978). Low urinary epinephrine levels in Swedish boys at age 13 predicted unprovoked aggressive, destructive behavior and bullying behavior during early adolescence, and criminal activity when they were 18–26 years of age (Magnusson, 1987, 1996; Olweus, 1987). The lower epinephrine levels could represent a lack of autonomic stress responsiveness, which is a risk factor for antisocial behavior because if one is not stressed by dangerous situations one may indulge in more risky behavior. However, Magnusson (1996) reported that differences between persistent offenders and both adolescence-limited offenders and nonoffenders on epinephrine secretion (tested at age 13) were significant during *both* resting and stressful conditions, and all three groups showed the same magnitude of response to stress. The fact that only persistent offenders, and not adolescence-limited offenders, showed an underactive catecholamine system supports Moffitt's (1993) theory that these are different types with different etiologies.

Cortisol, produced by the adrenal cortex, is another hormone activated by stress. Urinary cortisol levels are lower in the group of habitually violent APDs than all other groups in the study by Virkkunen (1985). Corticotrophin pituitary hormone releases cortisol from the adrenal cortex. In a later study Virkkunen et al. (1994) found that low CSF corticotrophin levels were also characteristic of alcoholic offenders with psychopathic personality traits. However, corticotrophin releasing hormone from the hypothalamus was not different between psychopathic and nonpsychopathic offenders.

Testosterone has been associated with the marked differences in aggressivity in men and women, but this hormone is correlated with other more socialized traits in men, including sensation seeking, sociability, dominance, conventional masculinity, and activity (Daitzman & Zuckerman, 1980). It is also related to sexual experience. Olweus (1987) found that testosterone in adolescent boys was related to aggressive reactions to provocations, but not to unprovoked aggression of the type found in psychopaths.

Although criminal populations in general do not have elevated testosterone levels, subgroups of that population who have a history of very violent crimes do have higher testosterone levels than other criminals (Dabbs, Ruback, Frady, Hopper, & Sgoritas, 1988; Ehrenkranz, Bliss, & Sheard, 1974; Kreuz & Rose, 1972; Mattson, Schalling, Olweus, Low, & Svensson, 1980). CSF testosterone levels in alcoholic violent offenders with antisocial personality characteristics were higher than in normal controls and tended to be higher than in other types of offenders as well (Virkkunen et al., 1994).

Testosterone influences the development of many traits more characteristic of males than females, and aggressiveness is only one of these traits. In nonpsychopathic males it may be expressed in social dominance and competitiveness. But in some part it may account for the extreme sex difference in the rates of APD. It may also explain why psychopathic behavior peaks in late adolescence and tends to diminish with age after 40. Testosterone levels also peak in adolescence and fall with age.

Overreactive insulin mechanisms may produce an alcohol-induced hypoglycemic state that may lower the threshold for episodic alcohol-related violence. Virkkunen (1987) found that young habitually violent males diagnosed APD, or others with intermittent explosive disorders, tend to have very low cholesterol levels. Both groups were observed to have reactive hypoglycemia during the glucose tolerance test (GTT). Antisocial adults with a long history of aggressive conduct disorder tended to show enhanced and long-lasting insulin secretion during the GTT. This kind of heritable abnormal metabolic dysfunction could account for at least one subgroup of APDs, those who are irrationally violent.

AROUSAL THEORY

There are two kinds of arousal theories of psychopathy. The first asserts that psychopaths are generally underaroused and need extraordinary kinds of stimulation to bring themselves to an optimal level of arousal where they feel good (Quay, 1965). Underarousal is not a pleasant state except when trying to fall asleep. During a waking day, underarousal is often associated with boredom, because ordinary variation in stimulation maintains arousal level and the absence of stimulus variation reduces arousal. High sensation seekers are particularly susceptible to boredom and require either physical activity or varied stimulus input to reduce it, as when they are confined in monotonous, invariant environments (Zuckerman, 1979, 1994b). Most psychopaths are high sensation seekers, but most high sensation seekers are not psychopathic and find variation that is not antisocial in their work, social, or leisure activities.

Cleckley's (1976) criteria for primary psychopathy listed a number of traits suggesting a lack of strong or persistent emotional arousal: *superficial charm*, absence of nervousness, lack of remorse or shame, incapacity for love, and "general poverty in major affective reactions." All of these descriptions imply the lack of strong emotional arousal of either a positive or negative type. Among these criteria the absence of nervousness (anxiety) is perhaps the most significant because anticipatory anxiety is important in inhibiting behavior that could lead to punishment.

Some emotions (shame, guilt, empathy) reinforce moral restraint arousal, and conditioned emotion cues associated with punishment are a major factor in inhibition of antisocial behavior. The arousability hypothesis is more specific and suggests that the psychopath is specifically deficient in fear-arousal in response to such cues (Lykken, 1957). A broader version of the hypothesis includes reaction to unpleasant or negative stimuli, whether or not stimuli have been directly conditioned to punishment.

The arousal and arousability hypotheses have been tested using psychophysiological measures of arousal. The general arousal hypothesis should be tested using EEG measures of cortical arousal, although baseline measures of autonomic arousal such as basal skin conductance or heart rate have also been used. The specific fear-arousal hypothesis is most often tested by autonomic measures such as skin conductance or heart rate levels reached in response to novel stimuli or conditioned cues for punishment or loss.

Two kinds of abnormalities in EEG measures in psychopaths were frequently reported in the older literature (Syndulko, 1978). The most common was an excess of slow-wave activity and the other was 14- and 6-s positive spiking during drowsiness or light sleep. EEG recording is usually done with the subject reclining with eyes closed in a dimly lit soundproof room. Instructions to stay awake in this monotonous environment may conceivably have less impact on a psychopathic personality than on normals! Even so, laboratory studies have not always supported the underarousal hypothesis of APD (e.g., Blackburn, 1979; Fishbein et al., 1989). However, the latter study did show excessive slow-wave activity related to measures of aggressiveness in psychopaths and others. Two prospective studies described by Volavka (1987) showed that slow-wave activity in the EEGs of boys predicted subsequent theft offenses.

Weak differences between psychopaths and controls in basal levels of skin conductance (Hare, 1978) and heart rate (Venables, 1987) have been reported, but so have many failures of replication. The differences between psychopaths and control participants on skin conductance in one experiment became larger as the experiment progressed (Schalling, Lidberg, Levander, & Dahlin, 1973). Whether differences are found in basal arousal levels may depend upon the details and stage of the experiment. When psychopaths enter the novel laboratory situation, they may be just as aroused as the controls, but as the recording proceeds they may more quickly succumb to boredom and become dearoused while the controls are still interested or apprehensive.

Because of the problems in evaluating basal measures of arousal, interest has shifted to the evoked cortical potential as a measure of arousal or arousability in a task requiring the maintaining of attention to stimuli in order to detect the unpredictably occurring "target" or "odd-ball" stimulus. The P300 (P3) component of the EP has been regarded as the place where stimulus novelty or unexpectedness affects the reaction. Raine and Venables (1988) found that contrary to the underarousal hypothesis the psychopath had enhanced P3 amplitudes in response to target stimuli in the parietal region, but not in the temporal region. In contrast, another study showed no differences in P3 amplitudes in temporal or parietal areas but in two frontal areas the study showed that P3 amplitudes were smaller in persons diagnosed as having APD using *DSM-III* criteria (O'Connor,

Bauer, Tasman, & Hesselbrock, 1994). It should be remembered that the frontal lobes have been specifically emphasized as a likely neurological site for psychopathy.

Testing the broader stimulus arousability hypothesis, investigators have found that skin conductance responses (SCRs) to stimuli tend to be smaller in more psychopathic prisoners and delinquents, particularly among younger prisoners and using more intense stimuli (Hare, 1978; Venables, 1987). But SCRs do not differentiate between fearful or negative arousal (valence) and positive arousal. A psychopath and a conventional person might respond equally strongly to a stimulus, such as a picture of a nude or of a mutilated body, but the response of one might reflect interest or pleasure and the other fear or disgust.

Recently a new method has been developed to measure valence as well as arousal: the *fear-potentiated startle* (FPS). A loud noise elicits an unconditioned startle response (UCS) which may be measured by the amplitude of the eye-blink in humans. If a stimulus, such as a light, is paired with the loud noise, it becomes a conditioned stimulus (CS) for the startle response. When the CS and UCS are presented together, they produce an augmented FPS. The conditioned reactions to the CS+ are larger than reactions to a stimulus (CS−) not associated with the UCS.

Patrick (1994) applied the FPS method to a modified version of the Hare paradigm using a neutral visual cue as a CS and loud noise as the UCS. The UCR to noise during the intertrial intervals served as the baseline for responses to the visual cue CS when followed by the noise (anticipation). In this study, however, prisoners were classified by ratings on both factors of Hare's PCL. PCL Factor 1 was called "emotional detachment" because of the traits of lack of emotional reactivity, and Factor 2 was labeled antisocial behavior. Those low on both factors were called nonpsychopaths, and those high on both factors were called psychopaths. Factor 1 was negatively related, and Factor 2 was positively related to self-report measures of distress and fearfulness. As shown in Figure 5.2, the FPS was diminished in the detached and psychopathic groups relative to the nonpsychopathic and purely antisocial groups, demonstrating that the deficit in fear arousal is confined to that subgroup of the antisocial population with the emotional unresponsiveness of the primary psychopath. The experiment brings into question the DSM criteria, which exclude many of the PCL Factor 1 personality characteristics and rely more exclusively on antisocial behavior alone.

Normal subjects show a weak FPS to slides rated as pleasant (e.g., opposite sex nudes, food), a stronger reaction to slides that are neutral in valence, and the strongest FPS to unpleasant slides (e.g., mutilations, snakes), and a linear relationship between valence and response. In contrast, those with psychopathic personalities show equally weak responses to pleasant and unpleasant stimuli and a stronger reaction to neutral slides

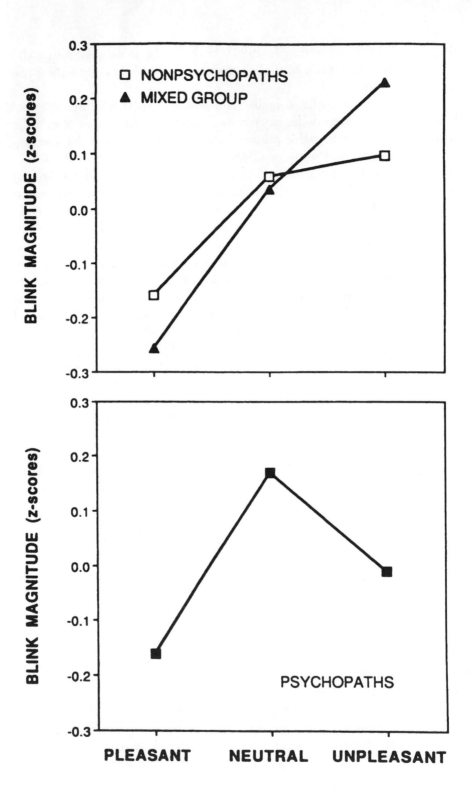

VULNERABILITY TO PSYCHOPATHOLOGY

(Patrick, Bradley, & Lang, 1993). It is as if the unpleasant slides are actually pleasant for them, although this is not shown in their valence ratings of the slides (perhaps a social desirability effect).

Nonpsychopathic high sensation seekers are attracted to scenes of horror in movies and other media, whereas "lows" are repelled by such stimuli (Zuckerman & Litle, 1986). Since most psychopaths are high sensation seekers, they may use arousal as the primary source of valence, that is, they value stimuli for their shock value rather than for their valence. The difference between a psychopath and a normal sensation seeker is that the former cannot confine themselves to vicarious arousal, but may seek to produce positive arousal by inflicting harm on real people. The lack of empathic inhibition in psychopaths is illustrated in a study in which psychopathic prisoners were exposed to portrayals of distress in slides (e.g., crying faces) and threat in other slides (Blair, Jones, Clark, & Smith, 1997). They did not differ from other prisoners in SCR responses to the threat slides but showed weaker responses to the distress cues. This may be an analogue of their lack of arousal by distress in their victims.

More direct evidence that APDs lack fear arousal comes from the so-called count-down experimental paradigm, which has been widely replicated (Hare, 1978). Participants watch or hear a descending sequence of numbers appearing on a revolving drum after being informed beforehand that they would be shocked or hear a painfully loud noise (UCS) at the count of zero, and this is demonstrated to them in practice trials. Hare (1978) classified prisoners as psychopathic or nonpsychopathic using raters and a scale of socialization (So). Prisoners classified as psychopaths by both the raters and by low scores on So showed a weaker SCR arousal gradient compared to other groups as the time approached for the anticipated UCS (see Fig. 5.3). Similar effects have been obtained using electric shock as the UCS.

The evidence is strong in support of the specific fear-arousal deficit, but weak in support of the more general underarousal hypothesis. H. J. Eysenck (1967) postulated that psychopaths are deficient in conditioning because of a general underarousal characteristic of extraverts in general. Gray (1982, 1987) suggests that psychopaths suffer from a more specific deficit in anxiety arousability and that their learning should only suffer when punishment or the withholding of reward are the reinforcers. In fact,

---

Figure 5.2. Mean startle response magnitude during pleasant, neutral, and unpleasant slide viewing in three groups of incarcerated male sexual offenders. Top panel: nonpsychopathic and mixed subjects. Bottom panel: psychopaths; n = 18 per group. Startle magnitude is expressed in z-score units, which were computed by standardizing raw blink magnitude scores within subjects. From "Emotion in the Criminal Psychopath: Startle Reflex Modulation," by C. J. Patrick et al., 1993, *Journal of Abnormal Psychology, 102*, p. 88. Copyright 1993 by American Psychological Association.

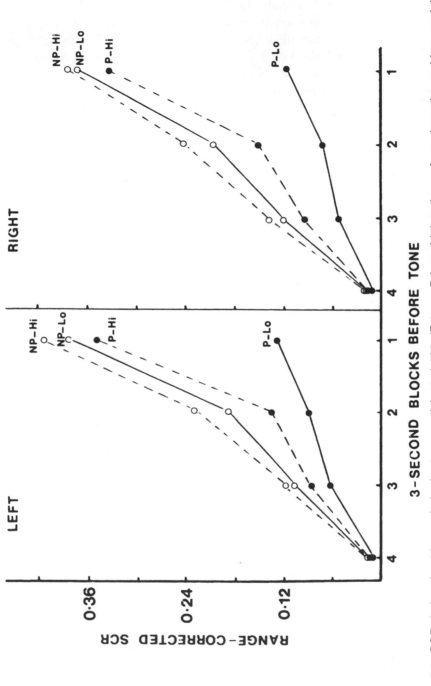

Figure 5.3. SCR during the 12-s period prior to an anticipated 120-dB tone. P-Lo = high ratings of psychopathy and low *socialization* scores; P-Hi = high ratings of psychopathy and high *socialization* scores; NP-low = low ratings of psychopathy and low *socialization* scores; NP-Hi = low ratings of psychopathy and high *socialization* scores. From "Electrodermal and Cardiovascular Correlates of Psychopathy" by R. D. Hare, in *Psychopathic Behaviour: Approaches to Research* (p. 123), edited by R. D. Hare & D. Schalling, 1978. New York: Wiley. Copyright 1978 by John Wiley & Sons. Reproduced by permission of John Wiley & Sons Limited.

Gray considers psychopathy to be the opposite pole of the anxiety dimension. Both theories would predict a lack of passive avoidance learning, or the failure to respond to cues associated with punishment. Classical and instrumental learning experiments bearing on these hypotheses are described later.

PERSONALITY

Unlike the descriptions of other personality disorders in terms of broad personality traits, the current DSM definition of antisocial personality disorder stresses a chronic pattern of antisocial behavior starting in preadolescence and persisting into adult life. Impulsivity, aggressiveness, lack of empathy, egocentricity, narcissism, and sensation seeking (boredom susceptibility), are typical traits used to describe the APD. H. J. Eysenck and Eysenck (1978) claim that psychopathy is related to all three of their factors, psychoticism (P), extraversion (E), and neuroticism (N), although they admit that the correlations of antisocial behavior are highest with P and lowest with N. Gray (1987) regards psychopathy as the opposite pole of a dimension that runs from anxiety at one end to psychopathy at the other. The psychopathy pole is defined by Eysenck's positions of high E and P, but low N. Cloninger (1987a) describes the antisocial personality as high on novelty-seeking (impulsive sensation seeking), and low on harm-avoidance and reward dependence.

In contrast to these multidimensional definitions of psychopathy, Zuckerman (1989) suggests that psychopathy represents the extreme of only Eysenck's broad P dimension, or Impulsive Unsocialized Sensation Seeking (ImpUSS), which is an amalgam of the narrower traits of impulsivity, sensation seeking, lack of socialization, irresponsibility, autonomy, and aggression.

Concurrent Studies

Costa and McCrae's measures of the Big Five personality factors have won wide acceptance in the normal personality field and recently have been used in studies of the personality disorders (Costa & Widiger, 1994). Harpur, Hart, and Hare (1994) examined the correlations between the Big Five and the PCL in samples of prison inmates and students. In the inmates only the major factor of agreeableness was negatively related to PCL ratings, but the facet scores of hostility and "excitement seeking" were positively related to the PCL. In the students, but not in the inmates, conscientiousness was negatively related to the PCL. Hare states:

> The fact remains that psychopathy is consistently related to these various aspects of impulsivity, broadly defined. We leave it to others to

consider these as individual facets of several dimensions within the FFM [five factor model] or as elements of a unitary, biologically based dimension of temperament (e.g., Zuckerman, 1989). (Harpur et al., 1994, p. 163)

Hare is referring here to the ImpUSS dimension. The sensation seeking component of this factor has been repeatedly shown to be associated with psychopathy, particularly its disinhibition aspect (Zuckerman, 1979, 1994b).

Correlations of personality scales with Hare's PCL showed no correlations with E and N and a low but significant correlation with P (Harpur, Hare, & Hakstian, 1989). However, N and various anxiety scales correlated negatively with the first factor of the PCL, and N actually correlated positively with the second factor. Sensation-seeking and socialization scales correlated with both the total and Factor 2 PCL scores. This is not surprising because "proneness to boredom," and impulsivity, are part of the PCL Factor 2 criteria. The Socialization scale has many items suggesting conduct disorder behavior when younger, and Factor 2 includes behavioral and criminal expressions of psychopathy. By definition, the antisocial behavioral traits must go back to childhood years (before age 15), and therefore, they describe the expression of a stable personality dimension: socialization. The capacity to conform to a reasonable degree to the rules of society is a behavioral trait. Regardless of whether one can verbalize the rules or how one regards them it is the actual conformance to them that defines the trait.

Longitudinal Studies

Before the age-of-onset criterion was built into the diagnosis of APD, nearly all of the boys in a longitudinal study who became adult APDs showed an onset of antisocial behavior as soon as they began attending school, and nearly 90% had established a pattern of such behavior by age 10 (L. N. Robins, 1978). The onset was later for girls with more than half of them showing an onset between 14 and 18 years of age, the time of puberty. Robins looked at many social and familial factors that played a role in prediction of adult APD, but the most powerful prognostic factor was the number of antisocial symptoms during childhood.

Can the antisocial personality be identified even before the school years? A study compared classifications of temperament of children made when they were only 3 years old with subsequent diagnoses (DSM-III-R) made when they were 21 years old (Caspi et al., 1996). The undercontrolled type of child was characterized as impulsive, restless, and distractible. The inhibited type of child was described as either shy or fearful, and easily upset. The well-adjusted type are capable of self-control when needed, are self-confident and not upset by new situations or meeting new people. At 18 years old, the undercontrolled types described themselves as "danger-seeking," impulsive, easily angered or upset by everyday events, and "enmeshed in adversarial relationships." At age 21, they were more frequently found among those adults diagnosed as having APD, they were more likely to be recidivist offenders, and to have been convicted of a violent offense. Unexpectedly, inhibited boys (but not girls) were also more likely than adjusted types to be later convicted of a violent offense, but unlike the undercontrolled types, they were not more likely to be recidivist offenders; they had "learned their lesson." A characteristic of the APD types is that they do not learn from the experience of punishment.

Lack of control (impulsivity) in children at ages 3–5 in interaction with having a single parent predicted later convictions for nonviolent crimes by age 18, but the control dimension of temperament alone predicted convictions for violent offenses (Henry, Caspi, Moffitt, & Silva, 1996). These findings suggest that the presence of a father with a temperamentally uncontrolled child may not prevent antisocial behavior, but may prevent this behavior from assuming the violent expressions found in the more severe delinquents. However, family factors may not moderate expression of aggressive antisocial behavior in the life course-persistent delinquent.

Another study predicted male antisocial behavior at age 13 from personality characteristics rated in kindergarten (Tremblay, Pihl, Vitaro, & Dobkin, 1994). Personality was rated within the context of Cloninger's (1987a) multifactor theory in order to test his multidimensional construct of APD. Novelty-seeking (NS) was labeled "impulsivity" in this study, and actually the NS scale, like Zuckerman's ImpSS scale is a mixture of impulsivity and sensation-seeking items. ImpSS and NS are highly correlated ($r = .68$; Zuckerman & Cloninger, 1996). Impulsivity (NS), assessed in kindergarten, was the strongest predictor of the onset of stable, highly delinquent behavior at age 13. Low anxiety and reward dependence were also significant but weaker predictors.

Noting the similarity of childhood predictors of psychopathy and symptoms observed in hyperactive children, Satterfield (1978) suggested that hyperactivity (ADHD, attention deficit–hyperactivity disorder) in children may be a precursor of adult psychopathy. Follow-up studies of hyperactive children showed a markedly higher arrest record of these children when they reached young adulthood (Satterfield, 1987). Other follow-up studies of children referred for hyperactivity at 6–12 years of age showed that at about 18 years of age one fourth to one third of them, in contrast to only 8% of controls, were diagnosed as having antisocial or conduct disorder (Mannuzza et al., 1991). About 40% of the subjects continued to manifest attentional difficulties, impulsivity, or hyperactivity as adults, and of these, nearly half had antisocial personality or conduct disorder in addition to ADHD.

An interesting comparison of the outcomes of children diagnosed as hyperactive between ages 6 and 12 with their own brothers showed that the adult outcome of antisocial personality was found in 45% of those who were hyperactive children but only in 18% of their brothers (Loney, Whaley-Klahn, Kossler, & Conboy, 1983). Differences between the brothers in conduct disorder types of symptoms were already apparent in childhood and persisted in unemployment, aggressive behavior, drug use (but not alcoholism), and impaired interpersonal relationships as adults.

Clearly, persistent ADHD is a risk factor for APD. Using activity monitors to record actual physical activity, Virkkunen et al. (1994) found that adult antisocial and impulsive alcoholics were more active over three 24-hour days spent in a research ward than were nonimpulsive alcoholics and normal controls. The traits of impulsivity and boredom susceptibility may produce individuals with strong needs for stimulation and activity, and when they are confined they become restless and discontented.

Summary

Both concurrent and predictive studies suggest that the APD is formed from a group of nuclear personality traits that include socialization, impulsive sensation seeking, and aggression. In a three-factor model, these are all part of a broad third dimension (the first two are extraversion and neuroticism/anxiety). The broad trait is highly heritable (Zuckerman, 1989, 1991), and its behavioral expressions in disinhibited behavior can be identified as early as 3 years of age. APD may be the extreme pathological end of this trait dimension. Differences in the other two dimensions may play a role in distinguishing subtypes among the disorder or other personality disorders. The borderline personality disorder, for instance, may represent a combination of P-ImpUSS and neuroticism or conscientiousness, agreeableness, and neuroticism in the NEO dimensions (Widiger, Trull, Clarkin, Sanderson, & Costa, 1994).

In a large-scale longitudinal study in Sweden, aggressiveness, as rated by teachers in boys 10–13 years of age, was a potent predictor of adult criminality, with the most aggressive youths constituting the majority of subjects who later in life committed offenses against persons, property, and the public at large (Magnusson, Stattin, & Dunner, 1983).

In sum, APD is associated with traits of impulsivity, sensation seeking, low socialization, hyperactivity, and aggression, and these traits tend to be manifested in behavior in childhood and preadolescence in those whom are likely to become adult criminals or psychopaths.

STRESS

APD is a long-standing personality disorder so current stress cannot be used to explain the origins of its characteristic antisocial behavior. The person with APD seems curiously indifferent to stress, except perhaps, to the stress of incarceration. However, borderline personality disorder, which shares some of the same behavioral traits, is characterized by frequent suicide attempts, which are sometimes fatal. According to Cleckley (1976), suicide is rarely carried out in psychopaths, but some studies have suggested otherwise. The difference between Cleckley's impressions and other studies may be that most of Cleckley's subjects were of the primary type (having little or no anxiety or depression), and were middle-class, and not incarcerated, whereas most other studies are of mixed (primary and secondary types) groups of lower-class psychopaths who have been incarcerated for long periods. Incarcerated inmates who were rated among the highest group on the PCL index of psychopathy had the highest incidents of attempted suicide and self-mutilation (Hare, 1991). They also had the highest levels of belligerence and fighting. The role of stress in both inward and outward directed aggression was not clear in this study, but it is likely that reactions to stress in prison can be directed either way by the psychopath.

One study investigated the relationship of life stress to depressive reactions in people with borderline and antisocial personality disorders recruited from clinical settings and the outside community (Perry, Lavori, Pagano, Hoke, & O'Connell, 1992). Those with borderline personalities were highly susceptible to depressive symptoms and major depression following stressful life events, particularly those events caused by the subjects themselves. None of the stressful events were signficantly related to depression in those with APD. Those subjects with both types of disorder actually seemed less vulnerable to depression after stressful events of any type. The authors speculate that such events provoke further antisocial behavior instead of depressive symptoms unless the subject's "acting-out" is restricted by incarceration. In the latter case the anger may be turned against the self with a suicide attempt if not a completed suicide. Some of the same biological factors (e.g., low serotonin levels) are common to impulsive aggression and impulsive suicide.

FAMILY AND SOCIAL RISK FACTORS

Antisocial individuals, particularly those found in the convicted criminal population, often come from lower socioeconomic disorganized communities and families, accounting for the common assumption that these are the primary factors that produce the disorder. Delinquent children often come from broken homes or those where there is violence, conflict, abuse, and neglect, suggesting that these produce antisocial behavior and violence in them as well as adult criminal violence later on (Widom, 1989). Children may model themselves after deviant parents or peers, doing the same things to their spouses and children as were done to them. Conflict resolution by the fist may be the only way they have learned. Abuse of themselves may lead to an added aggressive instigation, which is displaced to society in general.

But other observations raise questions about such easy extrapolations. Why are some children in the same family raised in the same homes by the same parents and exposed to the same "criminogenic" community environments law-abiding, whereas others follow the sociopathic route? Why do some adoption studies show greater influences of the biological parents than of the adoptive parents, who actually provide part of the social environment? Why is the environmental influence in antisocial traits largely the nonshared (nonfamilial) environment? Why do environmental factors play such a larger role in delinquency than in persistent adult criminality?

The Home

As L. N. Robins (1978) observed, having antisocial parents and low social status increases the risk of antisocial personality, but neither factor is a necessary precursor of APD. The major factor was early-appearing antisocial behavior tendencies in the children themselves:

> In neither Blacks nor Whites did having conforming parents reduce the risk of antisocial personality among highly antisocial children, nor did having extremely deviant parents increase the risk in very conforming children. In both Blacks and Whites it was in children in the middle range of antisocial behavior where the effects of parents was most apparent. (L. N. Robins, 1978, p. 266)

Broken homes, frequently blamed for criminality, was an important variable only because of its association with antisocial traits in the parents. Death of parents rather than loss due to separation led to no increased risk for antisocial behavior.

J. McCord (1990) compared the effects of parental behavior within three types of family structure: (a) *broken homes*, in which the father was replaced by a stepfather or the mother was absent; (b) *mother alone*, where no father was present in the home; and (c) *intact families*, in which both original parents remained in the home. Parental behavior clearly had a stronger influence than family structure. The latter influenced the rate of juvenile delinquency but not that of adult criminality, but parental behavior influenced the likelihood of adult criminality as well as the rate of juvenile delinquency. Among sons of competent mothers raising their children alone, only 20% became juvenile delinquents, and 23% ended as adult criminals. But among sons of incompetent single-parent mothers, 53% became juvenile delinquents, and 53% became adult criminals. The contrasts between outcomes of sons with competent and incompetent mothers in broken homes were even more extreme.

Henry et al. (1996) found that the number of parent changes during the child's development predicted nonviolent convictions, but not violent convictions, which were predicted solely from child temperament, particularly impulsivity or lack of control.

The results of the Cambridge-Somerville longitudinal study also suggest that the traits and childrearing practices of the mother alone can insulate the child against the long-term effects of a criminogenic environment. J. McCord (1986) found that under the worse family conditions in which boys were raised by aggressive quarreling parents and were exposed to fathers who were deviant (alcoholic or criminal) and unaffectionate and who did not respect the boys' mothers, 74% of the boys became criminals. But if the fathers were deviant but affectionate, only 22% of the boys became criminal. Boys whose fathers were nondeviant and affectionate and got along with their wives had only a 13% risk for criminality. The mother's affection for the boy, her self-confidence, and her ability to set firm rules also reduced the son's risks of criminality. The family environment provided by the primary caregiver can reduce the criminogenic effects of the father, whether this risk is genetically or environmentally mediated. Affectionless and punitive control or affectionless neglect may increase the risk of criminality, whereas affectionate control, even if only from one parent, may reduce the risks of antisocial behavior.

Child Abuse or Neglect

Child abuse or neglect is often blamed for antisocial behavior, especially when an offender is on trial for some heinous or vicious crime. Too often the evidence of the abuse depends upon the offenders' own retrospective accounts of their treatment during childhood and is rarely confirmed by records of outside agencies. Among adults who had been abused or neglected when they were children, as substantiated by records at the time, 13% (20% of males) were diagnosed as having APD (*DSM-III-R*) 20-years later, in contrast to 7% (10% of males) of nonabused, non-neglected children. Although child abuse or neglect doubled the risk of having APD, it is notable that 66% of abused or neglected children did not develop this personality type. Furthermore, because parents with APD are more likely to abuse their children than others, some of the subsequent antisocial traits of their children could be due to genetic factors rather than to the abuse itself.

Peer Influences

In a study by L. N. Robins (1978), early antisocial behavior predicted later antisocial personality regardless of whether that behavior occurred in gangs or independently. Black schoolboys were less affected by the delinquency rate in their neighborhoods than by their own early behavior and by having an antisocial parent, confirming again the primacy of the family interactions over the broader social environment in the etiology of APD. Moffitt's (1993) theory predicts that peer influences are more important in adolescence-limited delinquency than in life course-persistent delinquency, which starts in childhood. This idea is supported by findings that peer delinquency is related to adolescent but not to childhood delinquency (Bartusch, Lynam, Moffitt, & Silva, 1997).

Social Class

Poverty has long been implicated as a cause of crime, but most sociologists concede that the effects of poverty, to the extent that they do play a role in criminal behavior, work through other factors such as family disorganization and unemployment, which are so prevalent in the lowest socioeconomic classes.

Even in Denmark, where there is a smaller range of socioeconomic conditions and the poorest classes are buffered from the exacerbations of poverty by a generous welfare system, there were relationships between the socioeconomic status of the biological and the adoptive parents and the rates of criminality in their sons (Mednick et al., 1987; Van Dusen, Mednick, Gabrielli, & Hutchings, 1983). The relationship between social class of the biological parents and criminality in their sons confirms that there is a biological factor associated with lower social class and criminality, possibly the genetic component of intelligence. But the relationship with the adoptive parents' social class indicates a pure environmental effect. For males, the environmental effect was greater than the biological one, but for females, the biological effect was more important. Males appear to be more susceptible to the criminogenic effects of the social environment than females.

In the Swedish longitudinal study, social class interacted with the behavioral trait of aggressiveness in boys in producing criminality in adult life (Magnusson et al., 1983). Parental education was used as an indicator of social class. Boys who were moderate or high in aggressiveness and of lower social class were about twice as likely to commit criminal offenses in adolescence and adult life as boys who were equally aggressive but whose parents were more educated. Social class, or parental education, moderated the risk factor of the aggressiveness trait in these boys. Education probably acts through its effects on the childrearing methods used with such difficult children, as well as by providing other opportunities for expression in the children. Intelligence may also be a mediating factor.

If social class is related to risk for criminality in Scandinavian countries, then one would expect an even stronger relationship in the United States. L. N. Robin's (1978) study, conducted in St. Louis, found an interaction between social class and race when person and familial characteristics were controlled. Among White children, social class was unrelated to later antisocial behavior when their degree of early antisocial behavior was held constant. But among Black children, social class was significantly related to later criminal behavior even after controlling for antisocial behavior in the child and his father. Being a middle-class Black reduced the child's chances of developing an antisocial personality. In the previous section on personality I described the study by J. McCord (1987) showing how strictness combined with affection on the part of mothers can reduce risks for later criminality in their children.

The interactions of social class with other factors, such as personality, gender, and race, in these studies show that poverty alone is not a sufficient explanation for crime. However, to the extent that poverty causes social and familial disorganization and poor or indifferent parenting, it may play a major role in crime and perhaps even in producing antisocial personalities. It should be remembered that parents selected for adoption are usually at least middle class, and are usually highly motivated to raise children. If there was the same range of socioeconomic conditions and parental competence in the adopting parents as in the biological parents, the environmental part of the equation in adoption studies might be much stronger.

LEARNING

Classical Conditioning

The fear-potentiated startle (FPS) experiments are based on a classical conditioning paradigm and indicate a weakness of conditioning in the primary psychopath. Other conditioning studies of primary psychopaths using conditioning with either electric shock (Hare & Quinn, 1971) or loud noise (Hemming, 1981) have found that psychopathic prisoners condition less easily and extinguish conditioned responses more readily than nonpsychopathic prisoners. Hemming's study was unusual in its selection criteria, using only those criminals who came from middle-class unbroken homes (in which they were well treated) and who regarded their home lives as happy. This selection is likely to draw the primary psychopath rather than the "sociopathic" personality as distinguished by Lykken (1995).

Instrumental Conditioning

Why don't psychopaths learn from punishment experiences, such as prison or physical harm, that they experience repeatedly during their chronic criminal careers? Punishment which might deter nonpsychopaths from repeating their offenses usually occurs sometime after the criminal activity, and therefore, cannot be attributed to a deficit in classically conditioned fear in which the CS and UCS must overlap or occur in very close proximity. The lack of fear in anticipation of punishment, as illustrated in the countdown experiment, may be a factor in the moments before the execution of the crime, but it does not explain the long-term effects and the indifference to experience.

Lykken (1957) designed a test of passive-avoidance learning which has served as a model for many subsequent experiments. Subjects are presented with a panel with four levers and are required to learn a sequence of lever presses within 20 trials. Each time an error is made, the subject starts over. The procedure has been described as a "mental maze." However, there was a hidden passive-avoidance task within the experiment. Pressing one lever was always an error, but it also produced electric shock. In addition to learning the correct sequence of lever presses in the course of the trial and error, subjects also had to learn to avoid pressing the lever which shocked them. Primary psychopaths had the greatest problem in learning the avoidance reaction, but they learned the mental maze itself as well as secondary psychopaths and nonpsychopathic controls.

The experiment has been well replicated, although an experiment by Schmauk (1970) showed that by using loss of money as punishment, psychopaths were as able to learn avoidance of errors as were controls. However, studies by J. P. Newman and Kosson (1986) showed that punishment by loss of money could be a factor distinguishing types of psychopaths. Subjects in one condition were rewarded for correct responses and punished (loss of money) for making incorrect responses. They had a third option of not responding if they were unsure, in which case they would avoid punishment. The low-neurotic (primary) psychopaths did more poorly than nonpsychopathic prisoners in making more errors of commission (failures in passive avoidance) or in responding when they should not have.

Newman conceives of the psychopaths' problem as an inability to avoid responding in the pursuit of reward even when contingency cues change. If the psychopath has gotten rewarded for some antisocial behavior in the past, he will continue to behave in the same way even if the behavior no longer leads to reward, or even if it results in punishment. Thornquist and Zuckerman (1995) found that prisoners who were rated in the upper third of the sample on PCL psychopathy made more errors of commission in the Newman learning task than those in the average or low-scoring groups, but this finding only held for White and not for Black or Hispanic prisoners. Kosson, Smith, and Newman (1990) also could not replicate their results using Black prisoners. Only the Impulsive Sensation Seeking scale among Zuckerman's five major personality factors correlated significantly with errors of commission across all ethnic groups. Impulsivity may be the significant trait associated with the tendency to persist in response to nonrewarded or punished outcomes.

The particular experimental model described above has not worked in some replications by Newman, but more success has been achieved with a new experimental model (J. P. Newman, Patterson, & Kosson, 1987). Subjects gamble in a computer game which automatically generates winning or losing outcomes. The game is rigged so that the first block of trials provides 90% wins and 10% losses, the second block, 80% wins and 20% losses, and so on, down to the last block of trials in which there are no wins. The more psychopathic prisoners persisted longer and lost more money before quitting the game. However, the differences between these groups disappeared when subjects were required to pause for 5 seconds before deciding to play the next card, implicating the trait of impulsivity in the psychopath's failure of passive avoidance.

The learning studies tend to show that persons with APD do have difficulty in conditioning fear-arousal and anticipating imminent punishment. However, the studies also suggest a problem in learning from the outcomes of their experiences. In the presence of cues for reward, which may consist of material rewards or anything that is arousing, they tend to ignore and impulsively respond even in the presence of cues for punishment or loss of reward. Their major problem is learning when to restrain responding rather than when to respond. If the experimental paradigms are relevant to their real-life behavior, a training in deliberation and delay of response may be useful in helping them to cope with their impulsivity and maladaptive fearlessness and optimism. It is not likely that their basic defect in empathy can be retrained. The motivation to change their behavior must emerge from a realistic reappraisal of their life patterns, which for some consist of a major part of their lives spent in incarceration. For young psychopaths this is very difficult to do, because they must anticipate what will happen to them rather than understand their "losing" past pattern of behavior. One thing I noticed in working with young drug abusers with psychopathic personalities is that many of them quickly learn to verbalize the proper values and even conform their behavior to those values within a closely supervised environment. But after they return to the real (nontherapeutic) world, in which the reward and punishment contingencies are no longer guaranteed, they respond to the new cues for reward in drugs and crime, and revert to their old patterns of ignoring the possibilities of punishment. This is particularly likely to happen when the rewards of freedom, such as an interesting and profitable job, are not immediately given. Drugs, in particular, are a quick sensation-seeking reward because they go right to the brain's centers for pleasure.

SUMMARY

Psychopaths have a destructive effect on society, families, and their victims that is far out of proportion to their numbers. They represent the "selfish gene" out of control. Psychopathy is now defined as an antisocial personality disorder (APD), although the *DSM* criteria stress the expression in criminal behavior: "[of] repeatedly performing acts that are grounds for arrest" (*DSM-IV*, 1994). But in personality terms, it is clear that criminality and psychopathy are correlated but not synonymous. Personality traits of impulsivity, sensation seeking, aggression, and lack of empathy and socialization are combined in the APD, although any one of them in isolation from the others is not sufficient for its definition. Neuroticism and extraversion are not core traits in APD, but they may determine subtypes of the disorder. The primary type, in particular, shows little anxiety or other types of emotion, whereas the secondary type manifests a mixture of impulsive, antisocial behavior and dysphoric emotions and is less sociable. The disorder develops from an undercontrolled, impulsive, destructive childhood to conduct disorder or delinquency in adolescence, and finally to chronic criminality or other antisocial behavior in adulthood.

Both twin and adoption studies show that genetic factors play a role in chronic criminality, although there is disagreement on the role of the shared (family) environment. Delinquency seems to be explained by environmental factors, but a subgroup of the delinquents who showed antisocial behavior at preadolescent ages and go on to commit adult crimes have a stronger genetic component in their makeup. But even in this group, there is ample evidence that given the genetic predisposition the parental care and treatment of the child can enhance or reduce the likelihood of the disposition finding expression in a criminal career. Physical neglect of the child by the mother in the prenatal period and the first year of life may have irreversible biological consequences. Beyond that age the affectionate or rejecting relationships of the mother with the child may reduce or enhance the social and genetic effects of a deviant father. In intact families, the parenting competencies of both parents influence the outcomes, and one parent may compensate for the deficiencies of the other. Child abuse has significant consequences, but it cannot account for the majority of criminal outcomes.

Although broader social influences, such as social class, family structure, and neighborhoods may influence criminality, it is clear that their influence depends on their effects on the interactions among parents and children rather than on direct effects on the child. The lack of education and resultant lack of economic opportunity for the person with APD are both a cause and result of this personality disorder, in a vicious progression from rebellion against authority, through failure and truancy, to expulsion or drop-out from school, followed by lack of stable employment, boredom, use of drugs, and committing crimes.

Granted the genetic component in APD, what is inherited? Structural–physiological differences have been postulated in hypoactivity of frontal lobes and other structures necessary for the modulation of behavior, but there is little evidence to support these hypotheses. A general cortical arousal deficit is largely situation-dependent. A problem in atypical laterality of the cerebral hemisphere has been postulated to account for the way language is used by APDs, with some support from specific types of cognitive–perceptual tests, but the postulated defect is not manifested in other indices of laterality. Even if it were true it would explain only a limited aspect of the behavior of the psychopath.

More promising hypotheses have emerged from biochemical studies. The lack of regulation of behavior could be related to evidence of low levels of the enzyme monoamine oxidase (MAO) and the neurotransmitter serotonin. Both of these have been linked to personality traits of the psychopath such as sensation seeking, impulsivity, and aggressiveness. Low levels of cortisol and peripheral catecholamines have been found in psychopaths and may be related to their lack of responsiveness in reaction to situations that are stressful for normal individuals. High levels of testosterone are related to social assertiveness and sensation seeking in normal males, but are associated with a history of extreme aggressiveness in psychopaths.

Laboratory psychophysiological and learning studies involving reward and punishment demonstrate behavioral features of the APD and some of their intermediate causes. A lack of anticipatory anxiety is found in a subgroup of the people with APD in their weak physiological arousal gradient when expecting painful shock or noise. A failure of conditioned reactivity is illustrated by a weakness in the conditioned startle response. A deficit in empathy is shown in the lack of response to cues of distress or unpleasant social stimuli. A failure in inhibition is apparent in their failure in learning to inhibit responses associated with cues for punishment. These are interesting demonstrations, but studies are needed to link the psychophysiological and behavior tendencies of APDs with the genetic and brain mechanisms which may underlie them.

A purely genetic explanation of the emergence of perverse and cruel psychopaths within normal families has been termed *the bad seed*. Certainly this phenomenon is not unknown, because psychopaths can sometimes emerge from families where they were kindly and affectionately treated in spite of their early antisocial tendencies. However, the more common finding is that an antisocial disposition is aggravated by poor parenting or neglect and reinforced by a criminogenic environment to produce criminal manifestations. This is not to say that the APD will not come to fruition in a more benevolent environment, but it may express itself in narcissism, unstable interpersonal relationships, and substance abuse rather than through criminal acts. Unfortunately, spousal and child abuse, and driving when drunk are also manifestations of APD that are not infrequent in the middle-class psychopath as well as in those from lower socioeconomic classes.

6

SUBSTANCE ABUSE AND DEPENDENCE AND PATHOLOGICAL GAMBLING DISORDERS

DESCRIPTION

Substance abuse and dependence are the most prevalent psychiatric disorders for males in the United States. Apart from the toll they take on the affected individuals, they have more widespread effects in the victims of homicide, abuse, and motor vehicle accidents, and in the general disruption of family life these disorders create. The distinction between licit drugs, such as alcohol and nicotine, and illicit drugs results in a short supply for the latter and a large criminal industry involved in producing, transporting, and selling them. Local, state, and federal governments spend huge sums of money in trying to suppress the trade in drugs, with little success. An understanding of the biological, social, and psychological sources of substance abuse is necessary if we are to act intelligently in treating the affected individuals and establishing effective social policies to deal with the broader problems.

Diagnosis

The diagnostic problem in disorders dealing with substance is to distinguish use, abuse, and dependence. Only the latter two categories constitute pathologies. One may regard these as distinct disorders but it is clear that some individuals cross the borders between use, abuse, and dependence in both directions during their lifetimes. The *DSM-III* attempted to define abuse and dependence for every class of substance. Beginning with the *DSM-III-R* and extending to the *DSM-IV*, general definitions are provided for abuse and dependence. Specific substance criteria are given only for the states of intoxication and withdrawal that have characteristic features for each of the substances.

Just as there are social drinkers (the majority of American adults), there are drug users who only use illicit drugs occasionally without significant impact on their life adjustments. Use becomes abuse, according to *DSM-IV*, when within a 12-month period: (a) recurrent substance use leads to irresponsibilities in meeting obligations at work, school, or home; (b) recurrent substance use takes place in situations where it is hazardous, as in driving an automobile; (c) substance use results in recurrent legal problems; and (d) substance use results in recurrent interpersonal problems as a result of their use, as in arguments or physical fights with spouses or others.

There are many heavy drinkers or drug users who do not meet these criteria. If one drinks primarily at home and does not commit spousal or child abuse, manages to get to work and not drink on the job, has a spouse tolerant of the drinking, and does not create a financial drain on the family by drinking, then heavy drinking has not crossed the line to abuse. Much depends on the social context of the drinking. In some cultures weekend binging is acceptable, whereas in others it would be regarded as alcoholism.

Substance dependence is a substitute for the older term *addiction* that referred to the physiological need for the substance. The term *dependence* recognizes that the need for the substance and the resultant dysphoric reactions when it is not ingested may have psychological as well as physiological sources. The major criteria for dependence are tolerance and withdrawal symptoms.

Tolerance is defined in *DSM-IV* as either an increasing dosage of the substance required to achieve the desired intoxication effect or a markedly diminished effect of the original amount of the substance that had achieved the desired state. *Withdrawal* is defined by (a) a characteristic unpleasant syndrome which occurs when substance use is suddenly discontinued, or (b) when the same substance is taken to relieve or avoid the withdrawal reaction.

Five other criteria related to the compulsive use of the substance are specified, including (a) the substance is taken in larger amounts than intended; (b) the user would like to cut down or control substance use but cannot do so; (c) a great deal of time is spent in obtaining, using, and recovering from the use of the substance; (d) important life activities are sacrificed or reduced because of the substance use; and (e) the user continues to use the substance knowing that it is producing persistent physical or psychological problems. If either tolerance or withdrawal is present it may be specied as either "with" or "without physiological dependence."

Use, abuse, and dependence could be regarded as a developmental continuum with abstinence at one end and dependence at the other, but the prevalence statistics by *DSM-III-R* criteria (Kessler et al., 1994) show that abuse without dependence is only a little more than half of the prevalence of dependence. This would suggest that whereas one must usually pass through the phase of abuse to reach dependence (dependence alone is rare), many or most abusers of substances do go on to dependency at some stage in their lives. In a longitudinal study over 4 years, only 30% of alcohol abusers were reclassified as alcohol dependent; the remainder were either in remission or still diagnosed as alcohol abusers (Haskin, Grant, & Endicott, 1990). But the definition for dependency has been so broadened that it leaves abuse as a residual category. The constructors of *DSM-IV* actually considered removing the diagnosis of substance abuse from the manual (Helzer, 1994). As it stands now, *abuse* refers primarily to the social consequences, and *dependence* to the compulsive aspects of substance disorder.

ALCOHOL DISORDERS

Alcoholism remains the most prevalent of all the substance disorders with the possible exception of nicotine use. This is probably due to a combination of its legality, wide availability, and social acceptance of moderate and even heavy drinking. Symptoms shown by a majority of alcohol abusers and dependents include drinking a fifth of whiskey or its equivalent in one day, having periods of weekly heavy drinking and blackouts, having family objections to drinking, and having physical fights when drinking (Helzer, Burnam, & McElvoy, 1991). Symptoms shown only in those who are alcohol dependent and not at all in abusers (by *DSM-III* definitions) include having periods of daily heavy drinking, showing severe withdrawal symptoms such as delirium tremens, and drinking before breakfast. Almost a third of alcohol dependents but only 6% of abusers had job or school problems or been fired or expelled from school because of drinking.

Comorbidity

The high comorbidity of alcohol disorder and APD was discussed in chapter 6 of this volume. Almost half of alcoholics have a second diagnosis (Helzer et al., 1991). Female alcoholics are even more likely than male alcoholics to have a second diagnosis. About 12 times as many men and 30 times as many women with alcoholic disorders (*DSM-III*) as those with nonalcoholic disorders have a codiagnosis of APD on Axis II. About a quarter of male alcoholics and a tenth of female alcoholics have an APD (*DSM III-R*) diagnosis (Kessler et al., 1997). Alcoholism is prevalent in a majority of those using hard drugs and reaches a high of 84% in cocaine users (Helzer et al., 1991). Major depression is comorbid with many other disorders, but it is two to three times more prevalent among alcoholics with a rate of 36%. Panic disorder is more than four times as frequent among alcoholics as among nonalcoholics. Many panic disorder patients use alcohol in an attempt to reduce their panic and anticipatory anxiety. Alcohol has been shown to decrease state anxiety in panic disorder patients responding to 35% CO_2 inhalation, a panic-provoking procedure (Kushner et al., 1996).

The order of precedence of the two disorders gives some indication of which disorder is a risk for the other. APD by definition almost always precedes alcoholism, even though the type of alcoholic with APD starts drinking at a relatively young age. Alcoholism precedes depression in the majority of cases for men, but in two thirds of women, the depression precedes the alcoholism. This finding is congruent with a number of findings suggesting a different type of etiology for alcoholism in most men and women. Mania and schizophrenia also have relatively high rates of comorbidity with alcoholism, considering their rarity of occurrence in the population.

Prevalence and Demographic Correlates

Table 6.1 shows the rates of alcohol abuse and dependence in the ECA (*DSM-III*), and the NCS studies (*DSM-III-R*) by gender. The rates of dependence and abuse for men and women are higher in the more recent NCS study (Kessler et al., 1994) than in the ECA study (L. N. Robins & Regier, 1991), probably because of the changed diagnostic criteria or the methods used in the studies. Both studies, however, show a very high rate of lifetime prevalence, particularly among men.

There is evidence of an increase in alcoholism in the United States

TABLE 6.1
Lifetime Prevalence Rates (%) for Alcoholism

	Abuse and Dependence		Abuse Only		Dependence[a]	
	Men	Women	Men	Women	Men	Women
DSM-III ECA study	23.8	4.8	10.3	1.8	13.5	2.8
DSM-III-R NCS study	32.6	14.6	12.5	6.4	20.1	8.2

Note. ECA = epidemiologic catchment area; NCS = national comorbidity survey.
[a]With or without abuse.

and Sweden, as well as evidence for an increase in total alcohol consumption in the United States and Europe beginning in the years after World War II (Cloninger, Reich, Sigvardsson, von Knorring, & Bohman, 1988). Men and women born in the United States since 1953 show higher rates and earlier onsets of alcoholism than those born before 1938.

Alcohol use can be classified along a continuum from total abstention to dependence. The ECA study (Helzer et al., 1991) classified 11% of the population as lifelong abstainers, 61% as social drinkers, 14% as heavy drinkers, and 14% as alcohol abusers or alcohol dependent. In the 1994 study (Kessler et al., 1994), the rates for male alcohol abuse or dependence were about twice those for women (33% vs. 15%), but in the 1991 study (Helzer et al., 1991), the rates were five times as high among men (25% vs. 5%). The change in female diagnoses may be due to the different diagnostic criteria used in *DSM-III-R* or to differences in the sampling or data collection methods of the studies. However, male gender is a prominent risk factor for alcoholism in both studies.

One-year prevalence rates for alcoholism are highest in the 18–29-year range for both men and women and decline thereafter (Helzer et al., 1991). The lifetime prevalence rates for ethnic groups were similar, although Hispanic men were somewhat higher, and Hispanic women were somewhat lower than Black or White groups of the same gender. However, there was an interaction between age and ethnicity. The lifetime and 1-year prevalence rates for Whites in the youngest age group (18–29) are nearly twice that for Blacks, whereas the rates for Blacks in the next age group are slightly higher than those for Whites, and the differences become even larger with each older age group until in the oldest group the difference is completely reversed from what it is in the youngest group. From young adult ages to middle-age, there is an increase in Black groups compared to the decrease of rates in the White groups. Blacks on welfare have a higher rate of alcoholism than those not on public assistance. Alcoholism among Blacks at middle-age and older may be due to the cumulative effects of poverty in many of them.

The 1-year prevalence rate of alcoholism is much higher in unskilled and skilled labor groups than in professionals and managers, with service and sales workers intermediate (Helzer et al., 1991). Those who are underemployed have higher rates than those who are employed. Mean income is negatively correlated with 1-year prevalence rates in income categories for men ($r = -.91$), but not for women.

The relationship between education and rates of alcoholism shows the same irregular pattern as do rates of APD (Helzer et al., 1991). The highest rates are in high school and grade school dropouts, and the lowest rates are found in those who graduate from college, grade school, or high school. Those who have maintained a stable marriage have the lowest rates of alcoholism, and those who have only cohabited or who have had more than one divorce or separation have the highest rates. Alcohol itself may be the cause or a contributing factor to these demographic correlates. Alcoholics are not good educational or marital risks.

A large series of cross-cultural studies were done using the *DSM-III* criteria and the DIS standard interview, and the results on alcoholism were published in a volume edited by Helzer and Canino (1992). One should be wary of making national comparisons because of the sampling differences and the problems of using a standardized interview in cultures for which it was not designed. However, the very high correlations between rankings of symptom frequencies from 13 sites suggest some validity for the data.

Table 6.2 shows the lifetime prevalence rates for alcoholism (alcohol abuse or dependence) in nine cultures in the United States, Europe, and Asia. The highest rates of alcoholism are in Native Americans sampled from three reservations. Half of all the members of the community were alcoholic at some point in their lives, and an astounding 80% of males were so diagnosed! The phenomenon of alcoholism among reservation-dwelling Native Americans has been been blamed on economic and social factors and even on genetic vulnerability. The lowest rates were found in Taiwan (5–10%). There has been speculation about a genetic protection mediated by the lack of an enzyme needed for the metabolism of alcohol. But in Asian ethnic stocks, the two highest rates of alcoholism were found in American Indians (of Asiatic origin) and Koreans. If we disregard the two extreme groups (American Indians and Taiwanese), the range of alcoholism in the remaining groups is not great: 13–22% overall, 25–43% for males, and 2–6% for females. In every culture, many more males than females are diagnosed as alcoholic. The male to female ratio is extremely high in Korea and Taiwan (about 20:1) and very high in Puerto Rico (12.5: 1). In the other five cultures, the ratio ranges from 4:1 to 6:1. The cultural prohibition against heavy drinking in women is particularly strong in the two Asiatic cultures and in Puerto Rico and probably accounts for the high gender ratios in these places. But even in more permissive societies, such as the United States and Western Europe, the ratio is very high, suggesting that something more than social–cultural factors is operating to produce gender differences in alcoholism.

Course

Vaillant (1996) examined the outcomes of alcoholism in two samples of males ranging from ages 40 to 60 or 70. One was a group of Harvard undergraduates, and the other was an inner-city nondelinquent group. At the last contact, or at their time of death, if this had occurred, only 19% of the college group and 37% of the inner-city group had achieved abstinence. An additional 23% of the college group and 20% of the inner-city

TABLE 6.2
Lifetime Prevalence Rates (%) for Alcoholism (Alcohol Abuse and Dependence) in Nine Cultures

Ethnicity	Samples Taken From	All	Men	Women	ns	M:F ratio
Native American	3 reservations	51	81	40	197	2:1
Korean	Seoul & rural areas	22	43	1.6–2.6	5,100	20:1
New Zealander	urban area	19	32	6	1,498	5:1
Mexican American	Los Angeles, CA	18	31	5	1,244	6:1
Canadians	Edmonton, Canada	18	29	7	3,258	4:1
American (USA): ECA study	5 sites, 90% urban	14	24	5	20,862	5:1
German	Munich	13	25	2	455	4:1
Puerto Rican	Demo. Pop. Rep.	13	25	2	1,551	12.5:1
Taiwanese (Chinese)	urban, townships, villages	5–10	9–14	0.2–0.9	11,004	21:1

Note. Data derived from Helzer & Canino, 1992, Alcoholism in North America, Europe and Asia. New York: Oxford University Press.

group had either returned to controlled drinking or had been reclassified as social drinkers. About 59% of the college group and 43% of the inner-city group were described as suffering from chronic alcohol abuse. Strangely, the prognosis was better for the inner-city group than for the university group despite the advantages of a Harvard education and the high IQ levels and socioeconomic status of that group. However the author noted that sustained alcohol abuse in the college group seldom led to job loss or alcohol dependence.

DIATHESIS

Genetics

Alcoholism runs in families. About one-half of alcoholic men and women seeking treatment have at least one alcoholic close relative (Schukitt, 1994). There is stronger assortative mating for female alcoholics (56% have alcoholic husbands) than for male alcoholics (13% with alcoholic wives). To the extent that genetic–familial relationships reflect the genetic aspects, these data would suggest that the genetic risk is higher for males than for females. Twin studies tend to confirm this.

Twin Studies

Table 6.3 shows the concordance rates for male and female identical and fraternal twins in recent studies that used *DSM-III* or *DSM-III-R* criteria for the diagnosis of alcoholism. Among identical male twins, 68–76% are concordant for alcoholism. The concordance rates for female identical twins range from 32% to 47%. Heritabilities for males range from .36 to .54, whereas there is no evidence of heritability in 2 of the 4 female twin samples, and minimal evidence in a third one. In discussing these and other studies, McGue concluded that alcoholism is moderately heritable in males

TABLE 6.3
Concordance Rates (%) in Recent Twin Studies of
Alcohol Abuse or Dependence

	Males		Females		Heritability	
	IT	FT	IT	FT	M	F
Pickens et al. (1991)	76	61	36	25	.36	.26
McGue et al. (1992)	77	54	39	42	.54	.00
Caldwell & Gottesman (1991)	68	46	47	42	.49	.10
Kendler et al. (1992)	—	—	32	24	—	.56

Note. IT = identical twins; FT = fraternal twins; M = male; F = female. Data adapted from *Seminars in Psychiatric Genetics* (p. 163), by P. McGuffin, M. J. Owen, M. C. Donovan, A. Thapar, & I. Gottesman, 1994, London: Gaskell. Copyright 1994 by Gaskell. Adapted with permission.

and "very modestly" heritable in females. But even among males, early onset of problem drinking (before age 25 yielded a very high heritability, .73, whereas late-onset males show only a weak and insignificant heritability of .30). Shared and nonshared environmental factors are of somewhat more importance in the late-onset alcoholics and nondependent abusers.

Adoption Studies

Goodwin et al.'s (1974) study, conducted in Denmark, showed a rate of alcoholism (18%) of male children whose biological fathers were alcoholic as contrasted with a rate of 5% for those whose biological father was not alcoholic. The adoptees never knew their biological fathers so that the nearly fourfold difference represents a purely genetic effect. Furthermore, the rates of alcoholism among adoptees with an alcoholic biological father were not higher than the rates of males raised by their biological alcoholic fathers. The same group (Goodwin, Schulsinger, Knopf, Mednick, & Guze, 1977) found no differences between those with genetic risk and those without such risk among female adoptees: The rate of alcoholism was only 4% in both groups.

A study conducted in Sweden (Sigvardsson, Bohman, & Cloninger, 1996) showed increased rates of alcoholism in adopted men and women whose biological parents were diagnosed as alcoholic abusers, but the risk for men increased when either parent was alcoholic, whereas only alcoholism in the biological mother increased the risk for women (see Table 6.4). A replication study confirmed the results for men, but not for women, perhaps because of the infrequency of women who had alcoholic biological mothers. Of course, a biological mother who is alcoholic could have influenced her child through the prenatal environment if she drank during pregnancy.

A study of American adoptees using *DSM-III* criteria for alcohol abuse or dependency found that if a biological first-degree relative was an alcoholic, 62% of their male and 33% of their female adopted-away children became alcoholics, in contrast to 24% of the men and 5% of the women without biological alcoholic relatives (Cadoret, O'Gorman, Troughton, & Haywood, 1985). But even when the genetic influence from the biological relatives was controlled, there was also a significant but somewhat weaker influence of alcoholism in adoptive relatives. The genetic factor was significant in women as well as in men, but the risk was lower for women. APD was also studied and a genetic risk was found for it, but analyses showed there were different genetic dispositions for APD and alcoholism. These results were replicated in another study (Cadoret, Troughton, & O'Gorman, 1987).

TABLE 6.4
Inheritance of Susceptibility to Alcohol Abuse in Stockholm and Replication Adoption Studies

Alcohol Abuse in Biological Parents		Alcohol Abuse in Adoptees (%)	
Father	Mother	Stockholm	Replication Study
Adopted men			
No	No	14.7	12.8
Yes	No	22.4[a]	23.1[a]
No	Yes	26.0[a]	31.8[a]
Yes	Yes	33.3[a]	12.5[a]
Adopted women			
No	No	2.8	1.1
Yes	No	3.5	0.9
No	Yes	10.3[b]	0.0
Yes	Yes	9.1[b]	0.0

Note. From "Replication of the Stockholm Adoption Study," by S. Sigvardsson, M. Bohman, & R. Cloninger, 1996, in *Archives of General Psychiatry, 53,* p. 683. Copyright 1996 by American Medical Association. Reprinted by permission.
[a] Sons with alcoholic biological parents significantly more likely than others to abuse alcohol in the Stockholm *and* replication studies.
[b] Daughters with alcoholic biological mothers significantly more likely than others to abuse alcohol in the Stockholm study, but not in the replication study. However, *n*s for two groups with alcoholic mothers were very low in replication study (7 for No–Yes, and only 1 for Yes–Yes combinations).

Alcoholic Subtypes and Genetic Risk

Cloninger (1987b) introduced a method subclassifying alcoholics by patient characteristics which has proven useful in genetic and prognostic studies. Table 6.5 describes the Type 1 and Type 2 alcoholics. Type 1, found in both male and female alcoholics, has a later age of onset, a psychological dependence on alcohol that leads to a loss of control over drinking after periods of abstention, and guilt and fear engendered by the alcoholic dependence. Type 2, found primarily in men, is characterized by an inability to abstain at all, and by fighting and arrests when drinking. The personality traits will be discussed later. Summarizing the two types in diagnostic generalities, Type 1 seems to have neurotic, dependent, and anxious traits, whereas Type 2 has antisocial, impulsive, sensation seeking, and aggressive traits.

The effects of the socioeconomic levels of the adoptive parents on Types 1 and 2 were studied by Sigvardsson et al. (1996). Severe environments (equated with adoption into a lower socioeconomic class home) were considered a risk only for the Type 1 alcoholism. Genetic background or environmental liability alone were not sufficient to produce an increased risk of Type 1 alcoholism in the sons. Only the combination of genetic Type 1 and lower class environment increased this type of alcoholism. Type 2 alcoholism, however, was increased (17–18% vs. 2–4%) if the biological

TABLE 6.5
Distinguishing Characteristics of Two Types of Alcoholism

Characteristic Features	Type of Alcoholism	
	Type 1	Type 2
Alcohol-related problems		
Usual age of onset (years)	After 25	Before 25
Spontaneous alcohol-seeking (inability to abstain)	Infrequent	Frequent
Fighting and arrests when drinking	Infrequent	Frequent
Psychological dependence (loss of control)	Frequent	Infrequent
Guilt and fear about alcohol dependence	Frequent	Infrequent
Personality traits		
Novelty-seeking	Low	High
Harm avoidance	High	Low
Reward dependence	High	Low

Reprinted with permission from Cloninger, C. R. (1987b). "Neurogenetic Adaptive Mechanisms in Alcoholism," *Science, 236*, 410–416 (Table 1, p. 411). Copyright 1987. American Association for the Advancement of Science.

fathers had Type 2 alcoholism, regardless of the social background of the home. One might conclude from this study that the Type 2 alcoholic is more strongly influenced by genetics than the Type 1, which requires an environmental factor in addition to some genetic vulnerability.

Molecular Genetics

Many genes are probably involved in alcoholism, but linkage studies have attempted to find major genes associated with the disorder (McGue, 1993). Alcoholism may be due to the absence of protective mechanisms as well as the presence of genetic traits which might make alcohol more attractive to some people than to others. Those who get immediately ill after ingesting one or two drinks are unlikely to become alcoholics because aversive conditioning will make alcohol unattractive to them, just as Antabuse interacts with alcohol to produce nausea and conditioned aversion. The immediacy of the reaction is important because the more typical hangover, which is delayed until the following morning, cannot be effective in aversive conditioning. A gene that affects the alcohol metabolizing liver enzyme acetaldehyde dehydrogenase (ALDH) has been used to account for the low rate of alcoholism in people of Asian relative to European descent. One allelic variant of this gene results in deficient ALDH activity, producing sickness when a person ingests alcohol. About half of Japanese and Chinese people have this variant form of the gene, but only about 2% of Japanese alcoholics have it. Although this gene might explain the difference between abstainers and heavy drinkers, it does not explain what prevents most social drinkers and some heavy drinkers from becoming alcoholics.

Another gene, the A1 form of the D2 dopamine receptor gene, has been linked to alcoholism in some studies but not in others (Noble, 1996; Uhl, Persico, & Smith, 1992). The selection of this gene was an extrapolation from the results of animal studies. Some species of rats and mice will drink alcohol in solution, and others will not. Positive alcohol reactions in rodents are associated with other traits such as explorativeness, fearlessness, and aggressiveness, suggestive of the traits associated with Type 2 alcoholism in humans. Individuals with the A1 allele seem to have fewer D2 dopamine receptors than others. Noble suggests that they attempt to compensate for this deficiency by stimulating dopamine release in the reward circuits of the mesolimbic system through alcohol and other drugs. This hypothesis is similar to those that propose an "endogenous deficit" theory of drug abuse (see Zuckerman, 1986). The dopamine system is involved in alcohol self-administration in rodents. The variant of the D4 receptor gene associated with novelty (sensation) seeking in humans (Ebstein et al., 1996; Ebstein & Belmaker, 1997) is another potential gene because of the involvement of this trait in Type 2 alcoholism (Cloninger, 1987b). The D4 receptor exon III has been found to occur significantly more often in alcoholics than in controls in two out of six studies reviewed by Ebstein and Belmaker (1997). In one of these studies the effect of the D4 allele was only found in alcoholics with the ALDH2 gene version, suggesting a polygenetic and interactive effect of genes in alcoholism. Since the D2 gene is also found in other types of substance abuse (Smith et al., 1992), it may represent a broad vulnerability, perhaps mediated by personality traits, whereas the ALDH2 gene may represent the specific vulnerability to alcohol as a substance.

Taken together the genetic data suggest a moderate heritability for alcoholism of about the magnitude found for some personality traits (50%). Of course, there is the possibility that there are no specific genes for alcoholism, but only genes that predispose broad personality traits such as impulsivity, sensation seeking, and neuroticism.

Biological Factors

Surprisingly little is known about the biochemical basis for the actions of alcohol in the brain considering that it is the oldest and most widespread drug of abuse. Unlike other psychotropic drugs, alcohol has no distinct receptor in the CNS (Tabakoff & Hoffman, 1987). Instead, alcohol interacts with receptors from other systems including the GABA-benzodiazepine complex, catecholamine, serotonin, and opiate receptors. Alcohol's reinforcing properties may occur through the dopamine system as alcohol increases dopamine concentrations in the nucleus accumbens, a center for intrinsic reward (O'Brien, Eckart, & Linnoila, 1995).

More extensive evidence from studies of rats and humans links the endogenous opioid system to the reinforcing effects of alcohol. In subjects with a family history of alcoholism, baseline levels of beta-endorphin are lower than in those without such family history, but a dose of alcohol produces a rise in beta-endorphin in the high-risk subjects to the level of the low-risk subjects (Gianoulakis, Angelogianni, Meany, Thavundayil, & Tawar, 1990). A later study (Gianoulakis, Krishman, & Thavundayil, 1996) showed that plasma beta-endorphin is more sensitive to alcohol in the high-risk subjects. Alcoholics given the opiate blocker Naltrexone reduced their drinking below abuse levels, but the effects did not persist beyond 1-month posttreatment (O'Malley et al., 1996). Naltrexone probably reduced alcohol intake by blocking the opiate receptors, which are a source of reinforcement. Thus low levels of endorphins may constitute a vulnerability to alcoholism, and the release of endorphin through alcohol ingestion may be particularly reinforcing to those with this deficit. This deficit would also explain the high comorbidity of alcohol and opiate use, because both interact with the same receptors.

Serotonin may also play a role in the reinforcing effects of alcohol. Low doses of alcohol increase the firing rate of serotonin neurons and increase extracellular concentrations of serotonin in the nucleus accumbens in rats. Serotonin reuptake inhibitors reduce the amount of alcohol consumed in alcoholic volunteers (O'Brien et al., 1995). Alcohol-preferring rats have lower serotonin concentrations in the nucleus accumbens and frontal cortex. Early-onset alcoholics (Type 2) have lower concentrations of the serotonin metabolite 5-HIAA in CSF (Fils-Aime et al., 1996). Of course, certain antidepressants are serotonin reuptake inhibitors, and their efficacy in treatment of alcoholism is being explored. A natural deficit in serotonin could explain the comorbidity of alcoholism with both antisocial personality and depression because both disorders have also been associated with serotonin deficits.

Several biological markers are associated with alcoholism. Low levels of the enzyme MAO have been discussed in relation to APD and borderline personality disorder. Low platelet MAO levels have also been found in alcoholics (Major & Murphy, 1978; L. von Knorring, Oreland, & von Knorring, 1987). This association might be attributed to alcohol itself, because it can lower MAO, but studies have shown that low MAO is also found in those with a family history of alcoholism and in nonalcoholic sensation seekers (Schukitt, 1988; Sher, 1993) suggesting that low MAO is a biological marker for alcoholism or other disorders characterized by disinhibition.

The psychophysiological findings on the relationship between the cortical-evoked P300 and psychopathy were discussed in chapter 5. Begleiter and Porjesz (1988) found that alcoholics show reduced P300 amplitudes or even absence of this component in response to unpredictable and infrequent stimuli. They also report reduced amplitudes of an earlier EP component, the P100, related to the orienting response. As with the

MAO marker, we may ask whether the reduced EPs are states, related to the clinical condition, or stable traits of the alcoholic that preceded the alcoholism. Begleiter answers this by showing that the EP deficits do not change after recovery and abstinence and are also found in about one third of the young sons of alcoholics. Future studies will show whether these same sons develop alcoholism at older ages.

Studies of alcohol tolerance among sons of alcoholics provide another marker, one based on subjective and behavioral rather than physiological reactions to alcohol. Blood alcohol concentrations in sons of alcoholics and sons of nonalcoholics are similar over time after ingestion of alcohol, but the sons of alcoholics rate themselves as less intoxicated and show less impairment on cognitive and behavioral tasks (Schukitt, 1988). An 8-year follow-up of these young men showed that (a) more of those with a family history of alcoholism met the criteria for alcohol abuse or dependence (43%) than those with no family history of alcoholism (17%); and (b) level of reactivity to alcohol (subjective, body-sway test, and cortisol reactions) at age 20 was negatively related to the diagnosis of alcohol abuse or dependence and the number of alcohol dependence symptoms 8 years later (Schukitt & Smith, 1996).

Alcoholics in the making frequently brag about how they can "hold their liquor," meaning they do not show the effects in speech or incoordination at moderate doses. This capacity may be their undoing, because it allows them to drink larger quantities of alcohol before becoming impaired, and therefore, to develop a tolerance for alcohol. Genetic factors contribute to these alcohol reactivity variables (Heath & Martin, 1992).

It is interesting that many of the biochemical and psychophysiological markers for alcoholism are the same as those for APD. Perhaps what is inherited by most male alcoholics is the tendency toward antisocial personality if not the full-blown syndrome.

PERSONALITY

Alcoholics who are admitted for treatment represent heterogeneous personality types (Nerviano, 1976). Cloninger's (1987b) classification specified three personality traits distinguishing Type 1 and Type 2 alcoholics (see Table 6.5). The Type 1 personality is characterized as low in novelty (sensation) seeking, high in harm-avoidance (anxious), and high in reward dependence (dependent). In contrast, the Type 2 personality is high in sensation seeking, low in harm-avoidance (fearless), and low in reward dependence (autonomous). He is less of a compulsive drinker and more of an "alcohol-seeker." Type 1 drinks to reduce anxiety and distress, whereas Type 2 drinks because he enjoys the disinhibition produced by alcohol and is more likely to engage in fighting and other antisocial behavior.

Sensation seeking has been related to heavy drinking and early onset of drinking in preadolescents, adolescents, young adults, and adult alcoholics (Zuckerman, 1987, 1994b). Type 2 alcoholics do score higher on the Sensation Seeking scale (SSS) than Type 1, as predicted from Cloninger's model (Oreland, Hallman, von Knorring, & Edman, 1988). Among alcoholics, those who are high sensation seekers tend to be sociable, self-confident, and engaging in "risky, stimulating, and/or uninhibited behavior" (O'Neil et al., 1983). Alcoholic drivers arrested for drunken driving score higher on the SSS than do nonalcoholic drivers (Mookerjee, 1986). Chronic alcoholics frequently arrested for public drunkenness score higher on the SSS than do acute alcoholics (Malatesta, Sutker, & Treiber, 1981). A high sensation seeking group of alcoholics were younger and used more drugs other than alcohol than low sensation seekers. Sensation seeking is associated with the more aggressive, psychopathic type of alcoholic, as predicted from Cloninger's typology.

If a substantial subgroup of alcoholics (Type 1) is characterized by harm avoidance or anxiety, then unselected groups should score high on this measure. Alcoholics in a Veterans Administration hospital scored higher than occasional users of alcohol and than nonusers on measures of anxiety and neuroticism, but the latter two groups did not differ on these measures (Kilpatrick, Sutker, & Smith, 1976). Note that these studies used participants who were *voluntary* hospital admissions. Studies of heavy drinking among adolescents and young adults show little concurrent or predictive value for scales of neuroticism and anxiety (Zuckerman, 1987, 1994b). The only way to really determine if anxiety and depression are traits that are antecedent and possibly etiological to alcoholism is to examine longitudinal studies in which the personality assessments were made in childhood or early adolescence, before the onset of alcoholism.

In the Oakland growth study, children were first assessed at the age of 10, then again in junior high school, high school, and finally 30 years later when the subjects were 43 years old (Jones, 1968, 1971). "Problem drinkers" were those with a history of excessive drinking that had created problems for themselves, their families, or their employers. At the minimum they were alcohol abusers. They were compared with moderate drinkers and abstainers on ratings made when they were in junior high school. At that age the male problem drinkers had been rated as more undercontrolled, rebellious, hostile, limit-pushing, self-indulgent, sensuous, negativistic, expressive, assertive, talkative, humorous, and "other-directed" than moderate drinkers or abstainers. They were rated lower than the moderate drinkers on overcontrol, emotional blandness, dependability, objectivity, fastidiousness, dependency (and acceptance of dependency), submissiveness, vulnerability, and considerateness. Personality trait differences related to future alcoholism were similar for high school and adult periods of their lives. Young, prealcoholic men were already showing the Type 2 alcoholic personality traits (impulsive, sensation seeking, aggressive). They did not show any of the traits of the Type 1 alcoholic (anxious, dependent, low sensation seeking). The personality pattern was apparent even at the junior high school prealcoholic stage.

The "problem drinking" women showed many of the same traits as the males during adolescence, being described as unstable, impulsive, unpredictable, and highly interested in the opposite sex. Unlike male prealcoholic boys, they were also described as anxious and depressed, self-defeating, vulnerable, pessimistic, irritable, and sensitive to criticism. The girls showed a mixture of Type 1 and Type 2 alcoholic personality types.

W. McCord and McCord (1960) reported a longitudinal study of boys from high delinquency urban areas near Boston. They were first studied at about 9 years of age and then again in their 30s, by which time about 10% had become alcoholic and had been arrested two or three times for drunkenness, joined AA, or had been treated for alcoholism. They sound like chronic alcohol dependent types. Prealcoholic boys had been rated as outwardly self-confident, undisturbed by abnormal fears, indifferent toward their siblings, disapproving of their mothers, highly aggressive and even sadistic, and hyperactive. They were fearless, self-sufficient, and aggressive, typifying the adult Type 2 personality. However as adult alcoholics, some of them became more dependent and withdrawn in contrast to their preadolescent personalities.

In the Swedish longitudinal study of boys, severe aggressiveness and hyperactivity at age 13 predicted both criminality and alcohol abuse in adults (Magnusson & Bergman, 1990). Its authors did not look at a broader range of personality traits; however, the aggressiveness finding is consistent with the two studies previously described.

A short-term prediction study from personality traits assessed at age 18 to alcohol dependence (*DSM-III-R*) at age 21 found that those persons who were alcohol-dependent at age 21 were characterized by low scores on scales of Traditionalism, Harm Avoidance, Control, and Social Closeness, and by high scores on Aggression, Alienation, and Stress Reaction (Caspi et al., 1997). With the exception of the last two of these scales, the pattern was the same for those who had convictions for violent crimes and engaged in risky sexual behaviors. The traits characterizing all of these groups consist of the same nonconforming, risk-taking, impulsive, and aggressive traits seen in the other longitudinal studies of alcoholism, particularly among males.

STRESS

Alcoholics and others drink to reduce stress and the tension it engenders, but they also drink when they are in a good mood, so that the drinking cannot be blamed on the immediate stress. The question is whether their drinking started with severe stress provoked by major kinds of trauma or chronic stress of the type found in dysfunctional families. Part of the evidence must come from longitudinal studies of the environmental stresses and of the prealcoholic personality. There is little point in studying the stress in currently alcoholic individuals, because much of the stress is produced by the consequences of their alcoholism. Alcohol itself may aggravate the depression produced by stress. The effects of alcohol on stress hormones such as corticosterone are biphasic, first producing a reduction and then, at higher doses, an increase (Pohorecky & Brick, 1987). Many humans exhibit a similar biphasic reaction in mood over the course of a drinking session, first becoming euphoric and relaxed and then depressed and anxious.

Alcoholism has a comorbidity with some anxiety and depressive disorders (see chaps. 3 & 4, respectively, this volume). Males with posttraumatic stress disorder have an extraordinary rate of comorbid alcoholism (52%) and the rate is elevated in women as well (Kessler et al., 1995). Alcohol represents one way of coping with chronic stress like that felt in PTSD or following a job loss or marital separation. But extreme kinds of stress do not necessarily increase rates of alcoholism. The death or serious illness of a spouse did not increase alcohol consumption in the well partner (Kasl, Ostfeld, Berkman, & Jacobs, 1987). Unless there has been some previous history of alcoholism, a life stress is unlikely to trigger alcoholism or even increase alcohol consumption. Many of those who drink to excess during a life crisis return to their normal drinking patterns when the crisis is resolved. But some do not recover. Perhaps the Type 1 alcoholic, with a later onset and neurotic rather than antisocial traits, is the most likely to have a stress-precipitated alcoholism.

Stress has been narrowly defined as environmental events that produce negative moods or general tension. But as Selye (1956) observed, stress can be produced by positive as well as negative events. Powers (1987) distinguished three kinds of stress. The first, *distress*, refers to events ranging from mildly negative to catastrophic. Mild distress might be situations which produce loneliness or boredom, whereas catastrophic stress would be events such as deaths, separations, or sudden job losses. The second, *mesostress*, refers to events which are neutral in hedonic tone but produce strain, such as job pressures, minor frustrations, day-to-day "hassles," or maintaining defenses against internal conflicts, conscious or unconscious. The third, *eustress*, is produced by events ranging from mildly to extremely positive, such as a job promotion or a new relationship.

Powers (1987) interviewed male alcohol-dependent patients and normal social drinkers, and asked about drinking in response to these three kinds of stresses. Mesostress relief was the most frequently reported stimulus for drinking in both groups. The two groups differed significantly only on drinking to alleviate distress: The alcoholics reported more drinking in response to distress. Regardless of the role of stress in the etiology of alcoholism, it accounts for about half of the incidents of relapse in those who have temporarily quit drinking (Hore, 1971). Lisman (1987), reviewing the naturalistic and laboratory research on the stress-reduction explanation of alcoholism, concludes that stress reduction by alcohol depends on other factors, including the attitudes toward alcohol and personalities of the subjects.

FAMILY AND SOCIAL RISK FACTORS

Like other studies, the Cambridge-Somerville study found a higher incidence of alcoholism among fathers of boys who grew up to become alcoholics than among fathers of controls (W. McCord & McCord, 1960). They also found more family conflict and evidence of rejection or indifference in the parents of alcoholics. But they also found differences between the family factors predisposing toward criminal and noncriminal alcoholism. Boys given punitive discipline were more likely to become criminal than alcoholic. Parental antagonism was related to future alcoholism, whereas parental indifference was predictive of criminality. Unambiguous rejection is more likely to produce aggressive criminal behavior, whereas ambivalent emotional interactions between parents and children are more likely to produce alcoholism in the children.

More recent analyses of outcomes when the boys had reached 45–53 years of age, used cluster analysis to group the parental variables into three factors: mother's competence (consistency, self-confidence, affection), father's interaction (esteem for mother, affection for son, aggressiveness, parental conflict), and family control (restrictiveness, supervision, demands) (J. McCord, 1990). All three factors (Low Maternal Competence, Bad Father Interaction, and Weak Family Control) predicted juvenile delinquency, juvenile deviancy, and adult criminality, but none of them significantly predicted an outcome of alcoholism in the boys. The father's status as an alcoholic predicted the son's alcoholism, but the father's criminality did not. The only interaction predicting alcoholism was that between family structure and an alcoholic father: An alcoholic father increased the son's chance of becoming alcoholic only if the father was part of an intact family. Despite the contradictory conclusions from adoption studies, the results of this study suggest a social role of the father's alcoholism as well as a genetic influence in producing alcoholism in a son, because his presence in the family does seem to increase the risk for the son.

DRUG DISORDERS

Other than alcohol, the substances of abuse, dependence, or intoxication listed in the *DSM-IV* include amphetamines, caffeine, cannabis (marijuana), cocaine, opioids, hallucinogens, inhalants, nicotine, phencyclidine, sedatives, hypnotics or anxiolytics, and a residual category for all others. Probably the most widely used of these are caffeine and nicotine. Among the illegal drugs, cannabis is the most widely used and abused. Although it has a potential for dependence, there are no withdrawal symptoms associated with its discontinuance. It is proscribed by our society as a step on the pathway to the use of more dangerous and addictive drugs, but one could say the same for nicotine or alcohol, usually the first drugs of abuse (L. N. Robins & Regier, 1991).

Both cocaine and heroin are drugs said to produce dependence, but a study comparing daily cocaine users with daily heroin users found that smaller percentages of the cocaine users ever felt dependent, developed tolerance, or felt a lack of control over drug use (J. C. Anthony, 1992). Only 13% of the cocaine users reported having ever experienced withdrawal, compared to 75% of the heroin users. Although cocaine abusers may not experience withdrawal in the physiological sense, they do report high levels of anxiety, hostility, fatigue, depression, confusion, sleep disturbance, and craving for cocaine after the cessation of its use, and these symptoms decrease gradually over a month of abstinence (Weddington et al., 1990).

After alcohol there is a typical life sequencing of the onset of other drug use: cannabis and inhalants at 13–16 years; amphetamines and hallucinogens at 16–18 years; barbiturates and opioids other than heroin at 17–21 years; heroin at 20–22 years; and cocaine at 21–25 years of age (Cottler, Price, Compton, & Mager, 1995). Naturally, there is a great deal of variation in individual histories as a function of cultural and ethnic subgroups, drug availability, and individual preferences among drugs. Women show about the same ordering of drugs, but later onset of use.

In this section I focus primarily on cocaine and opioids. These are the drugs that have the greatest potential for abuse and dependence, intoxication, and withdrawal. Excluding alcohol, cocaine and opioids are currently the major sources of individual and societal problems in the Western world.

Are alcohol and drug abusers from the same population? Weisner (1992) compared subjects seeking alcohol treatment with another group seeking drug treatment. The two groups did not differ in age, but those seeking drug treatment contained fewer older clients, a higher proportion of White persons, and more married or cohabiting persons, whereas more of those seeking treatment for alcoholism were separated or divorced, college educated, and employed full-time. Of course, those seeking treatment for alcohol reported drinking more frequently (every day) and copiously, and those seeking drug treatment reported using a larger number of different types of drugs, but a majority of those in the alcohol treatment group reported using drugs, and in most cases the drugs were used with alcohol. The drug treatment group often used alcohol with drugs but less frequently than the alcohol group. The alcohol group tended to attribute their problems to alcohol *and* drugs, whereas the drug group tended to blame drugs alone for their life complications. A higher proportion of the drug group admitted criminal behavior in nearly every category of crime than in the alcohol group, suggesting more antisocial tendencies among these patients. This last difference could be due to the illegality of drugs, making them expensive and forcing the nonaffluent drug users to sell them and engage in prostitution or robbery to support their habits.

Stabenau (1992) compared nonhospitalized or treated subjects using, abusing, or dependent on only alcohol, or only drugs, or on both. The diagnosis of antisocial personality disorder was more common in the combination alcohol and drug group than in all other groups. A family history of drug abuse was most common in the drug-only group, and a family history of alcoholism was most common in the alcohol-only group, suggesting specific genetic or shared environmental influences in alcohol or drug abuse, with the antisocial personality predisposing toward both kinds of substance abuse.

Comorbidity

Among Substances

Many drug abusers have had problems with alcohol as well as with drugs other than their primary one. In the ECA community study (L. N. Robins & Regier, 1991), 60% of the males and 30% of the females diagnosed as having drug abuse or drug dependence also had a lifetime comorbidity of alcohol abuse or dependence. Among treatment-seeking opioid addicts, 35% were diagnosed as alcoholic in one study (Rounsaville et al., 1991), 50% were diagnosed as alcohol dependent, and 13% as alcohol abusers in another (Brooner, King, Kidorf, Schmidt, & Bigelow, 1997). Alcoholism is even more frequent in cocaine addicts seeking treatment (Rounsaville et al., 1991) with 62% showing a lifetime diagnosis of alcoholism (71% of male and 41% of female cocaine abusers).

Table 6.6 shows the lifetime rates of drug and alcohol dependence and abuse (*DSM-III-R*) among opioid abusers seeking treatment (Brooner et al., 1997). Despite the different pharmacological and physiological actions of opioids and cocaine, nearly two thirds of the opioid abusers had a life history of cocaine dependence and another 12% of abuse only. Even current rates of cocaine abuse were high (40%). There was also a high

TABLE 6.6
Lifetime Prevalence Rates (%) of Other Drug and Alcohol Disorders in
Opioid Abusers

Diagnostic Category	Lifetime Rates (%)		
	Men (n = 378)	Women (n = 338)	Total (N = 716)
Opioid dependence	100	100	100
Cocaine dependence	66.1	63.0	64.7
Cocaine abuse	13.0	11.8	12.4
Cannabis dependence	58.7	42.0	50.8
Cannabis abuse	17.7	11.8	14.9
Alcohol dependence	56.6	43.2	50.3
Alcohol abuse	16.1	9.5	13.0
Sedative dependence	47.9	40.8	44.6
Sedative abuse	15.3	10.4	13.0
Stimulant dependence	19.0	19.2	19.1
Stimulant abuse	15.6	7.1	11.6
Hallucinogen dependence	21.2	14.2	17.9
Hallucinogen abuse	12.7	5.6	9.4
Other Substances dependence	15.1	12.7	14.0
Other Substances abuse	7.9	4.7	6.4

Note. From "Psychiatric and Substance Use Comorbidity Among Treatment-Seeking Opioid Abusers," by R. K. Brooner et al., 1997, *Archives of General Psychiatry, 54,* p. 75. Copyright 1997 by American Medical Association. Adapted with permission.

lifetime dependence diagnosis for other depressant drugs (sedatives, 45%), and significant frequencies of diagnoses for stimulants and hallucinogens as well.

The high comorbidity among the different types of substance abuse and dependence suggests the reality of the "addictive personality" and explains the changes in patterns of drug use among different populations at different points in time (J. C. Anthony, 1992). Much depends on availability of a particular drug at a particular time and the appearance of cheaper or more potent forms of the drug, such as crack cocaine (Musto, 1992).

Between Drugs and Axis I Diagnoses

Those patients diagnosed with drug abuse or dependence in the ECA community study (L. N. Robins & Regier, 1991) were found to be at higher risk for every Axis I disorder except cognitive impairment. Table 6.7 contrasts the lifetime diagnoses of treatment-seeking opioid and cocaine abusers and those meeting the *DSM-III* criteria for selected Axis I and Axis II disorders (Rounsaville et al., 1991). Both drug-abuse disorders showed higher rates of nearly all psychiatric disorders than the general population sampled in the ECA study. The notable exception was schizophrenia, for which the rates in the drug abusing groups were lower. Contrasting the two types of drug abusers, the opioid abusers had a higher rate of major

TABLE 6.7
Lifetime Diagnoses (RDC Criteria) of Treatment-Seeking Opioid and Cocaine Abusers and Members of the Community (ECA Study)

Disorder	Opioid ($n = 533$)	Cocaine ($n = 298$)	ECA ($n = 3,058$)[a]
Any psychiatric disorder	86.9	70.1	28.8
Major depression	53.9	30.5	6.7
Minor depression	8.4	11.7	0.0
Intermittent depressive personality	18.8	11.1	0.0
Mania	0.6	3.7	1.1
Hypomania	6.6	7.4	0.0
Any mood disorder	74.3	60.7	9.5
Panic disorder	1.3	1.7	1.4
Generalized anxiety disorder	5.4	7.0	0.0
Obsessive–compulsive disorder	1.9	0.3	2.6
Phobia	16.1	13.4	7.8
Any anxiety disorder	34.5	20.8	10.4
Schizophrenia	0.8	0.3	1.9
Schizoaffective, depressed	1.7	0.7	0.0
Schizoaffective, manic	0.4	0.3	0.0
Alcoholism	34.5	61.7	11.5
Antisocial personality disorder (APD)	26.5	7.7	0.0
APD without adult drug exclusion	54.1	32.9	2.1
Childhood attention deficit disorder	22.0	34.9	0.0

Note. From "Psychiatric Diagnoses of Treatment-Seeking Cocaine Addicts," by B. J. Rounsaville et al., 1991, *Archives of General Psychiatry, 48,* p. 48. Copyright 1991 by American Medical Association. Reprinted with permission.
[a]Numbers are percentages meeting *DSM-III* criteria. ECA Catchment Area of New Haven only.

depression, whereas the cocaine abusers had higher rates of mania and alcoholism. J. C. Anthony (1992) found a very high risk rate for a *DSM*-defined manic episode in cocaine users relative to the general population. Such episodes may be precipitated by cocaine, although it is also possible that people with bipolar disorder are attracted to cocaine in their manic phases because of its stimulant properties. Panic attacks and panic disorder were also found, and these also could be a function of the stimulant effects of cocaine.

Cocaine users in general, particularly those who smoke crack cocaine, show more distress and depression, temper and violent behavior, suspiciousness, and hallucinations than heroin users (Flynn et al., 1995; Sterling, Gottheil, Weinstein, & Shannon, 1994). They also tend to be more socially inhibited and self-defeating. It is difficult to say how much of this psychopathology is a function of cocaine itself and how much preceded the cocaine abuse. Violence toward themselves as well as others is not uncommon in cocaine addicts. Cocaine may induce psychotic disorders with delusions and hallucinations, and mood and anxiety disorders during intoxication or withdrawal (*DSM-IV*).

Recent use of cocaine was found to increase the relative risk of suicide attempts by an astounding factor of 62 (J. C. Anthony, 1992). More than one fifth of those who committed suicide in New York City in 1985 were found to have traces of cocaine metabolites in their urine or blood (Marzuk et al., 1992). Persons who used firearms to commit suicide were twice as likely to have used cocaine just prior to suicide. Chronic users are at greatest risk of suicide during withdrawal.

Comparing the ages of onset of the disorders with the age of onset of drug abuse, substance abuse more often preceded major and minor depression, mania, and alcoholism, whereas phobias preceded the onset of substance abuse, and generalized anxiety disorder was equally divided between precedent and subsequent development relative to substance abuse (Rounsaville, Anton, et al., 1991).

Carroll and Rounsaville (1992) compared a treatment-seeking sample of cocaine abusers with those in the community feeling no need for treatment. The incidences of the various lifetime diagnoses in the community and treatment-seeking samples were quite similar. The only difference in current diagnoses was a slightly higher incidence of major depression in the treatment-seeking group compared to the community group.

Between Drugs and Axis II Disorders

Table 6.7 also shows the incidence of the APD disorder and childhood attention deficit disorder in the abuser and ECA control groups. About half of the opioid abusers and a third of the cocaine abusers were diagnosed as APD personalities, compared to 2% in the general population. APD was more prevalent among the opioid addicts, whereas childhood attention deficit disorder was more common among the cocaine abusers.

Brooner et al. (1997) diagnosed a more complete array of personality disorders in 716 opioid abusers. Among the males, 34% were diagnosed with APD and no other personality disorder had an incidence higher than 5%. Among the females, APD was also the most frequently diagnosed personality disorder (15%) with a second-place for borderline disorder (9.5%). Other studies using the DSM-III-R criteria for APD show about the same or even higher rates of APD among drug abusers: intravenous drug users, 44% (Brooner, Greenfield, Schmidt, & Bigelow, 1993); methadone maintenance clients, 61% (Darke, Hall, & Swift, 1994); substance abusers admitted to treatment, 44% men, 27% women (Cottler et al., 1995); and cocaine abusers in treatment, 53% (Carroll, Ball, & Rounsaville, 1993). Intravenous drug users have a particularly high incidence of APD. The lifetime prevalence of APD was found to be about 6% among nonusers of drugs, 21% among those using cannabis only, 35% among those using other drugs, and 69% among abusers practicing intravenous drug use (Dinwiddie, Reich, & Cloninger, 1992). The ECA community survey (L. N. Robins & Regier, 1991) found that about 22% of men and 10% of women with either drug abuse or dependence were diagnosed with APD with a risk ratio of 7.3 for men and 26.6 for women! The high ratio for women is a function of the lower rate of drug abuse for them in the general population.

A comparison of cocaine and heroin abusers on personality disorder diagnoses (Fieldman, Woolfolk, & Allen, 1995) indicated a higher proportion of APD in the heroin abusers (45%) than in cocaine abusers (25%). Both groups were predominantly male, but there was a somewhat higher proportion of men in the heroin group. The incidence of diagnoses of borderline PD was nearly the same in both groups (31–32%).

As was noted for alcoholism, the presence of an antisocial personality in a drug abuser has predictive implications for the type of behavioral and drug history and symptoms. APD diagnoses in drug abusers are associated with an earlier onset of drug abuse (Brooner et al., 1993; K. M. Carroll, Ball, & Rounsaville, 1993; Cottler et al., 1995); more severe dependence (Carroll et al., 1993); a greater abuse of alcohol and other drugs in addition to the primary drug of abuse (Brooner et al., 1993; Cacciola et al., 1994; Cottler et al., 1995); and a poorer outcome of treatment (Carroll et al., 1993).

Substance abusers with APD showed more chronic lying, use of weapons, felony arrests and involvement in criminal activities, violent impulses and aggressive criminal behavior, and less monogamy and more infidelity than non-APD abusers. Cocaine abusers with an APD diagnosis (*DSM-III-R*) had more severe family, social, and psychological problems and a higher comorbidity for affective and alcoholic (but not anxiety) disorders than non-APD abusers (Carroll et al., 1993).

Needle-sharing by intravenous drug users raises the risk of HIV infection. Intravenous drug abusers with APD reported more drug injection and sharing of needles with many partners than did non-APDs (Brooner et al., 1993). Not surprisingly, blood tests for HIV showed about twice the HIV infection rate among the APD drug abusers (17.6%) compared with non-APD abusers (7.8%).

The importance of APD in both alcoholism and drug abuse led Alterman and Cacciola (1991) to consider whether APD substance abuse might be used as a diagnostic subtype of substance abuse. They concluded that although APD substance abusers satisfy many of the criteria for a clinical subtype, the controversies about the APD diagnosis itself would make its use in a subtype of substance abuse problematic.

Extending Alcoholism Types 1 and 2 to Other Substances

Feingold, Ball, Kranzler, and Rounsaville (1996) have attempted to extend Cloninger's (1987a) typology for alcoholism (see Table 6.5) to other psychoactive substances. Subjects were drawn from clinics treating opiate, cocaine, and alcohol abuse, as well as from community and psychiatric samples. Cluster analysis showed that about 60% of the subjects primarily abusing each of four types of substance—alcohol, cocaine, opiates, and marijuana—could be classified as Type As (equivalent to Type 1 alcoholics) and 40% as type Bs (as in Type 2s). However, unlike the classification for alcoholism Types 1 and 2, this classification was not based on family history of drug abuse or recency of onset but was best defined by the use of drugs for relief from unpleasant states, and severity of psychiatric symptoms. A later study showed that the Type Bs had a higher incidence of all types of personality disorders but especially those in the *DSM* cluster that includes APD, borderline, histrionic, and narcissistic types (S. A. Ball, Kranzler, Tennen, Poling, & Rounsaville, in press).

The authors examined the possibility that their A–B distinction might be a function of APD (Type B) vs. non-APD subtypes. Their A–B distinctions remained even after APD-diagnosed individuals were removed from the analysis. However, within cocaine abuse samples, antisocial personality and alcohol dependence severity were the best independent dimensions predicting Type B status (S. A. Ball, Carroll, Barbor, & Rounsaville, 1995). Other variables differentiating the types within cocaine abusers were an earlier age of onset for cocaine abuse, more aggression, criminality, violence, and impairment of social adjustment, and higher scores on sensation seeking in the Type Bs. Within the cocaine group, the type Bs certainly show all the characteristics typical of the APD.

Prevalence and Demographics

Table 6.8 shows the lifetime prevalence rates of use, abuse, and dependence of drugs from the ECA and NCS community surveys. About one third of the men and one fourth of the women in the ECA study (L. N.

TABLE 6.8
Lifetime Prevalence Rates (%) of Drug Use, Abuse, and Dependence
From ECA and NCS Studies

Drug	ECA Study		NCS Study	
	Men	Women	Men	Women
Use	36.6	25.4	55.8	46.4
Abuse only	3.2	2.1	12.5	6.4
Dependence	4.6	2.6	9.2	5.9
Abuse or dependence	7.7	4.8	14.6	9.4

Note. Data derived from *Psychiatric Disorders in America: The Epidemiological Catchment Area Study,* edited by L. N. Robins and D. H. Regier, 1991, New York: The Free Press. Copyright 1991 by The Free Press; and from "Prevalence and Correlates of Drug Use and Dependence in the United States: Results From the National Comorbidity Study," by L. A. Warner et al., 1995, *Archives of General Psychiatry, 52,* pp. 219–229. Copyright 1995 by American Medical Association. Adapted by permission.

NCA study (Warner, Kessler, Hughes, Anthony, & Nelson, 1995) reported having tried an illegal drug at least once in their lives. Cannabis (marijuana, hashish) was by far the drug of highest usage. Despite the fallacious idea that use inevitably leads to abuse and dependence, the prevalence of drug abuse or dependence is only about one fifth of the prevalence of users. There are a lot of casual users out there.

Both community prevalence studies and abuser population studies show higher rates of use, abuse, and dependence for men than for women. The age differences for 12-month prevalences are largest in the youngest age groups and tend to diminish with increasing ages. Age and cohort (generational) differences are often confounded in epidemiological analyses. There is a powerful inverse relationship between age and 12-month usage of drugs, from a 24% usage rate in the 15- to 24-year-old group, to a 5.5% use of drugs in the 45- to 54-year-old group in the NCS study. The ECA study shows a similar decline in both use and abuse of drugs. The cohort born between 1936 and 1945 who finished high school before the drug revolution of the mid-1960s had the lowest rates of drug use, whereas the group who reached their teens in the middle of that revolution had the highest rates of drug use, beginning in their teens and persisting through later ages (Warner et al., 1995). The cohort trends for drug dependence are even stronger. The most recent cohort, coming of age in the 1980s and 1990s, shows the strongest rates of dependence during the middle and late teens. The onset of drug use was about 16 in the earlier cohorts, but in the more recent cohorts, the subjects started using drugs in their preteen years.

The ECA study found higher rates of drug use and abuse or dependence among Whites than among Blacks and higher rates among Blacks than among Hispanics. The NCS study found that although Blacks and Hispanics used drugs less than Whites, those who did use them had a higher rate of lifetime dependence than White users. There is evidence of a stronger tendency toward polydrug use in Whites than in Blacks. Those who can substitute one drug for another or who use drugs for "highs" rather than to normalize feelings are less likely to become dependent on a particular drug.

The ECA study showed the highest rates of drug abuse or dependence in high school and college dropouts and the lowest rates in those who only got through grade school. Similar patterns have been reported for alcohol abuse and antisocial personality, probably reflecting the antagonism between sensation seeking through substances and the completion of educational goals. The NCS study showed more use of drugs in the college-educated groups but more lifetime dependence in the non-college-educated groups.

Drug abuse or dependence was not related to employment status in the ECA study, and in the NCS study was highest in the lowest income group, but this could be a confound with age and probably only reflects legal sources of income.

In the ECA study conducted in selected urban centers, Los Angeles had the highest rates of drug abuse or dependence, Durham (the most rural area) had the lowest rates, and Baltimore and New Haven had intermediate rates. In the NCS study, regions of the United States were compared, and the western part of the country had the highest rates of dependence.

Not surprisingly, the lowest rates of drug disorders were found among stably married people, and the highest rates were in those who were divorced, separated, or cohabiting without benefit of marriage. Drug abuse does not make for stable relationships, particularly if only one of the partners is involved in drugs.

Course

Long-term follow-up studies of substance abusers, whether treated or not, are not encouraging. A large-scale study followed 581 narcotics addicts who entered a treatment program between 1962 and 1964 for 24 years (Hser, Anglin, & Powers, 1993). The first follow-up interviews and urine analyses were done about 12 years later in the mid-1970s, and the second follow-up was conducted in the mid-1980s after another 12 years had elapsed. The average age at which the subjects began using narcotics was 19. They were about 25 when they first entered the program, about 37 at the first follow-up, and about 48 years old at the second one.

Figure 6.1 shows the status of the group members during the years between 1956 and 1986. Between 1956 and 1964 the group showed increases in narcotic use and incarceration. About half of the incarcerations were for drug-related crimes, and another 30% were for property crimes, usually in response to the expense of supporting drug habits. After 1965 there was an increase in abstinence, a decrease in incarceration, and an increase in occasional use as compared to daily use. Methadone maintenance entered the picture in the early 1970s, although it did not account for a large proportion of the group and showed some decline in engagement over the subsequent years. Early deaths began cumulating in the 1970s and 1980s. About 29% of these deaths were due to homicide, suicide, or accident, about 32% to drug overdose, and the remainder were due to alcohol, smoking-related diseases, or other causes. Among the variables predicting an early death were heavy use of alcohol, number of arrests, and the level of cigarette smoking.

A comparison of the addicts who were still drug active with those who were inactive (confirmed by drug tests) was that the active users were heavier smokers, engaged in more polydrug use (including cocaine) in addition to narcotics, had a heavier criminal involvement, and were less often employed (in legal jobs). Based on these differences, one would guess that

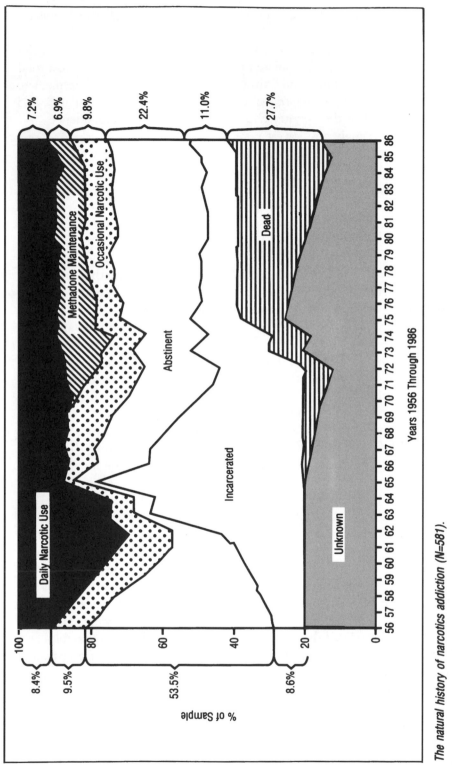

The natural history of narcotics addiction (N=581).

Figure 6.1. The natural history of narcotics addiction over 30 years (*N* = 581). From "A 24-Year Follow-Up of California Narcotics Addicts," by Y.-I. Hser et al., 1993, p. 580. Copyright 1993 by American Medical Association. Reprinted by permission.

employed (in legal jobs). Based on these differences, one would guess that more of the "actives" were antisocial personalities. One sobering finding is that there were no differences between the active and inactive groups in participation in methadone maintenance, therapeutic communities, or other treatment programs.

DIATHESIS

Genetics

A twin study of drug abuse or dependence (*DSM-III*) found a concordance of 63% for identical and 44% for fraternal male twins, and 22% for identical and 15% for fraternal female twins (Pickens et al., 1991). The difference between identical and fraternal twins was significant for men but not for women. The role of genetic factors in drug abuse was modest for men and negligible and unreliable for women. Drug abuse in men was more strongly influenced by shared environmental than by genetic factors, and in women it was primarily a function of specific or nonshared environmental factors. The results were similar to those obtained for alcohol abuse or dependence in the same study, although a breakdown of the alcohol diagnosis showed a stronger genetic factor for alcohol dependence in males. A large study of male twins who served in the U.S. military during the Vietnam era showed that abuse or dependence on any illicit drug could be accounted for by proportions of variance for genetic (.34), for shared environment (.28), and for nonshared environment (.38, Tsuang et al., 1996). In both studies drug abuse in males showed some influence of heredity, but shared environment was of nearly equal or greater influence.

A twin study done with a 5-point substance abuse scale and using a more age-heterogeneous sample found strong effects for age, but weak effects overall for genetic and shared environmental factors (Gynther, Carey, Gottesman, & Vogler, 1994). However, looking at male and female twins separately, it is apparent that males showed genetic and shared environmental effects, but females showed no evidence of genetic effects and strong indications of shared environmental effects.

Taken together, the twin studies suggest that male drug abuse, within the most vulnerable age cohorts, has some genetic sources plus an equal or greater influence of shared environment. Women, however, show little genetic influence on their drug abuse. The explanation for the discrepant findings for men and women might be that drug abuse is mediated by the antisocial and sensation seeking personality traits, which are stronger in men. This would also account for the higher use, abuse, and dependence on drugs in men.

Family studies cannot separate shared environment and genetic influ-

instance, does having an alcoholic parent or sibling produce a higher risk for alcoholism than for drug abuse in children or siblings, or are alcoholic parents and siblings only found in families of drug abusers who have a comorbid alcohol disorder?

Studies are in fair agreement that alcoholism, drug abuse or dependence, antisocial personality disorder, and major depression all occur with greater frequency in the first-degree relatives of persons with drug abuse disorders, both opioid and cocaine abusers (Handelsman et al., 1993; Luthar, Anton, Merikangas, & Rounsaville, 1992; Luthar, Merikangas, & Rounsaville, 1993; Rounsaville et al., 1991). Rates of drug abuse in siblings are much higher than those in parents, and rates in male relatives are higher than those in female relatives. Table 6.9 from the Luthar et al. (1992) study of siblings shows the diagnoses in male and female siblings of opiate abusers and the relative risk ratios compared to the ECA community study. Drug abuse, alcoholism, and antisocial personality disorder are all high risks for siblings of drug abusers, and major depression is also a high risk disorder, particularly for males. The question of specificity was answered by comparing rates of the disorders in relatives of probands with and without the particular comorbid disorders. For instance, the incidence of alcoholism in the siblings of opioid abusers with comorbid alcohol abuse was 47%, compared to 42% in the siblings of opioid abusers without comorbid alcoholism. Similar data for anxiety and depressive disorders and APD revealed no evidence of specificity for the disorders linked to their

TABLE 6.9
Rates of Psychiatric Disorders Among Interviewed Siblings of Opiate Dependents (RDC Criteria) Compared With Rates in the Community

| | Rates per 100 Relatives | | | | | |
| | Siblings | | ECA Community Sample | | Relative Risk | |
Diagnoses	M (%)	F (%)	M (%)	F (%)	M (%)	F (%)
Ns	57	76	4,391	4,948		
Major depression	38.6	31.6	2.6	7.0	14.9	4.5
Any anxiety disorder	24.6	31.6	—	—	—	—
Panic	1.8	7.9	1.2	2.5	1.5	3.2
Phobia	8.8	6.6	10.8	19.4	0.8	0.3
OCD	3.5	5.3	2.6	3.7	1.4	1.4
Alcoholism	49.2	42.1	13.4	3.6	3.7	11.7
Drug abuse	70.2	59.2	7.1	4.3	9.9	13.8
Antisocial personality	40.4	15.8	6.2	1.3	6.5	12.2

Note. M = male; F = female; OCD = obsessive–compulsive disorder. From "Vulnerability to Substance Abuse and Psychopathology Among Siblings of Opioid Abusers," by S. S. Luthar et al., 1992, *Journal of Nervous and Mental Disease, 180,* p. 156. Copyright 1992 by Williams & Wilkins. Reprinted with permission.

presence in the probands. However, the likelihood of alcoholism, APD, and major depression was highly related to drug abuse in the siblings.

The same effects were found for siblings of cocaine abusers as for siblings of opioid abusers: higher rates of alcoholism, drug abuse, and APD, but rates of major depresson and anxiety and minor depressive disorders were lower in siblings of cocaine abusers than in the siblings of opioid abusers (Luthar et al., 1993). Parents of cocaine and opiate abusers had low rates of drug abuse and APD relative to siblings of abusers, but rates of alcoholism and major depression were high compared to the ECA sample (see Table 6.10). The lack of drug disorders in the parents may be a function of the cohort differences. The parents came from a generation in which alcohol abuse was common, but drug abuse was rare. The relation between parental alcoholism and offspring drug abuse (both cocaine and opioids) varied with the extent of parental alcoholism: The lowest rate of drug abuse was found in offspring when neither parent was alcoholic, a higher rate when either parent was alcoholic, and the highest rate in children in families where both parents were alcoholic. The results show that the vulnerabilities to alcoholism and drug abuse share a familial cause, possibly mediated by antisocial personality disorder. For the precise separation of shared environmental and genetic causes we must turn to adoption studies.

The first adoption study compared influences from biological and adoptive parents in alcohol and drug abusers adopted shortly after birth (Cadoret, Troughton, O'Gorman, & Haywood, 1986). Alcohol problems in the biological relatives were related to both alcohol and drug abuse in the adoptees, and antisocial behavior in the biological relatives was related to antisocial personality and alcohol abuse in the adoptees. Parental divorces and separations and disturbance in parents in the adoptive home (alcohol, antisocial, or psychiatric problems) also were related to drug abuse in the adoptees. Figure 6.2 describes a model best fitting the relationships

TABLE 6.10
Rates of Psychiatric Disorders (RDC Criteria) Among Parents of
Cocaine and Opioid Abusers

Diagnoses	Parents, Cocaine		Parents, Opioid		ECA Sample	
	M	F	M	F	M	F
Ns	236	256	190	201	4,391	4,948
Major depression	8.4	13.9	11.1	21.9	2.6	7.0
Alcoholism	42.4	16.8	36.7	15.4	13.4	3.6
Drug abuse	5.8	4.3	4.0	2.5	7.1	4.3
Antisocial personality	4.8	0.8	2.0	0.0	6.2	1.3

Note. M = male; F = female. Based on proband reports rather than direct interviews with parents. Adapted from "Parental Psychopathology and Disorders in Offspring," by S. S. Luthar et al., 1993, *Journal of Nervous and Mental Disease, 181*, p. 353. Copyright 1993 by Williams & Wilkins. Reprinted with permission.

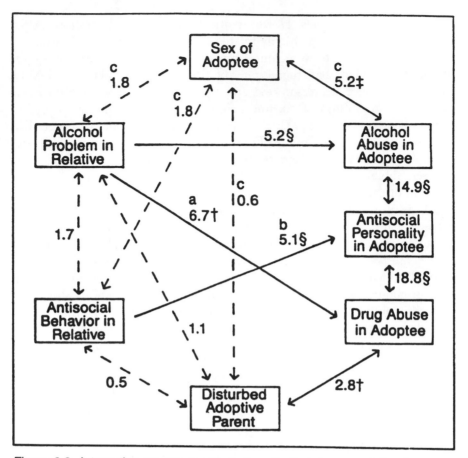

Figure 6.2. Interaction among genetic factors (in first-degree relatives), environmental factors (in adoptive family), and adoptee problems. Disturbed adoptive parents include those with alcohol, antisocial, or psychiatric problems, or divorced, or separated. Dagger indicates $p < .01$, double dagger, $p < .001$; and section mark, $p < .0001$. From "An Adoption Study of Genetic and Environmental Factors in Drug Abuse," by R. J. Cadoret et al., 1986, *Archives of General Psychiatry, 43,* p. 1135. Copyright American Medical Association. Reprinted by permission.

among the genetic (biological relatives) and environmental (adoptive parents) influences on drug and alcohol abuse in the adoptees. The figure shows two genetic pathways to drug abuse: one directly from alcoholism in the biological relatives to drug abuse in the adoptees, the other more indirectly from antisocial behavior in the biological relatives to antisocial personality in the adoptee, which in turn leads to either drug abuse, alcohol abuse, or both.

The second adoption study compared adoptees whose biological parents were known to have alcohol abuse or dependence or antisocial personalities, judged from hospital or prison records, with matched control adoptees whose biological parents did not have such disorders (Cadoret et al., 1995).

A model showing the relationships between substance abuse, personality, and diagnostic variables was constructed from the data (see Fig. 6.3). One pathway leads directly from alcohol abuse in the biological parent to drug abuse in the adoptee, a relationship observed in the family studies and now shown to be genetic. The other pathway is from a biological parent's antisocial personality through aggressivity and antisocial personality in the adoptee to drug abuse or dependency. The disturbance (anxiety or depression) in the adoptive parent is also an indirect influence in abuse through its relationship to APD in the adoptee. The main difference between this model and the one developed from the earlier study (see Fig. 6.2) is that the relationship between antisocial personality in the biological parent and the adopted-away child is mediated through aggressivity in the adoptee, and the nature of disturbance in the adoptive parents seems to be mainly anxiety and depression rather than directly related problems in the adopted parents such as alcoholism and antisocial behavior or marital

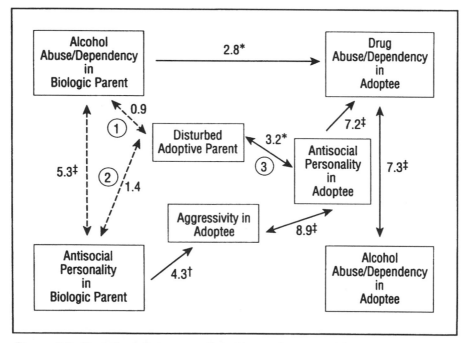

Figure 6.3. Genetic pathways mediated by environmental factors in drug and alcohol abuse. Log-linear interaction diagram of male sample. Asterisk indicates odds ratio significant at 5% level, dagger at 1% level; and double dagger at 0.1% level. Solid arrows indicate relationship found in data; dashed arrows relationship forced into the model to control for selective placement. From "Adoption Study Demonstrating Two Genetic Pathways to Drug Abuse," by Cadoret et al., 1995, *Archives of General Psychiatry, 52,* p. 49. Copyright 1995 by American Medical Association. Reprinted by permission.

problems. Are these problems in the adoptive parents potentiating or interacting causes in producing the antisocial personalities in the adoptees, or are they reactions to the antisocial expressions in them? One cannot say for sure, but given the early appearance of the antisocial personality, it is hard to blame the adopting parents. However, it may be that disturbances in the adopting parents make them less capable of coping with the emerging antisocial tendencies in their child.

The findings of an association between certain alleles of the D2 receptor dopamine receptor gene and alcoholism have been extended to drug abuse (Uhl et al., 1992). Both polydrug abusers and cocaine-dependent males show higher frequencies of either the A1, B1, or both alleles than do nondrug users and those in the general population (Noble et al., 1993; Smith et al., 1992). The cocaine-dependent subjects also had a very high comorbidity for alcoholism (70%) and a high prevalence of alcoholism in their parents. It is possible that these alleles are involved in the broad genetic susceptibility to alcohol *or* drug abuse found in the adoption studies.

Another dopamine gene variant, the allele of the D4 receptor gene which has been associated with the personality trait of sensation (novelty) seeking (Ebstein et al., 1996; Ebstein & Belmaker, 1997), occurs with significantly greater frequency in heroin-dependent subjects than in controls in three studies (Geijer et al., 1997; Kottler et al., 1997; Mel, Kramer, Gritsenko, Kottler, & Ebstein, unpublished, reported in Ebstein & Belmaker, 1997). The association of the D4 receptor gene polymorphism with both the trait of sensation (novelty) seeking in normals and opiate dependence is interesting in view of the finding that most opiate users are high sensation seekers (Craig, 1986; Platt & Labate, 1976), as are most illegal drug users.

Although we know that genes are activated at different stages of life, we normally think of the causal effects from genes as proceeding in one direction. But various *immediate early genes* (IEGs), which are expressed in neurons in response to neurotropic stimuli, have been recently discovered (Grzanna & Brown, 1993). IEGs could regulate the expression of structural genes involved in the formation of synapses or provide a reset mechanism which functions to replenish or restore neurotransmitters already used. Drugs such as cocaine and amphetamine that release dopamine or prevent its reuptake also increase an IEG in the striatum through dopamine D1 receptors. D2 receptor agonists also activate these IEGs (Robertson, 1993). Morphine also may release IEGs in the mesolimbic dopamine system. There is a strong possibility that the vulnerability to the reinforcing qualities of these drugs in some individuals is a function of these IEGs once they are released by the first use of the drugs (Nestler, Bergson, Guitart, & Hope, 1993). This inherited vulnerability might explain why only some of the users of drugs go on to become drug dependent. However, a less direct pathway to drug abuse and dependence may be through inheritance of broad personality traits.

Biological Factors

Even if we did not know the biological mechanisms of drug reward, it would be apparent from the potency of such reward that drugs trigger an unconditioned positive reinforcer. Nearly all of the drugs abused by humans can serve as reinforcers in other species, although susceptibility to "addiction" varies between strains of rodents. The discovery of intrinsic reward areas in the brain by Olds and Milner (1954) proved to be the key to explaining the reinforcing power of drugs, which enables them to compete successfully with all other basic and acquired motives.

The medial forebrain bundle (MFB) shown in Figures 6.4a and 6.4b, is a pathway containing nuclei from which the highest rates of intracranial electrical self-stimulation are elicited from rats, with particular sensitivity in the nucleus accumbens (NA) at one end of this pathway and the ventral tegmental (VT) area at the other end. The curious thing about direct

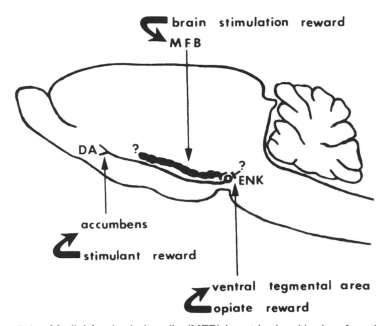

Figure 6.4a. Medial forebrain bundle (MFB) in rat brain with sites for stimulant and opiate reward, activating the ascending mesolimbic dopamine (DA) system in the nucleus accumbens, and opiate reward activating the system in the ventral tegmental area, possibly through enkephalinergic system (ENK). Brain stimulation reward activates descending fibers within the MFB, which transsynaptically activate the ascending DA system. From "Ventral Tegmental Reward System," by M. A. Bozarth, 1987, in *Brain Reward Systems and Abuse* (p. 13), edited by J. Engel et al., New York: Raven Press. Copyright 1987 by Raven Press. Reprinted by permission.

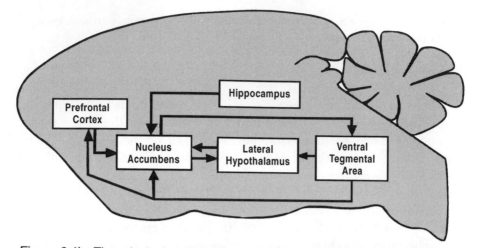

Figure 6.4b. The principal nuclei of the limbic-motor reinforcement system. Sagitta! section from a rat brain. From "Drug Reward and Brain Circuitry: Recent Advances and Future Directions," by K. A. Trujillo et al., 1993, in S. G. Korenman & J. D. Barchas (Eds.), *Biological Basis of Substance Abuse,* Figure 9.1. Copyright 1993 by Oxford University Press, Inc. Used by permission of Oxford University Press, Inc.

stimulation of these areas is that animals do not seem to satiate as they do to natural rewards, rather, they press levers continuously to stimulate these areas, ignoring natural rewards such as food and water, analogous to the fixation on drug reward by addicts. Most classes of drugs abused by humans, including amphetamine, cocaine, opiates, cannabis, ethanol, phencycladine, barbiturates, and benzodiazepines, increase lever-pressing rewarded by brain stimulation in nuclei in the MFB (Wise, Bauco, Carlezon, & Trojniar, 1992). Rats may be trained to press levers to directly infuse many drugs into these nuclei. The stimulant drugs, such as amphetamine, are avidly self-administered by rats in the NA, whereas opiate drugs have their major reinforcement effects in the VT as indicated in Figure 6.4a. However, opiates are also self-administered in the NA and the lateral hypothalamus. The medial prefrontal cortex is another site where rats will self-administer cocaine. As shown in Figure 6.4b these areas constitute an interconnected "limbic-motor reinforcement circuit" (Trujillo et al., 1993) with the NA playing a central role. Apart from its inputs from the other parts of the reinforcement system and other limbic areas, the NA has projections to motor areas which may influence the drive aspects of reward stimulation. Thus, animal models inform us of the basic biological mechanisms involved in drug abuse. Human drug abuse may be influenced by many social factors not shared with other species, but we do share the basic biological mechanisms through which drugs exert their powerful motivating effects.

The MFB contains a major dopaminergic pathway in the brain. Although cocaine and amphetamine potentiate the noradrenaline system as well as the dopaminergic ones, it is the effects on the mesolimbic dopamine systems which are the source of primary reinforcement and subjective euphoria. By inhibiting dopamine reuptake in the reward areas, cocaine prolongs the postsynaptic action of the dopamine in the synaptic cleft (Bloom, 1993; Johanson & Schuster, 1995). Chemical lesions that deplete dopamine in the NA disrupt intravenous self-stimulation through amphetamine or cocaine (Bozarth, 1987).

Sensitization with repeated exposure to a fixed dose of cocaine results in increased locomotor and stereotypic effects (Post, Weiss, Fontana, & Pert, 1992). Repeated administration of cocaine results in elevations of dopamine levels in the NA and increased locomotive activity. Sensitization may account for the initial tendency to become addicted to a drug. Of interest is the fact that the D2 dopamine receptor, which is linked in genetic studies to substance abuse, decreases in sensitivity in response to increased release of dopamine. Because these receptors normally inhibit neuronal firing, their decreased sensitivity results in increases in extracellular dopamine in the NA (Kalivas, Striplin, Steketee, Klitenick, & Duffy, 1992). Depletion of serotonin in the MFB seems to increase the reinforcing effects of cocaine, whereas drugs that are serotonin agonists reduce cocaine self-stimulation.

The pharmacological effects of opioids such as heroin are suppressant rather than stimulant, but they also act on the MFB to release dopamine, although their effects are localized to cells at the VT end of the MFB (Bozarth, 1987). Perhaps the release of dopamine and norepinephrine produces the "rush," an intense euphoria experienced through injection of heroin, which lasts a short time but has been compared to sexual orgasm. The suppressant effects of the drug follow the rush and are more prolonged. The opiates act on endogenous opiate receptors (mu class) which suppress spontaneous discharge in inhibitory neurons, thereby disinhibiting some systems from their control. This kind of disinhibition could occur in the ventral tegmental area (Bloom, 1993). Activation of opioid receptors in the VTA region causes release of dopamine in the VTA terminus in the nucleus accumbens (Trujillo et al., 1993).

Although the secondary effects of cocaine and opiates are quite different, this is probably due to their effects on other systems: the noradrenergic arousal system for cocaine and general suppressant effects of opioids on the brainstem and elsewhere. However, PET scans of polydrug users after injection of cocaine (London et al., 1990a) or morphine (London et al., 1990b) show reduced cerebral metabolism or glucose utilization in most brain regions. Both drugs, however, probably have rewarding or pleasurable effects through direct stimulation or disinhibition of dopamine in the reward centers of the MFB, which are too small to see on PET scans. Thus, the reason for the high comorbidity of abuse among all types of drugs may be partly due to a common biological pathway and the genes for the receptors (such as the D2) which are involved in this pathway. The other pathway is through the personality traits that are associated with disinhibition of behavior and the readiness to take risks of punishment in pursuit of short-term rewards.

In the past, positive reinforcement was blamed for initial drug abuse, but drug dependence was attributed to noxious physiological withdrawal effects. The theory was that one starts taking drugs for pleasure but ends by taking them to avoid pain. But physical withdrawal symptoms are not part of cocaine dependence, and users of diluted heroin also do not suffer from very severe physical withdrawal. Many drug abusers undergo voluntary withdrawal when their habit becomes too expensive or involuntary withdrawal during incarceration. But most relapse even after they no longer face the "pain" of withdrawal. Conditioned cues associated with drug use and inevitable life stress may reactivate drug-taking habits. Dependence on drugs to avoid dysphoria is more characteristic of modern-day abusers. The loss of pleasure and positive feelings is the source of much dependence. The drug abuser has found a direct biochemical pathway to positive mood and can no longer tolerate the indirect and delayed gratifications of life rewards.

PERSONALITY

Antisocial personalities are frequently found within the population of substance abusers so that the traits which are characteristic of the APD should also be found in many drug abusers. These traits include poor socialization, sensation seeking, impulsivity, and aggression. However, major depression is also frequently found in the lifetime comorbid prevalence for drug abuse, although it is not clear whether it is primary or secondary to drug abuse. The Type A and Type B classifications of alcoholics and drug abusers suggest that one subtype (B) should have a likely background of antisocial personality and more history of delinquency and criminality, whereas the other type (A) may have a more neurotic personality, and the substance abuse may be triggered by some traumatic or chronically stressful life events. The Type A substance abuse is particularly frequent among women.

Concurrent studies of drug abusers who are entering or were recently involved in treatment programs often reveal a high degree of neuroticism, anxiety, and depression, but these cannot be assumed to be parts of the pre-drug-abuse personality. A study of drug abusers before and after treatment in a therapeutic community showed abnormal peaks on depression, psychasthenia, schizophrenia, psychopathic deviate (Pd), and mania (Ma) using MMPI scales, but after 3–6 months in the program, scores on most of these were dramatically reduced except for the Pd and Ma scales (Zuckerman et al., 1975). High two-point scale codes involving Pd and Ma, with normal scores on other scales, constitute the classical psychopathic personality profile. When the subjects first entered the program, only 21% showed this type of profile, but by 6 months in the program, 63% of the residents (and 93% of the female residents) were left with this type of profile because scores on the other scales had lowered.

In contrast to the mixed types of MMPI profiles in the above-described group entering inpatient treatment, 61% of a group of outpatient cocaine abusers had the psychopathic profile (Pd–Ma peaks; S. A. Ball, Carroll, Robinson, & O'Malley, 1997) shortly after starting treatment. The rest of the group had high scores on nearly all scales suggestive of severe distress and some with psychotic traits as well. Ratings of severity of psychiatric symptoms were higher for this group than for the group with the uncomplicated psychopathic profiles. It appears that nearly two thirds of drug abusers who are not involved in the immediate stress of a confrontational inpatient drug program, and an even higher proportion of the women who abuse drugs, have an antisocial type of personality even if they do not all meet the diagnostic criteria for the APD diagnosis.

Prospective studies are useful in distinguishing preexistent personality traits from reactive changes. A prospective study over 8 years from early adolescence to young adulthood showed that low law abidance, early use of drugs, and general lack of social conformity were major predictors of late adolescent and early adult use of drugs including cocaine (Newcomb & Bentler, 1990). Antisocial traits precede and predict drug use. A study following a cohort of Swedish children from birth to 28 years of age found that childhood ratings of high novelty (sensation) seeking, low harm-avoidance, and low reward dependence predicted adult alcoholism (Cloninger, Sigvardsson, & Bohman, 1988). A similar study of French-speaking children in Canada included a drug abuse as well as an alcohol abuse outcome (Masse & Tremblay, 1997). Teachers' ratings of high novelty-seeking and low harm-avoidance in children at ages 6 and 10 predicted drug and alcohol abuse at ages 11–15. Prediction at 6 years of age was nearly as effective as that from 10 years of age. However, reward dependence was not predictive of later substance abuse.

Another longitudinal study in New Zealand assessed personality at age 18 and psychopathology at 15 and 21 years of age (Krueger, Caspi, Moffitt, Silva, & McGee, 1996). The authors compared a substance dependent group, a substance dependent group with other comorbid disorders, and a control group free of any disorders. The pure substance-dependent group scored higher than the disorder-free group on alienation (a sense of victimization and betrayal), aggression, and lower on control, harm-avoidance, and traditionalism, the three traits making up the superfactor of constraint. The group with comorbid Axis I disorders in addition to substance dependence were also higher on stress reaction and alienation than the pure substance abuse group and the disorder-free group. These two scales are part of a negative emotionality or neuroticism factor. The results suggest that differences in general neuroticism stem from the co-morbid disorders rather than from the substance abuse disorder itself. There were no differences between pure and comorbid substance disorder groups on the constraint factor, indicating that impulsivity and nonconformity are central traits in the substance-abusing personality. The negative emotion-ality and constraint factors at age 18 were predictive of drug abuse at age 21.

Trull and Sher (1994) did a concurrent study of psychopathology and personality using the Costa and McCrae (1992) Five-Factor Model test and *DSM-III-R* criteria for diagnosis. Profile shapes of alcohol and drug abuse or dependent disorders on the five factors look alike, but the scores on the scales were more extreme in the drug abuse or dependent group. Drug abuse or dependence was characterized by high scores on openness and low scores on conscientiousness. Openness to experience is related to at least one type of sensation seeking (experience seeking), and consci-entiousness has a moderately high negative correlation with impulsive sen-sation seeking in the alternative five-factor system (Zuckerman et al., 1993).

Sensation seeking has been studied in relation to substance abuse since the early 1970s. Studies of adolescent high school students in several countries and young draftees in Sweden have shown correlations between sensation seeking and drug use in general, and between all types of illegal abused drugs, including marijuana, hashish, stimulants, depressants, hallu-cinatory drugs, inhalants, tranquilizers and others (research summarized in Zuckerman, 1979; 1983, 1986, 1994). Studies that also used scales of neu-roticism or anxiety usually found no relationship to drug use or a restricted one to use of barbiturates or other depressant drugs. Among the four SSS subscales, the disinhibition (Dis) and experience seeking (ES) subscales are most consistently related to drug use.

A prospective study in Israel found that sensation seeking predicted use of alcohol, hashish, and depressant drugs, but trait and state anxiety and depression were only related to the use of depressant drugs (Teichman, Barnes, & Rahav, 1989). A multiple regression showed that only the sen-sation seeking trait added significantly to the prediction of drug use.

A study of American adolescents attempted to predict initiation or changes in drug use 3 years later using the Disinhibition (Dis) subscale of the SSS (Bates, Labourie, & White, 1985). Initial levels of Dis and changes in Dis over the 3 years predicted drug use. Those whose Dis scores rose tended to increase drug usage, whereas those who had initially high Dis scores which decreased and who already had used drugs at the earlier time of assessment tended to level off in substance abuse. Those who were low in Dis at both periods simply never used drugs.

Studies of college students and other young adult populations have yielded similar results over the years. Zuckerman, Neary, & Brustman (1970) found that 74% of high and 23% of low sensation seekers among college students reported having used at least one illegal drug. Twenty years later, at a university in the same area, Kumar, Pekala, and Cummings (1993) found that 69% of high and 23% of low sensation seekers used an illegal drug. SSS scores, particularly ES and Dis, are highest in polydrug users and lowest in nonusers, with marijuana users somewhere in between (Galizio, Rosenthal, & Stein, 1983; Segal, Huba, & Singer, 1980). Marijuana is on the pathway to abuse of other drugs, but alcohol precedes marijuana on the pathway. Sensation seeking first distinguishes the heavy users of alcohol from normal social drinkers and then those who use illegal drugs from those who stick to alcohol or marijuana.

Sensation seeking is related to the number or variety of drugs used but not to use of specific drugs. However, those who use drugs to self-medicate for anxiety or depression tend to abuse nonprescriptive tranquilizers, particularly among medical students and physicians who have easy access to these drugs (Golding & Cornish, 1987; McAuliffe et al., 1984). Both high and low sensation seekers prefer the stimulant amphetamine to the tranquilizer diazepam in blind testing in experimental settings, suggesting that diazepam does not provide much in the way of pleasurable sensations (E. N. Carrol, Zuckerman, & Vogel, 1982; De Wit, Uhlenhuth, & Johanson, 1986).

Among young adult drug abusers, high sensation seekers tend to abuse all types of drugs, including heroin (Craig, 1982, 1986; Platt & Labate, 1976), marijuana, cocaine, amphetamines, and barbiturates (S. A. Ball et al., 1994; Kohn, Barnes, & Hoffman, 1979). The highest sensation seekers are polydrug abusers, characterized by the number and variety of drugs they use concurrently or over their life history rather than by the particular drugs they abuse (S. A. Ball et al., 1994; Galizio, Rosenthal, & Stein, 1983; Kern, Kenkell, Templer, & Newell, 1986; Sutker, Archer, & Allain, 1978). White substance abusers tend to abuse more drugs than Black or Hispanic drug abusers, so that sensation seeking correlates less with number of drugs in the latter two populations (Kaestner, Rosen, & Apel, 1977).

Although most young drug users use more than one drug, some of the older users do fixate on one drug, such as heroin or cocaine, and only use that type of drug. Spotts and Shontz (1984) screened over 1,000 drug abusers in the community who were not in drug programs to find exclusive one-drug abusers of four types of drugs: amphetamines, barbiturates or sedatives, opiates, and cocaine. An optimal level-of-arousal theory suggested that exclusive stimulants users (amphetamine and cocaine) should score higher than non-drug-using controls, whereas exclusive users of depressants (opiates and barbiturates) should score lower than normal. Exclusive chronic amphetamine users were the highest sensation seekers, as predicted, but cocaine users were the lowest, and opiate and sedative users were not different from controls. Chronic cocaine users often undergo considerable personality changes, becoming more socially withdrawn, anxious, and paranoid. These users scored lower on an extraversion scale than the other groups. After 6 years of daily cocaine use, they were not looking for novel experiences from the drug. The motives of early drug users tend to be novelty and excitement seeking, and the drugs are used to enhance social and sexual activities. Chronic daily drug users tend to seek only the sensations provided by the drug itself or just to feel normal and avoid withdrawal symptoms such as anxiety and depression.

Personality variables such as sensation seeking also have diagnostic and behavioral significance within substance abuser groups. Cocaine abusers were classified as Type As and Bs (as described previously, Type Bs represent the more severe addictions and antisocial types) and the B types scored higher than the As on all of the Sensation Seeking subscales (S. A. Ball et al., 1995). The higher sensation seekers among cocaine abusers have more comorbid substance abuse on alcohol and other drugs and are more likely to have an APD diagnosis themselves, as well as a family history of conduct disorder, or attention deficit, *but not of drug or alcohol abuse or affective disorders*, in their first-degree relatives.

The family studies previously discussed suggested that inheritance of a tendency toward substance abuse represented a different pathway to drug abuse than inheritance of an APD tendency. These data suggest that the sensation seeking trait is in the APD pathway. Sensation seeking may also be in the alternate pathway to opioid addiction. Opioid abusers and their siblings who also abused drugs scored higher than their non-drug-abusing siblings on both the general and all five of the sensation seeking subscales (Kosten, Ball, & Rounsaville, 1994).

S. A. Ball (1995) has also used the broader alternative five-factor questionnaire (Zuckerman et al., 1993) in studies of cocaine abusers. The Impulsive Sensation Seeking (ImpSS), Neuroticism–Anxiety (N-Anx), and Aggression–Hostility (Agg-Host) scales were all correlated with interview-based ratings of severity of drug abuse. The ImpSS had the highest correlation with severity of drug abuse and was the only scale correlated with severity of alcohol abuse. ImpSS, N-Anx, and Agg-Host also correlated with rated severity of psychiatric impairment, and N-Anx alone correlated with severity of family and social problems.

The cocaine abusers who scored high on Agg-Host had a greater history of violence and suicidality. High scores on ImpSS and N-Anx were found in those who continued to use drugs throughout treatment and who had a higher percentage of positive urine samples. Similar but marginal effects were found for Agg-Host. Those who scored high on ImpSS kept fewer treatment appointments, were less likely to stay in treatment for at least 1 month or to complete treatment. Those who scored high on N-Anx and Agg-Host were more likely to be referred for inpatient treatment.

The Type Bs were higher than the Type As on ImpSS, N-Anx, and Agg-Host, and lower on Sociability (Sy). The Type Bs were more commonly men involved in the criminal justice system, who began using cocaine earlier and were relatively free of psychiatric symptoms other than those connected with drug abuse. A contrast of the Type A and Bs on the NEO Big Five personality factors (Costa & McCrae, 1992) and Cloninger's (1987a) Temperament and Character Inventories showed similar personality differences (S. A. Ball et al., in press). Type Bs were higher on Novelty Seeking, Neuroticism, and Harm Avoidance, and Type As were higher on Agreeableness, Conscientiousness, and Self-Directedness. The major inconsistency with the conceptualization of the Type Bs as antisocial personality types is their high scores on neuroticism and harm-avoidance scales. This could be a function of their greater current stress because of situational factors in their lives at the time of testing.

The alternative five personality traits were used in a study of pregnant cocaine abusers (S. A. Ball & Schottenfeld, 1997). Both ImpSS and Agg-Host were related to a history of violence and N-Anx was strongly related to anxiety, depression, and suicidality. In addition, those with a history of many sex partners and those who had a history of exchanging sex for drugs and money were higher on ImpSS and Agg-Host. N-Anx was also high in those with many sex partners, as well as those who engaged in prostitution, putting them at greater risk for HIV infection. Women who reported being tested many times for HIV scored higher on N-Anx and Agg-Host with a marginal tendency on ImpSS.

STRESS

As with alcoholism, stress may be a contributing cause of drug abuse, a result of drug abuse, or both. Stress may not be the cause of drug abuse, but it is an important factor in those seeking treatment. Treatment-seeking abusers did not differ from the untreated users in the community in severity of cocaine use, rates of other comorbid disorders, or strategies used to limit or cope with the consequences of their addiction (K. M. Carroll & Rounsaville, 1992). The main difference between the two groups was that the treatment-seekers were experiencing more problems with their families, friends, and coworkers, and were reacting to these stresses with serious depression and anxiety. Members of the group seeking treatment were more likely to be married and living with a spouse or other family, and more likely to hold full-time jobs. In other words, they were more involved with others who would pressure them to seek treatment. Their stress was a function of their abuse of drugs in non-accepting social environments.

Deykan and Buka (1997) examined the role of posttraumatic stress disorder (PTSD) in young adolescents who already met the full *DSM-III-R* criteria for substance dependence. Most were using drugs and alcohol. Two thirds to three fourths of them had a parent who had been treated for alcohol abuse, nearly half had a parent who had been treated for drug abuse, and two thirds of the females and 42% of the males had a parent treated for mental health problems. It is likely that much of the trauma they experienced was in their own homes as well as in the community. Rates of PTSD were about 30% overall, but nearly twice as high in the females as in the males. PTSD was the most common diagnosis in the group, exceeding that for depressive disorders. Reported trauma was even more frequent, reported by 75% of the subjects. The most frequent kinds of trauma were seeing someone hurt or killed, threats of injury, physical assault, sudden injury or accident, and rape (for the females). Females were more likely to develop PTSD after a trauma than males. The investigators examined the sequences of trauma and the beginning of substance dependence. Females were more likely to have experienced the trauma before they became substance dependent, whereas males were more likely to have had the traumatic event after they became dependent. Substance dependence appeared to be the primary disorder in males, leading to behaviors and interactions in which violence became more likely. As was the case with alcoholism, the Type 1 (or Type A of substance abuse), which comes from depressive or anxious reactions to early stressful events, is more characteristic of females (and some males) than of most males who become drug dependent.

Alcohol abuse may be a more common method of coping with stressful experiences than other types of drug abuse. Breslau and Davis (1992) studied persons from the community who had experienced trauma. Only 9% had a PTSD. They compared those with chronic (more than a year) PTSD with those experiencing a nonchronic PTSD episode. The chronic group had higher comorbid rates of most major disorders including mood and anxiety disorders *and* alcohol abuse or dependence, but drug abuse or dependence rates were higher in the nonchronic cases. Either drugs are more effective than alcohol in getting over PTSD or, more likely, drugs are generally used for pleasure rather than for self-medication after stressful life events. Barbiturates or tranquilizers would be more likely candidates for dealing with anxiety than would cocaine or heroin, but these suppressant drugs have effects similar to alcohol, and alcohol is both legal and cheaper.

FAMILY AND SOCIAL FACTORS

Because availability of drugs, price, and prevalence of use are strong determinants of usage in any society, they determine the likelihood of use by the person who is vulnerable by genetic and personality factors. But even in families in which drug abuse is prevalent, some of the children may abjure drugs and seek a more conforming and productive role in society. Sometimes it may be simply a matter of being able to afford the drugs. In two U.S. communities, there was an increased risk of starting or increasing cocaine use in persons who had recently gotten a job after a period of unemployment or who had a sudden increase in income (J. C. Anthony, 1992). In those persons who are not employed, the willingness to engage in criminal activities or in prostitution to pay for drugs is a crucial factor. Marriage lowers the risk factor unless one is married to a drug user, although it could simply be that drug users are less likely to be married or to stay married.

Concordance in drug use between best friends in adolescence and adult spouse or partner dyads is high and is higher for illicit than for licit drugs at both stages of life (Kandel, Davies, & Baydar, 1990). To some extent this must be due to selection of like-minded friends and partners, but two persons may be attracted for reasons other than their propensity to use drugs. Once one member of a dyad or larger group starts to use drugs, both observational learning and social reinforcement may cause the other to start drug use. The trait of sensation seeking is a strong source of assortative mating (Farley & Mueller, 1978; Lesnik-Oberstein & Cohen, 1984), and if two partners share this trait, they might be both open to drugs in their search for new experiences.

Experiences within the family may be important because alcoholism or drug abuse in parents has been shown to be a direct risk factor in drug abuse in children. But even when there is no such direct influence, poor relationships with parents and lack of social support from them can negate their potential prosocial antidrug influences (Newcomb & Bentler, 1990). Early adolescent drug use leads to less academic orientation, less social conformity, and more emotional distress; by late adolescence it causes more drug and cocaine involvement, decreased grades, and lack of social support from the family. Finally, increased cocaine involvement may lead to dealing cocaine, other criminal activities, and prostitution. Early drug use thus may initiate a vicious cycle leading to social alienation and drug dependence. For those who attempt to break out of the cycle, employment possibilities may be limited to low-paid and boring jobs because of their low educational attainment. Such jobs are unsatisfying to high sensation seekers.

PATHOLOGICAL GAMBLING

Pathological gambling (PG) is included in a *DSM* category called "Impulse Control Disorders Not Elsewhere Classified," along with disorders such as kleptomania, pyromania, and intermittent explosive disorder.

Clearly this is a "wastebasket" category. PG cannot be included in the substance abuse disorder category for the obvious reason that it does not involve a substance. But the characteristics of the disorder, its comorbidities, and even its genetic and biochemical influences shared with substance abuse disorders suggest that it would be classified with them in a more rational taxonomy, perhaps under the label of "habit disorder." Like alcoholism, PG begins with a socially and legally acceptable (now in most communities in the United States) habit which stays within the limits of normal recreation for most persons, but progresses to abuse and dependence in a minority.

Gambling as recreation begins before substance abuse. Children gamble for marbles, playing cards, and even money. They bet on the outcome of events. There is something in the power to predict the outcome of essentially uncontrollable events which makes gambling appealing beyond the tangible rewards that come from winning. Capitalism depends upon small groups of bookies called stockbrokers, and the millions of people who gamble through them in the stock markets. In the past decades, we have seen a remarkable expansion of legalized gambling in casinos and state-sponsored lotteries. Millions of people who would only occasionally gamble with each other can now go to legal gambling casinos or card rooms in their own communities. A minority of them will become pathological gamblers. Just as availability influences the prevalence of substance abuse, ease of gambling inevitably increases the prevalence of PG. Lester (1994) tested this hypothesis by correlating the number of legal gambling opportunities in each state with the number of chapters of Gamblers Anonymous (GA) per capita in the states. The total number of outlets was significantly correlated with GA chapters, but correlations of GA with some types of outlets were high (slot machines, sports betting, casinos, cardrooms), whereas others were low (bingo, charitable gambling, most lottery forms, and off-track betting). The differences in correlations probably reflect the preferences of pathological as opposed to social gamblers.

When does such a universal activity become "pathological?" What makes some persons vulnerable to abuse? The answers to such questions can only be answered by research, but the amount of research in this area is minuscule compared to the millions of dollars spent on alcohol and drug abuse research. Perhaps the recognition of this disorder in books such as this one will change this state of scientific neglect.

Diagnosis

PG was introduced as an official diagnosis in *DSM-III*, although psychoanalysts, beginning with Freud (1928/1959), regarded PG as a neurotic disorder. The original definition of PG in *DSM-III* defined it in terms of two major criteria: (a) an inability to resist impulses to gamble, and (b) disruption of family, personal, or work relationships and activities. The *DSM-IV* symptoms of PG are given below along with my comparisons with substance abuse disorders, which appear in parentheses. Note that the last two criteria, particularly 10, are more unique to PG:

1. A preoccupation in thinking, time, and money with gambling activities (like the substance abuser whose activities revolve around getting and using the drug).
2. A need to gamble with increasing amounts of money in order to reach the sought for state of euphoria (analogous to the development of tolerance in substance dependence).
3. Unsuccessful attempts to stop gambling (like dependence in substance abuse).
4. Restlessness or irritability when attempting to stop gambling (like withdrawal symptoms in substance dependence).
5. Gambling used to escape from stress or relieve negative moods (as substances are used for this purpose).
6. Lying to family or therapist to conceal continuing heavy involvement in gambling (also a characteristic of many substance abusers in regard to their use of the substance).
7. Committing illegal acts such as forgery, fraud, theft, or embezzlement to finance gambling (like the need for criminal activity to finance expensive drug habits).
8. Risking or losing significant relationships, jobs, educational or career opportunities because of gambling (similar to the risks of substance abuse).
9. Using others to help extricate oneself from a desperate financial situation due to gambling losses (e.g., inability to pay the rent or meet basic family expenses).
10. Urgent needs to keep gambling or return another day to recoup the losses of the previous day. This pattern is called "chasing," and it is a basic part of pathological gambling which distinguishes it from normal gambling. The compulsion to get even and the belief that if one just keeps gambling, one's luck is bound to change are fatal flaws in the pathological gambler's strategy. Increasingly larger bets at greater risks are characteristic in this desperate "end-game."

Prevalence and Comorbidity

PG was not surveyed in the ECA or NCS national prevalence studies, but a number of smaller surveys have been done in selected states in the United States and in some other countries. These studies are listed in Table 6.11 along with the prevalence rates in selected psychiatric, substance

TABLE 6.11
Prevalence Rates of Pathological Gamblers Among Community, Substance Abuser, and General Psychiatric Populations

	Samples Taken From	n	Subjects	Ages	M (%)	Crit.	PG (%)
Community surveys							
Volberg (1994)	5 states, U.S.	4,500	community	>18	43	SOGS	1.3
Volberg & Steadman (1988)	NY state, U.S.	1,000	community	>18	44	SOGS	1.4
Ladoucer (1991)	Quebec, Canada	1,002	community	>18	46	SOGS	1.2
Legarda et al. (1992)	Seville, Spain	598	community	>18	45	SOGS	1.7
Sommers (1988)	So. PA & NJ, U.S.	164	community	>17	52	DSM-III	3.4
Becona et al. (1996)	Galicia, Spain	1,615	community			DSM-IV	1.5
Chen et al. (1993)	Hong Kong, China	1,691	community	>18	48	DSM-III	1.6
Student surveys							
Lesieur & Klein (1987)	4 NJ high schools	892	students	16–18		DSM-III	5.7
Lesieur et al. (1991)	6 colleges in 5 states	1,771	students	$M = 22$	44	SOGS	5.5
Lumley & Roby (1995)	urban university	1,147	students	Median = 19	40	SOGS	3.1
Substance abusers							
Feigelman et al. (1995)	methadone clinic	220	opiate abusers	>30	67	SOGS	7.0
Spunt et al. (1995)	methadone clinic	117	opiate abusers	$M = 39$	60	SOGS	16.0
Daghestani et al. (1996)	veterans hospital	276	substance abusers	$M = 41$	98	SOGS	33.0
Lesieur & Heineman (1988)	2 therapeutic communities	100	young substance abusers	$M = 17$	81	SOGS	14.0
Miller & Westmeyer (1996)	veterans hospital	211	alcoholics			SOGS	17.0
Lesieur et al. (1986)	psychiatric hospital	458	alcoholics		71	DSM-III	9.0
General psychiatric							
Miller & Westmeyer (1996)	veterans hospital	201	gen. psychiatric patients			SOGS	12.0
Lesieur & Blume (1990)	psychiatric hospital	105	mostly mood disorders	18–65		SOGS	6.7

Note. M (%) = percentage of males in sample; PG = pathological gambling; Crit. = criteria used for definition of pathological gambling; SOGS = South Oaks Gambling Screen.

abuse, and offender samples. Most of these studies have used a self-report instrument developed by Lesieur and Blume (1987) for the diagnosis of PG: the South Oaks Gambling Screen (SOGS). The SOGS has demonstrated good reliability and validity in terms of relationship to ratings based on interviews with clients and the *DSM-III* criteria, and based on ratings of counselors and family members. However, it does depend on accuracy of self-report and trust in confidentiality since some of the admissions concern illegal activities.

The largest survey, done in five states in the United States with a total of 4,500 respondents, shows an incidence of 1.3% for PG (Volberg, 1994). An earlier study in New York state had yielded a PG prevalence of 1.4% (Volberg & Steadman, 1988). These and other studies with the SOGS use a cutting score of 5 or higher to define "probable" PG. Other broad community surveys using the SOGS criteria in Quebec, Canada (Ladoucer, 1991), Seville, Spain (Legarda, Babio, & Abreu, 1992), Galicia, Spain (Becona, Lorenzo, & Fuentes, 1996), and Hong Kong (C.-N. Chen et al., 1993) have shown remarkably similar prevalences of PG ranging from 1.2% to 1.7%. A community study in southern Pennsylvania and New Jersey used a different criterion for PG (the ISR Questionnaire) and found a higher prevalence rate of 3.4% (Sommers, 1988). In most of these studies, the rates for men are at least twice as high as those for women.

Studies of younger adolescent populations in high schools and colleges have shown higher rates of PG than broad community surveys. Lesieur et al. (1991) found a PG prevalence of 5.5% among students at six universities in five states (PG range 4–8%) of the United States using the SOGS criterion. Lumley and Roby (1995), also using the SOGS, reported a prevalence of PG of 3.1% among midwestern urban university students in Detroit. Using questionnaire criteria based on the *DSM-III*, Lesieur and Klein (1987) found a PG prevalence of 5.7% among students from four high schools in New Jersey. Overall, rates of PG in adolescent school populations using the SOGS criterion range from 3% to 8% compared to the range of 1% to 2% in community surveys. The most popular forms of gambling for college students are playing slot and poker machines, playing cards for money, and playing casino games (Lesieur et al., 1991). For high school students card playing, casino gambling, and sports betting are the gambling forms of choice (Lesieur & Klein, 1987).

Comorbidity

The question of comorbidity of PG and substance abuse can be first addressed by comparing the rates of PG among groups of substance abusers and dependents in treatment units shown in Table 6.11. These rates range from 7% to 33% with most outside of the range of the rates given above for community and college populations. The highest rate (33%) of PG was found in a Veterans Administration inpatient hospital for substance abuse (Daghestani, Elenz, & Crayton, 1996). The patients diagnosed as pathological gamblers reported earlier ages of first drug use, alcohol use, and gambling, and more frequent alcohol use than the non-PG substance abusers. The lowest PG comorbidity rate (7%) was found in a methadone outpatient treatment center (Feigelman, Kleinman, Lesieur, Millman, & Lesser, 1995). The measure of PG correlated with lifetime comorbid alcohol abuse and current alcohol use, major drug problems in past year, and current use of heroin (despite participation in the methadone program). A majority of the pathological gamblers in another methadone clinic reported that they had used heroin or alcohol most of the time or always when they were gambling, and that they used heroin, alcohol, and cocaine prior to or while gambling (Spunt, Lesieur, Hunt, & Cahill, 1995). Many describe the high from drugs as adding to the excitement derived from gambling, but nearly all of them said that the drug use was more important than the gambling. Among young drug abusers being treated in a therapeutic community, 40% said that they had gambled while drinking or doing drugs some of the time, and 25% said they had all of the time (Lesieur & Heineman, 1988). Although the rate of PG in a substance abuse hospital was only 9%, it was 13% among cocaine users, and 18% among heroin users (Lesieur, Blume, & Zoppa, 1986).

Those who treat specific forms of drug abuse are usually aware of the strong tendency to substitute one drug for another, but they often are not as aware of the comorbid gambling disorder. A cure of the drug abuse problem can leave even more money for gambling, and the consequences of PG can be as severe as those associated with drug abuse. At some phase of PG when the gamblers are chasing their losses and have exhausted the patience and resources of those they have borrowed from in the past, they may turn to white-collar crime, if in a business occupation, or theft if otherwise employed or unemployed.

To what extent is the criminal activity a function of comorbidity between PG and APD? Among a PG group defined by *DSM-III* criteria, 15.5% met the full *DSM-III* criteria for APD, 10% met the childhood but not the adult criteria, and 25% met the adult but not the childhood criteria (Blaszczynski, Steel, & McConaghy, 1997). The APD rate of 15.5% is much higher than would be expected in the general population, but not extraordinary compared to the rates of APD among male alcoholics or drug abusers. Those meeting the adult criteria were probably only engaging in crime as a consequence of their pathological gambling. Criminal activity is highly correlated with the SOGS index of PG (Lesieur & Heineman, 1988), but the rate of PG among young imprisoned offenders in one study was quite low (2.2%) although 12% were classified as "excessive gamblers" (Madden, Swinton, & Gunn, 1992). Theft or burglary, rather than robbery or crimes of violence, were characteristic of the gamblers. A higher proportion of the gambler offenders had early criminal convictions and more extensive records prior to the current conviction.

High rates of major depression have been reported for gamblers in treatment (Berg & Kühlhorn, 1994). Nearly three fourths of a group of gamblers reported an episode of major depression around the time that they first stopped gambling, but these episodes are likely to be reactive rather than indications of a predisposition to depression (Linden, Pope, & Jonas, 1986). Gamblers in treatment are those who are most likely to become dysphoric as a consequence of their life stresses. What of those not in treatment?

A group of pathological gamblers from a prevalence study along with others in that study were given the Beck Depression Inventory (BDI). Using a conventional cut-off score for depression, 21% of the gamblers could be classified as suffering from a depressive disorder as compared with 9% of the nongamblers. The difference in depression scores was particularly marked for the women. A study using American college students also found that BDI-measured depression was higher among problem gamblers than in the remainder of the population (Lumley & Roby, 1995).

Although larger studies are needed, it is likely that there is some comorbidity between PG and depression even in those who never sought treatment. But the question remains: Is depression primary to gambling or secondary to it? One would expect that the rates of PG in acute psychiatric hospitals would be high considering the prevalence of depression in these places, but, although they are higher than those in the general population, they are not extraordinary (Lesieur & Blume, 1990; Miller & Westermeyer, 1996). The gambler tends to be restless, bored, and irritable when not gambling, excited and elated during gambling, and depressed after major losses. Apart from the loss of money, losing seems to challenge the basis of their self-esteem and feelings of power and control. One might say they have a bipolar mood disorder linked to their gambling outcomes rather than to endogenous factors.

Alexithymia is a newly defined disorder, characterized by difficulties in identifying and communicating feelings and a concrete externally oriented cognitive style, which has been found with significant frequency in patients with alcoholism and other addictive disorders. A general sample of university students was screened with a standard scale for alexythymia and the SOGS (Lumley & Roby, 1995). Among the 3% classified as PG using the SOGS, nearly a third were classified as having alexithymia compared with only 11% of control participants. As with depression, we cannot be sure whether the emotional problem is a cause or a result of PG.

Pathological gamblers are notably restless and easily bored when not gambling. This suggests that many may have had a background of attention-deficit hyperactivity disorder (ADHD) when younger. Ideally one should have a longitudinal study to test this hypothesis, but only a retrospective study has been done. Male pathological gamblers completed a questionnaire describing their childhood traits which included some of the classical signs of ADHD and reported more primary and associated signs related to ADHD than did controls (Carlton et al., 1987). Follow-ups of childhood ADHD-diagnosed children are needed to check this result.

Demographic Characteristics

Community-wide and high school and college studies all show more men than women among those identified as PG. Volberg's (1994) community sample was 43% male; however, males constituted 76% of the group identified as PG. Among those coming into professional treatment programs, over 90% are male, suggesting that female gamblers are less likely to seek treatment or their problems are less severe. The latter is unlikely considering the extreme criteria of dysfunction in the SOGS instrument.

Most community surveys show that although the majority of pathological gamblers are White, non-Whites are overrepresented in the GP population, but underrepresented and even rare in the treatment population. People of Jewish descent are underrepresented in alcohol treatment groups, but overrepresented in gambling treatment groups (Comings et al., 1996; Lorenz & Shuttlesworth, 1983; Lowenfeld, 1979). The GP population tends to be less educated, and more of them lack a high school degree with the exception of the sample from Quebec (Ladoucer, 1991) where more of the problem and pathological gamblers have a high school education. Relatively more people in the PG population are unmarried than in the general population, which is fortunate, considering the negative impact of the pathological gamblers on their spouses (Lorenz & Shuttlesworth, 1983). Income is lower among members of the PG group, which is not surprising considering their lower education. Those who can afford to lose less are most involved in PG, contrary to the stereotype of the middle-class gambler.

Among high school and college students, there is little association of PG with parental social class, although there is some with the general social class of the neighborhood (Lesieur & Klein, 1987). Not surprisingly, grades are inversely related to PG. Proximity of the high schools to Atlantic City (where the casinos are) had no relationship to PG rates in the schools, but many students diagnosed with PG had managed to get into the casinos with fake identification cards and even have drinks and gamble there. However, over the 50 states there is a significant relationship between the number of Gamblers Anonymous chapters per capita and the availability of casinos (Lester, 1994).

Course

The longest follow-up of PG is on a group of 120 gamblers who had been given a brief 5-day behavioral treatment for PG (Blaszczynski,

McConaghy, & Frankova, 1991). The follow-up periods ranged from 2 to 9 years posttreatment with an average interval of 5½ years. Those who consented to a follow-up were asked to retake some tests and classify themselves as abstinent (for at least a month preceding the follow-up), controlled (gambling without a sense of impaired control or adverse financial consequences), or uncontrolled. Reports of abstinence or controlled gambling were checked with informants from the family.

At follow-up, 29% of the group was abstinent, but only 14% had been abstinent since the treatment. The others had experienced brief relapses in the interval but came back to abstinence. Of the remainder, 29% engaged in controlled gambling, and 33% were still uncontrolled in their gambling. However, 17 participants had refused to be restudied or were incarcerated at the time of the follow-up, usually for gambling-related crimes. If we count the latter group as probably uncontrolled, then the percentages of outcome are reduced to 23% abstinent, 30% controlled, and 48% uncontrolled. The results are not unlike those for treated substance abuse discussed previously in this chapter. How one regards the prognosis depends upon opinion of the controlled group. If this is regarded as a successful outcome, then a majority of the cases of PG will recover. But if this group is regarded as problematic and likely to revert to uncontrolled gambling, then the prognosis is bleak.

DIATHESIS

Genetics

Eisen et al. (1998), using a large sample of male twins, found that heavy gambling without PG symptoms had a heritability of .35, but this increased to .54 when there were at least two symptoms of PG from the *DSM-III* present. Systematic family prevalence studies for PG of the type done for other disorders could not be found, but some of the studies of prevalence and comorbidity already discussed included questions about parental or general family involvement in PG. None of these studies actually interviewed the parents or applied the standard PG diagnostic techniques. In Lesieur et al.'s (1991) study of university students, the subjects were asked about gambling problems in their parents. Among the students who said either of their parents had a gambling problem, 19% were rated as having a PG disorder themselves, as compared to 5% of the rest of the sample not reporting gambling problems in their parents. Parental overeating and drug use were also associated with PG in the students.

Only 1% of the first-degree relatives of a group of members of GA were described as pathological gamblers, although 11% were said to have major mood disorders, and 9% alcohol disorders (Linden et al., 1986).

However, those with PG in substance abuse treatment programs describe much higher prevalences of PG in their parents, particularly in their fathers. In an alcohol and drug abuse treatment center, 39% of the fathers of substance abusers with PG were described as pathological gamblers and an additional 23% as "abusive" gamblers (Lesieur, Blume, & Zoppa, 1986). Among the patients in a drug abuse therapeutic community, 10% said either their father or mother (generally the father) had a gambling problem, but among those with PG themselves, 50% describe a gambling problem in their parents (Lesieur & Heineman, 1988). A similar figure was obtained from a group with PG in a substance abuse hospital where 49% of those with PG reported a family member with a gambling problem (Daghestani et al., 1996). In this study there was evidence of probable learning of gambling behavior from family members: Of those with PG, 68% described gambling with other family members compared to only 22% of the other residents.

The higher incidence of familial PG reported in substance abuse treatment groups may simply reflect the retrospective bias of these clients or may be because of the higher comorbidity of PG in substance abusers. Unfortunately, most of these studies do not report other comorbid disorders in their relatives.

Twin and adoption studies, which could separate the genetic and shared environmental influences in the families, have not been done with this disorder, but a molecular genetic study of pathological gambling provides strong evidence of a shared genetic source for both substance abuse and PG (Comings et al., 1996). It will be recalled that the Taq A1 variant of the human DRD2 (dopamine receptor) gene has been associated with drug addiction and some forms of severe alcoholism. In one study, a group of non-Hispanic, White pathological gamblers from multiple sites of GA donated blood samples, were interviewed, and filled out questionnaires to define PG by *DSM-III-R* criteria.

About 51% of the pathological gamblers carried the D2A1 allele compared to 26% of control participants. Furthermore, the frequency of the allele varied with the severity of the gambling problem. Of those in the upper half of the PG score distribution, 64% carried the allele compared to 41% in the less severe range of PG. Comorbid alcohol or drug abuse also increased the frequency of the allele: In the group with comorbid alcohol or drug abuse, 61% had the allele contrasted with 44% in the PG group without substance abuse. Major depression was also associated with presence of the allele but in a different direction. Those with PG who did *not* have major depressive episodes had a greater incidence of the allele (63%), whereas those with a history of major depression had a lower incidence (41%). These differences were particularly striking in the female PG group (83% vs. 9%). This suggests that although major depression is often comorbid with PG, particularly in women, it represents an alternate, nongenetic association with the disorder. Another interesting sidelight is that the prevalence of the allele in Jewish gamblers (25% of the PG sample) was lower than in non-Jewish groups. Only 7 of the controls were Jewish, and none of them had the allele. Alcohol abuse is lower in ethnic Jews than in other groups, and comorbid alcoholism increased the frequency of the allele in this PG population. The gene which may protect Jews from alcoholism does not seem to protect them from PG.

What is linked to the D2A1 allele, which seems to be involved in a broad spectrum of subtance abuse and impulsive disorders? One might speculate that this is one of a polygenetic set of genes involved in the personality traits and biological factors common to these disorders. In a subsequent section, I review the personality traits of pathological gamblers to see which they share with those already described for the antisocial personality and substance abuse disorders.

Biological Factors

Hare and McPherson (1984) hypothesized that in psychopaths, the left hemisphere is not as specialized for linguistic processing as in "normals" and this lack of mature lateralization might account for the dissociation between cognitive and emotional functioning. Hare and Connolly (1987) found that psychopathic criminals even showed a reversal of the usual processing of verbal stimuli in the left hemisphere, showing better processing when the stimuli were presented in the left visual field (right hemisphere). An EEG study showed that pathological gamblers had less differential hemispheric activation and even showed a reversal with greater left hemisphere activation during a nonverbal task (L. Goldstein, Manowitz, Nora, Swartzburg, & Carlton, 1985).

The enzyme monoamine oxidase (MAO) is one of the most reliable biological markers for sensation seeking and impulsivity traits and disinhibitory disorders such as APD, borderline personality disorder, alcohol and substance abuse, and other disorders characterized by poor impulse control. Low MAO levels were also found in a group of male pathological gamblers in treatment (Blanco, Orensanz-Munoz, Blanco-Jerez, & Saiz-Ruiz, 1996).

Findings on MAO point to possible differences in monoamine levels, particularly of dopamine. A. Roy et al. have explored basal levels of monoamine metabolites in a group of pathological gamblers (1988). Results of metabolites measured from CSF, plasma, and urine were not always in agreement. Another problem is that most of the participants met the lifetime criteria for affective or anxiety disorders, and 58% of them had a current major depressive episode. The investigators used the *DSM-III* criteria which exclude those with PG problems who also had APD, but do not exclude those with major depressive or anxiety disorders. This kind of selective exclusion is almost guaranteed to select out the more typical impulsive gamblers and give a different picture of the biochemistry of the disorder. The gamblers had signficantly lower plasma MHPG (norepineph-rine metabolite), and it was the nondepressed gamblers who accounted for this difference. But the entire PG group had higher CSF MHPG and higher urinary norepinephrine than controls. Gamblers were also higher than con-trols on CSF HVA (the dopamine metabolite), and the nondepressed gam-blers were even higher on HVA, but these differences were not significant. Mean values for the serotonin metabolite (5-HIAA) were almost exactly the same in the two groups. The sample sizes and confounding of PG with depressive disorder make these results difficult to interpret. The low levels of plasma MHPG would suggest underarousal in gamblers as postulated for high sensation seekers, but the high levels of CSF MHPG and urinary NE suggest that these participants were in high states of arousal at the time they were assessed. The dopamine metabolite results were in the predicted direction for high sensation seekers, but there was too much variability to reach significance. More psychopharmacological research is needed, pref-erably using nondepressed pathological gamblers who are not in treatment programs.

PERSONALITY

Custer and Milt (1985) described the pathological gambler as one who needs intense stimulation, excitement, and change and loves risk, challenge, and adventure. The pathological gambler is also said to be easily bored. What they have described is the essence of sensation seeking (Zuck-erman, 1979, 1994b). Sensation seeking is also relevant to the arousal theory of gambling which suggests that it is the excitement of betting and risking at high stakes, rather than money per se, which is the reward for the pathological gambler (Anderson & Brown, 1984).

Sensation seeking is strong in antisocial personalities (see chap. 5, this volume) so that another hypothesis is that socialization (or lack of it) is a prominent feature in PG. Sensation seeking is also closely linked with the trait of impulsivity or the tendency to act quickly without much thought or restraint. This is certainly a trait that distinguishes pathological gamblers from social or professional gamblers, particularly when they are recklessly "chasing" their losses. Sensation seeking and impulsivity are both related to the broad trait of psychoticism as defined by Eysenck (Zuckerman et al., 1988, 1993). But those who are impressed with the neurotic aspects of pathological gambling and its frequent association with depression would probably bet on an elevation of neuroticism as well as psychoticism.

Gamblers depend on external outcomes for their rewards so it has been hypothesized that they will show an external locus of control. This assumption, however, ignores the fact that many or even most gamblers do not believe just in luck but assume they have special powers to control or predict outcomes, even those events which are objectively a function of chance (M. B. Walker, 1992). To the extent they do believe in their own gambling abilities, they would have an internal locus of control. Or, more likely, they have an external locus of control for losses ("bad luck") and an internal locus of control for wins.

Much of the research on the personality of gamblers has not distinguished the forms of gambling: the game played, the size of the bet, the amount of time and preoccupation with gambling, and the types of "action." There are obviously differences between the little old ladies playing bingo and the "high rollers" in the casinos, or between those who bet at the off-track parlors and those who go to the racetrack.

The most salient scale peak in the MMPI profile of the pathological gambler is on the Psychopathic Deviate (Pd) scale. In a group of pathological gamblers in a treatment facility, the average T score on the Pd scale was 80 (3 SDs above the norm), and the most frequent profile was one with peaks on the Pd and Hypomania (Ma) scales, the characteristic profile of APDs (Graham & Lowenfeld, 1986). However, other profile types were also found which incorporated measures of neuroticism and anxiety along with psychopathy. These kinds of profiles have been found in alcoholics and drug abusers, particularly in those entering treatment programs.

A study using the California Personality Inventory (CPI) compared pathological gamblers and alcoholics admitted to treatment programs for these disorders and with medical controls within a VA medical center (McCormick, Taber, Kruedelbach, & Russo, 1987). The PG and alcoholic groups had similar profiles on the CPI, and both were different from the medical controls being significantly higher on a scale of Flexibility and lower on scales of Socialization (So), Self-Control, Ego Control, and Good Impression. Gamblers who also abused substances scored even lower than other gamblers on Ego Control. The general picture for PGs is one of unsocialized impulsivity and a lack of concern over how others view them. In another study, lower scores on So were found in pathological gamblers compared to the norms for the scale, and those who met the DSM-III APD diagnostic criteria were the lowest on this scale (Blaszczynski et al., 1997). Similarly, the PG group scored higher than the norms on the EPQ Psychoticism (P) scale and the APD-diagnosed group of gamblers scored the highest among the gamblers on this scale. As previously discussed (see chap. 5, this volume) the P scale may measure psychopathy rather than psychoticism, and P is positively related and So is negatively related to Psychopathy.

Studies of sensation seeking in pathological gamblers seeking or in treatment have either shown lower scores than norms, or scores not different than those of control participants (Allcock & Grace, 1988; Blanco et al., 1996; Blaszczynski, McConaghy, & Frankova, 1990; Blaszczynski, Wilson, & McConaghy, 1986).

Studies of active gamblers not in treatment programs have shown more relationships between certain types of gambling and sensation seeking. Kuley and Jacobs (1988) tested active gamblers recruited from ads and notices posted in gambling places or handed to persons boarding buses for the racetracks. Problem gamblers within this group, identified by a standard list of questions, scored higher than social gamblers on the total and all of the subscales of the SSS except TAS. The percentage of their incomes they reported spending on gambling also correlated with the Disinhibition and Boredom Susceptibility subscales. Kusyszyn and Rutter (1985) also solicited gamblers not involved in treatment programs and classified them by frequency of gambling and money spent in gambling into groups of heavy and light gamblers, nongamblers, and lottery players exclusively. A risk-taking scale, similar to sensation seeking scales, was highest in the heavy gamblers and lowest in lottery players and nongamblers.

Coventry and Brown (1993) studied gamblers from off-course betting offices and a sample from the general population evaluated for gambling behavior as well as for personality. Gamblers who participated only in off-course betting scored even lower than nongamblers on sensation seeking, but gamblers who participated in at least two different forms of gambling, or those who went to casinos or racetracks among their other gambling activities, scored higher on the SSS and all of its subscales than did exclusive off-track bettors and nongamblers. Sensation seeking varied directly with the number of different types of gambling activities, just as it has been found to vary with the number of different drugs used in drug-abusing populations. The disinhibition and boredom susceptibility scales of the SSS were significantly correlated with typical bet sizes, expenditures on gambling, subjective awareness of arousal, loss of control (a scale for PG), and chasing behavior. All of the SSS subscales correlated with awareness of arousal, bet size, and expenditure.

Sensation seeking is related to PG and its attributes such as chasing behavior in the active gambling population, but not in those gamblers in treatment or posttreatment groups. There are two possibilities. Either a subgroup of low sensation seekers are the ones who seek treatment, or treatment itself lowers sensation seeking tendencies. SSS scores before and after treatment were assessed in a study by Blaszczynski et al. (1991). The pretreatment scores on the SSS were about equivalent to those found for the modal gambling group in the Coventry and Brown (1993) study, and they did not predict the outcomes of treatment. Sensation seeking showed a marked drop in the group who stopped gambling, a smaller drop in those who gambled in a more controlled fashion after treatment, and no change at all in those who remained uncontrolled gamblers.

PG was placed in the major category of impulse-control disorders, which assumes that impulsivity is a major characteristic of PG. There is increasing evidence that this assumption is accurate. Gamblers seeking treatment and members of GA scored higher than norms for the Impulsivity and Non-planning subscales of the Eysenck Impulsivity scale (Blaszczynski et al., 1997). The gamblers scored lower than norms on Risk-taking and at the normative level on Liveliness. Gamblers in treatment scored even higher than alcoholics and cocaine abusers in treatment on the Barrett Impulsivity scale, and on the NEO scale of neurotic impulsivity (Castellani & Rugle, 1995). The groups did not differ on the NEO Excitement Seeking scale, a scale similar to sensation seeking.

Both of these aforementioned studies used gamblers in treatment and found differences in impulsivity but no differences or even lower scores on sensation seeking types of measures. Perhaps gamblers in treatment are more willing to concede their impulsivity but not their need for excitement and variety. But another recent study suggests that impulsivity may be more basic than sensation seeking to the abnormal betting behavior involved in chasing, which is specific to the pathological gambler as opposed to the social gambler.

Breen and Zuckerman (in press) constructed a laboratory model for short-term chasing consisting of a gambling task in which subjects are given a $10 stake which they may keep or choose to gamble in a computer controlled card-cutting game. Although the subjects have a choice of betting high or low and on the size of the bet, the outcomes are controlled in a seemingly random schedule, but one which actually consists of a decreasing ratio of wins beginning at 70% in the first block of trials and decreasing by 10% with each subsequent block of trials. Subjects may quit at any time, but those who persist long enough through the trials (chasers) will eventually lose all of their money. The Impulsive Sensation Seeking (ImpSS) scale from the Zuckerman-Kuhlman Personality Questionnaire was used, and the ImpSS scores were found to be higher in those who chased (lost all their stake) than in those who played and quit while they were ahead. But when the ImpSS was analyzed in terms of its two subscales, impulsivity and sensation seeking, only the impulsivity scale was found to be predictive of chasing.

Sensation seeking and impulsivity may be related to two different phases of PG. Sensation seeking may be what involves young gamblers in varied forms of gambling for high stakes, but impulsivity may be what governs their compulsive need to persist when they are losing. However, sensation seeking may predict other aspects of pathological gambling not assessed in the Breen and Zuckerman experiment in which subjects always thought they were making bets at 50% chance. Vuchinich and Calamas (1997) used a laboratory task in which the riskiness of the gamble was varied. Pathological gamblers are said to make more risky bets when chasing, hoping that a long-odds bet with a bigger payoff will recoup their losses quickly. A variety of impulsivity measures and the SSS were used in the study. Only the sensation seeking scales and a risk-taking impulsivity subscale predicted risky gambling behavior, whereas all of the Barrett and Eysenck impulsivity scales (except risk-taking) did not.

Another line of evidence on impulsivity comes from a neuropsychological study of attention problems in pathological gamblers (Rugle & Melamed, 1993). The gamblers had low scores on tests such as the Porteus Mazes, which are indicative of lack of inhibitory capacity stemming from a frontal lobe deficit.

Some psychodynamic theorists see gambling as a way of dealing with anxiety and depression stemming from basic conflicts, rather than from desperation in losing at games and the stresses engendered by spiralling debt. Gamblers seeking treatment score very high on scales of neuroticism and depression and a psychiatric symptom checklist (Blaszczynski et al., 1997), but the problems with testing for psychopathology in groups entering treatment have been discussed. Gamblers who have been successfully treated in a program and who stopped gambling show a marked reduction in measures of neuroticism and anxiety, whereas those who are still engaged in uncontrolled gambling show no reduction in levels of these traits or states (Blaszczynski et al., 1991). Probably the initially high pretreatment levels were a function of the stresses in the gamblers' lives produced by uncontrolled gambling.

Locus of control (LC) has been suggested as a relevant trait for PG on the assumption that gamblers would have a high external locus of control. Some studies (e.g., Hong & Chiu, 1988) tended to confirm this but many others could not (e.g., Kusyszyn & Rutter, 1985; Malkin & Syme, 1986).

A PG group entering treatment was given the EPPS scales of Murray needs (Moravec & Munley, 1983). Compared to norms they showed very high scores on needs for achievement, dominance, heterosexuality, exhibitionism, and autonomy, and very low scores on needs for order, endurance, and deference. The profile very much resembles that for high sensation seekers on the EPPS and Jackson PRF, also based on the Murray need classification (Zuckerman, 1979).

STRESS

There is not much published on the role of stress in PG. Whereas abuse of alcohol and drugs has been attributed to an attempt to self-medicate after stressful experiences, gambling is not seen as an anxiety reducer. Conceivably, gambling could be a means of dealing with dysphoric emotions produced by life stress. Gamblers tend to blot out all other preoccupations when gambling, and their moods are entirely a function of the specific game they are engaged in rather than of the larger game of life. The association between PG and alexythymia, previously discussed, could represent the defensive role of gambling as suggested by psychodynamic theorists.

The role of traumatic events in the symptoms and traits of gamblers admitted to an inpatient gambling program for veterans was evaluated by Tabler, McCormick, and Ramirez (1987). About one fourth of the group reported severely traumatic events, 16% reported moderately heavy trauma, 30% reported less severe trauma, and 32% reported no severe life trauma. From these data alone one could question the importance of stress from traumatic events in PG because nearly two thirds of the group did not report trauma of significant severity. Patients were required to read their autobiographies aloud in group sessions so there was an implicit demand for significant life trauma. The patients who did report experiencing severe life stressors showed more anxiety and depression in questionnaires, and more abuse of alcohol than did the nonstressed group. The authors claim that in 9 of the 10 cases reporting severe life trauma, the traumatic experiences occurred before gambling became compulsive, but this does not prove the etiological role of stress in pathological gambling. Possibly the alcohol and drug involvement or antisocial activities could have played a role in the stressful events. Longitudinal studies are needed to clarify the role of stress in PG.

SUMMARY

All three types of disorders share many features, although each has some specific characteristics as well. All of the disorders start with an activity (drinking, taking drugs, gambling) which is reinforced by pleasurable sensations, such as getting "high" or excited. All are within the range of normal pleasure-seeking even if sometimes illegal. At some point the activity goes beyond the normal limits, and negative social, physical, or economic consequences begin to accrue, at which point we say that the person is "abusing" or entering the "problem" stage. At some further point, the person's life centers on the maladaptive activity to the detriment of other normal life activities and pleasures, and attempts to cease the activity lead to unpleasant feelings or physical discomforts that are only terminated by reengaging in the activity (dependence).

But even more fundamental similarities exist. There is a great deal of comorbidity, particularly between alcohol and drug abuse and between abuse of different drugs. Pathological gambling disorder is very common among alcohol and drug abusers. Diagnoses of antisocial personality disorder are much more frequent among these disorders, particularly among the abusers of heroin and cocaine, than in the general population. Men are more vulnerable than women to these disorders. A substantial proportion of the men who develop the disorders have a background personality characterized by traits of poor socialization, high impulsivity, sensation seeking, and aggressiveness. Among the substance abusers and gamblers who show these traits, we see a more severe form of the disorder and more cross-addictions than in those who do not have these traits. A minority of the men but a larger number of women with these disorders show some of these traits such as impulsivity, but also have the neurotic traits, anxiety and depression which precede the "addictive" or disinhibitory disorders. They often have a history of trauma and stress preceding the disorder. Some of these distinctions between personality types have been encoded in the Type 1 and 2 (or A and B) characteristics for substance abuse disorders. The more antisocial, impulsive, sensation seeking B types usually have a worse prognosis and a greater criminal involvement as well as more severe drug, alcohol, and general psychiatric problems.

Parallel distinctions can be seen at the genetic level. Alcoholism and drug abuse seem to be accounted for by heredity more in men than in women. The same genetic marker, the A1 allele of the Dopamine D2 receptor gene, has been found more frequently in alcoholics, drug abusers, and pathological gamblers than in controls, and its presence is related to severity of abuse and cross-addictions, including one between pathological gambling and substance abuse. One of the biological markers for all three disorders and APD as well, the enzyme MAO-B type, is highly heritable and is lower in males than in females in the general population, which might be part of the explanation for the greater prevalence of cases for males among the APD, substance abuse, and pathological gambling disorders.

Family studies show relationships between the disorders in probands and their first-degree relatives, and these relationships are not specific, for instance, the relative of a drug abuser may be an alcoholic rather than a drug abuser. Adoption studies are particularly informative on the pathways to drug abuse and alcoholism (Cadoret et al., 1986, 1995). They show two genetic pathways: The first is a direct one from substance abuse (more usually alcoholism) in the biological parent to substance abuse in the adopted child, and the second is an indirect one from antisocial personality in the biological parent to aggressiveness and antisocial personality in the adopted children, predisposing them to substance abuse.

Figure 6.5 shows my postulated and highly speculative pathway model which attempts to link the diatheses with two end types of substance abuse. Common to both is a specific reward sensitivity (RS) mechanism mediated by the mesolimbic reinforcement pathway and possibly involving the D2 receptor gene among others. This is the genetic mechanism that makes some strains of rodents particularly susceptible to the reinforcements of drugs. The same mechanism may be involved in the vulnerability to path-

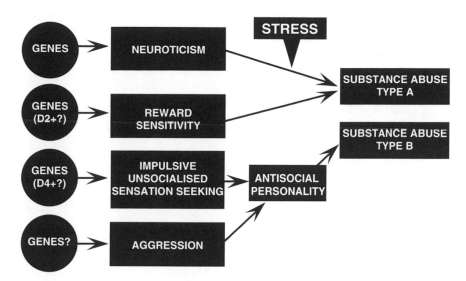

Figure 6.5. Pathways to substance abuse.

ological gambling. The other two diatheses involve the genetic dispositions to neuroticism and impulsive unsocialized sensation-seeking (ImpUSS). ImpUSS, of course, may consist of a general genetic factor plus some specific ones for its three components: impulsivity, sensation seeking, and socialization. A fourth factor of aggression is often combined with ImpUSS in the form of the antisocial personality disorder (APD). These traits combine with the RS mechanism to produce either Type B substance abuse or pathological gambling. The broad trait of neuroticism, activated by life stressors and interaction with the RS mechanism, predisposes one toward the Type A substance abuse. The other influences of shared and unshared environments are not shown here, although genetic studies show that they do play a role in developing substance abuse, particularly drug abuse and pathological gambling, through observational learning and social reinforcement.

7

SCHIZOPHRENIA

DIAGNOSIS

Historical Changes

Schizophrenia is not among the more prevalent disorders, with a typical lifetime prevalence of only about 1%, but its severity and chronicity make it the most terrible. In the anxiety and mood disorders there may be disability for periods of acute effects with intermittent periods of return to the predisorder personality. Too often in schizophrenia, function is severely limited, even after recovery from the acute phase of the psychosis, and the personality is changed forever. The research literature of recent years shows an exponential expansion of our knowledge of the biological mechanisms involved in the disorder, but no necessary cause that could account for all cases.

Schizophrenia emerged from the general classification of "madness" and was distinguished from the more ancient medically defined disorders of melancholia and mania in the 19th century. Kraepelin (1919) used the term *dementia praecox* to describe what he believed to be a brain disorder with a deteriorative, chronic course (*dementia*) beginning relatively early (*praecox*) in adolescence or adult life. In a tautological fashion, the disorder was defined by its characteristic symptoms but primarily by its course. Kraepelin recognized that some patients had a later onset and recovered, but

319

these cases were classified as *paraphrenias*, another disorder with a different etiology. Previous psychiatrists had described discrete catatonic, paranoid, and hebephrenic disorders, but Kraepelin believed that all of these were syndromes of one underlying disorder. The primary symptoms of the disorder were delusions, hallucinations, catatonic motor expressions, incoherence, and bizarre behavior. His emphasis was on the observable (positive) symptoms rather than on the more general loss of motivation and interest in normal activities, social withdrawal, and absence of affect (negative symptoms), which also characterized the disorder. His main distinction between dementia praecox and other mental disorders, however, was the early onset, and long course with poor outcome in the former. This pessimistic view of the disorder resulted in reduced efforts at therapy and the "warehousing" of chronic patients in the back wards of large mental hospitals.

Bleuler (1911/1950) used the term *schizophrenias* instead of dementia praecox to describe the disorder. The plural was not meant to deny the unity of the syndrome but to suggest that there were probably different causes for the disorder, rather than the single neurological dementia suggested by Kraepelin (Gottesman, 1991). In fact Bleuler described the disorder in much broader terms than Kraepelin with altered functions of (a) *association*, a loosening of associative connections; (b) *affect*, "flatness" or inappropriate affect; (c) *ambivalence* of affect, will, or ideas; (d) *autism*, or living in a world of fantasy; (e) *avolition*, the lack of motivation, and (f) *attention*, primarily impaired. Items b, c, e, and f would be described today as negative symptoms, or the loss of normal behavior. Bleuler regarded the more florid positive symptoms, such as hallucinations and delusions, as products of the more basic disturbed psychological functions. His more abstract definition of the disorder allowed clinicians more latitude in diagnosis because they could detect an association disorder in peculiar thinking even in the absence of bizarre delusions and hallucinations. Many of the signs, such as avolition, could be seen in other kinds of disorders, particularly major depressions. Psychotic delusions, particularly mood-related ones, are also not uncommon among major mood disorders.

This broad definition was particularly influential in American psychiatry and resulted in a blurring of the distinction between schizophrenia and major mood disorders. The former was described as a "thought disorder" and the latter as a "mood disorder," but most American psychiatrists used a hierarchal decision process so that any trace of a thought disorder (altered associations) was enough to tilt the decision toward a diagnosis of schizophrenia. Schizophrenia was the more common diagnosis in North America until 1979, when the definitions began to change in anticipation of *DSM-III*. The dissatisfaction of researchers with the unreliability of diagnosis led to the formulation of more explicit and objective diagnostic criteria in *DSM-III* (see chap. 2, this volume). For the study of schizophrenia, this meant a return to the narrower diagnostic signs of Kraepelin and away from Bleuler's broader definitions of schizophrenic process. Although the changes resulted in improved reliability for the diagnosis, some researchers feel they have reduced the validity of the diagnosis by neglecting the negative or deficit symptoms in favor of the positive symptoms such as delusions (Andreasen & Carpenter, 1993; Andreasen & Flaum, 1991). There has been some attempt to redress this deficiency in *DSM-IV* by adding negative symptoms as a fifth category in the symptom criteria below in which the other four categories are positive symptoms.

DSM-IV Definitions

The *DSM-IV* diagnosis of schizophrenia requires that two of five characteristic symptoms be manifest for a significant portion of the time during a 1-month period. The characteristic symptoms are delusions, hallucinations, disorganized speech, grossly disorganized or catatonic behavior, and negative symptoms.

1. *Delusions* are defined as erroneous beliefs in spite of evidence to the contrary, which are not accepted by other members of the person's culture or subculture (Maher & Spitzer, 1993). Bizarre or "clearly implausible" delusions are said to be especially diagnostic of schizophrenia, as differentiated from delusional disorders (Spitzer, First, Kendler, & Stein, 1993). Schneider (1959) described delusions supposedly specific to schizophrenia. "First-rank" delusional symptoms include beliefs that one's thoughts, feelings, impulses, or actions are not one's own but are inserted by external forces and that one's thoughts may be withdrawn and broadcast to the world.

2. *Hallucinations* are sensory impressions that patients believe originate from outside of themselves when there is no tangible evidence for an external source (Heilbrun, 1993). They may occur in any of the sensory modalities, but the most common are auditory hallucinations consisting of voices that are not recognized as one's own thoughts. Schneider's (1959) first-rank hallucinations include voices that keep up a running commentary on one's behavior or thoughts, or two or more voices conversing with each other.

3. *Disorganized speech* is symptomatic of the thought disorder that Bleuler (1911/1950) regarded as the most fundamental symptom. Whereas delusions represent a disturbance in the content of thought, disorganization is a disruption in the *process* of thought. The thought disorder is manifested in loose associations (derailment), so that the connection between one expressed thought and another is not apparent, and the topics of speech are tangential and rapidly shifting, making for generally incoherent speech (Marengo, Harrow, & Edell, 1993).

4. *Catatonic behavioral signs* which were common prior to the introduction of antipsychotic drugs at mid-century, such as catalepsy, mutism,

stupor, unresponsiveness, or muscular rigidity, are not often seen today (Manschreck, 1993). Although these dramatic catatonic symptoms are rarely seen, the generally passive, uncommunicative, and retarded behaviors of many schizophrenics constitute a major syndrome, loosely described as "negative symptoms." These symptoms represent the absence of normal behavior rather than the presence of abnormal or bizarre behaviors, like those seen in the person with classical catatonic schizophrenia.

5. *Negative symptoms*, the fifth category of symptom in *DSM-IV*, includes the absence of variation in emotional expression (affective flattening), poverty of speech (alogia), or a disinterest in engaging in goal-directed work, recreational, or social activities (avolition). Two other kinds of negative symptoms described by others (Andreasen & Olsen, 1982) are not listed in *DSM-IV*: *anhedonia*, or the inability to experience pleasure, and *asociality*, or the lack of interest in social interchange or intimacy with others. Both of these may be the source or the result of avolition, because they concern the emotional sources of reward motivation.

The diagnosis requires the presence of at least two of the above categories of symptoms for at least 1 month, and negative symptoms only or subclinical forms of the positive symptoms, such as odd beliefs instead of delusions, for at least 6 months. There is often a prodromal period to the onset of acute schizophrenia characterized by a loss of interest in former activities and social contacts, loss of concern over appearance, and some peculiar ideas and behaviors.

Subtypes and Syndromes

The *DSM* has retained most of the traditional subtypes of schizophrenia that Kraepelin originally incorporated into the basic disorder of dementia praecox. The *DSM-IV* subtypes include the following five types:

1. The *paranoid type* has one or more delusions or frequent auditory hallucinations as primary symptoms but does not have disorganized speech or behavior, catatonic symptoms, or flat or inappropriate affect. Delusions are usually organized around a coherent theme, and hallucinations are usually related to that theme. People with this paranoid type of schizophrenia are better integrated and less disorganized than those with other types, but their delusions tend to be more bizarre than those of delusional disorders. Essentially, their disorder is in the content but not in the form of thinking.

2. The symptoms of the *catatonic type* include catalepsy, stupor, or excessive motor activity, extreme rigidity, or negativism in movement, posturing, echolalia or echopraxia. They may have delusions in the form of morbid and irrational fears but be unable to communicate them.

3. The symptoms of the *disorganized type* include disorganized speech and disorganized behavior, and flat or inappropriate affective expression. From Kraepelin to the *DSM*, the subtype was called "hebephrenic," noting

its early onset and poor prognosis. Delusions and hallucinations may occur, but they are fragmentary and not organized into a coherent theme. Grimacing, silliness, and other odd behavior is characteristic.

4. The label *undifferentiated type* is used when the criteria for schizophrenia are met but the symptoms do not fit the other subtypes or are a mixture of them. The acute undifferentiated type may be found in the early stages of schizophrenia when the delusions are not well formed, and the patient is confused but still not disorganized. The chronic undifferentiated type is now likely to be described as a residual type.

5. The designation *residual type* is used to describe the aftereffects of at least one prior episode of schizophrenia in which the positive psychotic symptoms such as delusions and hallucinations or disorganized speech and behavior have subsided or persist in an attenuated form, but the negative symptoms, such as flat affect, alogia, or avolition, are still present, leaving the patient functioning at a lower level than that prior to the onset.

Other Psychotic Disorders

The schizoaffective disorder has already been described with the mood disorders (see chap. 4, this volume), but it is neither a mood nor a schizophrenic disorder but something between the two. The major depressive or manic symptoms occur concurrently with the psychotic symptoms during a subtantial part of the time, but the delusions and hallucinations also occur for at least 2-weeks duration in the absence of the mood symptoms.

Delusional disorder is defined solely by delusions that are "nonbizarre" and persist for at least 1 month. *Nonbizarre delusions* are described as involving situations which could occur in real life, such as being followed, deceived, poisoned, or having a disease. There are no "prominent" auditory hallucinations like those in paranoid schizophrenia. There is less impairment and disorganization than in schizophrenia, and the subject usually appears quite normal when not discussing the delusions. The subject must not meet any of the other symptomatic criteria for schizophrenia other than that of the delusions. Subtypes of delusional disorder are defined by the type of delusion, that is, erotomanic, grandiose, jealous, persecutory, or somatic.

Brief psychotic disorder is characterized by a sudden onset of at least one of the schizophrenic symptoms and lasting between 1 day and 1 month with full return to the premorbid level after the episode. Diagnosis may specify if the onset was with a marked life stressor or without one, and if the onset followed the birth of a child (e.g., "with postpartum onset"). *Schizophreniform disorder* also may meet the symptomatic criteria for schizophrenia, but lasts between 1 and 6 months. Diagnoses may specify with or without good prognostic features such as rapid onset of psychosis and good premorbid functioning.

Personality Disorders

Meehl's (1962) diathesis–stress theory proposed that the schizotaxic neural basis of schizophrenia inevitably led to the development of a schizotypic personality type from which some developed later into a full-blown schizophrenia. Meehl (1990) views both schizotypy and schizophrenia as a taxon, or a natural category of disorder rather than an endpoint on a dimension, but even those who, like H. J. Eysenck (1986), advocate a dimensional view of psychosis, suggest that there is an underlying personality dimension to schizophrenia and other disorders called "psychoticism." The Cluster A personality types in the DSM embody different aspects of the premorbid personality characteristics often associated with schizophrenia.

Persons with the *paranoid personality disorder* tend to be suspicious and distrustful of others and to attribute malevolent motives to their actions short of actual delusions. They have persistent doubts about the loyalty of friends, are reluctant to confide in others, tend to see hidden meanings in casual remarks or events, and develop persistent antipathies in reaction to real or fancied insults or slights. They tend to be easily angered by imagined attacks on their reputation. They have unjustified jealous suspicions of lovers.

Persons with a *schizoid personality disorder* lead isolated lives with only superficial contacts with others because they prefer being alone. Unlike those people with avoidant personality disorders or normal introverts, they avoid any intimate relationships except with close relatives. They have little interest in sexual relationships, enjoy few if any activities and then only solitary ones (anhedonia), and appear to be indifferent to praise or criticism. They are cold and detached in relating to others and show signs of the "flattened affect" found in more extreme form in schizophrenics.

Schizotypal personality disorder, as described in the DSM, shares many features with paranoid and schizoid disorders, such as suspiciousness and paranoid ideation, a lack of desire for intimate friends other than relatives, and a constricted range of emotional expression. But in addition to these traits, people with schizotypal personality disorder also show some tendencies toward schizophrenic thinking. They have ideas of reference, but not delusions of reference; perceptual alterations, but not actual hallucinations; eccentric or odd beliefs in the supernatural, but not bizarre delusions; and beliefs in their own special powers of clairvoyance, telepathy, and magical control, but not grandiose delusions. Their speech is odd, digressive, or vague, but not derailed or incoherent. Words may be used in unusual ways, but they do not form neologisms. They may even cross the line at times with very brief psychotic episodes not lasting long enough (1 day) to qualify as brief psychotic disorder.

Schizophrenic Syndromes

The subtypes of schizophrenia in the *DSM* are based on those rationally developed by Kraepelin and his predecessors in the 19th century. Other ways of organizing symptoms into syndromes or types have been suggested over the years. Some are based on theoretical, some on rational–clinical, and some on empirical statistical analyses of covariations between symptoms. Some typologies are organized around cross-sectional analyses of symptoms at given points in time, some around the premorbid characteristics and onset (process vs. reactive, good vs. poor prognosis), and some around the post-onset course (acute vs. chronic).

Lorr, Klett, and McNair (1963) used the statistical approach of factor analysis to identify syndromes among psychotics. He found 10 such syndromes:

1. Excitement (excess in speech, activity, and euphoric mood)
2. Paranoid projection (delusions of reference, persecution, and control)
3. Hostile belligerence
4. Perceptual distortion (hallucinations)
5. Anxious intropunitiveness (guilt, anxiety, and depression)
6. Retardation and apathy (slowed speech, movement, flat affect, blocking)
7. Motor disturbances (peculiar posturing, grimacing, repetitive gestures)
8. Conceptual disorganization (irrelevant, incoherent speech, derailment, neologisms, word or phrase repetitions
9. Disorientation (of place, time, person) and
10. Grandiose expansiveness (grandiose delusions and hallucinations)

A higher-order analysis of the 10 syndromes revealed 3 major syndromes: (X) excitement and hostile belligerence versus retardation and apathy, (Y) paranoid projection, and (Z) conceptual disorganization.

A more recent study used the method of latent class analysis (LCA) to search for diagnostic groupings among patients with schizophrenia and mood disorders (Kendler, Karkowski, & Walsh, 1998). Factor analysis groups symptoms into syndromes, whereas LCA groups patients into diagnostic classes. The resulting classification of six classes was highly related to the *DSM-III-R* classifications. Of those in the class labeled "classic schizophrenia," 84% were classified schizophrenia by *DSM-III-R*. Nearly all patients classified as having "major depression" by the LCA were given the same diagnosis by *DSM-III-R* criteria. Those in the LCA class of "hebe-phrenia" received *DSM* diagnoses of schizophrenia or schizoaffective disorder. Although these results support the classical distinction between schizophrenia and major mood disorder, they also yield mixed classifications: bipolar-schizomania and schizodepression, recognized in the *DSM* as schizoaffective disorders, manic and depressive subtypes. The authors claim that their results argue against a unitary dimension of psychosis containing both mood and schizophrenic disorders. Presumably, the mixed schizoaffective diagnoses represent combinations of mood and schizoid types. But why should such mixtures exist if these represent pure disorders with different etiologies? A dimensional view could more easily accommodate such mixtures.

The history of the positive–negative symptom distinction in schizophrenia can be found in several reviews (Andreasen, 1990; Andreasen & Carpenter, 1993). The distinction between positive and negative symptom (or deficit vs. nondeficit) types of schizophrenia started with a theoretical distinction made by Jackson (1889/1931). Negative symptoms, characterized by the loss of normal functions, represented a loss of higher mental functioning produced by brain disease, whereas positive symptoms, like hallucinations and delusions, were conceived as release phenomena secondary to the loss of higher cortical control. Jackson regarded the distinction as a way of classifying symptoms, not subtypes of schizophrenia. Syndromes as types carries the assumption of stability of the classification of a patient over time, whereas the definition of syndromes as related symptoms only requires that they be intercorrelated at a given time during the course of the disorder.

Crow (1980, 1985) used the positive–negative symptom distinction to define two schizophrenic syndromes, as described in Table 7.1.

TABLE 7.1
Crow's Two Syndromes in Schizophrenia

	Type I	Type II
Characteristic symptoms	Hallucinations, delusions, thought disorder (positive symptoms)	Affective flattening, poverty of speech, loss of drive (negative symptoms)
Type of illness in which most commonly seen	Acute schizophrenia	Chronic schizophrenia, the "defect" state
Response to neuroleptics	Good	Poor
Outcome	Reversible	Irreversible?
Intellectual impairment	Absent	Sometimes present
Postulated pathological process	Increased dopamine receptors	Cell loss and structural changes in the brain

Note. From "Molecular Pathology of Schizophrenia," by T. J. Crow, 1980, *British Medical Journal,* *280,* p. 67. Copyright 1980 by British Medical Association. Adapted by permission.

The Type I schizophrenic is defined by a predominance of positive symptoms, such as hallucinations and delusions, an acute course with a reversible process (good prognosis), a good response to neuroleptic drugs, and the absence of intellectual impairment. The Type II is characterized by negative symptoms, affective flattening, and alogia. This type tends to be chronic and irreversible, although not inevitably so, with a poor response to neuroleptic drugs, and intellectual impairment and abnormal involuntary movements sometimes present. Type I represents a pathological process resulting in increased dopamine receptors, explaining the effectiveness of the neuroleptic drugs (dopamine receptor blockers) in reducing or temporarily eliminating the positive symptoms. In contrast, Type II is related to cell loss and structural brain changes in temporal lobe structures. The brain damage might be due to viral infections, pre- or perinatal factors, or later brain trauma.

Psychometric, genetic and biochemical, and brain imaging studies have generally not supported the associations predicted from the theory or the reliable grouping of positive and negative syndromes into two basic types. However, Crow (1985) says that he is not postulating distinctive schizophrenic disorders with distinctive causes, but only "different manifestations of the activity of a single pathogen" (p. 482). It is difficult to conceive of a single "pathogen" which would result in dopamine receptor excess and brain damage in temporal lobe and limbic structures. But whatever the presumed basis for typologies of symptoms or patients, the adequacy of correlational studies depends on the reliability of the diagnostic criterion, the positive–negative symptom type classification.

Andreasen and Olsen (1982) developed scales for rating symptoms in order to derive syndrome types. Positive symptom types were defined by the presence of severe hallucinations, delusions, marked positive formal thought disorder, and repeated instances of bizarre or disorganized behavior, as well as the absence of any prominent signs of negative schizophrenia. The signs of negative schizophrenia include alogia, affective flattening, anhedonia–asociality, avolition–apathy, and attentional impairment, and the absence of prominent signs of positive schizophrenia. A third group of mixed schizophrenia was formed by patients who did not meet the criteria for positive or negative schizophrenia or who met the criteria for both. About a third of the patients fell into each of the three groups. Crow (1985) criticized Andreasen's criteria for negative symptoms as too broad and inclusive of symptoms such as apathy and asociality which might be a reaction to the positive symptoms or might be related to depression.

The initial results of the factor analysis of symptoms suggested a bipolar factor with positive symptoms at one pole and negative symptoms at the other (Andreasen & Olsen, 1982). A later factor analysis on a larger sample of cases showed the independence of positive and negative symptom factors and the existence of two, rather than one, bipolar symptom factors

(Andreasen, Arndt, Alliger, Miller, & Flaum, 1995). The three empircally derived factors are

1. Negative symptoms (avolition, anhedonia–asociality, and affective flattening)
2. Disorganization (inappropriate affect, thought disorder, and bizarre behavior)
3. Psychoses (delusions and hallucinations).

Figure 7.1 represents the results of this factor analysis in a hierarchal fashion from specific symptoms to higher order factors.

The disorganized factor closely resembles the classical subtype of hebephrenia (*DSM-IV*, disorganized), and the psychotic factor corresponds to paranoid schizophrenia. The negative symptom syndrome would now be classified as residual type schizophrenia if it followed a schizophrenic episode when positive symptoms were more prominent, although in milder form, it would correspond to the category of schizotypal personality or simple schizophrenia which was dropped in *DSM-III*.

The symptoms of schizotypal personality disorder have also been factor analyzed to derive syndromes from ratings made from interviews with nonpsychotic patients and normal controls (Battaglia, Cavallini, Macciardi, & Bellodi, 1997; Bergman et al., 1996). Both studies found a cognitive–perceptual factor (magical thinking, perceptual aberrations) and a social withdrawal factor (social anxiety, no close friends). Both also found a disorganization factor (odd behavior, odd speech), but the Bergman et al. study found an alternative paranoid factor (ideas of reference, suspiciousness, social anxiety) for the disorganization, one which yielded a somewhat better fit in the confirmatory factor analysis.

Many self-report scales have been developed to measure different aspects of the schizotypal personality and these have been factor analyzed in studies nearly all of which used "normals" as subjects (Claridge, McCreery, & Mason, 1996; see Vollema & van den Bosch, 1995, for a review of 9 studies). All studies found a psychotic-like schizotypy factor (magical thinking and perceptual aberrations) resembling the cognitive–perceptual factor found in the interview studies. An introverted anhedonia factor that resembles the social withdrawal factor found in ratings was found in a number of studies. A third factor of asocial, impulsive, nonconformity and borderline personality disorder tendency does not resemble anything found in the clinical interview studies, but is highly related to Eysenck's Psychoticism scale, which the Eysencks conceive of as a measure of schizotypal tendencies underlying psychosis. Its absence in the clinical interview data would suggest that its relevance is limited to antisocial personality and that it is not a basic schizotypal factor (Claridge et al., 1996; Zuckerman, 1989). The two other factors could be interpreted as mild positive (cognitive–perceptual) and negative (introverted anhedonia) symptom factors.

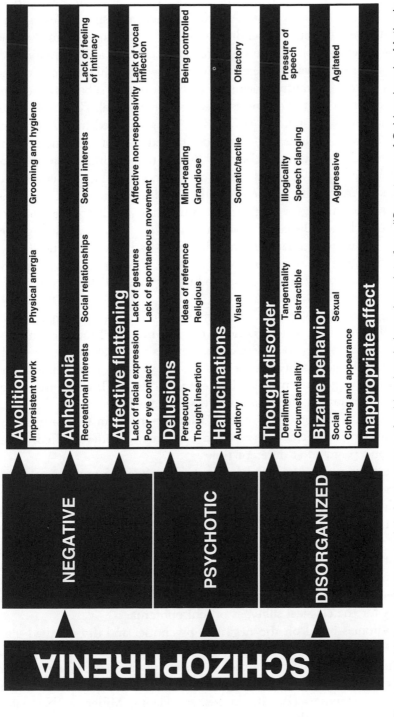

Figure 7.1. Major syndromes and their symptoms of schizophrenia based on data from "Symptoms of Schizophrenia: Methods, Meanings, and Mechanisms," by N. C. Andreasen et al., 1995, *Archives of General Psychiatry, 52,* p. 348. Copyright 1995 by American Medical Association. Adapted by permission.

Stability and Reliability of the Syndrome Subtypes

The first question that must be answered concerns the reliability of subtype classification over time. Are these syndromes simply descriptions of individuals that change depending on phase of the disorder, medication status, or other factors? Or are these reliable classifications of individuals perhaps indicative of valid differences in etiology, effective treatments, and outcomes? Before attempting to answer this question for subtypes, one must pose the question for the diagnosis of schizophrenia itself. The stability of the diagnosis of schizophrenia (*DSM-III-R*) was analyzed in a 7-year longitudinal study of patients who were hospitalized at least four times during that period (Chen, Swann, & Burt, 1996). Of those initially diagnosed as having schizophrenia, 22% had a different diagnosis during a later episode. The cases where this happens could either be due to errors in diagnosis at the first admission, or to an incorrect assumption about the permanence of the schizophrenic disorder. More women's than men's initial diagnoses of schizophrenia were changed, and Hispanics had a higher rate of diagnostic change (44%!) than Caucasian or African American subjects. The last finding suggests that misunderstandings of cultural differences might account for many misdiagnoses.

The classical subtypes of schizophrenia are known to change within individuals over time, which is one of the reasons that Kraepelin thought they were all manifestations of one disorder. As a case example, see Table 7.2 for the subtype diagnoses over time in the Genain quadrupulets, who are identical in genetic makeup (Rosenthal, 1963). Three of the quads began with a catatonic diagnosis, whereas the fourth, Nora, was diagnosed as having acute schizophrenia at first examination. From there on all the four quads' diagnoses changed between catatonic, undifferentiated, hebephrenic, and paranoid at different times.

Comparing initial and index admissions after a 5-year interval, researchers found about two thirds of a group of schizophrenic patients retained their initial diagnosis of paranoid, hebephrenic, or undifferentiated type (Fenton & McGlashan, 1991a). The kappa coefficients of reliability were .52 for paranoid, .40 for hebephrenic, and .39 for undifferentiated schizophrenia, and .44 for all patients. The most frequent change, in about one third of the patients diagnosed as paranoid, was from paranoid to undifferentiated schizophrenia. The results do not indicate much temporal reliability for the classical subtypes of schizophrenia.

Syndromes based on the negative, psychotic, and disorganized classification of symptoms (Andreasen et al., 1995) were moderately reliable from admission to discharge, although there was a marked reduction in psychotic and disorganized syndromes and a significant but lesser reduction in negative symptoms (Arndt, Andreasen, Flaum, Miller, & Nopoulos, 1995). A year later, the reliability of the negative symptoms remained

TABLE 7.2
Subtype Diagnoses of the Genain Quadruplets
(Arranged Chronologically)

Nora	Iris	Myra	Hester
acute	catatonic	catatonic	catatonic
acute	undifferentiated	undifferentiated	catatonic
undifferentiated	catatonic	catatonic	hebephrenic
catatonic	undifferentiated		undifferentiated
catatonic	undifferentiated		undifferentiated
catatonic	catatonic		undifferentiated
hebephrenic features	catatonic		paranoid features
hebephrenic features	catatonic		hebephrenic
hebephrenic features	hebephrenic		undifferentiated
undifferentiated	catatonic and hebephrenic features		hebephrenic
undifferentiated	catatonic and paranoid features		hebephrenic
undifferentiated	hebephrenic		hebephrenic
	hebephrenic or undifferentiated		hebephrenic features
	hebephrenic or undifferentiated		hebephrenic features

Note. From *The Genain Quadruplets*, edited by D. Rosenthal, 1963, p. 519. New York: Basic Books.

significant ($r = .54$), but those for the psychotic and disorganized syndromes were close to zero. After 2 years, the negative syndrome reliability dropped slightly, to .47, the disorganized syndrome was still low and insignificant, but the psychotic symptom reliability increased slightly, to .31. Moderate reliability was found for most of the negative symptoms, particularly alogia, affective flattening, and attention deficit, and negligible reliabilities were shown for disorganized behavior and positive thought disorder. The study confirms the theory that the deficit type is the most persistent and traitlike type of schizophrenia. Of course, this may be due to the fact that treatment affects the positive abnormal behaviors more than the negative deficits of behavior, and treatment effects and their durations vary among patients.

Comorbidity

The diagnosis of schizophrenia takes precedence over other types of disorder in diagnosing symptoms. But anxiety and depression often precede, accompany, or follow acute schizophrenia to an extent that would qualify for an independent diagnosis of anxiety or mood disorder if regarded independently of the psychotic symptoms. Table 7.3 shows the lifetime comorbidity of nonaffective psychoses (schizophrenia, schizophreniform,

TABLE 7.3
Patterns of Lifetime Comorbidity for Clinician Diagnosis of
Nonaffective Psychosis

Diagnoses	Prevalence of Other Disorders	Odds Ratio
Mood disorders		
Major depression	66.6	9.4
Dysthymia	28.3	5.4
Mania	20.9	15.7
Any mood disorder	73.4	10.7
Anxiety disorders		
Generalized anxiety disorder	30.9	8.0
Agoraphobia	27.5	5.1
Simple phobia	30.8	3.4
Social phobia	39.5	4.1
Panic disorder	25.5	9.1
Posttraumatic stress disorder	28.9	4.9
Any anxiety disorder	71.4	5.9
Substance use disorder		
Alcohol dependence	43.2	4.4
Drug dependence	37.7	7.1
Alcohol abuse or dependence	57.0	4.2
Drug abuse or dependence	44.8	6.2
Any substance use disorder	58.5	3.7

Note. From "Lifetime Prevalence, Demographic Risk Factors, and Diagnostic Validity of Nonaffective Psychosis as Assessed in a US Community Sample," by K. S. Kendler et al. 1994, *Archives of General Psychiatry, 51,* p. 12. Copyright 1994 by American Medical Association. Reprinted by permission.

schizoaffective, and delusional disorders, and atypical psychosis) with other disorders in the NCS Community Survey (Kendler, Gallagher, et al., 1996).

All of the listed disorders showed significantly increased comorbidity with the primary diagnosis of schizophrenic (spectrum) disorder. Nearly three fourths of those patients with a nonaffective psychosis also had symptoms meeting the criteria for mood disorder, and 71% had at least one anxiety disorder during their lifetime. Two thirds of the mood disorder cases were major depression, 28%, dysthymia, and 21%, mania. Although the prevalence of mania is lower than that for major depression, the odds ratio in relation to the general population is higher. The most prevalent comorbid anxiety disorder was social phobia, and the one with the highest odds ratio was panic disorder. All substance abuse disorders were also common in these psychoses, with the highest odds ratio for drug dependence.

It has been suggested that the depression in schizophrenia is a residual symptom in reaction to the prolonged psychotic condition. However, major depression has been found to occur in 22–75% of first-episode schizophrenia cases, depending on strictness of the diagnostic criteria (Koreen et al., 1993). In nearly all of the depressed schizophrenics, the depression resolved as the psychosis remitted, justifying the assumption that the depression was secondary to the schizophrenic psychosis. However, a prospective study of schizophrenia found that *DSM-III* diagnoses of social phobia, specific phobias of small animals, obsessive–compulsive disorder, and panic attacks, were made before the first schizophrenic episode (Tien & Eaton, 1992). The anxiety disorders in these cases are precursors of the schizophrenic disorder. Clinicians dealing with these disorders should be careful about excluding schizophreniform disorder as a possibility.

Given the high comorbidity between major mood disorders and schizophrenia, one must ask if they can really be distinguished in terms of symptoms and course. It has been suggested by some researchers that both are similar on a broad dimension of psychoticism (Crow, 1990; H. J. Eysenck & Eysenck, 1976). A large study conducted by the World Health Organization (1973) showed that although schizophrenics and psychotic depressives shared many symptoms in common, delusions of being controlled, flatness of affect, auditory hallucinations, and lack of insight (of having a mental disorder) were more characteristic of patients with schizophrenia, and depression and elation were more common in patients with psychotic mood disorders.

Andreasen (1990) compared *DSM-III*-diagnosed schizophrenics, manics, and major depressives using a discriminant function. When positive symptoms alone were used, a majority of the manics were misclassified as schizophrenics, and when negative symptoms alone were used, many depressives were classified as schizophrenics. Using both positive and negative symptoms, over 80% of depressives and schizophrenics were correctly classified, but 42% of the manics were still classified as schizophrenics. However, when mood symptoms were added, 94% of the manics, 96% of the depressives, and 98% of the schizophrenics were correctly classified. The mood symptoms worked so well because manics were high on euphoria and low on dysphoria, the depressives showed the opposite pattern, and the schizophrenics were low on both types of affect. However, these were mostly chronic schizophrenics. Patients diagnosed with acute schizophrenia during their first episode are more likely to be high on dysphoria, which might make the depression versus schizophrenia discrimination harder, particularly if some of the depressives were also psychotic.

Recent studies using *DSM-III-R* criteria for schizophrenia and other disorders have confirmed the discriminant validity of the diagnoses. A study found that a discriminant function, based on symptoms and course of the disorders, could correctly distinguish 98% of the subjects in two groups, those with schizophrenia and bipolar disorders (Maziade et al., 1995). Schizophrenics had higher scores on negative and positive symptom (hallucinations and delusions) factor scores and worse functioning during interepisode intervals than did the bipolar patients. In another study, psychotic and nonpsychotic depressives did not differ significantly on a scale of depression, but both were higher than a schizophrenic group on this scale (Jeste et al., 1996). Amador et al. (1994) found that 57% of a group of schizophrenics showed a moderate to severe lack of awareness of having a mental illness, and 32% had severe unawareness. In contrast, patients with schizoaffective disorders and major depressives with or without psychosis all showed relatively more insight, with severe unawareness ranging from only 7% in those with nonpsychotic major depression to 18% in those with schizoaffective disorders. Patients with bipolar disorders, however, did not differ significantly frrom schizophrenics in awareness, with 23% denying mental illness. However, the bipolars did show more awareness than schizophrenics in doubting the reality of their delusions, with only 34% showing severe unawareness of the falsity of their ideas in contrast to 58% of the schizophrenics.

Although depression occurs in schizophrenia and psychosis in major mood disorders, the former is more intense in mood disorders and the latter in schizophrenic disorders. But this leaves open the possibility that the distinctions are quantitative rather than qualitative, with major mood disorder falling between schizophrenia and normalcy on a psychosis dimension, and schizophrenia falling between major mood disorder and minor mood disorder on a depression or dysphoria dimension.

Prevalence

A worldwide study of prevalence of schizophrenia in seven locations including one each in Denmark, Ireland, the United States, Russia, Japan, and England, yielded world rates of about 1% for a broad definition of schizophrenia, and about .3% for a narrow definition based on the Schneider's first-rank symptoms of schizophrenia (Sartorius et al., 1986). There was much more variation in the broad signs, ranging from about .5% in Denmark and Honolulu to about 1.75% in a rural region of India. There was much less variation in the narrowly defined schizophrenia (about .25–.50%).

In the United States, the ECA Community Study (L. N. Robins & Regier, 1991) using *DSM-III* criteria found a rate of 1.5% for a combination of schizophrenia (1.3%) and schizophreniform disorder (0.2%). The NCS Community Study (Kessler et al., 1994) reported a rate of 0.7% for a broad spectrum of "non-affective psychoses," including schizophrenia, schizophreniform, schizoaffective, and delusional disorders and atypical psychosis. It is surprising that the NCS study came up with a lower rate than the ECA study, considering the fact that they used a broader spectrum of schizophrenic-like disorders, and reported higher rates for most other disorders. However, the rates in both studies are close to the usual 1% lifetime prevalence rate for broad definitions of schizophrenia.

Demographic Factors

Gender

The overall lifetime prevalence of schizophrenia in men and women does not differ significantly, but since the time of Kraepelin and Bleuler, a later onset in women than in men has been noted, and recent community studies in the United States and Germany confirm this (Häfner et al., 1995; Kendler, Gallagher, et al., 1996; L. N. Robins & Regier, 1991). In a Greek sample, the mean age of onset was 23.0 years for men and 26.6 years for women, a difference of 3.6 years (Beratis, Gabriel, & Hoidas, 1994). In Germany, the average age for the first nonspecific or negative symptom of schizophrenia was 22.6 years for men and 25.6 years for women, a difference of 3 years (Häfner et al., 1995). This difference in the German study is maintained for the patient's assessment of onset (usually later), the first positive symptom, the first episode, and the first admission at 28.2 years for men and 32.2 years for women. Late onset disorders after age 40 rarely appear in men, but women show a smaller secondary peak of the disorder between ages 45 and 49. These are mainly paranoid type disorders. Beratis et al. (1994) found that the mean age of onset was lower for males for the paranoid and undifferentiated types of schizophrenia, but the disorganized type began earlier in females.

Häfner et al. (1998) hypothesized that the later onset in women is due to a protective effect of estrogen which reduces the sensitivity of D2 dopamine receptors. Lowering of estrogen levels during menopause in women is the source of the secondary peak of onset between ages 45 and 49, according to this theory. Would men with high estrogen levels also have a later onset? Some evidence from young college-age males suggests the opposite: estradiol is associated with MMPI measures of schizophrenic tendencies and general deviance (Daitzman & Zuckerman, 1980).

Age

The American community studies (ECA and NCS) both found the highest concentrations of schizophrenia in the younger age groups (18–44 years), but these are for schizophrenia at all stages. Looking only at first admissions in the German sample, Häfner et al. (1995) found that the modal age of the prepsychotic prodromal signs was 15–19 years, and the first positive symptoms appeared 5 years later at 20–24 years. The interaction between gender and age was described above and is shown in Figure 7.2. For the earliest signs of mental disorder, frequencies for males exceed those for females between ages 15 and 24, the two genders have about the same frequencies between ages 25 and 39, but frequencies for females exceed those for males between ages 40 and 49. After age 50, few new cases are seen in either gender.

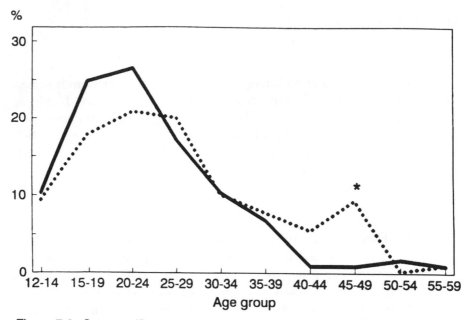

Figure 7.2. Sex-specific age distributions in the earliest course of schizophrenia of a broad definition at earliest sign of mental disorder. Data obtained in Mannheim, Heidelberg, and Rhein-Neckar-District, eastern Palatinate, Germany. Solid line, males, *n* = 117; dotted line, females, *n* = 131. **p* < .05. From *Search for the Causes of Schizophrenia* (Vol. III, p. 49) by H. Häfner & W. F. Gattaz, 1995, Berlin: Springer-Verlag. Copyright 1995 by Springer-Verlag. Reprinted by permission.

Marital Status

Both American community studies found a higher lifetime prevalence for schizophrenic disorders among single and divorced groups than among marrieds. Schizophrenic males remain single more frequently than females, probably as a function of their earlier onset of the disorder with its anhedonic, asocial characteristics. But more female schizophrenics tend to get divorced, probably because of the behavioral effects of the positive symptoms, which occur after marriage.

Education

Both American community studies show a slightly higher incidence of schizophrenics who have some college education, but a pronounced lower number of those who graduate college. The same tendency is seen for grade school and high school completion. The tendency for patients with antisocial and substance abuse disorders is similar and probably represents the interference of the disorder with completion of educational goals at all levels of academic potential. Schizophrenia often has its onset during a person's late teens or early 20s, the early years of college, accounting for the larger "drop-out effect" at the upper range of the educational progression.

Socioeconomic Status and Income

Studies finding a high concentration of people with schizophrenia in the lowest social class have been published beginning mid-century. The ECA study also found an inverse relation between social class and lifetime prevalence of schizophrenia with the disorder five times as frequent in the lowest as in the highest class. The NCS study only analyzed income and found an excess number of schizophrenics at the lowest income level, compared to the nonclinical population, but this was more at the expense of a lower incidence in the middle-income than in the high-income range. There is less question of the finding of an inverse relationship between class and schizophrenia than of its interpretation as a cause or effect of schizophrenia. Is low socieconomic status a source of stress in the diathesis–stress relationship, or do schizophrenics show *drift* into the lowest social class because of their pervasive disability? Evidence discussed by Gottesman (1991) suggests that the latter hypothesis is more likely to be true. Most schizophrenics have a lower social class than that achieved by their fathers. In a society where children are expected to exceed their parents or at least equal them in social class, a drop in social class represents an anomaly that is often related to disability. The failure in educational goals also supports this notion. The ECA data show that schizophrenics are overrepresented among the unemployed and among those living on disability or welfare income.

Ethnicity

The ECA study found a higher lifetime prevalence for schizophrenia in Blacks than in Whites or Hispanics in their primarily urban samples, but this difference between Black and White Americans disappeared when the data were statistically controlled for age, sex, marital status, and socioeconomic level. The rate for Hispanics became significantly lower than that for the other two groups. The NCS study found no differences between the three ethnic groups in the stratified sample.

Religion

Only the NCS study analyzed this variable and found a relatively lower prevalence among patients who were Catholics than among those with other religions, or those with no religious preference.

Geographical Region and Urban Versus Rural Settings

The NCS study found relatively higher rates of schizophrenia in the western United States, and lower rates in the midwestern parts of the United

States. The study also found higher rates in those raised in cities, and lower rates in those raised in rural settings. Unlike one's education and socio-economic status, one has no role in choosing where one is raised, so the relationship here is more likely to be due to the stress of urban as opposed to rural environments. The alternative "selective migration" hypothesis, often invoked to explain the lower IQs in rural settings, would predict a result opposite to that found: Schizophrenics would be *less* likely to leave rural environments where they can find a nondemanding protected life among farm families.

A very high prevalence of schizophrenia has been found among people of African Caribbean origin residing in London, relative to White or Asian Londoners, Trinidadians residing in their Caribbean island, and population samples from nine other countries (Bhurgra et al., 1996). A study of relatives of schizophrenic patients of African Caribbean origins living in Manchester showed an increased risk for the male African Caribbeans born in the United Kingdom, but not for those born in the West Indies (Sugarman & Crawford, 1994). Furthermore, the increased risk was for siblings and not for parents. The specificity of the findings to second-generation males and their siblings suggests environmental stress factors rather than selective hereditary sources for the increased risk for schizophrenia. Discrimination, prejudice, and depressed economic conditions usually have their strongest effects on the second generation, who are between cultures and have frustrated expectations. However, because the incidence of schizophrenia in the parents of immigrants was not different from that in the parents of White British-born schizophrenics, the added environmental stress is probably interacting with a genetic vulnerability, as it is in the other schizophrenics. If it were solely environmental stress, the incidence of schizophrenia in the parents and sisters should have been lower than in the parents of the White British schizophrenics.

Course

Before First Acute Episode

Figure 7.3 shows a schematic plot of the earlier phases of schizophrenic onset based on the German study by Häfner et al. (1995). The first signs of the schizophrenic disorder in the prodromal phase begin with a mixure of nonspecific and negative signs. The most frequent earliest signs of the disorder were restlessness, depression, anxiety, trouble with thinking and concentration, worrying, lack of self-confidence and energy, poor work performance, and social withdrawal, with distrust and reduction of communication. All but the last two of these could also be signs of anxiety or mood disorders. These nonspecific and negative symptoms typically persist

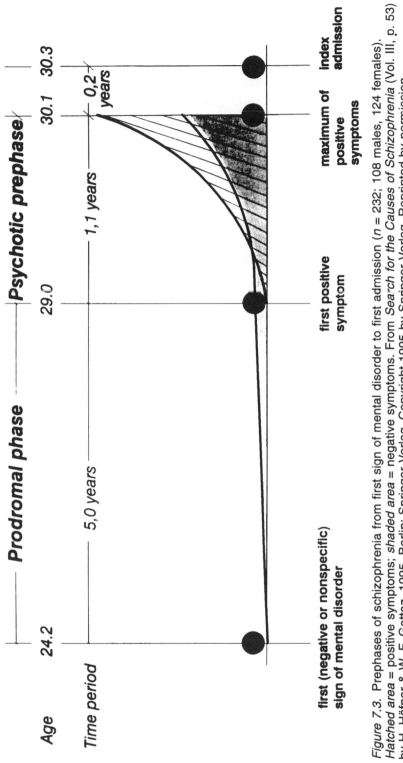

Figure 7.3. Prephases of schizophrenia from first sign of mental disorder to first admission (*n* = 232; 108 males, 124 females). *Hatched area* = positive symptoms; *shaded area* = negative symptoms. From *Search for the Causes of Schizophrenia* (Vol. III, p. 53) by H. Häfner & W. F. Gattaz, 1995, Berlin: Springer-Verlag. Copyright 1995 by Springer-Verlag. Reprinted by permission.

for about 5 years prior to the appearance of the first positive symptom. Positive symptoms tend to increase at a greater rate than negative symptoms over the next year until they reach a peak shortly before the index admission. Positive correlations between positive and negative symptoms begin to increase about 2 years prior to the first hospital admission, but then decrease during the months prior to admission until the correlation is almost nil at the time of admission. The positive correlations in the year prior to admission are not typical, although other studies finding little correlation have generally been done shortly after admission.

Hebephrenic (disorganized) and undifferentiated types of schizophrenia both have an early and insidious onset beginning in adolescence and resulting in some disability prior to the index admission (Fenton & McGlashan, 1991a). The paranoid subtype tends to have a later and more acute onset and to have attained a higher premorbid level of social and occupational functioning prior to the onset. The onset tends to be partly in reaction to stressful life events, more so than that for the other two types.

During Index Admissions

Table 7.4 shows the base rates of positive and negative symptoms in a sample of consecutive admissions to a psychiatric hospital in Iowa during the first week after admission when symptoms were generally at their most acute state (Andreasen & Flaum, 1991). The most common symptoms found in severe or extreme form are the two negative ones of avolition–apathy and anhedonia–asociality, and the two positive psychotic symp-

TABLE 7.4
Symptoms of 111 Consecutively Admitted Patients to a Psychiatric
Hospital in Iowa

| | Ratings (%) | | |
Symptoms	Absent or Questionable	Mild– Moderate	Severe– Extreme
Negative symptoms			
Affective flattening	12	55	33
Alogia	48	35	18
Avolition-Apathy	10	24	66
Anhedonia-Asociality	13	31	57
Positive symptoms			
Bizarre behavior	74	16	10
Thought disorder	58	36	7
Inappropriate affect	50	29	22
Attention deficit	34	44	22
Hallucinations	30	20	49
Delusions	15	19	65

Note. From "Schizophrenia: The Characteristic Symptoms," by N. C. Andreasen and M. Flaum, 1991, *Schizophrenia Bulletin, 49*, 16–17.

toms, delusions and hallucinations. Formal thought disorder and bizarre behavior are extremely rare, found in extreme in only 7–10% of the admissions and completely absent or questionable in 58–74% of the patients. Affective flattening is found in one third of the admissions, and inappropriate affect and attention deficit in about one fifth of the group. A large percentage of cases recover from the first episode after about 36 weeks of drug treatment (Lieberman et al., 1993) but relapse comes soon for most (in 1 or 2 years), and about 61% have continued episodes with varying degrees of recovery between episodes (Mason, Harrison, Glazebrook, Medley, & Croudace, 1996).

Post Episode

Following discharge and in the years following the episode, negative, positive, and disorganized symptoms are significantly reduced except during periods of relapse (Arndt et al., 1995; Eaton et al., 1995; Häfner et al., 1995). By 5 years after the first onset, about 70% of patients in Holland had suffered a relapse (Wiersma, Nienhuis, Sloof, & Giel, 1998). However, positive and disorganized symptoms are reduced more than negative symptoms (Arndt et al., 1995). The only symptom that increases over the years is self-neglect. This often leaves the patient with a residual psychosis consisting mainly of negative symptoms with an occasional mild positive symptom intruding itself. Figure 7.4 shows the relationship between positive and negative symptoms from the admission 0 to 36 months after the admission to the hospital (Häfner et al., 1995). At first admission positive symptoms tend to dominate the picture, but beginning at 6 months after admission positive symptoms fall off and negative symptoms predominate. Anhedonia is the most persistent negative symptom likely to continue after the episode. After 12 months, the moderate positive correlations between positive and negative symptoms, which were typical in the 2 years prior to admission, reappear, suggesting that the underlying disorder has a unity of symptomatology seen in the premorbid and residual phases.

A 5-year follow-up of schizophrenic patients admitted to hospitals at eight sites around the world showed full remission in 17%, partial remission with no further episodes in 13%, further episodes with full remission between episodes in 15%, further episodes without full remission between episodes in 33%, and continuation of the episode without remission in 19% (Leff et al., 1991). However, the outcomes differed in developed and underdeveloped countries. In Agra (India) and Ibadan (Nigeria) the most frequent course was a full remission after the first episode and no further episodes during the 5-year follow-up. The most frequent pattern in the developed countries (Denmark, England, Russia, Czechoslovakia, the United States) was a chronic residual state punctuated by acute psychotic episodes. The better outcomes were in the underdeveloped countries for

VULNERABILITY TO PSYCHOPATHOLOGY

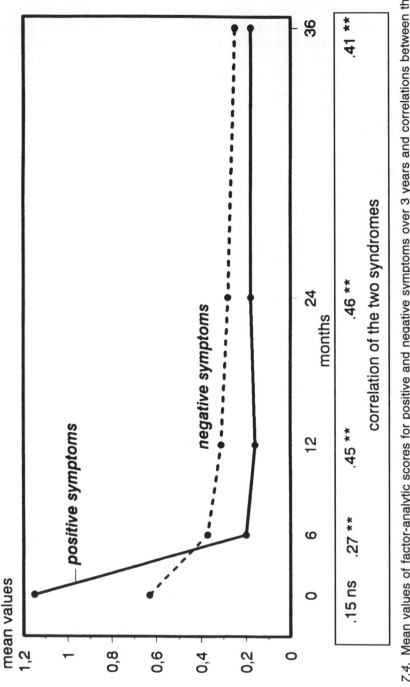

Figure 7.4. Mean values of factor-analytic scores for positive and negative symptoms over 3 years and correlations between the scores for the two types of symptoms at each time period. ns = not significant; ** *p* < .01. From *Search for the Causes of Schizophrenia* (Vol. III, p. 56) by H. Häfner & W. F. Gattaz, 1995, Berlin: Springer-Verlag. Copyright 1995 by Springer-Verlag. Reprinted by permission.

reasons which were not obvious! The same standardized interview was used, and the differences remained significant even when the usual predictor variables (sex, marital status, acuteness of onset, duration of symptoms before contact, premorbid personality, life event stress) were statistically controlled. The authors suggest that the greater tolerance of symptoms and lower expression of negative emotions in the families might account for the good outcomes in the patients. Another possibility is that symptoms such as delusions and hallucinations do not have the same significance as indicators of a chronic psychotic process in underdeveloped countries.

Outcome statistics over the years depend on two important factors: the definition of the disorder, and how it is treated. A meta-analysis of the international outcome literature in schizophrenia compared the percentage of patients rated as "improved" in (Hegarty, Baldessarini, Tohen, Waternaux, & Oepen, 1994): (a) studies using narrow Kraepelinian-type diagnostic criteria (e.g., *DSM-III* and *DSM-III-R*) and studies using broader Bleuler-type criteria (e.g., *DSM-II*, ICD-8, ICD-9), with (b) studies in which patients were treated with either neuroleptic drugs, convulsive shock treatments, lobotomy, or nonspecific methods. Follow-up periods averaged about 5.6 years, but in 57% of the studies, the outcome was assessed at 4 years or less after the index admission. *Improved* was defined as recovered, in remission, without residual symptoms or mildly symptomatic, socially recovered, or working or living independently. Table 7.5 shows the diagnostic by treatment results. Regardless of the decade in which the study was done, studies using narrow diagnostic criteria report poorer outcomes than studies using broader criteria, and studies of patients being treated with neuroleptic drugs yielded better outcomes than studies of patients receiving other treatments.

Because the drug treatment did not start until the 1950s, it is con-

TABLE 7.5
Percentages of Cohorts in Schizophrenia Outcome Studies Improved
at Follow-Up by Treatment and Diagnostic Systems

Treatment	Diagnosed by Kraepelinian Systems			Diagnosed by Non-Kraepelinian Systems		
	N	Mean (%)	SD	N	Mean (%)	SD
Neuroleptic	37	31.2	17.3	87	48.0	17.6
Convulsive Shock	13	26.9	13.8	7	42.2	19.8
Nonspecific	30	22.5	11.1	10	34.0	17.5
Total	80	27.3	15.1	104	46.5	17.3

Note. Adapted from "One Hundred Years of Schizophrenia: A Meta-Analysis of the Outcome Literature," by J. D. Hegarty, R. J. Baldessarini, M. Tohen, C. Waternaux, & G. Oepen, 1994, *American Journal of Psychiatry, 151*, table 2, p. 1413. Copyright 1994 by American Psychiatric Association, adapted with permission.

founded with the periods in which the studies were done, and with the changing diagnostic systems during those periods. Figure 7.5 shows the outcomes from the studies done in decades from before 1910 to the 1990s. Before 1920 diagnosis was primarily Kraepelinian, no specific treatments were used, and only 25–30% of patients were described as improved after a few years in the hospital. Convulsive therapies were introduced in the 1930s with some increase in recovery rates to about 35%. The antipsychotic drugs were introduced in the 1950s, and their effects are probably reflected in the follow-ups done in the 1960s, showing an increase to about 50% recovery. This increase held until the 1980s, when there is evidence of a decline, with a significant drop in the 1990s down to the 1930–1950 levels. Why should recovery rates decline even as drug treatments are being improved? The answer probably is the advent of the *DSM-III* definition of schizophrenia in 1980 which returned to "neo-Kraepelinian" narrow diagnoses of schizophrenia that have been widely adopted since then in most parts of the world. Insisting, for instance, on a 6-month duration for the

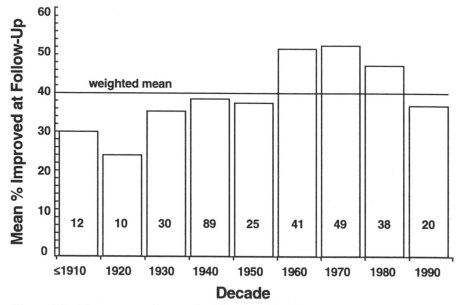

Figure 7.5. Mean percentages of schizophrenic patient cohorts considered improved in follow-ups of 10 years or more by decades of studies reviewed. Horizontal line indicates weighted overall mean for the century (40.1%; *N* = 314 cohorts). Numbers inside the bars indicate number of cohorts for each decade. Decades are defined by midpoint of the decade (e.g., the 1950 decade is 1946–1955). The year of a study is defined as the mean of the first and last years of follow-up. There was significant variation in outcome by decade. From "One Hundred Years of Schizophrenia: A Meta-Analysis of the Outcome Literature," by J. D. Hegarty et al., 1994, *American Journal of Psychiatry, 151,* Figure 1, p. 1412. Copyright 1994, the American Psychiatric Association. Reprinted by permission.

diagnosis means that more chronic- and fewer acute-onset cases will be diagnosed as schizophrenia.

What happens after 10 years? Twenty-two long-term follow-up studies of at least 10 years are included in a table by Johnston (1991). Outcomes were crudely classified as recovered, improved, and not improved. The studies span the years between 1932 and 1980, during which there were changes in diagnostic criteria and methods of treatment. The widespread use of antipsychotic drugs began in the mid-1950s. Comparing patients hospitalized before the advent of drug treatment with those hospitalized in later eras, shows little change in the category of full recovery with only about a quarter of the patients receiving this positive outcome. The major change is in the remaining two categories. In the earlier studies prior to 1952, 62% of the patients were rated as not improved. What this usually meant was that they spent most of their lives in back wards of large mental hospitals. The percentages of these patients fulfilling Kraepelin's description of dementia praecox, fell to about 50% in the 1957–1968 periods, when some of them may have been receiving drug treatments in the latter part of their course. But in the era of drug treatment (studies published 1970–1980) only a third of the patients fell into this category. The major change is in the intermediate category of "improved," which shows a threefold increase from the earliest studies to those in the 1970–1980 period. The patients in this category probably are those who are left with residual, negative symptoms and, although not acutely psychotic, have a reduced capacity to function independently outside of the family or a sheltered environment. The studies done by the World Health Organization (WHO, 1979) in 12 centers around the world show similar results, with 32% with good, 43% with intermediate, and 25% with poor outcomes. A recent Dutch study of 15-year outcomes found that 27% had remitted completely, 50% partially, and 11% were still chronically psychotic (Wiersma et al., 1998).

Describing outcomes at specified periods is inadequate for the full course of the disorder. Eight different types of course with the different combinations of acute or chronic onset, episodic or simple (no remissions) course, and recovered or nonrecovered end states are described by Mason et al. (1996) and Ciompi (1980). Table 7.6 shows the percentages of patients in each type of course. The most common are (a) acute onset with repeated episodes of psychosis and an end state of recovery or with mild residual symptoms; or (b) chronic onset with a longer premorbid history, a simple unchanging or deteriorating course, and generally with a moderate or severe outcome. Both the length of time between onset and hospitalization and the episodic or chronic course of the disorder (related to response to treatment) are clearly factors in the outcome. A year-to-year analysis shows that the disorder is at its worse during the first year or two, but stabilizes (in terms of time each year spent in the hospital) thereafter

TABLE 7.6
Percentages of Patients With Each Type of Onset and Course and Their End States (Recovered/Mild or Moderate/Severe)

Onset	Course	Mason et al. (1996)			Ciompi (1980)		
		Recovered/Mild	Moderate/Severe	Total	Recovered/Mild	Moderate/Severe	Total
Acute	Episodic	29	5	34	25	12	37
Acute	Simple	0	10	10	5	8	13
Chronic	Episodic	16	6	22	10	5	15
Chronic	Simple	2	33	35	10	24	34

Note. Adapted from "The Course of Schizophrenia Over 13 Years," by P. Mason, G. Harrison, C. Glazebrook, I. Medley, & T. Croudace, 1996, *British Journal of Psychiatry, 169,* p. 583. Copyright 1996 by the Royal College of Psychiatrists. Adapted with permission.

for the next 11–12 years. The most common course in the Dutch study over 15 years was two or more episodes followed by the negative symptom syndrome (Wiersma et al., 1998). The diagnostic group as a whole does not show either much long-term amelioration or deterioration, but individuals vary in their course, and it is worthwhile to learn which factors are predictive of the outcome.

Predictors of Outcome

This section is confined to symptom, syndrome, and diagnostic predictors of outcome. Other categories such as premorbid personality, prenatal and birth trauma, and social–familial factors will be discussed separately under those topics. Disorganized (hebephrenic) and catatonic subtypes of schizophrenia generally have earlier ages of onset and poorer long-term outcomes than the paranoid subtype (Fenton & McGlashan, 1991a; Hultman et al., 1996; Loebel et al., 1992). The paranoid type has a later onset and a better prognosis. The undifferentiated type is intermediate in both age of onset and outcome. The illness course in the hebephrenic is generally continuous and deteriorative. Although their overall prognosis was good, paranoid males had one negative outcome in contrast to other types: They were more likely to commit suicide during the follow-up period. A diagnosis of schizoaffective disorder is associated with a high short-term relapse rate (within 2 years), probably because of their emotional instability (Doering, Müller-Spahn, Tegeler, & Schüssler, 1998). However their further episodes tend to be shorter with less social or work disabilities.

Negative symptoms are predictive of long-term (19 years) outcome (Fenton & McGlashan, 1991b). During the early course of the disorder, those patients with high negative symptom counts were more likely to have a continuous disorder or an intermittent one with only partial remissions. Over the long-term, those with pervasive negative symptoms at onset were more likely to spend more time in the hospital, less time at work outside of the hospital, have fewer social contacts, and be symptomatic for more of the time, than those with few negative symptoms. All of the negative symptoms were significantly associated with poor outcome, and anhedonia, avolition, and flat affect showed the highest correlations. Among the positive symptoms, hallucinations and delusions were not associated with long-term outcome, but bizarre behavior and thought disorder were predictive of negative outcomes. Most of these findings relating negative symptoms to outcome have been confirmed in other studies (McGlashan & Fenton, 1992). The Dutch study of 15-year outcomes found that acute onset, immediate treatment, married status, and good premorbid functioning predicted shorter first and subsequent psychotic episodes (Wiersma et al., 1998). Early and acute onset, prompt treatment, being married, and not being on welfare predicted a longer proportion of time in full or partial remission. The study emphasizes the importance of prompt treatment, especially for acute-onset cases.

Fenton and McGlashan (1994) define a "deficit syndrome" in schizophrenia by the presence of negative symptoms persisting for at least 12 months prior to the episode and continuously in the 3 months after hospital admission. Those with a deficit syndrome had a more insidious onset and a worse outcome after 7–8 years between onset and index admission: Of those with the deficit syndrome, 78% had a continuous course without remissions in contrast to 28% of those with nondeficit syndrome schizophrenia. Schizophrenics have a much longer duration (4–10 times as long) of the first episode than do patients of both psychotic mood disorder and schizoaffective disorder (Tsuang & Coryell, 1993). We may conclude that schizophrenia has a worse short-term outcome than all other disorders with psychosis, but has an equally poor outcome as schizoaffective disorder for the long term, particularly in regard to the persistence of the psychotic symptoms of the disorders (Grossman, Harrow, & Fichtner, 1991). Psychotic and nonpsychotic mood disorders have better outcomes than schizophrenic and schizoaffective disorders.

Most patients who are admitted to a hospital with a diagnosis of schizophrenia now receive antipsychotic medications. The initial response to the medications predicts the outcome over the longer course of the disorder, and symptoms after treatment are more predictive than symptoms observed before treatment (Breier, Schreiber, Dyer, & Pickar, 1991). However, this finding may not apply to new atypical types of antipsychotic drugs which affect the negative symptoms more than the older drugs did.

Meehl's (1990) diathesis–stress theory of schizophrenia suggests that all persons who inherit the neurological defect (schizotaxia) predisposing them to schizophrenia will develop a schizotypal personality, but only some of those with this type of personality will become schizophrenic. A prospective study of persons with very high scores on scales assessing schizotypic traits taken during their college years yielded some partial support of this hypothesis, linking schizotypy with schizophrenia (Chapman, Chapman, Kwapil, Eckblad, & Zinser, 1994). This was a 10-year follow-up of subjects then about 30 years old. The group had not yet passed through the period of risk for schizophrenia. At the follow-up, the subjects were interviewed and diagnosed for psychotic diagnoses using *DSM-III-R* criteria.

At the 10-year follow-up, 14 participants qualified for a psychotic diagnosis, and all but one had developed the psychosis during the follow-up period. Ten of these psychotic subjects were in the group who had scored at the extreme on perceptual aberration (Per), magical ideation (Mag), or both at the earlier age. The Per–Mag group was the only one exceeding control participants on the incidence of psychosis. Of the remaining four, two psychotics were in the extreme physical anhedonia group and two were in the control group. Although the participants were not selected on the basis of scores on the social–anhedonia (SocAnh) scale, most of those who scored high on Mag also scored high on SocAnh, and the combination of these two scores yielded a higher psychosis rate than Per–Mag alone.

The most predictive measures of schizotypical personality are those which measure psychotic-like experiences, particularly Mag, occurring years before the onset of actual psychosis, and the SocAnh scale. The latter symptom is also one which is among the highest predictors of outcome after the onset of schizophrenia. Schizotypal personality puts one at risk for psychosis as a broad category rather than for schizophrenia alone. This would be compatible with the psychosis dimensional theories of Crow (1990) and H. J. Eysenck and Eysenck (1976). But family and twin studies discussed below more directly test this idea.

The impulsive nonconformity (Noncon) scale, resembling Eysenck's factor of Psychoticism and Zuckerman's factor of Impulsive Unsocialized Sensation Seeking, did not predict psychosis, but both Per–Mag and Noncon predicted substance abuse disorders, alcohol, cannabis, and amphetamine abuse, and a combination of these scores resulted in a 58% rate of substance abuse compared to 18% in the control group during the follow-up period (Kwapil, 1996). An increased rate of substance abuse is also found in schizophrenia, so this finding in regard to schizotypy is not surprising.

DIATHESIS

Genetics

The popularity of genetic explanations of schizophrenia has waxed and waned as a function of the political attitudes toward the science of genetics. Kallmann is one of the reasons why many psychiatrists and psychologists in the 1950s rejected the evidence for a strong genetic predisposition in schizophrenia. He was an enthusiast for eugenics in Nazi Germany and advocated sterilization not only of schizophrenic patients but also of their relatives. Despite his compatibility with the eugenics of Nazi Germany, he lost his university position and had to emigrate to the United States in 1935 when the Nazis discovered that his father was Jewish. He did a large study of twins who were resident in state hospitals in New York (Kallmann, 1946). His methods were poor, without diagnostic assessment or establishment of zygosity on anything but physical appearance. His concordance rates, including "doubtful" cases, were 69% for identical and 10% for fraternal twins, which corrected for age, yielded rates of 86% for identical and 15% for fraternal twins, higher than all other studies before or after him. Probably more of a factor than the flawed methods and his scientific bias was the fact that his index cases were residents of state hospitals, and therefore, represented the most chronic cases. Subsequent studies have shown that the more chronic or deteriorative cases have the highest concordance rates. It is interesting that Kallmann's rates for fraternal twins were not different from the modern studies.

Gottesman (1991) reviewed twin studies done between 1963 and 1987. Studies done in the Scandinavian countries used national registers to find twins and health records to find those diagnosed as schizophrenic, whether or not hospitalized. Averaging the concordance rates from these studies done in Finland, Norway, and Denmark and one done from hospital records in the United Kingdom, he found probandwise concordance rates of 48% for identical twins and 17% for fraternal twins. However, he did not average in the large study done on male veterans in which both twins had served in the armed forces, most during World War II. Probandwise rates for a broadly defined diagnosis of schizophrenia were 31% for identical and 6% for fraternal twins (Kendler & Robinette, 1983).

A more recent twin study using a total population from a national register for mental disorders in Norway and a structured diagnostic interview and *DSM-III-R* criteria, found probandwise concordance rates of 48% for identical and 4% for fraternal twins (Onstad, Skree, Torgersen, & Kringlen, 1991). The rate for identical twins was exactly that found in Gottesman's weighted average even though he summarized studies done with pre-*DSM-III* criteria. It seems safe to say now that if one identical twin has schizophrenia, the chances are about 1 in 2 that the other one will also have the disorder. The chances for fraternal twins, however, are only about 1 in 10. But on a pairwise concordance rate, less than 1 out of 3 pairs (28%) of identical twins is concordant for the disorder, which is only half the rate found in bipolar disorder (Torrey, Bowler, Taylor, & Gottesman, 1994).

Concordance rates vary markedly depending on the characteristics of patients with schizophrenia (Gottesman & Shields, 1976). Severity of the disorder, as indicated by inability to work or hospitalization, was related to concordance rates: Of severely affected identical twins, 75% were concordant for schizophrenia, but only 17% of mildly affected identical twins were. Crow's Type I (positive type symptoms and good response to medication) had concordances of 53% for identical twins, and of 19% for fraternal twins, and for Type II (mixed) characterized by negative symptoms and treatment resistance, concordance rates were 64% for identical and 0% for fraternal twins. A different classification of the twin sample into a type "P" (paranoid-like), with a later illness onset, good premorbid adjustment, and well-organized delusions, and a type "H" (hebephrenic-like), with an earlier onset, poor premorbid adjustment, disorganization in behavior and speech, and flat affect, yielded identical twin concordance rates of 33% for the P type and 79% for the H type, and fraternal twin rates of 6% for the P type and 18% for the H type (Farmer, McGuffin, & Gottesman, 1984). McGuffin, Farmer, Gottesman, Murray, & Reveley (1984) calculated heritabilities of .44 for the paranoid type, and .68 for the hebephrenic type based on their differential concordance rates. These differences could be expressions of the dosage of schizophrenia genes, rather than different types of schizophrenia with strong and weak genetic etiologies.

The fact that at least half of identical twins are discordant for schizophrenia indicates that something other than genetics influences the development of schizophrenia. Since both twins have the same genetic code, and their own offspring are equally at risk for schizophrenia in the next generation, a pathogenetic genome may be a necessary but not a sufficient cause for schizophrenia. It is often erroneously assumed that everything which is not genetic in etiology is due to the social environment. But the environmental differences for identical twins may begin before they are born! All fraternal twins have separate chorionic sacs and placentas, and therefore, separate fetal circulation systems. Two thirds of identical twins share a single chorion and placenta, but the rest have the dual chorion-placental arrangement (Davis, Phelps, & Bracha, 1995). Monochorionic twins share the same circulation, and therefore, are generally exposed to the same viral, hormonal, and toxic influences, but in dichorionic twins, one twin might be affected by an infectious agent that the other twin's placenta filters out. Differences in circulation may develop, leading to one twin receiving a better blood supply and more nourishment than the other who may be smaller and lighter at birth.

Identical twin pairs who were concordant or discordant for schizophrenia were identified as dichorionic or monochorionic (Davis et al., 1995). Among those who were probably dichorionic, only 11% were concordant for schizophrenia, but among those who were monochorionic, 60% were concordant. The findings suggest that part of what makes one of a pair of identical twins schizophrenic happens in the womb during the fetal period.

Torrey et al. (1994) did a study of nonconcordant schizophrenic twins to find out what pre- and postnatal factors might account for their different fates. They found that complications during birth and pregnancy, especially prolonged labor and precipitous delivery, were more frequent in the twins who were discordant for schizophrenia than for normal controls. Those concordant were in between in frequency of birth complications. When complications occurred, it was usually the twin who subsequently developed schizophrenia whose birth had the most complications. Differences in finger-ridge counts between affected and nonaffected twins within pairs were also found, pointing to a prenatal factor perhaps associated with circulation difficulties or due to infections. Seven of the eight with perinatal differences were born in the winter and early spring months when viral infections in the mothers are more common. Prenatal influences in schizophrenia will be discussed in later sections referring to larger nontwin samples. Differences in size of specific brain structures were also found, which could be due to biological stress encountered early in life. These will also be discussed in later sections. The point to be remembered here is that what is not genetic is not necessarily social- or familial-environmental.

Some of the twin studies have attempted to examine the question of the genetic sources of comorbidity, but most have samples which are too small to do this effectively. Adoption and family prevalence studies have larger samples and are better for this purpose. Adoption studies are discussed first because they can separate the genetic from the shared environmental influences in the disorder.

Adoption Studies

Separated identical twins reared apart constitute a more definitive test of the genetic effect reflected in the identical twin correlation than do comparisons of identical and fraternal twins. These are quite rare in the literature, but a sample of 14 such pairs yielded a concordance rate of 64%, higher than the typical 48% found in the recent literature (Gottesman & Shields, 1982). Given the low number of cases it is parsimonious to assume that the larger concordance in separated identical twins than in those raised together is a variation due to error, and that the concordance in separated twins is the same as in twins raised together. The implication of this finding is that shared environment does not account for the 50-fold increased risk for a cotwin of one who has schizophrenia. Thus all of the theories of the 1960s which attributed schizophrenia *solely* to social influences in disturbed families must now be regarded as implausible.

The first adoption study of schizophrenia compared 47 offspring of schizophrenic mothers separated from them at birth to 50 children of mothers who placed them in foundling homes (Heston, 1966). Five of the forty-seven children of schizophrenic mothers (10.6%) became schizophrenic, and none of the controls was even psychotic. There was also an excess of antisocial personality disorders and other personality disorders or neuroses in the index group.

A study conducted in Denmark used the full adoption cross-fostering strategy, comparing children of "normals" adopted by parents one of whom became schizophrenic after the adoption, with children of schizophrenics adopted and raised by "normals" (Wender, Rosenthal, Kety, Schulsinger, & Welner, 1974). About 19% of the children whose biological parent was schizophrenic became schizophrenic compared with about 11% of the children of normals with schizophrenic adoptive parents. The difference was not significant due to the high rate of schizophrenia in those raised by schizophrenic parents. However, the rate in the latter group was about the same as the rate in children of normals adopted away (10%), perhaps due to too wide a definition of schizophrenia in this study (Gottesman & Shields, 1982). The rate in the adopted-away children of normals is remarkably high compared to the general population norms of 1%.

Another study done in Denmark compared the biological and adoptive relatives of parents of adoptees who had become schizophrenic and parents of a matched control sample of adoptees (Kety, Rosenthal, Wender, & Schulsinger, 1968). A recent update of the study extended it beyond Copenhagen to include the rest of Denmark (Kety et al., 1994), and the results were reanalyzed using the *DSM-III* criteria for disorders (Kendler, Gruenberg, & Kinney, 1994). About 8% of the first-degree biological relatives of the schizophrenic adoptees had a record of a schizophrenic disorder compared to 1% of the relatives of control adoptees. The rates of schizotypal personality disorder (13.2%) and paranoid personality disorder were also high, and the total rate of schizophrenic spectrum disorder in the first-degree biological relatives of schizophrenic adoptees (24%) was significantly higher than in the relatives of control adoptees (4.7%).

A Finnish adoption study used the RDC and *DSM-III-R* criteria applied to offspring of mothers who had given birth to their children while hospitalized for schizophrenia or paranoid psychosis compared with adopted children from normal parents (Tienari, 1991a; Tienari et al., 1994). Of the 136 adopted-away children of schizophrenic mothers six (4.4%) had a confirmed diagnosis of schizophrenia and another 2.2% had another schizophrenic spectrum diagnosis (schizoaffective, schizophreniform, or delusional disorder) for a total of 6.8% of spectrum disorders. Only one (0.5%) of the 186 control adoptees developed schizophrenia, and none had any of the other spectrum disorders.

The adoptees were rated on a scale of severity of disorders in which 1 and 2 were healthy, 3 was neurotic, 4 and 5 were severe personality disorders (like paranoid and schizotypal on *DSM-III-R*), and 6 was psychosis (whether schizophrenic, paranoid, or affective disorder psychosis). Among the adoptees whose biological mothers were schizophrenic, about 11% became psychotic (Category 6) in contrast to the usual population rate of about 1% in the adoptees whose biological mothers were not schizophrenic. An interaction was found between biologic parents' status (schizophrenic or control) and adoptive parents' status (both healthy vs. one or both disturbed, ratings 3–6) as shown in Table 7.7. If both of the adoptive parents were essentially healthy (ratings 1–3), there was a low incidence of schizophrenic spectrum disorders in the children regardless of the status of the biological mother. But if either of the adoptive parents was disturbed (ratings 4–6) a very high proportion of the children of psychotic mothers (62%) had severe disturbances including psychosis. Note that the rate is even high in the children of biological mothers who were not psychotic (34%) relative to the rates in those who were fortunate enough to get

TABLE 7.7

Interaction Between Diagnosis of Biological Mother and Mental Health or Disturbance in Adoptive Parents

Adoptees	Adoptees With Schizophrenic Spectrum Disorders (%)	
	Biological Parents Nonpsychotic	Biological Parents Schizophrenic
Adoptive parents healthy (1–3)	4.1	3.4
Adoptive parents disturbed (4–6)	34.0	61.7

Note. Data adapted from "Interaction Between Genetic Vulnerability and Family Environment: The Finnish Adoptive Study of Schizophrenia," by P. Tienari, 1991, *Acta Psychiatrica Scandinavica, 84,* p. 462. Copyright 1991 by Munksgaard International Publishers Ltd., Copenhagen, Denmark. Adapted with permission.

healthy adoptive parents. If both adoptive parents were disturbed, that effect was significantly stronger than if only one was disturbed. This is the first adoption study to show the effects of the adopting family environment and these effects appear to be substantial. If the results are accepted, it must be concluded that the diathesis is only detrimental to the children if the family environment is disturbed.

Family Studies

Family studies confound genetic and environmental influences, but one might assume that the social stress of having a schizophrenic in the family is worse when that member is a parent who has more control over a child than do siblings. From a genetic point of view, however, siblings, parents, and children are all first-degree relationships, and therefore, are equivalent in terms of the number of genes shared (50%) with the proband. On the assumption of an additive genetic model, second-degree relatives (grandparents, uncles and aunts, half-siblings, nephews and nieces, and grandchildren) share only 25% of their genes with the proband, and their genetic risk should be half that of first-degree relatives. Unless there is assortative mating for schizophrenia, spouses should share no schizophrenia genes, but if both should be schizophrenic, the risk would be 100% for their children if the disorder were totally genetic or the same as the concordance for identical twins if the disorder is only partly genetic in origin.

Table 7.8 is based on Gottesman's (1991) summary of family studies conducted on European populations between 1920 and 1987. Although first-degree relatives generally have higher concordance rates than second-degree relatives, and second-degree relatives higher than third-degree relatives, there are a number of anomalies within a purely additive genetic model. Concordance rates among the first-degree relatives vary from a low of 6% for parents of schizophrenics to 17% for fraternal twins. On a genetic basis alone fraternal twins should have no higher concordance than ordinary siblings. But unlike other siblings, they are born at the same time,

TABLE 7.8
Lifetime Averaged Risk Rates for Schizophrenia From Studies of Relatives of Different Degrees of Relatedness

Total Risk Relatedness	Risk of Relatives (%)			
	First-Degree	Second-Degree	Third-Degree	Unrelated
Two parents (46)	One parent (6)	Uncles/Aunts (2)	First-cousins (2)	General population (1)
Identical twins (48)	Fraternal twins (17)	Nephews/Nieces (4)		Spouses of patients (2)
	Siblings (9)	Half-siblings (6)		
	Children (13)	Grandchildren (5)		

Note. Adapted from *Schizophrenia Genesis: The Origins of Madness* (p. 96). Copyright 1991 by I. I. Gottesman. Used with permission of W. H. Freeman and Company.

and therefore, are exposed to the same family environment at the same ages. This may be what produces a concordance rate which is nearly twice that for ordinary siblings. Similarly, parents and children of schizophrenics have the same degree of genetic relatedness, but the rate for children is twice that for parents. The low rate for parents is attributed to the fact that many schizophrenics, particularly the men with their earlier age of onset, become disturbed before the age of marriage and are unable to participate in the kind of social interactions involved in courtship. In addition there is likely to be more social influence from parents to children than from children to parents. Schizophrenic parents are more likely to have had a later onset and a milder form of the disorder with a good prognosis (M. Bleuler, 1978). They are also more likely to be mothers than fathers, probably because of the later onset in women. The lack of social interest and passivity of young male schizophrenics, even before the onset of the disorder, would be a handicap in finding a mate. Half-siblings have a rate (6%) which is more than half that of full siblings (9%). This could be due to the fact that sharing the same family environment, even if only sharing one biological parent, has some influence in addition to that of genetics.

The case in which two parents are schizophrenic is interesting in view of the fact that the child receives all of his genes from these parents. If the trait were due to a single recessive gene, all of the children would be schizophrenic and if to a single dominant gene, 75% of the children would have the disorder (the one fourth receiving a recessive gene from each parent would not be affected). From an additive genetic model, with the number of critical genes exceeding the threshold in both parents, all of the children would presumably be affected. The actual result based on 134 cases from the literature is a parent–child concordance of 46% (actually about 33% before age corrections). This figure is almost exactly the same as the current best estimate for concordance in identical twins (48%).

Most of the studies surveyed by Gottesman were done before the advent of objective criteria for diagnosis as in the DSM-III, III-R, and IV and the RDC and Feighner systems which preceded them. Some of these studies have investigated other disorders in the schizophrenic spectrum and mood disorders as well in the families of schizophrenic probands. A number of these studies are listed in Table 7.9. The first listed study is the Danish adoption study (Kendler et al., 1994) for which only the disorders in the biological parents are listed. This and the other two family studies conducted in Ireland (Kendler, McGuire, et al., 1995) and Norway (Onstad, Skre, Edvardsen, Torgensen, & Kringlen, 1991) found rates of schizophrenia of 7–8% in the close relatives of schizophrenics, significantly higher than in controls.

All three studies also found significantly increased risks for schizotypal personality disorder in the relatives of schizophrenics, ranging from 7–13%.

TABLE 7.9
Rates of Schizophrenia and Other Disorders in First-Degree Relatives of Schizophrenics

Study	N	SZ	SAD	SPD	NAP	BP	UP
				Relatives (%)			
Kendler et al. (1994) Adoption	178	7.9	0	13.2	—	—	—
Kendler et al. (1995) Ireland	354	8.0	3.0	6.9	—	1.2	23.7
Onstad et al. (1991) Norway	215	7.4	—	7.0	3.7	—	—
Parnas et al. (1993) Denmark	188	16.2	0.5	20.8	3.6	—	—
Erlenmeyer-Kimling (1995) USA–NYC	54	11.1	5.6	4.5	5.6	0	14.0
Ingraham et al. (1995) Israel	50	8.0	—	—	—	—	20.7
Maier et al. (1993) Germany	589	5.2	3.5	2.1	2.2	2.1	14.7
Gershon et al. (1988) USA	97	3.1	5.0	—	—	1.3	2.7
Guze et al. (1983) USA	111	3.6	—	—	—	0	6.0
Kendler et al. (1985) USA	723	3.7	1.4	—	2.5	1.2	—
Bellodi et al. (1986) Italy	1,045	3.2	—	—	1.8	—	—
Kendler (1988)							
Paranoids	185	3.9	—	—	10.8	0.6	6.3
Hebephrenics	150	4.8	—	—	10.3	1.4	3.8
Catatonics	37	5.6	—	—	5.7	0	12.2
Undifferentiated	54	3.0	—	—	5.4	1.6	6.3

Note. N = number of subjects; SZ = Schizophrenia; SAD = Schizoaffective disorder; SPD = Schizotypal personality disorder; NAP = Non-affective psychosis; BP = Bipolar mood disorders; UP = Unipolar depressive disorder.

Not listed in the table is a study by Silverman et al. (1993) who found a rate of 12.3% of schizotypal personality disorder among nonpsychotic relatives of patients with schizophrenia, and Torgersen et al. (1993) who found that 7.5% of the first-degree relatives of schizophrenics, but none of the relatives of major depressives had a schizotypal personality disorder. Paranoid and schizoid personality disorders were found in nearly equal proportions in the relatives of schizophrenics and probands with major depression. In another study no schizophrenics were found among relatives of probands with paranoid personality disorder and only less than 3% of the relatives of those with schizoid personality disorder were diagnosed as schizophrenic (Fulton & Winokur, 1993). Schizotypal personality is more intrinsically related to schizophrenia than the other two Class A personality disorders (paranoid and schizoid).

The prevalence of mood and anxiety disorders in the relatives of schizophrenics in the Danish adoption study did not exceed those for relatives of controls. In the Norwegian family study they were significantly lower than those for relatives of mood disorders. In contrast to previously described rates in Table 7.8, the parents of schizophrenics in the Irish study (Kendler, Pederson, et al., 1993) had an incidence of schizophrenia (14%) which was twice that of the rate for siblings (7%). However, in the Italian study (Bellodi et al., 1986) results were more like those reported by Gottesman with a higher risk for siblings (9.1%) than for parents (4.8%).

The next three studies in Table 7.9 were longitudinal studies of high-risk children of schizophrenic parents who were not adopted away from the family home. The studies were conducted in Copenhagen, Denmark (Parnas et al., 1993), New York City (Erlenmeyer-Kimling et al., 1995), and Israel (Ingraham, Kugelmass, Frenkel, Nathan, & Mirsky, 1995). The children in these samples had first been assessed when they were 10–15 years of age. The last diagnostic assessments were made when they were in their 40s in the Danish study but with an average age of only about 30 in the other two. Thus, except for the Danish study, the subjects were still of the ages of risk. Schizophrenic outcomes in the children of schizophrenic parents ranged from 8–16% for the studies of high-risk children.

In the remaining five studies in Table 7.9, the rate of schizophrenia in first-degree relatives of schizophrenics was lower than that of those already discussed, ranging only from 3–5%. Most have used fairly large samples and one (Maier et al., 1993) used *DSM-III-R* criteria, while two others used *DSM-III*. All studies showed significantly higher incidence of schizophrenia in relatives of schizophrenics, and the three which diagnosed schizoaffective disorders also found these significantly higher in the relatives of schizophrenics. Broadly defined, bipolar disorder was generally not more frequent in relatives of schizophrenics than in controls, although it was more frequent in the relatives of schizoaffectives (Maier et al., 1993) than in controls. Unipolar depression was more frequent in relatives of schizo-phrenics and schizoaffectives than in controls in two studies (Gershon et al., 1988; Maier et al., 1993), did not differ from relatives of other disorders in another (Guze, Cloninger, Martin, & Clayton, 1983), and was only higher when psychosis accompanied the unipolar depression in a third (Kendler, Gruenberg, & Tsuang, 1985). In a much broader review of the familial relationships between schizophrenia and mood disorders, Taylor (1992) concluded that although the risk for schizophrenia in relatives of mood disorders is modest, there is evidence of a higher risk for mood dis-orders in relatives of schizophrenics. But a high risk for major mood disorders is found in nearly all types of psychopathology, particularly the anxiety disorders (see chap. 3, this volume). Considering the 17% preva-lence for major mood disorders in the most recent survey of the United States (Kessler et al., 1994), even the higher rates found in the relatives of schizophrenics in these studies do not seem out of the general population range. If one considers the depressing effect of a schizophrenic upon the immediate family, one might expect the rates to be even higher than they are.

Other disorders studied in the families of schizophrenics include anx-iety disorders and substance abuse. Alcoholism and drug abuse were not higher in relatives of schizophrenics in the Gershon et al. (1988) study, and alcoholism was significantly lower in the relatives of schizophrenics than in controls in the Kendler, Gruenberg, and Tsuang (1988) study. No differences were found for anxiety disorders in either study.

Since higher twin concordances have been reported for some schizo-phrenic subtypes (hebephrenic and catatonic) than for others, one might expect the family prevalences to differ among the subtypes in family stud-ies. An investigation of the prevalences for the different subtypes in the Iowa study showed a slightly higher rate of schizophrenia in relatives of hebephrenics and catatonics than in relatives of paranoid and undifferen-tiated schizophrenics, but these differences (shown in Table 7.9) and the differences in the other diagnoses were not significant (Kendler et al., 1988).

Genetic Models for Schizophrenia

One type of model suggests that there are different genetic factors underlying different types of schizophrenia. Another version of this het-erogeneity approach is that some forms of schizophrenia are primarily ge-netic and others are environmental in origin. The term *environmental* does not necessarily imply social environmental, but incorporates the kinds of nongenetic brain damage from prenatal or perinatal environments found in the schizophrenic twin in nonconcordant pairs (Torrey et al., 1994). Against this latter theory is the finding that the offspring of both the schizophrenic and well twins are equally at risk for schizophrenia (Gottesman & Bertelsen, 1989), and that brain anomalies in schizophrenia are unrelated to the presence or absence of a family history of schizophrenia (M. A. Roy & Crowe, 1994). McGuffin (1991) suggests that the subtypes of schizophrenia really represent points on a severity continuum of genetic liability with the more disorganized (hebephrenic) or incapacitated (catatonic) types further out on the continuum than the more intact types such as the paranoid and simple schizophrenics. W. Maier (1995) suggests that other disorders showing increased familial risk for schizophrenia, schizoaffective disorder, schizotypal personality, and nonschizophrenic psychoses lie further in on the continuum of liability, and even closer to the normal are traits which tend to aggregate in families of schizophrenics, such as unipolar depression, neuroticism, anhedonia, attentional deficits, abnormal evoked potentials and eye-pursuit movements. The genetic liability might depend on the "gene dosage" in polygenetic models.

Meehl (1990) still advocates a single dominant gene basis for the great majority of cases of schizophrenia, but allows polygenic "potentiators" in the form of personality traits. In some smaller proportion of cases, these potentiators in interaction with environmental potentiators may produce schizophrenia. If the dominant gene were fully penetrant (expressed) in schizophrenia, then every schizotaxic schizophrenic would have to have at least one schizophrenic parent. However, Meehl suggests that the gene is only 10% penetrant, which would mean that only 10% of schizophrenics would have a schizophrenic parent, and the overall rate for their parents would be 5%. This is close to the rate typically observed for parents of schizophrenics.

Reviewing the evidence from twin and family studies using model fitting methods, Gottesman (1991, 1993) and McGuffin (1991; McGuffin, Owen, Donovan, Thapar, & Gottesman, 1994) concluded that a single major gene for schizophrenia does not describe the data. A simple polygenetic additive model suggests that there are a number of genes that in quantitative combinations exceeding a liability threshold may produce schizophrenia. Gottesman (1991) proposes a multifactorial polygenetic model which combines several kinds of more limited genetic models. First, there are single rare genes of the Mendelian types, which might account for some special cases of schizophrenia associated with specific physical or physiological anomalies. Then, there are polygenes which in additive combinations and in interaction with environmental stress factors may produce schizophrenia. Finally, there are most common specific genes which produce specific major effects and when potentiated by polygenes and environment may produce clinical schizophrenia. Whatever the role of specific genes with major effects there is now a possibility of identifying them using the methods of molecular genetics.

Molecular Genetics

Linkage studies test for DNA markers in families or pairs of related individuals that might identify a region of the genome where differences are found between affected and nonaffected family members. Such studies could be successful if only one or a small number of specific genes have a major effect. Many such areas have been reported in familial studies of schizophrenia, but are not replicated in other families or by other studies (Karayiorgou & Gogos, 1997; Moldin, 1997). Areas of highly significant effects have been found on chromosomes 22, 8, and 6. A study of 265 Irish families reported evidence of a linkage of schizophrenia and a region on the distal end of the short arm of chromosome 6 in 15–30% of the families (Straub et al., 1995). There has been some replication of this finding. Although the strongest linkage evidence of loci for schizophrenic susceptibility are on chromosomes 6 and 8, the findings are not clearly confirmed (Moldin & Gottesman, 1997), perhaps because the effects of the genes are so small and difficult to detect without very large samples. But even if the chromosome 6p locus was definitely confirmed, it would only "narrow" the search to about 4,000 of the 9,000 genes on that chromosome.

Association studies are needed to test candidate genes whose locus is known or to narrow the areas of interest using known markers which might be linked with genes of interest. These studies do not require families and may be conducted by genetic testing of groups of individuals who manifest the disorder and of controls. However, ethnic subpopulations may have different distributions of genetic polymorphisms, confounding the search for associations of alleles with a disorder in a heterogeneous population. An approach that controls for such diversity contrasts individuals who have the disorder with their own unaffected parents. In either strategy the candidate genes are usually selected from those having a theoretical connection with the disorder. In the case of schizophrenia, there has been a great interest in dopamine receptor genes and the enzymes involved in their metabolism because a dysfunction in dopamine neurotransmission still constitutes the major biochemical theory of schizophrenia.

Negative or nonreplicable findings have been obtained with the D2 and D4 receptor genes, but some promising findings have emerged for the D3 receptor gene. An excess of allele 1 of this gene was found in subgroups of schizophrenics with a positive family history of schizophrenia (Maziade et al., 1997). The D3 receptor is particularly interesting because, unlike D1 and D2 receptors, which have a widespread distribution in the brain, it is more concentrated in dopaminergic transmissions in the limbic areas (such as the striatal complex, substantia nigra, hippocampus, and septum) which are involved in control of cognitive, emotional and reward processes, and some of which have been associated with schizophrenia in brain imaging and autopsy studies. Another gene candidate, a polymorphism of the gene for serotonin, has been associated with schizophrenia in a large European sample (Williams et al., 1996).

Although results in molecular genetics have been difficult to replicate in all populations, this might be expected if there are population differences in the frequencies of specific genes. The future promises ultimate identification of a few major genes connected with schizophrenia and an understanding of what these genes construct in the nervous system will bring us closer to the complete chain of causation from gene through biological abnormalities to abnormal behavior and cognition.

Biological Factors

Behavioral and Biological Markers for Vulnerability

The concept of vulnerability is even harder to define than stress. The children of schizophrenics have often been used to define vulnerable or "high-risk" groups as described above in adoption and family studies. However, there is a need to define vulnerability beyond the genetic factors. Investigators have searched for behavioral and psychophysiological markers which might have predictive value beyond that of the presence of schizophrenia in the immediate family. A marker should have a number of characteristics to differentiate it from characteristics produced by the acute disorder itself (Iacono, 1993). The marker should: (1) Have a low base rate in the general population, (2) be stable and reliable over time, (3) be genetically transmitted; (4) be frequently found among first-degree relatives of those with the disorder, (5) be specifically present in those with the disorder and their relatives compared to the frequency of presence in other disorders and the general population, (6) appear in patients with the disorder even when they are in remission, and (7) segregate with the disorder in relatives of the proband within families. To these six criteria we might add that the marker should predict the occurrence of the disorder in longitudinal studies starting with those at risk for the disorder. One could argue with the requirements of genetic transmission and presence in relatives because the disorder might be a function of nongenetic factors, such as prenatal or perinatal brain damage.

The marker which seems to come closest to meeting Iacono's criteria as applied to schizophrenia is smooth-pursuit oculomotor or *eye-tracking dysfunction* (ETD). The electro-oculogram (EOG) records eye movements from electrodes attached to the skin around the eyes. The most frequently used target is a dot slowly moving on a screen at a constant rate in a sinusoidal pattern as shown in A in Figure 7.6 (Levy, Holzman, Mathysse, & Mendell, 1993). Normal eye-tracking follows the pattern fairly closely (B), but not abnormal tracking (C). Saccades are fast eye movements that reposition the eye, sometimes showing the kind of irregularities pictured in C.

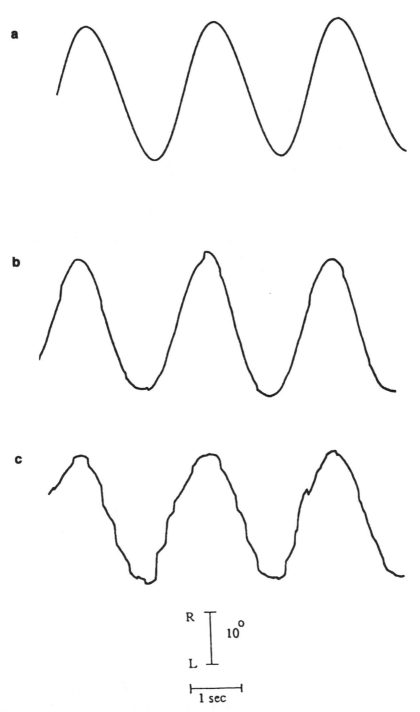

a

b

c

R ⊤ 10°
L ⊥

⊢——⊣
1 sec

Figure 7.6. Eye-tracking patterns in normal and abnormal pursuit. (a) sinusoidal pattern of the stimulus target; (b) normal tracking; (c) abnormal tracking. From "Eye Tracking Dysfunction and Schizophrenia: A Critical Perspective," by D. L. Levy et al., 1993, *Schizophrenia Bulletin, 19,* p. 462.

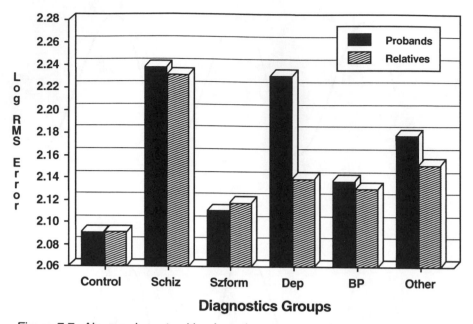

Figure 7.7. Abnormal eye-tracking in patient groups and their relatives. Mean log root mean square (RMS) error scores for each proband and relative group. Schiz = schizophrenia; Szform = schizophreniform disorder; Dep = major depressive disorder; BP = bipolar disorder; Other = other functional psychoses. From "Smooth Pursuit Eye Tracking in First-Episode Psychotic Patients and Their Relatives," by W. G. Iacono et al., 1992, *Journal of Abnormal Psychology, 101,* p. 108. Copyright 1992 by the American Psychological Association. Reprinted by permission.

Scores of studies without exception have found a higher incidence of ETD in schizophrenics than in normal populations (Levy et al., 1994), but the sensitivity is low: Only 20% of schizophrenics are classfied as deviant using a quantitative criterion (Iacono, 1993). Higher percentages of both schizophrenics and other psychiatric diagnostic groups show abnormal tracking using the qualitative criteria of Holzman. Iacono's study (Iacono, 1993; Iacono, Moreau, Beiser, Fleming, & Lin, 1992) used an epidemiological sample of first episode patients, their relatives, and normal controls. The mean ETD (RMS error) scores of the groups and their relatives are shown in Figure 7.7. Only 4% of the normal controls showed abnormal ETD. The only patient group besides the schizophrenics which significantly exceeded the control group in the measure of ETD was the major depressive patient group. In a post hoc analysis, most of the depressives who showed ETD were also diagnosable as schizoaffectives. Only the relatives of schizophrenics had higher ETD scores than did controls.

The results on specificity in this study differ in certain respects from other studies comparing incidence of ETD among schizophrenic and other patient groups. The findings are mixed but some studies have found incidences of ETD in bipolar and unipolar depressives which exceeded those in normal control groups (Levy et al., 1994), so the specificity of ETD for schizophrenia is still in question. The normal eye-tracking in patients with schizophreniform disorders and their relatives in the Iacono et al. study was surprising, because this group is usually regarded as part of the schizophrenic spectrum.

Assuming that the schizophrenics with ETD represent a subgroup of the schizophrenic population with a different etiology, they might be expected to show a different pattern of symptoms and specific neural defects. The neural mechanisms involved in eye-tracking include not only those in the visual and visual-motor systems, but also parts of the nonvisual cortex as well. Patients showing ETD were found to be impaired on neuropsychological performance tests measuring frontal lobe function and IQ, but not on specific tests of nonfrontal function (Katsanis & Iacono, 1991). However, no correlations were found between CAT scan measures of cortical atrophy and ETD. Those with ETD tended to have more negative symptoms and fewer positive schizophrenic symptoms than those with normal eye-tracking.

Schizotypal patients, relatives of schizophrenic patients, and others in the community with schizotypal traits tend to show impaired eye-tracking (Lencz et al., 1993; Siever et al., 1994; Thaker, Cassady, Adami, Moran, & Ross, 1996). Deficit or negative-type symptoms, such as social isolation, emotional restriction, and avolition, were related to ETD whereas psychotic or positive symptoms were not (Siever et al., 1994; Thaker, Cassady, Adami, Moran, & Ross, 1996). ETD seems to be a marker for the deficit-type of schizophrenic or schizotypal personality.

Tonic EEG recordings of schizophrenics typically show lower alpha power with increased variability of frequency, abnormal power in low-frequency bands, and excessive slow wave activity in frontal areas (Nuechterlein & Dawson, 1995). Slowed EEG patterns, particularly in the frontal lobes, are not specific to schizophrenics but are also found in antisocial personality disorders (see chap. 5, this volume).

The *event-related (evoked) potential* (ERP), derived from averaging the EEG over many presentations with a specific stimulus as shown in Figure 7.8, reflects the characteristics of the stimulus and biological responsiveness of the organism to the particular stimulus paradigms. Studies with schizophrenics usually show reduced amplitudes of the ERPs in the N1 (100 msec after the stimulus onset) and P3 (300 msec after stimulus onset; R. Cohen, 1991). These reduced amplitudes are related to decreased performance on tasks requiring stimulus discrimination and seem to reflect deficiencies in controlled or effortful processing of information. Decreased P300 has been found in the relatives of schizophrenics in some studies suggesting it might have the characteristics of a marker (Nuechterlein & Dawson, 1995), but it did not predict later pathological outcomes in the high-risk offspring of

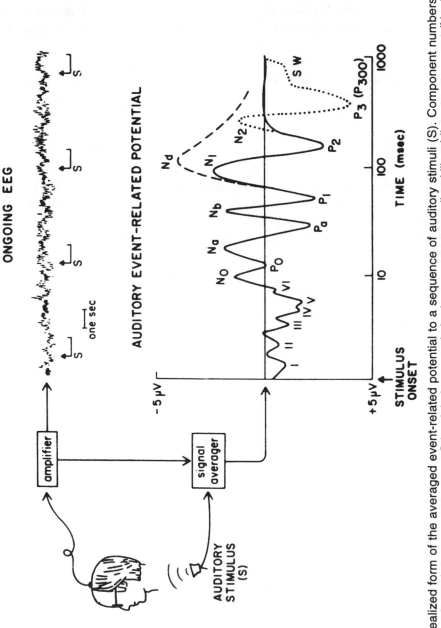

Figure 7.8. Idealized form of the averaged event-related potential to a sequence of auditory stimuli (S). Component numbers represent approximate latency × 100 msec. Other labels are early brainstem responses (I to VI), midlatent component (No, Po, Na, Pa, Nb) and slow wave (SW). Note log units on time axis. From "'Neurophysiological Approaches to Schizophrenia," by K. H. Nuechterlein & M. E. Dawson, in *Psychopharmacology: The Fourth Generation of Progress* (p. 1236), edited by F. E. Bloom & D. J. Kupfer, 1995, New York: Raven Press. Copyright 1995 by Raven Press. Reprinted by permission.

schizophrenic parents (Squires-Wheeler, Friedman, & Erlenmeyer-Kimling, 1993).

The earlier P50 component of the ERP reflects automatic processing and is used to study "sensory gating" deficits in schizophrenia. Many schizophrenics in the acute phase of the disorder seem to suffer from a failure of a filter mechanism to screen out irrelevant background noise. In the P50 gating paradigm, two tones are presented about 500 msec apart in a series of paired presentations. About 90% of normal subjects typically show a typical P50-ERP response to the first tone but a reduction of more than 50% in the amplitude of response to the second tone (Judd, McAdams, Budnick, & Braff, 1992; Nuechterlein & Dawson, 1995). In sharp contrast, about 85% of schizophrenics do not show this kind of normal stimulus inhibition, suggesting a failure of the gating mechanism. This kind of sensitivity is remarkable for markers for schizophrenia. The abnormality is also found in about half of the first-degree relatives (one parent or one sibling) of schizophrenics who are not schizophrenic themselves, but show schizotypal tendencies on the MMPI test (Siegel, Waldo, Mizner, & Adler, 1984). This marker has the possibility of association with a single dominant gene as suggested by Meehl (1989). It could serve to identify schizotaxia in clinically unaffected relatives.

The *prepulse inhibition* (PPI) of the startle reflex is a mechanism related to the gating deficit in the P50-ERP paradigm. The startle reflex in humans is measured by the eye-blink response to a loud noise. When a less intense prepulse stimulus is presented 30–300 msec before the intense stimulus, the startle reflex is reduced by 50% or more in normal subjects. In several studies of schizophrenics impaired PPI was seen with little reduction in the startle reflex (Nuechterlein & Dawson, 1995). The robust finding did not depend on the sensory modality of the starting stimulus or on whether the patients were currently symptomatic. A similar lack of normal PPI was found in asymptomatic schizophrenic outpatients, showing that the phenomenon is not limited to the schizophrenic symptom phase (Dawson, Hazlett, Filion, Nuechterlein, & Schell, 1993).

Attention deficit was noted by Bleuler (1911/1950) as one of the basic deficits in schizophrenia. Many behavioral tests have been used to assess this deficit, but the best candidate for a marker is the *Continuous Performance tests* (CPT). The task is to detect and respond to a target stimulus (a number) or a stimulus sequence by pressing a button (Nuechterlein et al., 1991). The stimuli move by in rapid succession on a screen over a period of 5–15 minutes. The subject may make errors of omission (missing targets) or errors of commission (responding to nontargets). High demands on information processing capabilities are made by using blurred stimuli and high rates of stimulus presentation. Chronic schizophrenics have lower target hit rates than do normal controls or chronic alcoholics, even on easier versions of the task. The deficit is apparent in schizophrenics even when they are in the remitted state, but only when using the more difficult versions. Children of schizophrenics also show the processing deficit, and children of nonschizophrenic psychiatric disorders do not. Some deficit appears in the CPT in patients with major mood disorders, but certain patterns of deficit are specific to schizophrenia (Cornblatt & Kelip, 1994). Thus, the CPT fulfills most of the requirements for a vulnerability marker. Another task, the span of attention, also requires attention, reveals deficits in schizophrenic patients and their nonaffected mothers, and is relatively specific to schizophrenia as contrasted with other psychiatric disorders (Asarow & Granholm, 1991).

Backward masking is another performance task assessing both sensory–perceptual processes and attentional capacities. A visual stimulus (the target) is briefly presented followed in rapid succession by a second stimulus (the mask). The mask interferes with identification of the target when the interstimulus interval is short even in normal subjects. Schizophrenic patients, however, need a longer interval between target and mask to identify the target. The deficit is found in nonpsychotic schizophrenic spectrum disorders as well as in schizophrenia. Those showing excessive interference from masking among schizophrenics tend to have more negative symptoms, poor premorbid functioning, poor prognosis, and a more chronic course. Unaffected siblings of schizophrenics show more deficit than do control participants on the sensory–perceptual component of the task, whereas schizophrenics show a deficit on both the sensory–perceptual and attentional components (Green, Nuechterlein, & Breitmeyer, 1997). Schizophrenics perform poorly on many other measures of cognitive abilities, including learning, psychomotor speed, motor skills, attention, and memory, but patients with major depression also show these deficits (Jeste et al., 1996).

Abnormalities in emotional response, such as blunted affect, are common in schizophrenia. Studies of electrodermal (skin conductance) basal activity and response to stimuli have revealed hyporeactivity in a significant proportion of schizophrenic patients. The skin conductance orienting response (SCOR) is represented by the amplitude of the skin conductance response (SCR) to the first presentation of a stimulus. Whereas 75–95% of normals show a strong SCOR to the first presentation of a tone, 40–50% of schizophrenics fail to show any indication of arousal in response to the tone or to those that follow it (Bernstein, 1991; Nuechterlein & Dawson, 1995). The orienting response (OR) is not necessarily an emotional response, except as an expression of heightened interest, but the SCOR is an index of autonomic reactivity (phasic arousability). Tonic levels of arousal are abnormally high during the psychotic phase of schizophrenia and fall during states of remission (Dawson, Nuechterlein, Schell, Gitlin, & Ventura, 1994). Many other diagnoses, such as anxiety and mood disorders, are characterized by elevated levels of tonic skin conductance

(SC) arousal. The phasic SCOR, however, shows even more impairment (less reactivity) in the remitted state than in the psychotic phase, thus qualifying as a predictive vulnerability factor. SCOR hyporesponsivity was predictive of later schizophrenic development in a study of high-risk adolescents in Israel (Kugelmass et al., 1995), and was characteristic of adolescents with early-onset schizophrenia, particularly those with negative types of symptoms (Zahn et al., 1997). Nonresponding in the SCOR among schizophrenics tends to be related to both negative symptoms and the disorganized types of positive symptoms (Nuechterlein & Dawson, 1995). Nonresponsivity is related to an early age of onset and more severe symptoms, and is a predictor of poor outcome in chronic schizophrenics (Katsanis & Iacono, 1994). Skin conductance hyporeactivity to stimuli shows some of the characteristics of a vulnerability marker.

The significance of these markers for the actual etiology of schizophrenia is unclear. Some of the neurological pathways mediating sensory-motor control, attention, and autonomic responsivity are known, but their role in schizophrenia is uncertain. Neuroimaging and psychopharmacological studies provide a more direct route to the understanding of possible abnormal structural or physiological brain characteristics in the schizophrenic disorder, discussed below.

Prenatal and Perinatal Factors

One source of the physiological and structural anomalies seen in some schizophrenic patients is not necessarily genetic, but due to damage to the brain from prenatal influences or complications during birth. Torrey et al. (1994) summarized the studies examining the connection between obstetrical complications in the prenatal period and birth of those children who later developed schizophrenia. Most of these studies found an increase in obstetrical complications in schizophrenics, whether using the original hospital records or the data based on maternal recall. A recent study using birth records has also found an excess of severe birth complications among the birth records of schizophrenics compared to normal control participants, although these complications were not more common in schizophrenic patients than in people with other types of psychotic reactions (Hultman, Öhman, Cnattingius, Wieselgren, & Lindstrom, 1997). Severe complications accounting for most of the difference between schizophrenics and controls, were found in only 11% of the schizophrenics.

Studies of identical twins who are discordant for schizophrenia are useful in evaluating the role of pregnancy and birth complications because they control for the genetic factor which might affect such problems. A review of studies of obstetrical complications in identical twins who are discordant for schizophrenia tends to show that these complications are more frequent for the twin who later developed schizophrenia (Torrey et al., 1994). However, Torrey et al. found no significant difference between the incidence of birth complications in the schizophrenic twins and their unaffected cotwins in their own study.

Possible sources of prenatal brain damage to the fetus include viral infections contracted by the mother during a critical phase of brain development (the second trimester), severe nutritional deprivation during pregnancy, and Rhesus (Rh) incompatibility between mother and child. All of these factors, plus many others, are potential sources of nonspecific damage to the brain of a developing fetus. Most large-scale studies investigating the relationship between birthdates and the rate of schizophrenia have found that future schizophrenics are more likely to be born in late winter or spring, indicating that their pregnancy coincided with the period when influenza epidemics are common in the northern latitudes (Bradbury & Miller, 1985). Mothers reporting having had influenza or having been exposed to influenza infection during the second trimester of pregnancy had more obstetrical complications and low-birth-weight babies. They were also more likely to have schizophrenic or schizotypal offspring than were controls (Venables, 1996; Wright, Takei, Rifkin, & Murray, 1995).

During the last winter of World War II in Nazi-occupied Holland the inhabitants of certain parts of that country were subjected to severe famine. During the critical months of the famine, the offspring of mothers who were pregnant and starved during the peak months of the famine showed a twofold increase in the rate of congenital neural defects and later schizophrenia (Susser et al., 1996). Either general malnutrition or a specific nutrient or vitamin deficiency might have produced the increased risk for schizophrenia.

Incompatibilities between the Rh-antigen in mother and child have been known to cause brain damage secondary to hemolytic disease of the fetus and newborn. These pathogenic effects are more frequent in later births than in earlier births of the mother. The rate of schizophrenia was found to be doubled in a large Rh-incompatible group of males (2.1%) compared with an Rh-compatible group (0.8%; Hollister, Laing, & Mednick, 1996). The rate among second and later born offspring (2.6%) was even higher. The authors suggest that fetal hypoxia resulting from the hemolysis in the Rh-incompatible infants may account for the vulnerability.

All of these prenatal risk factors account for only a small proportion of the schizophrenic population. Not much has been done on the specificity of these factors for schizophrenia, but they are unlikely to be highly specific because most result in a broad kind of brain damage which could be involved in many other kinds of disorder, such as mental deficiency. However, it has been suggested that some areas of the brain, such as the hippocampus, are particularly susceptible to hypoxic conditions resulting from pregnancy and birth complications. Prenatal and perinatal complications may be one of the causal factors in the kinds of structural brain anomalies discussed below. In the Danish high-risk study, delivery complications and the use of ether anaesthesia to the mother during childbirth were related to the enlargement of the spaces of the brain (ventricles) filled with cerebrospinal fluid in their children (Cannon et al., 1993). The degree of genetic risk, as assessed by schizophrenic spectrum diagnoses in both, one, or neither parent, was also related in a linear fashion to ventricular enlargement and widening of cortical sulci in the brain. Although some have suggested that detectable brain damage, in schizophrenia indicates a nongenetic cause of the disorder, these findings would suggest otherwise. Perhaps the brain damage is only a risk factor in those who have the genetic predisposition or perhaps some of the genetic factors directly produce brain developmental disorders.

Brain Imaging Studies

The *computed tomographic* (CT) method of brain imaging came on the scene in the 1970s and beginning in 1976 was applied to the study of schizophrenia. The CT method is used to picture the brain in the axial plane and to measure the CSF-filled cavities of the brain on the assumption that these are indicators of the loss of brain tissue in the areas surrounding them. Figure 7.9 shows the major spaces including the ventricles, sulci, and fissures. The measures are usually corrected for total brain volume. A review of the literature through 1991 showed that in about three fourths of the studies, schizophrenic patients have enlarged lateral ventricles, third ventrical, or enlarged sylvian fissures in comparison with normal control participants (Gattaz, Kohlmeyer, & Gassers, 1991). The schizophrenic patients with the greatest degree of brain loss tend to have a more chronic course, show more neuropsychological deficits, and have a poor response to neuroleptic therapy, but there are no relationships of brain loss to premorbid adjustment or negative symptomatology. The enlarged ventricles and sulci are not related to duration of the disorder, do not get worse over time, and are also observed in young, first-episode schizophrenics, suggesting that they originate early in life and develop during childhood and early adolescence before the onset of the disorder.

The Danish high-risk study had reported that obstetrical problems in the mothers with schizophrenia were related to enlarged ventricles in their high-risk children (Cannon et al., 1993). The high-risk children in the study who developed schizophrenia had larger ventricles than those who developed schizotypical personality, nonspectrum psychiatric disorders, and low-risk subjects with or without psychiatric disorders. However, the schizophrenics and schizotypics did not differ on size of the sulci, and both exceeded all other groups on these (Cannon et al., 1993). The study shows that the ventricular deficit precedes and predicts the development of the disorder in the high-risk group. The previously mentioned study by Wright

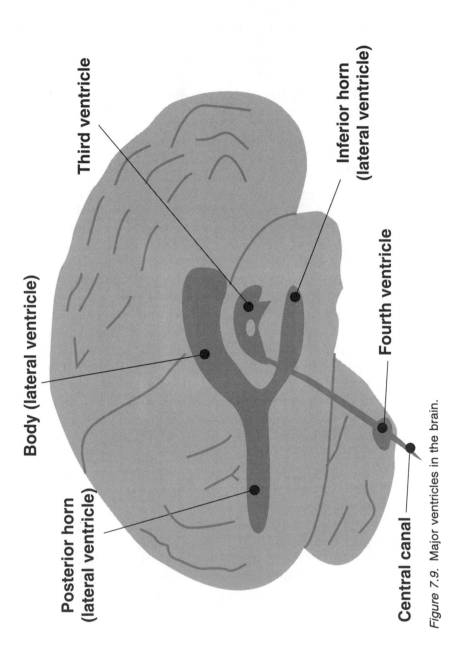

Third ventricle

Inferior horn
(lateral ventricle)

Body (lateral ventricle)

Fourth ventricle

Posterior horn
(lateral ventricle)

Central canal

Figure 7.9. Major ventricles in the brain.

et al. (1995) found a connection between influenza contacted in the second semester of pregnancy and birth complications. Exposure to influenza was also found to be associated with enlarged sulcal fluid spaces and sylvian fissures, but not with ventricular spaces, in the schizophrenic offspring of these mothers (Takei, Lewis, Jones, Harvey, & Murray, 1996). The relationship was not significant in normal controls or nonschizophrenic patients.

Both of these studies suggest a specificity of the ventricular enlargement for schizophrenia. A meta-analysis of studies comparing schizophrenic patients with those having mood disorders (primarily unipolar depression) showed that although nearly all studies found larger ventricles in the schizophrenics than in the mood disordered patients, the aggregated effect was significant but weak (Elkis et al., 1995). Like schizophrenics, the mood disorders patients show moderate and highly significant effects compared with normal controls on comparisons of ventricular and sulcal enlargement. The studies suggest that CT evidence of brain atrophy is a general risk factor for psychopathology rather than one specific to schizophrenia. However, studies comparing schizophrenics with their own unaffected first-degree relatives show within-family specificity with about 84% higher ventricle:brain ratios in the schizophrenics than in their unaffected relatives (Cannon & Marco, 1994).

The method of *magnetic resonance imaging* (MRI) appeared in the 1980s. Unlike the CT which uses ionizing X-ray radiation, MRI scans direct nonionized radio waves at brain tissue. The MRI produces much better resolution of soft brain tissue from many angles and allows for better imaging of the brain unimpeded by bony structures. For these reasons it is becoming the favored method of structural imaging among those who can afford it. A summary of MRI studies performed in the late 1980s confirmed the increased size of cerebral ventricles found in the CT studies and smaller total cerebral, frontal, and cerebellar areas in schizophrenic patients (Nasrallah, 1991). A summary of MRI studies conducted in the early 1990s found few showing reductions in frontal lobe size, but many finding reductions in temporal lobe size, particularly the left temporal lobe (Ebmeier, 1995). Smaller hippocampus and amygdala have also been found, confirming some postmortem studies of cell loss in these areas.

Gur et al. (1994) found that schizophrenics had smaller cranial and total brain volume, higher ventricular CSF volume, and a higher *ventricle to brain ratio* (VBR) than did controls. There were no differences between first-episode and other patients, indicating an earlier origin and a lack of progression on these global measures of brain damage. Analyzing differences in terms of symptom types, Gur et al. found that VBR was higher in patients with intense negative symptoms and in those with the Schneiderian primary signs of schizophrenia, but not in a subgroup of those with general paranoid symptoms who had essentially normal MRIs. In a subsequent study, this group investigated more specific brain structures and found selective decreases in left temporal and right frontal lobe regions in the schizophrenics (Turetsky et al., 1995). The left temporal lobe volume reductions were correlated with the severity of negative symptoms, and those with deficit syndrome (persistent negative symptoms) had greater lateral ventricular space. Reduction of right frontal lobe volume correlated with the duration of illness, suggesting that frontal lobe damage is progressive in contrast to temporal lobe damage.

MRI studies of first-episode schizophrenics already show enlarged lateral ventricles and loss of cortical gray matter (Lieberman et al., 1993; Lim et al., 1996; Zipursky, Lambe, Kapur, & Mikulis, 1998) and abnormalities in frontal–parietal and medial temporal lobe structures (Lieberman et al., 1993). Another study of first-episode schizophrenics showed increased ventricular and intersulcal CSF and reduced frontal lobe brain tissue but no reductions in parietal, temporal, or occipital lobes (Nopoulos et al., 1995). These studies show that the structural brain abnormalities in schizophrenia predate the onset of the active psychosis.

Studies of progression in brain tissue loss in adults over time are still rare. Schizophrenic and schizoaffective patients showed a significantly greater rate of loss of tissue in left and right hemispheres, right cerebellum, and one region of the corpus callosum than did controls over a 4- to 5-year period following their first hospitalization, but no differences were found for rate of loss in temporal lobes, hippocampus, and caudate volumes (DeLisi et al., 1997). Another study done with fewer patients showed a significantly greater ventricular space expansion in patients than in controls over a 2- to 3-year period, but the distribution of rate of expansion appeared to be bimodal in the patients with about half of the patients showing ventricular expansion in the same range as normals, while the rest showed marked expansion outside of the range of normals (Nair et al., 1997). There were no differences in age, age of onset, or other clinical characteristics of the two groups. Both studies found some evidence for increased brain deterioration over time in at least a subgroup of patients.

In recent years findings on subcortical structures have received some prominence. Never-medicated patients with schizophrenia showed both a diminished metabolic rate and a reduction in size of part of the thalamus (Buchsbaum et al., 1996). The authors suggest that a disruption in a cortical-thalamic pathway may cause the defective sensory filtering mechanism seen in many schizophrenics, with the consequent loss of ability to filter task-relevant from irrelevant information. Other investigators have repeatedly found smaller left thalamus volume in schizophrenics (Flaum et al., 1995). They also found larger lateral and third ventricles, smaller superior temporal, and smaller hippocampal volumes. Hippocampal size has been found to be related to severity of thought disorder, and superior temporal volume to severity of auditory hallucinations.

An MRI study showed that schizophrenics had a smaller amygdala-hippocampus complex than controls as well as prefrontal white matter suggesting an abnormality in prefrontal-limbic connections (Breier et al., 1992). Torrey et al. (1994) conducted MRI investigations on identical twins discordant for schizophrenia. They found that about 80% of the affected twins in the pairs had smaller bilateral hippocampal-amygdala (HA) complexes than their own unaffected paired twins. Because the genetic matching rules out a genetic source of the diminished HA, an environmental source is probable. The mother's obstetrical complication score correlated negatively and significantly with the HA size, providing one explanation for the source of the HA differences. Performance on the Wisconsin Card Sort Test is generally impaired in schizophrenics and is associated with activation of the frontal lobes during performance. Frontal cortical activation is associated with anterior hippocampal size; therefore, defective cortical-hippocampal function could underlie the cognitive defects found in schizophrenics, particularly deficits in concept formation.

Unlike the imaging methods just discussed, which are used to study structure of the brain, *positron emission tomography* (PET) is used to study activity of the brain during a specified period of time ranging from 2–45 minutes depending on the particular radioactive tracer used. Radioactive tagged glucose has an uptake period of 30–45 minutes. After that the rapidly decomposing ions produce gamma rays that are detected by scanners which surround the head and can be adjusted to produce images of relative activity or glucose uptake in the parts of the brain that are responding during the period of uptake of the tagged glucose. What is happening during the uptake period determines what parts of the brain will be activated. Investigators have differed on what should be done during the uptake period. Some, like Gur (1995), have favored a resting baseline with the subject simply resting with eyes open and ears unoccluded. Others, like Buchsbaum, Haier, et al. (1992) have administered performance tasks during the uptake period. The results could very well depend on the cognitive activity during the period when the brain is taking up glucose.

One of the most commonly reported results is a relatively low level of activity in the frontal lobes, or *hypofrontality*, particularly when activity in the uptake period is assessed while the subject is attempting to take tests associated with frontal lobe function such as the Continuous Performance Test (CPT, see description above), the Tower of London (a test involving planning and attention), or the Wisconsin Card Sorting Task (WCST), a measure of concept formation (Ebmeier, 1995). As with other types of psychophysiological measures, one must ask whether the differences observed are chronic or dependent on the psychotic state. This is less of a problem with the structural measures. Although the brain may deteriorate over time, it cannot regenerate. Since antipsychotic drugs may normalize PET responses in some brain areas (see, e.g., Buchsbaum, Potkin, et al.,

1992) there is certainly a state component to these reactions. This is why it is important to use nonmedicated and preferably first-admission subjects in PET studies and to repeat the studies on the same patients before and after treatment. Some of the inconsistencies in the literature may be a function of the small numbers of participants characteristic in most studies. Few studies meet all of these criteria. Two relatively large recent studies were done by Gur et al. (1995) and B. V. Siegel et al. (1993).

Gur et al. (1995) used both first-episode (FE) patients never treated with drugs as well as previously treated (PT) patients not currently receiving drugs. They used the resting PET condition without any task during the uptake period. There were no differences between schizophrenic and control participants in whole brain metabolism or in regional ratios, but left midtemporal metabolism was relatively higher than that in right hemisphere in both FE and PT schizophrenic patients, whereas in controls, right midtemporal metabolism was higher. This difference in laterality was more pronounced in patients with predominantly negative symptoms and in those with the Schneiderian core signs for schizophrenia. In contrast, paranoid patients showed normal activity in the left temporal region.

In contrast to the relatively circumscribed difference found in the Gur et al. study, B. V. Siegel et al. (1993), when giving the CPT during the uptake period to drug-free schizophrenic subjects, found a number of specific regional differences. Low metabolic rates were found in the schizophrenic patients' medial frontal cortex, cingulate gyrus, medial temporal lobe, corpus callosum, and ventral caudate nucleus; and increased metabolism was found in the left lateral temporal and occipital cortices. Of these findings only the difference in the left temporal cortex resembles that found in the Gur et al. study. Their results suggest a deficit in the cortical–striatal–thalamic pathway, loss of normal lateralization patterns, and a relationship between underactivity of medial frontal cortex and negative symptoms. Both positive and negative symptoms correlated negatively with activity in the caudate nucleus. Andreasen et al. (1992) also found lower activation of the left mesial frontal cortex and anterior cingulate gyrus using a different type of PET tag (Xenon 133) and a different experimental task (the Tower of London).

The cingulate gyrus has been called the cerebral cortex of the mammalian (limbic) brain. It is the transmission pathway from the frontal lobes to the limbic brain. The anterior cingulate gyrus is involved in motivational, attentional, and memory functions which are altered in schizophrenia. A Mt. Sinai group focused on glucose metabolism in the cingulate cortex and found lower relative metabolic rates in the anterior cingulate and higher rates in the posterior cingulate in unmedicated male schizophrenics while taking the CPT (Hazneder et al., 1997).

A study of identical twins discordant for schizophrenia, using the

Xenon inhalation method, found that in *every pair* of discordant twins, the schizophrenic twin had a relatively lower index of prefrontal activation when performing the WCST than did the nonschizophrenic cotwin (Berman, Torrey, Daniel, & Weinberger, 1992). Twin pair differences in activation correlated highly with differences in performance on the WCST. There were no differences between unaffected discordant and normal twins in the prefrontal index. These results suggest that hypofrontality does not originate in genetic sources, but is a function of something that happens to one twin that does not affect the other.

Postmortem Studies

Descending to a molecular level, investigators have looked for cellular abnormalities in schizophrenic brains postmortem. For many years Mednick (1970; Mednick, Machon, & Huttunen, 1988) has suggested that one of the sources of schizophrenia might be damage to the hippocampal formation during a critical period of fetal development (the second trimester) or during the birth process. MRI studies discussed above show smaller hippocampus and amygdala in schizophrenics even in comparison with their nonschizophrenic identical twins (Torrey et al., 1994). Studies of the neurons in the hippocampus have shown differences in size and shape with smaller sizes and altered shapes of neurons in brains of schizophrenics compared to controls (Talamini, Louwerens, Sloof, & Korf, 1995; Zaidel, Esiri, & Harrison, 1997). An earlier report of differences in cell orientation in the hippocampus (Conrad, Abebe, Austin, Forsythe, & Scheibel, 1991) was not confirmed in later studies including the one by Zaidel et al. (1997). The neurons of the parahippocampal gyrus containing the entorhinal cortex, which is the main source of input to the hippocampus, have also been found to be reduced in volume, cell number, and organization in schizophrenic patients (Talamini et al., 1995).

Abnormal cellular morphometric characteristics have also been found in the prefrontal and temporal cortices, and in the thalamus, but consistent findings have not emerged from studies of the amygdala or basal ganglia. However, increased dopamine levels and binding to D2 receptors have been found in the caudate, putamen, and nucleus accumbens of schizophrenics. Both structural and binding abnormalities occurring in most of these structures are in the upper layers of cells through which interconnections between areas run. Talamini et al. (1995) suggest that the cellular defects suggest a circuit (Fig. 7.10) which is involved in negative symptoms and cognitive deficits found in schizophrenia. Figure 7.11 shows some of the areas of brain implicated in imaging and postmortem studies.

Summarizing the research on brain abnormalities in schizophrenia, Weinberger (1995) says that it suggests that damage to prefrontal and limbic cortices and their connections that originate before the disorder are

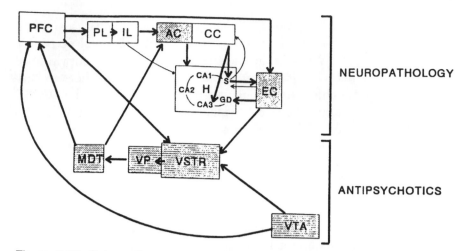

NEUROPATHOLOGY

ANTIPSYCHOTICS

Figure 7.10. Schematic representation of the projections between a number of limbic and prefrontal areas likely to be primarily (arched) or secondarily (dotted) involved in the pathogenesis of schizophrenia. Also illustrated are the connections between the aforementioned areas and the ventral tegmental area, which may be involved in the therapeutic action of antipsychotic drugs (stripes). AC = anterior cingulate cortex; CA1-CA3 = various subdivisions of Ammon's horn; CC = cingulate cortex; EC = entorhinal cortex; GD = dentate cortex, H = hippocampus; IL = intralimbic cortex; MDT = mediodorsal thalamic nucleus; PFC = prefrontal cortex; PL = prelimbic cortex; VP = ventral pallidum; VSTR = ventral striatum; VTA = ventral tegmental area. From "PET Versus Postmortem Studies in Schizophrenia Research: Significance for the Pathogenesis and Pharmacotherapy," by L. M. Talamini et al., 1995, in J. A. den Boer et al. (Eds.), *Advances in the Neurobiology of Schizophrenia*, Figure 1, p. 165. Copyright 1995 by John Wiley & Sons, Ltd. Reproduced with permission of John Wiley & Sons, Ltd.

static rather than degenerative and are consistent with a developmental defect occurring in the second trimester of pregnancy and involving a failure of neuronal migration during that period. If crucial connections between brain areas are not formed or are abnormally formed, future cognitive and emotional development may be put at risk. Whatever the source of these deviations, their consequences in cognitive functions are manifold.

Soft Neurological Signs

"Soft" neurological signs include, for example, lateral gaze impersistence, problems in face–hand test, right–left discrimination, incoordination, involuntary movements, and tremors. "Hard" signs might include the persistence or absence of developmental reflexes and the absence of motor tone or strength. Soft signs have been found in 36–75% of schizophrenic patients in various studies (L. J. Seidman, 1983) and 50–60% in a later review (Heinrichs & Buchanan, 1988). To what extent are these signs due to the antipsychotic drugs which may impair the dopamine functions in the striatal motor systems? A comparison of schizophrenics who never re-

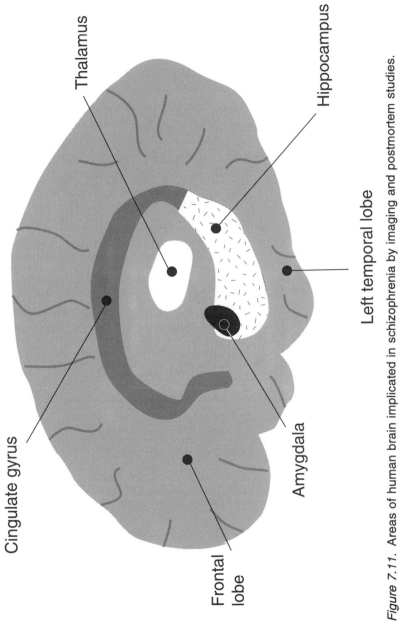

Thalamus

Hippocampus

Cingulate gyrus

Frontal lobe

Amygdala

Left temporal lobe

Figure 7.11. Areas of human brain implicated in schizophrenia by imaging and postmortem studies.

ceived neuroleptic drugs, those currently on these drugs, and normal controls showed soft signs present in none of the normals, in 23% of the neuroleptic-naive, and in 46% of those currently on neuroleptic drugs (Gupta et al., 1995). The results indicate that these signs may occur in schizophrenia without any drug influence, but also that the neuroleptic drugs may increase their prevalence in this group. Comparisons of identical twins discordant for schizophrenia show that in 59–77% of the pairs, the twin with schizophrenia showed more signs of neurological impairment than the nonaffected twin (Mosher, Pollin, & Stabenau, 1971; Torrey et al., 1994).

Signs of neurobehavioral dysfunctioning were investigated at birth and during the first year of life, and later at school age in the Jerusalem study of high-risk participants. These signs were then related to later disorders (Marais et al., 1993). Only 15% of the children of normal parents displayed poor neurobehavioral functioning in contrast to 24% of children of parents with nonschizophrenic disorders, and to 44% of the children of schizophrenic parents. Only perceptual–cognitive signs, and not motoric defects, were linked to parental diagnosis of schizophrenia, but only motoric signs were related to birth and pregnancy complications in the mothers. Results suggested a genetically influenced cognitive defect that is not attributable to pregnancy and birth sources in the children of schizophrenics. The implications of soft signs for impairments of function on neuropsychological tests were explored in a study by Flashman, Flaum, Gupta, and Andreasen (1996). They found that the presence of soft signs in schizophrenia was related to poor performance on tests that measured motor coordination and timed motor speed, coordination and sequencing, but they were not related to a more global, cognitive impairment as assessed by other kinds of tests.

Neuropsychological Tests

Batteries of neuropsychological tests given to schizophrenic participants generally show a broad range of impairments relative to normal control participants. Saykin et al. (1991) compared schizophrenics and controls on 11 major categories of tests. Schizophrenics showed major impairment on tests of semantic memory, visual memory, and verbal learning; moderate impairment on tests of verbal intelligence, abstraction–flexibility (e.g., Wisconsin Card Sorting Test), auditory processing and attention, attention-vigilance (e.g., Continuous Performance Test), and motor tests; and no impairment on tests of spatial organization, language, and visual-motor processing and attention. The findings were similar in first-episode, never-medicated schizophrenics and previously but not currently medicated patients. Both groups scored well below normals on most tests in the battery (Saykin et al., 1994). Deficits in verbal learning and memory accounted for most of the variance between patients and controls over all types of tests. The authors attribute the pattern to impairment in temporal–hippocampal system connections against a background of diffuse dysfunction.

In a test of specificity of the neuropsychological deficits in schizophrenia, T. E. Goldberg et al. (1993) compared schizophrenic and affective disorder patients on a neuropsychological battery. The patients with schizophrenia scored lower than did those with unipolar and bipolar mood disorders on measures of intelligence, verbal and visual memory, abstraction, problem solving, attention, and psychomotor speed. In accord with many previous studies, Goldberg et al. found an average IQ of 90 in schizophrenics, 10 points below the normal population. Contrasting this with a higher score on a reading test, they concluded that IQ must have undergone some deterioration in the schizophrenic group. But another study which actually had childhood IQs on record at average age 13 and retested those who had become schizophrenic in the next 20 years, found no difference in early adolescent and adult full scale, verbal, or performance IQs, suggesting that the intellectual deterioration occurred before the onset of the disorder (Russell, Munro, Jones, Hemsley, & Murray, 1997). Typically there is a lack of correlation between IQ and other cognitive measures and duration of illness or age of onset suggesting that these deficits do not reflect a deteriorative process but one which began early and remains stable.

Comparisons of schizophrenics, their unaffected siblings, and normal controls suggest that the impaired information processing in schizophrenics is at least partly a function of a genetic vulnerability to the disorder (Cannon et al., 1994). Both schizophrenics and their unaffected siblings scored lower than controls on most tests with the well siblings scoring intermediate between the schizophrenics and the controls. As in previous studies, the functions most affected were verbal learning and memory, abstraction, attention, and language. The differences between schizophrenics and their siblings were quantitative rather than qualitative because their profiles over the test battery were quite similar, differing only in elevation. Noting that medial temporal lobe structures (hippocampus, entorhinal cortex, and parahippocampal gyrus) have been shown to play an important role in explicit or declarative memory, as in learning and recall of words, they found abnormal regional activation in the temporal lobes during recall testing and a relationship between activation and poorer memory performance. The finding of left temporal lobe dysfunction in schizophrenics is consistent with the neurological deficits in verbal learning and language.

Neuropsychological Impairment, Syndromes, and PET Studies

On the basis of his PET studies of cerebral blood flow with the subjects at rest, Liddle (1995; Liddle, Friston, Hirsch, Jones, & Frackowiak,

1992) outlined correlational associations between the three major syndromes found in schizophrenia, the areas of neuropsychological impairment associated with these, and their associations with area blood flow patterns (see Table 7.10, Fig. 7.12). Psychomotor poverty or negative symptoms are associated with tests assessing initiation and planning and low activation of the prefrontal cortex and the left parietal cortex, and high activation of the caudate nucleus. This is interesting in view of the inhibitory action of dopamine systems in the prefrontal cortex on dopamine systems in the striate (including the caudate nucleus). Disorganization is associated with tests measuring selection of activity and is correlated with lowered activity in the right ventral prefrontal cortex, insula, and parietal cortex, as well as in the left parietal cortex. This syndrome is correlated positively with activity in the right anterior cingulate cortex, thalamus, and left temporal cortex. Reality distortion (delusions and hallucinations) is associated with incapacity for internal correction of errors and low activity in the left lateral temporal lobe and right posterior cingulate, and with positive correlation with activity in the left medial temporal lobe and left lateral frontal cortex. Of course, activity during the resting state is assumed to be trait characteristic, whereas it may be a function of the general levels of tension or specific reactions when the subject is in the resting state. The changes in cortical activation during the specific activities are more relevant. For instance, recordings of CBF during actual hallucinations show increased blood flow in Broca's area in nearly all of the patients, and in the left medial temporal lobe and left anterior cingulate cortex (McGuire, Shah, & Murray, 1993). Studies showing hypofrontality or diminished activity in the prefrontal lobes during the WCST have been previously described.

The brain imaging and neuropsychological studies have pointed to areas of the brain where structural or functional abnormalities are linked with symptoms and specific kinds of deficits in information processing. But the crucial next step is to identify the specific neurochemical bases of the neural dysfunctions. The putative association between hypofrontality and dopamine in prefrontal and striate cortex is one instance linking the structural, behavioral, and pharmacological functions. This carries us beyond simple correlation of structure and function into an area where effective treatment may emerge from basic knowledge. It is easier to remedy a chemical imbalance than to repair a damaged neuron.

Psychopharmacology

Dopamine Hypothesis

The dopamine hypothesis for schizophrenia was originally quite simple: excessive dopaminergic activity causes schizophrenia (Matthysse, 1973), but it has become more complex over time in order to accommodate

TABLE 7.10
Neuropsychological Impairments Associated With Schizophrenic Syndromes

Syndrome	Impairment	Process	Neg. r with rCBF	Pos. r with rCBF
Psychomotor poverty	Word generation Wisconsin categories Recall of memories	Initiation/planning	Prefrontal cortex Left parietal cortex	Caudate nucleus (left and right)
Disorganization	Stroop test Trails B (Halstead) Wisconsin perseverative errors	Selection of activity	Right ventral prefrontal cortex Right insula Parietal cortex	Right anterior cingulate cortex Thalamus Left temporal cortex
Reality distortion	Internal correction of errors	Monitoring	Left lateral temporal lobe Right posterior cingulate	Left medial temporal lobe Left lateral frontal cortex

Note. From "Regional Cerebral Blood Flow and Subsyndromes of Schizophrenia" by P. F. Liddle, in *Advances in the Neurobiology of Schizophrenia* (pp. 193, 194), edited by J. A. Den Boer et al., 1995, Chichester, UK: Wiley. Copyright 1995 by John Wiley & Sons Limited. Reproduced by permission of John Wiley and Sons Limited. Neg. r with rCBF = negative correlation with cerebral blood flow. Pos. r with rCBF = positive correlation with cerebral blood flow.

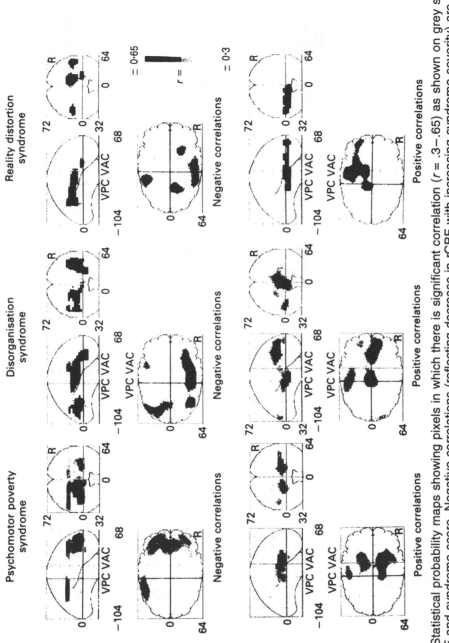

Figure 7.12. Statistical probability maps showing pixels in which there is significant correlation (*r* = .3–.65) as shown on grey scales between rCBF and syndrome score. Negative correlations (reflecting decrease in rCBF with increasing syndrome severity) are presented above, positive correlations below. Each map is presented in three orthogonal projections of the brain viewed from the right-hand side (top left), from behind (top right), and from above (bottom left). From "Patterns of Cerebral Blood Flow in Schizophrenia," by P. F. Liddle et al., 1992, *British Journal of Psychiatry, 160*, p. 182. Copyright 1992 by Royal College of Psychiatry. Reprinted by permission.

negative, mixed, and contradictory findings (K. L. Davis, Kahn, Ko, & Davidson, 1991; Kahn & Davis, 1995). The initial hypothesis was based on inferences from what seemed to be solid data at that time:

1. All of the neuroleptic drugs used at that time blocked dopamine receptors, and their capacity to displace dopamine antagonists in vitro was directly related to their clinical potency. These drugs dramatically reduced the positive symptoms (hallucinations and delusions) of schizophrenia, but were less effective in ameliorating the negative symptoms.

2. Drugs that increase dopamine activity, such as amphetamine, cocaine, and L-dopa, usually made the symptoms of schizophrenia worse. These drugs often precipitated a psychosis in chronic drug abusers which resembled paranoid schizophrenia with delusions of persecution, intense hostility, and sometimes violence. Psychoses could be produced in non-psychotic abusers in the laboratory by frequent amphetamine dosage over a relatively short period of time (Griffith, Cavanaugh, Held, & Oates, 1972).

3. Postmortem studies have found increased levels of dopamine or its metabolite, homovanyllic acid (HVA), in the brains of schizophrenics compared to those of controls, but the results have varied across brain regions and when the schizophrenics were on or off medication before death (K. L. Davis et al., 1991).

4. Postmortem studies consistently found increased D2 (but not D1) dopamine receptors in the striatum of schizophrenics, even in those who never had drugs or were drug-free for at least a year prior to death (Kahn & Davidson, 1995).

Subsequent studies have raised complications for the simple dopamine hypothesis:

1. Three new dopamine sites, D3, D4, and D5 were identified, and new atypical neuroleptics acted at sites other than the D2, where most of the early neuroleptics had their effects. Furthermore, two atypical antipsychotics, clozapine and risperidone, have significant affinities for serotonin receptor sites as well (Den Boer & Westenberg, 1995; Kahn & Davis, 1995; Roth & Meltzer, 1995). Whereas the typical drugs had their effects mostly on the positive psychotic symptoms, the atypical drugs were also effective for reducing the negative symptoms.

2. Baseline or resting studies of HVA in the CSF or plasma have generally failed to find differences between schizophrenics and controls (Kahn & Davidson, 1995). However, HVA does have some interesting correlates within the schizophrenic group. Antipsychotic drugs reduce plasma HVA in schizophrenics and baseline HVA is higher in responders than in nonresponders to the drugs (Kahn & Davis, 1995). HVA in CSF is related to the severity of psychotic symptoms in schizophrenia or even in nonschizophrenic psychoses (Maas et al., 1997). Elevated HVA in plasma and CSF was found in schizotypal personality disorders and within

this group HVA correlated with extent of psychotic-like symptoms (Siever et al., 1991, 1993).

3. The density of dopamine D2 receptors, as revealed in PET scans, is higher in schizophrenics *and* in psychotic bipolar patients than in non-psychotic bipolar patients and in controls (Pearlson et al., 1995). D2 receptors correlate with psychotic but not with nonpsychotic symptoms among the bipolars. Thus both HVA and D2 receptors seem to be related to degree of psychosis rather than specifically to schizophrenia. HVA might be a correlate of the psychotic state rather than a trait marker for psychosis. After all, antipsychotic drugs do decrease the HVA concentrations. Longitudinal studies are needed to resolve this question.

4. Studies in monkeys show that CSF HVA correlates with the concentration of HVA in the frontal cortex and thus reflects mesocortical dopamine activity (Davis et al., 1991). Other experiments on animals suggest that there is an inverse relationship between dopamine reactions to stress in the prefrontal cortex and the striatum (Kahn & Davis, 1995). Cortical hypoactivity during the WCST task and poor performance on the task are related to low CSF HVA, suggesting a decreased dopaminergic prefrontal cortical function. The dopamine agonist amphetamine increases blood flow in the prefrontal cortex in schizophrenics, contrary to its purported effect in increasing psychotic symptoms. The hypothesis from these findings is this: Whereas negative symptoms and some cognitive deficits in schizophrenia are related to decreased dopaminergic activity in the frontal lobes, positive psychotic symptoms are related to increased activity in the striatal, mesolimbic, and temporal lobe dopaminergic systems. The conventional antipsychotic drugs act primarily on the latter areas, and this would explain why they do not have as robust effects on negative symptoms as they have on positive symptoms. Drugs that have a selective stimulant effect on the D1 and D5 receptors in the prefrontal cortex, and not the D2 receptor in the mesolimbic and striatal system, might be more effective in treating the deficit syndrome in schizophrenia without worsening psychotic symptoms.

5. The action of the new atypical antipsychotics on serotonergic as well as dopamine receptors suggests that both neurotransmitters are involved in a reciprocal manner in schizophrenia. Lewine et al. (1991) found that although HVA and HIAA were not independently related to the ventricle:brain ratio (VBR), the ratio of HVA to 5-HIAA was strongly and negatively associated with VBR. These findings have revived a serotonin hypothesis of schizophrenia (in a different form).

Serotonin (5-HT) Hypothesis

A serotonin hypothesis of schizophrenia predated the dopamine hypothesis (Iqbal & van Praag, 1995; Roth & Meltzer, 1995). It was based on the observation of psychotic-like reactions to the drug lysergic acid diethylamide (LSD), including visual hallucinations and illusions, paranoid delusions, and some conceptual disorganization, collectively summarized in the vernacular as a "bad trip." LSD was regarded as a serotonin antagonist, and it was assumed that the psychotic-like reactions to it were the result of a serotonin deficit. This hypothesis had to be revised when it was discovered that a specific 5-HT antagonist did not produce psychotic symptoms and that LSD had some 5-HT agonist as well as antagonist properties. A second hypothesis suggested that some endogenous error of metabolism produced a methylated indoleamine which produced the psychotic effects. However, no such products could be found in schizophrenics, and no differences were reported between methylated indoleamines in schizophrenics and controls. Furthermore, the psychotic-like reactions to LSD differed from those of paranoid schizophrenics, including producing visual hallucinations which are rare in schizophrenics, but not eliciting auditory hallucinations, which are common in schizophrenics. But with the recognition of the role of dopamine in the drugs used to treat schizophrenia, the serotonin hypothesis was relegated to the junkyard of discarded theories.

What revived the hypothesis was the development of the atypical antipsychotic drugs, with inhibiting effects on 5-HT receptor subtypes as well as on specific dopamine receptors. There are currently 14 distinct 5-HT receptors. Hallucinogens have their effects mainly on the 5-HT2A or 5-HT2C receptors, and the same sites are primary ones for the 5-HT antagonistic effects of the atypical drug clozapine. The new hypothesis suggests that schizophrenia or psychosis may be due to defects in the serotonergic modulation of dopaminergic activity in the mesencephalon and cortex (Meltzer, 1989). Clozapine is supposed to normalize the interactions between 5-HT and dopamine in relevant brain regions. This is not a strictly serotonin hypothesis but a systems serotonin–dopamine one. The relevant findings are confused by the differential effects of 5-HT receptors on dopaminergic activity: 5-HT1 receptors reduced dopamine activity by affecting GABA release, but 5-HT2A and 2C receptors increase dopaminergic activity. The antagonistic action of clozapine on the latter receptors may be what modulates excessive dopamine activity.

As is the case for dopamine, simple comparisons of levels of activity of CSF or platelet 5-HT in the basal state yield negative or inconclusive findings. Comparisons of schizophrenics and controls on the 5-HT metabolite 5-HIAA in the CSF generally fail to reveal any differences. Curiously, 5-HIAA and the dopamine metabolite HVA in CSF are positively correlated at a high level that would be regarded as indicating near similarity in the realm of psychometric tests. On the other hand, the ratio of CSF HVA to 5-HIAA correlates negatively with the ventricular brain ratio in schizophrenics (Lewine et al., 1991), and low ratios predict positive responses to clozapine. These results suggest an abnormality of the interactive function of dopamine and serotonin, although the metabolite CSF measures may not be the optimal way to measure central brain activity of these neurotransmitters.

Neuroendocrine challenge studies in which 5-HT is stimulated with an agonist and endocrine indices of response are measured have yielded more interesting results. For instance, Meltzer claims that prolactin and cortisol responses to a 5-HT agonist are consistent with a blunted reactivity of the 5-HT2A or 2C receptors in unmedicated schizophrenics (Roth & Meltzer, 1995). Roth and Meltzer regard this as a compensatory down-regulation of activity in the system and thus regard the blocking effect of clozapine as a therapeutic furthering of the natural defenses. Increased serotonergic activity in peripheral platelet measures may be related to paranoid types of schizophrenia, whereas diminished activity could be related to deficit syndromes.

The results on 5-HT receptor densities in specific brain areas in postmortem studies are as equivocal as those for CSF metabolites. Differences in receptor types and areas of the brain offer too many possibilities for interaction to make any sense of these results. Diminished serotonergic activity is found in depression, impulsive suicidal, and homicidal cases. One wonders if evidence of deficit in some schizophrenics is secondary to these other kinds of mood and impulse control problems. What the new research does suggest is that one must consider more than a single neurotransmitter system in relation to a complex disorder such as schizophrenia. One must also be specific about which areas or brain pathways are involved and which receptors are abnormal in the disorder. Other transmitters and neuropeptides outside of the monoamines may also be involved. The following theories open new areas of possibility.

Glutamate Receptor Dysfunction (GRD)

Like the influence of the LSD psychomimetic reactions in pointing to serotonin, the impetus to the GRD hypothesis came from unfortunate informal experiments conducted by polydrug abusers on themselves. Phencyclidine (PCP) was originally developed as an anesthetic agent, but was withdrawn when psychotic reactions to the drug were observed (Olney & Farber, 1995a). Unfortunately, word of the drug had spread to the illegal street market where it acquired the ironic name of "angel dust." Users of PCP began to show up in psychiatric hospitals where they were first taken for schizophrenics. Unlike LSD in which the hallucinations are mostly visual, PCP produces primarily auditory hallucinations resembling those in schizophrenia as well as delusions (Olney & Farber, 1995b). Given to stabilized chronic schizophrenics, PCP reactivated symptoms and produced an acute active psychosis which lasted several weeks, instead of the very brief reaction produced by LSD.

PCP produces its effects through blocking the ion channel of the glutamate N-methyl-D-aspartic Acid (NMDA) receptor. Glutamate is a major neurotransmitter mediating fast excitatory activity throughout the central nervous system (Henn, 1995). PCP and other NMDA antagonists, which also can cause psychotic reactions, produce neurodegenerative changes in corticolimbic regions of rat brain, the extent of damage depending on dosage (Olney & Farber, 1995a). The first effects are in the posterior cingulate and retrosplenial cortex (PC/RS). Higher doses produce damage to neurons in anterior cingulate, parietal, temporal, piriform, and entorhinal cortices, hippocampus, parahippocampus, and amygdala. Most of these areas have been shown to be diminished in some of the MRI and PET studies of schizophrenia. Drugs that are effective in treating schizophrenia, including the typical and atypical antipsychotics, and GABA facilitators, such as benzodiazepines and barbiturates, were found to block the neurotoxic effects of NMDA antagonists.

Based on these kinds of findings Olney and Farber (1995a) offer a theory of schizophrenia that suggests that NMDA hypofunction can cause psychosis by reducing inhibitory control over excitatory inputs to the PC/RS and the feedback mechanisms by which it monitors and restrains its own discharge activity. The result would be disorganization of the psychological functions mediated by the PC/RS as well as the anterior thalamus and basal forebrain. When NMDA receptors are hypofunctional, they fail to activate GABA receptors and inhibitory control over the corticolimbic circuits is impaired. Because these circuits are normally not fully developed until late adolescence, the dysfunctional effects of the unmodulated circuits would not be fully expressed until that time, explaining the adolescent- or early-adult onset typical in schizophrenia. Rats given NMDA antagonists prenatally or in early infancy do not show the neurotoxic effects until an age that would correspond to puberty in the human. Since the function of the NMDA receptors is expressed through GABAnergic neurons, anything which produces loss of these neurons could have the same effects (Benes, 1995). A loss of GABAnergic neurons in the cerebral cortex of schizophrenics has been reported by Benes and her colleagues. Their model also involves dopamine. One action of dopamine release is inhibition of glutamate release so that DA hyperactivity would result in excessive suppression of glutamate release at NMDA receptors. This would explain why the antipsychotic drugs that block dopamine receptors relieve the symptoms produced by NMDA receptor blocking. But they go further and suggest that NMDA receptor hypofunction is the mechanism by which dopamine hyperactivity produces symptoms.

Like many psychopharmacological theories, this one is specific on proximal causes but vague on distal causes as pointed out by Crow (1995). In utero causes of neural damage such as viral infections cannot account for a significant number of schizophrenic cases and would not explain the constancy of incidence across societies around the world. Crow regards schizophrenia as a genetic disorder that affects the higher nervous functions in the cerebral cortex which affect language (left temporal lobe) and socialization forms which are unique to the human primate. In response to Crow's criticisms, Olney and Farber (1995b) present a schematic model that attributes early alterations of the NMDA state to gene defects in the NMDA or GABA systems, gene defects in the dopamine system, or developmental excitotoxic events such as viruses and fetal ischemia. The hypofunction of the NMDA system during late adolescent or early adult life is the cause of the subsequent psychological dysfunctions expressed in symptoms and structural brain changes which in turn affect the symptoms. The nature of the symptoms, positive, negative, or disorganized cognition, depends upon the specific neural pathways affected by the NMDA syndrome or the structural brain changes it results in. But as Henn (1995) asks, does the NMDA receptor malfunction play a primary or secondary role in schizophrenia? Is the PCP psychosis an adequate model for schizophrenia, particularly for the persistent negative symptoms? Do patients with chronic schizophrenia continue to show progressive cell loss? Henn takes the view that there are different forms of schizophrenia with diverse etiological causes despite the sharing of some common core of symptoms.

The theory of Gray and his colleagues is even more specific than that of Olney and Farber regarding the neural pathways that are malfunctioning in schizophrenia (Gray, 1998; Gray, Feldon, Rawlens, Hemsley, & Smith, 1991). Glutamate and GABA as well as dopamine play a central role as neurotransmitters in these pathways, as in the Olney and Farber model. Another similarity is the use of animal models and experiments to explore the basis for the disorder and the relative emphasis on subcortical nuclei and pathways. As a psychological generalization about schizophrenic cognition, they suggest that the schizophrenic shows a weakened influence of "stored memories or regularities of previous input on current perceptions" and a lack of monitoring of behavior in terms of "willed intentions" (Gray et al., p. 2). Attention is taken up by task-irrelevant stimuli, and the capacity to inhibit or habituate responses to such stimuli is impaired. As a consequence, automatic processing of such stimuli fails, and they break into conscious processing of other stimuli which should be in the focus of attention. The intrusion of irrelevant stimuli from external or internal sources could result in delusions, hallucinations, and thought disorganization, the positive symptoms. The theory has little to say about the negative symptoms, except as a consequence of the enduring cognitive deficits. In contrast to Gray's (1982) theory of anxiety, this one is more concerned with cognitive rather than motivational or emotional mechanisms.

The neurological basis for the cognitive abnormalities is described in a complex model involving the frontal and temporal neocortex, the hippocampal formation and the nucleus accumbens, seen as the "gateway to a basal ganglia motor programming system." At the heart of the system is the projection from the prefrontal cortex to the entorhinal cortex (EC) and then to the septohippocampal system by way of the subiculum to the nucleus accumbens (NA). Another input is from the A10 dopamine nuclei in the ventral tegmental area. The enhanced dopamine release in the NA activates thalamocortical systems that pass on stimuli which seem novel although they are not. The result is intrusions of irrelevant stimuli into normal conscious processing. "Normals" ignore such stimuli because they unconsciously process them as having no immediate associative connection with current events and their consequences. Ideas of reference are an example of external stimuli that are taken as significant to the schizophrenic and to his intentions.

Gray does not speculate on where in this complex information processing system the pathology occurs or what the distal source of the dysfunction might be. This is a process theory that attempts to link the cognitive traits of the schizophrenic to brain systems that mediate the normal functions altered in schizophrenia. Curiously, it says little about the emotional dysfunction in schizophrenia, even though the circuits described are much of the same ones used to describe the neuropsychology of anxiety and depression (Gray, 1982). The NA, which is at the core of the cognitive defect, has also been described as a major source of positive reinforcement from electrical stimulation or drugs, although it is also responsive to negative stress. Gray regards its function as a marker of salience or associability of the stimuli that elicit it. But couldn't hypofunction of the NA produce the negative symptoms of anhedonia and avolition that often persist beyond the active phase of the disorder?

Each biological theory of schizophrenia seems to deal with only part of the characteristics of the disorder. Is this because there is not one disorder but many with different etiologies? Or is there a core pathology which may affect different functions depending upon other factors? One of these factors might be the preexisting personality and cognitive traits of the preschizophrenic individual.

PERSONALITY

According to Meehl's (1962) earlier diathesis–stress theory, a schizotypic personality, characterized by "cognitive slippage," anhedonia, ambivalence, and social anxiety, is an inevitable result of the inheritance of the "schizogene" and its neurological consequences. His later theory suggests that traits such as introversion, anxiety, and submissiveness, with polygenic origins, may both potentiate the development of the schizotype and the decompensation of the schizotype into the schizophrenic. In combination with stressful environmental events, they may also result in schizophrenia without the inheritance of the major schizogene and a schizotaxic brain. Twin and family studies have shown a significant aggregation of schizotypical personalities (*DSM-III* defined) among the relatives of schizophrenics, but such personalities might simply represent the early stages of schizophrenia. The basic question is this: How far back do we see distinctive premorbid personality traits in the schizophrenics that distinguish them from those who do not develop the disorder? How specific are these traits? Are they merely anxiety and depression, which might be found in the background of other types of disorders, or are they an early version of Bleuler's signs? For many years these questions were addressed only by retrospective case studies, but now they can be answered by the longitudinal studies of "high-risk" individuals, which are presently coming to fruition.

A meta-analysis of studies comparing the contemporary personalities of schizophrenics with those of normal controls and neurotic patients showed that schizophrenics are usually found to be more introverted, neurotic, and peculiar than normal controls, but less neurotic and more peculiar than neurotics (Berenbaum & Fujita, 1994). There were no differences between schizophrenics and neurotics on introversion. Only the peculiarity traits, like the Perceptual Aberration and other scales used to define the schizotypical personality, distinguish schizophrenics from neurotics. But these scales do not distinguish schizophrenics from individuals with major depression or bipolar disorder with psychotic features (Katsanis, Iacono, & Beiser, 1990). The question becomes are these measures of a personality dimension or early symptoms of psychotic disorders? Eysenck's P scale, which purports to measure a personality dimension that shades into psychoticism at the extreme does not predict psychosis as do the perceptual aberration and magical ideation types of scales (Chapman et al., 1994).

Although the personality differences between schizophrenics and normal controls do not depend on the current acuteness of their psychosis, they might be caused by schizophrenia and not be reflective of the basic personality that existed before the onset of the disorder. On the assumption of a continuous dimension from normal personality to psychosis, the relatives of schizophrenics should differ from normals on the personality measures distinguishing schizophrenics from normals. But studies of the relatives of schizophrenics show that their personality profiles are normal on these dimensions (Berenbaum & Fujita, 1994). A study which divided the schizophrenic probands into those with "core" (negative symptoms such as emotional blunting), and noncore types found one weak difference between the relatives of core types only and normals: The former were lower on a measure of "social closeness" (Berenbaum, Taylor, & Cloninger, 1994). A study of discordant twins, who shared their complete set of genes with a schizophrenic twin but who were themselves without psychosis, showed that they differed from normals on measures of traditionalism, absorption, stress reaction, and the general factor of neuroticism (negative emotionality), but in the nonpredicted direction they were lower on these measures than normals (DiLalla & Gottesman, 1995)! They scored higher on extraversion and lower on neuroticism than did their schizophrenic twins. Their cotwins who were schizophrenic, however, scored significantly higher than the normal population on alienation, negative emotionality, and stress reaction, and lower on well-being, positive emotionality, social closeness, and achievement. The studies of contemporary schizophrenics and their relatives indicate that the differences on personality dimensions are probably a result rather than a precursor of the disorder. At least they are not directly linked to the genes involved in schizophrenia. Furthermore, only the dimension of "peculiarity" (if one regards this as a normal personality dimension) is specific to psychosis. But longitudinal studies offer more direct evidence on this question.

The Danish high-risk study is currently the most mature, with the subjects now in their 40s, having passed through most of the high-risk period (Olin et al., 1997; Parnas et al., 1993). Behavioral data were obtained at the onset of the study when the children of schizophrenic mothers (high-risk) group were about 15 years of age. A recent follow-up using *DSM-III-R* criteria found that 31 members of the high-risk group had become schizophrenic at some time during the 24–27 years between the initial and last evaluation, and 30 had developed schizotypal personalities (Olin et al., 1997). At the time of initial evaluation (age 15) those who later became schizophrenic were described by teachers as disruptive and hyperexcitable (males only), passive and unengaged, and hypersensitive to criticism. Passivity and hypersensitivity tended to be characteristic of the schizotypal personality disorders as well as of those members who developed a schizophrenic disorder. However, disruptive and excitable behavior was less common in the children who were to become schizotypal in contrast to those who became schizophrenic. Retrospective parental reports of infancy described the future schizophrenics as passive babies with a short attention span during play (Parnas, Schulsinger, Schulsinger, Mednick, & Teasdale, 1982).

The psychiatrist's early report showed that those who later developed schizophrenia showed more cognitive disturbance (distracted, confused, absent-minded, inattentive), eccentricity and peculiarity (silly, clownish, bizarre, strange, eccentric), but *not* more schizoid behavior (shy, inhibited, introverted, shut-in, nervous, reserved, withdrawn, evasive, anxious). The first two categories describe early schizotypic traits on a continuum with psychosis, but the schizoid dimension, on which the preschizophrenics did not differ from the good outcome high-risk group, is a combination of neuroticism-anxiety and introversion dimensions.

In the New York project children of schizophrenic parents were first evaluated when they were 7- to 12-years old and last followed up at ages 9, 12, and 15 before most had entered the age of risk (Dworkin et al., 1991). Offspring of parents with schizophrenia were compared to those of parents with affective disorders, and to normal comparison children. During childhood (mean age 9) there were no differences between the offspring in the three groups. But at early adolescence (mean age 12), those at risk for schizophrenia had poorer social competence and more signs of thought disorder than did members of the other groups. By adolescence (mean age 15) those at risk for schizophrenia had more signs of thought disorder, poorer social competence, greater affective flattening, and poverty of speech than did members of the other groups. The study shows a gradual development of schizophrenic signs beginning in early adolescence, but not before in childhood.

The Israeli study of high-risk children began with children of schizophrenic parents, with the sample equally divided between a kibbutz and town environments, and followed them over 25 years (Mirsky, Kugelmass, Ingraham, Frenkel, & Nathan, 1995). At ages 11 and 17, children from the schizophrenic spectrum group did not get along well with parents, teachers, or peers, were rated as undesirable by peers, had poor self-regard, were suspicious and withdrawn, and had poor communication skills. The picture resembles that in the Denmark study with the future schizophrenics making themselves unpopular with teachers and peers through their inappropriate and asocial behavior.

The National Child Developmental Study started with a population of all births in the United Kingdom registered during one week in March, 1958 (Crow, Done, & Sacker, 1995). The children were followed over the next 23 years, and those who had a record of psychiatric hospitalization for schizophrenia, affective psychosis, or neurosis were compared with a control group of normals from the cohort on ratings made by teachers when the children were 7 and 11 years old. The preschizophrenic males at both ages 7 and 11 were rated as more anxious for acceptance by other children, as shown by "buffoonery," bravado, showing off, and bragging; more hostile to children and adults; less conscientious (showing poor concentration), a lack of perseverance, carelessness; more untidyness and mischievousness; more depression and apathy; and showing more "miscellaneous" nervous habits including stuttering, twitching, and nail-biting. Of these behaviors, anxiety over acceptance by peers, nervous habits, hostility toward adults, and inattentiveness and lack of conscientiousness did not differentiate preaffective or preneurotic boys from controls at those ages. Preschizophrenic girls were not significantly different from controls at age 7, but at age 11, they showed more withdrawal, depression, lack of willingness to work, and miscellaneous nervous symptoms than controls. All of these behaviors except nervous habits were also found in excess in the 11-year-old preneurotic girls. As in the Danish study, the preschizophrenic boys showed a pattern of disagreeableness, defiance of authority, and signs of disorganization, whereas the 11-year-old girls showed a pattern of shyness, withdrawal, and depression similar to that seen in preneurotic girls at that age.

The Atlanta (Georgia) study compared offspring of schizophrenic parents to controls from families with no mental illness at ages 10 and 11, using parental behavioral ratings of their children (Walker, Weinstein, Baum, & Neumann, 1995). As in the previously described studies, there was a gender difference in the patterns of behavior in high-risk children (schizophrenic outcomes had not yet been determined). Male children of schizophrenics had the highest externalizing behavior (lack of inhibition, aggression, hyperactivity), and this behavior pattern markedly increased over the 1-year interval in contrast to control and high-risk female groups. High-risk females showed the highest rate of internalizing behavior problems (social withdrawal, anxiety, and depression particularly), and these problems increased at 11 years of age, becoming significantly higher than those of controls. The internalizing pattern in 11-year-old high-risk females is similar to the pattern seen in the studies conducted in Denmark and the United Kingdom. A retrospective study based on maternal reports showed that the 8- to 12-year-old period is the time when male preschizophrenics increased in externalizing behavior problems, and females markedly increased in the internalizing problems (Neumann, Grimes, Walker, & Baum, 1995).

Emotional behavior is less obvious than social behavior and sometimes difficult for observers—even parents—to rate. The Atlanta group has developed an ingenious way of evaluating childhood emotional expression in preschizophrenics and in their healthy siblings by examining home movies and using a standardized method for rating emotional facial expressions from films (Walker, Grimes, Davis, & Smith, 1993). Lower expressions of joy were seen in the films of preschizophrenic female subjects compared to their healthy siblings at ages 4–8 months, 1–4 years, and 10–16 years. Male preschizophrenics showed no differences in expressions of positive emotions, but manifested more negative emotions than did their healthy siblings from birth to 4 years and from 8–12 years of age. The preschizophrenic girls also showed more negative emotions than did sibling controls during the preadolescent period of 12–16 years.

The preschizophrenic pattern for boys does not show a specifically neurotic or introverted pattern such as that seen in later assessments after the onset of the disorder. Rather, it is the peculiar asocial and antisocial (relative to adults) behavior of the preschizophrenic boy that sets him apart from his peers and leads to peer rejection. The preschizophrenic girls, however, do show traits of withdrawal, anxiety, and depression that are not unlike those seen in girls who will become neurotic in later life. Emotional expressions follow the same gender lines, with absence of positive emotions in the preschizophrenic girls and the presence of negative emotions, particularly hostility, in the boys. Girls show many aspects of Meehl's (1989) SHAI (submissive, hypohedonic, anxious, introverted) personality, but boys do not. Meehl (personal communication) says that he had thought of including "excessive anger" as a major personality potentiator but decided not to do so, which he now regrets. The expressions of negative emotions begin earlier in the boys but are not intensified in the girls until the pre- and early adolescent period. The personality changes parallel the gender difference in onset of the clinical disorder. Of course, some of the differences in peculiar behavior, nervous mannerisms, and attentional problems may be early manifestations of the disorder rather than extremes of normal personality dimensions. Unless one regards disorganized thinking as a normal dimension of personality, the dimensional view of schizophrenia is harder to maintain than for the anxiety and mood disorders which do emerge at the extreme of the dimension of neuroticism.

On the basis of intensive case studies, Bleuler (1978) classified only about one fourth of his schizophrenic patients as having a pathological schizoid personality before they became psychotic. Another 30% were said to have had an aberrant schizoid personality "within the norm." Early emotional and behavioral problems may be potentiating factors for schizophrenia, but they are not the core factor, and they are not specific to schizophrenia. The boy's externalizing behaviors are shared with early antisocial personality development, and the girl's emotional problems are similar to those in neurotic development.

In their review of the high-risk, life-span studies, Gooding and Iacono (1995) note that the most consistently replicated finding is the presence of attention deficits and related information processing deficits across all ages in the at-risk individuals. Impaired attention is found in signal detection, attention span, and stimulus-discrimination tasks. The neurological theories already discussed have attempted to explain the neurobiological bases of this problem.

STRESS

The stress–vulnerability model for schizophrena of Zubin and Spring (1977) was described in chapter 1. According to that model, the impact of stress depends upon where one falls on a continuum of vulnerability and upon the intensity of the "challenging events." *Vulnerability* was defined as the genetic inheritance plus acquired propensities. For a person with high vulnerability, only slightly stressful events may trigger the initial psychotic episode or subsequent relapse episodes, whereas a person with low vulnerability can endure the most extreme kinds of stress with only a brief episode at the maximum and no decompensation in most cases. The early-onset schizophrenic, who breaks down with little provocation, has a worse prognosis than the late-onset cases which are more often provoked by definite environmental stressors. Some of the methodological issues involved in the definition of stress were discussed in chapter 1. They are particularly salient in the study of schizophrenia because of the likelihood of reciprocal influences between stress and symptoms (Norman & Malla, 1993a). The preschizophrenic male provokes rejection by his peers and teachers, and sometimes by his own family as well, through his hostile and asocial behavior. At the same time, preschizophrenic males are hypersensitive to criticism, nervous, and excitable. One of the major factors predicting relapse in schizophrenics is a family atmosphere where there is open expression of negative emotions toward the patient. How do we separate the worsening symptoms that are so provocative to the family from the stress to the patient produced by negative emotional expressions in the family?

A review of the research literature on stressful life events and schizophrenia (Norman & Malla, 1993b) concluded that there is much more evidence that variation in stress within patients is associated with changes in their symptoms than for the hypothesis that schizophrenics are exposed to more severe life stress than persons in the general population or those with other types of disorders. These conclusions are compatible with the diathesis–stress model which suggests that many schizophrenics have a low threshold for stress provocation. Meehl (1990) says that "unlucky" events, such as loss of a close relative during adult life, can precipitate schizophrenia in a genetically vulnerable person. The kind of stress that might trigger a disorder in a schizophrenic might have little effect on a normal or neurotic one, so that an objective description of life event stressors might reveal little difference between schizophrenics and others in their occurrence.

The life stress in these studies is that immediately preceding the onset or acute exacerbation of symptoms. But it is possible that schizophrenia is partly due to long past stressful events as in posttraumatic stress disorders. In that case the stress might be part of the vulnerability determinant of reactions to future stressors. Meehl (1990) suggests that either major trauma during the developmental period (such as being raped) or minor traumas (such as continued verbal rejections) could increase the risk for later schizophrenia in a genetically vulnerable child. One of the life situations rated very highly on stress scales is the loss of a parent, particularly before the age of 15. M. Bleuler (1978) compared the incidence of parental loss by ages 15 and 18 of schizophrenics, depressives, and male controls (draftees for Swiss army). There was no normal control group for the female patients. Comparing among the groups the only outstanding differences were the loss by death of the father—which was somewhat higher in the male schizophrenics than in depressives and controls—and the death of the mother—which was higher in both male and female depressed groups compared to male schizophrenics and controls. Parental loss is a more important factor in the background of depression than in schizophrenia.

In chapter 1, the question is whether severe prolonged traumatic experiences can produce psychosis in the absence of a predisposition. The answer was equivocal in studies of concentration camp victims, although a case-by-case analysis suggested that there were a small number of cases where a psychosis followed the camp experience in individuals who showed no signs of predisposition prior to their incarceration.

Studies done by the Veterans Administration on American soldiers who were prisoners of war (POWs) during World War II and the Korean War showed that posttraumatic stress disorders were very prevalent among these former POWs, with 71% of them suffering from this anxiety disorder (Eberly & Engdahl, 1991). Depression and alcoholism were also high in this group. However, the rate of schizophrenia and schizophreniform disorder among the POWs was 1.9%, not much higher than the rate of 1.5% for these two disorders in the general population (see ECA study, L. N. Robins & Regier, 1991). There was a wide range of conditions in the POW camps with prisoners starved and tortured, particularly in the Japanese camps during World War II. The percentage of body-weight loss was used to provide an index of the severity of camp conditions. The rate of subsequent schizophrenia in those who lost more than 35% of their weight was 4.2% compared to 0.4% of those who lost less than 35% of their weight, an eightfold difference. Apparently the overall 2% rate of schizophrenia in the POWs is entirely accounted for by the more severe camp conditions. Another possibility is that starvation itself may increase vulnerability through irreversible brain damage, although such effects are more common in young children in whom the developing brain is affected.

Psychotic symptoms, including hallucinations, delusions, and bizarre behavior, do occur in combat veterans with PTSD and are usually ascribed to re-experiencing the trauma (Butler, Mueser, Sprock, & Braff, 1996). But in some cases the phenomena seem to bear no relationship to the traumatic experiences. Negative symptoms are not characteristic except for the symptom of anhedonia.

Apparently, only the most severe and prolonged types of stress can increase the vulnerability to schizophrenia. Given the rarity of such severe stress in the general population, it cannot account for the great majority of cases. However, later stress may act as the immediate releasing factor for schizophrenic episodes.

A retrospective study of the influence of stressful life events in the months preceding the onset of disorders compared the rates of severe and mildly stressful events in patients with schizophrenia, mania, and depressive psychosis and screened normal controls using DSM-III criteria for diagnoses (Bebbington et al., 1993). Unlike most prospective studies which find a sharp increase in stressful experiences in the month preceding onset (e.g.,

Nuechterlein et al., 1992; Pallanti, Quercioli, & Pazzagli, 1997), this one found only a steady gradual increase in stressful life events in the 4 months preceding the onset in schizophrenics and manics, and a sharper increase in the last 2 months for the psychotic depressives. Controls, as expected, showed no gradient and a low frequency of any kind of severe events overall. Severe events were more frequent in all patient groups than in the controls. There was little difference between frequencies of events in the schizophrenic and manic groups, but the psychotic depressives had more severe events than both of these groups. Only about half the members of the schizophrenic group experienced any event, and only about a third experienced an independent stressful event in the prodromal period. For less severe, independent events there was no difference between schizophrenics and controls.

A controlled prospective study of schizophrenics during a standard drug treatment period followed by a drug-withdrawal and placebo period found that the relationship between stressful life events and relapse was only found for patients on antipsychotic drugs (Nuechterlein et al., 1992). Nearly all patients who relapsed during the drug-free period did so without any obvious provocation from life events, whereas in half of the cases of patients who relapsed while on drugs, there was a significant life event occurring in the month before relapse. Thus the internal process of the disorder itself accounts for most relapse in untreated patients, whereas stress becomes the crucial factor during treatment that controls the physiological brain state.

The untreated schizophrenic is highly vulnerable to even minor stress, which might not be classified as stressful by nonschizophrenics. The subjective stress of schizophrenics was related more to the cumulative effect of daily minor stresses, such as family demands, money, and transportation problems, than to major crises or life changes (Norman & Malla, 1991). Of course these patients were stabilized on medication, and probably not many major changes were occurring in their lives. The study does show, however, how the minor kinds of hassles that everyone must contend with seem so overwhelming to the schizophrenic patient. This is partly a function of their sensitivity and vulnerability, but may be also due to their lack of coping effort and ability and sense of competence in dealing with these problems (Zubin & Spring, 1977).

Schizophrenic patients under high stress tend to use non-problem-centered highly emotional ways of coping (Wiedl, 1992). Patients with negative type symptoms use more emotional and non-problem-focused ways of coping, whereas those with positive type symptoms use relatively more cognitive coping. Both types of patients used little social coping, trying to solve their problems on their own.

Medicated patients who relapse without the provocation of severe life events show less problem-centered coping and more non-problem-solving coping including withdrawal, avoidance, suppression, or other ineffective cognitive methods (Pallanti et al., 1997). They were also less cognitively able, as shown by their lower educational levels, worse levels of global functioning in the year preceding onset, and weaker capacity for information processing.

The mythology of the "schizophrenogenic mother" probably emerged from the frequent clinical observation of negative interactions between mothers and their schizophrenic sons. Supposedly, a pattern of lack of affection combined with subtle rejection, as in the "double-bind" message conveying love on the surface and hostility and rejection below, confused and infuriated the schizophrenic (Bateson, Jackson, Haley, & Weakland, 1956). Family studies have shown that a pattern of *expressed emotion* (EE) in relatives of schizophrenics is a major factor in relapse of patients sent home after hospital treatment. EE is not the subtle kind of rejection postulated by early dynamic theories, but is openly expressed criticism, hostility, and guilt-inducement directed toward the patient and an emotional overinvolvement in the patient's behavioral problems (Valone, Norton, Goldstein, & Doane, 1983; Vaughn & Leff, 1976). High EE parents show both benign and harsh types of criticism. This kind of open criticism and rejection by parents is not uncommon in other disorders or even in the family backgrounds of those who manage to emerge sound and psychologically unscarred. If critical parents alone could cause one to become schizophrenic, there would be a higher proportion than 1% of schizophrenics in the general population. However, once one develops schizophrenia, the probability of relapse is increased by a high EE family atmosphere, particularly if patients are not taking their medication (Vaughn & Leff, 1976). In low EE families, the relapse rates were 12–15% compared to high EE families in frequent contact with the patients in which the relapse rate was 53% for those on medication and 92% for those not on medication! A meta-analysis of 27 studies of EE found overall relapse rates of 65% in high EE families compared to 35% in low EE families (Butzlaf & Hooley, 1998).

The recognition of the importance of the family emotional climate in the maintenance of recovery led to the development of successful family treatments that reduced relapse rates from 28–40% to 0–9% when combined with antipsychotic medications (Strachen, 1986). This is a remarkable contrast to the ineffectiveness of traditional individual psychotherapy with schizophrenia, with or without drug treatment.

What implications do these findings have for the etiology of schizophrenia? First, it must be recognized that the EE pattern is a reciprocal one. High rates of criticism and hostility in parents are associated with similar reactions in the patients, so we cannot distinguish family reactivity to deficit or disturbance in the patient from family disturbance itself as a cause of relapse in the patient (Milkowitz & Goldstein, 1993). Parents who have high EE are more likely to be psychiatrically disturbed than low

EE parents, but their diagnoses are not specifically in the schizophrenic spectrum, and also include depression and nonspectrum personality disorders. The EE pattern may be regarded as another type of stressor within the diathesis–personality–stress model. If high EE family atmospheres are a factor in relapse, they may also be the stress factor that triggers the first onset of schizophrenia in a vulnerable individual. The particular reaction to a negative family atmosphere depends upon the specific diatheses and can be anxiety, depression, substance abuse, or schizophrenia. Even stronger effect sizes for EE are found in mood and eating disorders than in schizophrenia (Butzlaf & Hooley, 1998). However, the cognitive dysfunction in schizophrenics may make them even less able to cope with the hostility of parents. The dependency of a partially recovered schizophrenic with negative symptoms such as avolition is a stress on the family, and their intolerance is understandable. This is why family therapies focus on the problems of dealing with the patients' reentry and means of coping as well as the patients' problems and skill deficits.

FAMILY AND SOCIAL RISK FACTORS

The reaction against the concepts of *schizophrenogenic* (the term implying sufficient cause) mothers or families has led some researchers to deny any role of parental and family environments in the stress part of the diathesis model. McGuffin, Asherson, Owen, and Farmer (1994) ask: "Is there room for an environmental influence in the aetiology of schizophrenia?" (p. 593). They argue that the environmental component is small and may consist entirely of changes in gene structure or expression that are not transmissible. Meehl (1989, 1993) continues to argue that there is still a major role for schizophrenogenic mothers as potentiators for subsequent schizophrenia. He cites the evidence for EE and relapse and says that the mother's child-rearing practices and "subtle attitudes" must have also influenced the developing predisposition before the child became schizotypic and schizophrenic. But EE refers to the family's *openly expressed* hostility toward the patient, and thus, is not specifically a trait of mothers and is not at all subtle! There is, however, other evidence now suggesting that we need to take another look at the role of parental influences other than genetic or prenatal and perinatal events.

The Finnish adoption study discussed previously found that psychologically healthy adoptive families reduce the risk of a genetically predisposed child from becoming schizophrenic or even schizotypic, whereas severe psychopathology in adoptive families increased the risk in genetically vulnerable children (Tienari, 1991a, 1991b). One negative type of influence in schizotypical parents is their peculiar kinds of communication.

Communication deviance (CD) is defined as "unclear, unintelligible, or oddly worded communications during family transactions" (Milkowitz & Goldstein, 1993, p. 313). CD is more common in parents of schizophrenics than in parents of controls. *Affective style* (AS) refers specifically to emotional-verbal behavior of key relatives during a family interaction test and consists of criticisms of the child by the relatives or intrusions (contradictions of what the child actually feels). A 15-year longitudinal study of disturbed, but not yet schizophrenic, adolescents showed that CD, AS, and EE in the parents predicted which children developed schizophrenic spectrum disorders (M. J. Goldstein, 1987).

Among the high-risk adoptees (children of schizophrenic mothers) in the Finnish adoption study, there was a strong relationship between CD *in the adoptive parents* and thought disorder in the adoptees, but among the low-risk adoptees, there was no relationship between these variables (Wahlberg et al., 1997). There is a problem in this study in that CD in the adoptive parents was determined after the adoptee had been schizophrenic for some years. It is possible, but not likely, that the CD in the adoptive parent was induced by living with a schizophrenic child rather than the obverse. But assuming the influence went from parent to child, the dismissal of the evidence of CD in the parents of schizophrenics in intact families as merely reflecting the influence of genetically shared schizotypy in parents and children is unwarranted, because the adoptive parental influence is social and not genetic. But those who suggest that the communication disturbance in parents is itself sufficient to induce thought disorder in their children are also wrong, because the influence was only evident in those children at genetic risk. The remaining interpretation is the diathesis–stress model proposed by Meehl (1989): The schizotypic mother induces "primary aversive drift" and social fear in a child who already has "synaptic slippage" on a genetic basis, but not in other children.

If problems of parent–child bonding and frustration of the need for affection and attachment are important factors in schizophrenia, as maintained by many psychodynamic theorists, then institutional rearing would be the type of environment most likely to produce schizophrenia in a genetically predisposed child. The effect of institutional rearing was examined in the Danish high-risk study (Parnas, Teasdale, & Schulsinger, 1985). The children whose mothers were schizophrenic and who became schizophrenic themselves were found to have spent more time in institutions (orphanages) than those who became schizotypes, had other diagnoses, or had no mental disorders. This effect was stronger in males than in females. A confounding problem was that the time spent in institutions was inversely related to the contact time these children had with their parents and the mother's age at first hospitalization (a possible index of the severity of her disorder). But even when these factors were statistically controlled, the time the child spent in institutions was higher in the group who became schizophrenic than in all other groups. A further analysis revealed that the years in institutions between the ages of 1 and 5 years accounted for the effect, whereas institutionalization between ages 6 and 10 years had little effect on subsequent diagnoses. The authors note that Danish institutions for rearing children were characterized by good physical care, but were deficient in stable emotional contact and support. Although this type of cold early environment may not be sufficient to produce severe personality or clinical disorders in most children, the early emotional deprivation may be the crucial factor that turns a schizotype into a schizophrenic.

However, the quality of the relationship between parent and child may also account for some of the increased vulnerability in those children who were raised by their own parents, one of whom was disturbed at some parts of the childhood experience. At the beginning of the Danish study the parents and children were interviewed regarding the quality of the parent–child relationships and the interviews were rated for perceived qualities of the relationships (Burman, Mednick, Machon, Parnas, & Schulsinger, 1987). Both the children who later became schizophrenic and their parents perceived their relationships to be significantly less satisfactory than those perceived by parents and schizotypal children of those without disorders. Actually the ratings were much less negative for fathers than for mothers, which is not surprising in view of the fact that the mothers were schizophrenic at some stages of the children's lives. In a household with a disorganized, disturbed mother, a supportive father could make the difference in the vulnerability of the child and the ultimate difference between a compensated schizotype and a decompensated schizophrenic when the child reaches adolescence.

Studies of children raised at home with schizophrenic parents do not always show separate family environmental and genetic effects, but considered together with the adoption studies, the recent work suggests a significant role for the family environment as the early stress factor in a diathesis–stress model. Deficient parent–child bonding and nonaffectionate relationships now assume significance within a diathesis–stress framework, not as sufficient or even necessary causes but as contributory ones. Institutionalization in early life is a drastic procedure for a child whose personality is undeveloped. Even a schizophrenic mother may be better than no mother at all, if the father is sufficiently supportive in times of family stress.

The kibbutz method of child-rearing in Israel is far from institutional rearing because the children are raised by others during the day and sleep in a dormitory, but interact with their parents at night after they return from work. This is not unlike the current situation of many in the United States at this time where both parents work full-time and the children are in the charge of a "nanny" and attend preschool during the day. A high-risk study in Israel contrasted the children of schizophrenics (index) raised in a kibbutz with those raised in towns in the usual family arrangement (Ingraham et al., 1995). All of the children who became schizophrenic over the 25-year study were from the index group, but an equal number were raised in kibbutz and town. However, an unexpected finding was that of those who developed major mood disorders most were raised in the kibbutz. Although the kibbutz rearing did not increase or decrease vulnerability for schizophrenia, it may have done so for mood disorder, particularly among those at risk for schizophrenic disorders.

SUMMARY

Statistical analyses of symptoms have usually shown three basic syndromes: (a) deficit (negative) symptoms, (b) cognitive disorganization, and (c) psychotic symptoms (delusions and hallucinations). Similar syndromes are found for schizotypical personality: (a) social withdrawal and anhedonia (deficit symptoms), (b) oddness or peculiarity (disorganization), and (c) magical thinking or perceptual aberration (resembling psychotic symptoms and the best predictors of psychosis). The deficit symptoms are the most reliable over the course of the disorder which is why they are often described as "residual symptoms." But they are often part of the prodromal phase even though they are not as likely to precipitate admission to the hospital as the more dramatic disorganized or psychotic symptoms. Some researchers have suggested that there is more than one disorder involved. But heterogeneity of symptoms is found in many medical disorders such as general paresis or AIDS depending on which organ system is infected at a given time during the course of the disorder. The variability in the symptoms of schizophrenia may also depend upon which parts of the brain are affected at a given time during the course of the disorder.

Among the personality disorders, the schizotypical personality disorder has the greatest comorbidity as a disorder usually preceding the development of full-blown schizophrenia. However, only about 10% of schizotypes decompensate to schizophrenia during their lifetimes. The prevalence of this type in the relatives of schizophrenics suggests that it is actually a milder but persistent form of the schizophrenic disorder itself.

The precedence given to schizophrenia in a diagnostic decision hierarchy hides its high comorbidity with other diagnoses in terms of shared symptoms. Major depression and anxiety disorders are found in schizophrenia, although the anxiety disorders, such as social phobia and panic disorder, generally precede the schizophrenia, whereas the major depression is a reaction to the schizophrenic disorder and usually recedes with the remission of the schizophrenic disorder. Schizophrenia also overlaps with bipolar disorder, particularly where the latter is accompanied by psychotic delusions. The schizoaffective psychosis represents a puzzling, intermediate type of disorder with a mixture of schizophrenic psychotic and mood symptoms. The comorbidity of schizophrenia and severe mood disorders suggests that they might share a common etiology or at least a dimension of pathology. However, persons diagnosed with schizophrenia, mania, and major depression can be distinguished with a greater than high accuracy by symptoms, types of emotions, course of the disorders, degree of recovery between episodes, and relative degree of insight or awareness of being "sick."

The prodromal phase of schizophrenia usually begins with a mixture of nonspecific signs, such as anxiety and distractibility, and negative symptoms such as lack of energy and motivation, poor work performance, and social withdrawal. The first positive symptoms appear about 5 years later. Disorganized types usually have an earlier onset and a worse prognosis, whereas paranoid types usually have a later onset and more acute course. Those with severe deficit syndromes have a much worse outcome than those without those symptoms. Since the advent of antipsychotic drug treatment, the most common type of outcome is further psychotic episodes and residual deficit symptoms between episodes of psychotic behavior. However, a curious finding is a much higher incidence of full remissions in many of the underdeveloped countries. But outcomes depend upon how schizophrenia is defined and treated. Broader definition of the disorder and drug treatment, particularly when combined with family therapy, lead to better outcomes.

Twin, adoption, and family prevalence studies show a significant genetic factor in schizophrenia, although the strength of this factor varies among the types of schizophrenia. It is strongest in the disorganized, or deficit syndrome early-onset types that do not respond to medication, and still significant but weaker in the paranoid, late-onset types with good response to medication. Either there are different etiologies with some depending more on inherited liabilities, or the types simply represent degrees of severity of the single underlying disorder based on different amounts of "genetic dosage." The contribution of familial rearing environment has been downplayed in recent years, but an adoption study in Finland, which examined the adoptive parents more closely, suggests that the presence of severe disorders in the adopting parents can be a crucial factor in determining which of the genetically disposed children actually develop schizophrenia. Most behavior geneticists have abandoned the single necessary gene theory of schizophrenia and subscribe to a polygenetic model. However, some have proposed a multifactorial model with some specific genes producing major effects and polygenes potentiating or insulating against the effects of the specific genes. A search is underway for some specific major genes that might be crucial in the disorder.

Differences between future schizophrenics and their "at-risk" peers who were unaffected by the disorder do not usually appear until early adolescence. In boys, the preschizophrenic does not show the withdrawn schizoid pattern described in the clinical literature, but is described as disruptive, eccentric, and as manifesting peculiar behavior. They tend to be rejected by peers and teachers because of their peculiar behavior. Some are also described as passive and unengaged and these are more likely to develop into schizotypes, whereas the more disorganized types are more likely to develop schizophrenia. Preschizophrenic girls show more of the withdrawal, depression, and anxiety than boys, but preneurotic girls show much of the same pattern. Preschizophrenic boys tend to "externalize," whereas preschizophrenic girls tend to "internalize." Both boys and girls show more evidence of negative affect than do their siblings.

There is little evidence of any greater traumatic stress in the background of schizophrenics than in other patients or in normals. Traumatic events or familial stress alone cannot account for the schizophrenic disorder. However, familial stress is clearly an important factor in the relapse of patients after they have become schizophrenic and probably is a factor in the onset as well. Although preschizophrenic children probably experience no more stress than others, they are more sensitive to criticism, hostility, and rejection, and therefore, may react in disorganized or psychotic ways to such stress from parents or peers. Institutional rearing during the early years of childhood constitutes a significant risk factor for children with a genetic disposition to schizophrenia. The results of these and other studies best fit a diathesis–stress model of schizophrenia.

Psychophysiological and behavioral markers supplement the genetic risk markers of a parent with schizophrenia in defining vulnerability to this disorder. In addition to being present in schizophrenic spectrum disorders, they are generally found to be present in many of their relatives as well (suggesting genetic linkage) and to be independent of the clinical status of the patient. Such markers include eye-tracking dysfunction, reduced amplitude of the P300 evoked potential, failure to show normal stimulus inhibition in response to a second stimulus in the P50 evoked potential, and the prepulse inhibition of the startle reflex, attention failure in the Continuous Performance Test (CPT), backward masking, and hyporesponsivity of the skin conductance response to a novel stimulus. Most of these lack full sensitivity, being only present in a subgroup of schizophrenics, but most show fair specificity.

Nongenetic prenatal influences have been implicated in some cases. Such influences include maternal influenza infection or starvation during the second trimester of pregnancy, mother–child Rh incompatibility, and other pregnancy and birth complications which could cause damage to the brain during a vulnerable period of its development. These factors could cause some of the brain damage found in imaging studies.

Both CT and MRI studies have shown enlarged ventricular and sulcal spaces in brains of schizophrenics compared to those of patients with mood disorders and normal controls, and these signs of brain deterioration cannot be attributed to the effects of medications because they are found in first admissions as well as in more chronic types. They are associated with negative symptoms and primary signs of schizophrenic psychosis. MRI volumetric studies of brain also show tissue loss in frontal and temporal cortical lobes, thalamus, amygdala, and hippocampus. In identical twins discordant for schizophrenia the subcortical tissue loss usually is found in the affected twin, indicating a nongenetic source for the damage and a link with the schizophrenic symptoms. PET studies show reduced metabolic rates in frontal lobe, temporal lobe, and cingulate gyrus, during performance on tasks such as the CPT. Postmortem studies of the cells in the prefrontal and temporal cortices, thalamus, hippocampus, and parahippocampal gyrus in schizophrenics tend to show reductions in cell sizes and numbers, and abnormal cell shapes. The pattern of brain abnormalities suggests damage to prefrontal and temporal cortices and their connections with the limbic system orginating early in development but manifesting themselves in early adolescence.

"Soft" neurological signs are present in about one fourth of schizophrenics who have never been on antipsychotic drugs, and the drugs increase the incidence. The signs are linked to the presence of schizophrenia in identical twins discordant for the disorder. Schizophrenics show a broad range of impairments over a variety of types of performance tests and a lower IQ than normal control participants. Tests of semantic learning, verbal and visual memory, and abstraction are particularly vulnerable. IQ seems to be affected before the disorder and shows no evidence of further deterioration during its course.

The actions of the major antipsychotic drugs used during the past 40 years suggest that a dysfunction in the dopamine neurotransmitter system is central to the schizophrenic symptoms, at least to the positive ones, because they reduce such symptoms by blocking dopamine receptors. But excessive dopaminergic activity does not explain the negative symptoms which, if anything, would be related to a lack of dopaminergic activity. New drugs that act on different dopamine receptors and also affect serotonin receptors have shown effectiveness in reducing negative as well as positive symptoms with fewer neurological side effects from actions in the striatum. Some current thinking suggests an interaction between dopaminergic and serotonergic systems in producing schizophrenic symptoms. New theories also involve the role of damaged glutamate receptors and their failure to activate GABA release, and glutamate and dopamine interactions in the system which runs from the prefrontal to the entorhinal cortex and then into the septohippocampal system and the nucleus accumbens.

Meehl (1962, personal communication, 1998) asserts that schizophrenia is primarily a neurological disorder, not a psychiatric one. The schizotaxia pathology is said to be operating everywhere in the brain "from the sacral cord to the frontal lobes" (Meehl, 1990). Such widespread damage would be expected to have profound, general cognitive effects, but in the majority of schizophrenic patients, the defects are more specific. Brain imaging studies suggest more localization. The designation of the precise neurological locus of the schizophrenic dysfunction may be premature, because there are such widespread areas of dysfunction and damage throughout the brain. Still, there is evidence of localization as in the prefrontal and temporal cortices, the septal–hippocampal system, and the cingulate pathway. In their focus on the information processing deficit in schizophrenia many current theorists seem to neglect the role of the primary affective disturbances, which seem to be the first nonspecific signs of the disorder. Older theories attributed a primary role to unmanageable anxiety as a precursor to the disorder, but could not explain why anxiety led to psychotic symptoms in the schizophrenic but not in those with anxiety disorders. Perhaps the neuropharmacological deficit is one that interferes with the normal inhibition of anxiety.

Diathesis–Personality–Stress

There are adequate grounds for regarding anxiety and mood disorders as the end of a normal continuum of the basic personality trait of neuroticism or negative emotionality, and antisocial personality disorder as the extreme end of the impulsive unsocialized sensation seeking dimension (Zuckerman, 1989). But can we identify a normal dimension of personality that underlies schizophrenia or, in a broader sense, psychosis? Or is schizophrenia and related disorders such as schizotypic personality disorder a taxon in the sense of a qualitatively distinct medical syndrome with a unique etiology? Meehl (1962, 1989) has argued against the mainstream of dimensional psychopathologists, that schizophrenia and its precursor schizotypical personality are a taxon based on an inherited neurological defect, "schizotaxia."

In view of the imaging evidence of damage in brains of at least a subgroup of schizophrenic patients, their performance on neuropsychological tests, and the suppressant effect of neuroleptic drugs on psychotic symptoms, it is hard to deny that schizophrenia is a manifestation of a brain disease, albeit a sometimes reversible one. It has been argued that schizotypal personality can provide the continuity between schizophrenia and normal "eccentricity." But new methods devised to detect the presence of a taxon in the distribution of a continuous measure have indicated that the schizotypy is itself a taxon. There may be some continuity between schizotypy, schizophreniform, and schizophrenic disorders, but together they constitute a different population than the normal.

The extreme heterogeneity among schizophrenic symptoms has led some researchers to postulate that there are different disorders with different etiologies, or "schizophrenias" rather than "schizophrenia." This would take us back to the pre-Kraepelinian days when catatonia, hebephrenia, and paranoia were regarded as different disorders. The negative symptoms or deficit syndrome seem to provide the only constancy in the syndrome, particularly since the antipsychotic drugs have been successful in suppressing the positive symptoms in many patients. The variety of possible etiological factors in schizophrenia has suggested to some a disorder like mental deficiency in which the same syndrome can have different origins, some genetic and some due to nongenetic organic factors. Indeed, many of the structural abnormalities in brain and neurological problems are found more frequently in the schizophrenic twin in discordant pairs showing that they cannot be attributed to the genetic causes for the disorder. But it is also possible that the different causes may have a common pathway, like dysfunction in dopaminergic pathways in the brain. The process in some might be due to a genetic abnormality leading to a developmental abnormality in the system, whereas in others it could be produced by damage incurred in utero or subsequently.

The genetic diathesis itself might not be the same for all cases of schizophrenia. The major genes involved could be different in the three major syndromes: the deficit, the psychotic, and the disorganized. There is some evidence in the MRI and PET studies that different brain patterns are associated with the major syndromes. But the finding of some localization for particular syndromes of schizophrenia does not mean that these are distinct disorders. There are probably some common biological substrates among the different syndromes.

Figure 7.13 shows some of the possibilities for the etiology of schizophrenia. Essentially this is the modified Meehl model shown in Figure 1.7 (chap. 1, this volume) in which early stress (biological in this case) acts on the genetically vulnerable brain systems, while familial–interpersonal stress is involved in shaping the vulnerable personality. The genetic factors are prominent, but not completely determinant in producing the disorder. Prenatal and perinatal biological factors may increase the risk created by genetic factors or create their own risk through their damage to the brain systems involved. The particular brain pathologies (*schizotaxia* in Meehl's terms) produce certain abnormal personality tendencies (*schizotypy*) which

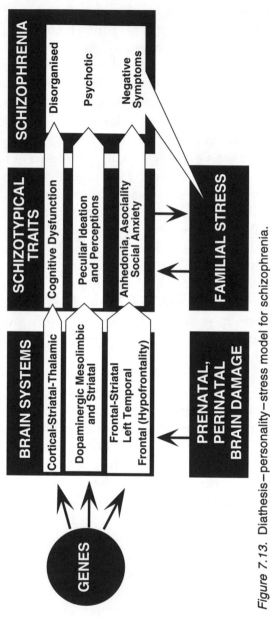

Figure 7.13. Diathesis–personality–stress model for schizophrenia.

are the potential substrate for the three major syndromes in the clinical disorder. Familial pathology or the absence of positive social-emotional interactions during the early years can intensify the inappropriate social behavior and communication disturbance, which in turn, can lead to peer and family rejection which will intensify the cognitive and behavioral disturbance in a positive feedback loop. At this stage there is also interaction between cognitive disturbances, such as the inability to draw logical conclusions from preceding events, leading to peculiarities in the content of thought. The main point of this diathesis–personality–stress model is that negative social influences are only instrumental in producing schizophrenia in those individuals with the biological vulnerabilities.

8

PROGNOSIS FOR THE SCIENCE OF PSYCHOPATHOLOGY

A half century ago when I began my studies in clinical psychology, the textbooks of psychopathology contained a mixture of diagnostic description and dubious psychoanalytic theories of etiology. Genetics was a curiosity, thought to be relevant only for schizophrenia and manic–depressive psychosis. The gene itself was a hypothetical construct. Freud (1922/1961) suggested that someday all of the mysteries of mental disorders might be understandable in biological terms, and he postulated an undefined "constitutional" factor for every kind of disorder. But most of his followers ignored this "reductionistic" kind of explanation, even as a possibility for the future. Even at the psychological level there was a large chasm between the studies of scientific psychology and its new clinical branch. Selective observations in individual cases were offered as evidence, and case histories filtered through the distortive prisms of therapists' perceptions were passed off as proofs of theories. The only challenge to the psychoanalytic viewpoint came from another extreme, behaviorism. Experiments with other species furnished a theoretical basis for anxiety and planted the theoretical seeds which would eventually bloom into the practice of behavioral therapy. One thing that both behavioral and post-Freudian psychoanalytic theories had in common was the conviction that learning and life experiences alone could account for all disorders, even schizophrenia. At that time, it would have been impossible to write this kind of book on psychopathology, restricted mostly to research on humans with disorders and theories based on research findings. At most it would have been a very slim volume.

DIAGNOSIS

Now there are almost too many findings, particularly in the biological field, and too little integration between the behavioral and the biological findings. Most research centers on the designated diagnostic categories rather than on the psychopathological thought and behavior. We know a lot about the biology of schizophrenia but little about the biological basis of a delusion or the apathy of avolition and anhedonia. Much of the research depends on the validity of the diagnostic definitions in the current *DSM*. Diagnostic definitions have undergone radical changes beginning with the *DSM-III* in 1980. The data on heritability and prognosis are widely variable, depending on whether one uses a broad or a narrow definition of schizophrenia. Certainly there was a need to improve the reliability of diagnosis. Before *DSM-III*, the diagnosis of schizophrenia versus something else was about as good as the toss of a coin. It was the researchers, not the clinicians, whose concerns about reliability led to the development of more objective criteria. Reliability has improved for most diagnoses but is still far from optimal, particularly when one does not use a semistructured interview and computer programs. But as many have observed, reliability is no guarantee of validity, and sometimes an excessive concern with the former may lead to a loss of the latter. Actually the most reliable systems are dimensional rather than categorical. The medical-model categorical diagnosis is based on the assumption of a distinctive etiology for every disorder, even though there may be extensive overlap in symptoms between disorders. High comorbidities have been found between many of the disorders discussed in this volume, and genetic analyses suggest that some of these are based on shared genetic factors. Anxiety disorders and unipolar mood disorders, for instance, share much of a common genetic diathesis, but the diagnostic system insists on separate major categories leading to the stated need for a "mixed anxiety–depression" disorder. The problem now is that not enough is known about shared pathology and its significance for etiology.

Many voices, particularly coming from clinical psychology, advocate the dimensionalization of diagnosis. It is clear that the current diagnostic system is slicing up dimensions of psychopathology into arbitrary diagnoses. Does a "depressive personality disorder" (a suggested addition to the *DSM*), differ in anything but intensity from a "dysthymic disorder," and does the latter differ qualitatively from a "major mood disorder?" Is a melancholic depressive disorder anything but a more severe version of the major mood disorder? The data argue for a shared major category of "dysphoric disorders" with subcategories for the purer forms such as panic disorder and melancholic depression, rather than mixed categories. The mixture of anxiety and depression is probably more common than the purer forms of the disorders.

Personality diagnoses are assumed to be longer lasting and clinical disorders episodic, but in actual terms of reliabilities over time, many of the personality disorders are reactive to stress, and many of the clinical disorders can be chronic. Putting personality disorders on a separate and independent axis in the DSMs allows for dual diagnoses, but also takes us further away from the basic dimensional nature of mood traits such as anxiety and depression.

The DSM system also ignores the continuity between some personality traits in the normal range and personality disorders. Neuroticism as a dimension of personality is the precursor of anxiety and unipolar mood disorders. Impulsive unsocialized sensation seeking, low constraint, and low conscientiousness (overlapping and similar personality factors) are the background for the development of antisocial personality, and the latter is a basis for the development of some types of substance abusers. A dimensional system would allow for the mixtures of types without the need for special typologies within diagnoses. Type 1 alcoholism (Cloninger, 1987b) and borderline personality disorders, for instance, appear to be mixtures of impulsivity and neuroticism, whereas Type 2 alcoholism and antisocial personality disorders are purer extremes of the impulsive unsocialized sensation seeking dimension (Zuckerman, 1989).

My prognosis is that the multiplication of diagnostic categories will be reversed in the future, and most disorders will be defined in dimensional terms. Most dimensional models are currently based on self-report questionnaires, but there is no reason why rating scales cannot be used for the same purpose. Since the diagnosis of dysphoric disorders should be based in part on reports of mood which are only accessible through self-reports, these must remain part of the standard for diagnostic evaluation whether through test or interview. In fact, there is already a primitive kind of dimensionality in the polythetic format of some of the diagnostic categories in which a threshold for diagnosis depends on counting the number of signs or symptoms. The symptom descriptive terms of the DSM can be used for constructing dimensional systems based on empirical factor-analytic criteria rather than a priori clinical assumptions.

But the ultimate validity of diagnostic systems depends on the latent psychopathological traits underlying them, the etiologies, rather than the correlational structures based on surface symptom. Biological and behavioral tests such as the dexamethasone suppression test for melancholic depression, or the P50 evoked potential and eye-tracking dysfunction for schizophrenia, may be the first steps in delimiting basic dimensions of psychopathology. But this will depend on levels of sensitivity and specificity not yet achieved by most of them.

The assumption of continuity between normal personality dimensions, personality disorders, and clinical disorders may not be accurate for all disorders. It has been argued that schizophrenia is an extension of schizotypic personality, which is in turn, an extension of a normal dimension of "psychoticism." The concept of a "normal dimension of psychoticism" may be congruent with the popular idea that some people, like geniuses, are a little bit "crazy," but this confuses behavioral nonconformity with disorganized behavior, and original thinking with bizarre thinking. The only dimensional connection between schizophrenic and normal thinking is along dimensions of cognitive "peculiarity" which are not normal dimensions of personality, but milder forms of the psychopathologies in schizophrenia. The existence of a schizophrenic spectrum taxon, including schizophrenia, schizotypy, schizoaffective disorder, and delusional disorders, has been shown by taxometric methods (Meehl, 1995) and by genetic analyses. The preschizophrenic personality of the schizophrenic incorporates some elements of neuroticism and impulsive nonconformity, but the peculiarity comes later with the development of the early schizophrenia. The relatives of schizophrenics who are not schizotypic or schizophrenic themselves appear to be remarkably normal on the conventional dimensions of personality.

The gender differences in diagnoses revealed in large community studies in this country and by cross-cultural studies were at first attributed by some to diagnostic biases of the definitions of the disorders or to the biases of those who applied them. However, the universality of these differences suggests something more than stereotypes, biases, or cultural differences underlying them. More women have anxiety and mood disorders, and more men have substance-abuse and antisocial personality disorders. Similar differences have been found in personality traits related to these disorders: Women score higher on neuroticism-anxiety scales and men on sensation seeking and aggression scales. Are women simply subject to more stress everywhere, or are there some biological differences that account for the differential vulnerabilities? An example of the second possibility is the finding that the enzyme MAO-B which is lower in high sensation seekers than in low sensation seekers, and lower in alcoholics, drug-abusers, antisocial personality disorders, and criminals in general, is higher in women than in men at all ages. MAO-B is a very reliable and stable trait and varies little with experience, unlike testosterone which is also associated with sensation seeking and assertiveness in general.

In schizophrenia, there is no overall gender difference, but women tend to develop the disorder several years later than men. The basis for these kinds of gender and age differences may help to understand the disorders themselves. My prognosis is that most of them will be found to have a predominantly biological rather than a social basis.

DIATHESIS

The thesis of this volume is that all forms of psychopathology can be best explained within the framework of a diathesis–personality–stress model. The diathesis is the biological predisposition in terms of the biological traits which create a disposition or vulnerability to the development of psychopathology. Personality is a mediating factor, out of which psychopathology could develop. Biological or environmental stressors may contribute to the development of a disorder or may be the proximal trigger for the episodes of the disorder.

Causal factors may be described as sufficient, necessary, or contributing. A single gene with full "penetrance" could be a sufficient cause if its presence led to the inevitable development of a disorder, as the presence of a gene for Huntington's chorea invariably leads to the neurological disorder. An intensive and prolonged life experience could be a sufficient cause if it always resulted in a disorder. A type of personality which invariably progressed to a clinical disorder would be a sufficient cause. It is doubtful if any such sufficient causes exist in the realm of psychopathology.

Having an identical twin who is schizophrenic or two schizophrenic parents increases the risk of schizophrenia nearly fifty-fold, but the risk is still only 50%. If there were a single gene it must have a reduced "penetrance." Being exposed to conditions of social isolation, physical deprivation, torture, loss, and relentless fear over periods of years, as in concentration and prisoner-of-war camps, does not inevitably result in later severe disorders or even in posttraumatic stress disorder. An extremely strong trait of neuroticism does not inevitably result in an anxiety or mood disorder. The presence of a strong trait of impulsive sensation seeking or low conscientiousness does not make an antisocial personality inevitable, and an antisocial personality disorder does not necessarily lead to criminality or substance abuse. Only a minority of those with schizotypic personality disorders develop the full schizophrenic disorder. All of these preconditions increase the risk for the clinical disorders, and therefore, could be necessary, if not sufficient, causes.

Necessary causes are a more likely possibility than sufficient causes. Most diathesis–stress theories suggest that the diathesis is a necessary cause of the disorder. In the simplest dichotomous diathesis model, described in chapter 1 (see Fig. 1.3), if one has the diathesis factor, one is vulnerable to stress which in combination with the diathesis can produce the disorder. But if one does not have the specific gene(s) involved in the diathesis, one cannot develop the disorder regardless of the degree of stress encountered.

Single gene models, like Meehl's (1989) for schizophrenia, are most congenial to this kind of diathesis model, although viral infection and brain pathology models, whether genetic or not, could fit it. Model-fitting tests have not supported any single gene model for any kind of psychopathology discussed in this volume, and viral infections and brain pathologies account for only a minority of cases.

Polygenetic heritability would be compatible with the second diathesis model, involving the interaction of a continuously variable degree of stress and a quasicontinuous diathesis (see Fig. 1.4), as in Zubin's model of vulnerability (see Fig. 1.1). The presence of a variable degree of genetic "dosage" with a variable degree of stress produces the disorder. A threshold effect may be postulated so that below a certain level of diathesis, no amount of stress can produce the disorder. Above this level the interaction between degree of stress and strength of diathesis is responsible for the disorder. This model could be compatible with the data on most of the disorders, since chronic or early-developing cases seem to have a stronger genetic component than acute or late-developing ones. But the question is this: Do all disorders require either stress or genetic diathesis, and is the stress an independent factor or is it related to the diathesis itself?

The stress in antisocial personality disorder and substance abuse in men seems to be largely produced by the consequences of their behaviors rather than an initial cause of these behaviors. Although concurrent studies reveal a great deal of stress, prospective studies show that the stress was largely generated by their own behaviors. The substance abusers are stressed by the social, legal, and physical consequences of their drinking or drug use, and this stress, and the dysphoric reactions it produces, increases the substance abuse itself. Anxiety and depressive disorders that are comorbid with the substance abuse are reactions rather than causes in most cases of early-onset substance abuse in men. The pattern is different in women where early family problems and depression antedate the substance abuse.

In schizophrenia, stress is often a consequence of the impact of the disorder itself on family and peers, which exacerbates the disorder. Schizotypics who are less obviously disturbed may remain unstressed unless something beyond their control happens, such as the disruption of the family by death or separation. The schizophrenic encounters no more independent stress than do other people, but is particularly sensitive to such stress. This vulnerability is revealed when the schizophrenic is returned to the family after remission of the psychotic symptoms but relapses when the family is overtly hostile and critical.

Depression fits the independent diathesis–stress model somewhat better because there is evidence that the first and subsequent episodes of unipolar major depression are triggered by stressful events in the social environment, many of which are independent of reactions to the patients themselves. Chronic economic and familial stress also play a role in this disorder. Social support and personality strengths and weaknesses are important in determining the reactions to stress. Early occurring stress in the form of parental loss through separation or divorce or abandonment creates a vulnerability through the mechanism of "learned helplessness." But learning is not the entire source of the helplessness. There is a genetic mechanism as well as life experiences underlying learned helplessness. Strains of rats have been bred based on their reactions of "active avoidance" or passive freezing when exposed to stress. In humans, the impact of stress is greater in genetically vulnerable than in less vulnerable persons.

Do all forms of psychopathologies have a genetic diathesis? One is tempted to answer affirmatively in view of the finding that all major personality traits have some genetic component ranging from 30–60% as calculated from twin studies. But for a few disorders the evidence of a genetic component is not strong. Generalized anxiety disorder, if defined by the current 6-month duration criterion, shows no evidence of heritability, some weak influence of shared environment, and a large influence of nonshared environment in twin studies (Kendler et al., 1992a, 1992b). Situational type-specific phobias show a similar pattern. Other anxiety disorders show weak heritabilities, little or no influence of shared environments, and major influence from nonshared environment. Although neuroticism as a trait generally has a heritability of about .5, the anxiety disorders that have any heritability range from .2 to .4. Independent stress factors are presumably represented in the strong nonshared environment factor. The suggestion from these data is that the inherited diathesis of the anxiety disorders is largely a function of the broader diathesis of the personality traits which underlie and precede them. Another implication is that stressful life experiences acting on those with a vulnerable personality have a major role in the development of the clinical anxiety disorders. In the case of the generalized anxiety disorder, the genetic vulnerability may not even be necessary if stress is intense and persistent. The GAD is characterized by chronic worrying and tension rather than autonomic arousal, and such a pattern may be produced by real-life circumstances and a lack of coping skills. Similarly, the less severe depressions, such as dysthymic disorder, show less genetic influence than the more severe major depressions. Specific environmental stress in interaction with a weaker diathesis may be what turns a general trait of neuroticism into a GAD or dysthymic disorder. Perhaps genetic factors are relatively more important at the extreme ends of the continua of all psychopathologies.

The simple diathesis–stress models assume that personality develops from the basic genotype involved in the disorder and that the psychopathology stems from the interaction of that personality with life stressors, as in Meehl's (1962) model in which the schizogene results in the schizotaxic neurological dysfunction which leads to the schizotypic personality. But it is possible that for some disorders the genotypes for the clinical disorder and its symptoms are independent. This is a strong possibility for substance abuse in which one genetic pathway leads from alcoholism in the parent to alcoholism or drug abuse in the child, whereas another leads from antisocial personality in the parents to aggressiveness and antisocial personality in the child and then to substance abuse (Cadoret et al., 1986, 1995). In another type of substance abuse, unrelated to antisocial personality, neuroticism may be the personality trait interacting with the genetic vulnerability to substance abuse. Many schizophrenics do not show evidence of the schizotypic personality prior to their first psychotic episode. Conceivably the cognitive disorganization in schizophrenia may have a different genotype than the personality characteristics such as social fear, avolition, and anhedonia, which could be predisposing antecedents of neuroticism or depression as well as of schizophrenia.

The brain structural and physiological mediators of psychopathology have been investigated using CAT and MRI scans for structural investigations, and functional MRIs, PET scans, EEG, and evoked potentials for physiological studies. In an ideal situation, these kinds of studies should advance us beyond the need to analogize from animal models of psychopathology for the study of brain and behavioral relationships. In actual practice, the limitations of the imaging methods hinder progress in this area. EEG and evoked potentials are too imprecise as to origin of the signals, particularly for the subcortical areas. The resolution of the functional imaging methods is insufficient to view small areas such as the nucleus accumbens or the locus coeruleus or specific neural pathways which are postulated to be of vital importance in psychopathologies. Since the PET can only give data for a relatively long period of time, what is happening during that period is crucial to the activation patterns in the brain. Different results are obtained during resting states and task stimulation conditions, and in the latter too much depends on the nature of the task.

Structural studies of schizophrenia have revealed areas of brain damage such as a loss of neuronal tissue in the frontal and temporal lobes and the hippocampal-amygdala complex in some schizophrenics. Not enough studies of other types of psychopathology have been done to be sure of the specificity of these findings. If they are due to brain damage during the fetal periods or during difficult birth, they may not be specific to schizophrenia, because such brain damage is common in other disorders. As such, they may be contributing but not necessary causes, particularly because they are only found in a minority of schizophrenics. The tasks used in the active condition are tests on which schizophrenics do poorly; therefore, the differences in brain activation patterns may reflect only the difficulty in performing the tasks rather than any intrinsic defect in the brain systems involved. However, there are some interesting congruencies between structural and functional studies, such as the signs of damage to the frontal lobes and hypofrontality during performance on tasks, which are difficult for the schizophrenic, and the smaller hippocampal areas revealed in MRIs and the postmortem findings of cellular abnormalities in the hippocampus and parahippocampal gyrus and in frontal and temporal cortices.

Most of the research on the biological basis of the anxiety and mood disorders has been psychopharmacological. Here again, the limitations of the methods of investigating the physiology of the neurotransmitter systems in the brain are barriers to progress, depending largely upon metabolites, once, twice, or thrice removed from the changes in the brain itself. Metabolites of neurotransmitters or enzymes of peripheral origin, such as MAO, are imperfect estimations of what is happening in specific areas of the brain itself. However, coordinating data on the actions of drugs used to treat the disorders with study of levels of indirect activity in the neurotransmitter systems has yielded some viable hypotheses about the source of these disorders in dysregulations of the monoamine systems. It is not clear how many of these disturbances are purely state related (episode markers) and how many of them are biological traits (vulnerability markers). Longitudinal studies in psychopharmacology are rare. My hopeful prognosis is that future high-risk studies of the offspring of persons with disorders will include more psychopharmacological assessments.

Neurochemically selective brain scans would be optimal because they could be used in studying the responses of persons with disorders to tasks or stimuli that are theoretically of interest in those disorders. For instance, positive and negative emotion-provoking stimuli could be used to examine the monoaminergic responses in people with anxiety, mood, and antisocial personality disorders. These kinds of studies have been done with peripheral psychophysiological and psychopharmacological response measures, but it is reactions in the brain itself which are of primary interest. The prognosis is excellent for the pay-off from such studies, given the advances in methodology, which are likely. The "decade of the brain" will be extended over the millenium year into many more decades of discovery.

The kind of reductionism predicted by Freud is unlikely. Many problems of psychopathology will be most conveniently approached from the behavioral–cognitive or psychosocial levels, and others will best be treated by a combined biopsychosocial approach. Emotional traits are at the root of most basic personality traits, and disordered emotions are the basis of most psychopathologies. Emotional reactions are basically neurochemical responses, but it cannot be denied that they mostly arise from a combination of external events and internal perceptions of these events and their significance. As such, they can often be altered by psychological interventions, either by reconditioning or cognitive changes.

PERSONALITY

Discussing the frustrating search for major genes for major disorders such as schizophrenia and bipolar disorder, Plomin (1995) suggested that it might be easier to find major genes associated with the personality traits that underlie these disorders. The higher heritabilities found for neuroticism as a personality trait than for specific anxiety disorders tend to support this suggestion. A search is underway for major genes connected with anxiety-depressive neurotic disorders. I predict that these will be the same genes involved in the trait of neuroticism. In chapter 6, I discussed the recent findings of a gene common to sensation seeking and opiate abuse, and another gene common to alcohol and drug abuse and pathological gambling. Sensation seeking trait is also related to substance abuse, bipolar disorder, alcohol and drug abuse, and antisocial and borderline disorders directly and through a common biological substrate, to monoamine oxidase (MAO). Low levels of MAO-B type, assessed from blood platelets, are common to all types of disinhibitory disorders. Genes for MAO types A and B have been located on the X chromosome, but as yet no one has looked at the frequency of their polymorphisms in sensation seeking or the disinhibitory disorders. My prognosis is that the associations between major genes and their functions in the nervous system will result in the understanding of the biological basis of personality and its role in psychopathology.

Personality dimensions can be described in either three or five-factor (or more) hierarchal models depending on how narrow or specific the component factors need to be (Zuckerman, 1991, 1995). My own analyses have shown reliable and replicable three-factor (Sociability, Neuroticism-Anxiety, and Impulsive Unsocialized Sensation Seeking) and five-factor models (these three plus Aggression-Hostility and Activity; Zuckerman et al., 1988, 1991). Anxiety and unipolar depressive disorders represent an extreme expression of the Neuroticism factor, and antisocial personality disorders and some proportion of the substance abuse disorders represent the extreme expression of the Impulsive Unsocialized Sensation Seeking factor which includes Aggression in the three-factor model. The personality of the bipolar mood disorder incorporates impulsive sensation seeking rather than the neuroticism in the background of the unipolar disorder. This difference in the personality background of people with bipolar and unipolar disorders explains why bipolar patients are found only in the families of bipolars, whereas major unipolar depression is found in the families of both bipolar and unipolar patients. Some elements of neuroticism may be involved in the depressive component of the bipolar patient, but only the trait of impulsive sensation seeking is found in the manic component. Longitudinal studies of the personalities of people with disinhibitory disorders prior to the manifestation of the clinical disorder support their association with impulsive unsocialized sensation seeking.

Sociability does not seem to be involved in any of the major disorders, despite predictions of low sociability in people with schizophrenia and high sociability in those with bipolar mood disorders. Prior to longitudinal studies, investigators may have assumed that the social withdrawal in schizotypy or schizophrenia or that in social phobics or agoraphobics was long-standing and preceded the disorders themselves. Actually, there is little evidence of an association between schizoid personality disorder and schizophrenia.

Aggression-hostility is a characteristic of many but not all antisocial personalities. Possibly it determines the expression of antisocial tendencies rather than being intrinsic to the personality type itself. The sadistic, violent psychopath has a strong aggressive component in addition to the basic impulsivity, hedonistic sensation seeking, and lack of empathy which constitute the central personality components of the trait. Sadistic aggression for psychopaths is an antisocial way of seeking sensation through the suffering of their victims.

The need for Activity does not seem to be intrinsic to any disorder except for the person with "Type A" compulsive disorder, who needs to be doing something in work or active recreation all the time, and becomes restless, bored, and hostile during periods of enforced inactivity or waiting. But Type A is not an official diagnosis. Actually athletes all manifest a strong Activity need, and they are also lower than normal in neuroticism (O'Sullivan, Zuckerman, & Kraft, 1998).

My prognosis is that the coming years will see the identification of more major genes associated with personality traits, and many of these will be the same as or covariant with the genes associated with the forms of psychopathology discussed in this volume. The functions of these genes will help us understand the biological bases of personality. For instance, MAO-B seems to be involved primarily in the regulation of dopamine in the neurons in the brain. Dopamine in the mesocorticolimbic system is involved in intrinsic reward produced by drugs or novel and exciting experiences. Reward seeking may be one of the basic mechanisms involved in substance abuse and could be a function of an unregulated or overreactive dopaminergic system. If a form of the MAO-B gene can be found in excess in the high sensation seeker, and the function of the gene and MAO-B in dopamine regulation can be elucidated, we can better understand the disinhibitory disorders.

The relevance of the science of personality to psychopathology is only now becoming apparent in the growing interest in personality disorders. Psychopathologies are often thought of as evil spirits which are suddenly released from Pandora's box (or brain) by mishap. The view here is that they are the developmental outcomes of personality traits which begin in the differences of temperament seen in young children. Isolating them from clinical disorders on a separate axis of the DSM is a mistake which I prognosticate will be corrected if and when the final switch is made to dimensional approaches to diagnosis.

STRESS

In order to be meaningfully studied independent of other factors involved in the disorders, *stress* must be independently defined as that which happens to individuals rather than as their reactions to these events. Their reactions are functions of their vulnerabilities as well as of the events themselves. We must also distinguish between distal stress, which may have persistent effects throughout life, and proximal stress, which occurs just prior to the clinical episode of the disorder. Another primary distinction must be made between stressful events that are independent of persons and those that are a direct consequence of the behaviors characteristic in the disorders. Genetic factors have been found to influence the occurrence of nonindependent, but not independent types of stressful events, although they certainly influence the vulnerabilities or reactions to both types of events. When these distinctions are made, it is clear that independent stress plays a larger role in anxiety and mood disorders than in substance-abuse and schizophrenic disorders. In these latter two disorders the stress is most usually generated by the disorders themselves, such as the frightening delusions in the schizophrenic or the social reactions of others to the behavior in both of the disorders. But even though the stress may originate in the disorders, it exacerbates them, causing schizophrenics to relapse and the substance abusers to increase their use of the substance. Although stress may not have been an important source of the disorder, it becomes a major factor in its course and in the outcome of psychological or drug therapies.

Distal stress is of two types: biological and environmental. Biological distal stress refers to nongenetic stresses on the developing nervous system, usually occurring during the prenatal period, during birth, or in early infancy. Viral infections or alcohol and drug use of the pregnant mother may affect the fetus. Damage during the birth process may affect the fetus, and even in twins may affect one and not the other. Some drugs taken later in life may exacerbate the schizotypic tendencies and precipitate active psychoses. These kinds of factors have been found in excess in many studies of schizophrenic patients, but they only account for a minority of cases. They may be related to the kinds of brain damage found in a number of schizophrenics early in the course of their disorder, before exposure to the antipsychotic drugs. However, findings such as enlarged ventricles are not entirely specific to schizophrenics but are found in major mood disorders as well. These kinds of stressors may be nonspecific and increase the risks for many kinds of disorder.

Stress from family interactions used to carry most of the theoretical burden in explaining all kinds of psychopathologies including schizophrenia as well as the anxiety and mood disorders. The lack of significant shared environmental effects in most studies of personality and psychopathology challenges the theories involving abnormal family interactions as a major source of distal or proximal stress. But few of these studies have looked at the family interactions directly, and the interpretations of a lack of shared family influences were based on the presence or absence of the particular disorder in the parents or siblings of the person with the disorder. A parent with the disorder may be a source of stress in the child's environment, but that is not necessarily the case, particularly if the other parent is competent and loving and assumes major responsibility for the child-rearing. Conversely, even though the parent may not have the disorder, they may be a major source of stress in the home through neglect, irrational discipline, or open marital conflict.

It has been suggested that stress is relatively nonspecific, that any kind of stress may interact with specific diatheses to produce any kind of disorder. However, there is some evidence that both distal and proximal stress may have some specificity. Uncertain threat of loss or harm in the future are more likely to produce anxiety, whereas actual loss or separation is more likely to provoke depression. A background of familial loss by separation or divorce of parents may increase the risk for future depression, particularly if the later stress is a reinstatement of the earlier one. Persons with antisocial personality disorder may be immune to stress produced by threat of interpersonal loss, because they do not value the esteem or love of others. But the threat of loss of tangible rewards, such as money or drugs, or restriction of freedom by imprisonment (actual not threatened) are particularly stressful to them. Schizophrenics seem particularly sensitive to signs of anger or hostility directed toward them from within the family.

FAMILY AND SOCIAL FACTORS

Studies that have looked more closely at the actual home situation suggest that the general family climate may make a substantial difference in the risk of a son of a criminal father becoming a criminal, or of the child of a schizophrenic mother becoming schizophrenic. Perhaps the importance of the family environment is in the learning of strengths and coping skills rather than the stress produced by a disruptive or disorganized parent. Children can develop these strengths or learn these skills not only from the healthy parent or siblings, but from children and adults outside of the home. Of course, some of these adaptive traits come from partly inherited traits loosely described under the term *ego-strength*.

The adoption studies assume that the adoptive parent acts as a model for the learning of pathological behavior, but this influence may be attenuated by two factors. If the relationship between the affected parent and the child is not a rewarding one for the child, he or she is less likely to identify with and imitate the behavior of that parent. In fact, if the behavior of the parent is seen as injurious to the parent or the child, the parent is likely to become a negative role model. This is the case when an alcoholic father is abusive to his spouse and children or neglectful of them and the children come to see drinking as the source of the father's behavior. They may even become total abstainers. This kind of reaction appears to be more common in the daughters of alcoholics who have less of the genetic risk and are more likely to develop depression in later life as the outcome of living with an alcoholic father.

Many of the disorders are most frequent in the lowest socioeconomic level, and this has been interpreted as a sign of the stress produced by poverty. On closer examination, in many cases studied, patients have "drifted" down into the lower class from their class of origin, because of their disorder. However, even the social class of adoptive parents influences risk for antisocial behavior. Moreover, social class tends to be associated with outcome of treatment. Some of these relationships may be due to genetic linkages between class and vulnerabilities to disorders. But it is my opinion that much of the correlation is a function of the greater possibilities for coping and family social support in the middle and upper classes. A family concerned with meeting the basic survival needs for themselves and their children often do not have the time, energy, or interest to meet the emotional needs and solve the interpersonal problems of their children. The problems of the child may be dealt with by immediate punishment rather than by understanding and instruction. Of course, this is not true for all families in poverty, and some manage to give the emotional support and discipline that is meaningful to the child because it is in the context of a caring relationship. Outcomes for schizophrenia are actually better in the poorer underdeveloped countries than in the developed ones, possibly because of the familial acceptance and support for a recovered patient. A schizophrenic with residual symptoms of avolition is perhaps more likely to elicit a climate of negative emotionality in a Western middle-class home because of his failure to resume the kinds of independence and employment valued by Western society. This kind of emotional climate has been shown to be a powerful factor in relapse.

THERAPY

Therapy is a topic that has been deliberately neglected in this volume. However, a diathesis–personality–stress approach has implications for therapy. If all of these disorders are functions of a disordered nervous system, particularly if they depend upon biochemical disorders rather than gross brain damage, then drug therapy may play an important role in ameliorating them. There has been an ideological resistance among some psychotherapists to the use of drugs, although it is diminishing as evidence of their efficacy increases. In the United States, clinical psychologists are lobbying for the right to prescribe drugs, a right which would have been unthinkable 20 years ago.

Most drugs are "stupid" in two senses. The first is that one learns nothing from them, and their symptom amelioration is only effective as long as they are taken. This means that for some patients the drugs must be taken for the rest of their lives in order to prevent relapse. This is not necessarily unique to psychotropic drugs. People with diabetes must continue to take insulin to prevent remission because there is nothing to correct the basic deficiency in the production of insulin by the pancreas. Problems arise when the drugs like the phenothiazines, taken to suppress the psychotic symptomatology of schizophrenia, have serious potential side effects like Parkinson's syndrome and Tardive Dyskinesia. This occurs because of the second type of "stupidity" of many drugs. They affect an entire neurochemical system, like the dopaminergic one, instead of just that part of the system which is the source of the abnormal behavior. The phenothiazines and butyrophenomes, for instance, reduce the psychotic symptoms by blocking dopamine receptors in the mesolimbic systems, but they also block receptors in the nigrostriatal system and that is the source of the motoric neurological problems. "Smarter" drugs, such as clozapine and thioridazine, target the specific types of receptors in the mesolimbic system alone. In the area of depression some drugs act on both the noradrenergic and serotonergic neurons, whereas others specifically target one or the other. Because patients may suffer from a deficit in only one of the two systems, it is best to target the one involved. There are many kinds of receptors in these systems (10 or more in the serotonergic). Even smarter drugs may be developed to address only one or two of the receptors, when we understand which types are involved in specific depressive symptoms.

My prognosis is that as we learn more about the functions of the receptors, much more effective drugs with fewer side effects will be developed for the treatment of anxiety and mood disorders and schizophrenia. For the most part, these drugs are not curative because they cannot change the underlying diathesis which may cause future relapse without the suppressant effects of the drugs. It may take some drastic prophylactic treatment, such as gene replacement, to actually cure or prevent the disorder without the need for continual drug treatment, but these are probably far into the future. In the meantime, the manic may have to stay on lithium, the depressive on Prozac, and the schizophrenic on risperidone or clozipine (two of the smarter drugs) for the foreseeable future.

For the antisocial personality disorder and substance abusers there is currently little available in the form of drug treatment. There is some possibility that serotonin enhancers might reduce the impulsivity element in antisocial behavior. Dopamine and opiate receptor blockers may reduce the reinforcing effects of these drugs, but they depend on the motivation to quit the drug and by reducing the basic neurochemical sources of pleasure, they make it unlikely that they can be accepted by the drug abuser. The main drug treatment is replacement of one addictive drug by another. Methadone treatment is not very successful in treating heroin addiction, but it is just as effective as other therapies and much cheaper. But given the reward-seeking personality of the substance abuser, drug substitution may be the only answer in pharmacological terms. Legalization of less harmful but more rewarding substitutes would remove the terrible social consequences of drug abuse by making the drugs less expensive for the user and unprofitable for criminal organizations. But this is a solution that politicians are not ready to face.

Until recently, the traditional psychodynamic psychotherapies were also "stupid" in the sense that they had only one answer for all disorders: transference, insight, and catharsis. Although there was some specificity in theories of etiology of specific disorders, there was little corresponding specificity in therapeutic technique. The assumption was that when patients "understood" the source of their problems in past or current conflicts, they would be freed from anxiety and be able to devise new and more adaptive ways of coping. The success of behavioral and cognitive therapy is a function of their focus on symptoms, or the proximal cognitions involved in the symptoms. They also developed strategies for the patients to cope with their problems by suggesting alternatives and providing exercises. New interpersonal therapies have been developed for depression and anxiety, and these seem as effective as the behavioral–cognitive ones. They differ from older kinds of psychotherapy and simpler behavioral treatments primarily in their focus on the problems in current interpersonal relationships rather than on long past relationships, "unconscious" conflicts, or symptoms alone.

Theoretically, one does learn something of use from psychotherapies, which should carry over to prevent future relapse. This may happen for some individuals, but studies of the outcome of therapies for depression suggest that continuous or periodic sessions beyond remission may be as necessary for psychotherapies as for drug therapies. Psychotherapies particularly address the stress aspect of the diathesis–personality–stress model. Long-term psychoanalysis was the only therapy that ever claimed to change the personality of the patient, but considering the outcome statistics, it is questionable whether it really accomplished this, and considering the cost, it was limited to those of extensive means. But by helping patients cope with their own symptoms and the life stress problems, behavioral–cognitive therapies reduce the patient's vulnerability to disorganization or immobilization by stress. Interpersonal therapy focuses on dealing with the stress arising from interpersonal problems, and family therapies treat the stress engendered by the complex family interactions.

Freud assumed that schizophrenic patients could not benefit from psychoanalytic therapy, but those of other psychodynamic schools, such as the followers of Harry Stack Sullivan, thought they could treat them. Research on the effects of psychodynamic psychotherapy with or without drugs has proven Freud's assumption correct. However, nondynamic family therapy has been very efficacious when combined with drug treatment in preventing relapse in schizophrenia. Social skills training for the patients themselves has also been effective in helping them to function in the outside world and prevent relapse.

My prognosis is that psychotherapies will become smarter, by addressing the specific problems producing the stress that provokes the disorders. The behavioral–cognitive therapies have focused too much on the symptoms and cognitions and not enough on the current interpersonal sources of disturbance in the family. Most affective disorders arise in an interpersonal context and must be solved by more than an analysis of the patient's own perceptions and behavior. Another prognosis is that there will be increasing combination of drug and psychotherapies. Drugs are often essential in the initial phases of therapy when the patient is too upset to think or behave rationally, or to do the "homework" and bookkeeping required by cognitive therapy. As Dollard and Miller (1950) once observed, anxiety is like a blow on the head, it makes one temporarily stupid. As the patient settles down, the therapist can reduce the drug dosage and begin to work on the current sources of stress using the behavioral and cognitive methods developed specifically for the particular kinds of disorders. Of course the most convenient way of doing this is for the same person to give both drugs and psychotherapy. If the efforts of clinical psychologists to legalize their right to prescribe drugs is successful, we will need to revise their training to include more background in psychopharmacology and biopsychology in general. A "quickie" postgraduate seminar will not be adequate. A "cookbook" approach to drug therapy is an invitation to litigious disaster for ourselves and harm to our patients. We must redesign the basic graduate training program in clinical psychology to include the brain as well as behavior and the mind.

Students often reproach me for wasting their time on research information and theory not immediately applicable to their practical work with patients. Students in clinical psychology are particularly impatient with didactics on the biological basis of mental disorders, although this may change as they become more interested in prescribing drugs. The reason I start my psychopathology course with some history of psychopathology is to give them perspective on the prescientific past from which we are just emerging. Over the centuries those patients with mental disorders have been purged, drugged (with opiates), suppurated, lobotomized, exorcised, and psychoanalyzed, because of medical theories based on pseudoscience. Treatment in the absence of a sound scientific basis is folly, at best morale building and at worst harmful to the natural processes of recovery.

The past half-century has witnessed the first real scientific understanding of the physiology of the brain and its disorders. We are on the verge of understanding the role of genes in creating the vulnerabilities to the stressors of life that result in the compensations we call psychopathology. The past 50 years have also seen the emergence of psychosocial treatment methods based on direct approaches to life problems, maladaptive behaviors, and disordered emotions, rather than on indirect treatment methods based upon dubious theories of limited applicability to the problems of the great majority of sufferers from psychopathologies.

REFERENCES

Abramson, L. Y., Metalsky, G. I., & Alloy, L. B. (1989). Hopelessness depression: A theory-based subtype of depression. *Psychological Review, 96*, 358–372.

Abramson, L. Y., Seligman, M. E. P., & Teasdale, J. (1978). Learned helplessness in humans. Critique and reformulation. *Journal of Abnormal Psychology, 87*, 49–74.

Alden, L. E., & Wallace, S. T. (1995). Social phobia and social appraisal in successful and unsuccessful social interactions. *Behavior Research and Therapy, 33*, 497–505.

Allcock, C. C., & Grace, D. M. (1988). Pathological gamblers are neither impulsive or sensation seekers. *Australian and New Zealand Journal of Psychiatry, 22*, 307–311.

Alnaes, R., & Torgersen, S. (1991). Personality and personality disorders among patients with various affective disorders. *Journal of Personality Disorders, 5*, 107–121.

Alnaes, R., & Torgersen, S. (1993). Mood disorders: Developmental and precipitating events. *Canadian Journal of Psychiatry, 38*, 217–224.

Alpert, J. E., Maddocks, A., Rosenbaum, J. F., & Farva, M. (1994). Childhood psychopathology retrospectively assessed among adults with early onset major depression. *Journal of Affective Disorders, 31*, 165–171.

Altemus, M., Pigott, T., Kalogeras, K. T., Demitrack, M., Dubbert, B., Murphy, D. L., & Gold, P. W. (1992). Abnormalities in the regulation of vasopressin and corticotropin releasing factor secretion in obsessive-compulsive disorder. *Archives of General Psychiatry, 49*, 9–20.

Altemus, M., Swedo, S. E., Leonard, H. L., Richter, D., Rubinow, D. R., Potter, W. Z., & Rapoport, J. L. (1994). Changes in cerebrospinal fluid neurochemistry during treatment of obsessive-compulsive disorder with clomipramine. *Archives of General Psychiatry, 51*, 794–803.

Alterman, A. I., & Cacciola, J. S. (1991). The antisocial personality diagnosis in substance abusers. *The Journal of Nervous and Mental Disease, 179*, 401–409.

Amador, X. F., Flaum, M., Andreasen, N. C., Strauss, D. H., Yale, S. A., Clark, S. C., & Gorman, J. M. (1994). Awareness of illness in schizophrenia and schizoaffective and mood disorders. *Archives of General Psychiatry, 51*, 826–836.

American Psychiatric Association. (1952). *Diagnostic and statistical manual of mental disorders* (1st ed.). Washington, DC: Author.

American Psychiatric Association. (1968). *Diagnostic and statistical manual of mental disorders* (2nd ed.). Washington, DC: Author.

American Psychiatric Association. (1980). *Diagnostic and statistical manual of mental disorders* (3rd ed.). Washington, DC: Author.

American Psychiatric Association. (1987). *Diagnostic and statistical manual of mental disorders* (3rd ed., rev.). Washington, DC: Author.

American Psychiatric Association. (1994). *Diagnostic and statistical manual of mental disorders* (4th ed.). Washington, DC: Author.

Anderson, G., & Brown, R. I. (1984). Real and laboratory gambling, sensation seeking, and arousal. *British Journal of Psychology, 75*, 401–410.

Andreasen, N. C. (1990). *Schizophrenia: Positive and negative symptoms and syndromes.* Basel, Switzerland: Karger.

Andreasen, N. C., Arndt, S., Alliger, R., Miller, D., & Flaum, M. (1995). Symptoms of schizophrenia: Methods, meanings, and mechanisms. *Archives of General Psychiatry, 52*, 341–351.

Andreasen, N. C., & Carpenter, W. T., Jr. (1993). Diagnosis and classification of schizophrenia. *Schizophrenia Bulletin, 19*, 199–214.

Andreasen, N. C., & Flaum, M. (1991). Schizophrenia: The characteristic symptoms. *Schizophrenia Bulletin, 17*, 27–49.

Andreasen, N. C., & Olsen, S. (1982). Negative vs. positive schizophrenia. *Archives of General Psychiatry, 39*, 789–794.

Andreasen, N. C., Rezai, K., Alliger, R., Swayze V. W. II, Flaum, M., Kirchner, P., Cohen, G., & O'Leary, D. S. (1992). Hypofrontality in neuroleptic-naive patients and in patients with chronic schizophrenia. *Archives of General Psychiatry, 49*, 943–958.

Andrews, G., Freed, S., & Teeson, M. (1994). Proximity and anticipation of a negative outcome in phobics. *Behaviour Research and Therapy, 32*, 643–645.

Andrews, G., Neilson, M., Hunt, C., Stewart, G., & Kiloh, L. R. (1990). Diagnosis, personality and the long-term outcome of depression. *British Journal of Psychiatry, 157*, 13–18.

Andrews, G., Stewart, G., Allen, R., & Henderson, A. S. (1990). The genetics of six neurotic disorders: A twin study. *Journal of Affective Disorders, 19*, 23–29.

Andrews, G., Stewart, G., Morris-Yates, A., Holt, P., & Henderson, S. (1990). Evidence for a general neurotic syndrome. *British Journal of Psychiatry, 157*, 6–12.

Angst, J., & Clayton, P. (1986). Premorbid personality of depressive, bipolar, and schizophrenic patients with special reference to suicidal issues. *Comprehensive Psychiatry, 27*, 511–532.

Anthony, J. C. (1992). Epidemiological research on cocaine use in the USA. In G. R. Bock & J. Whelan (Eds.), *Cocaine: Scientific and social dimensions* (pp. 20–33). Chichester, England: Wiley.

Antony, M. M., & Barlow, D. M. (1990). Emotion theory as a framework for explaining panic attacks and panic disorder. In R. M. Rapee (Ed.), *Current controversies in the anxiety disorders* (pp. 55–76). New York: Guilford Press.

Arana, G. W., & Baldessarini, R. J. (1987). Clinical use of the dexamethasone suppression test in psychiatry. In H. Y. Meltzer (Ed.), *Psychopharmacology: The third generation of progress* (pp. 607–615). New York: Raven Press.

Arndt, S., Andreasen, N. C., Flaum, M., Miller, D., & Nopoulos, P. (1995). A longitudinal study of symptom dimensions in schizophrenia. *Archives of General Psychiatry, 52*, 352–360.

Asarow, R. F., & Granholm, E. (1991). The contributions of cognitive psychology to vulnerability models. In H. Häfner & W. F. Gattaz (Eds.), *Search for the causes of schizophrenia* (Vol. 2, pp. 205–220). Berlin, Germany: Springer-Verlag.

Asherson, P., Mant, R., Williams, N., Cardno, A., Jones, L., Murphy, K., Collier, D., Nanko, S., Criddock, N., Morris, S., Muri, W., Blackwood, B., McGuffin, P., & Owen, M. J. (1998). *Molecular Psychiatry, 3,* 310–320.

Austin, M. P., & Mitchell, P. (1996). Melancholia as a neurological disorder. In G. Parker & D. Hadzi-Pavlovic (Eds.), *Melancholia: A disorder of movement and mood* (pp. 223–236). New York: Cambridge University Press.

Aylward, E. H., Harris, G. J., Hoehm-Saric, R., Barta, P. E., Machlin, S. R., & Pearlson, G. D. (1996). Normal caudate nucleus in obsessive-compulsive disorder assessed by quantitative neuroimaging. *Archives of General Psychiatry, 53,* 577–584.

Baer, L., Jenike, M. A., Black, D. W., Treece, C., Rosenfeld, R., & Greist, J. (1992). Effect of axis II diagnoses on treatment outcome with clomipramine in 55 patients with obsessive-compulsive disorder. *Archives of General Psychiatry, 49,* 862–866.

Baer, L., Rauch, S. L., Ballantine, T., Jr., Martuza, R., Cosgrove, R., Cassem, E., Giriunas, I., Manzo, P. A., Diminino, C., & Jenike, M. A. (1995). Cingulotomy for intractable obsessive-compulsive disorder: Prospective long-term follow-up of 18 patients. *Archives of General Psychiatry, 52,* 384–392.

Bagby, R. M., Schuller, D. R., Parker, J. D. A., Levitt, A., Joffe, R. T., & Shafir, S. (1994). Major depression and the self-criticism and dependency of personality dimensions. *American Journal of Psychiatry, 151,* 597–599.

Ball, S. A. (1995). The validity of an alternative five-factor measure of personality in cocaine abusers. *Psychological Asssessment, 7,* 148–154.

Ball, S. A., Carroll, K. M., Barbor, T. F., & Rounsaville, B. J. (1995). Subtypes of cocaine abusers: Support for a Type A-Type B distinction. *Journal of Consulting and Clinical Psychology, 63,* 115–124.

Ball, S. A., Carroll, K. M., Robinson, J. E., & O'Malley, S. S. (1997). Addiction severity and MMPI-derived typologies in cocaine abusers. *The American Journal on Addictions, 6,* 83–86.

Ball, S. A., Carroll, K. M., & Rounsaville, B. J. (1994). Sensation seeking, substance abuse, and psychopathology in treatment-seeking and community cocaine abusers. *Journal of Consulting and Clinical Psychology, 62,* 1053–1057.

Ball, S. A., Kranzler, H. R., Tennen, H., Poling, J. C., & Rounsaville, B. J. (1998). Personality disorder and dimension differences between Type A and B substance abusers. *Journal of Personality Disorders, 12,* 1–12.

Ball, S. A., & Schottenfeld, R. S. (1997). A five-factor model of personality and addiction, psychiatric, and AIDS risk severity in pregnant and postpartum cocaine misusers. *Substance Use and Misuse, 32,* 25–41.

Ball, S. A., Tennen, H., Poling, J. C., Kanzler, H. R., & Rounsaville, B. J. (1997). Personality, temperament, and character dimensions and the DSM-IV personality disorders in substance abusers. *Journal of Abnormal Psychology, 106,* 545–553.

Ball, S. G., Baer, L., & Otto, M. W. (1996). Symptom subtypes of obsessive-compulsive disorder in behavioral treatment studies: A quantitative review. *Behaviour Research and Therapy, 34,* 47–51.

Bandura, A. (1977). *Social learning theory.* Englewood Cliffs, NJ: Prentice-Hall.

Barlow, D. H. (1988). *Anxiety and its disorders.* New York: Guilford Press.

Barlow, D. H. (1991). The nature of anxiety: Anxiety, depression, and emotional disorders. In R. M. Rapee & D. H. Barlow (Eds.), *Chronic anxiety, generalized anxiety disorder, and mixed anxiety-depression* (pp. 1–28). New York: Guilford.

Barlow, D. H., Blanchard, E. B., Vermilyea, J. A., Vermilyea, B. E., & DiNardo, P. A. (1986). Generalized anxiety and generalized anxiety disorder: Description and reconceptualization. *American Journal of Psychiatry, 143,* 40–44.

Barlow, D. H., Brown, T. A., & Craske, M. G. (1994). Definitions of panic attacks and panic disorder in the DSM-IV: Implications for research. *Journal of Abnormal Psychology, 103,* 553–563.

Barlow, D. H., & Craske, M. G. (1988). The phenomenology of panic. In S. Rachman & J. D. Maser (Eds.), *Panic: Psychological perspectives* (pp. 11–35). Hillsdale, NJ: Erlbaum.

Barlow, D. H., & DiNardo, P. A. (1991). The diagnosis of generalized anxiety disorder: Development, current status, and future directions. In R. M. Rapee & D. H. Barlow (Eds.), *Chronic anxiety, generalized anxiety disorder and mixed anxiety-depression* (pp. 95–118). New York: Guilford Press.

Baron, M. (1998). Mapping genes for personality: Is the saga sagging? *Molecular Psychiatry, 3,* 106–108.

Bartusch, D. R. J., Lynam, D. R., Moffitt, T. E., & Silva, P. A. (1997). Is age important? Testing a general versus a developmental theory of antisocial behavior. *Criminology, 35,* 13–48.

Bates, M. E., Labourie, E. W., & White, H. R. (1985). *A longitudinal study of sensation seeking needs and drug use.* Paper presented at the 93rd Annual Convention of the American Psychological Association, Los Angeles, CA, August 23–27. (Available from EDRS reproduction services [MF01/PC02])

Bateson, G., Jackson, D. D., Haley, J., & Weakland, J. (1956). Toward a theory of schizophrenia. *Behavioral Science, 1,* 251–264.

Battaglia, M., Cavallini, M. C., Macciardi, F., & Bellodi, L. (1997). The structure of DSM-III-R schizotypal personality disorder diagnosed by direct interviews. *Schizophrenia Bulletin, 23,* 83–92.

Bauer, M. S., Whybrow, P. C., & Winokur, A. (1990). Rapid cycling bipolar affective disorder. *Archives of General Psychiatry, 47,* 427–432.

Baxter, L. R. (1991). PET studies of cerebral function in major depression and obsessive-compulsive disorder. *Annals of Clinical Psychiatry, 3,* 103–109.

Baxter, L. R., Schwartz, J. M., Bergman, K. S., Szuba, M. P., Guze, B. H., Mazziotta, J. C., Alazraki, A., Selin, C. E., Ferng, H. K., Munford, P., & Phelps, M. E.

(1992). Caudate glucose metabolic rate change with both drug and behavior therapy for obsessive-compulsive disorder. *Archives of General Psychiatry, 49,* 681–689.

Baxter, L. R., Schwartz, J. M., Phelps, M. E., Mazziotta, J. C., Guze, B. H., Selin, C. E., Gerner, R. H., & Sumida, R. M. (1989). Reduction in prefrontal glucose metabolism common to three types of depression. *Archives of General Psychiatry, 46,* 243–250.

Bebbington, P., Williams, S., Jones, P., Foerster, A., Murray, R., Toone, B., & Lewis, S. (1993). Life events and psychosis: Initial results from the Camberwell collaborative psychosis study. *British Journal of Psychiatry, 162,* 72–79.

Beck, A. T. (1967). *Depression: Clinical, experimental, and theoretical aspects.* Philadelphia: University of Pennsylvania Press.

Beck, A. T. (1972). *Depression: Causes and treatment.* Philadelphia: University of Pennsylvania Press.

Beck, A. T. (1976). *Cognitive therapy and the emotional disorders.* New York: International Universities Press.

Beck, A. T. (1983). Cognitive therapy of depression: New perspectives. In P. J. Clayton & J. E. Barrett (Eds.), *Treatment of depression: Old controversies and new approaches* (pp. 265–284). New York: Raven Press.

Beck, A. T. (1987). Cognitive models of depression. *Journal of Cognitive Psychotherapy, 1,* 5–37.

Beck, A. T., Emery, G., & Greenberg, R. L. (1985). *Anxiety disorders and phobias: A cognitive perspective.* New York: Basic Books.

Becona, E., Lorenzo, C., & Fuentes, M. J. (1996). Pathological gamblers and depression. *Psychological Reports, 78,* 635–640.

Begleiter, H., & Porjesz, B. (1988). Neurophysiological dysfunction in alcoholism. In R. M. Rose & J. E. Barrett (Eds.), *Alcoholism: Origins and outcome* (pp. 157–172). New York: Raven Press.

Bellodi, L., Bussoleni, C., Scorza-Smeraldi, R., Gorassi, G., Zacchetti, L., & Smeraldi, E. (1986). Family study of schizophrenia: Exploratory analysis for relevant factors. *Schizophrenia Bulletin, 12,* 120–128.

Bellodi, L., Sciuto, G., Diaferia, G., Ronchi, P., & Smeraldi, E. (1992). Psychiatric disorders in the families of patients with obsessive-compulsive disorder. *Psychiatry Research, 42,* 111–120.

Belmaker, R. H., & Biederman, J. (1994). Genetic markers, temperament and psychopathology. *Biological Psychiatry, 36,* 71–72.

Benes, F. M. (1995). Altered glutamatergic and GABAergic mechanisms in the cingulate cortex of the schizophrenic brain. *Archives of General Psychiatry, 52,* 1015–1018.

Benjamin, J., Li, L., Patterson, C., Greenberg, B. D., Murphy, D. L., & Hammer, D. H. (1996). Population and familial association between the D4 dopamine receptor gene and measures of sensation seeking. *Nature Genetics, 12,* 81–84.

Benkelfut, C., Ellenbogen, M. A., Dean, P., Palmour, R. M., & Young, S. N.

(1994). Mood-lowering effect of tryptophan depletion: Enhanced susceptibility in young men at genetic risk for major affective disorders. *Archives of General Psychiatry, 51,* 687–697.

Beratis, S., Gabriel, J., & Hoidas, S. (1994). Age at onset in subtypes of schizophrenic disorders. *Schizophrenia Bulletin, 20,* 287–296.

Berenbaum, H., & Fujita, F. (1994). Schizophrenia and personality: Exploring the boundaries and connections between vulnerability and outcome. *Journal of Abnormal Psychology, 103,* 148–158.

Berenbaum, S. A., Taylor, M. A., & Cloninger, C. R. (1994). Family study of schizophrenia and personality. *Journal of Abnormal Psychology, 103,* 475–484.

Berg, C., & Kühlhorn, E. (1994). Social, psychological and physical consequences of pathological gambling in Sweden. *Journal of Gambling Studies, 10,* 275–285.

Bergman, A. J., Harvey, P. D., Mitropoulou, V., Aronson, A., Marder, D., Silverman, J., Trestman, R., & Siever, L. J. (1996). The factor structure of schizotypal symptoms in a clinical population. *Schizophrenia Bulletin, 22,* 501–509.

Berman, K. F., Torrey, E. F., Daniel, D. G., & Weinberger, D. R. (1992). Regional cerebral blood flow in monozygotic twins discordant and concordant for schizophrenia. *Archives of General Psychiatry, 49,* 927–934.

Bernstein, A. S. (1991). The autonomic orienting response as a possible vulnerability marker in schizophrenia? In H. Häfner & W. F. Gattaz (Eds.), *Search for the causes of schizophrenia* (Vol. 2, pp. 321–341). Berlin, Germany: Springer-Verlag.

Bertelson, A., Harvald, B., & Hauge, M. (1977). A Danish twin study of manic-depressive disorders. *British Journal of Psychiatry, 130,* 330–351.

Bhurgra, D., Hilwig, M., Hossein, B., Marceau, H., Neehall, J., Left, J., Mallet, R., & Der, G. (1996). First contact incidence rates of schizophrenia in Trinidad and one-year follow-up. *British Journal of Psychiatry, 169,* 587–592.

Bifulco, A., Brown, G. W., & Adler, Z. (1991). Early sexual abuse and clinical depression in adult life. *British Journal of Psychiatry, 159,* 115–122.

Black, D. W., Noyes, R., Jr., Goldstein, R. B., & Blum, N. (1992). A family study in obsessive-compulsive disorder. *Archives of General Psychiatry, 49,* 362–368.

Blackburn, R. (1979). Cortical and autonomic arousal in primary and secondary psychopaths. *Psychophysiology, 16,* 143–150.

Blackwood, D. H. R., He, L., Morris, S. W., McLean, A., Whitton, C., Thomson, M., Walker, M. T., Woodburn, K., Sharp, C. M., Wright, A. F., Shibasaki, Y., St. Clair, D. M., Porteous, D. J., & Muir, W. J. (1996). A locus for bipolar affective disorder on chromosome 4p. *Nature Genetics, 12,* 427–430.

Blair, R. J. R., Jones, L., Clark, F., & Smith, M. (1997). The psychopathic individual: A lack of responsiveness to distress cues? *Psychophysiology, 34,* 192–198.

Blanco, C., Orensanz-Munoz, L., Blanco-Jerez, C., & Saiz-Ruiz, J. (1996). Pathological gambling and platelet MAO activity: A psychobiological study. *American Journal of Psychiatry, 153,* 119–121.

Bland, R., & Orn, H. (1986). Family violence and psychiatric disorder. *Canadian Journal of Psychology, 31,* 129–137.

Blashfield, R. K. (1984). *The classification of psychopathology: Neo-Kraepelinian and quantitative approaches.* New York: Plenum.

Blaszczynski, A., McConaghy, N., & Frankova, A. (1990). Boredom proneness in an impulse control disorder. *Psychological Reports, 67,* 35–42.

Blaszczynski, A., McConaghy, N., & Frankova, A. (1991). Control versus abstinence in the treatment of pathological gambling: A two to nine year follow-up. *British Journal of Addiction, 86,* 299–306.

Blaszczynski, A., Steel, Z., & McConaghy, N. (1997). Impulsivity in pathological gambling: The antisocial impulsivist. *Addiction, 92,* 75–87.

Blaszczynski, A., Wilson, A. C., & McConaghy, N. (1986). Sensation seeking and pathological gambling. *British Journal of Addiction, 81,* 113–117.

Bleuler, E. (1950). *Dementia praecox or the group of schizophrenias* (J. Zinkin, Trans.). New York: International Universities Press. (Original work published 1911)

Bleuler, M. (1978). *The schizophrenic disorders: Long term patient and family studies.* New Haven, CT: Yale University Press.

Bloom, F. E. (1993). The neurobiology of addiction: An integrated view. In S. G. Korenman & J. D. Barchas (Eds.), *Biological basis of substance abuse* (pp. 3–16). New York: Oxford University Press.

Bloom, F. E., & Kupfer, D. J. (Eds.). (1995). *Psychopharmacology: The fourth generation of progress.* New York: Raven Press.

Blouin, J., Spindler, E., Perez, E., Blouin, A., Hotz, S., & Hakkaku, J. (1992). The role of stress in interpreting the dexamethasone suppression test. *Canadian Journal of Psychiatry, 37,* 724–727.

Bohman, M. (1996). Predisposition to criminality: Swedish adoption studies in retrospect. In G. R. Bock & J. A. Goode (Eds.), *Genetics of criminal and antisocial behaviour* (pp. 99–109). Chichester, England: Wiley.

Borkovec, T. D., Shadnick, R. N., & Hopkins, M. (1991). The nature of normal and pathological worry. In R. M. Rapee & D. H. Barlow (Eds.), *Chronic anxiety: Generalized anxiety disorder and mixed anxiety-depression* (pp. 29–51). New York: Guilford Press.

Boster, J., & Fabrega, H. (1993). Semantic structures and psychiatric diagnosis. *Journal of Nervous and Mental Disease, 181,* 54–58.

Bouchard, T. J., Lykken, D. T., McGue, M., Segal, N. L., & Tellegen, A. (1990). Sources of human psychological differences. *Science, 250,* 223–228.

Bowlby, J. (1951). *Maternal care and mental health.* Geneva, Switzerland: World Health Organization.

Bowlby, J. (1977). The making and breaking of affectional bonds. *British Journal of Psychiatry, 130,* 201–210.

Boyce, P., & Hadzi-Pavlovic, D. (1996). Issues in classification: I. Some historical aspects. In G. Parker & D. Hadzi-Pavlovic (Eds.), *Melancholia: A disorder of movement and mood* (pp. 9–19). New York: Cambridge University Press.

Boyce, P., Parker, G., Barnett, B., Cooney, M., & Smith, F. (1991). Personality as a vulnerability factor to depression. *British Journal of Psychiatry, 159,* 106–114.

Boyd, J. H., Burke, J. D., Jr., Gruenberg, E., Holzer, C. E., III, Rae, D. S., George, L. K., Karno, M., Stoltzman, R., McEvoy, L., & Nestadt, G. (1984). Exclusion criteria of DSM-III. *Archives of General Psychiatry, 41,* 983–989.

Bozarth, M. A. (1987). Ventral tegmental reward system. In J. Engel, L. Oreland, B. Pernor, S. Rössner, & L. A. Pelhorn (Eds.), *Brain reward systems and abuse* (pp. 1–17). New York: Raven Press.

Bradbury, T. N., & Miller, G. A. (1985). Season of birth in schizophrenia: A review of evidence, methodology, and etiology. *Psychological Bulletin, 98,* 569–594.

Bradwejn, J., Koszycki, D., & Couetoux-de-Terte, A. (1992). The cholecystokinin hypothesis of pain and anxiety disorders: A review. *Journal of Psychopharmacology, 6,* 345–351.

Breen, R. B., & Zuckerman, M. (in press). Chasing in gambling behavior: Personality and cognitive determinants. *Personality and Individual Differences.*

Breier, A., Buchanan, R. W., Elkashef, A., Munson, R. C., Kirkpatrick, B., & Gellad, F. (1992). Brain morphology and schizophrenia: A magnetic resonance imaging study of limbic, prefrontal cortex, and caudate structures. *Archives of General Psychiatry, 49,* 921–924.

Breier, A., Schreiber, J. D., Dyer, J., & Pickar, D. (1991). National Institute of Mental Health longitudinal study of chronic schizophrenia. *Archives of General Psychiatry, 48,* 236–246.

Bremner, J. D., Randall, P., Scott, T. M., Bronen, R. A., Seibyl, J. P., Southwick, S. M., Delaney, R. C., McCarthy, G., Charney, D. S., & Innis, R. B. (1995). MRI-based measurements of hippocampal volume in patients with combat-related posttraumatic stress disorder. *American Journal of Psychiatry, 152,* 973–981.

Brennan, S. A., Mednick, S. A., & Jacobsen, B. (1996). Assessing the role of genetics in crime using adoption cohorts. In G. R. Bock & J. A. Goode (Eds.), *Genetics of criminal and antisocial behaviours* (pp. 115–123). Chichester, England: Wiley.

Breslau, N., & Davis, G. C. (1992). Posttraumatic stress disorder in an urban population of young adults: Risk factors for chronicity. *American Journal of Psychiatry, 149,* 671–675.

Breslau, N., Davis, G. C., & Andreski, P. (1995). Risk factors of PTSD-related traumatic events: A prospective analysis. *American Journal of Psychiatry, 152,* 529–535.

Breslau, N., Davis, G. C., Andreski, P., & Peterson, E. (1991). Traumatic events and posttraumatic stress disorder in an urban population of young adults. *Archives of General Psychiatry, 48,* 216–222.

Breslau, N., Davis, C. G., Peterson, E. L., & Schultz, L. (1997). Psychiatric sequelae of posttraumatic stress disorder in women. *Archives of General Psychiatry, 54*, 81.

Breuer, J., & Freud, S. (1955). Studies on hysteria. In J. Strachey (Ed. & Trans.), *Standard edition of the collected works of Sigmund Freud*. London: Hogarth Press. (Original work published 1895)

Brodarty, H., Peters, K., Boyce, P., Hickie, I., Parker, G., Mitchell, F., & Wilhelm, K. (1991). Age and depression. *Journal of Affective Disorders, 23*, 137–149.

Brooner, R. K., Greenfield, L., Schmidt, C. W., & Bigelow, G. E. (1993). Antisocial personality and HIV infection among intravenous drug abusers. *American Journal of Psychiatry, 150*, 53–58.

Brooner, R. K., King, V. L., Kidorf, M., Schmidt, C. W., & Bigelow, G. E. (1997). Psychiatric and substance use comorbidity among treatment-seeking opioid abusers. *Archives of General Psychiatry, 54*, 71–79.

Brown, G. W. (1993). Life events and affective disorder: Replications and limitations. *Psychosomatic Medicine, 55*, 248–259.

Brown, G. W., Andrews, B., Bifulco, A., & Veiel, H. (1990). Self esteem and depression. I: Measurement issues and prediction of onset. *Social Psychiatry and Psychiatric Epidemiology, 25*, 200–209.

Brown, G. W., & Harris, T. (1978). *Social origins of depression*. New York: The Free Press.

Brown, G. W., Harris, T., & Heyworth, C. (1994). Life events and endogenous depression: A puzzle reconsidered. *Archives of General Psychiatry, 51*, 525–534.

Brown, T. A., & Barlow, D. H. (1992). Comorbidity among anxiety disorders: Implications for treatment and DSM-IV. *Journal of Consulting and Clinical Psychology, 60*, 835–844.

Brown, T. A., Barlow, D. H., & Liebowitz, M. R. (1994). The empirical basis of generalized anxiety disorder. *American Journal of Psychiatry, 151*, 1272–1280.

Bruner, H. G. (1996). MAO-A deficiency and abnormal behavior: Perspectives on an association. In G. R. Bock & J. A. Goode (Eds.), *Genetics of criminal and antisocial behaviour* (pp. 155–164). Chichester, England: Wiley.

Bryant, R. A., & Harvey, A. G. (1995). Processing threatening information in posttraumatic stress disorder. *Journal of Abnormal Psychology, 104*, 537–541.

Buchsbaum, M. S., Haier, R. J., Potkin, S. G., Nuechterlein, K., Bracha, H. S., Katz, M., Lohr, J., Wu, J., Lottenberg, S., Jerabek, P. A., Trenary, M., Tafalla, R., Reynolds, C., & Bunney, W. E., Jr. (1992). Frontostriatal disorder of cerebral metabolism in never-medicated schizophrenics. *Archives of General Psychiatry, 49*, 935–942.

Buchsbaum, M. S., Potkin, S. G., Siegel, B. V., Lohr, J., Katz, M., Gottschalk, L. A., Gulasekaram, B., Marshall, J. F., Lottenberg, S., Teng, C. Y., Abel, L., Plony, L., & Bunney, W. E., Jr. (1992). Striatal metabolic rate and clinical response to neuroleptics in schizophrenia. *Archives of General Psychiatry, 49*, 966–974.

Buchsbaum, M. S., Someya, T., Teng, C. Y., Abel, L., Chin, S., Najafi, J. A., Haier,

R. J., Wu, J., & Bunney, W. E., Jr. (1996). PET and MRI of the thalamus in never-medicated patients with schizophrenia. *American Journal of Psychiatry, 153,* 191–199.

Buchsbaum, M. S., Wu, J., Haier, R., Hazlett, E., Bull, R., Katz, M., Sokolski, K., Lagunas-Solar, M., & Langer, D. (1987). Positron emission tomography assessment of effects of benzodiazepines on regional glucose metabolic rate in patients with anxiety disorder. *Life Sciences, 40,* 2393–2400.

Burke, K. C., Burke, J. D., Jr., Rae, D. S., & Regier, D. A. (1991). Comparing age at onset of major depression and other psychiatric disorders by birth cohorts in five US community populations. *Archives of General Psychiatry, 48,* 789–795.

Burman, B., Mednick, S. A., Machon, R. A., Parnas, J., & Schulsinger, F. (1987). Children at high risk for schizophrenia: Parent and offspring perceptions of family relationships. *Journal of Abnormal Psychology, 96,* 364–366.

Butler, R. W., Mueser, K. T., Sprock, J., & Braff, D. L. (1996). Positive symptoms of psychosis in posttraumatic stress disorder. *Biological Psychiatry, 39,* 839–844.

Butzlaf, R. L., & Hooley, J. M. (1998). Expressed emotion and psychiatric relapse: A meta-analysis. *Archives of General Psychiatry, 55,* 547–552.

Cacciola, J. S., Rutherford, M. J., Alterman, A. I., & Snider, E. C. (1994). An examination of the diagnostic criteria for antisocial personality disorder in substance abusers. *The Journal of Nervous and Mental Disease, 182,* 517–523.

Cadoret, R. J., O'Gorman, T. W., Troughton, E., & Haywood, E. (1985). Alcoholism and antisocial personality: Interrelationships, genetic and environmental factors. *Archives of General Psychiatry, 42,* 161–167.

Cadoret, R. J., Troughton, E., & O'Gorman, T. W. (1987). Genetic and environmental factors in alcohol abuse and antisocial personality. *Journal of Studies on Alcoholism, 48,* 1–8.

Cadoret, R. J., Troughton, E., O'Gorman, T. W., & Haywood, E. (1986). An adoption study of genetic and environmental factors in drug abuse. *Archives of General Psychiatry, 43,* 1131–1136.

Cadoret, R. J., Winokur, G., Langbehn, D., Troughton, E., Yates, W. R., & Stewart, M. A. (1996). Depression spectrum disease. I: The role of gene-environment interaction. *American Journal of Psychiatry, 153,* 892–899.

Cadoret, R. J., Yates, W. R., Troughton, E., Woodworth, G., & Stewart, M. A. (1995). Adoption study demonstrating two genetic pathways to drug abuse. *Archives of General Psychiatry, 52,* 42–52.

Campbell, R. J. (1989). *Psychiatric dictionary* (6th ed.). New York: Oxford University Press.

Cannon, T. D., & Marco, E. (1994). Structural brain abnormalities as indicators of vulnerability to schizophrenia. *Schizophrenia Bulletin, 20,* 89–99.

Cannon, T. D., Mednick, S. A., Parnas, J., & Vestergaard, A. (1994). Developmental brain abnormalities in the offspring of schizophrenic mothers. II:

Structural brain characteristics of schizophrenic and schizotypal personality disorder. *Archives of General Psychiatry, 51*, 955–962.

Cannon, T. D., Mednick, S. A., Parnas, J., Schulsinger, F., Praestholm, J., & Vestergaard, A. (1993). Developmental brain abnormalities in the offspring of schizophrenic mothers. I: Contributions of genetic and perinatal factors. *Archives of General Psychiatry, 50*, 551–564.

Carey, G. (1992). Twin imitation for antisocial behavior: Implications for genetic and family environmental research. *Journal of Abnormal Psychology, 101*, 18–25.

Carey, G., & Gottesman, I. I. (1981). Twin and family studies of anxiety, phobic, and obsessive disorders. In D. F. Klein & J. Rabkin (Eds.), *Anxiety: New research and changing concepts* (pp. 117–134). New York: Raven Press.

Carlton, P. L., Manowitz, P., McBride, H., Nora, R., Swartzburg, M., & Goldstein, L. (1987). Attention deficit disorder and pathological gambling. *Journal of Clinical Psychiatry, 48*, 487–488.

Carr, D. B., Sheean, D. V., Surman, O. S., Coleman, J. H., Greenblatt, D. J., Heninger, G. R., Jones, K. J., Levine, P. H., & Watkinds, D. (1986). Neuroendocrine correlates of lactate-induced anxiety and their response to chronic alprazolam therapy. *American Journal of Psychiatry, 143*, 483–494.

Carrol, E. N., Zuckerman, M., & Vogel, W. H. (1982). A test of the optimal level of arousal theory of sensation seeking. *Journal of Personality and Social Psychology, 42*, 572–575.

Carroll, B. J. (1989). Diagnostic validity and laboratory studies: Rules of the game. In L. N. Robins & J. E. Barrett (Eds.), *The validity of psychiatric diagnoses* (pp. 229–245). New York: Raven Press.

Carroll, B. J., Feinberg, M., Greden, J. F., Tarika, J., Albala, A. A., Haskett, R. F., James, N., Kronfeld, Z., Lohr, N., Steiner, M., De Vigne, J. P., & Young, E. (1981). A specific laboratory test for the diagnosis of melancholia. *Archives of General Psychiatry, 38*, 15–22.

Carroll, K. M., Ball, S. A., & Rounsaville, B. J. (1993). A comparison of alternate systems for diagnosing antisocial personality disorder in cocaine abusers. *The Journal of Nervous and Mental Disease, 181*, 436–443.

Carroll, K. M., & Rounsaville, B. J. (1992). Contrast of treatment-seeking and untreated cocaine abusers. *Archives of General Psychiatry, 49*, 464–471.

Carter, M. M., Hollon, S. D., Carson, R., & Shelton, R. C. (1995). Effects of a safe person on induced distress following a biological challenge in panic disorder with agoraphobia. *Journal of Abnormal Psychology, 104*, 156–163.

Carton, S., Jouvent, R., Bungener, C., & Widlöcher, D. (1992). Sensation seeking and depressive mood. *Personality and Individual Differences, 7*, 843–849.

Caspi, A., Begg, D., Dickson, N., Harrington, H. L., Langley, J., Moffitt, T. E., & Silva, P. A. (1997). Personality differences predict health-risk behaviors in young adulthood: Evidence from a longitudinal study. *Journal of Personality and Social Psychology, 73*, 1052–1063.

Caspi, A., Moffitt, T. E., Newman, D. L., & Silva, P. A. (1996). Behavioral observations at age 3 years predict adult psychiatric disorders: Longitudinal evidence for a birth cohort. *Archives of General Psychiatry, 53,* 1033–1039.

Castellani, B., & Rugle, L. (1995). A comparison of pathological gamblers to alcoholics, and cocaine misusers on impulsivity, sensation seeking, and craving. *The International Journal of the Addictions, 30,* 275–289.

Chambless, D. L. (1988). Cognitive mechanisms in panic disorder. In S. Rachman & J. D. Maser (Eds.), *Panic: Psychological perspectives* (pp. 205–217). Hillsdale, NJ: Erlbaum.

Chapman, L. J., Chapman, J. P., Kwapil, T. R., Eckblad, M. E., & Zinser, M. C. (1994). Putatively psychosis-prone subjects 10 years later. *Journal of Abnormal Psychology, 103,* 171–183.

Charney, D. S., Deutch, A. Y., Krystal, J. H., Southwick, S. M., & Davis, M. (1993). Psychobiologic mechanisms of posttraumatic stress disorder. *Archives of General Psychiatry, 50,* 294–304.

Charney, D. S., & Heninger, G. R. (1986). Abnormal regulation of noradrenergic function in panic disorders. *Archives of General Psychiatry, 43,* 1042–1054.

Charney, D. S., Heninger, G. R., & Jatlow, P. I. (1985). Increased anxiogenic effects of caffeine in panic disorders. *Archives of General Psychiatry, 42,* 233–243.

Charney, D. S., Woods, S. W., Goodman, W. K., & Heninger, G. R. (1987). Serotonin function in anxiety. II: Effects of the serotonin agonist mCPP in panic disorder patients and healthy subjects. *Psychopharmacology, 92,* 14–24.

Charney, D. S., Woods, S. W., Price, L. H., Goodman, W. K., Glazer, W. M., & Heninger, G. R. (1990). Noradrenergic dysregulation in panic disorder. In J. C. Ballenger (Ed.), *Neurobiology of panic disorder* (pp. 245–270). New York: Wiley-Liss.

Chen, C.-N., Wong, J., Lee, N., Chan-Ho, M. W., Lau, J. T. F., & Fung, M. (1993). The Shatin community mental health survey in Hong Kong. *Archives of General Psychiatry, 50,* 125–133.

Chen, Y. R., Swann, A. C., & Burt, D. B. (1996). Stability of diagnosis in schizophrenia. *American Journal of Psychiatry, 153,* 682–686.

Chess, S., & Thomas, A. (1984). *Origins and evolution of behavior disorders.* New York: Bruner/Mazel.

Christiansen, K. O. (1977). A review of studies of criminality among twins. In S. A. Medinick & K. O. Christiansen (Eds.), *Biosocial bases of criminal behavior* (pp. 45–88). New York: Gardner Press.

Ciompi, L. (1980). Catamnestic long-term study on the course of life and aging of schizophrenics. *Schizophrenia Bulletin, 6,* 608–618.

Claridge, G., McCreery, C., & Mason, O. (1996). The factor structure of schizotypal traits: A large replication study. *British Journal of Clinical Psychology, 35,* 103–115.

Clark, D. M. (1988). A cognitive model of panic attacks. In S. Rachman & J. D. Maser (Eds.), *Panic: Psychological perspectives* (pp. 71–89). Hillsdale, NJ: Erlbaum.

Clark, L. A. (1993). *SNAP, Schedule for nonadaptive and adaptive personality: Manual for administration, scoring and interpretation*. Minneapolis, MN: University of Minnesota Press.

Clark, L. A. (1995). The challenge of alternative perspectives in classification: A discussion of basic issues. In W. J. Livesley (Ed.), *The DSM-IV personality disorders* (pp. 482–496). New York: Guilford Press.

Clark, L. A., & Watson, D. (1991). Tripartite model of anxiety and depression: Psychometric evidence and taxonomic implications. *Journal of Abnormal Psychology, 100*, 316–336.

Clarkin, J. F., & Kendall, P. C. (1992). Comorbidity and treatment planning: Summary and future directions. *Journal of Consulting and Clinical Psychology, 60*, 904–908.

Cleckley, H. (1976). *The mask of sanity* (5th ed.). St. Louis, MO: Mosby.

Cloitre, M., Cancienne, J., Heimberg, R. G., Holt, C. S., & Liebowitz, M. (1995). Memory bias does not generalize across anxiety disorders. *Behavior Research and Therapy, 33*, 305–307.

Clomipramine Collaborative Study Group. (1991). Clomipramine in the treatment of patients with obsessive compulsive disorder. *Archives of General Psychiatry, 48*, 730–738.

Cloninger, C. R. (1987a). A systematic method for clinical description and classification of personality variants. *Archives of General Psychiatry, 44*, 573–588.

Cloninger, C. R. (1987b). Neurogenetic adaptive mechanisms in alcoholism. *Science, 236*, 410–416.

Cloninger, C. R., & Gottesman, I. I. (1987). Genetic and environmental factors in antisocial behavior. In S. A. Mednick, T. E. Moffitt, & S. A. Stack (Eds.), *The causes of crime: New biological approaches* (pp. 92–109). Cambridge, MA: Cambridge University Press.

Cloninger, C. R., Reich, T., Sigvardsson, S., von Knorring, A. L., & Bohman, M. (1988). Effects of changes in alcohol abuse. In R. M. Rose & J. E. Barrett (Eds.), *Alcoholism, origins, and outcomes* (pp. 49–74). New York: Raven Press.

Cloninger, C. R., Sigvardsson, S., & Bohman, M. (1988). Childhood personality predicts alcohol abuse in young adults. *Alcoholism: Clinical and Experimental Research, 12*, 494–505.

Coccaro, E. F., Kavoussi, R. J., Sheline, J. I., Lish, J. D., & Csernansky, J. G. (1996). Impulsive aggression in personality disorder correlates with triated peroxetine binding in the platelet. *Archives of General Psychiatry, 53*, 531–536.

Coffey, C. E., Wilkinson, W. E., Weiner, R. D., Parashos, I. A., Djang, W. T., Webb, M. C., Figiel, G. S., & Spritzer, C. E. (1993). Quantitative cerebral anatomy in depression: A controlled magnetic resonance imaging study. *Archives of General Psychiatry, 50*, 7–16.

Cohen, J. (1960). A coefficient of agreement for nominal scales. *Educational and Psychological Measurement, 20*, 37–46.

Cohen, R. (1991). Event-related potentials and cognitive dysfunction in schizophrenia. In H. Häfner & W. F. Gattaz (Eds.), *Search for the causes of schizophrenia* (Vol. II, pp. 342–360). Berlin, Germany: Springer-Verlag.

Collins, D., Dimsdale, J. E., & Wilkins, D. (1992). Consultation liaison psychiatry utilization patterns in different cultural groups. *Psychosomatic Medicine, 54,* 240–245.

Comings, D. E., Rosenthal, R. J., Lesieur, H. R., Rugle, L. J., Muhleman, D., Chiu, C., Dietz, G., & Gade, R. (1996). A study of the D2 receptor gene in pathological gambling. *Pharmacogenetics, 6,* 223–234.

Conrad, A. J., Abebe, T., Austin, R., Forsythe, S., & Scheibel, A. B. (1991). Hippocampal pyramidal cell disarray in schizophrenia as a bilateral phenomena. *Archives of General Psychiatry, 48,* 413–417.

Cornblatt, B. A., & Kelip, J. G. (1994). Impaired attention, genetics, and the pathophysiology of schizophrenia. *Schizophrenia Bulletin, 20,* 31–43.

Corty, E., Lehman, A. F., & Myers, C. P. (1993). Influence of psychoactive substance use on the reliability of psychiatric diagnosis. *Journal of Consulting and Clinical Psychology, 61,* 165–170.

Coryell, W., Akiskel, H. S., Leon, A. C., Winokur, G., Maser, J. D., Mueller, T. I., & Keller, M. B. (1994). The time course of nonchronic major depressive disorder. *Archives of General Psychiatry, 51,* 405–410.

Coryell, W., & Winokur, G. (1992). Course and outcome. In E. S. Paykel (Ed.), *Handbook of affective disorders* (2nd ed., pp. 89–108). New York: Guilford Press.

Costa, P. T., Jr., & McCrae, R. R. (1992). *NEO-PI-R: Revised NEO Personality Inventory (NEO-PI-R).* Odessa, FL: Psychological Assessment Services.

Costa, P. T., Jr., & Widiger, T. A. (Eds.). (1994). *Personality disorders and the five-factor model of personality.* Washington, DC: American Psychological Association.

Cottler, L. B., Price, R. K., Compton, W. M., & Mager, D. E. (1995). Subtypes of adult antisocial behavior among drug abusers. *The Journal of Nervous and Mental Disease, 183,* 154–161.

Coventry, K. R., & Brown, I. F. (1993). Sensation seeking, gambling and gambling addictions. *Addiction, 88,* 541–554.

Cowley, D. S., & Arana, G. W. (1990). The diagnostic utility of lactate sensitivity in panic disorder. *Archives of General Psychiatry, 47,* 277–284.

Cowley, D. S., Dager, S. R., McClellan, J., Roy-Byrne, P. P., & Dunner, D. L. (1988). Response to lactate infusion in generalized anxiety disorder. *Biological Psychiatry, 24,* 409–414.

Cowley, D. S., & Roy-Byrne, P. P. (1991). The biology of generalized anxiety. In R. M. Rapee & D. H. Barlow (Eds.), *Chronic anxiety, generalized anxiety disorder and mixed anxiety-depression* (pp. 52–75). New York: Guilford Press.

Cox, B. J., Endler, N. S., & Swinson, R. P. (1995). An examination of levels of agoraphobic severity in panic disorder. *Behavior Research and Therapy, 33,* 57–62.

Craig, R. J. (1982). Personality characteristics of heroin addicts: Review of empirical research 1976–1979. *International Journals of the Addictions, 17*, 227–248.

Craig, R. J. (1986). The personality structure of heroin addicts. *National Institute on Drug Abuse Research Monograph, 74*, 25–36.

Craske, M. G., Rapee, R., Jackel, L., & Barlow, D. H. (1989). Qualitative dimensions of worry in DSM-III-R generalized anxiety disorder subjects and non-anxious controls. *Behaviour Research and Therapy, 27*, 397–402.

Cronbach, L. J., & Meehl, P. E. (1955). Construct validity in psychological tests. *Psychological Bulletin, 52*, 281–302.

Cronin, C., & Zuckerman, M. (1992). Sensation seeking and bipolar affective disorder. *Personality and Individual Differences, 13*, 385–387.

Crow, T. J. (1980). Molecular pathology of schizophrenia: More than one disease process? *British Medical Journal, 280*, 66–68.

Crow, T. J. (1985). The two syndrome concept: Origins and current status. *Schizophrenia Bulletin, 11*, 471–485.

Crow, T. J. (1990). The continuum of psychosis and its genetic origins. *British Journal of Psychiatry, 156*, 788–797.

Crow, T. J. (1995). Constraints on concepts of pathogenesis: Language and the speciation process as the key to the etiology of schizophrenia. *Archives of General Psychiatry, 52*, 1011–1014.

Crow, T. J., Done, D. J., & Sacker, A. (1995). Birth cohort study of the antecedents of psychosis: Ontogeny as witness to phylogenetic origins. In H. Häfner & W. T. Gattaz (Eds.), *Search for the causes of schizophrenia* (Vol. III, pp. 3–20). Berlin, Germany: Springer-Verlag.

Cui, X., & Vaillant, G. E. (1996). Antecedents and consequences of negative life events in adulthood: A longitudinal study. *American Journal of Psychiatry, 152*, 21–26.

Custer, R. L., & Milt, H. (1985). *When luck runs out.* New York: Facts on File.

Dabbs, J. M., Jr., Ruback, R. B., Frady, R. L., Hopper, C. H., & Sgoritas, D. S. (1988). Saliva testosterone and criminal violence among women. *Personality and Individual Differences, 9*, 269–275.

Dager, S. R., Strauss, W. L., Marro, K. I., Richards, T. L., Metzger, G. D., & Artu, A. A. (1995). Proton magnetic resonance spectroscopy investigation of hyperventilation in subjects with panic disorder and comparison subjects. *American Journal of Psychiatry, 152*, 666–672.

Daghestani, A. N., Elenz, E., & Crayton, J. W. (1996). Pathological gambling in hospitalized substance abusing veterans. *Journal of Clinical Psychiatry, 57*, 360–363.

Daitzman, R. J., & Zuckerman, M. (1980). Personality, disinhibitory sensation seeking and gonadal hormones. *Personality and Individual Differences, 1*, 103–110.

Dalgaard, O. S., & Kringlen, E. (1976). A Norwegian twin study of criminality. *British Journal of Criminality, 16*, 213–232.

Darke, S., Hall, W., & Swift, W. (1994). Prevalence of symptoms and correlates of antisocial personality disorder among methadone maintenance clients. *Drug and Alcohol Dependence, 34*, 253–257.

Davidson, J. R. T., Hughes, D. C., George, L. K., & Blazer, D. G. (1994). The boundary of social phobia. *Archives of General Psychiatry, 51*, 975–983.

Davidson, R. J. (1992). Emotion and affective style: Hemispheric substrates. *Psychological Science, 3*, 39–43.

Davis, J. O., Phelps, J. A., & Bracha, H. S. (1995). Prenatal development of monozygotic twins and concordance for schizophrenia. *Schizophrenia Bulletin, 21*, 357–366.

Davis, K. L., Kahn, R. S., Ko, G., & Davidson, M. (1991). Dopamine in schizophrenia: A review and reconceptualization. *American Journal of Psychiatry, 148*, 1474–1483.

Dawson, M. E., Hazlett, E. A., Filion, D. L., Nuechterlein, K. H., & Schell, A. M. (1993). Attention and schizophrenia: Impaired modulation of the startle reflex. *Journal of Abnormal Psychology, 102*, 633–641.

Dawson, M. E., Nuechterlein, K. H., Schell, A. M., Gitlin, M., & Ventura, J. (1994). Autonomic abnormalities in schizophrenia: State or trait indicators? *Archives of General Psychiatry, 51*, 813–824.

De Jong, P. J., Merckelbach, H., Arntz, A., & Nijman, H. (1992). Covariation and detection in treated and untreated spider phobics. *Journal of Abnormal Psychology, 101*, 724–727.

Delgado, P. L., Charney, D. S., Price, L. H., Aghajanian, G. K., Landis, H., & Heninger, G. R. (1990). Serotonin function and the mechanism of antidepressant action. *Archives of General Psychiatry, 47*, 411–418.

Delgado, P. L., Price, L. H., Miller, H. L., Salomon, R. M., Aghajanian, G. K., Heninger, G. R., & Charney, D. S. (1994). Serotonin and the neurobiology of depression. *Archives of General Psychiatry, 51*, 865–874.

DeLisi, L. E., Sakuma, M., Tew, W., Kushner, M., Hoff, A. L., & Grimson, R. (1997). Schizophrenia as a chronic active brain process: A study of progressive structural changes subsequent to the onset of schizophrenia. *Psychiatry Research: Neuroimaging Section, 74*, 129–140.

Den Boer, J. A., & Westenberg, H. G. M. (1995). Atypical antipsychotics in schizophrenia: A review of recent developments. In J. A. Den Boer, H. G. M. Westenberg, & H. M. van Praag (Eds.), *Advances in the neurobiology of schizophrenia* (pp. 275–302). Chichester, England: Wiley.

Depue, R. A., & Iacono, W. G. (1988). Neurobehavioral aspects of affective disorder. *Annual Review of Psychology, 40*, 457–492.

Dewhurst, K. (1982). *Hughlings Jackson on psychiatry*. Oxford, England: Sanford.

De Wit, H., Uhlenhuth, E. H., & Johanson, C. E. (1986). Individual differences in the reinforcing and subjective aspects of amphetamine and diazepam. *Drug and Alcohol Dependence, 16*, 341–360.

Deykan, E. Y., & Buka, S. L. (1997). Prevalence and risk factors for posttraumatic stress disorder among chemically dependent adolescents. *American Journal of Psychiatry, 154,* 752–757.

DiLalla, D. L., & Gottesman, I. I. (1995). Normal personality characteristics in identical twins discordant for schizophrenia. *Journal of Abnormal Psychology, 104,* 490–499.

Dinwiddie, S. H., Reich, T., & Cloninger, C. R. (1992). Psychiatric comorbidity and suicidality among intravenous drug users. *Journal of Clinical Psychiatry, 53,* 364–369.

Doering, S., Müller-Spahn, F., Tegeler, J., & Schüssler, G. (1998). Predictors of relapse and rehospitalization in schizophrenia and schizoaffective disorder. *Schizophrenia Bulletin, 24,* 87–98.

Dohrenwend, B. P., Shrout, P. E., Linki, B. G., Skodol, A. E., & Stueve, A. (1995). Life events and other possible psychosocial risk factors for episodes of schizophrenia and major depression. In C. M. Mazure (Ed.), *Does stress cause psychiatric illness?* (pp. 43–65). Washington, DC: American Psychiatric Press.

Dollard, J., & Miller, N. (1950). *Personality and psychotherapy: An analysis in terms of learning, thinking, and culture.* New York: McGraw-Hill.

DuPont, R. M., Jernigan, T. L., Butlers, N., Delis, D., & Hesselink, J. R. (1990). Subcortical abnormalities detected in bipolar affective disorder using magnetic resonance imaging. *Archives of General Psychiatry, 47,* 55–59.

Dworkin, R. H., Bernstein, G., Klaplansky, L. M., Lipsitz, J. D., Rinaldi, A., Slater, S. L., Cornblatt, B. A., & Erlenmeyer-Kimling, L. (1991). Social competence and positive and negative symptoms: A longitudinal study of children and adolescents at risk for schizophrenia and affective disorder. *American Journal of Psychiatry, 148,* 1182–1188.

Eaves, G., & Rush, A. J. (1984). Cognitive patterns in symptomatic and remitted major depression. *Journal of Abnormal Psychology, 93,* 31–40.

Eaves, L. J., & Young, P. A. (1981). Genetical theory and personality differences. In R. Lynn (Ed.), *Dimensions of personality* (pp. 129–179). Oxford, England: Pergamon.

Eberly, R. E., & Engdahl, B. E. (1991). Prevalence of somatic and psychiatric disorders among former prisoners of war. *Hospital and Community Psychiatry, 42,* 807–813.

Eberly, R. E., Harkness, A. R., & Engdahl, B. E. (1991). An adaptational view of trauma response as illustrated by the prisoner of war experience. *Journal of Traumatic Stress, 4,* 363–380.

Ebmeier, K. P. (1995). Brain imaging and schizophrenia. In J. A. Den Boer, H. G. M. Westenberg, & H. M. Van Praag (Eds.), *Advances in the neurobiology of schizophrenia* (pp. 131–155). Chichester, England: Wiley.

Ebstein, R. P., & Belmaker, R. H. (1997). Saga of an adventure gene: Novelty seeking, substance abuse and the dopamine D4 receptor (D4DR) exon III repeat polymorphism. *Molecular Psychiatry, 2,* 381–384.

Ebstein, R. P., Nemarov, L., Klotz, I., Gritsenko, I., & Belmaker, R. H. (1997). Additional evidence for an association between the dopamine D4 receptor

(D4DR) exon III repeat polymorphism and the human personality trait of novelty seeking. *Molecular Psychiatry, 2,* 472–477.

Ebstein, R. P., Novick, O., Umansky, R., Priel, B., Osher, Y., Blaine, D., Bennett, E. R., Nemanov, L., Katz, M., & Belmaker, R. H. (1996). Dopamine D4 receptor (D4DR) exon III polymorphism associated with the human personality trait of novelty seeking. *Nature Genetics, 12,* 78–80.

Eckert, E. D., Heston, L. L., & Bouchard, T. J. (1981). Monozygotic twins reared apart: Preliminary findings of psychiatric disturbances and traits. In L. Gedda, P. Parsi, & W. E. Nance (Eds.), *Twin research-3: Intelligence, personality and development* (pp. 179–188). New York: Alan Liss.

Egeland, J. A. (1994). An epidemiologic and genetic study of appetite disorders among the old order Amish. In D. F. Papolos & H. M. Lackman (Eds.), *Genetic studies in affective disorders* (pp. 70–90). New York: Wiley.

Ehrenkranz, J., Bliss, E., & Sheard, M. H. (1974). Plasma testosterone: Correlation with aggressive behavior and social dominance in man. *Psychosomatic Medicine, 36,* 469–475.

Eisen, S. A., Lin, N., Lyons, M. J., Scherrer, J. F., Griffith, K., True, W. R., Goldberg, J., & Tsuang, M. T. (1998). Familial influences on problem gambling: Analysis of 3,359 twin pairs. *Addiction, 93,* 1375–1384.

Eitinger, L. (1972). *Concentration camp survivors in Norway and Israel.* The Hague, Holland: Martinus Nijhoff.

Eitinger, L. (1985). *The psychological and medical effects of concentration camps and related persecutions on survivors of the Holocaust: A research bibliography.* Vancouver, Canada: University of British Columbia Press.

Eitinger, L., & Strom, A. (1973). *Mortality and morbidity after excessive stress: A follow-up investigation of Norwegian concentration camp survivors.* Oslo, Norway: Universitetsforlaget.

Elkis, H., Friedman, L., Wise, A., & Meltzer, H. Y. (1995). Meta-analyses of studies of ventricular enlargement and cortical sulcal prominence in mood disorders. *Archives of General Psychiatry, 52,* 735–746.

Enright, S. J. (1996). Obsessive-compulsive disorder: Anxiety disorder or schizotype? In R. M. Rapee (Ed.), *Current controversies in the anxiety disorders* (pp. 161–190). New York: Guilford Press.

Erlenmeyer-Kimling, L., Squires-Wheeler, E., Adamo, U. H., Bassett, A. S., Roberts, S. A., & Gottesman, I. I. (1995). The New York high-risk project: Psychoses and Cluster A personality disorders in offspring of schizophrenic parents at 23 years of follow-up. *Archives of General Psychiatry, 52,* 857–865.

Ernberg, G., Leff, J., & Gulbinat, W. (1987). Course of schizophrenia in different countries: Some results of a WHO international 5-year study. In H. Häfner, W. F. Gattaz, & J. Zarik (Eds.), *Search for the causes of schizophrenia* (pp. 107–113). Berlin, Germany: Springer-Verlag.

Epstein, S. (1979). The stability of behavior: I. On predicting most of the people most of the time. *Journal of Personality and Social Psychology, 37,* 1097–1126.

Eysenck, H. J. (1947). *Dimensions of personality.* New York: Praeger.

Eysenck, H. J. (1957). *The dynamics of anxiety and hysteria*. New York: Praeger.

Eysenck, H. J. (1967). *The biological basis of personality*. Springfield, IL: Charles C Thomas.

Eysenck, H. J. (1986). A critique of contemporary classification and diagnosis. In T. Millon & G. L. Klerman (Eds.), *Contemporary directions in psychopathology: Toward the DSM-IV* (pp. 73–98). New York: Guilford Press.

Eysenck, H. J. (1992). The definition and measurement of psychoticism. *Personality and Individual Differences, 13*, 757–785.

Eysenck, H. J., & Eysenck, M. W. (1985). *Personality and individual differences: A natural science approach*. New York: Plenum Press.

Eysenck, H. J., & Eysenck, S. B. G. (1976). *Psychoticism as a dimension of personality*. New York: Crane, Russak.

Eysenck, H. J., & Eysenck, S. B. G. (1978). Psychopathy, personality and genetics. In R. D. Hare & D. Schalling (Eds.), *Psychopathic behavior approaches to research* (pp. 197–223). Chichester, England: Wiley.

Eysenck, S. B. G., Eysenck, H. J., & Barrett, P. (1985). A revised version of the psychoticism scale. *Personality and Individual Differences, 6*, 21–29.

Fabrega, H. (1987). Psychiatric diagnosis: A cultural perspective. *Journal of Nervous and Mental Disease, 175*, 383–394.

Fabrega, H. (1994). International systems of diagnosis in psychiatry. *Journal of Nervous and Mental Disease, 182*, 256–263.

Farley, F. H., & Mueller, C. B. (1978). Arousal, personality, and assortative mating in marriage: Generalizability and cross-cultural factors. *Journal of Sex and Marital Therapy, 4*, 50–53.

Farmer, A. E., McGuffin, P., & Gottesman, I. I. (1984). Searching for the split in schizophrenia: A twin study perspective. *Psychiatry Research, 13*, 109–118.

Fava, M., Alpert, J. E., Borus, J. S., Nierenberg, A. A., Pava, J. A., & Rosenbaum, J. F. (1996). Patterns of personality disorder comorbidity in early-onset versus late-onset major depression. *American Journal of Psychiatry, 10*, 1308–1312.

Fedoroff, J., Starkstein, S., Forrester, A., Geisler, F. H., & Jorge, R. E. (1992). Depression in patients with acute traumatic brain injury. *American Journal of Psychiatry, 149*, 918–923.

Feigelman, W., Kleinman, P. H., Lesieur, H. R., Millman, R. B., & Lesser, M. L. (1995). Pathological gambling among methadone patients. *Drug and Alcohol Dependence, 39*, 75–81.

Feighner, J. P., Robins, E., Guze, S. B., Woodruff, R. A., Winokur, G., & Munoz, R. (1972). Diagnostic criteria for use in psychiatric research. *Archives of General Psychiatry, 26*, 57–63.

Feingold, A., Ball, S. A., Kranzler, H. R., & Rounsaville, B. J. (1996). Generalizability of the Type A/Type B distinction across different psychoactive substances. *American Journal of Drug and Alcohol Abuse, 22*, 449–462.

Fenton, W. S., & McGlashan, T. H. (1991a). Natural history of paranoid, hebephrenic, and undifferentiated schizophrenia. *Archives of General Psychiatry, 48,* 969–977.

Fenton, W. S., & McGlashan, T. H. (1991b). Natural history of schizophrenic subtypes II: Positive and negative symptoms and long-term course. *Archives of General Psychiatry, 48,* 978–986.

Fenton, W. S., & McGlashan, T. H. (1994). Antecedents, symptoms, progression and long-term outcome of the deficit syndrome in schizophrenia. *American Journal of Psychiatry, 151,* 351–365.

Fieldman, N. P., Woolfolk, R. L., & Allen, L. A. (1995). Dimensions of self-concept: A comparison of heroin and cocaine addicts. *American Journal of Drug and Alcohol Abuse, 21,* 315–326.

Fils-Aime, M.-L., Eckardt, M. J., George, G. T., Brown, G. L., Mefford, I., & Linnoila, M. (1996). Early-onset alcoholics have lower cerebrospinal fluid 5-hydroxyindoleacetic acid levels than late-onset alcoholics. *Archives of General Psychiatry, 53,* 211–216.

Fishbein, D. H., Herning, R. I., Pickworth, W. B., Haertzen, C. A., Hickey, J. E., & Jaffe, J. H. (1989). EEG and brainstem auditory evoked response potentials in adult male drug abusers with self-reported histories of aggressive behavior. *Biological Psychiatry, 26,* 595–611.

Flashman, L. A., Flaum, M., Gupta, S., & Andreasen, N. C. (1996). Soft signs and neuropsychological performance in schizophrenia. *American Journal of Psychiatry, 153,* 526–532.

Flaskerud, J. H., & Hu, L. (1992). Relationship of ethnicity to psychiatric diagnosis. *Journal of Nervous and Mental Disease, 180,* 296–303.

Flaum, M., Swayze, V. W., O'Leary, D. S., Yuh, W. T. C., Ehrhardt, J. C., Arndt, S. V., & Anderson, N. C. (1995). Effects of diagnosis, laterality and gender on brain morphology in schizophrenia. *American Journal of Psychiatry, 152,* 704–714.

Flick, S. N., Roy-Byrne, P. P., Cowley, D. S., Shores, M. M., & Dunner, D. L. (1993). DSM III-R personality disorders in a mood and anxiety disorders clinic: Prevalence, comorbidity, and clinical correlates. *Journal of Affective Disorders, 27,* 71–79.

Flor-Henry, P. (1976). Lateralized temporal-limbic dysfunction and psychopathology. *Annals of the New York Academy of Sciences, 280,* 777–797.

Flynn, P. M., Luckey, J. W., Brown, B. S., Hoffman, J. A., Dunteman, G. H., Theisen, A. C., & Hubbard, R. L. (1995). Relationship between drug preference and indicators of psychiatric impairment. *American Journal of Drug and Alcohol Abuse, 21,* 153–166.

Foa, E. B., Feske, U., Murdock, T. B., Kozak, M. J., & McCarthy, P. R. (1991). Processing of threat-related information in rape victims. *Journal of Abnormal Psychology, 100,* 156–162.

Foa, E. B., McNally, R. J., Steketee, G. S., & McCarthy, P. R. (1991). A test of preparedness theory in anxiety disordered patients using an avoidance paradigm. *Journal of Psychophysiology, 5,* 159–163.

Foucault, M. (1965). *Madness and civilization: A history of insanity in the age of reason.* New York: Pantheon Books.

Fowles, D. C. (1992). Schizophrenia: Diathesis-stress revisited. *Annual Review of Psychology* (Vol. 43, pp. 303–336). Palo Alto, CA: Annual Reviews.

Frances, A. J., Widiger, T. A., & Pincus, A. (1989). The development of the DSM IV. *Archives of General Psychiatry, 46,* 373–375.

Francis, G., & Radka, D. F. (1995). Social anxiety in children and adolescents. In M. B. Stein (Ed.), *Social phobia: Perspectives* (pp. 119–143). Washington, DC: American Psychiatric Press.

Frank, E., Anderson, B., Reynolds, C. F., Ritenour, A., & Kupfer, D. J. (1994). Life events and the research diagnostic criteria for endogenous subtype. *Archives of General Psychiatry, 51,* 519–534.

Frank, E., Kupfer, D. J., Perel, J. M., Cornes, C., Jarrett, D. B., Mallinger, A. G., Thase, M. E., McEachran, A. B., & Grochocinski, V. J. (1990). Three-year outcomes for maintenance therapies in recurrent depression. *Archives of General Psychiatry, 47,* 1093–1099.

Fredrikson, M., Annas, P., Fisher, H., & Wik, G. (1996). Gender and age differences in the prevalence of specific fears and phobias. *Behavior Research and Therapy, 34,* 33–39.

Freedman, R. R., Ianni, P., Ettedgui, E., & Puthezhath, N. (1985). Ambulatory monitoring of panic disorder. *Archives of General Psychiatry, 42,* 244–248.

Freud, S. (1957). Mourning and melancholia. In J. Strachey (Ed. and Trans.), *Standard edition of the collected works of Sigmund Freud* (Vol. 14, pp. 243–258). London: Hogarth Press. (Original work published 1917)

Freud, S. (1959). Inhibitions, symptoms, and anxiety. In J. Strachey (Ed. and Trans.), *The standard edition of the complete psychological works of Sigmund Freud* (Vol. 20, pp. 87–156). London: Hogarth Press. (Original work published 1926)

Freud, S. (1959). Doestoevsky and parricide. In J. Strachey (Ed. and Trans.), *The standard edition of the complete psychological works of Sigmund Freud* (Vol. 21, pp. 177–194). London: Hogarth Press. (Original work published 1928)

Freud, S. (1961). Beyond the pleasure principle. In J. Strachey (Ed. and Trans.), *The standard edition of the complete psychological works of Sigmund Freud* (Vol. 18, pp. 7–64). London: Hogarth Press. (Original work published 1922)

Fulton, M., & Winokur, G. (1993). A comparative study of paranoid and schizoid personality disorders. *American Journal of Psychiatry, 150,* 1313–1367.

Fyer, A. J., Mannuza, S., Chapman, T. F., Liebowitz, M. R., & Klein, D. F. (1993). A direct interview family study of social phobia. *Archives of General Psychiatry, 50,* 286–293.

Fyer, A. J., Mannuza, S., Gallops, M. S., Martin, L. Y., Aaronson, C., Gorman, J. M., Liebowitz, M. R., & Klein, D. F. (1990). Familial transmission of simple phobia and fears. *Archives of General Psychiatry, 47,* 252–256.

Galizio, M., Rosenthal, D., & Stein, F. (1983). Sensation seeking, reinforcement and student drug use. *Addictive Behaviors, 8,* 243–252.

Gater, R., Tansella, M., Korten, A., Tremens, B. G., Mavreas, V. G., & Olatawura, M. O. (1998). Sex differences in the prevalence and detection of depressive and anxiety disorders in general health care settings. *Archives of General Psychiatry, 55*, 405–413.

Gattaz, W. F., Kohlmeyer, K., & Gassers, T. (1991). Computer tomographic studies in schizophrenia. In H. Häfner & W. F. Gattaz (Eds.), *Search for the causes of schizophrenia* (Vol. II, pp. 242–256). Berlin, Germany: Springer-Verlag.

Gatz, M., Pederson, N. L., Plomin, R., Nesselroade, J. R., & McClearn, G. E. (1992). Importance of shared genes and shared environments for symptoms of depression in older adults. *Journal of Abnormal Psychology, 101*, 701–708.

Geijer, T., Jonsson, E., Persson, M. L., Brene, S., Gyllander, A., Sedvall, G., Rydberg, U., Wasserman, D., & Terenius, L. (1997). Tyrosine hydroxylase and dopamine D4 receptor allelic distribution in Scandinavian chronic alcoholics. *Alcoholism: Clinical and Experimental Research, 21*, 35–39.

Gelernter, J., & Gershon, E. S. (1989). Psychiatric diagnosis in the age of molecular genetics. In L. N. Robins & J. E. Barrett (Eds.), *The validity of psychiatric diagnosis* (pp. 143–161). New York: Raven Press.

Gerardi, R. J., Keane, T. M., Cahoon, B. J., & Klauminzer, G. W. (1994). An in vivo assessment of physiological arousal in posttraumatic stress disorder. *Journal of Abnormal Psychology, 103*, 825–827.

Gerlsma, C., Emmelkamp, P. M. G., & Arrindell, W. A. (1990). Anxiety, depression and perception of early parenting: A meta-analysis. *Clinical Psychology Review, 10*, 251–277.

Gershon, E. S., DeLisi, L. E., Hamart, J., Nurnberger, J. I., Jr., Maxwell, M. E., Schreiber, J., Daupkhinais, D., Dingman, C. W., & Guroff, J. J. (1988). A controlled family study of chronic psychoses. *Archives of General Psychiatry, 45*, 328–336.

Gershon, E. S., Hanovit, J., Guroff, J. J., Dibble, E., Leckman, J. F., Nurnberger, J. I., Jr., Goldin, L. R., & Bunney, W. E., Jr. (1982). A family study of schizoaffective bipolar I, bipolar II, unipolar, and normal control probands. *Archives of General Psychiatry, 39*, 1157–1167.

Gershon, E. S., & Soares, J. C. (1997). Current therapeutic profile of lithium. *Archives of General Psychiatry, 54*, 16–20.

Gianoulakis, C., Angelogianni, P., Meany, M., Thavundayil, J., & Tawar, V. (1990). Endorphins in individuals with high and low risk for development of alcoholism. In L. D. Reid (Ed.), *Opioids, bulimia, alcohol abuse, and alcoholism* (pp. 229–246). New York: Springer-Verlag.

Gianoulakis, C., Krishman, B., & Thavundayil, J. (1996). Enhanced sensitivity of pituitary beta-endorphin to ethanol in subjects at high risk of alcoholism. *Archives of General Psychiatry, 53*, 250–257.

Ginns, E. I., Ott, J., Egeland, A., Allen, C. R., Fann, C. S. J., Pauls, D. L., Keith, T. P., & Paul, S. M. (1996). A genome-wide search for chromosomal loci linked to bipolar affective disorder in the Old Order Amish. *Nature Genetics, 12*, 431–435.

Gittleman, R., & Klein, D. F. (1985). Childhood separation, anxiety and adult agoraphobia. In A. H. Tuma & J. D. Maser (Eds.), *Anxiety and the anxiety disorders* (pp. 389–402). Hillsdale, NJ: Erlbaum.

Goetz, R. R., KIein, D. F., Gully, R., Kahn, J., Liebowitz, M. R., Fyer, A. J., & Gorman, J. M. (1993). Panic attacks during placebo procedures in the laboratory. *Archives of General Psychiatry, 50,* 280–285.

Goisman, R. M., Warshaw, M. G., Steketee, G. S., Fierman, E. J., Rogers, M. P., Goldenberg, I., Weinshenker, N. J., Vasile, R. G., & Keller, M. B. (1995). DSM-IV and the disapppearance of agoraphobia without a history of panic disorder: New data on a controversial diagnosis. *American Journal of Psychiatry, 152,* 1438–1443.

Goldberg, T. E., Gold, J. M., Greenberg, R., Griffin, S., Schultz, C., Pickar, D., Kleinman, J. E., & Weinberger, D. R. (1993). Contrasts between patients with affective disorders and patients with schizophrenia on a neuropsychological test battery. *American Journal of Psychiatry, 150,* 1355–1362.

Golden, R. R., & Meehl, P. E. (1979). Detection of the schizoid taxon with MMPI indicators. *Journal of Abnormal Psychology, 88,* 217–233.

Golding, J. F., & Cornish, A. M. (1987). Personality and life-style in medical students: Psychopharmacological aspects. *Psychology and Health, 1,* 287–301.

Goldman, D., Lappalainen, J., & Ozaki, N. (1996). Direct analysis of candidate genes in impulsive behaviours. In G. R. Bock & J. A. Goode (Eds.), *Genetics of criminal and antisocial behaviour* (pp. 139–152). Chichester, England: Wiley.

Goldstein, A. J., & Chambless, D. L. (1978). A reanalysis of agoraphobia. *Behavior Therapy, 9,* 47–59.

Goldstein, L., Manowitz, P., Nora, R., Swartzburg, M., & Carlton, P. L. (1985). Differential EEG activation and pathological gambling. *Biological Psychiatry, 20,* 1232–1234.

Goldstein, M. J. (1987). The UCLA high-risk project. *Schizophrenia Bulletin, 13,* 505–514.

Goldstein, R. B., Weissman, M. M., Adams, P. B., Horwath, E., Lish, J. D., Charney, D., Woods, S. W., Sobin, C., & Wickramaratne, P. J. (1994). Psychiatric disorders in relatives of probands with panic disorders and/or major depression. *Archives of General Psychiatry, 51,* 383–394.

Goodall, J. (1986). *The chimpanzees of Gombe.* Cambridge, MA: Harvard University Press.

Gooding, D. C., & Iacono, W. G. (1995). Schizophrenia through the lens of a developmental psychopathology perspective. In D. Cicchetti & D. J. Cohen (Eds.), *Developmental psychopathology. Vol. 2: Risk, disorder, and adaptation* (pp. 535–580). New York: Wiley.

Goodwin, D. W., Schulsinger, F., Knopf, J., Mednick, S., & Guze, S. B. (1977). Alcoholism and depression in adopted daughters of alcoholics. *Archives of General Psychiatry, 34,* 1005–1009.

Goodwin, D. W., Schulsinger, F., Molley, N., Hermansen, L., Winokur, G., & Guze,

S. B. (1974). Drinking problems in adopted and non-adopted sons of alcoholics. *Archives of General Psychiatry, 31,* 164–169.

Goodwin, F. K., & Jamison, K. R. (1990). *Manic-depressive illness.* New York: Oxford University Press.

Gorenstein, E. E. (1982). Frontal lobe functions in psychopaths. *Journal of Abnormal Psychology, 91,* 368–379.

Gorenstein, E. E., & Newman, J. P. (1980). Disinhibitory psychopathology: A new perspective and a model for research. *Psychological Review, 87,* 301–315.

Gorman, J. M., Fyer, M. R., Goetz, R., Askanazi, J., Liebowitz, M. R., Fyer, A. J., Kinney, J., & Klein, D. F. (1988). Ventilatory physiology of patients with panic disorder. *Archives of General Psychiatry, 45,* 31–39.

Gorman, J. M., Fyer, M. R., Liebowitz, A. J., & Klein, D. F. (1987). Pharmacologic provocation of panic attacks. In H. Y. Meltzer (Ed.), *Psychopharmacology: The third generation of progress* (pp. 985–993). New York: Raven Press.

Gorman, J. M., Liebowitz, M. R., Fyer, A. J., Dillon, D., Davies, S. O., Stein, J., & Klein, D. F. (1985). Lactate infusions in obsessive–compulsive disorder. *American Journal of Psychiatry, 142,* 864–866.

Gorman, J. M., & Papp, L. A. (1990). Respiratory physiology of panic. In J. C. Ballenger (Ed.), *Neurobiology of panic disorder* (pp. 187–203). New York: Wiley-Liss.

Gotlib, I. H., Lewinsohn, P. M., Seeley, J. R., Rohde, P., & Redner, J. E. (1993). Negative cognitions and attributional style in depressed adolescents. An examination of stability and specificity. *Journal of Abnormal Psychology, 102,* 607–615.

Gotlib, I. H., & McCabe, S. B. (1992). An information processing approach to the study of cognitive functioning in depression. In E. F. Walker, R. H. Dworkin, & B. A. Cornblatt (Eds.), *Progress in experimental personality and psychopathology research* (Vol. 15, pp. 131–161). New York: Springer.

Gottesman, I. I. (1991). *Schizophrenia genesis: The origins of madness.* New York: W. H. Freeman.

Gottesman, I. I. (1993). Origins of schizophrenia: Past as prologue. In R. Plomin & G. E. McClearn (Eds.), *Nature nurture and psychology* (pp. 231–244). Washington, DC: American Psychological Association.

Gottesman, I. I., & Bertelsen, A. (1989). Confirming unexpressed genotypes for schizophrenia. *Archives of General Psychiatry, 46,* 867–872.

Gottesman, I. I., & Shields, J. (1967). A polygenic theory of schizophrenia. *Proceedings of the National Academy of Sciences, 58,* 199–205.

Gottesman, I. I., & Shields, J. (1976). A critical review of recent adoption, twin, and family studies of schizophrenia: Behavioral genetics prospective. *Schizophrenia Bulletin, 2,* 360–401.

Gottesman, I. I., & Shields, J. (1982). *Schizophrenia: The epigenetic puzzle.* Cambridge, England: Cambridge University Press.

Graham, J. R., & Lowenfeld, B. H. (1986). Personality dimensions of the pathological gambler. *Journal of Gambling Behavior, 2,* 58–66.

Gray, J. A. (1982). *The neuropsychology of anxiety: An enquiry into the functions of the septohippocampal system.* New York: Oxford University Press.

Gray, J. A. (1987). The neuropsychology of emotion and personality. In S. M. Stahl, S. D. Iverson, & E. C. Goodman (Eds.), *Cognitive neurochemistry* (pp. 171–190). Oxford, England: Oxford University Press.

Gray, J. A. (1998). Integrating schizophrenia. *Schizophrenia Bulletin, 24,* 249–266.

Gray, J. A., Feldon, J., Rawlens, J. N. P., Hemsley, D. R., & Smith, A. D. (1991). The neuropsychology of schizophrenia. *Behavioral and Brain Sciences, 14,* 1–84.

Green, B. L., Lindy, J. D., Grace, M. C., & Leonard, A. C. (1992). Chronic posttraumatic stress disorder and diagnostic comorbidity in a disaster sample. *Journal of Nervous and Mental Disease, 180,* 760–766.

Green, M. F., Nuechterlein, K. H., & Breitmeyer, B. (1997). Backward masking performance in unaffected siblings of schizophrenic patients. *Archives of General Psychiatry, 54,* 465–472.

Greenberg, D. B. (1990). Neurasthenia in the 1980's: Chronic mononucleosis, chronic fatigue syndrome and anxiety and depressive disorders. *Psychosomatics, 31,* 129–137.

Griffith, J. D., Cavanaugh, J., Held, J., & Oates, J. A. (1972). Dextroamphetamine: Evaluation of psychomimetic properties in man. *Archives of General Psychiatry, 26,* 97–100.

Grossman, L. S., Harrow, J. F. G., & Fichtner, C. B. (1991). Outcome of schizoaffective disorder at two long-term follow-ups: Comparisons with outcome of schizophrenia and affective disorders. *American Journal of Psychiatry, 148,* 1359–1365.

Grove, W. M., & Andreasen, N. C. (1989). Quantitative and qualitative distinctions between psychiatric disorders. In L. N. Robbins & J. E. Barrett (Eds.), *The validity of psychiatric diagnoses* (pp. 127–141). New York: Raven Press.

Grove, W. M., & Andreasen, N. C. (1992). Concepts, diagnosis, and classification. In E. S. Paykel (Ed.), *Handbook of the affective disorders* (2nd ed., pp. 25–41). New York: Guilford Press.

Grzanna, R., & Brown, R. M. (Eds.). (1993). *Activation of immediate early genes by drugs of abuse* (NIDA Research Monograph No. 125). Rockville, MD: National Institute of Drug Abuse.

Gupta, S., Andreasen, N. C., Arndt, S., Flaum, M., Schultz, S. K., Hubbard, W. E., & Smith, M. (1995). Neurological soft signs in neuroleptic-naive and neuroleptic-treated schizophrenic patients and in normal comparison subjects. *American Journal of Psychiatry, 152,* 191–196.

Gur, R. E. (1995). Functional brain-imaging studies in schizophrenia. In F. E. Bloom & D. J. Kupfer (Eds.), *Psychopharmacology: The fourth generation of progress* (pp. 1185–1192). New York: Raven Press.

Gur, R. E., Mozley, D., Resnick, S. M., Mozley, H., Shtasel, P. L., Gallacher, F., Arnold, S. E., Karp, J. S., Alavi, A., Reivich, M., & Gur, R. C. (1995). Resting cerebral glucose metabolism in first episode and previously treated patients with schizophrenia relates to clinical features. *Archives of General Psychiatry, 52,* 657–667.

Gur, R. E., Mozley, D., Shtasel, D. L., Cannon, T. D., Gallacher, F., Turetsky, B., Grossman, R., & Gur, R. C. (1994). Clinical subtypes of schizophrenia: Differences in brain and CSF volume. *American Journal of Psychiatry, 151,* 343–350.

Guze, S. B., Cloninger, R., Martin, R. L., & Clayton, P. J. (1983). A follow-up and family study of schizophrenia. *Archives of General Psychiatry, 40,* 1273–1276.

Gynther, L. M., Carey, G., Gottesman, I. I., & Vogler, G. P. (1994). A twin study of non-alcohol substance abuse. *Psychiatry Research, 56,* 213–220.

Häfner, H. (1987). Epidemiology of schizophrenia. In H. Häfner, W. F. Gattaz, & J. Zarik (Eds.), *Search for the causes of schizophrenia* (pp. 47–74). Berlin, Germany: Springer-Verlag.

Häfner, H., an der Heiden, W., Behrens, S., Gattaz, W. F., Hambrecht, M., Löffler, W., Mawrer, K., Mumk-Jorgensen, P., Nowotny, B., Riecher-Kössler, A., & Stein, A. (1998). Causes and consequences of the gender difference in age at onset of schizophrenia. *Schizophrenia Bulletin, 24,* 99–113.

Häfner, H., Maurer, K., Löffler, W., Bustamante, S., an der Heiden, W., Reicher-Rösler, A., & Nowotny, B. (1995). Onset and early course of schizophrenia. In H. Häfner & W. F. Gattaz (Eds.), *Search for the causes of schizophrenia* (Vol. III, pp. 43–66). Heidelberg, Germany: Springer-Verlag.

Hammer, C. L. (1995). Stress and the course of unipolar and bipolar disorders. In C. M. Mazure (Ed.), *Does stress cause psychiatric illness?* (pp. 87–110). Washington, DC: American Psychiatric Press.

Handelsman, L., Branchey, M. H., Buijdens-Branchey, L., Gribromont, B., Holloway, K., & Silverman, J. (1993). Morbidity risk for alcoholism and drug abuse in relatives of cocaine addicts. *American Journal of Alcohol Abuse, 19,* 347–357.

Hare, R. D. (1978). Electrodermal and cardiovascular correlates of psychopathy. In R. D. Hare & D. Schalling (Eds.), *Psychopathic behaviour: Approaches to research* (pp. 107–143). Chichester, England: Wiley.

Hare, R. D. (1984). Performance of psychopaths on cognitive tasks related to frontal lobe function. *Journal of Abnormal Psychology, 93,* 133–140.

Hare, R. D. (1986). Twenty years of experience with the Cleckley psychopath. In W. H. Reid, D. Dorr, J. I. Walker, & J. W. Bonner III (Eds.), *Unmasking the psychopath* (pp. 3–27). New York: W. W. Norton.

Hare, R. D. (1991). *The Hare psychopathy checklist revised.* Toronto, Canada: Multi-Health Systems.

Hare, R. D., & Connolly, J. F. (1987). Perceptual asymmetries and information processing in psychopaths. In S. A. Mednick, T. E. Moffitt, & S. A. Stack (Eds.), *The causes of crime: New biological approaches* (pp. 218–238). Cambridge, England: Cambridge University Press.

Hare, R. D., & Cox, D. N. (1978). Clinical and empirical correlates of psychopathy and the selection of subjects for research. In R. D. Hare & D. Schalling (Eds.), *Psychopathic behaviour: Approaches to research* (pp. 1–22). Chichester, England: Wiley.

Hare, R. D., & Hart, S. D. (1995). Commentary on antisocial personality disorders: The DSM-IV field trial. In W. J. Livesley (Ed.), *The DSM-IV personality disorders* (pp. 127–134). New York: Guilford Press.

Hare, R. D., Hart, S. D., & Harpur, T. J. (1991). Psychopathy and the DSM-IV criteria for antisocial personality disorder. *Journal of Abnormal Psychology, 100,* 391–398.

Hare, R. D., & Jutai, J. W. (1983). Criminal history of the male psychopath: Some preliminary data. In K. T. Van Dusen & S. A. Mednick (Eds.), *Prospective studies of crime and delinquency* (pp. 225–236). Boston: Kluwer-Nijhoff.

Hare, R. D., & McPherson, L. M. (1984). Violent and aggressive behavior by criminal psychopaths. *International Journal of Law and Psychiatry, 7,* 35–50.

Hare, R. D., McPherson, L. M., & Forth, A. E. (1988). Male psychopaths and their clinical careers. *Journal of Consulting and Clinical Psychology, 56,* 710–714.

Hare, R. D., & Quinn, M. J. (1971). Psychopathy and autonomic conditioning. *Journal of Abnormal Psychology, 77,* 223–235.

Harkness, A. R., & McNulty, J. L. (1994). The personality psychopathology five (Psy-5): Issue from the pages of a diagnostic manual instead of a dictionary. In S. Strachey & M. Lorr (Eds.), *Differentiating normal and abnormal personality.* New York: Springer.

Harpur, T. J., Hakstian, A. R., & Hare, R. D. (1988). Factor structure of the psychopathy check list. *Journal of Consulting and Clinical Psychology, 56,* 741–747.

Harpur, T. J., & Hare, R. D. (1994). Assessment of psychopathy as a function of age. *Journal of Abnormal Psychology, 103,* 604–609.

Harpur, T. J., Hare, R. D., & Hakstian, R. (1989). Two-factor conceptualization of psychopathy: Construct validity and assessment implications. *Psychological Assesssment, 1,* 6–17.

Harpur, T. J., Hart, S. D., & Hare, R. D. (1994). The personality of the psychopath. In P. T. Costa & T. A. Widiger (Eds.), *Personality disorders and the five-factor model of personality* (pp. 198–216). Washington, DC: American Psychological Association.

Harris, G. T., Rice, M. E., & Quinsey, V. L. (1994). Psychopathy as a taxon: Evidence that psychopaths are a discrete class. *Journal of Consulting and Clinical Psychology, 62,* 387–397.

Harrow, M., Goldberg, J. F., Grossman, L. S., & Meltzer, H. Y. (1990). Outcome in manic disorders: A naturalistic follow-up study. *Archives of General Psychiatry, 47,* 665–671.

Hart, S. D., Forth, A. E., & Hare, R. D. (1990). Performance of criminal psychopaths on selected neuropsychological tests. *Journal of Abnormal Psychology, 99,* 374–379.

Haskin, S., Grant, B., & Endicott, J. (1990). The natural history of drug abuse. *American Journal of Psychiatry, 147,* 1537–1546.

Hazen, A. L., & Stein, M. B. (1995). Clinical phenomenology and comorbidity. In M. B. Stein (Ed.), *Social phobia: Clinical and research perspectives* (pp. 3–41). Washington, DC: American Psychiatric Press.

Haznedar, M. M., Buchsbaum, M. S., Luu, C., Hazlett, E. A., Siegel, B. V., Jr., Lohr, J., Wu, J., Haier, R. J., & Bunney, W. E., Jr. (1997). Decreased anterior cingulate gyrus metabolic rate in schizophrenia. *American Journal of Psychiatry, 154,* 682–684.

Heath, A. C., & Martin, G. (1992). Genetic differences in psychomotor performance and alcohol tolerance decrement after alcohol: A multivariate analysis. *Journal of Studies on Alcohol, 53,* 262–271.

Hegarty, J. D., Baldessarini, R. J., Tohen, M., Waternaux, C., & Oepen, G. (1994). One hundred years of schizophrenia: A meta-analysis of the outcome literature. *American Journal of Psychiatry, 151,* 1409–1416.

Heilbrun, A. B., Jr. (1993). Hallucinations. In C. G. Costello (Ed.), *Symptoms of schizophrenia* (pp. 56–91). New York: Wiley.

Heimberg, J. D., Hope, D. A., Dodge, C. S., & Becker, R. E. (1990). DSM III-R subtypes of social phobia. Comparison of generalized social phobics and public speaking phobics. *The Journal of Nervous and Mental Disease, 178,* 172–179.

Heinrichs, D. W., & Buchanan, R. W. (1988). Significance and meaning of neurological signs of schizophrenia. *American Journal of Psychiatry, 145,* 11–18.

Helzer, J. E. (1994). Psychoactive substance abuse and its relation to dependence. In T. A. Widiger, A. J. Francis, H. A. Pincus, M. B. First, R. Ross, & W. Davis (Eds.), *DSMIV-Sourcebook* (Vol. I, pp. 21–32). Washington, DC: American Psychiatric Association.

Helzer, J. E., Burnam, A., & McElvoy, L. T. (1991). Alcohol abuse and dependence. In L. N. Robins & D. A. Regier (Eds.), *Psychiatric disorders in America: The epidemiologic catchment area study* (pp. 81–115). New York: The Free Press.

Helzer, J. E., & Canino, G. V. (1989). The implications of cross-national research for diagnostic validity. In L. N. Robins & J. E. Barrett (Eds.), *The validity of psychiatric diagnosis* (pp. 247–261). New York: Raven Press.

Helzer, J. E., & Canino, G. V. (1992). *Alcoholism in North America, Europe and Asia.* New York: Oxford University Press.

Helzer, J. E., Clayton, P. J., Pambakian, R., Reich, T., Woodruff, R. A., Jr., & Reveley, M. A. (1977). Reliability of psychiatric diagnosis: II. The test retest reliability of diagnostic classification. *Archives of General Psychiatry, 34,* 136–141.

Hemming, J. H. (1981). Electrodermal indices in a selected prison sample and students. *Personality and Individual Differences, 3,* 37–46.

Henn, F. A. (1995). The NMDA receptor as a site for psychopathology: Primary or secondary role? *Archives of General Psychiatry, 52,* 1008–1010.

Henry, B., Caspi, A., Moffitt, T. E., & Silva, P. A. (1996). Temperamental and familial predictors of violent and nonviolent criminal convictions: Age 3 to age 18. *Developmental Psychology, 32,* 614–623.

Herbert, J. D., Hope, D. A., & Bellack, A. S. (1992). Validity of the distinction between generalized social phobia and avoidant personality disorder. *Journal of Abnormal Psychology, 101,* 332–339.

Hesselbrock, M. N. (1991). Gender comparison of antisocial personality disorder and depression in alcoholism. *Journal of Substance Abuse, 3,* 205–219.

Heston, L. L. (1966). Psychiatric disorders in foster home reared children of schizophrenic mothers. *British Journal of Psychiatry, 112,* 819–825.

Hickie, I., Wilhelm, K., Parker, G., Boyce, P., Hadzi-Pavlovic, D., Brodaty, H., & Mitchell, P. (1990). Perceived dysfunctional intimate relationships: A specific association with the non-melancholic depression type. *Journal of Affective Disorders, 19,* 99–107.

Hirshfeld, D. R., Rosenbaum, J. F., Biederman, J., Bolduc, E., Faraone, S. V., Snidman, N., Reznick, J. S., & Kagan, J. (1992). Stable behavioral inhibition and its association with anxiety disorder. *Journal of the American Academy of Child and Adolescent Psychiatry, 31,* 103–111.

Hirschfeld, R. M. A. (1994). Major depression, dysthymic and depressive personality disorder. *British Journal of Psychiatry, 165,* 23–30.

Hirschfeld, R. M. A., Klerman, G. L., Clayton, P. J., Keller, M. B., McDonald-Scott, P., & Larkin, B. H. (1983). Assessing personality: Effects of the depressive state on trait measurement. *American Journal of Psychiatry, 140,* 695–699.

Hirschfeld, R. M. A., Klerman, G. L., Lavori, P., Keller, M. B., Griffith, P., & Coryell, W. (1989). Premorbid personality assessments of first onset of major depression. *Archives of General Psychiatry, 46,* 345–350.

Hirschfeld, R. M. A., & Shea, M. T. (1992). Personality. In E. S. Paykel (Ed.), *Handbook of affective disorders* (2nd ed., pp. 185–194). New York: Guilford Press.

Hoehn-Saric, R., McLeod, D. R., & Hipsley, P. (1995). Is hyperarousal essential to obsessive-compulsive disorder? *Archives of General Psychiatry, 52,* 688–693.

Hoehn-Saric, R., McLeod, D. R., & Zimmerli, W. D. (1989). Somatic manifestations in women with generalized anxiety disorder. *Archives of General Psychiatry, 46,* 1113–1119.

Hoffman, S. G., Ehlers, A., & Roth, W. T. (1995). Conditioning theory: A model for the etiology of public speaking anxiety? *Behavior Research and Therapy, 33,* 567–571.

Hoffman, S. G., Newman, M. G., Ehlers, A., & Roth, W. T. (1995). Psychophysiological differences between subgroups of social phobia. *Journal of Abnormal Psychology, 104,* 224–231.

Hollander, E., DeCaria, C. M., Nitescu, A., Gully, R., Suckow, R. F., Cooper, T. B., Gorman, J. M., Klein, D. F., & Liebowitz, M. R. (1992). Serotonergic function in obsessive-compulsive disorder. *Archives of General Psychiatry, 49,* 21–28.

Hollander, E., Schiffman, E., Cohen, B., Rivera-Stein, M. A., Rosen, W., Gorman, J. M., Fyer, A. J., Papp, L., & Liebowitz, M. R. (1992). Signs of central nervous system dysfunction in obsessive-compulsive disorder. *Archives of General Psychiatry, 47,* 27–32.

Hollister, J. M., Laing, P., & Mednick, S. A. (1996). Rhesus incompatibility as a risk factor for schizophrenia in male adults. *Archives of General Psychiatry, 53,* 19–24.

Holsboer, F. (1995). Neuroendocrinology of mood disorders. In F. E. Bloom & D. J. Kupfer (Eds.), *Psychopharmacology: The fourth generation of progress* (pp. 957–969). New York: Raven Press.

Hong, Y.-Y., & Chiu, C.-Y. (1988). Sex, locus of control, and illusion of control in Hong Kong as correlates of gambling involvement. *Journal of Social Psychology, 128,* 667–673.

Hore, B. D. (1971). Life events and alcoholic relapse. *British Journal of Addictions, 66,* 83–88.

Horwath, E., Lish, J. D., Johnson, J., Hornig, C. D., & Weissman, M. M. (1993). Agoraphobia without panic: Clinical reappraisal of an epidemiologic finding. *American Journal of Psychiatry, 150,* 1496–1501.

Horwath, E., Wolk, S. I., Goldstein, R. B., Wickramatne, P., Sobin, C., Adams, P., Lish, J. D., & Weissman, M. M. (1990). *Journal of Affective Disorders, 19,* 23–29.

Hser, Y.-I., Anglin, D., & Powers, K. (1993). A 24-year follow-up of California narcotics addicts. *Archives of General Psychiatry, 50,* 577–584.

Hultman, C. M., Öhman, A., Cnattingius, S., Wieselgren, I.-M., & Lindstrom, L. H. (1997). Prenatal and neonatal risk factors for schizophrenia. *British Journal of Psychiatry, 170,* 128–133.

Hultman, C. M., Öhman, A., Öhlund, L. S., Wieselgren, I.-M., Lindstrom, L. H., & Öst, L.-G. (1996). Electrodermal activity and social network as predictors of outcome of episodes in schizophrenia. *Journal of Abnormal Psychology, 105,* 626–636.

Husain, M., MacDonald, W., Doraiswamy, P., Figiel, G. S., Na, C., Escalona, R., Boyko, O. B., Nemeroff, C. B., & Krishman, R. R. (1991). A magnetic resonance imaging study of putamen nuclei in major depression. *Psychiatry Research, 40,* 95–99.

Hyler, S. E., Williams, J. B. W., & Spitzer, R. L. (1982). Reliability in the DSM-III field trials: Interview vs. case summary. *Archives of General Psychiatry, 39,* 1275–1278.

Iacono, W. G. (1993). Smooth pursuit oculomotor dysfunction as an index of schizophrenia. In R. L. Cromwell & C. R. Snyder (Eds.), *Schizophrenia: Origins, processes, treatment, and outcome* (pp. 76–97). New York: Oxford University Press.

Iacono, W. G., Moreau, M., Beiser, M., Fleming, J. A. E., & Lin, T.-Y. (1992). Smooth-pursuit eye tracking in first-episode psychotic patients and their relatives. *Journal of Abnormal Psychology, 101,* 104–116.

Information Please Almanac: Atlas and yearbook. (1986). Boston, MA: Houghton Mifflin.

Ingraham, L. J., Kugelmass, S., Frenkel, E., Nathan, M., & Mirsky, A. F. (1995). Twenty-five year followup of the Israeli high-risk study: Current and lifetime psychopathology. *Schizophrenia Bulletin, 21,* 183–192.

Ingram, R. E., Miranda, J., & Segal, Z. V. (1998). *Cognitive vulnerability to depression* (pp. 134–161). New York: Guilford Press.

Insel, T. R., Zahn, T., & Murphy, D. L. (1985). Obsessive-compulsive disorder. An anxiety disorder? In A. H. Tuma & J. Maser (Eds.), *Anxiety and the anxiety disorders* (pp. 577–589). Hillsdale, NJ: Erlbaum.

Iqbal, N., & van Praag, H. M. (1995). The role of serotonin in schizophrenia. In H. G. M. Westenberg & H. M. van Praag (Eds.), *Advances in the neurobiology of schizophrenia* (pp. 221–243). Chichester, England: Wiley.

Jackson, J. H. (1931). *Selected writings of J. H. Jackson.* London: Hodder & Stoughton. (Original work published 1889)

Jackson, S. W. (1986). *Melancholia and depression: From Hippocratic times to modern times.* New Haven, CT: Yale University Press.

Jaffe, L., & Schukitt, M. A. (1981). The importance of drug use history in a series of alcoholics. *Journal of Clinical Psychology, 42,* 224–227.

Jamison, K. R. (1993). *Touched with fire: Manic-depressive illness and the artistic temperament.* New York: The Free Press.

Jansen, M. A., Arntz, A., Merckelbach, H., & Mersch, P. A. (1994). Personality disorders and features in social phobia and panic disorder. *Journal of Abnormal Psychology, 103,* 391–395.

Jenike, M. A., Baer, L., Ballatine, T., Martuza, R. L., Tynes, S., Giriunas, I., Buttolph, L., & Cassen, N. H. (1991). Cingulotomy for refractory obsessive-compulsive disorder: A long-term follow-up of 33 patients. *Archives of General Psychiatry, 48,* 548–555.

Jeste, D. V., Heaton, S. C., Paulsen, J. S., Ercoli, L., Harris, J., & Heaton, R. K. (1996). Clinical and neuropychological comparison of psychotic depression and nonpsychotic depression and schizophrenia. *American Journal of Psychiatry, 153,* 490–496.

Johanson, C. E., & Schuster, C. R. (1995). Cocaine. In P. E. Bloom & D. J. Kupfer (Eds.), *Psychopharmacology: The fourth generation of progress* (pp. 1685–1697). New York: Raven Press.

Johnston, E. C. (1991). What is crucial for the long-term outcome of schizophrenia? In H. Häfner & W. F. Gattaz (Eds.), *Search for the causes of schizophrenia* (Vol. II, pp. 67–76). Berlin, Germany: Springer-Verlag.

Jones, M. C. (1968). Personality correlates and antecedents of drinking patterns in adult males. *Journal of Consulting and Clinical Psychology, 32,* 2–12.

Jones, M. C. (1971). Personality antecedents and correlates of drinking patterns in women. *Journal of Consulting and Clinical Psychology, 36,* 61–69.

Jordan, B. K., Schlenger, W. E., Hough, R., Kulka, R. A., Weiss, D., Fairbanks,

J. A., & Marmar, C. R. (1991). Lifetime and current prevalence of specific psychiatric disorders among Vietnam veterans and controls. *Archives of General Psychiatry, 48,* 207–215.

Judd, L. L., McAdams, L., Budnick, B., & Braff, D. L. (1992). Sensory gating deficits in schizophrenia: New results. *American Journal of Psychiatry, 149,* 488–493.

Jutai, J. W., Hare, R. D., & Connolly, J. F. (1987). Psychopathy and event-related brain potentials: ERPs associated with attention to speech stimuli. *Personality and Individual Differences, 8,* 175–184.

Kaestner, E., Rosen, L., & Apel, P. (1977). Patterns of drug abuse: Relationships with ethnicity, sensation seeking and anxiety. *Journal of Consulting and Clinical Psychology, 45,* 462–468.

Kagan, J. (1994). *Galen's prophecy: Temperament in human nature.* New York: Basic Books.

Kagan, J., & Moss, H. A. (1962). *Birth to maturity.* New York: Wiley.

Kagan, J., Reznick, J. S., & Snidman, N. (1988). Biological bases of childhood shyness. *Science, 240,* 167–171.

Kagan, J., Reznick, J. S., Snidman, N., Johnson, M. O., Gibbons, M., Gersten, M., Biederman, J., & Rosenbaum, J. A. (1990). Origins of panic disorder. In J. C. Ballenger (Ed.), *Neurobiology of panic disorder: Frontiers of clinical neuroscience* (Vol. 8, pp. 71–87). New York: Wiley-Liss.

Kahn, R. S., & Davidson, M. (1995). Dopamine in schizophrenia. In J. A. Den Boer, H. G. M. Westenberg, & H. M. van Praag (Eds.), *Advances in the neurobiology of schizophrenia* (pp. 205–243). Chichester, England: Wiley.

Kahn, R. S., & Davis, K. L. (1995). New developments in dopamine and schizophrenia. In F. E. Bloom & D. J. Kupfer (Eds.), *Psychopharmacology: The fourth generation of progress* (pp. 1193–1203). New York: Raven Press.

Kahn, R. S., van Praag, H. M., Wetzler, S., Asnis, G. M., & Barr, G. (1988). Serotonin and anxiety revisited. *Biological Psychiatry, 15,* 189–208.

Kalivas, P. W., Striplin, C. D., Steketee, J. D., Klitenick, M. A., & Duffy, P. (1992). Cellular mechanisms of behavioral sensitization to drugs of abuse. In P. W. Kalivas & H. H. Sanson (Eds.), *The neurobiology of drug and alcohol addictions* (pp. 128–135). New York: New York Academy of Sciences.

Kallmann, F. J. (1946). The genetic theory of schizophrenia: An analysis of 691 schizophrenic twin index families. *American Journal of Psychiatry, 103,* 309–322.

Kandel, D., Davies, M., & Baydar, N. (1990). The creation of interpersonal contexts: Homophily in dyadic relationships in adolescence and young adulthood. In L. Robins & M. Rutter (Eds.), *Straight and devious pathways from childhood to adulthood* (pp. 221–241). Cambridge, England: Cambridge University Press.

Karayiorgou, M., & Gogos, J. A. (1997). Dissecting the genetic complexity of schizophrenia. *Molecular Psychiatry, 2,* 211–223.

Karno, M., Golding, J. M., Sorenson, S. B., & Burnham, A. (1988). The epidemiology of obsessive-compulsive disorder in five US communities. *Archives of General Psychiatry, 45*, 1094–1099.

Karowski, L. M., & Kendler, K. S. (1997). An examination of the genetic relationship between bipolar and unipolar illness in an epidemiological study. *Psychiatric Genetics, 7*, 159–163.

Kasl, S. V., Ostfeld, A. M., Berkman, L. F., & Jacobs, S. C. (1987). Stress and alcohol consumption: The role of selected social and environmental factors. In E. Gotheil, K. A. Druley, S. Pashko, & S. P. Weinstein (Eds.), *Stress and addiction* (pp. 40–60). New York: Bruner/Mazel.

Katon, W., & Roy-Byrne, P. P. (1991). Mixed anxiety and depression. *Journal of Abnormal Psychology, 100*, 337–345.

Katsanis, J., & Iacono, W. G. (1991). Clinical neuropsychological and brain structural correlates of smooth pursuit eye tracking performance in chronic schizophrenia. *Journal of Abnormal Psychology, 100*, 526–534.

Katsanis, J., & Iacono, W. G. (1994). Electrodermal activity and clinical status in chronic schizophrenia. *Journal of Abnormal Psychology, 103*, 777–783.

Katsanis, J., Iacono, W. G., & Beiser, M. (1990). Anhedonia and perceptual aberration in first-episode psychotic patients and their relatives. *Journal of Abnormal Psychology, 99*, 202–206.

Keller, M. B., Lavori, P. W., Mueller, T. I., Endicott, J., Coryell, W., Hirschfeld, R. M. A., & Shea, T. (1992). Time to recovery, chronicity, and levels of psychopathology in major depression: A 5-year prospective follow-up of 431 subjects. *Archives of General Psychiatry, 49*, 809–816.

Kelly, D. (1980). *Anxiety and emotions.* Springfield, IL: Charles C Thomas.

Kendell, R. E. (1989). Clinical validity. In L. N. Robins & J. E Barrett (Eds.), *The validity of psychiatric diagnosis* (pp. 305–323). New York: Raven Press.

Kendell, R. E., Cooper, J. E., Gourlay, A. J., Copeland, J. R. M., Sharpe, L., & Gurland, B. J. (1971). Diagnostic criteria of American and British psychiatrists. *Archives of General Psychiatry, 25*, 123–130.

Kendler, K. S., Davis, C. G., & Kessler, R. C. (1997). The familial aggregation of common psychiatric and substance use disorders in the National Comorbidity Survey: A family history study. *British Journal of Psychiatry, 170*, 541–548.

Kendler, K. S., Eaves, L. J., Walters, E. E., Neale, M. C., Heath, A. C., & Kessler, R. C. (1996). The identification and validation of distinct depressive syndromes in a population-based sample of female twins. *Archives of General Psychiatry, 53*, 391–399.

Kendler, K. S., Gallagher, T. J., Abelson, J. M., & Kessler, R. C. (1996). Lifetime prevalence, demographic risk factors, and diagnostic validity of nonaffective psychosis as assessed in a US community sample. *Archives of General Psychiatry, 53*, 1022–1031.

Kendler, K. S., Gruenberg, A. M., & Kinney, D. K. (1994). Independent analysis of adoptees and relatives as defined by DSM-III in the provincial and national samples of the Danish adoption study of schizophrenia. *Archives of General Psychiatry, 51*, 456–468.

Kendler, K. S., Gruenberg, A. M., & Tsuang, M. T. (1985). Psychiatric illness in first degree relatives of schizophrenia and surgical control patients. *Archives of General Psychiatry, 42,* 770–778.

Kendler, K. S., Gruenberg, A. M., & Tsuang, M. T. (1988). A family study of the subtypes of schizophrenia. *American Journal of Psychiatry, 145,* 57–62.

Kendler, K. S., Heath, A. C., Martin, N. G., & Eaves, L. J. (1987). Symptoms of anxiety and symptoms of depression: Same genes different environments? *Archives of General Psychiatry, 44,* 451–457.

Kendler, K. S., Karkowski, L. M., & Walsh, D. (1998). The structure of psychosis. *Archives of General Psychiatry, 55,* 492–499.

Kendler, K. S., Kessler, R. C., Walters, E. E., MacLean, C., Neale, M. C., Heath, A. C., & Eaves, L. J. (1995). Stressful life events, genetic liability, and onset of an episode of major depression in women. *American Journal of Psychiatry, 152,* 833–842.

Kendler, K. S., McGuire, M., Gruenberg, A. M., O'Hare, A., Spellman, M., & Walsh, D. (1993). The Roscommon Family Study III: Schizophrenia-related personality disorders in relatives. *Archives of General Psychiatry, 50,* 781–788.

Kendler, K. S., McGuire, M., Gruenberg, A. M., & Walsh, D. (1995). Examining the validity of DSM-III-R schizoaffective disorder and its putative subtypes in the Roscommon family study. *American Journal of Psychiatry, 152,* 755–764.

Kendler, K. S., Neale, M. C., Kessler, R. C., Heath, A. C., & Eaves, L. J. (1992a). The genetic epidemiology of phobias in women. *Archives of General Psychiatry, 49,* 273–281.

Kendler, K. S., Neale, M. C., Kessler, R. C., Heath, A. C., & Eaves, L. J. (1992b). Major depression and generalized anxiety disorder: Same genes (partly) different environments? *Archives of General Psychiatry, 49,* 716–722.

Kendler, K. S., Neale, M. C., Kessler, R. C., Heath, A. C., & Eaves, L. J. (1992c). A population based twin study of major depression in women: The impact of varying definitions of illness. *Archives of General Psychiatry, 49,* 257–266.

Kendler, K. S., Neale, M. C., Kessler, R. C., Heath, A. C., & Eaves, L. J. (1993a). Twin studies of recent life events. *Archives of General Psychiatry, 50,* 789–796.

Kendler, K. S., Neale, M. C., Kessler, R. C., Heath, A. C., & Eaves, L. J. (1993b). A longitudinal twin study of personality and major depression in women. *Archives of General Psychiatry, 50,* 853–862.

Kendler, K. S., Pederson, N., Johnson, L., Neale, M. C., & Mathe, A. A. (1993). A pilot Swedish twin study of affective illness, including hospital- and population-ascertained subsamples. *Archives of General Psychiatry, 50,* 699–706.

Kendler, K. S., & Robinette, C. D. (1983). Schizophrenia in the National Academy of Sciences National Research Council Twin Registry: A 16 year update. *American Journal of Psychiatry, 140,* 1551–1563.

Kendler, K. S., Walters, E. E., Neale, M. C., Kessler, R. C., Heath, A. C., & Eaves,

L. J. (1995). The structure of the genetic and environmental risk factors for six major psychiatric disorders in women. *Archives of General Psychiatry, 52,* 374–383.

Kern, M. F., Kenkell, M. B., Templer, D. I., & Newell, T. G. (1986). Drug preference as a function of arousal and stimulus screening. *International Journal of the Addictions, 21,* 255–265.

Kessler, R. C., Crum, R. M., Warner, L. A., Nelson, C. B., Schulenberg, J., & Anthony, J. C. (1997). Lifetime co-occurrence of DSM-III-R alcohol abuse and dependence with other psychiatric disorders in the National Comorbidity Survey. *Archives of General Psychiatry, 54,* 313–321.

Kessler, R. C., McGonagle, K. A., Zhao, S., Nelson, C. B., Hughes, M., Eshleman, S., Wittchen, H.-U., & Kendler, K. S. (1994). Lifetime and 12-month prevalence of DSM-III-R psychiatric disorders in the United States. *Archives of General Psychiatry, 51,* 8–19.

Kessler, R. C., Sonnega, A., Bromet, E., Hughes, M., & Nelson, C. B. (1995). Posttraumatic stress disorder in the National Comorbidity Survey. *Archives of General Psychiatry, 52,* 1048–1060.

Kety, S. S., Rosenthal, D., Wender, P. H., & Schulsinger, F. (1968). The types and prevalence of mental illness in the biological and adoptive families of adopted schizophrenics. *Journal of Psychiatric Research, 6*(Suppl.), 345–362.

Kety, S. S., Wender, P. H., Jacobsen, B., Ingraham, L. J., Jansson, L., Faber, B., & Kinney, D. K. (1994). Mental illness in the biological and adoptive relatives of schizophrenic adoptees: Replication of the Copenhagen study in the rest of Denmark. *Archives of General Psychiatry, 51,* 442–455.

Kilpatrick, D. G., Sutker, P. B., & Smith, A. D. (1976). Deviant drug and alcohol use: The role of anxiety, sensation seeking and other personality variables. In M. Zuckerman & C. D. Spielberger (Eds.), *Emotions and anxiety: New concepts, methods and applications* (pp. 247–278). Hillsdale, NJ: Erlbaum.

Kim, L. S., & Chun, C. (1993). Ethnic differences in psychiatric diagnosis among Asian-American adolescents. *Journal of Nervous and Mental Disease, 181,* 612–617.

Kinney, D. K., Yurgelun-Todd, D. A., Levy, D. L., Medoff, D., Lajonchere, C. M., & Radford-Paregol, M. (1993). Obstetrical complications in patients with bipolar disorder and their siblings. *Psychiatry Research, 48,* 47–56.

Kirby, K. C., Menzies, R. G., Daniels, B. A., & Smith, K. L. (1995). Aetiology of spider phobia: Classificatory differences between two origins. *Behaviour Research and Therapy, 33,* 955–958.

Kirk, S. A., & Kutchins, H. (1992). *The selling of DSM: The rhetoric of science in psychiatry.* New York: Aldine de Gruyter.

Klein, D. F. (1967). Importance of psychiatric diagnosis in prediction of anxiety attacks: Clinical drug effects. *Archives of General Psychiatry, 16,* 118–126.

Klein, D. F. (1981). Anxiety reconceptualized. In D. F. Klein & J. Rabkin (Eds.), *Anxiety: New research and changing concepts* (pp. 235–265). New York: Raven Press.

Klein, D. F. (1989). The pharmacologic validation of psychiatric diagnosis. In L. N. Robins & J. E. Barrett (Eds.), *The validity of psychiatric diagnoses* (pp. 203–216). New York: Raven Press.

Klein, D. F. (1993). False suffocation alarms, spontaneous panics and related conditions: An integrative hypothesis. *Archives of General Psychiatry, 50,* 306–317.

Klein, D. F., & Rosen, B. (1973). Premorbid asocial adjustment and response to phenothiazine treatment among schizophrenic inpatients. *Archives of General Psychiatry, 29,* 480–485.

Klein, D. N. (1990). Depressive personality: Reliability, validity, and relation to dysthymia. *Journal of Abnormal Psychology, 99,* 412–421.

Klein, D. N., Clark, D. C., Dansky, L., & Margolis, E. (1988). Dysthymia in the offspring of parents with primary unipolar affective disorder. *Journal of Abnormal Psychology, 97,* 265–274.

Klein, D. N., Depue, R. A., & Slater, J. F. (1986). Inventory identification of cyclothymia: IV. Validation in offspring of bipolar I patients. *Archives of General Psychiatry, 43,* 441–445.

Klein, D. N., & Miller, G. A. (1993). Depressive personality in nonclinical subjects. *American Journal of Psychiatry, 150,* 1718–1724.

Klein, D. N., Riso, L. P., Donaldson, S. K., Schwartz, J. E., Anderson, R. L., Ouimette, P. C., Lizardi, H., & Aronson, T. A. (1995). Family study of early-onset dysthymia. *Archives of General Psychiatry, 52,* 487–496.

Kleinknecht, R. A. (1994). Acquisition of blood injury, and needle fears and phobias. *Behaviour Research and Therapy, 32,* 817–823.

Klerman, G. L. (1978). The evolution of a scientific nosology. In J. C. Shershow (Ed.), *Schizophrenia: Science and practice* (pp. 99–121). Cambridge, MA: Harvard University Press.

Klerman, G. L. (1990). Approaches to the phenomenon of comorbidity. In J. D. Maser & C. R. Cloninger (Eds.), *Comorbidity of mood and anxiety disorders* (pp. 13–37). Washington, DC: American Psychiatric Press.

Knowles, J. A., Mannuzza, S., & Fyer, A. J. (1995). Heritability of social anxiety. In M. B. Steen (Ed.), *Social phobia: Clinical and research perspectives* (pp. 147–161). Washington, DC: American Psychiatric Press.

Ko, G. N., Elsworth, J. D., Roth, R. H., Rifkin, B. G., Leigh, H., & Redmond, E. (1983). Panic-induced elevation of plasma MHPG levels in phobic-anxious patients: Effects of clonidine and imipramine. *Archives of General Psychiatry, 40,* 425–430.

Koenigsberg, H. W., Kaplan, R. D., Gilmore, M. M., & Cooper, A. M. (1985). The relation between syndrome and personality disorder in DSM III: Experience with 2,412 patients. *American Journal of Psychiatry, 142,* 207–212.

Kohn, P. M., Barnes, G. E., & Hoffman, F. M. (1979). Drug-use history and experience seeking among male correctional inmates. *Journal of Consulting and Clinical Psychology, 47,* 708–715.

Koreen, A. R., Siris, S. G., Chakos, M., Alvir, J., Mayerhoff, D., & Lieberman, J.

(1993). Depression in first-episode schizophrenia. *American Journal of Psychiatry, 150,* 1643–1647.

Korfine, L., & Lenzenweger, M. F. (1995). The taxonicity of schizotypy: A replication. *Journal of Abnormal Psychology, 104,* 26–31.

Kosson, D. S., Smith, S. S., & Newman, J. P. (1990). Evaluation of the construct validity of psychopathy in black and white male inmates: Three preliminary studies. *Journal of Abnormal Psychology, 99,* 250–259.

Kosten, T. A., Ball, S. A., & Rounsaville, B. J. (1994). A sibling study of sensation seeking and opiate addiction. *The Journal of Nervous and Mental Disease, 182,* 284–289.

Kosten, T. A., & Rounsaville, B. J. (1992). Sensitivity of psychiatric diagnosis based on the best estimate procedure. *American Journal of Psychiatry, 149,* 1225–1227.

Kottler, M., Cohen, H., Segman, R., Gritsenko, I., Nemanov, L., Lerer, B., Kramer, I., Zer-Zion, M., Kletz, I., & Ebstein, R. P. (1997). Excess dopamine D4 receptor (D4DR) exon III seven repeat allele in opioid-dependent subjects. *Molecular Psychiatry, 2,* 251–254.

Kraemer, H. C., Pruyen, J. P., Gibbons, R. D., Greenhouse, J. B., Grochocinski, V. J., Waternaux, C., & Kupfer, D. J. (1987). Methodology in psychiatric research. *Archives of General Psychiatry, 44,* 1100–1106.

Kraepelin, E. (1921). *Manic-depressive insanity and paranoia.* Edinburgh, Scotland: Livingston.

Kraepelin, E. (1919). *Dementia praecox and paraphrenia.* New York: Krieger.

Kraft, M. R., Jr., & Zuckerman, M. (in press). Perceived parental behavior of biological parents and stepparents reported by young adults, and relationships between perceived parenting and personality. *Journal of Personality and Individual Differences.*

Kreitman, N. (1961). The reliability of psychiatric diagnosis. *Journal of Mental Science, 107,* 878–886.

Kreuz, L. E., & Rose, R. M. (1972). Assessment of aggressive behavior and plasma testosterone in a young criminal population. *Psychosomatic Medicine, 34,* 321–332.

Krishnan, K. R. R., McDonald, W. M., Escalona, P. R., Doraiswamy, P. M., Na, C., Husain, M. M., Figiel, G. S., Boyho, O. B., Ellinwood, E. H., & Nemeroff, C. B. (1992). Magnetic resonance imaging of the caudate nuclei in depression. *Archives of General Psychiatry, 49,* 553–557.

Krueger, R. F., Caspi, A., Moffitt, T. E., Silva, P. A., & McGee, R. (1996). Personality traits are differentially linked to mental disorders: A multitrait-multidiagnosis study of an adolescent birth cohort. *Journal of Abnormal Psychology, 105,* 299–312.

Kruesi, M. J. P., Rapoport, J. L., Hamburger, S., Hibbs, E., Potter, W. Z., Lenane, M., & Brown, G. L. (1990). Cerebrospinal fluid monoamine metabolites, aggression, and impulsivity in disruptive behavior disorders of children and adolescents. *Archives of General Psychiatry, 47,* 419–426.

Krystal, H. (1969). *Massive psychic trauma*. New York: International Universities Press.

Kugelmass, S., Faber, N., Ingraham, L., Frenkel, E., Nathan, M., Mirsky, A. F., & Shakar, G. B. (1995). Reanalysis of SCOR and anxiety measures in the Israeli high-risk study. *Schizophrenia Bulletin, 21*, 205–217.

Kuley, N. B., & Jacobs, D. F. (1988). The relationships between dissociative-like experiences and sensation seeking among social and problem gamblers. *Journal of Gambling Behavior, 4*, 197–207.

Kumar, V. K., Pekala, R. J., & Cummings, J. (1993). Sensation seeking, drug use, and reported paranormal beliefs, and experiences. *Personality and Individual Differences, 14*, 685–691.

Kupfer, D. J., & Thase, M. E. (1989). Laboratory studies and validity of psychiatric diagnosis: Has there been progress? In L. N. Robbins & J. E. Barrett (Eds.), *The validity of psychiatric diagnosis* (pp. 177–201). New York: Raven Press.

Kushner, M. G., MacKenzie, T. B., Fiszdon, J., Valentiner, D. P., Foa, E., Anderson, N., & Wangensteen, D. (1996). The effects of alcohol consumption on laboratory-induced panic and state anxiety. *Archives of General Psychiatry, 53*, 243–249.

Kusyszyn, I., & Rutter, R. (1985). Personality characteristics of heavy gamblers, light gamblers, non-gamblers and lottery players. *Journal of Gambling Behavior, 1*, 59–64.

Kwapil, T. R. (1996). A longitudinal study of drug and alcohol use by psychosis-prone and impulsive-nonconforming individuals. *Journal of Abnormal Psychology, 105*, 114–123.

Lachman, H. M. (1994). Basic principles in linkage analysis. In D. F. Paplos & H. M. Lachman (Eds.), *Genetic studies in affective disorders* (pp. 46–69). New York: Wiley.

Lader, M. H. (1975). The psychophysiology of anxious and depressed patients. In D. C. Fowles (Ed.), *Clinical applications of psychophysiology* (pp. 12–41). New York: Columbia University Press.

Ladoucer, R. (1991). Prevalence estimates of pathological gambling in Quebec. *Canadian Journal of Psychiatry, 36*, 732–734.

Lang, P. J. (1988). Fear, anxiety, and panic: Context, cognition, and visceral arousal. In S. Rachman & J. D. Maser (Eds.), *Panic: Psychological perspectives* (pp. 219–236). Hillsdale, NJ: Erlbaum.

Leckman, J. F., Goodman, W. K., North, W. G., Chappell, P. B., Price, L. H., Pauls, D. L., Anderson, G. M., Riddle, M. A., McSwiggan-Harden, M., McDougle, C. J., Barr, L. C., & Cohen, D. J. (1994). Elevated cerebrospinal fluid levels of oxytocin in obsessive-compulsive disorder: Comparison with Tourette's syndrome and healthy controls. *Archives of General Psychiatry, 51*, 782–792.

Lee, K. A., Vaillant, G. E., Torrey, W. C., & Elder, G. H. (1995). A 50-year prospective survey of the psychological sequelae of World War II combat. *American Journal of Psychiatry, 152*, 516–522.

Leff, J., Sartorius, N., Jablensky, A., Anker, M., Korten, A., Gulbinat, W., & Ernberg, G. (1991). The international pilot study of schizophrenia: Five-year follow-up findings. In H. Häfner & W. F. Gattaz (Eds.), *Search for the causes of schizophrenia* (Vol. II, pp. 57–66). Heidelberg, Germany: Springer-Verlag.

Legarda, J. J., Babio, R., & Abreu, J. M. (1992). Prevalence estimates of pathological gambling in Seville (Spain). *British Journal of Addiction, 87,* 767–770.

Lencz, T., Raine, A., Scerbo, A., Redmon, M., Brodish, S., Holt, C., & Bird, L. (1993). Impaired eye tracking in undergraduates with schizotypal personality disorder. *American Journal of Psychiatry, 150,* 152–154.

Lesieur, H. R., & Blume, S. B. (1987). The South Oaks Gambling Screen (SOGS): A new instrument for the identification of pathological gamblers. *American Journal of Psychiatry, 144,* 1184–1188.

Lesieur, H. R., & Blume, S. B. (1990). Characteristics of pathological gamblers identified among patients in a psychiatric admissions service. *Hospital and Community Psychiatry, 41,* 1009–1012.

Lesieur, H. R., Blume, S. B., & Zoppa, R. M. (1986). Alcoholism, drug abuse, and gambling. *Alcoholism: Clinical and Experimental Research, 40,* 33–38.

Lesieur, H. R., Cross, J., Frank, M., Welch, M., White, C. M., Rubenstein, G., Moseley, K., & Mark, M. (1991). Gambling and pathological gambling among university students. *Addictive Behaviors, 16,* 517–527.

Lesieur, H. R., & Heineman, M. (1988). Pathological gambling among youthful multiple substance abusers in a therapeutic community. *British Journal of Addiction, 83,* 765–771.

Lesieur, H. R., & Klein, R. (1987). Pathological gambling among high school students. *Addictive Behaviors, 12,* 129–135.

Lesnik-Oberstein, M., & Cohen, L. (1984). Cognitive style, sensation seeking, and assortative mating. *Journal of Personality and Social Psychology, 46,* 112–117.

Lesser, I. M., Mena, I., Boone, K. B., Miller, B. L., Mehringer, C. M., & Wohl, M. (1994). Reduction of cerebral blood flow in older depressed patients. *Archives of General Psychiatry, 51,* 677–686.

Lester, D. (1994). Access to gambling opportunities and compulsive gambling. *The International Journal of the Addictions, 29,* 1611–1616.

Levin, A. P., Saoud, J. B., Straiman, T., Gorman, J. M., Fyer, A. J., Crawford, R., & Liebowitz, M. R. (1993). Response of 'generalized' and 'discrete' social phobics during public speaking. *Journal of Anxiety Disorders, 7,* 207–221.

Levy, D. L., Holzman, P. S., Mathysse, S., & Mendell, N. R. (1993). Eye tracking dysfunction and schizophrenia: A critical perspective. *Schizophrenia Bulletin, 19,* 461–497.

Levy, D. L., Holzman, P. S., Mathysse, S., & Mendell, N. R. (1994). Eye tracking and schizophrenia: A selective review. *Schizophrenia Bulletin, 20,* 47–62.

Lewine, R. R. J., Risch, S. C., Risbe, E., Stipetic, M., Jewart, D., Eccard, M., Caudle, J., & Pollard, W. (1991). Lateral ventricle-brain ratio and balance between CSF HVA and 5-HIAA in schizophrenia. *American Journal of Psychiatry, 148,* 1189–1194.

Lewinsohn, P. M., Hoberman, H., & Rosenbaum, M. (1988). A prospective study of risk factors for unipolar depression. *Journal of Abnormal Psychology, 97,* 251–264.

Lewinsohn, P. M., Roberts, R. E., Seeley, J. R., Rohde, P., Gotlib, I. H., & Hops, H. (1994). Adolescent psychopathy: II. Psychosocial risk factors for depression. *Journal of Abnormal Psychology, 103,* 302–315.

Lewinsohn, P. M., Steinmetz, J. L., Larson, D. W., & Franklin, J. (1981). Depression-related cognitions: Antecedent or consequence? *Journal of Abnormal Psychology, 91,* 213–219.

Lewis, C. E., Rice, J., & Helzer, J. E. (1983). Diagnostic interactions: Alcoholism and antisocial personality. *Journal of Nervous and Mental Disease, 171,* 105–113.

Lewis, C. E., Robins, E. N., & Rice, J. (1985). Association of alcoholism with antisocial personality in urban men. *Journal of Nervous and Mental Disease, 173,* 166–174.

Lewis-Fernández, R., & Kleinman, A. (1994). Culture, personality, and psychopathology. *Journal of Abnormal Psychology, 103,* 67–71.

Lezenweger, M. F., & Korfine, L. (1992). Confirming the latent structure and base rate of schizotypy: A taxometric analysis. *Journal of Abnormal Psychology, 101,* 567–571.

Lezenweger, M. F., & Moldin, S. O. (1990). Discerning the latent structure of hypothetical psychosis proneness through admixture analysis. *Psychiatry Research, 33,* 243–257.

Lidberg, L., Levander, S. E., Schalling, D., & Lidberg, Y. (1978). Urinary catecholamines, stress, and psychopathy: A study of arrested men awaiting trial. *Psychosomatic Medicine, 40,* 116–125.

Lidberg, L., Modlin, I., Oreland, L., Tuck, J. R., & Gillner, A. (1985). Platelet monoamine oxidase activity and psychopathy. *Psychiatry Research, 16,* 339–343.

Liddle, P. F. (1995). Regional cerebral blood flow and subsyndromes of schizophrenia. In J. A. den Boer, H. G. M. Westenberg, & H. M. van Praag (Eds.), *Advances in the neurobiology of schizophrenia* (pp. 189–204). Chichester, England: Wiley.

Liddle, P. F., Friston, K. J., Hirsch, S. R., Jones, T., & Frackowiak, R. S. J. (1992). Patterns of cerebral blood flow in schizophrenia. *British Journal of Psychiatry, 160,* 179–186.

Lieberman, J. A., Jody, D., Alvir, M. J., Ashtari, M., Levy, D. L., Bogerts, B., Degreef, G., Mayerhoff, D. I., & Cooper, T. (1993). Brain morphology, dopamine, and eye-tracking abnormalities in first episode schizophrenia: Prevalence and clinical characteristics. *Archives of General Psychiatry, 50,* 357–368.

Liebowitz, M. R., Gorman, J. M., Fyer, A. J., Levitt, M., Dillon, D., Levey, G., Appleby, I. L., Anderson, S., Paly, M., Davies, S. O., & Klein, D. F. (1985).

Lactate provocation of panic attacks. II. Biochemical and physiologic findings. *Archives of General Psychiatry, 42*, 709–719.

Lim, K. O., Tein, W., Kushner, M., Chow, K., Matsumoto, B., & DeLisi, L. E. (1996). Cortical gray matter volume deficit in patients with first-episode schizophrenia. *American Journal of Psychiatry, 153*, 1548–1553.

Linden, R. D., Pope, H. G., & Jonas, J. M. (1986). Pathological gambling and major affective disorder: Preliminary findings. *Journal of Clinical Psychology, 47*, 201–203.

Lisman, S. A. (1987). Alcohol and human stress: Closer to the truth or time to ask some new questions? In E. Gotheil, K. A. Druley, S. Pashko, & S. P. Weinstein (Eds.), *Stress and addiction* (pp. 61–74). New York: Bruner/Mazel.

Littlewood, R. (1992). Psychiatric diagnosis and racial bias: Empirical and interpretive. *Social Science and Medicine, 34*, 141–149.

Lloyd, G. (1989). Somatization: A psychiatrist's perspective. *Journal of Psychosomatic Research, 33*, 665–669.

Loebel, A. D., Lieberman, J. A., Alvir, J. M. J., Meyerkoff, D. I., Geisler, S. H., & Szymankski, S. R. (1992). Duration of psychosis and outcome in first-episode schizophrenia. *American Journal of Psychiatry, 149*, 1183–1188.

London, E. D., Broussole, E. P. M., Links, J. M., Wong, D. F., Cascella, N. G., Dennals, R. F., Sano, M., Herning, R., Snyder, F. R., Rippetoe, L. R., Toring, T. J. K., Jaffe, J. H., & Wagner, H. N. (1990a). Morphine-induced metabolic changes in human brain. *Archives of General Psychiatry, 47*, 73–80.

London, E. D., Cascella, N. G., Wong, D. F., Phillips, R. L., Dennals, R. F., Links, J. M., Herning, R., Grayson, R., Jaffe, J. H., & Wagner, H. N. (1990b). Cocaine-induced reduction of glucose utilization in human brain. *Archives of General Psychiatry, 47*, 567–574.

Loney, J., Whaley-Klahn, M. A., Kossler, T., & Conboy, J. (1983). Hyperactive boys and their brothers at 21: Predictors of aggressive and antisocial outcome. In K. T. Van Dusen & S. A. Mednick (Eds.), *Prospective studies of crime and delinquency* (pp. 181–207). Boston: Kluwer-Nijhoff.

Loranger, A. W., Sartorius, N., Andreoli, A., Berger, P., Buchheim, P., Channabasavanna, S. M., Coid, B., Dahl, A., Diekstra, R. F. W., Ferguson, B., Jacobsberg, L. B., Mombour, W., Pull, C., Ono, Y., & Regier, D. A. (1994). The interactional personality disorder examination: The World Health Organization/Alcohol, Drug Abuse and Mental Health Administration International Pilot Study of Personality Disorders. *Archives of General Psychiatry, 51*, 215–224.

Lorenz, V. C., & Shuttlesworth, D. E. (1983). The impact of pathological gambling on the spouse of the gambler. *Journal of Community Psychology, 11*, 67–76.

Lorr, M. (1986). Classifying psychotics: Dimensional and categorical approaches. In T. Millon & G. L. Klerman (Eds.), *Contemporary directions in psychopathology: Towards the DSM-IV* (pp. 331–345). New York: Guilford Press.

Lorr, M., Klett, C. J., & McNair, D. M. (1963). *Syndromes of psychosis.* Oxford, England: Pergamon Press.

Lowenfeld, B. H. (1979). Personality dimensions of the pathological gambler. Ph.D. dissertation, University of Kent State. *Dissertation Abstracts International, 40*, 456B.

Lubin, B., Van Witlock, R., & Zuckerman, M. (in press). Affect traits in differential diagnosis of anxiety, depressive, and schizophrenic disorders using the Multiple Affect Adjective Check List-Revised. *Assessment*.

Luborsky, L., Diguer, L., Luborsky, E., McLellan, A. T., Woody, G., & Alexander, L. (1993). Psychological health-sickness (PHS) as a predictor of outcomes in dynamic psychotherapies. *Journal of Consulting and Clinical Psychology, 61*, 542–548.

Lumley, M. A., & Roby, K. J. (1995). Alexithymia and pathological gambling. *Psychotherapy and Psychosomatics, 63*, 201–206.

Luntz, B. K., & Widom, C. S. (1994). Antisocial personality in abused and neglected children grown up. *American Journal of Psychiatry, 151*, 670–674.

Luria, A. R. (1980). *Higher cortical function in man* (2nd ed.). New York: Basic Books.

Luthar, S. S., Anton, S. F., Merikangas, K. R., & Rounsaville, B. J. (1992). Vulnerability to substance abuse and psychopathology among siblings of opioid abusers. *Journal of Nervous and Mental Disease, 180*, 153–161.

Luthar, S. S., Merikangas, K. R., & Rounsaville, B. J. (1993). Parental psychopathology and disorders in offspring. *Journal of Nervous and Mental Disease, 181*, 351–357.

Lykken, D. T. (1957). A study of anxiety in the sociopathic personality. *Journal of Abnormal and Social Psychology, 55*, 6–10.

Lykken, D. T. (1982). Research with twins: The concept of emergenesis. *Psychophysiology, 19*, 361–373.

Lykken, D. T. (1995). *The antisocial personality disorders*. Hillsdale, NJ: Erlbaum.

Lyons, M. J. (1996). A twin study of self-reported criminal behaviour. In G. R. Bock & J. A. Goode (Eds.), *Genetics of criminal and antisocial behaviours* (pp. 61–70). Chichester, England: Wiley.

Lyons, M. J., Eisen, S. A., Goldberg, J., True, W., Lin, N., Meyer, J. M., Toomey, R., Faraone, S. V., Merla-Ramos, M., & Tsuang, M. T. (1998). A registry-based twin study of depression in men. *Archives of General Psychiatry, 52*, 906–915.

Lyons, M. J., True, W. R., Eisen, S. A., Goldberg, J., Meyer, J. M., Faraone, S. V., Eaves, L. J., & Tsuang, M. T. (1995). Differential heritability of adult and juvenile antisocial traits. *Archives of General Psychiatry, 52*, 906–915.

Maas, J. W., Bowden, C. L., Miller, A. L., Javors, M. A., Funderburg, L. G., Berman, N., & Weintraub, S. T. (1997). Schizophrenia, psychosis, and cerebral spinal fluid homovanillic acid concentrations. *Schizophrenia Bulletin, 23*, 147–154.

Maas, J. W., Koslow, S. H., Katz, M. M., Bowden, C. L., Gibbons, R. L., Stokes, P. E., Robins, E., & Davis, J. M. (1984). Pretreatment neurotransmitter metabolite levels and the response to tricyclic antidepressant drugs. *American Journal of Psychiatry, 141,* 1159–1171.

Machizawa, S. (1992). Neurasthenia in Japan. *Psychiatric Annals, 22,* 190–191.

Maden, T., Swinton, M., & Gunn, J. (1992). Gambling in young offenders. *Criminal Behaviour and Mental Health, 2,* 300–308.

Maes, M., Jacobs, M. P., Suy, E., Minner, B., Leclercq, C., Christiaens, F., & Raus, L. (1990). Suppressant effects of dexamethasone on the availability of plasma L-tryptophan and tyrosine in healthy controls and in depressed patients. *Acta Psychiatrica Scandinavica, 81,* 19–23.

Maes, M., & Meltzer, H. Y. (1995). The serotonin hypothesis of major depression. In C. E. Bloom & D. J. Kupfer (Eds.), *Psychopharmacology: The fourth generation of progress* (pp. 933–944). New York: Raven Press.

Magnusson, D. (1987). Individual development in an interactional perspective. In D. Magnusson (Ed.), *Paths through life.* Hillsdale, NJ: Erlbaum.

Magnusson, D. (1996). The patterning of antisocial behavior and autonomic reactivity. In D. M. Stoff & R. B. Cairns (Eds.), *Aggression and violence: Genetic and biosocial perspectives* (pp. 291–308). Hillsdale, NJ: Erlbaum.

Magnusson, D., & Bergman, L. R. (1988). Individual and variable-based approaches to longitudinal research on early risk-factors. In M. Rutter (Ed.), *Studies of psychosocial risk: The power of longitudinal data.* Cambridge, England: Cambridge University Press.

Magnusson, D., & Bergman, L. R. (1990). A pattern approach to the study of pathways from childhood to adulthood. In L. Robins & M. Rutter (Eds.), *Straight and devious pathways from childhood to adulthood* (pp. 101–115). Cambridge, England: Cambridge University Press.

Magnusson, D., Stattin, H., & Dunner, A. (1983). Aggression and criminality in a longitudinal perspective. In K. T. Van Dusen & S. A. Mednick (Eds.), *Prospective studies of delinquency* (pp. 277–301). Boston: Kluwer-Nijhoff.

Maher, B. A., & Spitzer, M. (1993). Delusions. In C. G. Costello (Ed.), *Symptoms in schizophrenia* (pp. 92–120). New York: Wiley.

Maier, S. F., & Seligman, M. E. P. (1976). Learned helplessness: Theory and evidence. *Journal of Experimental Psychology, 103,* 3–46.

Maier, W. (1995). Genetic heterogeneity and phenotype variation of schizophrenia. In H. Häfner & W. F. Gattaz (Eds.), *Search for the causes of schizophrenia* (Vol. III, pp. 157–185). Berlin, Germany: Springer-Verlag.

Maier, W., Lichtermann, D., Mingus, J., Hallmayer, J., Heun, R., Benkert, O., & Levinson, D. F. (1993). Continuity and discontinuity of affective disorders and schizophrenia: Results of a controlled family study. *Archives of General Psychiatry, 50,* 871–883.

Major, L. F., & Murphy, D. L. (1978). Platelet and plasma amine oxidase activity in alcoholic individuals. *British Journal of Psychiatry, 132,* 548–554.

Malatesta, V. J., Sutker, P. B., & Treiber, F. A. (1981). Sensation seeking and chronic public drunkenness. *Journal of Consulting and Clinical Psychology, 49,* 292–294.

Malkin, D., & Syme, G. J. (1986). Personality and problem gambling. *The International Journal of the Addictions, 21,* 267–272.

Mannuzza, S., Klein, R. G., Bonagura, N., Malloy, P., Giampino, T. L., & Addalli, K. A. (1991). Hyperactive boys almost grown up. *Archives of General Psychiatry, 48,* 77–83.

Mannuzza, S., Schneier, F. R., Chapman, T. F., Liebowitz, M. R., Klein, D. F., & Fyer, A. J. (1995). Generalized social phobia: Reliability and validity. *Archives of General Psychiatry, 52,* 230–237.

Manschreck, T. C. (1993). Psychomotor abnormalities. In C. G. Costello (Ed.), *Symptoms of schizophrenia* (pp. 261–290). New York: Wiley.

Manu, P., Lane, T. J., & Matthews, D. A. (1988). The frequency of the chronic fatigue syndrome in patients with symptoms of persistent fatigue. *Annals of Internal Medicine, 109,* 554–556.

Marais, J., Hans, S. L., Auerbach, J. G., & Auerbach, A. G. (1993). Children at risk for schizophrenia: The Jerusalem infant development study. *Archives of General Psychiatry, 50,* 797–809.

Marengo, J. T., Harrow, M., & Edell, W. S. (1993). Thought disorganization. In C. G. Costello (Ed.), *Symptoms of schizophrenia* (pp. 27–55). New York: Wiley.

Marks, I. M. (1987). Behavioral aspects of panic disorder. *American Journal of Psychiatry, 144,* 1160–1165.

Marks, I. M. (1990). Learning and unlearning fear: A clinical and evolutionary perspective. *Neuroscience and Behavioral Reviews, 14,* 365–384.

Marzuk, P. M., Tardiff, K., Leon, A. C., Stajic, M., Morgan, E. B., & Mann, J. J. (1992). Prevalence of cocaine use among residents of New York City who committed suicide during a one-year period. *American Journal of Psychiatry, 149,* 371–375.

Maser, J. D., Kaelber, C., & Weise, R. E. (1991). International use and attitudes toward DSM-III and DSM-III-R: Growing consensus. *Journal of Abnormal Psychology, 100,* 271–279.

Mason, J. W., Kosten, T. R., & Giller, E. L. (1991). Multidimensional hormonal discrimination of paranoid schizophrenic from bipolar manic patients. *Biological Psychiatry, 29,* 457–466.

Mason, P., Harrison, G., Glazebrook, C., Medley, I., & Croudace, T. (1996). The course of schizophrenia over 13 years. *British Journal of Psychiatry, 169,* 580–586.

Mason, P., & Wilkinson, G. (1996). The prevalence of psychiatric morbidity: OPCS survey of psychiatric morbidity in Great Britain. *British Journal of Psychology, 168,* 1–3.

Masse, L. C., & Tremblay, R. E. (1997). Behavior of boys in kindergarten and the onset of substance abuse during adolescence. *Archives of General Psychiatry, 54,* 62–68.

Mathews, A. M., Gelder, M. G., & Johnston, D. W. (1981). *Agoraphobia: Nature and treatment.* New York: Guilford Press.

Mathews, A. M., Mogg, K., Kentish, J., & Eysenck, M. (1995). Effect of psychological treatment on cognitive bias in generalized anxiety disorder. *Behaviour Research and Therapy, 33,* 293–303.

Mathysse, S. (1973). Antipsychotic drug actions: A clue to the neuropathology of schizophrenia? *Federation Proceedings, 32,* 200–205.

Mattson, A., Schalling, D., Olweus, D., Low, H., & Svensson, J. (1980). Plasma testosterone, aggressive behavior, and personality dimensions in young male delinquents. *Journal of the American Academy of Child Psychiatry, 19,* 476–490.

Mayberg, H. S. (1994). Frontal lobe dysfunction in secondary depression. *Journal of Neuropsychiatry, 6,* 428–442.

Maziade, M., Martinez, M., Rodrigue, C., Gauthier, B., Trembley, G., Fournier, C., Bissonnette, L., Simard, C., Roy, M. H., Rouillard, E., & Merette, C. (1997). Childhood early adolescence-onset and adult-onset schizophrenia. *British Journal of Psychiatry, 170,* 27–30.

Maziade, M., Roy, M.-A., Martinez, M., Cliche, D., Fournier, J.-P., Garneau, Y., Nicole, L., Montgrain, N., Dion, C., Ponton, A.-M., Potrin, A., Lavalle, J.-C., Pires, A., Bouchard, S., Boutin, P., Brisebois, F., & Merette, C. (1995). *American Journal of Psychiatry, 152,* 1458–1463.

Mazure, C. M. (1995). *Does stress cause mental illness?* Washington, DC: American Psychiatric Press.

McAuliffe, W. F., Rohman, M., & Wechsler, H. (1984). Alcohol, substance use, and other risk factors of impairment in a sample of physicians in training. *Advances in Alcohol and Substance Abuse, 4,* 67–87.

McCord, J. (1986). Instigation and insulation: How families affect antisocial aggression. In D. Olweus, J. Block, & M. Radke-Yarrow (Eds.), *Development of antisocial and prosocial behavior: Research, theories, and issues* (pp. 343–357). New York: Academic Press.

McCord, J. (1990). Long-term perspectives on parental absence. In L. Robins & M. Rutter (Eds.), *Straight and devious pathways from childhood to adulthood* (pp. 116–134). Cambridge, England: Cambridge University Press.

McCord, W., & McCord, J. (1960). *Origins of alcoholism.* Stanford, CA: Stanford University Press.

McCormick, R. A., Taber, J., Kruedelbach, N., & Russo, A. (1987). Personality profiles of hospitalized pathological gamblers: The California Personality Inventory. *Journal of Clinical Psychology, 43,* 521–527.

McCrady, B. S. (1994). Alcoholics anonymous and behavior therapy: Can habits be treated as diseases? *Journal of Consulting and Clinical Psychology, 62,* 1159–1166.

McGlashan, T. H., & Fenton, W. S. (1992). The positive-negative distinction in schizophrenia: Review of natural history validations. *Archives of General Psychiatry, 49,* 63–72.

McGue, M. (1993). From proteins to cognitions: The behavioral genetics of alcoholism. In R. Plomin & G. E. McClearn (Eds.), *Nature, nurture, and psy-*

chology (pp. 245–268). Washington, DC: American Psychological Association.

McGuffin, P. (1991). Models of heritability and genetic transmission. In H. Häfner & W. F. Gattaz (Eds.), *Search for the causes of schizophrenia* (Vol. II, pp. 109–125). Berlin, Germany: Springer-Verlag.

McGuffin, P., Asherson, P., Owen, M., & Farmer, A. (1994). The strength of the genetic effect. Is there room for an environmental influence in the aetiology of schizophrenia? *British Journal of Psychiatry, 164*, 593–599.

McGuffin, P., Farmer, A. E., Gottesman, I. I., Murray, R. M., & Reveley, A. M. (1984). Twin concordance for operationally defined schizophrenia. *Archives of General Psychiatry, 41*, 541–545.

McGuffin, P., & Katz, R. (1989). The genetics of depression and manic-depressive disorder. *British Journal of Psychiatry, 155*, 294–304.

McGuffin, P., & Katz, R. (1993). Genes, adversity, and depression. In R. Plomin & G. E. McClearn (Eds.), *Nature, nurture, and psychology* (pp. 217–230). Washington, DC: American Psychological Association.

McGuffin, P., Katz, R., Watkins, S., & Rutherford, J. (1996). A hospital-based twin register of the heritability of DSM-IV unipolar depression. *Archives of General Psychiatry, 53*, 129–136.

McGuffin, P., Owen, M. J., Donovan, M. C., Thapar, A., & Gottesman, I. I. (1994). *Seminars in psychiatric genetics.* London: Gaskell.

McGuire, P. K., Shah, G. M. S., & Murray, R. M. (1993). Increased blood flow in Broca's area during auditory hallucinations. *The Lancet, 342*, 703–706.

McLellan, A. T., Alterman, A. I., Metzger, D. S., Grissom, G. R., Woody, G. E., Luborsky, L., & O'Brien, C. P. (1994). Similarity of outcome predictors across opiate, cocaine, and alcohol treatments: Role of treatment services. *Journal of Consulting and Clinical Psychology, 62*, 1141–1158.

McLeod, J. D. (1994). Anxiety disorders and marital quality. *Journal of Nervous and Mental Disease, 180*, 760–766.

McNally, R. J. (1990). Psychological approaches to panic disorder: A review. *Psychological Bulletin, 108*, 403–419.

McNally, R. J. (1994). *Panic disorder: A critical analysis.* New York: Guilford Press.

McNally, R. J. (1996). Anxiety sensitivity is distinguishable from trait anxiety. In R. M. Rapee (Ed.), *Current controversies in the anxiety disorders* (pp. 214–227). New York: Guilford Press.

McNally, R. J., Kaspi, S. P., Riemann, B. C., & Zeitlin, S. B. (1990). Selective processing of threat cues in posttraumatic stress disorder. *Journal of Abnormal Psychology, 99*, 396–402.

Mednick, S. A. (1970). Breakdown in individuals at high risk for schizophrenia: Possible predispositional perinatal factors. *Mental Hygiene, 54*, 50–63.

Mednick, S. A., Gabrielli, W. F., Jr., & Hutchings, B. (1987). Genetic factors in the etiology of criminal behavior. In S. A. Mednick, T. E. Moffitt, & S. A. Stack (Eds.), *The causes of crime: New biological approaches* (pp. 74–91). New York: Cambridge University Press.

Mednick, S. A., Machon, R. A., & Huttunen, M. O. (1988). Adult schizophrenia following prenatal exposure to an influenza epidemic. *Archives of General Psychiatry, 45,* 189–192.

Meehl, P. E. (1962). Schizotaxia, schizotypy, schizophrenia. *American Psychologist, 12,* 827–838.

Meehl, P. E. (1986). Diagnostic taxa as open constructs: Metatheoretical and statistical questions about reliability and construct validity in the grand strategy of nosological revision. In T. Millon & G. L. Klerman (Eds.), *Contemporary directions in psychopathology: Toward the DSM-IV* (pp. 215–231). New York: Guilford Press.

Meehl, P. E. (1989). Schizotaxia revisited. *Archives of General Psychiatry, 46,* 935–944.

Meehl, P. E. (1990). Toward an integrated theory of schizotaxia, schizotypy, and schizophrenia. *Journal of Personality Disorders, 4,* 1–99.

Meehl, P. E. (1993). The origins of some of my conjectures concerning schizophrenia. In L. J. Chapman, J. P. Chapman, & D. C. Fowles (Eds.), *Progress in experimental personality and psychopathology research* (Vol. 16, pp. 1–10). New York: Springer.

Meehl, P. E. (1995). Bootstraps taxometrics: Solving the classification problem in psychopathology. *American Psychologist, 50,* 266–275.

Meehl, P. E., & Rosen, A. (1955). Antecedent probability and the efficiency of psychometric signs, patterns, or cutting scores. *Psychological Bulletin, 52,* 194–216.

Mel, H., Kramer, I., Gritsenko, I., Kottler, M., & Ebstein, R. P. (1997). Association between dopamine receptor (D4DR) exon III repeat polymorphism and drug abuse. Unpublished manuscript cited in Ebstein & Belmaker, 1997.

Meltzer, H. Y. (1989). Clinical studies on the mechanism of action of clozapine: The dopamine-serotonin hypothesis of schizophrenia. *Psychopharmacology, 99,* 518–527.

Meltzer, H. Y., & Lowry, M. T. (1987). The serotonin hypothesis of depression. In H. Y. Meltzer (Ed.), *Psychopharmacology: The third generation of progress* (pp. 513–526). New York: Raven Press.

Mendelson, M. (1992). Psychodynamics. In E. S. Paykel (Ed.), *Handbook of affective disorders* (2nd ed. pp. 195–207). New York: Guilford Press.

Mendlewicz, J. (1994). Molecular genetic studies in affective illness. In D. F. Papolos & H. M. Lachman (Eds.), *Genetic studies in affective disorders* (pp. 105–116). New York: Wiley.

Mendlewicz, J., Papdimitroiu, G., & Wilmotte, J. (1993). Family study of panic disorder: Comparison with generalized anxiety disorder, major depression and normal subjects. *Psychiatric Genetics, 3,* 73–78.

Menzies, R. G., & Clarke, J. C. (1993). The etiology of childhood water phobia. *Behaviour Research and Therapy, 31,* 499–501.

Menzies, R. G., & Clarke, J. C. (1995). The etiology of acrophobia and its relationship to severity and individual response patterns. *Behaviour Research and Therapy, 33,* 795–803.

Merckelbach, H., Arntz, A., Arrindele, W. A., & De Jong, P. J. (1992). Pathways to spider phobia. *Behaviour Research and Therapy, 30,* 543–546.

Merckelbach, H., Arntz, A., & De Jong, P. (1991). Conditioning experiences in spider phobics. *Behaviour Research and Therapy, 32,* 643–645.

Milgram, P., Mancl, L., King, B., & Weinstein, P. (1995). Origins of childhood dental fear. *Behaviour Research and Therapy, 33,* 313–319.

Milkowitz, D. J., & Goldstein, M. J. (1993). Mapping the intrafamilial environment of the schizophrenic patient. In R. L. Cromwell & C. R. Snyder (Eds.), *Schizophrenia: Origins, processes, treatment, and outcome* (pp. 313–332). New York: Oxford University Press.

Miller, H. L., Delgado, P. L., Salomon, R. M., Berman, R., Krystal, J. H., Heninger, G. R., & Charney, D. S. (1996). Clinical and biochemical effects of catecholamine depletion on antidepressant induced remission of depression. *Archives of General Psychiatry, 53,* 117–128.

Miller, I. W. III, & Norman, W. H. (1986). Persistence of depressive cognitions within a subgroup of depressed inpatients. *Cognitive Therapy and Research, 10,* 211–224.

Miller, M. A., & Westermeyer, J. (1996). Gambling in Minnesota. *American Journal of Psychiatry, 153,* 845.

Millon, T. (1991). Classification in psychopathology: Rationale, alternatives and standards. *Journal of Abnormal Psychology, 100,* 245–261.

Mineka, S., Davidson, M., Cool, M., & Kier, R. (1984). Observational conditioning of snake fear in Rhesus monkeys. *Journal of Abnormal Psychology, 93,* 355–372.

Mineka, S., & Zinbarg, R. (1995). Conditioning and ethological models of phobia. In R. Heimberg, M. Liebowitz, D. Hope, & F. Schneier (Eds.), *Social phobia: Diagnosis, assessment and treatment* (pp. 134–161). New York: Guilford Press.

Mirowski, J., & Ross, C. E. (1989). Psychiatric diagnosis as reified measurement. *Journal of Health and Social Behavior, 30,* 11–25.

Mirsky, A. F., Kugelmass, S., Ingraham, L. J., Frenkel, E., & Nathan, M. (1995). Overview and summary: Twenty-five year followup of high risk children. *Schizophrenia Bulletin, 21,* 227–239.

Mitchell, P. (1996). Validity of the CORE: I. A neuroendocrinological strategy. In G. Parker & D. Hadzi-Pavlovic (Eds.), *Melancholia: A disorder of movement and mood* (pp. 138–148). Cambridge, England: Cambridge University Press.

Moffitt, T. E. (1993). Adolesence-limited and life-course persistent antisocial behavior: A developmental taxonomy. *Psychological Review, 100,* 674–701.

Mogg, K., Bradley, B. P., Millon, N., & White, J. (1995). A follow-up study of cognitive-bias in generalized anxiety disorder. *Behavior Research and Therapy, 33,* 927–935.

Moldin, S. O. (1997). Maddening hunt for madness genes. *Nature Genetics, 17,* 127–129.

Moldin, S. O., & Gottesman, I. I. (1997). At issue: Genes, experience, and chance in schizophrenia—Positioning for the 21st century. *Schizophrenia Bulletin, 23*, 547–561.

Monroe, S. M., & Simons, A. D. (1991). Diathesis-stress theories in the context of life-stress research: Implications for the depressive disorders. *Psychological Bulletin, 110*, 406–425.

Mookerjee, H. N. (1986). Comparison of some personality characteristics of male problem drinkers in rural Tennessee. *Journal of Alcohol and Drug Education, 31*, 23–28.

Moras, K., & Barlow, D. H. (1992). Dimensional approaches to diagnosis and the problem of anxiety and depression. In W. Fiegenbaum, A. Ehlers, J. Margraf, & I. Florin (Eds.), *Perspectives and promises of clinical psychology* (pp. 23–37). New York: Plenum Press.

Moravec, J. D., & Munley, P. H. (1983). Psychological test findings in pathological gamblers in treatment. *The International Journal of the Addictions, 18*, 1003–1009.

Mosher, L. R., Pollin, W., & Stabenau, J. R. (1971). Identical twins discordant for schizophrenia: Neurologic findings. *Archives of General Psychiatry, 24*, 422–430.

Moss, H. B., Yao, J. K., & Panzak, G. L. (1990). Serotonergic responsivity and behavioral dimensions in antisocial personality disorder with substance abuse. *Biological Psychiatry, 28*, 325–338.

Mowrer, O. H. (1950). *Learning theory and personality dynamics.* New York: Arnold Press.

Mueser, K. T., Bellack, A. S., & Blanchard, J. J. (1992). Comorbidity of schizophrenia and substance abuse: Implications for treatment. *Journal of Consulting and Clinical Psychology, 60*, 845–856.

Muramatsu, T., Higuchi, S., Murayama, M., Matsushita, S., & Hayashida, M. (1996). Association between alcoholism and the dopamine D4 receptor gene. *Journal of Medical Genetics, 33*, 113–115.

Muris, P., Steerneman, P., Merckelbach, H., & Meesters, C. (1996). The role of parental fearfulness and modeling in children's fear. *Behaviour Research and Therapy, 34*, 265–268.

Murphy, D. L., Aulakh, C. S., Garrick, N. A., & Sunderland, T. (1987). Monoamine oxidase inhibitors as antidepressants: Implications for the mechanism of action of antidepressants and the psychology of affective disorders and some related disorders. In H. Y. Meltzer (Ed.), *Psychopharmacology: The third generation of progress* (pp. 545–552). New York: Raven Press.

Musto, D. F. (1992). Cocaine's history, especially the American experience. In G. R. Bock & J. Whelan (Eds.), *Cocaine: Scientific and social dimensions* (pp. 7–14). Chichester, England: Wiley.

Nachon, I. (1988). Hemispheric function in violent offenders. In T. E. Moffitt & S. A. Mednick (Eds.), *Biological contributions to crime* (pp. 55–67). Dordrecht, The Netherlands: Martinus Nijhoff.

Naftolowitz, D. F., Vaughn, E. V., Ranc, J., & Tancer, M. E. (1993). Response to alcohol in social phobia. *Anxiety, 1,* 96–99.

Nair, T. R., Christensen, J. D., Kingsbury, S. J., Kumar, N. G., Terry, W. M., & Garver, D. L. (1997). Progression of cerebroventricular enlargement and the subtyping of schizophrenia. *Psychiatry Research: Neuroimaging Section, 74,* 141–151.

Nasrallah, H. A. (1991). Magnetic resonance imaging of the brain: Clinical and research applications in schizophrenia. In H. Häfner & W. F. Gattaz (Eds.), *Search for the causes of schizophrenia* (Vol. II, pp. 257–281). Berlin, Germany: Springer-Verlag.

Negrao, A. B. (1997). Mood disorder across the continents. *Molecular Psychiatry, 2,* 439–441.

Neighbors, H. W., Jackson, J. S., Campbell, L., & Williams, D. (1989). The influence of racial factors on psychiatric diagnosis: A review and suggestions for research. *Community Mental Health Journal, 25,* 301–311.

Neiswanger, K., Hill, S. Y., & Kaplan, B. B. (1995). Association and linkage studies of the TAQIA1 allele at the dopamine D2 receptor gene in samples of female and male alcoholics. *American Journal of Medical Genetics, 60,* 267–271.

Nelson-Gray, R. O. (1991). DSM-IV: Empirical guidelines from psychometrics. *Journal of Abnormal Psychology, 100,* 308–315.

Nerviano, J. (1976). Common personality problems among alcoholic males: A multivariate study. *Journal of Consulting and Clinical Psychology, 44,* 104–110.

Nesse, R. M., Curtis, G. C., Thyer, B. A., McCann, D. S., Huber-Smith, M. J., & Knopf, R. F. (1985). Endocrine and cardiovascular responses during phobic anxiety. *Psychosomatic Medicine, 47,* 320–332.

Nestadt, G., Romanski, A. J., Brown, C. H., Chahal, R., Merchast, A., Folstein, M. F., Gruenberg, E. M., & McHugh, P. R. (1991). DSM-III compulsive personality disorder: An epidemiological survey. *Psychological Medicine, 21,* 461–471.

Nestadt, G., Romanski, A. J., Samuels, J. F., Folstein, M. F., & McHugh, P. R. (1992). The relationships between personality and DSM-III Axis I disorders in the population: Results from an epidemiological survey. *American Journal of Psychiatry, 149,* 1228–1233.

Nestler, E. J., Bergson, C. M., Guitart, X., & Hope, B. T. (1993). Regulation of neural gene expression in opiate and cocaine addiction. In R. Grzanna & R. M. Brown (Eds.), *Activation of immediate early genes by drugs of abuse* (pp. 92–116). (Research Monograph No. 125.) Rockville, MD: National Institute of Drug Abuse.

Newcomb, M. D., & Bentler, P. (1990). Antecedents and consequences of cocaine use: An eight-year study from early adolescence to young adulthood. In L. Robbins & M. Rutter (Eds.), *Straight and devious pathways from childhood to adulthood* (pp. 158–181). Cambridge, England: Cambridge University Press.

Newman, C. S., Grimes, K., Walker, E. F., & Baum, K. (1995). Developmental pathways to schizophrenia: Behavioral subtypes. *Journal of Abnormal Psychology, 104*, 558–566.

Newman, J. P., & Kosson, D. S. (1986). Passive avoidance learning in psychopathic and nonpsychopathic offenders. *Journal of Abnormal Psychology, 95*, 252–256.

Newman, J. P., Patterson, C., & Kosson, D. (1987). Response perseveration in psychopaths. *Journal of Abnormal Psychology, 96*, 145–148.

Noble, E. P. (1996). The gene that rewards alcoholism. *Scientific American,* 52–61.

Noble, E. P., Blum, B., Khalsa, M. E., Ritchie, T., Montgomery, A., Wood, R. C., Fitch, R. J., Ozkaragoz, T., Sheridan, P. J., Anglin, M. D., Paredes, A., Treiman, L. J., & Sparkes, R. S. (1993). Allelic association of the D2 dopamine receptor gene with cocaine dependence. *Drug and Alcohol Dependence, 33*, 271–285.

Nobler, M. S., Sackheim, H. A., Prohovnik, I., Moeller, J. R., Mukherjee, S., Schnur, D. B., Prudic, J., & Devanand, D. P. (1994). Regional blood flow in mood disorders III: Treatment and clinical response. *Archives of General Psychiatry, 51*, 884–897.

Noelen-Hoeksemi, S. (1990). *Sex differences in depression.* Stanford, CA: Stanford University Press.

Nopoulos, P., Torres, I., Flaum, M., Amdreasen, N. C., Ehrhardt, J. C., & Yuh, W. T. C. (1995). Brain morphology in first episode schizophrenia. *American Journal of Psychiatry, 152*, 1721–1806.

Nordahl, T. E. (1990). Cerebral glucose differences in patients with panic disorder. *Neuropsychopharmacology, 3*, 261–272.

Norman, R. M. G., & Malla, A. K. (1991). Subjective stress in schizophrenia. *Social Psychiatry and Psychiatric Epidemiology, 26*, 212–216.

Norman, R. M. G., & Malla, A. K. (1993a). Stressful life events and schizophrenia II: Conceptual and methodological issues. *British Journal of Psychiatry, 162*, 166–174.

Norman, R. M. G., & Malla, A. K. (1993b). Stressful life events and schizophrenia I: A review of the literature. *British Journal of Psychiatry, 162*, 161–166.

Noyes, R., Clancy, J., Hoenk, P. R., & Slymen, D. J. (1980). The prognosis of anxiety neurosis. *Archives of General Psychiatry, 37*, 173–178.

Noyes, R., Clarkson, C., Crowe, R. R., Yates, W. R., & McChesney, C. M. (1987). A family study of generalized anxiety disorder. *American Journal of Psychiatry, 144*, 1019–1024.

Noyes, R., Crowe, R. R., Harris, E. L., Hamra, B. J., McChesney, C. M., & Chaudry, D. R. (1986). Relationship between panic disorder and agoraphobia: A family study. *Archives of General Psychiatry, 43*, 227–232.

Nuechterlein, K. H. (1987). Vulnerability models for schizophrenia: State of the art. In H. Häfner & W. F. Gattaz (Eds.), *Search for the causes of schizophrenia* (pp. 297–316). Berlin, Germany: Springer-Verlag.

Nuechterlein, K. H., & Dawson, M. E. (1995). Neuropsychological and psychophysiological approaches to schizophrenia. In F. E. Bloom & D. J. Kupfer (Eds.), *Psychopharmacology: The fourth generation of progress* (pp. 1235–1244). New York: Raven Press.

Nuechterlein, K. H., Dawson, M. E., Gitlin, M., Ventura, J., Goldstein, M. J., Snyder, K. S., Yee, C. M., & Mintz, J. (1992). Developmental processes in schizophrenic disorders: Longitudinal studies of vulnerability and stress. *Schizophrenia Bulletin, 18,* 387–425.

Nuechterlein, K. H., Dawson, M. E., Ventura, J., Fogelson, D., Gitlin, M., & Mintz, J. (1991). Testing vulnerability models: Stability of potential vulnerability indicators across clinical state. In H. Häfner & W. F. Gattaz (Eds.), *Search for the causes of schizophrenia* (Vol. II, pp. 177–191). Berlin, Germany: Springer-Verlag.

Nurnberger, J. I., Jr., & Gershon, E. S. (1992). Genetics. In E. S. Paykel (Ed.), *Handbook of affective disorders* (pp. 131–148). New York: Guilford Press.

Nurnberger, J. I., Jr., Hamovit, J., Hibbs, E. D., Pellegrini, D., Guroff, J. J., Maxwell, M. E., Smith, A., & Gershon, E. S. (1988). A high-risk study of primary affective disorder: Selection of subjects, initial assessment and 1- to 2-year follow-up. In D. L. Dunner, E. S. Gershon, & J. E. Barrett (Eds.), *Relatives at risk for mental disorder* (pp. 161–177). New York: Raven Press.

Nutt, D. J., Glue, P., Lawson, C. W., & Wilson, S. (1990). Flumazenil provocation of panic attacks: Evidence for altered benzodiazepine receptor sensitivity in panic disorder. *Archives of General Psychiatry, 47,* 917–925.

O'Brien, C. P., Eckart, M. J., & Linnoila, M. I. (1995). Pharmacotherapy of alcoholism. In F. E. Bloom & D. J. Kupfer (Eds.), *Psychopharmacology: The fourth generation of progress* (pp. 1745–1755). New York: Raven Press.

O'Connor, S., Bauer, L., Tasman, A., & Hesselbrock, V. (1994). Reduced P3 amplitudes are associated with both a family history of alcoholism and antisocial personality disorder. *Progress in Neuro-Psychopharmacology and Biological Psychiatry, 18,* 1307–1321.

O'Hara, B. F., Smith, S. S., Bird, G., Persico, A. M., Suare, B. K., Cutting, G. R., & Uhl, G. R. (1993). Dopamine D2 receptor RFLPs, haplotypes and their association with substance use in black and caucasian research volunteers. *Human Heredity, 43,* 209–218.

Öhman, A. (1986). Face the beast and fear the face: Animal and social fears as prototypes for evolutionary analyses of emotion. *Psychophysiology, 23,* 123–145.

Oke, A. F., Carver, L. A., & Adams, R. N. (1993). Dopamine initiated disturbances of thalamic information processing in schizophrenia? In R. L. Cromwell & C. R. Snyder (Eds.), *Schizophrenia: Origins, processes, treatment, and outcome* (pp. 31–47). New York: Oxford University Press.

Oldham, J. M., Skodol, A. E., Kellman, H. D., Hyler, S. E., Doidge, N., Rosnick, L., & Gallaher, P. E. (1995). Comorbidity of axis I and axis II disorders. *American Journal of Psychiatry, 152,* 571–578.

Olds, J., & Milner, P. (1954). Positive reinforcement produced by electrical stimulation of septal area and other regions of the rat brain. *Journal of Comparative and Physiological Psychology, 47,* 419–427.

Olin, S., Raine, A., Cannon, T. D., Parnas, J., Schulsinger, F., & Mednick, S. A. (1997). Childhood behavior precursors of schizotypal personality disorder. *Schizophrenia Bulletin, 23,* 93–103.

Olney, J. W., & Farber, N. B. (1995a). Glutamine receptor dysfunction and schizophrenia. *Archives of General Psychiatry, 52,* 998–1007.

Olney, J. W., & Farber, N. B. (1995b). Response to commentaries and to the challenge of building a perfect theory to explain schizophrenia. *Archives of General Psychiatry, 52,* 1019–1024.

Olweus, D. (1987). Testosterone and adrenaline: Aggressive antisocial behavior in normal adolescent males. In S. A. Mednick, T. E. Moffitt, & S. A. Stack (Eds.), *The causes of crime: New biological approaches* (pp. 263–282). Cambridge, England: Cambridge University Press.

O'Neil, P. M., Giacinto, J. P., Woud, L. R., Roitzsch, J. C., Miller, W. C., & Kilpatrick, D. G. (1983). Behavioral, psychological, and historical correlates of MacAndrew scale scores among male alcoholics. *Journal of Behavioral Assessment, 5,* 261–273.

Onstad, S., Skre, I., Torgersen, S., & Kringlen, E. (1991). Twin concordance for DSM-III-R schizophrenia. *Acta Psychiatrica Scandinavica, 83,* 395–401.

Onstad, S., Skre, I. Edvardsen, J., Torgensen, S., & Kringlen, E. (1991). Mental disorders in first-degree relatives of schizophrenics. *Acta Psychiatrica Scandinavica, 83,* 463–467.

Ontiveros, A., Fontaine, R., Breton, G., Fontaine, E. R., & Dery, R. (1989). Correlation of severity of panic disorder and neuroanatomical changes on magnetic resonance imaging. *Journal of Neuropsychiatry and Clinical Neuroscience, 1,* 404–408.

Oreland, L., Hallman, J., von Knorring, L. V., & Edman, G. (1988). Studies of monoamine oxidase in relation to alcohol abuse. In K. Kurujama, A. Takeda, & H. Ishu (Eds.), *Biomedical and social aspects of alcohol and alcoholism* (pp. 207–210). New York: Elsevier Science Publishers.

Ormel, J., Koeter, M. W., Van den Brink, W., & Van de Willige, G. (1991). Recognition, management and course of anxiety and depression in general practice. *Archives of General Psychiatry, 48,* 700–706.

Ormel, J., von Korff, M., Van den Brink, W., Katon, W., Brilman, E., & Oldehinkel, T. (1993). Depression, anxiety, and social disability show synchrony of change in primary care patients. *American Journal of Public Health, 83,* 385–390.

Orr, S. P., Lasko, N. B., Shalev, A. Y., & Pittman, R. K. (1995). Physiologic responses to loud tones in Vietnam veterans with posttraumatic stress disorder. *Journal of Abnormal Psychology, 104,* 75–82.

Orr, S. P., Pittman, R. K., Lasko, N. B., & Herz, L. R. (1993). Psychophysiological assessment of posttraumatic stress disorder imagery in World War II and Korean combat veterans. *Journal of Abnormal Psychology, 102,* 152–159.

Öst, L. G. (1987). Age of onset in different phobias. *Journal of Abnormal Psychology, 96*, 223–229.

Öst, L. G. (1991). Acquisition of blood and injection phobia and anxiety response patterns in clinical patients. *Behaviour Research and Therapy, 29*, 323–332.

Öst, L. G. (1992). Blood and injection phobia: Background and cognitive, physiological, and behavioral variables. *Journal of Abnormal Psychology, 101*, 68–74.

O'Sullivan, D. M., Zuckerman, M., & Kraft, M. (1998). Personality characteristics of male and female participants in team sports. *Personality and Individual Differences, 25*, 119–128.

Pallanti, S., Quercioli, L., & Pazzagli, A. (1997). Relapse in young paranoid schizophrenic patients. A prospective study of stressful life events, P300 measures and coping. *American Journal of Psychiatry, 154*, 792–798.

Papolos, D. F., & Lachman, H. M. (Eds.). (1994). *Genetic studies in affective disorders.* New York: Wiley.

Papp, L. A., Klein, D. F., Martinez, J., Schneier, F., Cole, R., Liebowitz, M. R., Hollander, E., Fyer, A. J., Jorddan, F., & Gorman, J. M. (1993). Diagnostic and substance specificity of carbon-dioxide-induced panic. *American Journal of Psychiatry, 150*, 250–257.

Parker, G. (1979). Parental characteristics in relation to depressive disorders. *British Journal of Psychiatry, 134*, 138–147.

Parker, G. (1992). Early environment. In E. S. Paykel (Ed.), *Handbook of affective disorders* (2nd ed., pp. 171–183). New York: Guilford Press.

Parker, G., & Hadzi-Pavlovic, D. (1996). Development and structure of the CORE system. In G. Parker & D. Hadzi-Pavlovic (Eds.), *Melancholia: A disorder of movement and mood* (pp. 82–129). New York: Guilford Press.

Parker, G., Hadzi-Pavlovic, D., & Boyce, P. (1996). Issues in classification II. Classifying melancholia. In G. Parker & D. Hadzi-Pavlovic (Eds.), *Melancholia: A disorder of movement and mood* (pp. 20–37). New York: Cambridge University Press.

Parker, G., Hadzi-Pavlovic, D., Brodaty, H., Boyce, P., Mitchell, P., Wilhelm, K., & Hickie, I. (1992). Predicting the course of melancholic and nonmelancholic depression: A naturalistic comparison study. *Journal of Nervous and Mental Disease, 180*, 693–702.

Parnas, J., Cannon, T. D., Jacobsen, B., Schulsinger, H., Schulsinger, F., & Mednick, S. A. (1993). Lifetime DSM-III-R diagnostic outcomes in the offspring of schizophrenic mothers. *Archives of General Psychiatry, 50*, 707–714.

Parnas, J., Schulsinger, F., Schulsinger, H., Mednick, S. A., & Teasdale, T. W. (1982). Behavioral precursors of schizophrenic spectrum. *Archives of General Psychiatry, 39*, 658–664.

Parnas, J., Teasdale, T. W., & Schulsinger, H. (1985). Institutional rearing and diagnostic outcome in children of schizophrenic mothers. A prospective high-risk study. *Archives of General Psychiatry, 42*, 762–769.

Patrick, C. J. (1994). Emotion and psychopathy: Startling new insights. *Psychophysiology, 31,* 319–330.

Patrick, C. J., Bradley, M. M., & Lang, P. J. (1993). Emotion in the criminal psychopath: Startle reflex modulation. *Journal of Abnormal Psychology, 102,* 82–92.

Pauls, D. L., Towbin, K. E., Leckman, J. F., Zahner, G. E. P., & Cohen, D. J. (1986). Gilles de la Tourette's syndrome and obsessive-compulsive disorder. *Archives of General Psychiatry, 43,* 1180–1182.

Paykel, E. S., & Cooper, Z. (1992). Life events and social stress. In E. S. Paykel (Ed.), *Handbook of affective disorders* (2nd ed., pp. 149–170). New York: Guilford Press.

Pearlson, G. D., & Schlaepfer, T. E. (1995). Brain imaging in mood disorders. In F. E. Bloom & D. J. Kupfer (Eds.), *Psychopharmacology: The fourth generation of progress* (pp. 1019–1028). New York: Raven Press.

Pearlson, G. D., Wong, D. F., Tune, L. E., Ross, C. A., Chase, G. A., Links, J. M., Dannals, R. F., Wilson, A. A., Ravert, H. T., Wagner, N. N., Jr., & De Paulo, R. (1995). In vivo D2 dopamine receptor density in psychotic and nonpsychotic patients with bipolar disorder. *Archives of General Psychiatry, 52,* 471–477.

Perna, G., Cocchi, S., Bertani, A., Arancio, C., & Bellodi, L. (1995). Sensitivity to 35% CO_2 in healthy first-degree relatives of patients with panic disorder. *American Journal of Psychiatry, 152,* 623–625.

Perris, C. (1992). Bipolar-unipolar distinction. In E. S. Paykel (Ed.), *Handbook of affective disorders* (2nd ed., pp. 57–75). New York: Guilford Press.

Perry, J. C., Lavori, P. W., Pagano, C. J., Hoke, L., & O'Connell, M. E. (1992). Life events and recurrent depression in borderline and antisocial personality disorders. *Journal of Personality Disorders, 6,* 394–407.

Persons, J. B., Burns, D. D., Perloff, J. M., & Miranda, J. (1993). Relationships between symptoms of depression and anxiety and dysfunctional beliefs about achievement and attachment. *Journal of Abnormal Psychology, 102,* 518–524.

Peterson, C., & Seligman, M. E. P. (1984). Causal explanations as a risk factor for depression: Theory and evidence. *Psychological Review, 91,* 347–374.

Pichot, P. (1978). Psychopathic behavior: An historical overview. In R. D. Hare & D. Schalling (Eds.), *Psychopathic behaviour: Approaches to research* (pp. 55–70). Chichester, England: Wiley.

Pickens, R. W., Svikis, D. S., McGue, M., Lykken, D. T., Heston, L. L., & Clayton, P. J. (1991). Heterogeneity in the inheritance of alcoholism: A study of male and female twins. *Archives of General Psychiatry, 48,* 19–41.

Pigott, T. M., Myers, K. R., & Williams, D. A. (1996). Obsessive-compulsive disorder: A neuropsychiatric perspective. In R. M. Rapee (Ed.), *Current controversies in the anxiety disorders* (pp. 134–160). New York: Guilford Press.

Platt, J. J., & Labate, C. (1976). *Heroin addiction: Theory, research, and treatment.* New York: Wiley.

Plomin, R. (1995). Molecular genetics and psychology. *Current Directions in Psychological Science, 4*, 114–117.

Plomin, R., DeFries, J. C., McClearn, G. E., & Rutter, M. (1997). *Behavioral genetics* (3rd ed.). New York: W. H. Freeman.

Plomin, R., Owen, M. J., & McGuffin, P. (1994). The genetic basis of complex human behaviors. *Science, 264*, 1733–1739.

Pohl, R., Yeragani, V., Balon, R., Ortiz, A., & Aleem, A. (1990). Isoproterenol-induced panic: A beta-adrenergic model of panic anxiety. In J. C. Ballenger (Ed.), *Neurobiology of anxiety disorder* (pp. 107–120). New York: Wiley-Liss.

Pohl, R., Yeragini, V., Balon, R., Rainey, J. M., Lycaki, H., Ortiz, A., Berchou, R., & Weinberg, P. (1988). *Biological Psychiatry, 24*, 891–902.

Pohorecky, L. A., & Brick, J. (1987). Characteristics of the interaction of ethanol and stress. In E. Gottheil, K. A. Druley, S. Pashko, & S. P. Weinstein (Eds.), *Stress and addiction* (pp. 75–100). New York: Bruner/Mazel.

Post, R. M., Weiss, R. B., Fontana, D., & Pert, A. (1992). Conditioned sensitization to the psychomotor stimulant cocaine. In P. W. Kalivas & H. H. Samson (Eds.), *The neurobiology of drug and alcohol addiction* (pp. 386–399). New York: The New York Academy of Sciences.

Poulton, R. G., & Andrews, G. (1992). Personality as a cause of adverse life events. *Acta Psychiatrica Scandinavica, 85*, 35–38.

Powers, R. J. (1987). Stress as a factor in alcohol use and abuse. In E. Gottheil, K. A. Druley, S. Pashko, & S. P. Weinstein (Eds.), *Stress and addiction* (pp. 248–260). New York: Bruner/Mazel.

Prange, A. J., Jr., Garbutt, J. C., & Loosen, P. T. (1987). The hypothalamus pituitary thyroid axis in affective disorders. In H. Y. Meltzer (Ed.), *Psychopharmacology: The third generation of progress* (pp. 629–636). New York: Raven Press.

Pulkkinen, L. (1988). Delinquent development: Theoretical and empirical considerations. In M. Rutter (Ed.), *Studies of psychosocial risk: The power of longitudinal data* (pp. 184–199). Cambridge, England: Cambridge University Press.

Purcell, R. Maruff, P., Kyrios, M., & Pantelis, C. (1998). Neuropsychological deficits in obsessive-compulsive disorder. *Archives of General Psychiatry, 55*, 415–423.

Purris, B., Brandt, R., Rouse, C., Wilfredo, V. (1988). Students' attitudes toward hypothetical chronically and acutely mentally and physically ill individuals. *Psychological Reports, 62*, 627–630.

Quay, H. C. (1965). Psychopathic personality as pathological stimulation seeking. *American Journal of Psychiatry, 122*, 180–183.

Rachman, S. (1977). The conditioning theory of fear acquisition: A critical examination. *Behaviour Research and Therapy, 15*, 375–387.

Raine, A., Brennan, P., & Mednick, S. A. (1994). Birth complications combined with early maternal rejection at age 1 year predispose violent crime at age 18 years. *Archives of General Psychiatry, 51*, 984–988.

Raine, A., Brennan, P., Mednick, B., & Mednick, S. A. (1996). High rates of violence, crime, academic problems, and behavioral problems in males with both early neuromotor deficits and unstable family environments. *Archives of General Psychiatry, 53*, 544–549.

Raine, A., & Venables, P. H. (1984). Electrodermal nonresponding, antisocial behavior, and schizoid tendencies in adolescents. *Psychophysiology, 21*, 424–433.

Raine, A., & Venables, P. H. (1988). Enhanced P3 evoked potentials and longer P3 recovery times in psychopaths. *Psychophysiology, 25*, 30–38.

Rapee, R. M. (1986). Differential response to hyperventilation in panic disorder and generalized anxiety disorder. *Journal of Abnormal Psychology, 95*, 24–28.

Rapee, R. M. (1991). Psychological factors involved in generalized anxiety. In R. M. Rapee & D. H. Barlow (Eds.), *Chronic anxiety, generalized anxiety disorder and mixed anxiety-depression* (pp. 76–94). New York: Guilford Press.

Rapee, R. M., Brown, T. A., Antony, M. M., & Barlow, D. H. (1992). Response to hyperventilation and inhalation of 5.5% carbon dioxide-enriched air across the DSM-III-R anxiety disorders. *Journal of Abnormal Psychology, 101*, 538–552.

Rapee, R. M., & Lim, L. (1992). Discrepancy between self- and observer ratings of performance in social phobics. *Journal of Abnormal Psychology, 101*, 728–731.

Rapee, R. M., McCallum, S. L., Melville, L. F., Ravenscroft, H., & Rodney, J. M. (1994). Memory bias in social phobia. *Behaviour Research and Therapy, 32*, 89–99.

Rapoport, J. L., Giedd, J., Kumra, S., Jacobsen, L., Smith, A., Lee, P., Nelson, J., & Hamburger, S. (1997). Childhood-onset schizophrenia. *Archives of General Psychiatry, 54*, 897–903.

Rasmussen, S. A., & Tsuang, M. T. (1984). The epidemiology of obsessive-compulsive disorder. *Journal of Clinical Psychiatry, 45*, 450–457.

Rauch, S. L., Jenike, M. A., Alpert, N. M., Baer, L., Breiter, H. C. R., Savage, C. R., & Fischman, A. J. (1994). Regional cerebral blood flow measure during symptom provocation in obsessive-compulsive disorder using oxygen-15-labeled carbon dioxide and positron emission tomography. *Archives of General Psychiatry, 51*, 62–70.

Rauch, S. L., Savage, C. R., Alpert, N. M., Miguel, E. O., Baer, L., Breiter, H. C., Fischman, A. J., Mango, P. A., Morette, C., & Jenike, M. A. (1995). A positron emission tomographic study of simple phobia. *Archives of General Psychiatry, 52*, 20–28.

Razran, G. (1961). The observable unconscious and the inferable conscious in current Soviet psychophysiology. Interoceptive conditioning, semantic conditioning, and the orienting reflex. *Psychological Review, 68*, 81–147.

Redmond, D. E., Jr. (1987). Studies of locus coeruleus in monkeys and hypotheses for neuropsychopharmacology. In H. Y. Meltzer (Ed.), *Psychopharmacology: The third generation of progress* (pp. 967–975). New York: Raven Press.

Regier, D. A., Farmer, M. E., Rae, D. S., Looke, B. Z., Keith, S. J., Judd, L. L., &

Goodwin, F. K. (1990). Comorbidity of mental disorders with alcohol and other drug abuse. *Journal of the American Medical Association, 264*, 2511–2518.

Regier, D. A., Narrow, W. E., & Rae, D. S. (1990). The epidemiology of anxiety disorders. *Journal of Psychiatric Research, 24*, 3–14.

Reich, J., Black, D. W., & Jarjoua, D. (1987). Architecture of research in psychiatry, 1953 to 1983. *Archives of General Psychiatry, 44*, 311–313.

Reich, J., & Green, A. (1991). Effect of personality disorders on outcome of treatment. *Journal of Nervous and Mental Disease, 179*, 74–82.

Reiman, E. M. (1990). PET, panic disorder and normal anticipatory anxiety. In J. C. Ballenger (Ed.), *Neurobiology of panic disorder* (pp. 245–270). New York: Wiley-Liss.

Reiman, E. M., Raiche, M. E., Robins, E., Mintun, M. A., Fusselman, M. J., Fox, P. T., Price, J. L., & Hashman, K. A. (1989). Neuroanatomical correlates of a lactate induced anxiety attack. *Archives of General Psychiatry, 46*, 493–500.

Reist, C., Haier, R. J., DeMet, E., & Cicz-DeMet, A. (1990). Platelet MAO activity in personality disorders and normal controls. *Psychiatry Research, 30*, 221–227.

Rey, J. M., Plapp, J. M., & Stewart, G. W. (1989). Reliability of psychiatric diagnosis in referred adolescents. *Journal of Child Psychology and Psychiatry and Allied Disorders, 30*, 879–888.

Rice, J. P., Rochberg, N., Endicott, J., Lavori, P. W., & Miller, C. (1992). Stability of psychiatric diagnoses. *Archives of General Psychiatry, 49*, 824–830.

Riso, L. P., Klein, D. N., Fervio, T., Kasch, K. L., Pepper, C. M., Schwartz, J. E., & Aronson, T. A. (1996). Understanding the comorbidity between early-onset dysthymia and cluster B personality disorders: A family study. *American Journal of Psychiatry, 153*, 900–906.

Robertson, H. A. (1993). Immediate early gene activation and long-term changes in neural-function: A possible role in addiction? In R. Grzanna & R. M. Brown (Eds.), *Activation of immediate early genes by drugs of abuse* (NIDA Research Monograph No. 125). Rockville, MD: National Institute of Drug Abuse.

Robins, E., & Guze, S. B. (1970). Establishment of diagnostic validity in psychiatric illness: Its application to schizophrenia. *American Journal of Psychiatry, 126*, 107–111.

Robins, L. N. (1978). Aetiological implications in studies of childhood histories relating to antisocial personality. In R. D. Hare & D. Schalling (Eds.), *Psychopathic behavior: Approaches to research* (pp. 255–272). Chichester, England: Wiley.

Robins, L. N., Helzer, J. E., Croughan, J., & Ratcliff, K. S. (1981). National Institute of Mental Health Diagnostic Interview schedule: Its history, characteristics, and validity. *Archives of General Psychiatry, 38*, 381–389.

Robins, L. N., Helzer, J. E., Weissman, M. M., Orvaschel, H., Gruenberg, E., Burke, J. D., Jr., & Regier, D. A. (1984). Lifetime prevalence of specific psychiatric disorders in three sites. *Archives of General Psychiatry, 41*, 949–958.

Robins, L. N., Locke, B. Z., & Regier, D. A. (1991). An overview of psychiatric disorders in America. In L. N. Robins & D. A. Regier (Eds.), *Psychiatric disorders in America: The epidemiological catchment area study* (pp. 328–366). New York: The Free Press.

Robins, L. N., & Regier, D. A. (Eds.). (1991). *Psychiatric disorders in America: The epidemiological catchment area study.* New York: The Free Press.

Robinson, D., Wu, H., Munne, R. A., Ashtari, M., Alvir, J. M. J., Lerner, G., Koreen, A., Cole, K., & Bogerts, B. (1995). Reduced caudate nucleus volume in obsessive-compulsive disorder. *Archives of General Psychiatry, 52,* 393–406.

Roccatagliata, G. (1986). *A history of ancient psychiatry.* New York: Greenwood Press.

Rohde, P., Lewinsohn, P. M., & Seely, J. R. (1990). Are people changed by the experience of having an episode of depression? *Journal of Abnormal Psychology, 99,* 264–271.

Rose, D. T., Abramson, L. Y., Hodulik, C. J., Halberstadt, L., & Leff, G. (1994). Heterogeneity of cognitive style among depressed inpatients. *Journal of Abnormal Psychology, 103,* 419–429.

Rosen, G. (1968). *Madness in society.* Chicago: University of Chicago Press.

Rosenbaum, J. F., Biederman, J., Hirshfeld, D. R., Bolduc, E. A., Faraone, S. V., Kagan, J., Snidman, N., & Resnik, J. S. (1991). Further evidence of an association between behavioral inhibition and anxiety disorders: Results from a family study of children from a non-clinic sample. *Journal of Psychiatric Research, 25,* 49–65.

Rosenthal, D. (Ed.). (1963). *The Genain quadruplets.* New York: Basic Books.

Rosenthal, D. (1967). An historical and methodological review of genetic studies of schizophrenia. In J. Romano (Ed.), *The origins of schizophrenia: Proceedings of the first Rochester International Conference on Schizophrenia* (pp. 15–26). Amsterdam: Exerpta Medica Foundation.

Roth, B. L., & Meltzer, H. Y. (1995). The role of serotonin in schizophrenia. In F. E. Bloom & D. J. Kupfer (Eds.), *Psychopharmacology: The fourth generation of progress* (pp. 1215–1227). New York: Raven Press.

Rounsaville, B. J., Anton, S. F., Carroll, K., Budde, D., Prusoff, D., & Gawin, F. (1991). Psychiatric diagnosis of treatment-seeking cocaine abusers. *Archives of General Psychiatry, 48,* 43–51.

Rounsaville, B. J., Kosten, T. R., Weissman, M. M., Prusoff, B., Pauls, D., Anton, S. F., Merikangas, K. (1991). Psychiatric disorders in relatives of probands with opiate addiction. *Archives of General Psychiatry, 48,* 33–42.

Rowe, D. C. (1986). Genetic and environmental components of antisocial behavior: A study of 265 twin pairs. *Criminology, 24,* 513–532.

Roy, A., Adinoff, B., Roehrich, L., Lamparski, D., Custer, R., Lorenz, V., Barbaccia, M., Guidotti, A., Costa, E., & Linnoila, M. (1988). Pathological gambling: A psychobiological study. *Archives of General Psychiatry, 45,* 369–373.

Roy, A., Jimerson, D. C., & Pickar, D. (1986). Plasma MHPG in depressive disorders and relationship to the dexamethasone suppression test. *American Journal of Psychiatry, 143*, 846–851.

Roy, A., Karoum, F., & Pollack, S. (1992). Marked reduction in indexes of dopamine transmission among patients with depression who attempt suicide. *Archives of General Psychiatry, 49*, 447–450.

Roy, M. A., & Crowe, R. R. (1994). Validity of the familial and sporadic subtypes of schizophrenia. *American Journal of Psychiatry, 151*, 805–814.

Roy, M. A., Neale, M. C., Pedersen, N. L., Mathé, A. A., & Kendler, K. S. (1995). A twin study of generalized anxiety disorder and major depression. *Psychological Medicine, 25*, 1037–1049.

Rugle, L., & Melamed, L. (1993). Neuropsychological assessment of attention disorder problems in pathological gamblers. *Journal of Nervous and Mental Disorders, 181*, 107–112.

Russell, A. J., Munro, J. C., Jones, P. B., Hemsley, D. R., & Murray, R. M. (1997). Schizophrenia and the myth of intellectual decline. *American Journal of Psychiatry, 154*, 635–639.

Rutherford, M. J., Alterman, A. I., Cacciola, J. S., & Snider, E. C. (1995). Gender differences in diagnosing antisocial personality disorder in methadone patients. *American Journal of Psychiatry, 152*, 1309–1316.

Rutter, M. (1987). Temperament, personality, and personality disorder. *British Journal of Psychiatry, 150*, 443–458.

Rutter, M. (1994). Beyond longitudinal data: Causes, consequences, changes and continuity. *Journal of Consulting and Clinical Psychology, 62*, 928–940.

Sackheim, H. A., Prohovnik, I., Moeller, J. R., Brown, R. P., Apter, S., Prudic, J., Devan, D. P., & Mukherjee, S. (1990). Regional cerebral blood flow in mood disorders. *Archives of General Psychiatry, 47*, 60–70.

Salkovskis, P. M. (1996). Cognitive-behavioral approaches to the understanding of obsessional problems. In R. M. Rapee (Ed.), *Current controversies in the anxiety disorders* (pp. 103–133). New York: Guilford Press.

Sandberg, D. P., & Liebowitz, M. R. (1990). Potential mechanisms for sodium lactate induction of panic. In J. C. Ballenger (Ed.), *Neurobiology of panic disorder* (pp. 155–172). New York: Wiley-Liss.

Sanderson, W. C., Beck, A. T., & Beck, J. (1990). Syndrome comorbidity in patients with major depression or dysthymia: Prevalence and temporal relationships. *American Journal of Psychiatry, 147*, 1025–1028.

Sanderson, W. C., DiNardo, P. A., Rapee, R. M., & Barlow, D. H. (1990). Syndrome comorbidity in patients diagnosed with a DSM-III-R anxiety disorder. *Journal of Abnormal Psychology, 99*, 308–312.

Sanderson, W. C., Rapee, R. M., & Barlow, D. H. (1989). The influence of an illusion of control on panic attacks induced via inhalation of 5.5% carbon dioxide-inhaled air. *Archives of General Psychiatry, 46*, 157–162.

Sanderson, W. C., & Wetzler, S. (1991). Chronic anxiety and generalized anxiety disorder: Issues in comorbidity. In R. M. Rapee & D. H. Barlow (Eds.), *Chronic anxiety, generalized anxiety disorder and mixed anxiety-depression* (pp. 119–135). New York: Guilford Press.

Sanderson, W. C., Wetzler, S., Beck, A. T., & Betz, F. (1992). Prevalence of personality disorders in patients with major depression and dysthymia. *Psychiatry Research, 42,* 93–99.

Sanderson, W. C., Wetzler, S., Beck, A. T., & Betz, F. (1994). Prevalence of personality disorders among patients with anxiety disorders. *Psychiatry Research, 51,* 167–174.

Sargeant, J. K., Bruce, M. L., Floris, L. P., & Weissman, M. M. (1990). Factors associated with 1-year outcome of major depression in the community. *Archives of General Psychiatry, 47,* 519–526.

Sartorius, N., Jablensky, A., Korten, A., Ernberg, G., Anker, M., Cooper, J. E., & Day, R. (1986). Early manifestations and first-contact incidence of schizophrenia in different cultures. *Psychological Medicine, 16,* 909–928.

Sato, T., Sakado, K., Sato, S., & Morikawa, T. (1994). Cluster A personality disorder: A marker of worse treatment outcome of major depression? *Psychiatry Research, 53,* 153–159.

Satterfield, J. H. (1978). The hyperactive child syndrome: A precursor of adult psychopathy? In R. D. Hare & D. Schalling (Eds.), *Psychopathic behaviour: Approaches to research* (pp. 329–346). Chichester, England: Wiley.

Satterfield, J. H. (1987). Childhood diagnostic and neurophysiological mediators of teenage arrest rates: An eight-year prospective study. In S. A. Mednick, T. E. Moffitt, & S. A. Stack (Eds.), *The causes of crime: New biological approaches* (pp. 146–167). Cambridge, England: Cambridge University Press.

Saykin, A. J., Gur, R. C., Gur, R. E., Mozley, D., Mozley, L. H., Resnick, S. M., Kester, D. B., & Stafiniak, P. (1991). Neuropsychological function in schizophrenia. *Archives of General Psychiatry, 48,* 618–624.

Saykin, A. J., Shtasel, D. L., Gur, R. E., Kester, D. B., Mozey, L. H., Stafiniak, P., & Gur, R. C. (1994). Neuropsychological deficits in neuroleptic naive patients with first-episode schizophrenia. *Archives of General Psychiatry, 51,* 124–131.

Schalling, D., Lidberg, L., Levander, S. E., & Dahlin, Y. (1973). Spontaneous autonomic activity as related to psychopathy. *Biological Psychology, 1,* 83–97.

Schatzberg, A. F., & Schildkraut, J. J. (1995). Recent studies on norepinephrine systems in mood disorders. In F. E. Bloom & D. J. Kupfer (Eds.), *Psychopharmacology: The fourth generation of progress* (pp. 911–920). New York: Raven Press.

Schildkraut, J. J. (1965). The catecholamine hypothesis of affective disorders: A review of supporting evidence. *American Journal of Psychiatry, 122,* 509–522.

Schmauk, F. J. (1970). Punishment, arousal, and avoidance learning in sociopaths. *Journal of Abnormal Psychology, 76,* 325–335.

Schneider, K. (1959). *Clinical psychopathology.* New York: Grune & Stratton.

Schneier, F. R., Johnson, J., Hornig, C. D., Liebowitz, M. R., & Weissman, M. M.

(1992). Social phobia: Comorbidity and morbidity in an epidemiological sample. *Archives of General Psychiatry, 49*, 282–288.

Schraeder, G. (1994). Chronic depression: State or trait? *Journal of Nervous and Mental Disease, 182*, 552–555.

Schuckit, M. A. (1988). A search for biological markers in alcoholism: Applications to psychiatric research. In R. M. Rose & J. E. Barrett (Eds.), *Alcoholism: Origins and outcome* (pp. 143–154). New York: Raven Press.

Schuckit, M. A. (1994). Familial alcoholism. In T. A. Widiger, A. J. Francis, H. A. Pincus, M. B. First, R. Ross, & W. Davis (Eds.), *DSMIV-Sourcebook* (Vol. I, pp. 159–167).

Schuckit, M. A., & Smith, T. L. (1996). An 8-year follow-up of 450 sons of alcoholic and control subjects. *Archives of General Psychiatry, 53*, 202–210.

Schumaker, D. N., Namerow, M. J., Parker, B., & Fox, P. (1986). Prospective payment for psychiatry—feasibility and impact. *New England Journal of Medicine, 315*, 1331–1336.

Segal, B. S., Huba, G. J., & Singer, J. F. (1980). *Drugs, daydreaming and personality: Studies of college youth.* Hillsdale, NJ: Erlbaum.

Seidman, L. J. (1983). Schizophrenia and brain dysfunction: An integration of recent neurodiagnostic findings. *Psychological Bulletin, 94*, 195–238.

Seligman, M. E. P. (1971). Phobias and preparedness. *Behavior Therapy, 307*–320.

Seligman, M. E. P. (1975). *Helplessness: On depression, development and death.* New York: W. H. Freeman.

Seligman, M. E. P. (1988). Competing theories of panic. In S. Rachman & J. D. Maser (Eds.), *Panic: Psychological perspectives.* Hillsdale, NJ: Erlbaum.

Seligman, M. E. P., Peterson, C., Kaslove, N. J., Tannenbaum, R. L., Alloy, L. B., & Abramson, L. Y. (1984). Attributional style and depressive symptoms among children. *Journal of Abnormal Psychology, 93*, 235–238.

Selye, H. (1956). *The stress of life.* New York: McGraw-Hill.

Shagass, C., Roemer, R. A., Straumanis, J. J., & Josiassen, R. C. (1985). Combinations of evoked potential amplitude measurements in relation to psychiatric diagnosis. *Biological Psychiatry, 20*, 701–722.

Shalev, A. Y., Orr, S. P., Peri, T., Schreiber, S., & Pitman, R. K. (1992). Physiologic responses to loud tones in Israeli patients with posttraumatic stress disorder. *Archives of General Psychiatry, 49*, 870–875.

Shapiro, R. W. (1970). A twin study of non-endogenous depression. *Acta Jutlandica, XLII* (Monograph 2). Copenhagen, Denmark: Munksgaard.

Shea, M. T., Elkin, I., Imber, S. D., Sotsky, S. M., Watkins, J. T., Collins, J. F., Pilkonis, P. A., Beckham, E., Glass, D. R., Dolan, R. T., & Parloff, M. B. (1992). Course of depressive symptoms over follow-up: Findings from the National Institute of Mental Health treatment of depression collaborative research program. *Archives of General Psychiatry, 49*, 809–816.

Shea, M. T., Leon, A. C., Mueller, T. I., Solomon, D. A., Warshaw, M. G., &

Keller, M. B. (1996). Does major depression result in lasting personality change? *American Journal of Psychiatry, 153,* 1404–1410.

Shea, M. T., Widiger, T. A., & Klein, M. H. (1992). Comorbidity of personality disorders and depression: Implications for treatment. *Journal of Consulting and Clinical Psychology, 60,* 857–868.

Shekim, W. O., Bylund, D. B., Alexson, J., Glaser, R. D., Jones, S. B., Hodges, K., & Perdue, S. (1986). Platelet MAO and measures of attention and impulsivity in boys with attention disorder deficit and hyperactivity. *Psychiatry Research, 18,* 179–188.

Sher, K. J. (1993). Children of alcoholics and the intergenerational transmission of alcoholism: A biopsychosocial perspective. In J. S. Baer, A. Marlatt, & R. J. McMahon (Eds.), *Addiction behaviors across the life span* (pp. 3–33). Newbury Park, NJ: Sage.

Sher, K. J., Bylund, D. B., Walitzer, K. S., Hartmann, J., & Ray-Prenger, C. (1994). Platelet monoamine oxidase (MAO) activity: Personality, substance abuse, and the stress-response-dampening effect of alcohol. *Experimental and Clinical Psychopharmacology, 3,* 53–81.

Shields, J., & Slater, E. (1971). Diagnostic similarity in twins with neuroses and personality disorders. In J. Shields & J. J. Gottesman (Eds.), *Man, mind, and heredity: Selected papers of Elliot Slater on psychiatry and genetics* (pp. 252–257). London: Johns Hopkins Press.

Shrout, P. E., Spitzer, R. L., & Fleiss, J. L. (1987). Quantification of agreement in psychiatric diagnosis revisited. *Archives of General Psychiatry, 44,* 172–177.

Siddle, D. A. T., & Bond, N. N. (1988). Avoidance learning, Pavlovian conditioning and the development of phobias. *Biological Psychology, 27,* 167–183.

Siegel, B. V., Jr., Buchsbaum, M. S., Bunney, W. E., Gottschalk, L. A., Haier, R. J., Lohr, J. B., Lottenberg, S., Najafi, A., Nuechterlein, K. H., Potkin, S. G., & Wu, J. C. (1993). Cortical-striatal-thalamic circuits and brain glucose metabolic activity in 70 unmedicated male schizophrenic patients. *American Journal of Psychiatry, 150,* 1325–1336.

Siegel, C., Waldo, M., Mizner, G., & Adler, L. E. (1984). Deficits in sensory gating in schizophrenic patients and their relatives. *Archives of General Psychiatry, 41,* 607–612.

Siever, L. J., Amin, F., Coccaro, E. F., Bernstein, D., Kavoussi, R. J., Kalus, O., Horvath, T. B., Warne, P., & Davidson, M. (1991). Plasma homovanillic acid in schizotypal personality disorder. *American Journal of Psychiatry, 148,* 1246–1248.

Siever, L. J., Amin, F., Coccaro, E. F., Trestman, R., Silverman, J., Horvath, T. B., Mahon, T. R., Knott, P., & Altstiel, K. L. (1993). CSF homovanillic acid in schizotypal personality disorder. *American Journal of Psychiatry, 150,* 149–151.

Siever, L. J., Friedman, L., Moskowitz, J., Mitropoylow, V., Keefe, R., Roitman, S. L., Merhige, D., Trestman, R., Silverman, J., & Mohs, R. (1994). Eye movement impairment and schizotypal personality. *American Journal of Psychiatry, 151,* 1209–1215.

Siever, L. J., & Trestman, R. L. (1993). The serotonin system and aggressive personality. *International Clinical Psychopharmacology, 8*(Suppl. 2), 33–39.

Sigvardsson, S., Bohman, M., & Cloninger, C. R. (1996). Replication of the Stockholm adoption study: Confirmatory cross-fostering analysis. *Archives of General Psychiatry, 53,* 681–687.

Silverman, J. M., Siever, L. J., Horvath, T. B., Coccaro, E. F., Klar, H., Davidson, M., Pinkham, L., Apter, S. H., Mohs, R. C., & Davis, K. L. (1993). Schizophrenia-related and affective personality disorder traits in relatives of probands with schizophrenia and personality disorders. *American Journal of Psychiatry, 150,* 435–442.

Silverman, J. S., Silverman, J. A., & Eardley, D. A. (1984). Do maladaptive attitudes cause depression? *Archives of General Psychiatry, 41,* 28–30.

Simon, G. E., & Von Korff, M. (1991). Somatization and psychiatric disorder in the NIMH epidemiologic catchment area study. *American Journal of Psychiatry, 148,* 1494–1500.

Smith, S. S., & Newman, J. P. (1990). Alcohol and drug abuse/dependence disorders in psychopathic and nonpsychopathic criminal offenders. *Journal of Abnormal Psychology, 99,* 430–439.

Smith, S. S., O'Hara, B. F., Persico, A. M., Gorelick, D. A., Newlin, D. B., Vlahov, D., Solomon, L., Pickens, R., & Uhl, G. R. (1992). Genetic vulnerability to drug abuse. *Archives of General Psychiatry, 49,* 723–727.

Soares, J. J. F., & Öhman, A. (1993). Preattentive processing, preparedness and phobias: Effects of instruction on conditioned electrodermal responses to masked and non-masked fear-relevant stimuli. *Behaviour Research and Therapy, 31,* 89–95.

Sommers, I. (1988). Pathological gambling: Estimating prevalence and group characteristics. *International Journal of the Addictions, 23,* 477–490.

Soubrié, P. (1986). Reconciling the role of central serotonin neurons in human and animal behavior. *Behavioral and Brain Sciences, 9,* 319–364.

Southwick, S. M., Krystal, J. H., Morgan, A., Johnson, D., Nagy, L. M., Nicolaou, A., Heninger, G. R., & Charney, D. S. (1993). *Archives of General Psychiatry, 50,* 266–274.

Spielberger, C. D. (1966). *Theory and research on anxiety.* In C. D. Spielberger (Ed.), *Anxiety and behavior* (pp. 3–20). New York: Academic Press.

Spitzer, R. L. (1980). Introduction. In *Diagnostic and statistical manual of mental disorders* (pp. 1–12). Washington, DC: American Psychiatric Association.

Spitzer, R. L., Cohen, J., & Endicott, J. (1967). Quantification of agreement in psychiatric diagnosis. *Archives of General Psychiatry, 17,* 83–87.

Spitzer, R. L., Endicott, J., & Robins, E. (1978). Research diagnostic criteria: Rationale and reliability. *Archives of General Psychiatry, 35,* 773–782.

Spitzer, R. L., First, M. B., Kendler, K. S., & Stein, D. J. (1993). The reliability of three definitions of bizarre delusions. *American Journal of Psychiatry, 150,* 880–884.

Spitzer, R. L., & Fleiss, J. L. (1974). A re-analysis of the reliability of psychiatric diagnosis. *British Journal of Psychiatry, 125,* 341–347.

Spotts, J. V., & Shontz, F. C. (1984). Correlates of sensation seeking by heavy chronic drug users. *Perceptual and Motor Skills, 58,* 427–435.

Spunt, B., Lesieur, H. R., Hunt, D., & Cahill, L. (1995). Gambling among methadone patients. *International Journal of the Addictions, 30,* 929–962.

Squires-Wheeler, E., Friedman, D., & Erlenmeyer-Kimling, L. (1993). A longitudinal study relating P3 amplitude to schizophrenia spectrum disorders and to global personality functioning. *Biological Psychiatry, 33,* 774–785.

Stabenau, J. R. (1992). Is risk for substance abuse unitary? *Journal of Nervous and Mental Disorder, 180,* 583–588.

Sterling, R. C., Gottheil, E., Weinstein, S. P., & Shannon, D. M. (1994). Psychiatric symptomatology in crack cocaine abusers. *Journal of Nervous and Mental Disease, 182,* 564–569.

Stevens, G. F. (1993). Applying the diagnosis antisocial personality to imprisoned offenders: Looking for hay in a haystack. *Journal of Offender Rehabilitation, 19,* 993.

Stoll, A. L., Tohen, M., Baldessarini, R. J., Goodwin, D. C., Stein, S., Katz, S., Geenens, D., Swinson, R. P., Goethe, J. W., & McGlashin, T. (1993). Shifts in diagnostic frequencies of schizophrenia and major affective disorders at six North American psychiatric hospitals, 1972–1988. *American Journal of Psychiatry, 150,* 1668–1673.

Strachen, A. M. (1986). Family intervention for the rehabilitation of schizophrenia: Toward protection and coping. *Schizophrenia Bulletin, 12,* 678–698.

Strakowski, S. M., Stoll, A. L., Tohen, M., Faedda, G. L., & Goodwin, D. C. (1993). The Tridimensional Personality Questionnaire as a predictor of six-month outcome in first episode mania. *Psychiatry Research, 48,* 1–8.

Straub, R. E., MacLean, C. J., O'Neill, A. O., Burke, J., Murphy, B., Duke, F., Shinkwin, R., Webb, B. T., Zhang, J., Walsh, D., & Kendler, K. S. (1995). A potential vulnerability locus for schizophrenia on chromosome 6p24-22: Evidence for genetic heterogeneity. *Nature Genetics, 11,* 287–292.

Strauss, J. S., Carpenter, W. T., Jr., & Bartko, J. J. (1974). The diagnosis and understanding of schizophrenia. Part III. Speculating on the processes that underlie schizophrenic symptoms and signs. *Schizophrenia Bulletin, 11,* 61–69.

Sugarman, P. A., & Crawford, D. (1994). Schizophrenia in the Afro-Caribbean community. *British Journal of Psychiatry, 164,* 474–480.

Sullivan, H. S. (1953). *The interpersonal theory of psychiatry.* New York: Norton.

Sullivan, P. F., Joyce, P. T., & Mulder, R. T. (1994). Borderline personality disorder in major depression. *Journal of Nervous and Mental Disease, 182,* 508–516.

Susser, E., Neugebauer, R., Hoek, H. W., Brown, A. S., Lin, S., Labovitz, D., & Gorman, J. M. (1996). Schizophrenia after prenatal famine: Further investigations. *Archives of General Psychiatry, 53,* 25–31.

Susser, E., & Wanderling, J. (1994). Epidemiology of nonaffective acute remitting psychosis vs. schizophrenia. *Archives of General Psychiatry, 51,* 294–301.

Sutherland, S. (1989). *Macmillan dictionary of psychology*. Worcester, England: Billing & Sons.

Sutker, P. B., Archer, R. P., & Allain, A. N. (1978). Drug abuse patterns, personality characteristics, and relationships with sex, race, and sensation seeking. *Journal of Consulting and Clinical Psychology, 46*, 1374–1378.

Sutker, P. B., Davis, J. M., Uddo, M., & Ditta, S. R. (1995). War zone stress, personal resources and PTSD in Persian Gulf war returnees. *Journal of Abnormal Psychology, 104*, 444–452.

Sutker, P. B., Moan, C. E., & Allain, A. N. (1983). Assessment of cognitive control in psychopathic and normal prisoners. *Journal of Behavioral Assessment, 5*, 275–287.

Sutker, P. B., Uddo, M., Brailey, K., Vasterling, J. J., & Errera, P. (1994). Psychopathology in war-zone deployed and nondeployed operation Desert Storm troops assigned graves registration duties. *Journal of Abnormal Psychology, 103*, 383–390.

Swedo, S. E., Leonard, H. L., Kruesi, M. J. P., Rettew, D. C., Listwak, S. J., Berrettini, W., Stipetic, M., Hamburger, S., Gold, P. W., Potter, W. Z., & Rapoport, J. L. (1992). Cerebrospinal fluid neurochemistry in children and adolescents with obsessive-compulsive disorder. *Archives of General Psychiatry, 49*, 29–36.

Syndulko, K. (1978). Electrocortical investigations of sociopathy. In R. D. Hare & D. Schalling (Eds.), *Psychopathic behaviour: Approaches to research* (pp. 145–156). Chichester, England: Wiley.

Szasz, T. S. (1961). *The myth of mental illness*. New York: Harper-Collins.

Tabakoff, B., & Hoffman, P. L. (1987). Biochemical psychopharmacology of alcohol. In H. Y. Meltzer (Ed.), *Psychopharmacology: The third generation of progress* (pp. 1521–1526). New York: Raven Press.

Tabler, J. I., McCormick, R. A., & Ramirez, L. F. (1987). The prevalence and impact of major life stressors among pathological gamblers. *The International Journal of the Addictions, 22*, 71–79.

Takei, N., Lewis, S., Jones, P., Harvey, I., & Murray, R. M. (1996). Prenatal exposure to influenza and increased cerebrospinal fluid spaces in schizophrenia. *Schizophrenia Bulletin, 22*, 521–534.

Talamini, L. M., Louwerens, J. W., Sloof, C. J., & Korf, J. (1995). PET versus postmortem studies in schizophrenia research: Significance for the pathogenesis and pharmacotherapy. In J. A. den Boer, H. G. M. Westenberg, & H. M. van Praag (Eds.), *Advances in the neurobiology of schizophrenia* (pp. 157–187). Chichester, England: Wiley.

Tancer, M. E., Lewis, M. H., & Stein, M. B. (1995). Biological aspects. In M. B. Steen (Ed.), *Social phobia: Clinical and research perspectives* (pp. 229–257). Washington, DC: American Psychiatric Press.

Taylor, M. A. (1992). Are schizophrenia and affective disorder related? A selective literature review. *American Journal of Psychiatry, 149*, 22–32.

Teichman, M., Barnes, Z., & Rahav, G. (1989). Sensation seeking, state and trait anxiety and depressive mood in adolescent substance users. *International Journal of the Addictions, 24,* 87–89.

Tellegen, A. (1985). Structures of mood and personality and their relevance to assessing anxiety with an emphasis on self-report. In A. H. Tuma & J. D. Maser (Eds.), *Anxiety and the anxiety disorders* (pp. 681–706). Hillsdale, NJ: Erlbaum.

Tennant, C. (1988). Parental loss in childhood: Its effect in adult life. *Archives of General Psychiatry, 45,* 1045–1051.

Thaker, G. K., Cassady, S., Adami, H., Moran, M., & Ross, D. E. (1996). Eye movements in spectrum personality disorders: Comparison of community subjects and relatives of schizophrenic patients. *American Journal of Psychiatry, 153,* 362–368.

Thornquist, M. H., & Zuckerman, M. (1995). Psychopathy, passive-avoidance learning and basic dimensions of personality. *Personality and Individual Differences, 19,* 525–534.

Thorpe, S. J., & Salkovkis, P. M. (1995). Phobics beliefs: Do cognitive factors play a role in specific phobias. *Behaviour Research and Therapy, 33,* 805–816.

Thrasher, S. M., Dalgesh, T., & Yule, W. (1994). Information processing in post-traumatic stress disorder. *Behaviour Research and Therapy, 32,* 247–254.

Tien, A. Y., & Eaton, W. W. (1992). Psychopathological precursors and sociodemographic risk factors for the schizophrenia syndrome. *Archives of General Psychiatry, 49,* 37–46.

Ticnari, P. (1991a). Gene-environment interaction in affective families. In H. Häfner & W. F. Gattaz (Eds.), *Search for the causes of schizophrenia* (pp. 126–143). Berlin, Germany: Springer-Verlag.

Tienari, P. (1991b). Interaction between genetic vulnerability and family environment. The Finnish adoptive family study of schizophrenia. *Acta Psychiatrica Scandinavica, 84,* 460–465.

Tienari, P., Wynne, L. C., Moring, J., Lahti, I., Naarala, M., Sorri, A., Wahlberg, K. E., Saarento, O., Seitamaa, M., Kaleva, M., & Kälesy, K. (1994). The Finnish adoptive family study of schizophrenia: Implications for family research. *British Journal of Psychiatry, 164*(Suppl. 23), 20–26.

Todd, R. D., & Reich, T. (1989). Linkage markers and validation of psychiatric nosology: Toward an etiologic classification of psychiatric disorders. In L. N. Robins & J. E. Barrett (Eds.), *The validity of psychiatric diagnosis* (pp. 163–175). New York: Raven Press.

Tohen, M., Waternaux, C. M., & Tsuang, M. T. (1990). Outcome in mania: A 4-year prospective follow-up of 75 patients utilizing survival analysis. *Archives of General Psychiatry, 47,* 1106–1111.

Torack, R. M., & Morris, J. C. (1988). The association of ventral tegmental areas of histopathology with adult dementia. *Archives of Neurology, 45,* 211–221.

Torgersen, S. (1983). Genetic factors in anxiety disorders. *Archives of General Psychiatry, 40,* 1085–1089.

Torgersen, S. (1986). Genetic factors in moderately severe and mild affective disorders. *Archives of General Psychiatry, 43,* 222–226.

Torgersen, S., Onstad, S., Skyre, I., Edvardsen, J., & Kringlen, E. (1993). "True" schizotypal personality disorder: A study of co-twins and relatives of schizophrenic probands. *American Journal of Psychiatry, 150,* 1661–1667.

Torrey, E. F., Bowler, A. E., Taylor, E. H., & Gottesman, I. I. (1994). *Schizophrenia and manic-depressive disorder.* New York: Basic Books.

Tremblay, R. E., Pihl, R. O., Vitaro, F., & Dobkin, P. L. (1994). Predicting early onset of male antisocial behavior from preschool behavior. *Archives of General Psychiatry, 51,* 732–739.

True, W. R., Rice, J., Eisen, S. A., Heath, A. C., Goldberg, J., Lyons, M. J., & Nowak, J. (1993). A twin study of genetic and environmental contributions to liability for posttraumatic stress symptoms. *Archives of General Psychiatry, 50,* 257–264.

Trujillo, K. A., Herman, J. P., Schäfer, M. K. H., Mansour, A., Meador-Woodruff, J. H., Watson, S. J., & Akil, H. (1993). Drug reward and brain circuitry: Recent advances and future directions. In S. G. Korenman & G. D. Barchas (Eds.), *Biological basis of substance abuse* (pp. 119–142). New York: Oxford University Press.

Trull, T. J., & Sher, K. J. (1994). Relationship between the five-factor model of personality and Axis I disorders in a nonclinical sample. *Journal of Abnormal Psychology, 103,* 350–360.

Trull, T. J., Widiger, T. A., & Guthrie, P. (1990). Categorical versus dimensional status of borderline personality disorder. *Journal of Abnormal Psychology, 99,* 40–48.

Tsuang, D., & Coryell, W. (1993). An 8-year follow-up of patients with DSM-III-R psychotic depression, schizoaffective disorder, and schizophrenia. *American Journal of Psychiatry, 150,* 1182–1188.

Tsuang, M. T., Faraone, S. V., & Green, R. R. (1994). Genetic epidemiology of mood disorders. In D. F. Papolos & H. M. Lachman (Eds.), *Genetic studies in affective disorders* (pp. 3–27). New York: Wiley.

Tsuang, M. T., Lyons, M. J., Eisen, S. A., Goldberg, J., True, W., Lin, N., Meyer, J. M., Toomey, R., Faraone, S. V., & Eaves, L. (1996). Genetic influences on DSM-III-R drug abuse and dependence: A study of 3,372 twin pairs. *American Journal of Medical Genetics (Neuropsychiatric Genetics), 67,* 473–477.

Turetsky, B., Cowell, P. E., Gur, R. C., Grossman, R. I., Shtasel, D. L., & Gur, R. E. (1995). Frontal and temporal lobe brain volumes in schizophrenia. *Archives of General Psychiatry, 52,* 1061–1070.

Turner, S. M., Beidel, D. C., Borden, J. W., Stanley, M. A., & Jacob, R. G. (1991). Social phobia: Axis I and II correlates. *Journal of Abnormal Psychology, 100,* 102–106.

Turner, S. M., Beidel, D. C., & Jacob, R. G. (1988). Assessment of panic. In S. Rachman & J. D. Maser (Eds.), *Panic: Psychological perspectives* (pp. 37–50). Hillsdale, NJ: Erlbaum.

Turley, B., Bates, G. W., Edwards, J., & Jackson, H. J. (1992). MCMI-II personality disorders. *Journal of Clinical Psychology, 48,* 320–329.

Tyrka, A. R., Cannon, T. D., Haslam, N., Mednick, S. A., Schulsinger, F., Schulsinger, H., & Parnas, J. (1995). The latent structure of schizotypy: I. Premorbid indicators of a taxon of individuals at risk for schizophrenia spectrum disorders. *Journal of Abnormal Psychology, 104,* 173–183.

Uhde, T. W. (1990). Caffeine provocation of panic: A focus on biological mechanisms. In J. C. Ballenger (Ed.), *Neurobiology of panic disorder* (pp. 219–242). New York: Wiley-Liss.

Uhl, G. R., Persico, A. M., & Smith, S. S. (1992). Current excitement with D2 dopamine receptor gene alleles in substance abuse. *Archives of General Psychiatry, 49,* 157–160.

Vaillant, G. E. (1996). A long-term follow-up of male alcoholic abuse. *Archives of General Psychiatry, 53,* 243–249.

Valone, K., Norton, J. P., Goldstein, M. J., & Doane, J. A. (1983). Parental expressed emotion and affective style in an adolescent sample at risk for schizophrenia spectrum disorders. *Journal of Abnormal Psychology, 92,* 399–407.

Van Ameringen, M., Mancini, C., Styan, G., & Donison, N. (1991). Relationship of social phobia with other psychiatric illnesses. *Journal of Affective Disorders, 21,* 93–99.

Van Dusen, K., Mednick, S. A., Gabrielli, W. F., & Hutchings, B. (1983). Social class and crime in an adoption cohort. *Journal of Criminal Law and Criminology, 74,* 249–269.

Van Oppen, P., Hoekstra, R. J., & Emmelkamp, P. M. G. (1995). The structure of obsessive-compulsive symptoms. *Behaviour Research and Therapy, 33,* 15–23.

Van Praag, H. M. (1993). Diagnosis, the rate limiting factor of biological depression research. *Neuropsychobiology, 28,* 197–206.

Vaugh, C. E., & Leff, J. P. (1976). The influence of family and social factors on the course of psychiatric illness. *British Journal of Psychology, 129,* 125–137.

Veith, R. C., Lewis, N., Linares, O. A., Barnes, R. F., Raskind, M. A., Villaacres, E. C., Murburg, M. M., Ashleigh, E. A., Castillo, S., Peskind, E. R., Pascualy, M., & Halter, J. B. (1994). Sympathetic nervous sytems activity in major depression. *Archives of General Psychiatry, 51,* 411–422.

Venables, P. H. (1987). Autonomic nervous system factors in criminal behavior. In S. A. Mednick, T. E. Moffitt, & S. A. Stack (Eds.), *The causes of crime: New biological approaches* (pp. 110–136). Cambridge, England: Cambridge University Press.

Venables, P. H. (1996). Schizotypy and maternal exposure to influence and to cold temperature: The Mauritius study. *Journal of Abnormal Psychology, 105,* 53–60.

Verma, R. M., & Eysenck, H. J. (1973). Severity and type of psychotic illness as a function of personality. *British Journal of Psychiatry, 122,* 573–585.

Virkkunen, M. (1985). Urinary free cortisol secretion in habitually violent offenders. *Acta Psychiatrica Scandinavica, 72,* 40–44.

Virkkunen, M. (1987). Metabolic dysfunctions among habitually violent offenders: Reactive hypoglycemia and cholesteral levels. In S. A. Mednick, T. E. Moffitt, & S. A. Stack (Eds.), *The causes of crime: New biological approaches* (pp. 292–311. Cambridge, England: Cambridge University Press.

Virkkunen, M., Goldman, D., & Linnoila, M. (1996). Serotonin in alcoholic violent offenders. In G. R. Bock & A. Goode (Eds.), *Genetics of criminal and antisocial behaviour* (pp. 168–177). Chichester, England: Wiley.

Virkkunen, M., Rawlings, R., Tokala, R., Poland, R. E., Guidotti, A., Nemeroff, C., & Bissette, G. (1994). CSF biochemistries, glucose metabolism, and diurnal activity in alcoholic, violent offenders, fire-setters, and healthy volunteers. *Archives of General Psychiatry, 51,* 20–27.

Volavka, J. (1987). Electroencephalography among criminals. In S. A. Mednick, T. E. Moffitt, & S. A. Stack (Eds.), *The causes of crime: New biological approaches* (pp. 137–145). Cambridge, England: Cambridge University Press.

Volberg, R. A. (1994). The prevalence and demographics of pathological gamblers: Implications for public health. *American Journal of Public Health, 84,* 237–241.

Volberg, R. A., & Steadman, H. J. (1988). Refining prevalence estimates of pathological gambling. *American Journal of Psychiatry, 145,* 502–505.

Vollema, M. G., & van den Bosch, R. J. (1995). The multidimensionality of schizotypy. *Schizophrenia Bulletin, 21,* 19–31.

Von Knorring, A. L., Bohman, M., von Knorring, L., & Oreland, L. (1985). Platelet MAO activity as a marker in subgroups of alcoholism. *Acta Psychiatrica Scandinavica, 72,* 51–58.

Von Knorring, L., Oreland, L., & von Knorring, A. L. (1987). Personality traits and platelet MAO activity in alcohol and drug abusing teenage boys. *Acta Psychiatrica Scandinavica, 75,* 307–314.

Von Knorring, L., Palm, U., & Andersson, H. E. (1985). Relationship between treatment outcome and subtype of alcoholism in men. *Journal of Studies on Alcohol, 46,* 388–391.

Vuchinich, R. E., & Calamas, M. L. (1997). Does the repeated gambles procedure measure impulsivity in social drinkers? *Experimental and Clinical Psychopharmacology, 5,* 157–162.

Wahlberg, K. E., Wynne, L. C., Oja, H., Keskitalo, P., Pykäläinen, L., Lahti, I., Moring, J., Naarala, M., Sorri, A., Seitanaa, M., Läksy, K., Lolassa, J., & Tienari, P. (1997). Gene-environment interaction in vulnerability to schizophrenia: Findings from the Finnish adoption family study. *American Journal of Psychiatry, 154,* 355–362.

Walker, E. F., Grimes, K. E., Davis, D. M., & Smith, A. J. (1993). Childhood precursors of schizophrenia: Facial expressions of emotion. *American Journal of Psychiatry, 150,* 1654–1660.

Walker, E. F., Weinstein, J., Baum, K., & Neumann, C. S. (1995). Antecedents of schizophrenia: Moderating effects of development and biological sex. In H. Häfner & W. F. Gattaz (Eds.), *Search for the causes of schizophrenia* (Vol. III, pp. 21–42). Berlin, Germany: Springer-Verlag.

Walker, J. R., & Stein, M. B. (1995). Epidemiology. In M. B. Stein (Ed.), *Social phobia: Clinical and research perspectives* (pp. 43–75). Washington, DC: American Psychiatric Press.

Walker, M. B. (1992). *The psychology of gambling.* New York: Pergamon.

Walton, H. (Ed.). (1985). *Dictionary of psychiatry.* Oxford, England: Blackwell Scientific Publications.

Ward, C. H., Beck, A. T., Mendelson, M., Mock, J. E., & Erbaugh, J. K. (1962). The psychiatric nomenclature. *Archives of General Psychiatry, 7,* 198–205.

Warner, L. A., Kessler, R. C., Hughes, M., Anthony, J. C., & Nelson, C. B. (1995). Prevalence and correlates of drug use and dependence in the United States: Results from the National Comorbidity Study. *Archives of General Psychiatry, 52,* 219–229.

Watson, J. B., & Rayner, R. (1920). Conditioned emotional reactions. *Journal of Experimental Psychology, 3,* 1–14.

Weddington, W. W., Brown, B. S., Haertzen, C. A., Cone, R. J., Dax, E. M., Herning, R. I., & Michaelson, B. S. (1990). Changes in mood, craving, and sleep during short-term abstinence reported in male cocaine addicts. *Archives of General Psychiatry, 47,* 861–868.

Weinberger, D. R. (1995). Neurodevelopmental perspectives on schizophrenia. In F. E. Bloom & D. J. Kupfer (Eds.), *Psychopharmacology: The fourth generation of progress* (pp. 1171–1183). New York: Raven Press.

Weine, S. M., Becker, D. R., McGlashan, T. H., Laub, D., Lazrove, S., Vojvoda, D., & Hyman, L. (1995). Psychiatric consequences of "ethnic cleansing": Clinical assessments and traumatic testimonies of newly resettled Bosnian refugees. *American Journal of Psychiatry, 152,* 536–542.

Weisner, C. (1992). A comparison of alcohol and drug treatment clients: Are they from the same population? *American Journal of Drug and Alcohol Abuse, 18,* 429–444.

Weissman, M. M., Wickramaratne, P., Adam, P. B., Lish, J. D., Horwath, E., Charney, D., Woods, S. W., Leeman, E., & Frosch, E. (1993). The relationship between panic disorder and major depression. *Archives of General Psychiatry, 50,* 767–780.

Weizman, R., Tanne, Z., Granek, M., Karp, L., Golomb, M., Tyano, S., & Gavish, M. (1987). Peripheral benzodiazepine binding sites on platelet membranes are increased during diazepam treatment of anxious patients. *European Journal of Pharmacology, 138,* 289–292.

Wender, P. H., Rosenthal, D., Kety, S. S., Schulsinger, F., & Welner, J. (1974). Cross-fostering: A research strategy for clarifying the role of genetic and experiential factors in the etiology of schizophrenia. *Archives of General Psychiatry, 30,* 121–128.

Wetzler, S., & Sanderson, W. C. (1995). In G. M. Asnis & H. M. van Praag (Eds.), *Pathogenic mechanisms of panic disorder*. New York: Wiley.

Whittal, M. L., & Goetsch, V. L. (1995). Physiological, subjective and behavioral responses to hyperventilation in clinical and infrequent panic. *Behaviour Research and Therapy, 33,* 415–422.

Widiger, T. A. (1991). Personality disorder models proposed for DSM-IV. *Journal of Personality Disorders, 5,* 386–398.

Widiger, T. A. (1992). Categorical versus dimensional classification: Implications from and for research. *Journal of Personality Disorders, 6,* 287–300.

Widiger, T. A., Cadoret, R., Hare, R., Robins, L., Rutherford, M., Zanarini, M., Alterman, A., Apple, M., Corbitt, E., Forth, A., Hart, S., Kulterman, J., Woody, G., & Frances, A. (1996). DSM-IV. Antisocial personality disorder field trial. *Journal of Abnormal Psychology, 105,* 3–16.

Widiger, T. A., & Shea, T. (1991). Differentiation of Axis I and Axis II disorders. *Journal of Abnormal Psychology, 100,* 399–406.

Widiger, T. A., Trull, T. J., Clarkin, J. F., Sanderson, C., & Costa, P. T., Jr. (1994). A description of the DSM-III-R and DSM-IV personality disorders with the five-factor model of personality. In P. T. Costa, Jr., & T. A. Widiger (Eds.), *Personality disorders and the five-factor model of personality* (pp. 41–127). Washington, DC: American Psychological Association.

Widiger, T. A., Trull, T. J., Hurt, S. W., Clarkin, J., & Frances, A. (1987). A multidimensional scaling of the DSM-III personality disorders. *Archives of General Psychiatry, 44,* 557–563.

Widom, C. S. (1989). Does violence beget violence? A critical examination of the literature. *Psychological Bulletin, 106,* 3–28.

Wiedl, K. H. (1992). Assessment of coping with schizophrenia: Stressors, appraisals, and coping behavior. *British Journal of Psychiatry, 161,* 114–122.

Wiersma, D., Nienhuis, F. J., Sloof, C. J., & Giel, R. (1998). Natural course of schizophrenic disorders: 15-year followup of a Dutch incidence cohort. *Schizophrenia Bulletin, 24,* 75–83.

Williams, J., Spurlock, G., McGuffin, P., Mallet, J., Nöthen, M. M., Gill, M., Aschauér, H., Nylander, P.-O., Macciardi, F., & Owen, M. J. (1996). Association between schizophrenia and T102c polymorphism of the S-hydroxytryptamine type 2a-receptor gene. *The Lancet, 347,* 1294–1296.

Williams, J. B. W., Gibbon, M., First, M. B., Spitzer, R. L., Davies, M., Borus, J., Howes, M. J., Kane, J., Pope, H. G., Jr., Rounsaville, B., & Wittchen, H.-U. (1992). The structured clinical interview for DSM-III-R (SCID) II. Multisite test-retest reliability. *Archives of General Psychiatry, 49,* 630–632.

Willner, P. (1995). Dopaminergic mechanisms in depression. In P. E. Bloom & D. J. Kupfer (Eds.), *Psychopharmacology: The fourth generation of progress* (pp. 921–931). New York: Raven Press.

Wilson, K. G., Sandler, L. S., Asmundson, G. J. G., Ediger, J. M., & Larsen, D. K. (1992). Panic attacks in the nonclinical population: An empirical approach to case identification. *Journal of Abnormal Psychology, 101,* 460–468.

Winokur, G. (1991). *Mania and depression: A classification of syndrome and disease*. Baltimore, MD: Johns Hopkins University Press.

Winokur, G., Coryell, W., Keller, M., Endicott, J., & Akiskal, H. (1993). A prospective follow-up of patients with bipolar and primary unipolar affective disorder. *Archives of General Psychiatry, 50,* 457–465.

Winokur, G., Coryell, W., Keller, M., Endicott, J., & Leon, A. (1995). A family study of manic-depressive (Bipolar I) disease. *Archives of General Psychiatry, 52,* 367–373.

Wise, R. A., Bauco, P., Carlezon, A., & Trojniar, W. (1992). Self-stimulation and drug reward mechanisms. In P. W. Kalivas & H. H. Samson (Eds.), *The neurobiology of drug and alcohol addiction* (pp. 192–198). New York: The New York Academy of Science.

Wittchen, H. U., Zhao, S., Kessler, R. C., & Eaton, W. W. (1994). DSM-III-R generalized anxiety disorder in the National Comorbidity Study. *Archives of General Psychiatry, 51,* 355–364.

Wolpe, J., & Rowan, V. C. (1988). Panic disorder: A product of classical conditioning. *Behaviour Research Therapy, 26,* 441–450.

Woodman, D., Hinton, J., & O'Neill, M. (1977). Abnormality of catecholamine balance related to social deviance. *Perceptual and Motor Skills, 45,* 593–594.

Woods, S. W., Charney, D. S., McPherson, C. A., Gradman, A., & Henninger, G. R. (1987). Situational panic attacks: Behavioral, physiologic, and biochemical characterization. *Archives of General Psychiatry, 44,* 365–375.

Woods, S. W., Charney, D. S., Silver, J. M., Krystal, J. H., & Heninnger, G. R. (1991). Behavioral, biochemical, and cardiovascular responses to the benzodiazepine receptor antagonist flumazenil in panic disorder. *Psychiatry Research, 36,* 115–127.

World Health Organization (1967). *International classification of diseases* (8th ed.). Geneva, Switzerland: Author.

World Health Organization (1973). *The international pilot study of schizophrenia* (Vol. 1). Geneva, Switzerland: Author.

World Health Organization (1979). *Schizophrenia: An international follow-up study.* Chichester, England: Wiley.

Wright, P., Takei, N., Rifkin, L., & Murray, R. M. (1995). Maternal influenza, obstetric complications, and schizophrenia. *American Journal of Psychiatry, 152,* 1714–1720.

Yehuda, R., & McFarlane, A. C. (1995). Conflict between current knowledge about posttraumatic stress disorder and its original conceptual basis. *American Journal of Psychiatry, 152,* 1705–1713.

Yonkers, K. A., Warshaw, M. G., Massion, A. O., & Keller, M. B. (1996). Phenomenology and course of generalized anxiety disorder. *British Journal of Psychiatry, 168,* 308–313.

Zahn, T. P., Jacobsen, L. K., Gordon, C. T., McKenna, K., Frazier, J. A., & Rapaport, J. L. (1997). Autonomic nervous system markers of psychopathology in childhood-onset schizophrenia. *Archives of General Psychiatry, 54,* 904–911.

Zaidel, D. W., Esiri, M. M., & Harrison, P. J. (1997). Size, shape, and orientation of neurons in the left and right hippocampus: Investigation of normal assymmetries and alterations in schizophrenia. *American Journal of Psychiatry, 154,* 812–818.

Zalweski, C. E., & Gottesman, I. I. (1991). (Hu)man versus mean revisited: MMPI group data and psychiatric diagnosis. *Journal of Abnormal Psychology, 100,* 562–568.

Zanarini, M. C. (1993). Borderline personality disorder as an impulse spectrum disorder. In J. Parris (Ed.), *Borderline personality disorder: Etiology and treatment* (pp. 67–85). Washington, DC: American Psychiatric Press.

Zarin, D. A., & Earls, F. (1993). Diagnostic decision making in psychiatry. *American Journal of Psychiatry, 150,* 197–206.

Zimmerman, M. (1994). Diagnosing personality disorders. *Archives of General Psychiatry, 51,* 225–245.

Zimmerman, M., & Coryell, W. (1989). DSM-III personality disorder diagnoses in a non-patient sample. *Archives of General Psychiatry, 46,* 682–689.

Zimmerman, M., Coryell, W., & Pfohl, B. (1986). The validity of the dexamethasone suppression test as a marker for endogenous depression. *Archives of General Psychiatry, 43,* 347–355.

Zipursky, R. B., Lambe, E. K., Kapur, S., & Mikulis, D. J. (1998). Cerebral gray matter volume deficits in first episode psychosis. *Archives of General Psychiatry, 55,* 540–546.

Zohar, J., Mueller, E. A., Insel, T. R., Zohar-Kadovich, R. C., & Murphy, D. L. (1987). Serotonergic responsivity in obsessive-compulsive disorder: Comparison of patients and healthy controls. *Archives of General Psychiatry, 44,* 946–951.

Zonderman, A. B., Herbst, J. H., Schmidt, C., Jr., Costa, P. T., Jr., & McCrae, R. R. (1993). Depressive symptoms as a nonspecific graded risk for psychiatric diagnosis. *Journal of Abnormal Psychology, 102,* 544–552.

Zubin, J., & Spring, B. (1977). Vulnerability—A new view of schizophrenia. *Journal of Abnormal Psychology, 86,* 103–126.

Zuckerman, M. (1969). Hallucinations, reported sensations, and images. In J. P. Zubek (Ed.), *Sensory deprivation: Fifteen years of research.* New York: Appleton-Century-Crofts.

Zuckerman, M. (1974). The sensation seeking motive. In B. A. Maher (Ed.), *Progress in experimental personality research* (Vol. 7, pp. 79–148). New York: Academic Press.

Zuckerman, M. (1979). *Sensation seeking: Beyond the optimal level of arousal.* Hillsdale, NJ: Erlbaum.

Zuckerman, M. (1983a). The distinction between trait and state scales is not arbitrary: Comment on Allen and Potkay's "On the Arbitrary Distinction Between Traits and States." *Journal of Personality and Social Psychology, 44,* 1083–1086.

Zuckerman, M. (1983b). Sensation seeking: The initial motive for drug abuse. In

E. H. Gottheil, K. A. Druley, T. E. Skoloda, & H. M. Waxman (Eds.), *Etiological aspects of alcohol and drug abuse* (pp. 202–220). Springfield, IL: Charles C Thomas.

Zuckerman, M. (1986). Sensation seeking and the endogenous deficit theory of drug abuse. *National Institute on Drug Abuse Research Monographs Series, 74*, 59–70.

Zuckerman, M. (1987). Is sensation seeking a predisposing trait for alcoholism? In E. Gottheil, K. A. Druley, S. Pashkey, & S. P. Weinstein (Eds.), *Stress and addiction* (pp. 283–301). New York: Bruner/Mazel.

Zuckerman, M. (1989). Personality in the third dimension: A psychobiological approach. *Personality and Individual Differences, 10*, 391–418.

Zuckerman, M. (1991). *Psychobiology of personality*. Cambridge, England: Cambridge University Press.

Zuckerman, M. (1994a). Impulsive unsocialized sensation seeking: The biological foundations of a basic dimension of personality. In J. E. Bates & T. D. Wachs (Eds.), *Temperament: Individual differences at the interface of biology and behavior*. Washington, DC: American Psychological Association.

Zuckerman, M. (1994b). *Behavioral expressions and biosocial bases of sensation seeking*. New York: Cambridge University Press.

Zuckerman, M., & Cloninger, C. R. (1996). Relationships between Cloninger's, Zuckerman's, and Eysenck's dimensions of personality. *Personality and Individual Differences, 21*, 283–285.

Zuckerman, M., Kuhlman, D. M., & Camac, C. (1988). What lies beyond E and N? Factor analyses of scales believed to measure basic dimensions of personality. *Journal of Personality and Social Psychology, 54*, 96–107.

Zuckerman, M., Kuhlman, D. M., Joireman, J., Teta, P., & Kraft, M. (1993). A comparison of three structural models for personality: The big three, the big five, and the alternative five. *Journal of Personality and Social Psychology, 65*, 757–768.

Zuckerman, M., & Litle, P. (1986). Personality and curiosity about morbid and sexual events. *Personality and Individual Differences, 7*, 49–56.

Zuckerman, M., & Lubin, B. (1985). *Manual for the Multiple Affect Adjective Check List-Revised (MAACL-R)*. San Diego, CA: Educational and Industrial Testing Service.

Zuckerman, M., Neary, R. S., & Brustman, B. A. (1970). Sensation seeking scale correlates in experience (smoking, drugs, alcohol, "hallucinations," and sex) and preference for complexity (designs). *Proceedings of the 78th Annual Convention of the American Psychological Association* (pp. 317–318). Washington, DC: American Psychological Association.

Zuckerman, M., & Neeb, M. (1980). Demographic influences in sensation seeking and expressions of sensation seeking in religion, smoking, and driving habits. *Personality and Individual Differences, 1*, 197–206.

Zuckerman, M., Sola, S., Masterson, J., & Angelone, J. V. (1975). MMPI patterns in drug abusers before and after treatment in therapeutic communities. *Journal of Consulting and Clinical Psychology, 43*, 286–296.

AUTHOR INDEX

Caldwell, 262
Camac, C., 68
Campbell, R. J., 3, 4
Cancienne, J., 125
Canino, G. V., 79, 260, 261
Cannon, T. D., 371, 373, 381
Carey, G., 92, 93, 138, 224, 283
Carlezon, A., 290
Carlton, P. L., 306, 309
Carpenter, W. T., Jr., 321, 326
Carr, D. B., 111
Carrol, E. N., 295
Carroll, B. J., 73, 181, 278
Carroll, K. M., 215, 216, 277, 279, 293,
    297
Carson, R., 112
Carter, M. M., 112
Carton, S., 183
Caspi, A., 184, 242, 243, 270, 293
Cassady, S., 365
Castellani, B., 313
Cavallini, M. C., 328
Cavanaugh, J., 385
Chambless, D. L., 102, 112
Chapman, J. P., 348
Chapman, L. J., 348, 392
Chapman, T. F., 123
Charney, D. S., 105, 109, 110, 128, 146
Chen, C.-N., 302, 303
Chen, Y. R., 330
Chess, S., 97
Chiu, C.-Y., 314
Christiansen, K. O., 223
Cicz-DeMet, A., 232
Cimbolic, P., 108
Ciompi, L., 345
Clancy, J., 99
Claridge, G., 328
Clark, D. C., 166
Clark, D. M., 102, 113
Clark, F., 239
Clark, L. A., 60, 61, 68, 71, 72
Clarke, J. C., 134
Clarkin, J. F., 42, 70, 244
Clarkson, C., 119
Clayton, P., 185
Clayton, P. J., 359
Cleckley, H., 209, 211, 213, 231, 235,
    245
Cloitre, M., 125
Clomipramine Collaborative Study
    Group, 140

Cloninger, C. R., 222–224, 227, 229,
    241, 243, 259, 263–266, 268,
    277, 278, 293, 297, 359, 392,
    415
Cnattingius, S., 369
Coccaro, E. F., 233
Cocchi, S., 111
Coffey, C. E., 170
Cohen, D. J., 41, 49, 138
Cohen, L., 299
Cohen, R., 365
Comings, D. E., 306, 308
Compton, W. M., 273
Conboy, J., 244
Connolly, J. F., 231, 309
Conrad, A. J., 377
Cook, M., 134
Cooney, M., 185
Cooper, A. M., 65
Cooper, Z., 187, 190, 194
Cornblatt, B. A., 368
Cornish, A. M., 295
Coryell, W., 59, 65, 137, 165, 182, 191,
    192, 348
Costa, P. T., Jr., 71, 97, 194, 241, 244,
    294, 297
Cottler, L. B., 273, 277, 278
Coventry, K. R., 312
Covetoux-de-terte, A., 110
Cowley, D. S., 89, 109, 111, 119
Cox, B. J., 127–129
Cox, D. N., 212
Craig, R. J., 288, 295
Craske, M. G., 102, 103, 117
Craufurd, D., 338
Crayton, J. W., 304
Cronbach, L. J., 73
Cronin, C., 183
Croudace, T., 341, 346
Croughan, J., 52
Crow, T. J., 78, 326, 327, 333, 349, 389,
    394
Crowe, R. R., 119, 360
Csernansky, J. G., 233
Cui, X., 191
Culbertson,, 160
Cummings, J., 295
Custer, R. L., 310

Dabbs, J. M., Jr., 234
Dager, S. R., 111

Daghestani, A. N., 302, 304, 308
Dahlin, Y., 236
Daitzman, R. J., 234, 335
Dalgaarn, O. S., 223
Dalgesh, T., 148
Daniel, D. G., 377
Daniels, B. A., 133
Dansky, L., 166
Darke, S., 277
Davidson, M., 134, 385
Davidson, R. J., 231
Davies, M., 299
Davis, C. G., 118, 158, 165
Davis, D. M., 395
Davis, G. C., 145, 298
Davis, J. M., 146
Davis, J. O., 351
Davis, K. L., 385, 386
Davis, M., 146
Dawson, M. E., 365–369
Dean, P., 176
DeCaria, C. M., 140
DeFries, J. C., 168
De Jong, P., 133, 135
Delgado, P. L., 176
Delis, D., 170
DeLisi, L. E., 374
DeMet, E., 232
Den Boer, J. A., 385
Denno, 231
DePue, R. A., 13, 166
Dery, R., 105
Deutch, A. Y., 146
De Wit, H., 295
Deykan, E. Y., 298
Diaferia, G., 138
DiLalla, D. L., 393
DiNardo, P. A., 8, 59, 118, 131
Dinwiddie, S. H., 277
Ditta, S. R., 146
Doane, J. A., 400
Dobkin, P. L., 243
Dodge, C. S., 124
Doering, S., 347
Dohrenwend, B. P., 189, 190
Dollard, J., 429
Done, D. J., 394
Donison, N., 121
Duffy, P., 291
Dunner, A., 244
Dunner, D. L., 89, 111
DuPont, R. M., 170

Dworin, R. H., 394
Dyer, J., 348

Eardley, D. A., 199
Eaton, W. W., 91, 333, 341
Eaves, G., 199
Eaves, L. J., 93, 94, 100, 186
Eberly, R. E., 144, 398
Ebmeier, K. P., 373, 375
Ebstein, R. P., 169, 179, 229, 288
Eckardt, M. J., 266
Eckblad, M. E., 348
Eckert, E. D., 92, 93
Edell, W. S., 321
Ediger, J. M., 103
Edman, G., 269
Edvardsen, J., 356
Edwards, J., 158
Egeland, J. A., 160, 168
Egstein, R. P., 266
Ehlers, A., 124
Ehrenkranz, J., 234
Eitinger, L., 11
Elder, G. H., 144
Elenz, E., 304
Elkin, I., 192
Elkis, H., 170, 373
Ellenbogen, M. A., 176
Emery, G., 102
Emmelkamp, P. M. G., 137, 201
Endicott, J., 49, 50, 52, 53, 165, 191, 257
Endler, N. S., 127
Engdahl, B. E., 144, 398
Enright, S. J., 137, 141, 143
Epstein, S., 8
Erbaugh, J. K., 41
Erlenmeyer-Kimling, L., 357, 358, 367
Ertera, P., 145
Esiri, M. M., 377
Ettedgui, E., 103
Eysenck, H. J., 67–69, 71, 76, 97, 132, 210, 239, 241, 324, 333, 349
Eysenck, M. W., 68, 120
Eysenck, S. B. G., 210, 241, 333, 349

Fabrega, H., 79
Faedda, G. L., 184
Faraone, S. V., 168

Gottesman, I. I., 4, 13, 92, 93, 138, 222–224, 227, 229, 262, 283, 320, 337, 350, 351–356, 358, 360, 361, 393
Gottheil, E., 276
Grace, D. M., 311
Grace, M. C., 101
Gradman, A., 128
Graham, J. R., 311
Granholm, E., 368
Grant, B., 257
Gray, J. A., 13, 97, 98, 105, 120, 149, 230, 239, 241, 390, 391
Green, A., 77
Green, B. L., 101
Green, M. F., 368
Green, R. R., 168
Greenberg, D. B., 80
Greenberg, R. L., 102
Greenfield, L., 277
Griffith, J. D., 385
Grimes, K. E., 395
Gritsenko, I., 169, 288
Grossman, L. S., 192, 348
Grove, W. M., 67, 153
Gruenberg, A. M., 353, 359
Grzanna, R., 288
Guitart, X., 288
Gunn, J., 304
Gupta, S., 380
Gur, R. E., 373, 375, 376
Guthrie, P., 67
Guze, S. B., 55, 56, 72, 263, 357, 359
Gynther, L. M., 283

Hadzi-Pavlovic, D., 152, 153, 156, 182
Häfner, H., 335, 336, 338, 339, 341, 342
Haier, R. J., 375
Hakstian, A. R., 212, 242
Halberstadt, L., 200
Haley, J., 400
Hall, W., 277
Hallman, J., 269
Hammer, C. L., 189
Handelsman, L., 284
Hare, R. D., 210, 212, 213, 215, 219, 221, 222, 231, 236, 237, 239, 240–242, 245, 249, 309
Harkness, A. R., 71, 144
Harpur, T. J., 212, 219, 241, 242
Harris, T., 187, 188, 190, 200

Harrison, G., 341, 346
Harrow, J. F. G., 348
Harrow, M., 192, 321
Hart, S. D., 212, 213, 231, 241, 242
Harvald, B., 161
Harvey, A. G., 148
Harvey, I., 373
Haskin, S., 257
Hauge, M., 161
Haywood, E., 229, 285
Hazen, A. L., 121, 122
Hazender, M. M., 376
Hazlett, E. A., 367
Heath, A. C., 93, 100, 186, 268
Hegarty, J. D., 343, 344
Heilbrun, A. B., Jr., 321
Heimberg, J. D., 124
Heimberg, R. G., 125
Heineman, M., 302, 304, 308
Heinrichs, D. W., 378
Held, J., 385
Helzer, J. E., 52, 53, 65, 79, 216, 257–261
Hemming, J. H., 249
Hemsley, D. R., 381, 390
Henderson, S., 87
Henn, F. A., 389, 390
Henninger, G. R., 128
Henry, B., 243, 247
Hepworth, C., 188
Herbert, J. D., 89
Herbst, J. H., 194
Herz, L. R., 147
Hesselbrock, M. N., 217
Hesselbrock, V., 237
Hesselink, J. R., 170
Heston, L. L., 92, 352
Heywood, E., 263
Hickie, I., 202
Hinton, J., 233
Hipsley, P., 141
Hirsch, S. R., 381
Hirschfeld, R. M. A., 157, 183, 184
Hirshfeld, D. R., 96
Hoberman, H., 189
Hodulik, C. J., 200
Hoehn-Saric, R., 119, 141
Hoekstra, R. J., 137
Hoenk, P. R., 99
Hoffman, F. M., 295
Hoffman, P. L., 266
Hoffman, S. G., 124

McAdams, L., 367
McAuliffe, W. F., 295
McCabe, S. B., 199
McCallum, S. L., 125
McCarthy, P. R., 135, 148
McChesney, C. M., 119
McClearn, G. E., 163, 168
McClellan, J., 111
McConaghy, N., 304, 307, 312
McCord, J., 246, 247, 249, 270, 272
McCord, W., 270, 272
McCormick, R. A., 311, 315
McCrae, R. R., 97, 194, 241, 294, 297
McCreery, C., 328
McElvoy, L. T., 257
McFarlane, A. C., 143
McGee, R., 293
McGlashan, T. H., 330, 340, 347, 348
McGue, M., 5, 262, 265
McGuffin, P., 5, 161–163, 262, 351, 360,
    401
McGuire, M., 356
McGuire, P. K., 382
McHugh, P. R., 63
McLeod, D. R., 119, 141
McLeod, J. D., 101, 116
McNair, D. M., 69, 325
McNally, R. J., 103, 112–115, 135, 148
McNeal, E. T., 108
McNeill, M., 233
McNulty, J. L., 71
McPherson, C. A., 128
McPherson, L. M., 219, 222, 231, 309
Meany, M., 267
Medley, I., 341, 346
Mednick, S. A., 226, 227, 230, 248, 263,
    370, 377, 393, 403
Meehl, P. E., 4, 12, 13, 17, 18, 49, 55,
    65, 67, 73, 324, 348, 360, 367,
    391, 396, 397, 401, 402, 408,
    416, 418, 419
Mel, H., 288
Melamed, L., 314
Meltzer, H. Y., 170, 175–177, 192, 395–
    388
Melville, L. F., 125
Mendell, N. R., 362
Mendelson, M., 41, 200
Mendlewicz, J., 95, 119, 168
Menzies, R. G., 133, 134
Merckelbach, H., 122, 133–135
Merikangas, K. R., 284

Mersch, P. A., 122
Metalsky, G. I., 197
Mikulis, D. J., 374
Milgrom, P., 134
Milkowitz, D. J., 400, 402
Miller, C., 52
Miller, D., 328, 330
Miller, G. A., 157, 186, 370
Miller, H. L., 173, 176
Miller, I. W., III, 199
Miller, M. A., 302, 305
Miller, N., 429
Millman, R. B., 304
Millon, N., 120
Millon, T., 42
Milner, p., 289
Milt, H., 310
Mineka, S., 113, 124, 125, 134
Miranda, J., 208
Mirsky, A. F., 358, 394
Mitchell, P., 156
Mizler, G., 367
Moan, C. E., 231
Mock, J. E., 41
Modin, I., 232
Moffitt, T. E., 184, 219, 224, 226, 234,
    243, 248, 293
Mogg, K., 120
Moldin, S. O., 67, 361
Monroe, S. M., 3, 14–16
Mookerjee, H. N., 269
Moran, M., 365
Moras, K., 150
Moravec, J. D., 314
Moreau, M., 364
Morikawa, T., 158
Morris, J. C., 172
Morris-Yates, A., 87
Mosher, L. R., 380
Moss, H. A., 96
Moss, H. B., 232
Mowrer, O. H., 142
Moyes, R., 99
Mueller, C. B., 299
Mueller, E. A., 140
Mueser, K. T., 61, 398
Mulder, R. T., 64
Müller-Spahr, F., 347
Munley, P. H., 314
Munro, J. C., 381
Murdock, T. B., 148
Muris, P., 134

Perry, J. C., 245
Persico, A. M., 266
Pert, A., 291
Peterson, C., 196
Peterson, E. L., 145, 158
Pfohl, B., 182
Phelps, J. A., 351
Pichot, P., 209
Pickar, D., 173, 348
Pickens, R. W., 262, 283
Pigott, T. M., 139
Pihl, R. O., 243
Pincus, A., 43
Pittman, R. K., 147
Platt, J. J., 288, 295
Plomin, R., 5, 56, 76, 77, 163, 168, 169, 422
Pohl, R., 109–111
Pohotecky, L. A., 271
Poling, J. C., 279
Pollack, S., 179
Pollin, W., 380
Pope, H. G., 305
Porjesz, B., 267
Post, R. M., 291
Potking, S. G., 375
Poulton, R. G., 101
Powers, R. J., 271
Prange, A. J., Jr., 182
Price, R. K., 273
Pulkkinen, L., 227
Purcell, R., 140
Puthezhath, N., 103

Quay, H. C., 235
Quercioli, L., 399
Quinn, M. J., 249

Rachman, S., 133
Radka, D. F., 122
Rae, D. S., 89, 160
Rahav, G., 294
Raine, A., 230
Ramirez, L. F., 315
Rapee, R. M., 59, 109, 111, 112, 117, 120, 125
Rasmussen, S. A., 138
Ratcliff, K. S., 52
Rauch, S. L., 132, 139

Ravenscroft, H., 125
Rawlins, J. N. P., 390
Rayner, R., 133
Razran, G., 112
Redmond, D. E., Jr., 105
Redner, J. E., 198
Regier, D. A., 59, 61, 82, 89, 104, 160, 217–221, 258, 273–275, 277, 279, 334, 335, 398
Reich, J., 77
Reich, T., 76, 77, 259, 277
Reiman, E. M., 105, 139
Reimann, B. C., 148
Reist, C., 232
Reveley, A. M., 351
Reynolds, C. F., 188
Reznick, J. S., 96
Rice, J., 65, 216
Rice, J. P., 51–53
Riess, J. L., 51
Rifkin, L., 370
Riso, L. P., 167
Ritenour, A., 188
Robertson, H. A., 288
Robin, L. N., 248
Robinette, C. D., 350
Robins, E., 53, 55, 56, 72
Robins, L. N., 51, 52, 59, 65, 82, 216–221, 229, 242, 246, 247, 258, 273–275, 277, 279, 334, 335, 398
Robinson, D., 171
Robinson, J. E., 293
Roby, K. J., 302, 303, 305
Roccatagliata, G., 26, 27
Rochberg, N., 52
Rodney, J. M., 125
Roemer, R. A., 74
Rohde, P., 185, 198
Romanoski, A. J., 63
Ronchi, P., 138
Rose, D. T., 200
Rose, R. M., 234
Rosen, A., 49
Rosen, B., 78
Rosen, L., 295
Rosenbaum, J. F., 96
Rosenbaum, M., 189
Rosenthal, D., 4, 295, 330, 331, 352, 353
Ross, D. E., 365
Roth, B. L., 385, 386, 388
Roth, N. T., 124

SUBJECT INDEX

Antisocial personality disorder (APD)
 (*continued*)
  social class, 248–249
  and stress, 244–245
  treatment of, 427–428
Anxiety disorders, 85–150
 agoraphobia. *See* Agoraphobia
 antidepressants for treatment of, 57
 comorbidity of, 60, 62–63
  with alcoholism, 271
  with depressive disorders, 87
  with personality disorders, 87–90
 demographic characteristics, 89, 91–92
 in *DSM*, 94, 95, 102, 116–119, 121–
  123, 126, 127, 130, 137–138,
  143–145
 genetic influences in
  family aggregation studies, 95
  twin studies, 92–95
 obsessive-compulsive disorder. *See*
  Obsessive-compulsive disorder
  (OCD)
 panic disorder. *See* Panic disorder (PD)
 and personality, 96–99
 posttraumatic stress disorder. *See* Posttraumatic stress disorder (PTSD)
 prevalence of, 89
 and schizophrenia, 332
 social phobia. *See* Social phobia
 specific phobias. *See* Specific phobias
 and stress, 99–102
Anxiety sensitivity (AS), 113–114
Anxiety Sensitivity Index (ASI), 114
APD. *See* Antisocial personality disorder;
 Avoidant personality disorder
Arginine vasopressin (AVP), 140–141
Arousal theories, 235–241
Artistic temperament, 184
AS. *See* Anxiety sensitivity
ASI (Anxiety Sensitivity Index), 114
Attention-deficit hyperactivity disorder
 (ADHD), 243–244, 305–306
Autoimmune deficiency syndrome
 (AIDS), 26
Avoidant personality disorder (APD),
 88–89, 121–122
AVP. *See* Arginine vasopressin
Axis I, 42, 48, 52, 62–67, 275–277
Axis II, 42, 43, 48, 52, 62–67, 277–278
Axis III, 42
Axis IV, 42
Axis V, 42

Backward masking, 368

Barbiturates, 273, 295
BAS. *See* Behavioral approach system
BDI. *See* Beck Depression Inventory
Beck, A. T., 195
Beck Depression Inventory (BDI), 64,
 305
Behavioral approach system (BAS), 13–
 14
Behavioral inhibition system (BIS), 13–
 14, 97
Behavior genetics, 5
Benzodiazepine, 119
Big Five. *See* Five-factor model
Biochemical factors. *See* Psychopharma-
 cological approaches
Biological correlates, 6
Biological variables, 6
Bipolar depression, 154
Bipolar disorders, 44, 61, 155, 184
BIS. *See* Behavioral inhibition system
Black bile, 27, 29
Blacks, 80–81, 219–220, 337
Bleuler, E., 320
Blood, 27, 30
Bootstrap approach, 55, 73
Borderline personality disorder (BPD), 64
Brain damage, 17
Brain disorders, 27
Brain imaging studies. *See* Neuroimaging
 studies
Brief psychotic disorder, 323
Bulimia, 75
Byron, Lord, 184

Caffeine, 109–110
California Personality Inventory (CPI),
 311
Cannabis, 273
Carbon dioxide, 111–112, 114
Carroll, B. J., 73–74
Catatonic behavioral signs, 321–322
Catatonic type schizophrenia, 322
CBF. *See* Cerebral blood flow
CCK (cholecystokinin), 110
Cerebral blood flow (CBF), 105, 170
CFS (chronic fatigue syndrome), 80
Charcot, Jean-Martin, 33
Child abuse/neglect, and antisocial per-
 sonality disorder, 247
Childhood conduct disorder, 64
China, 79

275, 277–281, 334, 335, 337, 398
Epinephrine, 105
Episode markers, 6
ETD. *See* Eye-tracking dysfunction
Ethnicity
    and alcoholism, 259
    and antisocial personality disorder, 219–220
    and anxiety disorders, 91
    and mood disorders, 160
    and pathological gambling, 306
    and schizophrenia, 337
Extraversion, 67–68, 97, 146
Eye-tracking, 6
Eye-tracking dysfunction (ETD), 362–365
Eysenck, Hans, 68, 97
Eysenck Impulsivity scale, 313

False negatives, 56
False positives, 56
Family studies, 56, 95
    of drug abuse/dependence, 283–285
    of mood disorders, 164–167
    of schizophrenia, 354–359
Fear-potential startle (FPS), 237, 249
Five-factor model (Big Five), 71, 294
Flumazenil, 110
FPS. *See* Fear-potential startle
Fraternal twins, 5
Freud, Sigmund
    on biological basis for mental disorders, 413
    and diagnosis, 33
    on psychoses vs. neuroses, 77

GABA, 110, 119, 168, 266, 389–390
GAD. *See* Generalized anxiety disorder
GA (Gamblers Anonymous), 300
Galen, 27, 29, 30
Gamblers Anonymous (GA), 300
Gambling, pathological. *See* Pathological gambling
Gay Rights movement, 46
Gender differences, 81, 416
    alcoholism, 258, 259
    antisocial personality disorder, 217–218

bipolar depression, 154
mood disorders, 160
schizophrenia, 335
Generalized anxiety disorder (GAD), 8, 63, 65, 74–76, 87, 116–121, 419
    biological factors in, 119–120
    cognition in, 120–121
    comorbidity in, 59, 60, 117, 158
    genetic factors in, 92–95, 118–119
    phenomenology of, 116–117
    prevalence of, 118
Generalized social phobia (GSP), 88, 121
Genetic factors
    in agoraphobia, 127–128
    in alcohol disorders, 262–266
        adoption studies, 263–264
        molecular genetics, 265–266
        subclassifications, 264–265
        twin studies, 262–263
    in antisocial personality disorder
        adoption studies, 225–229
        specific genes, 229
        twin studies, 222–225
    in anxiety disorders
        family aggregation studies, 95
        twin studies, 92–95
    and comorbidity, 74–77
    in drug disorders, 283–289
        adoption studies, 285–287
        family studies, 283–285
        molecular genetic studies, 288
        twin studies, 283
    in generalized anxiety disorder, 92–95, 118–119
    in mood disorders, 189
        family aggregation studies, 164–167
        molecular genetic studies, 167–169
        twin studies, 161–164
    in obsessive-compulsive disorder, 138
    in panic disorder, 104
    in pathological gambling (PG), 307–309
    in posttraumatic stress disorder, 145
    in schizophrenia, 349–362
        adoption studies, 352–354
        family studies, 354–359
        models, genetic, 359–360
        molecular genetics, 361–362
        twin studies, 349–352
    in social phobia, 123
    in specific phobias, 131–132
Genetic markers, 77

Glucose tolerance test (GTT), 235
Glutamate receptor dysfunction (GRD), 388–391
Gonadotropin-releasing hormone (GRH), 181
Goodall, Jane, 210
GRD. *See* Glutamate receptor dysfunction
Greece, ancient, 26–29
GRH (gonadotropin-releasing hormone), 181
GSP. *See* Generalized social phobia
GTT (glucose tolerance test), 235

Hallucinations, 321
Hallucinogens, 273
Harvey, William, 30
Heroin, 273, 278, 291, 295
Hippocrates, 27–29
Hispanics, 81, 337
History of psychopathology
   diagnoses, 26–33
   mood disorders, 151–152
   schizophrenia, 319–321
HIV, 278, 297
Home environment, and antisocial personality disorder, 246–247
Homosexuality, 45–47
Homovanyllic acid (HVA), 179, 385–387
Hopelessness depression, 197
Hormones, 180–183
HPA (hypothalamic-pituitary-adrenal) system, 181
Humoral theory, 27–30, 180
Huntington's chorea, 4, 417
HVA. *See* Homovanyllic acid
Hypochondriasis, 31
Hypofrontality, 375
Hypomania, 53
Hypomanic episode, 44, 154, 155
Hypothalamic-pituitary-adrenal (HPA) system, 181
Hysteria, 27–28, 31

Identical twins, 5
Immediate early genes (IEGs), 288
Impulsive Sensation Seeking. *See* Sensation Seeking

Impulsive-Unsocialized Sensation Seeking, 68
Internal reliability, 48–49
International Classification of Diseases, 35, 79
Involutional melancholia, 32
IQ, 381
Isoproterenol, 110
Israel, 403–404

Jamison, K. R., 184
Japan, 79

Kallmann, F. J., 349–350
Kappa (reliability statistic), 41, 49–54
Kibbutz method of child-rearing, 403–404
Klein, D. F., 78, 114–115
Kraepelin, Emil, 31–32, 320, 325, 330

Laboratory studies, 55, 73–74
Latent dimensional approach, 53
Learned helplessness, 20, 195–196
Liability threshold, 13
Linkage studies, 76–77
Locus of control, 310–311, 314
Lorr, M., 69–70
Loss, 99
LSD, 387, 388

MAACL-R. *See* Multiple Affect Adjective Check List
Magnetic resonance imaging (MRI), 169–170, 373, 375, 421
Major depressive disorders, 53, 64, 155
   comorbidity of, 60
   and pathological gambling, 305
Major depressive episode, 154
Mania, 27, 29–32, 183
Manic episode, 155
MAO. *See* Monoamine oxidase
Marital status
   and alcoholism, 259–260
   and antisocial personality disorder, 221
   schizophrenia by, 335–336
Markers
   episode, 6
   genetic, 77
   vulnerability, 6

Masturbation, 29
Medial forebrain bundle (MFB), 289–291
Medical categorization approach to mental disorders, 57–58
Melancholia, 27–32, 181–182
Melancholic specifier, 155–156
Metachlorophenylpiperazine, 110
Meyer, Adolf, 34, 35
MFB. *See* Medial forebrain bundle
MHPG, 107, 111, 128, 132, 140, 172, 173, 233, 310
Middle Ages, diagnosis in, 29–30
Monoamine oxidase (MAO), 179, 231–232, 267–268, 309, 416, 421–423
Mood congruent delusions/hallucinations, 155
Mood disorders, 151–208
  cognitive factors in, 194–200
  comorbidity of, 158–159
  course, 191–193
  demographic characteristics, 160–161
  in *DSM*, 153–159, 162–163, 166, 182, 184, 186, 187, 193, 203
  and early environmental experiences, 200–202
  genetic influences in
    family aggregation studies, 164–167
    molecular genetic studies, 167–169
    twin studies, 161–164
  historical background, 151–152
  neuropsychological approaches to, 169–172
  outcomes, 193–194
  and personality, 183–187
  prevalence of, 159–160
  psychopharmacology of, 172–183
    dopamine, role of, 177–179
    hormones, 180–183
    norepinephrine, role of, 172–175
    serotonin, role of, 175–177
  and schizophrenia, 332, 333
  and stress, 187–191
    events, stressful, 187–189
    genetic factors, 189
    risk factors, 189–191
Morbidity risk, 81–82
MRI. *See* Magnetic resonance imaging
Multiple Affect Adjective Check List (MAACL-R), 60–61

NARP (nonaffective acute remitting psychosis), 80
National Comorbidity Study (NCS), 82, 91, 122, 160, 280, 281, 334, 335, 337
Neo-Kraepelinians, 41, 46
Neurasthenia, 29, 79–80
Neuroimaging studies, 104–105, 169–172, 371–377
Neuropsychological approaches
  to antisocial personality disorder, 229–231
  to panic disorder, 104–105
Neurosis, 18–20
Neuroticism, 67–68, 97, 146, 186–187
NGSP (nongeneralized social phobia), 121
NIMH Psychobiology study, 184–185
NMDA, 146, 389–390
Nonaffective acute remitting psychosis (NARP), 80
Nonbizarre delusions, 323
Nongeneralized social phobia (NGSP), 121
Nonsuppressors, 182
Norepinephrine, 105, 107, 109, 111, 146–147, 172–175, 291
Norms, 25–26
Novelty Seeking. *See* Sensation Seeking

Obsessive-compulsive disorder (OCD), 62, 63, 88, 89, 136–143, 171
  cognitive factors in, 142–143
  comorbidity of, 137–138
  conditioning in, 142
  demographic characteristics of, 138
  Freudian view of, 33
  genetic factors in, 138
  neuropsychological approach to, 138–140
  and personality, 142
  phenomenology of, 136–137
  prevalence of, 138
  psychopharmacological approach to, 140–141
  and psychophysiological arousal, 141
Obsessive-compulsive personality disorder (OCPD), 137
OCD. *See* Obsessive-compulsive disorder
OCPD (obsessive-compulsive personality disorder), 137
Opioids, 273–275, 291

Psychopharmacological approaches
  to antisocial personality disorder, 231–
    235
  to panic disorder, 105, 107–112
  to schizophrenia, 382, 385–391
Psychoticism, 67–68
PTSD. *See* Posttraumatic stress disorder

Quakers, 26

Rachman, S., 133
Rapid-cycling specifier, 157
RDC (research diagnostic criteria), 52
Reactions, 35, 40
Reliability, diagnostic, 47–55
  in *DSM-I & II* vs. *DSM-III & III-R*,
    50–53
  internal reliability, 48–49
  kappa, 49–50
  personality disorders, 54–55
  and validity, 47–48
Religion, and schizophrenia, 337
Renaissance, diagnosis in, 29–30
Research diagnostic criteria (RDC), 52
Residual type schizophrenia, 323
Risk factors, 425–426
  for alcohol disorders, 272
  for antisocial personality disorder, 245–
    249
    child abuse/neglect, 247
    home environment, 246–247
    peer influences, 247–248
    social class, 248–249
  for drug disorders, 298–300
  for posttraumatic stress disorder, 145–
    146
  and stress, 401–404
Rome, ancient, 29
Rush, Benjamin, 31

SAD. *See* Schizoaffective disorder
Schedule for Nonadaptive and Adaptive
    Personality (SNAP), 71, 72
Schizoaffective disorder (SAD), 61, 157,
    323
Schizoid personality disorder, 324
Schizophrenia, 4, 17, 319–411, 416–418
  biological factors in, 362–382

brain imaging studies, 371–377,
    381–382, 385
  markers, behavioral/biological, 362–
    369
  neuropsychological tests, 380–381
  postmortem studies, 377–379
  prenatal and perinatal factors, 369–
    371
  "soft" neurological signs, 378, 380
bipolar mood disorders, comorbidity
    with, 61
comorbidity of, 331–334
course of, 338–347
  before first acute episode, 338, 340
  during index admissions, 340–341
  post episode, 341, 343–345, 347
demographic factors in, 335–338
  age, 335–336
  education, 336–337
  ethnicity, 337
  gender, 335
  geographical region, 337–338
  marital status, 336
  religion, 337
  socioeconomic status, 337
diagnosis of, 319–331
  in *DSM-IV*, 321–331
  historical background, 319–321
diathesis-stress model for, 12–14
in DSM, 320–328, 330, 333, 334,
    343, 344, 348, 350, 353, 356,
    392, 393
genetic factors in, 349–362
  adoption studies, 352–354
  family studies, 354–359
  models, genetic, 359–360
  molecular genetics, 361–362
  twin studies, 349–352
outcome, predictors of, 347–349
panic disorder, comorbidity with, 58
and personality, 391–396
and personality disorders, 324–325
prevalence of, 334
psychopharmacology of, 382, 385–391
  dopamine hypothesis, 382, 385–386
  glutamate receptor dysfunction,
    388–391
  serotonin hypothesis, 386–388
and stress, 396–401
substance abuse/dependence disorders,
    comorbidity with, 61–62
Schizophreniform disorder, 323–324

Therapy, 426–430
Tolerance, drug, 256
Tourette's syndrome, 138–139
Traits, 6, 7, 97
Treatment outcomes, 56–57
Tryptophan, 175–176
Twin studies, 5, 75, 76
  of alcoholism, 262–263
  of antisocial personality disorder, 222–225
  of anxiety disorders, 92–95, 99–100
  of drug abuse/dependence, 283
  of mood disorders, 161–164
  of pathological gambling, 307–308
  of schizophrenia, 349–352
Tyrosine hydroxylase, 173

Unconditioned stimuli (UCS), 112–113
Undifferentiated type schizophrenia, 323
Unipolar depression, 154
Uterine theory, 27–29

Validity, diagnostic, 55–82
  class factors in, 80–81
  and comorbidity, 57–67
  cultural factors in, 79–80
  and dimensional approaches, 67–73

and gender, 81
genetic studies, 74–77
laboratory test results, 73–74
and outcome of treatment, 56–57
phases of validation, 55–56
and prevalence, 81–82
and prognosis/course of disorder, 77
and reliability, 47–48
and response to treatment, 77–78
Van Gogh, Vincent, 184
Ventricle to brain ratio (VBR), 373
Vietnam veterans, 100–101, 145, 163
Vital humors, 27
Vulnerability, 4
Vulnerability markers, 6

War neurosis, 32
WCST. *See* Wisconsin Card Sorting Task
WHO (World Health Organization), 345
Wisconsin Card Sorting Task (WCST),
    375, 377, 380, 382
Withdrawal, 256
World Health Organization (WHO), 345
Wundt, Wilhelm, 32

Yellow bile, 27, 29
Yohimbine, 105, 107, 109

ABOUT THE AUTHOR

Marvin Zuckerman is a professor at the University of Delaware where he has taught and conducted research for the last 30 years. He received his PhD from New York University in the area of clinical psychology. He worked for several years as a clinical psychologist in state hospitals before accepting a research position at the Institute of Psychiatry in the Indiana University Medical Center. There he began his experimental studies in sensory deprivation, which continued for the next 11 years at Brooklyn College, Adelphi University, and the Endocrinology Research Labs of Einstein Medical Center in Philadelphia. Curiosity about individual differences in reactions to sensory deprivation led to the development of the first Sensation Seeking Scale. Research and theory building around the sensation seeking trait has been the major part of his work to the present and resulted in two major books on that topic: *Sensation Seeking: Beyond the Optimal Level of Arousal* in 1979, and *Behavioral Correlates and Biosocial Bases of Sensation Seeking* in 1994. An interest in the biological bases of sensation seeking broadened to a more general interest in the *Psychobiology of Personality* (the title of his 1991 book). He is one of the founders and a past-president of the International Society for the Study of Individual Differences. Dr. Zuckerman's current interest is in molecular genetics and he is hoping for funding to collaborate with colleagues at the Institute for Psychiatry in London, where he spent his last sabbatical, in tracking down specific genes for impulsive sensation seeking and pathological gambling disorder.